CONNECT FEATURES

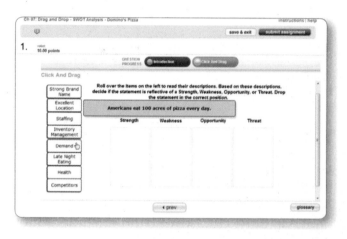

Interactive Applications

Interactive Applications offer a variety of automatically graded exercises that require students to **apply** key concepts. Whether the assignment includes a *click and drag*, *video case*, or *decision generator*, these applications provide instant feedback and progress tracking for students and detailed results for the instructor.

eBook

Connect Plus includes a media-rich eBook that allows you to share your notes with your students. Your students can insert and review their own notes, highlight the text, search for specific information, and interact with media resources. Using an eBook with Connect Plus gives your students a complete digital solution that allows them to access their materials from any computer.

Tegrity

Make your classes available anytime, anywhere. With simple, one-click recording, students can search for a word or phrase and be taken to the exact place in your lecture that they need to review.

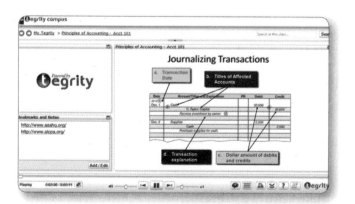

EASY TO USE

Learning Management System Integration

McGraw-Hill Campus is a one-stop teaching and learning experience available to use with any learning management system. McGraw-Hill Campus provides single sign-on to faculty and students for all McGraw-Hill material and technology from within the school website. McGraw-Hill Campus also allows instructors instant access to all supplements and teaching materials for all McGraw-Hill products.

Blackboard users also benefit from McGraw-Hill's industry-leading integration, providing single sign-on to access all Connect assignments and automatic feeding of assignment results to the Blackboard grade book.

POWERFUL REPORTING

Connect generates comprehensive reports and graphs that provide instructors with an instant view of the performance of individual students, a specific section, or multiple sections. Since all content is mapped to learning objectives, Connect reporting is ideal for accreditation or other administrative documentation.

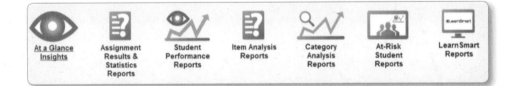

MARKETING

C. Shane Hunt
Arkansas State University

John E. Mello
Arkansas State University

Mc
Graw
Hill
Education

MARKETING

Published by McGraw-Hill Education, 2 Penn Plaza, New York, NY 10121. Copyright © 2015 by McGraw-Hill Education. All rights reserved. Printed in the United States of America. No part of this publication may be reproduced or distributed in any form or by any means, or stored in a database or retrieval system, without the prior written consent of McGraw-Hill Education, including, but not limited to, in any network or other electronic storage or transmission, or broadcast for distance learning.

Some ancillaries, including electronic and print components, may not be available to customers outside the United States.

This book is printed on acid-free paper.

1 2 3 4 5 6 7 8 9 0 DOW/DOW 1 0 9 8 7 6 5 4

ISBN   978-0-07-786109-4
MHID   0-07-786109-4

Senior Vice President, Products & Markets: *Kurt L. Strand*
Vice President, Content Production & Technology Services: *Kimberly Meriwether David*
Managing Director: *Paul Ducham*
Executive Brand Manager: *Sankha Basu*
Executive Director of Development: *Ann Torbert*
Development Editor: *Gabriela Gonzalez*
Marketing Manager: *Donielle Xu*
Director, Content Production: *Terri Schiesl*
Content Project Manager: *Lori Koetters*
Buyer II: *Debra R. Sylvester*
Design: *Debra Kubiak*
Lead Content Licensing Specialist: *Keri Johnson*
Typeface: *10/12 Palatino Roman*
Compositor: *Laserwords Private Limited*
Printer: *R. R. Donnelley*

All credits appearing on page or at the end of the book are considered to be an extension of the copyright page.

Library of Congress Cataloging-in-Publication Data

Hunt, C. Shane.
   Marketing/C. Shane Hunt, Arkansas State University, John E. Mello, Arkansas State University.
     pages cm
   Includes bibliographical references and index.
   ISBN-13: 978-0-07-786109-4 (alk. paper)
   ISBN-10: 0-07-786109-4 (alk. paper)
   1. Marketing. I. Mello, John E. II. Title.
HF5415.H872 2015
658.8—dc23

                                                                  2013031992

The Internet addresses listed in the text were accurate at the time of publication. The inclusion of a website does not indicate an endorsement by the authors or McGraw-Hill Education, and McGraw-Hill Education does not guarantee the accuracy of the information presented at these sites.

www.mhhe.com

BRIEF CONTENTS

iii

DEDICATION

To my children, Andrew and Sarah. You are the inspiration for everything I do, and I love you both very much.

Shane

To my wife, Sandra, for your support and patience. Without your help I could not have made it through a PhD program and achieved my dream of becoming a college professor.

John

C. SHANE HUNT

Dr. C. Shane Hunt received his PhD in marketing from Oklahoma State University where he was an AMA Sheth Foundation and National Conference in Sales Management Doctoral Fellow. Shane has won numerous awards for his teaching, including the 2010 National Inspire Integrity Award from the National Society of Collegiate Scholars, the 2010 Lt. Col. Barney Smith Award as Professor of the Year at Arkansas State University, and the 2011 Excellence in Undergraduate Teaching Award.

Shane's research has appeared in *The Journal of Personal Selling and Sales Management*, *The Journal of Business Logistics,* and other leading marketing journals, and he has presented to numerous organizations including the American Marketing Association and the National Conference in Sales Management. Shane also serves as the vice chair for an American Marketing Association special interest group in the area of personal selling and sales management.

After completing his bachelor's and MBA degrees at the University of Oklahoma, Shane went to work for a Fortune 500 company in Tulsa, Oklahoma, and spent eight years working as a pricing analyst, product manager, and business development manager overseeing numerous strategic initiatives. In addition to his role as a professor, Shane also serves as a consultant, speaker, and board member for businesses and nonprofit organizations across the country.

Shane is now an associate professor of marketing at Arkansas State University and lives in Jonesboro, Arkansas, with his wife Jenifer and their two children, Andrew and Sarah.

JOHN E. MELLO

Dr. John Mello received his PhD from the University of Tennessee. John is a well-respected educator at both the undergraduate and graduate levels and is the recipient of the 2012 Excellence in Teaching Award from the Arkansas State University College of Business. Prior to completing his PhD, John spent 28 years in the consumer packaged goods industry in a variety of positions at Unilever and Playtex Products. John holds a bachelor's degree from Central Connecticut State University and master's degrees from the University of New Haven and Wilmington College.

John's research has appeared in leading journals, including *The Journal of Business Logistics*, *Transportation Journal*, and the *International Journal of Physical Distribution and Logistics Management,* and he has presented to leading conferences, including the Decisions Sciences Institute and the Marketing Management Association. John serves on the editorial review boards of multiple leading journals, including *The Journal of Business Logistics* and *Transportation Journal*.

John is now an associate professor of marketing and the director for the Center for Supply Chain Management at Arkansas State University. He lives in Jonesboro, Arkansas, with his wife Sandra; they have two adult daughters, Abby and Katie.

Dear Students,

Wherever your life takes you after this course, you can be assured that knowing how to implement marketing principles will be an important part of your professional success. We have designed this product to demonstrate the connection between marketing and your career going forward, whether you choose to pursue a major in marketing or another field. As you begin this course, we encourage you not to look at the information as a collection of random concepts that you can forget about once you take your final exam. Instead, think about how each of the concepts you read about can help you market and position yourself as a student and as an employee. We have included a number of features to support your efforts, including career tips at the end of every chapter and a comprehensive marketing plan exercise that focuses on marketing the most important product and brand of your entire life: you.

If you are a marketing major, this product will give you a practical foundation in topics such as consumer behavior, professional selling, supply chain management, marketing research, and advertising—information that you will need as you move forward in your degree program. We have also included Today's Professional profiles in each chapter, which feature recent marketing graduates discussing their current jobs. You will see that a marketing major can open doors to a variety of opportunities in large companies, small businesses, and nonprofit organizations throughout the world.

If you are majoring in a field other than marketing, this might be the only marketing course you take. This product will help you understand the role marketing plays in the success of virtually every for-profit and nonprofit organization. Every chapter features a successful executive or entrepreneur who majored in something other than marketing, but who is using the principles you will learn in this course each day of his or her professional life.

Your future is bright, and this product can help you along the path of reaching your professional goals. The working world will continue to evolve and change, but no matter what part of the world you live in, how big your community is, or what the economy looks like, opportunities will always be available for people with marketing skills. We hope you enjoy this product, and we wish the very best for your future.

Sincerely,

C. Shane Hunt   John E. Mello

Hello, and welcome to Hunt and Mello's *Marketing*. Over the course of many conversations, we've heard from you, and instructors like you, about a number of the key challenges you face in your principles of marketing course. Though every instructor's situation is unique, some common themes emerged from our conversations.

1. Students, particularly non-marketing majors, struggle to understand how this course relates to them. They need guidance on how to put together the pieces and make it relevant.

2. Students come to the course expecting a high level of engagement. They need course materials that deliver on this expectation by providing them with engaging, interesting content.

3. Students want to know that what they are learning matters. Content must be presented in a logical, concise way that highlights its importance to encourage students to read and interact with the material as they prepare for class.

After listening to you discuss your challenges, we examined the other side—students' opinions—through surveys of principles students at several universities. Students from a variety of majors shared with us their primary complaints about existing course materials. Again, common themes emerged.

1. The content doesn't relate to students' individual goals and lives.

2. Products don't convey how marketing strategies can be used in students' future marketing careers.

3. There is a lack of order associated with the seemingly random inclusion of topics, terms, and chapters in most products.

Marketing meets the critical challenges voiced by both instructors and students. We deliver the most important content, in the most engaging way, to help students from all backgrounds and all career aspirations learn the science of marketing and how essential it is to their careers, their organizations, and society as a whole. *Marketing* was created with an emphasis on student engagement and relevance, a focus that's embodied in the following key benefits:

1. *Student career focus.* A number of pedagogical tools help students understand how marketing will support their career, whether they choose to major in marketing or something else. From the very first chapter, **"Why Marketing Matters to You,"** students learn about marketing as it relates to them, whatever their career path happens to be. The **Executive Perspective** features that begin

HELLO
my name is

Roberta Schultz
Western Michigan University

Very helpful addition of career focus. Students will benefit from the information and help in applying marketing to their own career search. Well-written, concise coverage of the concepts with current, relevant examples.

Erin Brewer
Managing Partner

RedPin Bowling Lounge and The Basement Modern Diner
http://www.bowlredpin.com/

REDPIN
RESTAURANT AND BOWLING LOUNGE

RedPin is a combination restaurant, bowling alley, and bar in Oklahoma City. It boasts 10 bowling lanes; a full-service bar; space for private parties; a menu of local, made-from-scratch fare; and a large canal-front patio.

every chapter connect to students' ultimate career goals and represent the importance of marketing to students from a wide range of majors, including computer science, anthropology, applied mathematics, and economics. Each chapter also includes a **Today's Professional** feature that connects to where students want to be in the near term. In these, recent graduates discuss various areas of marketing as an avenue for employment. Both of these features demonstrate marketing's relevance in a vivid and immediate way. In addition, **Career Tips** at the end of every chapter encourage students to think about their personal brand and how to market themselves effectively to future employers. Finally, instructors can choose to assign a personal **Marketing Plan Exercise** that asks students to apply principles concepts to create a marketing plan for the most important product they will ever market: themselves.

2. ***Relevant content integration.*** Coverage of **ethics, globalization, and social media has been integrated** throughout the chapters to emphasize the impact of these important topics on every marketing decision. Organizations don't have "ethical Tuesday" or celebrate "global Wednesday." Students must understand how these concepts integrate into key principles content. Finally, we've incorporated coverage of **marketing in nonprofit settings** throughout the text to appeal to students pursuing careers in this growing area.

3. ***Results-driven technology.*** Four **Interactive Assignments** in each chapter delivered via McGraw-Hill *Connect®* allow students to apply what they've just learned in a dynamic, interactive way. One of these, the **Social Media in Action** assignment, asks the student to view the chapter concepts as they relate to social media, an increasingly important tool in mar-keting as well as many other areas of business. In addition, each chapter has an associated **Video Case,** often featuring the executive that appears at the start of the chapter. The video case introduces students to marketing principles as they are practiced at both large corporations and the kind of small businesses at which most students will begin their careers.

HELLO my name is

Guy Lochiatto
MassBay Community College

. . . applying and integrating ethics, globalization, and social media makes it easier for the students to understand the impact of these on consumer behavior throughout marketing and makes them less generalized.

The global and social media icons highlight integrated coverage, allowing students and instructors to quickly locate relevant content within each chapter.

HELLO my name is

David Bourff
Boise State University

Powerful. Most of what I hear from students is that they'd like to hear more of the "how" when it comes to everything. This is a great way to show the how aspect in a fun way.

MAKING MARKETING PERSONAL

Marketing creates value by making it personal for both students and instructors. Students are always learning fundamental marketing principles through the lens of how they will apply those principles in the future. In addition, we have organized the material into 14 concise chapters to focus students on the fundamental principles topics they need to know rather than overwhelming them with details better suited to an advanced marketing course. This streamlined approach frees you up to personalize your course in various ways, by inviting guests to speak during class, assigning McGraw-Hill's Practice Marketing simulation, or incorporating other activities into your lectures.

The layout and terminology of the chapter content presented below clearly reflect the intent of the book to offer familiar topics in a way that relates to students. We have designed all of our chapters to maximize the most valuable content for a principles text.

PART ONE: Marketing in the Twenty-First Century

1. **Why Marketing Matters to You**
   Chapter 1 sets the stage by explaining to students the role and relevance of marketing to their lives. Students who have little affinity for marketing and are taking the course only because they "have to" will understand the relevance of marketing from the very first day of class.
2. **Strategic Planning for a Successful Future**
   Chapter 2 explains the importance of strategic marketing planning for businesses and nonprofit organizations. Students are introduced to the elements of a marketing plan and then allowed to apply their knowledge as they develop a marketing plan focused on the most important product of their lives: themselves.
3. **Analyzing Your Environment**
   In Chapter 3, students learn how the external environment influences marketing in an integrated way by examining how both local and global factors impact large companies, small businesses, and nonprofit organizations.

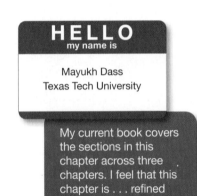

HELLO
my name is

Mayukh Dass
Texas Tech University

My current book covers the sections in this chapter across three chapters. I feel that this chapter is . . . refined and more useful than the ones I currently use.

PART TWO: Understanding Your Customer

HELLO
my name is

Rajiv Mehta
New Jersey Institute
of Technology

4. **Marketing Research**
   In addition to describing the importance of good marketing research and the marketing research process, Chapter 4 illustrates how quality marketing research can drive other marketing decisions, such as new product development and sales forecasts, that are critical to an organization's bottom line.
5. **Knowing Your Customer: Consumer and Business**
   Chapter 5 introduces students to the critical elements of buyer behavior for both consumers and businesses in one chapter to help them better understand the similarities and differences between B2C and B2B marketing.

   This chapter integrates information from two chapters on B2C and B2B into one concisely. Thus, it makes teaching issues related to target market consumers and industrial buyers a lot easier given that there [are] time constraints. What's more, this approach enables the discussion of the elements of marketing faster.

6. **Developing Your Product**
   Chapter 6 presents the product development process in a comprehensive way that reflects the real-world challenges in developing and marketing a new product. It also covers traditional product concepts like the consumer adoption process and the product life cycle and illustrates how factors such as ethics play a role in product decisions.
7. **Segmenting, Targeting, and Finding Your Market Position**
   In Chapter 7, students are exposed to the essential concepts of market segmentation and positioning in a dynamic way and learn about the challenges of segmenting and targeting markets in both the U.S. and in other parts of the world.

PART THREE: Reaching Your Customer

8. **Promotional Strategies**

   Chapter 8 makes students aware of the various tools they can use to communicate the value of their products to customers and the shifting dynamics of promotional strategies, ranging from social media to personal selling.

9. **Supply Chain and Logistics Management: Adding Value for Your Customers**

George Bass
Kennesaw State Technology

> You took the singularly most boring part of Principles and made it clear and interesting. You also showed via relevancy both sides of the buying/selling equation when it comes to price.

   Chapter 9 includes coverage of transportation and inventory management—practical topics that real-world professionals cite as necessary skills for new college graduates to possess. In addition, it has more coverage of logistics than any other book for a very practical reason: Logistics is one of the fastest growing and highest salary-generating fields in all of marketing.

HELLO my name is

Marilyn Liebrenz-Himes
The George Washington University

> The Hunt/Mello chapter really provides a readable condensation of promotional strategies, that touch on, I feel, the critical elements of this topic. Our past text devoted four chapters to this topic, going into such great detail that I feel the key points were obscured by all the details.

10. **Pricing for Profit and Customer Value**

    In response to market feedback on how instructors actually teach their course, pricing concepts have been consolidated into one chapter instead of two. Chapter 10 incorporates the most important elements of this topic into a concise chapter that engages students and introduces them to pricing terms and strategy without burdening them with the additional content that is more appropriate in an advanced marketing course.

11. **Building Successful Brands: Your Organization, Your Product, and Yourself**

    Chapter 11 shows how tools such as social media and product packaging can be helpful in building a successful brand. In addition to learning how to measure brand performance and how to successfully develop a brand for businesses and nonprofit organizations, students are also asked to consider how to manage their own personal brand.

PART FOUR: Responding to Your Customer

12. **Managing Your Customer Relationships**

    Chapter 12 focuses on one of the core aspects of any great marketing organization: customer service. Whether they work for a retailer, manufacturer, service provider, or nonprofit organization, the concepts and strategies discussed in this chapter will help students see the link between customer service and brand loyalty.

13. **Social Responsibility and Sustainability**

    Chapter 13 emphasizes the role social responsibility plays in marketing decisions by illustrating the economic and social benefits of developing sustainable marketing strategies. Finally, the chapter looks at the challenges marketers face in developing sustainable strategies across the globe.

Connie Golden
Lakeland Community College

> This is an excellent chapter to include! I have taught this course for many years, and this has been a huge shortfall in teaching the course. It is good to see some coverage of "Control."

14. **Measuring Marketing Performance**

    The final chapter wraps up the journey through marketing by teaching students how to measure marketing performance and compensate marketing employees. Ultimately, some of the strategies students implement will work and some will not, but it is essential that they be able to evaluate the success or failure of their ideas and make the appropriate adjustments.

EXECUTIVE PERSPECTIVE

Michael Friloux
Senior Vice President of Business Development
Citynet

Michael Friloux had a plan. He chose computer science as his major in college and intended to pursue a technical career in software development and software engineering. But Friloux quickly discovered that planning is a dynamic process and that meeting his objective of finding a job meant modifying his plans. After college, Friloux accepted a job with a communications firm, which allowed him to combine his technical skills with the marketing knowledge he had acquired during college. Over the course of his career as a product developer, sales engineer, and vice president of marketing and network planning, Friloux sharp-

recognize that knowledge is power. To you will also need social skills, integrit ethic, and determination. People with skills universally outperform their pee peers have superior technical abilities the best engineer, accountant, lawyer, the world, but if people don't like wor they won't.

How is marketing relevant to your at Citynet?

Developing marketing strategy and our organization's marketing plan is sor

Executive Perspective Each chapter opens with an executive's perspective on the role marketing plays in his or her business. The highly successful, senior-level executives who have been interviewed for these features purposefully come from backgrounds outside of marketing. Their perspectives illustrate the need for successful leaders in any organization to be effective marketers. In addition, in contrast to the in-chapter examples, which reference large, recognizable companies, the executives highlighted in the opening feature for the most part work for small, entrepreneurial companies,

HELLO
my name is

Shirley Arlene Green
Indian River State College

the kind of companies at which students are more likely to work after graduation. Finally, we link the Executive Perspective closely to the chapter content by including a tie-back feature at multiple points throughout the chapter. The tie-back feature presents the executive's perspective on how the chapter concepts relate to his or her personal and professional experience, once again allowing students to see the relevance of chapter concepts to their future careers.

HELLO
my name is

Timothy W. Aurand
Northern Illinois University

[The] [e]xecutive perspectives are excellent. Very current, well written.

WOW! . . . The integration of personalization from an executive perspective scattered throughout the text topics brings reality into the discussion and shows how these elements actually work in a business environment.

Forecast The Forecast at the start of each chapter sets the expectation for what students will encounter in the chapter and further reinforces the relevancy of the chapter concepts to students, whether they're marketing majors or not. The Forecast feature concludes with key questions—one for each learning objective—that students should keep in mind as they learn the topics in each chapter.

FORECAST

This chapter explores the importance of strategic planning in marketing. Executing a thoughtful strategic marketing plan is the most likely path to sustainable business success. The chapter examines the role of a mission statement, situation analysis, marketing strategy, global marketing strategy, and other elements of an effective marketing plan. As you read through the chapter, consider the following key questions:

1. Why is strategic planning important for marketing?
2. What elements should a marketing plan include?
3. How do I evaluate the effectiveness of a firm's mission statement?
4. What tools can I use to analyze my firm's situation externally and internally?

5. What strategic directions can a firm take?
6. How does globalization affect marketing strategy?
7. Why is strategic planning critical for nonprofit organizations?

STUDENT-FOCUSED FEATURES

Today's Professional Each chapter contains a profile of a recent (within five years) business graduate that focuses on how to market oneself. These professionals describe how developing their personal brand has helped advance their careers. We have found that profiles of these successful new professionals resonate just as much with our students as the chapter-opening descriptions of executives.

HELLO
my name is

Van Wood
Virginia Commonwealth
University

Theory and practice go hand in hand. The authors provide the theoretical basis for the importance of social media and then with the examples and exercises create a learning environment that is right on target.

Social Media in Action The Social Media in Action feature provides students with an example of social media at work in the real world. The feature discusses how a company is using social media to market its products. The online, interactive exercise that accompanies the feature asks students to make decisions about the best use of social media in a specific marketing scenario, effectively preparing them to make such decisions later in their careers.

connect | MARKETING
Interactive Assignment 3-1
Social Media in Action

Social media have become powerful tools for small business marketers looking to compete with larger firms. Jill Nelson is the founder of Oregon-based Ruby Receptionists, which provides virtual receptionists for other small businesses. She believes that social media level the playing field with bigger competitors. One of Nelson's biggest target markets is attorneys needing a virtual receptionist. When she hears via social media that an attorney has

SUMMARY

LO 3-1 Differentiate betwe[en] direct and indirect compet[itors.]

The competitive environmen[t] the direct competitors a firm faces and [di]rect competitors seeking to take mar[ket] and profits. The most commonly discus[sed] of competition is direct competition. Di[rect] petition occurs when products perfor[m the] same function compete against each o[ther.] rect competition occurs when product[s offer] an alternative solution to the same mar[ket.]

LO 3-2 Summarize the ma[jor] external factors that influe[nce the] marketing environment.

There are six major external factors t[hat influ]ence the marketing environment: e[conomic,] demographic, sociocultural, politica[l, legal,] and technological. Economic factors [...]

Interactive Assignment Each chapter includes several online exercises that provide students with an opportunity to apply the concepts they've just learned to a real-world scenario. These interactive assignments, available in McGraw-Hill *Connect* Marketing, are integrated into the chapters to offer students a total learning experience.

Summary Each chapter concludes with a summary section organized by learning objective that reemphasizes the key points made in the chapter. The summary provides a great study tool for students, particularly when used in conjunction with McGraw-Hill LearnSmart®, an adaptive learning program that helps students learn faster, study more efficiently, and retain more knowledge.

Personal Marketing Plan Exercise A Marketing Plan Exercise appears in each chapter. In a unique twist, students will learn the elements of the marketing plan in the context of marketing the most important product or brand of their life: themselves. In addition to really engaging students in understanding successful marketing plans, the project is also a fun alternative to more traditional class assignments.

MARKETING PLAN EXERCISE

In this chapter we discussed the importance of analyzing the marketing environment. In the next section of the marketing plan exercise, you will analyze the environment you will be entering upon graduation. Your assignment is to prepare a market summary for the job or graduate school program you discussed as your objective in Chapter 1. If your objective is a specific job or career, you need to answer questions like

- What is the average salary?
- What are the companies that are best positioned to offer the kind of job you want?
- Are there jobs in this field located where you want to live?
- What is the total size and growth rate of the industry you are planning to enter?
- What is the current unemployment rate in that field and what percentage of jobs are filled by new college graduates?

- What schools offer this program?
- What are those schools' admission statistics (percentage accepted, tuition and fees, financial aid available, etc.)?
- What are the average Grade Point Average (GPA) and entrance exam (LSAT, GMAT, MCAT, etc.) scores?
- What is the average starting salary for graduates of these programs?

It is important to conduct an honest environmental assessment. Students sometimes have unrealistic expectations of what their first job out of school or a graduate program may be like. The better you understand the environment you are entering, the better you will be able to market yourself and your skills to succeed in it.

HELLO
my name is

Laurel Cook
University of Arkansas

I would use this text especially for the social media applications. This is where college students are today & represents HOW they get & give information. I love it in each chapter in the H-M text!

Social Media Application Social Media Application features ask students to analyze the social media activities of the organizations with which they are most familiar. Rather than putting themselves in the position of the marketer, students evaluate social media strategies from the perspective of those being marketed to. In addition, the Social Media Application feature is designed to remain relevant even as technology evolves; thus it does not reference Facebook, Twitter, or other specific social media applications.

Ethical Challenge Ethics is an essential element in marketing and in AACSB assessment requirements. We include in each chapter real-world examples of business ethics that highlight how ethical issues permeate every marketing decision.

ETHICAL CHALLENGE

The economic environment has changed in the past decade due to stock market losses, rising health care costs, and declining property values. As a result, many seniors were forced to look for new ways to generate income after their working careers ended. One of the primary beneficiaries of this shift was firms marketing reverse mortgages.

Reverse mortgages allow older homeowners to tap into the equity of their home and receive payments against its value. Typically, when the homeowners die, their heirs must repay the loan, including interest and fees. For the past two decades, the vast majority of reverse mortgages have

Like many other industries, the reverse mortgage business contains two sides of an ethical dilemma. On one side are those marketers who are increasing profits by helping seniors access the equity in their home; on the other are those who are potentially taking advantage of desperate seniors who may not fully understand what a reverse mortgage is. Please use the ethical decision-making framework to answer the following questions:

1. Which parties are impacted by reverse mortgages marketing strategies?
2. If you are a bank hoping to increase profits, would

Video Case Video cases in each chapter, often tied to the executive featured throughout the chapter, provide an engaging way for students to see how the chapter concepts are applied in large and small corporations.

01:21 / 04:18

Career Tips We offer examples and ideas related to the chapter topic that can help students market themselves and develop their own personal brand. This feature reinforces the importance of marketing to the students' lives. The Career Tips often feature the executives introduced at the start of the chapter to further reinforce the connection between the feature and concepts discussed.

CAREER TIPS

Marketing Your Future

You have read in this chapter about the marketing environment and how external factors influence that environment for both for-profit and nonprofit organizations. As you think about your future, you may be considering a career in the nonprofit sector. Erin Brewer, who was featured in the Executive Perspective at the beginning of the chapter, spent a decade working for various nonprofit organizations and has some tips for securing a nonprofit position.

- **Gain experience.** Before you start interviewing for full-time positions, get some experience in charity work as a volunteer or an intern. The vast majority of nonprofits utilize both, so plenty of opportunities are available. A combination of volunteerism and internships provides the biggest advantage to a job seeker. It shows the hiring nonprofit that you're passionate about helping and that you know how similar organizations function. Some people begin their careers in the nonprofit world to gain significant hands-on experience

before making the leap to the corporate world. Others go the reverse route, getting their feet wet on the corporate side, and then taking on positions of greater responsibility in the charitable realm. The same principles of marketing apply to both sides of the spectrum and the smart professional can readily adapt.

- **Craft an effective resume.** Communicating who you are on a single piece of paper is a daunting task! Make sure that your resume conveys the right things about you. Be succinct, be compelling, be professional, and show a bit of personality. Highlight your unique accomplishments rather than simply listing your responsibilities, tailor your resume for each job you apply for, and always run spell check.

- **Put your intangibles to work.** Let your charm, gift for the spoken word, and passion for service shine. Once you have secured an interview, be prepared. Anticipate questions you may be asked and prepare a brief description of yourself and your goals. Be ready to ask some questions of your own. (To this day, I won't hire a candidate that doesn't ask a question.) Use your marketing coursework to your advantage by "spinning" your experience to suit the position you hope to attain. Be polite, be punctual, be honest, and most importantly, be yourself. And always send a thank you note.

Across the country, instructors and students continue to raise an important question: How can marketing courses further support students throughout the learning process to shape future business leaders? While there is no one solution, we see the impact of new learning technologies and innovative study tools that not only fully engage students in course material but also inform instructors of the students' skill and comprehension levels.

Interactive learning tools, including those offered through McGraw-Hill *Connect*, are being implemented to increase teaching effectiveness and learning efficiency in thousands of colleges and universities. By facilitating a stronger connection with the course and incorporating the latest technologies—such as McGraw-Hill LearnSmart, an adaptive learning program—these tools enable students to succeed in their college careers, which will ultimately increase the percentage of students completing their postsecondary degrees and create the business leaders of the future.

McGraw-Hill CONNECT

Connect is an all-digital teaching and learning environment designed from the ground up to work with the way instructors and students think, teach, and learn. As a digital teaching, assignment, and assessment platform, *Connect* strengthens the link among faculty, students, and coursework, helping everyone accomplish more in less time.

LearnSmart
The smartest way to get from B to A

LearnSmart is the most widely used and intelligent adaptive learning resource. It is proven to strengthen memory recall, improve course retention, and boost grades by distinguishing between what students know and what they don't know and honing in on the concepts that they are most likely to forget. LearnSmart continuously adapts to each student's needs by building an individual learning path. As a result, students study smarter and retain more knowledge.

SmartBook
A revolution in reading

Fueled by LearnSmart, SmartBook is the first and only adaptive reading experience available today. SmartBook personalizes content for each student in a continuously adapting reading experience. Reading is no longer a passive and linear experience, but an engaging and dynamic one where students are more likely to master and retain important concepts, coming to class better prepared.

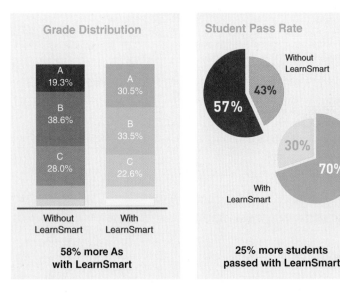

Grade Distribution

Without LearnSmart	With LearnSmart
A 19.3%	A 30.5%
B 38.6%	B 33.5%
C 28.0%	C 22.6%

58% more As with LearnSmart

Student Pass Rate

Without LearnSmart 43%
57%

30%
70%

With LearnSmart

25% more students passed with LearnSmart

LearnSmart Achieve
A revolution in learning

Leveraging a continuously adaptive learning path, the program adjusts to each student individually as he or she progresses through the program, creating just-in-time learning experiences by presenting interactive content that is tailored to each student's needs. This model is proven to accelerate learning and strengthen memory recall.

Interactive Assignments
A higher level of learning

Throughout the chapter, students will be prompted to complete a variety of interactive assignments that will require them to apply what they have learned in a real-world scenario. These online exercises will help students assess their understanding of the concepts.

Video Cases
Real-world assignments

Industry-leading video support helps students understand concepts and see how real companies and professionals implement marketing principles in the workplace. The video cases highlight companies from a broad range of industries, sizes, and geographic locations, giving students a perspective of marketing from a variety of businesses. In addition, five of the videos feature the executives profiled within the chapter (Chapters 1, 3, 8, 12, and 14).

Video Overviews
A multimedia learning experience

Specific to each learning objective, the video overviews in *Connect* are engaging, online, professional presentations covering the key concepts from the chapter. They teach students the core learning objectives in a multimedia format, bringing the content of the course to life.

McGraw-Hill Connect Plus

McGraw-Hill Education reinvents the textbook-learning experience for today's students with *Connect Plus*, providing students with a cost-saving alternative to the traditional textbook. A seamless integration of a media rich eBook and *Connect, Connect Plus* provides all of the *Connect* features plus the following:

- A web-optimized eBook, allowing for anytime, anywhere online access to the textbook.
- Powerful search function to pinpoint and connect key concepts in a snap.
- Highlighting and note-taking capabilities as well as access to shared instructors' notations.

Visit **www.huntmello.com** to learn more about how the author uses *Connect* and to register for your personal demonstration today!

CONNECT INTERACTIVE ASSIGNMENT GUIDE

Throughout this product, you will encounter Interactive Assignments that ask you to log onto McGraw-Hill *Connect* to complete exercises related to the concepts you just learned. The following guide provides you with a quick reference for locating the Interactive Assignments related to each chapter.

Hunt and Mello's *Marketing* offers you a complete package to prepare you for your course.

McGraw-Hill CONNECT

McGraw-Hill *Connect* strengthens the link between faculty, students, and course-work, helping everyone accomplish more in less time.

Efficient Administrative Capabilities

Connect offers you, the instructor, auto-gradable material in an effort to facilitate teaching and learning.

Reviewing Homework	Giving Tests or Quizzes	Grading
60 minutes without Connect → 15 minutes with Connect	60 minutes without Connect → 0 minutes with Connect	60 minutes without Connect → 12 minutes with Connect

Student Progress Tracking

Connect keeps instructors informed about how each student, section, and class is performing, allowing for more productive use of lecture and office hours. The progress tracking function enables instructors to:

- View scored work immediately and track individual or group performance with assignment and grade reports.
- Access an instant view of student or class performance relative to learning objectives.
- Collect data and generate reports required by many accreditation organizations, such as AACSB.

Connect and LearnSmart allow students to present course material to students in more ways than just the explanations they hear from me directly. Because of this, students are processing the material in new ways, requiring them to think. I now have more students asking questions in class because the more we think, the more we question.

Instructor at Hinds Community College

Instructor Library

Connect's instructor library serves as a one-stop, secure site for essential course materials, allowing you to save prep time before class. The instructor resources found in the library include:

- **Instructor's Manual.** The Instructor's Manual is a comprehensive resource designed to support you in effectively teaching your course. It includes learning objectives, lecture outlines, supplemental lectures, answers to discussion questions and end-of-chapter exercises, notes for video cases, and a guide on how to effectively integrate *Connect* into your course.

- **Test Bank.** The Test Bank offers more than 2,000 questions, which are categorized by topic, learning objective, level of difficulty, Bloom's Taxonomy, and accreditation standards (e.g., AACSB). The Test Bank contains true/false, multiple choice, and essay questions.

- **PowerPoint Presentations.** The PowerPoint presentations feature slides that you can personalize and use to help present concepts to the students effectively. Each set of slides contains figures and tables from the text.

- **Videos.** The video library allows instructors to access new, relevant videos covering a variety of companies and industries, all of which tie deeply to the content and often feature the executives profiled within each chapter. The videos can be used to support in-class or online lectures and are also available on DVD (ISBN: 0077636570).

Resources are also available on the secure instructor side of the book-specific Online Learning Center at **www.huntmello.com.**

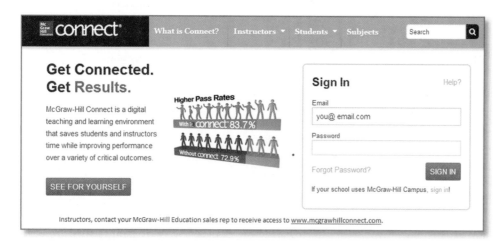

Create

Instructors can now tailor their teaching resources to match the way they teach! With McGraw-Hill Create, **www.mcgrawhillcreate.com,** instructors can easily rearrange chapters, combine material from other content sources, and quickly upload and integrate their own content, like course syllabi or teaching notes. Find the right content in Create by searching through thousands of leading McGraw-Hill textbooks. Arrange the material to fit your teaching style. Order a Create book and receive a complimentary print review copy in three to five business days or a complimentary electronic review copy via e-mail within one hour. Go to **www.mcgrawhillcreate.com** today and register.

Tegrity Campus

Tegrity makes class time available 24/7 by automatically capturing every lecture in a searchable format for students to review when they study and complete assignments. With a simple one-click start-and-stop process, you capture all computer screens and corresponding audio. Students can replay any part of any class with easy-to-use browser-based viewing on a PC or Mac. Educators know that the more students can see, hear, and experience class resources, the better they learn. In fact, studies prove it. With patented Tegrity "search anything" technology, students instantly recall key class moments for replay online or on iPods and mobile devices. Instructors can help turn all their students' study time into learning moments immediately supported by their lecture. To learn more about Tegrity, watch a two-minute Flash demo at **http://tegritycampus.mhhe.com.**

Blackboard® Partnership

McGraw-Hill Education and Blackboard have teamed up to simplify your life. Now you and your students can access *Connect* and Create right from within your Blackboard course—all with one single sign-on. The grade books are seamless, so when a student completes an integrated *Connect* assignment, the grade for that assignment automatically (and instantly) feeds your Blackboard grade center. Learn more at **www.domorenow.com.**

McGraw-Hill Campus™

McGraw-Hill Campus is a new one-stop teaching and learning experience available to users of any learning management system. This institutional service allows faculty and students to enjoy single sign-on (SSO) access to all McGraw-Hill Higher Education materials, including the award-winning McGraw-Hill *Connect* platform, from directly within the institution's website. With McGraw-Hill Campus, faculty receive instant access to teaching materials (e.g., eTextbooks, test banks, PowerPoint slides, animations, learning objects, etc.), allowing them to browse, search, and use any instructor ancillary content in our vast library at no additional cost to instructor or students.

In addition, students enjoy SSO access to a variety of free content (e.g., quizzes, flash cards, narrated presentations, etc.) and subscription-based products (e.g., McGraw-Hill *Connect*). With McGraw-Hill Campus enabled, faculty and students will never need to create another account to access McGraw-Hill products and services. Learn more at **www.mhcampus.com.**

Assurance of Learning Ready

Many educational institutions today focus on the notion of *assurance of learning,* an important element of some accreditation standards. *Marketing* is designed specifically to support instructors' assurance of learning initiatives with a simple yet powerful solution. Each test bank question for *Marketing* maps to a specific chapter learning objective listed in the text. Instructors can use our test bank software, EZ Test and EZ Test Online, to easily query for learning objectives that directly relate to the learning outcomes for their course. Instructors can then use the reporting features of EZ Test to aggregate student results in similar fashion, making the collection and presentation of assurance of learning data simple and easy.

AACSB Tagging

McGraw-Hill Education is a proud corporate member of AACSB International. Understanding the importance and value of AACSB accreditation, *Marketing* recognizes the curricula guidelines detailed in the AACSB standards for business accreditation by connecting selected questions in the text and the test bank to the six general knowledge and skill guidelines in the AACSB standards. The statements contained in *Marketing* are provided only as a guide for the users of this textbook. The AACSB leaves content coverage and assessment within the purview of individual schools, the mission of the school, and the faculty. While the *Marketing* teaching package makes no claim of any specific AACSB qualification or evaluation, we have within *Marketing* labeled selected questions according to the six general knowledge and skills areas.

McGraw-Hill Customer Experience Group Contact Information

At McGraw-Hill Education, we understand that getting the most from new technology can be challenging. That's why our services don't stop after you purchase our products. You can e-mail our Product Specialists 24 hours a day to get product training online. Or you can search our knowledge bank of Frequently Asked Questions on our support website. For Customer Support, call **800-331-5094** or visit **www.mhhe.com/support.** One of our Technical Support Analysts will be able to assist you in a timely fashion.

ACKNOWLEDGMENTS

We are deeply indebted to the many marketing scholars and instructors, business leaders and professionals, and colleagues and friends who have contributed their time, ideas, and insights to the development of this product. We appreciate your help and your shared passion for maximizing the educational experience of our students and future leaders.

We are also thankful to have had the privilege to work with all of the talented and thoughtful colleagues who reviewed each chapter throughout the development of this product, providing expert feedback to improve and refine the content. This product is much better and more beneficial to students because of the work that you did. We extend our sincere appreciation to all of the review and focus group participants who have contributed so much to our efforts.

Praveen Aggarwal,
University of Minnesota, Duluth

Bob Ahuja,
Xavier University

Mary Albrecht,
Maryville University

Keanon Alderson,
California Baptist University

Daniel Allen,
Utah State University

Cynthia Anderson,
Youngstown State University

Maria Aria,
Camden County College

Tim Aurand,
Northern Illinois University

Joe K. Ballenger,
Stephen F. Austin State University

Soumava Bandyopadhyay,
Lamar University

Jennifer Barr,
Richard Stockton College of New Jersey

Arne Baruca,
Sacred Heart University

George Bass,
Kennesaw State University

Charles Beem,
Bucks County Community College

Frank Benna,
Raritan Valley Community College

Tom Bilyeu,
Southwestern Illinois College

Nicholas Bosco,
Suffolk County Community College

David Bourff,
Boise State University

Michael Brady,
Florida State University

Cheryl Brown,
University of West Georgia

Kendrick Brunson,
Liberty University

Gary Brunswick,
Northern Michigan University

Kent Byus,
Texas A&M University, Corpus Christi

Kimberly Cade,
Houston Community College, Central

Carla Cardellio,
Schoolcraft College

Deborah Carter,
Coahoma Community College

Eric Carter,
California State University, Bakersfield

Debi Cartwright,
Truman State University

Gerald Cavallo,
Fairfield University

Piotr Chelminski,
Providence College

Haozhe Chen,
East Carolina University

Lisa Cherivtch,
Oakton Community College

Christina Chung,
Ramapo College of New Jersey

Janet Ciccarelli,
Herkimer County Community College

Reid Claxton,
East Carolina University

Steven Clinton,
Robert Morris University

Kyle Coble,
Lindenwood University

Kesha Coker,
Eastern Illinois University

Francisco Conejo,
University of Colorado, Denver

Mary Conran,
Temple University

Laurel Anne Cook,
University of Arkansas

Richard Cooper,
Lindenwood University

Tracy Cosenza,
University of Memphis

Ian Cross,
Bentley University

Anna Crowe,
University of San Diego

Mayukh Dass,
Texas Tech University

Larry Degaris,
University of Indianapolis

Beth Deinert,
Southeast Community College

George Deitz,
University of Memphis

Duleep Delpechitre,
University of Louisiana, Lafayette

Paul Dion,
Susquehanna University

Beibei Dong,
Lehigh University

Kathy Dougherty,
Maryville University

Howard Dover,
Salisbury University

Lawrence Duke,
Drexel University

Stu Dunlop,
Missouri Southern State University

Judy Eberhart,
Lindenwood University

Diane Edmondson,
Middle Tennessee State University

Ronald Feinberg,
Suffolk Community College

Troy Festervand,
Middle Tennessee State University

David Fleming,
Eastern Illinois University

Richard Flight,
Eastern Illinois University

Angel Fonseca,
Jackson College

Michael Fowler,
Brookdale Community College

Venessa Funches,
Auburn University, Montgomery

Carol Gaumer,
Frostburg State University

Connie Golden,
Lakeland Community College

Edward Gonsalves,
Boston College

Kimberly Grantham,
University of Georgia

Arlene Green,
Indian River State College

Mike Grier,
Central Piedmont Community College

Jamey Halleck,
Marshall University

Richard Hanna,
Northeastern University

Robert Harrison,
Western Michigan University

Kelli Hatin,
Adirondack Community College

Adrienne Hinds,
Northern Virginia Community College

Nasim Hosein,
Northwood University

Tarique Hossain,
California State Polytechnic University, Pomona

Jing Hu,
California State Polytechnic University, Pomona

Robert Hucks,
Bob Jones University

Janet Huetteman,
Fairfield University

Steven Huff,
Utah Valley University

Doug Hughes,
Michigan State University

James Jarrard,
University of Wisconsin, Platteville

Sean Jasso,
University of California, Riverside

Keith Jones,
Saint Leo University

Sungwoo Jung,
Columbus State University

Vishal Kashyap,
Xavier University

Sylvia Keyes,
Bridgewater State University

Tina Kiesler,
California State University, Northridge

Nancy Kimble,
Carroll Community College

Ann Kuzma,
Minnesota State University, Mankato

Jane Lang,
East Carolina University

Nikki Lee-Wingate,
Fairfield University

Fuan Li,
William Paterson University

Marilyn Liebrenz-Himes,
The George Washington University

Noah Lim,
University of Wisconsin, Madison

Guy Lochiatto,
MassBay Community College

Subhash Lonial,
University of Louisville

Pat Lupino,
Nassau Community College

Lisa Machado,
Southeast Community College, Lincoln

Deanna Mader,
Marshall University

Cesar Maloles,
California State University, East Bay

Gayle Marco,
Robert Morris University

Peter Maresco,
Sacred Heart University

Anil Mathur,
Hofstra University

William Matthews,
William Paterson University

Brian Mazur,
Schoolcraft College

Enda McGovern,
Sacred Heart University

Rajiv Mehta,
New Jersey Institute of Technology

Havva Meric,
East Carolina University

William Merkle,
Bob Jones University

Deborah Merrigan,
Rockland Community College

Marty Meyers,
University of Wisconsin, Stevens Point

Iris Mohr,
St. John's University

Detra Montoya,
University of Washington

Melissa Moore,
Mississippi State University

Jay Mulki,
Northeastern University

Thomas Myers,
Virginia Commonwealth University

Gergana Nenkov,
Boston College

Louis Nzegwu,
University of Wisconsin, Platteville

Matt O'Hern,
University of Oregon

Joanne Orabone,
Community College of Rhode Island

Judy Orfao,
Middlesex Community College

Karen Overton,
Houston Community College, Southwest

Debra Perosio,
Cornell University

Edward Petkus,
Ramapo College of New Jersey

Julie Pharr,
Tennessee Tech University

Warren Purdy,
University of Southern Maine

Sekar Raju,
Iowa State University

Bruce Ramsey,
Franklin University

Sampath Kumar Ranganathan,
University of Wisconsin, Green Bay

Mohammed Rawwas,
University of Northern Iowa

Timothy Reisenwitz,
Valdosta State University

Eddie Rhee,
Stonehill College

Brent Richard,
North Central Michigan College

David Robinson,
University of California, Berkeley

Jessica Rogers,
Texas A&M University

Ann Root,
Florida Atlantic University

Carol Rowey,
Community College of Rhode Island

Donald Roy,
Middle Tennessee State University

Catherine Ruggieri,
St. John's University

Alan Sandomir,
University of Utah

Kumar Sarangee,
Santa Clara University

Fritz Scherz,
Morrisville State College

Roberta Schultz,
Western Michigan University

Eric Schulz,
Utah State University

Joe Schwartz,
Georgia College and State University

Sandipan Sen,
Southeast Missouri State University

Ravi Shanmugam,
Santa Clara University

Rob Simon,
University of Nebraska, Lincoln

Ian Skurkik,
University of Utah

Rudy Soliz,
Houston Community College

Karen Stewart,
Richard Stockton College of New Jersey

Pete Stone,
Spartanburg Community College

Randy Stuart,
Kennesaw State University

Ramendra Thakur,
University of Louisiana, Lafayette

Scott Thorne,
Southeast Missouri State University

Patricia Todd,
Western Kentucky University

Deborah Toomey,
Northwest Missouri State University

Dennis Tootelian,
California State University, Sacramento

Hope Torkornoo,
Kennesaw State University

Ed Valenski,
Long Island University

Laura Valenti,
Nicholls State University

Sal Veas,
Santa Monica College

Ann Veeck,
Western Michigan University

Franck Vigneron,
California State University, Northridge

Jorge Villa,
Park University

Mary Walker,
Xavier University

Michael Walsh,
West Virginia University

Ursula Wefers,
Plymouth State University

Diane Whitney,
University of Maryland, College Park

Debbora Whitson,
California State Polytechnic University, Pomona

Natalie Winter,
California Baptist University

Van Wood,
Virginia Commonwealth University

Jefrey Woodall,
York College of Pennsylvania

Poh-Lin Yeoh,
Bentley University

Mark Yi-Cheon Yim,
Canisius College

James Zemanek,
East Carolina University

This product would not have been possible without the effort and expertise of many people. First and foremost, we would like to recognize and thank the entire editorial and marketing teams at McGraw-Hill Higher Education that have made this product possible. We are very thankful to our executive editor, Sankha Basu, who surrounded us with the best team in all of higher education publishing. We are thankful for our development editor, Gabriela Gonzalez, for keeping us on track and focused on all of the integrated aspects of the product. We are thankful for Donielle Xu, a truly amazing marketing manager, whose vision was instrumental in communicating the message of our product. We are thankful for Cortney Kieffer, who was our McGraw-Hill field representative when we came to Arkansas State University. Cortney was our first exposure to McGraw-Hill, and her professionalism, dedication to our students, and friendship made us want to be part of the McGraw-Hill family. We are thankful for Ann Torbert, Lori Koetters, Keri Johnson, Debra Kubiak, Doug Hughes, Paul Ducham, and all of the talented McGraw-Hill publisher's representatives whose guidance and feedback made the product much better.

Additionally, we are especially thankful for our content development editor, Emily Hatteberg, who has made every page of this product better through her counsel, advice, and extraordinary efforts. We cannot imagine writing this without her. It has been our pleasure and privilege to work with these incredibly talented and skilled professionals who have shaped the final product that you are about to read.

We also want to thank our colleagues in the College of Business at Arkansas State University. It is an honor every day to get to work with brilliant people who genuinely and passionately care about the education of our students. We want to give special thanks to our department chair, Gail Hudson, and our administrative assistant, Ricky Miller, for their help during this process. Their support and friendship is priceless, and we feel very thankful to be part of the Red Wolf Nation and professors at a truly world-class institution.

We want to thank our families for their love, support, and patience while we developed this product. We want to thank the great faculty members at Oklahoma State University and the University of Tennessee for the training and knowledge they gave us during our doctoral programs. We want to thank our many great colleagues in the private sector, at companies including Williams, Citynet, Playtex, and Unilever, who provided us with experiences that sharpened our focus on the practical applications of marketing and preparing our students for today's competitive job market.

Finally, we want to thank our students. Being a marketing professor is the best job in the world because of the students we get to teach, help, and learn from. The great students at Arkansas State University and throughout the country and the world drove our decision to create this product. Marketing is an extremely important topic for their careers and their lives, and we hope we have developed a product to help them succeed and achieve their dreams.

DETAILED CONTENTS

PART ONE
Marketing in the Twenty-First Century

Michael Friloux
Senior Vice President of Business Development

Citynet
http://citynet.com/

Citynet is a regional telecommunications company headquartered in West Virginia.

Steve DeVore
Senior Vice President and General Manager

Twin Oaks Integrated Marketing
http://www.thetwinoaks.com/

Twin Oaks is a strategic sales and marketing resource that delivers integrated shopper marketing solutions for consumer goods and retailer clients.

Erin Brewer
Managing Partner

RedPin Bowling Lounge and The Basement Modern Diner
http://www.bowlredpin.com/

RedPin is a combination restaurant, bowling alley, and bar in Oklahoma City. It boasts 10 bowling lanes; a full-service bar; space for private parties; a menu of local, made-from-scratch fare; and a large canal-front patio.

Chapter 1
WHY MARKETING MATTERS TO YOU

LEARNING OBJECTIVES

After reading this chapter, you should be able to

At the beginning of each chapter, you'll see a list of learning objectives that identify the key topics you need to master. You can also use the list as an outline for taking notes as you read through the chapter.

LO 1-1 Define marketing and describe a marketer's role in creating, communicating, and delivering value.

LO 1-2 Differentiate among the various eras in the history of marketing.

LO 1-3 Distinguish between consumer needs and consumer wants.

LO 1-4 Explain each of the four elements in the marketing mix.

LO 1-5 Discuss the importance of globalization in the field of marketing.

LO 1-6 Evaluate the potential benefits of corporate social responsibility.

LO 1-7 Demonstrate the relationship between ethical business practices and marketplace success.

LO 1-8 Analyze the functions of marketing beyond the for-profit firm.

EXECUTIVE PERSPECTIVE

Steve DeVore
Senior Vice President and General Manager
Twin Oaks Integrated Marketing

Steve DeVore came to marketing late. DeVore majored in journalism in college, but discovered a passion for marketing during an introductory marketing course he took his last year of college. He consequently pursued marketing internships to prepare for his career. After graduation, he worked for a traditional advertising agency for several years before joining Saatchi and Saatchi X, a creative communications company, where he worked with some of the largest companies in the world, including Walmart and Procter & Gamble, on their shopper marketing efforts. Shopper marketing is a rapidly growing area of marketing which is designed to drive sales growth by improving consumers' shopping experience. Today, DeVore leads Twin Oaks, a fully integrated shopper marketing agency.

What has been the most important thing in making you successful at your job?

Three things:

1. Success depends heavily on relationships. No one gets to the top on their own, and if people don't respect you for doing the right thing or think you're a jerk, you'll never be in a position to lead.
2. You have to be restless. If you get complacent and don't work every day like you have something to prove, you're dead. Always "play up a level"; meaning, if you're a manager, begin to think like a director. Try to understand the why behind everything: every idea, every decision, every behavior.
3. A little luck goes a long way. But here's the thing: People who work hard are luckier than those who don't. There is a direct correlation. It helps to be sharp, but sometimes, you just have to chalk it up to timing. Regardless, don't be a victim. Those who persevere come out the other side much stronger and more determined.

What advice would you give soon-to-be graduates?

It's not enough to do your job well. That just keeps you from getting fired. Advancing in your career means adding value above and beyond your job requirements. A good litmus test for how valuable of an asset you are is to imagine what would happen if you were to get pulled off of your team or out of your organization. Would they suffer?

How is marketing relevant to your role at Twin Oaks?

I am the leader of a team whose focus is developing great marketing to improve the shopping experience of consumers. Our clients realize the importance of marketing and ask for our help in giving consumers the best possible experience so that they will buy again and again from our clients. In addition, I'm always marketing myself to clients so they will want to work with me and my team.

What do you consider your personal brand to be?

I learned in college that a brand is a name, term, symbol, design, or any combination of these that identifies and differentiates a firm's products. Steve DeVore is a brand and reflects what those around me think of when they hear my name. I hope my brand is that I'm someone who does the right thing, is passionate about the things that matter the most, and has a positive influence on others. Former Dallas Cowboys receiver Michael Irvin once said that the ability to influence others is the greatest gift someone can have, and I truly believe that.

Steve DeVore
Senior Vice President and General Manager

TWINOAKS

neptune

Twin Oaks Integrated Marketing
http://www.thetwinoaks.com/

Twin Oaks is a strategic sales and marketing resource that delivers integrated shopper marketing solutions for consumer goods and retailer clients.

3

FORECAST

This chapter explores the importance of marketing to businesses of all sizes, nonprofit organizations, and individuals. Marketing matters to each of us regardless of our background, college major, or future plans. The chapter examines what marketing is, how it is being impacted by global forces, and the importance of corporate social responsibility and ethics in this dynamic field. As you read through the chapter, consider the following key questions:

1. Why does marketing matter to an organization?
2. How has marketing changed throughout the past century?
3. What is the difference between needs and wants?
4. What things can I do to influence consumer demand for my product?

5. How does globalization impact marketing activities?
6. Why is it important to be a good corporate citizen?
7. Why are ethical business practices so important to marketing?
8. How do nonprofit organizations market themselves?

The Forecast at the start of each chapter sets the expectation for what you will encounter in the chapter and further reinforces how the chapter concepts relate to you, whether you're a marketing major or not.

LO 1-1

Define marketing and describe a marketer's role in creating, communicating, and delivering value.

marketing

An organizational function and set of processes for creating, communicating, and delivering value to customers and managing customer relationships in ways that benefit the organization and its employees, customers, investors, and society as a whole.

THE VALUE OF MARKETING

Welcome to marketing. Wherever your life and career take you after reading this book, you can be assured that knowing how to implement marketing principles will be an important part of your professional success. In fact, there is a good chance you have already used marketing principles if you've ever had a job in retail sales or customer service. Marketing is an organizational function and set of processes for creating, communicating, and delivering value to customers and managing customer relationships in ways that benefit the organization and its employees, customers, investors, and society as a whole. This is a fairly lengthy definition, and it is important to understand the three components before we proceed.

Creating Value

Whether we are talking about a consumer product such as the iPad, social networking applications like Twitter, or educational software like the McGraw-Hill *Connect* package that accompanies this text, organizations today are constantly

Apple can charge higher prices than its competitors without fear of losing sales because of the value customers place on Apple products.

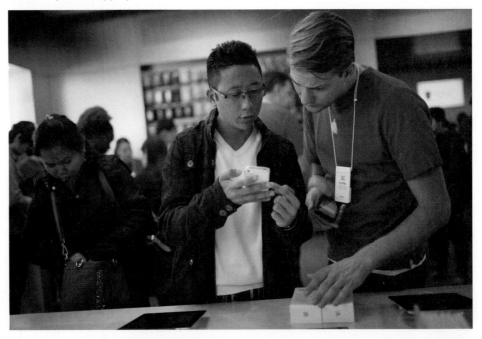

looking for new ways to create value for the customer. Customer value refers to the perceived benefits, both monetary and nonmonetary, that customers receive from a product—for example, making them safer (ADT home security), saving them money (GEICO), or making their lives easier (Apple iPhone)—compared to the cost associated with obtaining the product.

customer value
The perceived benefits, both monetary and nonmonetary, that customers receive from a product compared to the cost associated with obtaining it.

The key ingredient for creating value is providing consumers with benefits that meet their needs and wants. Merely creating a new product does not guarantee success. Over 80 percent of all new products fail, a percentage that remains consistent in good and bad economic conditions.[1] To create value, the new good, service, or idea must satisfy a perceived marketplace demand. Understanding marketplace demands before competitors do is one of the secrets of great marketing. We will explore specific strategies that support this effort, including analyzing the environment, conducting effective marketing research, and understanding customer behavior, in later chapters. Once a company has created a valuable product, it must communicate that value to potential customers.

Communicating Value

Business history is littered with failed companies that had a valuable offering, but lacked the capability to get that message out to potential customers. There may be a restaurant in the city where you live that serves great food; however, if the restaurant doesn't market itself well, you may never even know it exists. A firm must communicate not only what its product is but what value that product brings to potential customers. For example, a new Subway restaurant near your college campus might use online advertisements to communicate its convenient location, healthy alternatives, and monthly student specials.

Communicating value will be critical for you on a personal level as you begin looking for a job after you graduate. Imagine a human resources manager looking at a stack of 400 resumes, all from applicants with the same college degree as you, and trying to decide whom to interview. If your resume looks like every other resume in the stack, odds are your value will not be communicated. There are countless examples of job applicants who do not understand this fundamental point, then wonder why they are not getting the interviews and opportunities that others, who are better at marketing themselves, are getting. This book will help you learn to communicate your professional value in a variety of ways through features like the Career Tips section at the end of each chapter. In this chapter, the Career Tips feature focuses on moving your resume out of the stack and getting you into the interview. Once you've landed a job, delivering on the value you communicated will be key not only to keeping your job but also to moving up in your organization. In the same way, to be successful, firms must deliver on the value of the goods, services, and ideas they offer.

Many of the most successful firms in the world, including Coca-Cola, Walmart, and UPS, excel at managing their supply chains efficiently and have made delivering value a competitive advantage in their industries.

Delivering Value

Isn't it remarkable to think that you can buy Diet Coke at a grocery store in Chicago, a mall in San Francisco, a restaurant in Miami, a gas station in rural Arkansas, and practically everywhere in between? Millions

supply chain
A set of three or more companies directly linked by one or more of the upstream and downstream flows of products, services, finances, and information from a source to a customer.

logistics
That part of supply chain management that plans, implements, and controls the flow of goods, services, and information between the point of origin and the final customer.

LO 1-2
Differentiate among the various eras in the history of marketing.

production orientation
A marketing strategy in which the firm focused on efficient processes and production to create quality products and reduce unit costs.

of people throughout the world buy and enjoy Diet Coke, a phenomenon made possible by Coca-Cola's ability to deliver its product to countless places. Coca-Cola's supply chain is critical in delivering value. A firm's supply chain is "a set of three or more companies directly linked by one or more of the upstream and downstream flows of products, services, finances, and information from a source to a customer."[2] Members of the supply chain can include manufacturers, wholesalers, retailers, transportation companies, and other groups, depending on the specific industry. That part of supply chain management that plans, implements, and controls the flow of goods, services, and information between the point of origin and the final customer is called logistics. We will examine the challenges and strategies associated with logistics and supply chain management in a later chapter.

HISTORY OF MARKETING

Before we move beyond the definition and begin to understand modern marketing, it is important to understand how marketing has evolved.

Production Orientation

Prior to the 1920s, most firms throughout the United States and the rest of the developed world focused on production. Firms had a production orientation in which they focused on efficient processes and production to create quality products and reduce unit costs. Firms with a production orientation believed that quality products would simply sell themselves. The production era continued until the mid-1920s,

Henry Ford's production line innovation and success manufacturing the Model A automobile represents perhaps the height of the production orientation era, during which firms believed that quality products would sell themselves.

when consumer demand could not keep up with the growth in production and new strategies were needed to maximize success. In an effort to increase demand, firms sought to develop effective sales forces that could find customers for their growing production capacity.

Sales Orientation

As the size and impact of sales forces grew, many firms shifted to a sales orientation, in which personal selling and advertising were used to persuade consumers to buy new products and more of existing products. This strategy was especially important during the Great Depression when consumers did not have much money and firms competed intensely for their dollars. Firms such as Ford could no longer sell all of their products, even though they had reduced costs due to mass production. Ford increasingly had to rely on personal selling and advertising to get consumers to buy its products instead of the products of competitors such as General Motors. The selling era continued until the end of World War II.

sales orientation
A marketing strategy in which personal selling and advertising are used to persuade consumers to buy new products and more of existing products.

Marketing Concept

After two decades of economic depression and world war, the U.S. entered an era of expansion beginning in the early 1950s. Demand for goods and services increased significantly. Products that had been in limited supply during the war flooded the market, forcing firms to develop new strategies to compete. As a result, a strategy focused on the consumer called the *marketing concept* began to emerge. The marketing concept reflects the idea that a firm's long-term success must include a company-wide effort to satisfy customer needs. The marketing concept is characterized by a *customer orientation*, which stresses the idea that everyone in a firm, from salespeople to accountants to human resource managers to administrative assistants, should assess, then satisfy, a consumer's needs. Walmart's focus on customer satisfaction, whether it is the cashier checking out customers, the logistics department holding down costs, or a customer service representative handling product returns, is an example of the marketing concept in action. This customer orientation has helped Walmart succeed in a very competitive environment, even though very few of the products it sells are unique to its stores. Rather than offering unique products, it has focused on satisfying consumers' desire for lower prices, friendly service, and convenience better than its retail competitors.

marketing concept
A marketing strategy that reflects the idea that a firm's long-term success must include a company-wide effort to satisfy customer needs.

The marketing concept continues to evolve. Technology has allowed marketers to tailor their offerings in a way that has never before been possible. Dell became a market leader in the 1990s by allowing individual consumers to customize computers and purchase exactly what they wanted. Organizations today also focus on establishing, maintaining, and growing relationships with customers. Groupon allows local and national firms to offer special discounts in an effort to enhance customer relationships while driving profits. Groupon's website and mobile applications can help a firm offer shoppers with college-age children discounts on comforter sets or high-end bladeless fans. This type of custom outreach helps marketers sell products but, more importantly, helps the firm develop relationships with the customers who are most likely to buy its products. Relationship marketing, a strategy that focuses on attracting, maintaining, and enhancing customer relationships,[3] is of primary importance for today's most successful firms.

relationship marketing
A marketing strategy that focuses on attracting, maintaining, and enhancing customer relationships.

The Future of Marketing

More exciting than the history of marketing is thinking about how marketing will develop in the years ahead. As technology and other changes impact the business world, firms will need to explore new models that address what

FIGURE 1.1 Trends in News Consumption

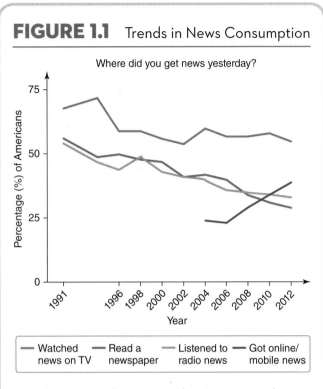

Where did you get news yesterday?

Legend:
— Watched news on TV
— Read a newspaper
— Listened to radio news
— Got online/ mobile news

Source: Pew Research Center, "In Changing News Landscape, Even Television Is Vulnerable," September 27, 2012, http://www.people-press.org/2012/09/27/in-changing-news-landscape-even-television-is-vulnerable/.

customers want and how they prefer to receive information. In 2010, for the first time in decades, the number of cable television subscribers in the United States declined,[4] while the number of Americans using the Internet to watch videos reached an all-time high. Newspaper circulation has decreased significantly over the past decade, while the amount of information consumed through websites, blogs, and other online content has soared exponentially, as illustrated in Figure 1.1. Products like Facebook and Twitter are changing how firms interact with customers. Regardless of how marketing evolves in the years ahead, remember that the basic goal of marketing we discussed earlier in the chapter—to create, communicate, and deliver value—doesn't change. To achieve this goal, marketers must use all the tools and strategies at their disposal to satisfy the needs and wants of customers.

NEEDS VERSUS WANTS

Marketers create value for customers when they develop products that allow consumers to satisfy their needs and wants through exchange relationships. Exchange happens when a buyer and seller trade things of value so that each is better off as a result. Firms, such as Sony, initiate their part of the exchange by creating products like a PS3 game console, communicating the value and enjoyment of owning a PS3 through television ads and online content, and delivering the PS3 consoles to locations like Best Buy and Amazon warehouses, where consumers can purchase them conveniently either at the store or online. Consumers complete the exchange by providing the money necessary to purchase the PS3. In addition to the financial exchange that has taken place, consumers have also likely exchanged information, such as their e-mail address or phone number.

The difference between consumer needs and wants is perhaps the most basic concept in marketing. Still, satisfying needs and wants can prove challenging for firms that do not fully appreciate the difference between the two and how that difference impacts the way they market their product to customers. Needs are states of felt deprivation. Consumers feel deprived when they lack something useful or desirable like food, clothing, shelter, transportation, and safety. Marketers do not create needs; they are a basic part of our human makeup. Regardless of whether you ever see an ad, talk to a salesperson, or receive an e-mail from an online retailer, you will still need food, water, shelter, and transportation.

Marketing's role is to match your need, for food perhaps, with a want, such as a desire for IHOP pancakes or french fries from McDonald's. Consumers need shelter because it gets cold or rains, but marketers work to turn that need into a want, perhaps for a large home with multiple bedrooms or a condo where someone else takes care of the lawn maintenance. Wants are the form that human needs take as they are shaped by personality, culture, and buying situation. Wants are influenced by numerous things, including a consumer's family, job, and background.

LO 1-3

Distinguish between consumer needs and consumer wants.

exchange
An activity that occurs when a buyer and seller trade things of value so that each is better off as a result.

needs
States of felt deprivation. Consumers feel deprived when they lack something useful or desirable like food, clothing, shelter, transportation, and safety.

wants
The form that human needs take as they are shaped by personality, culture, and buying situation.

For example, a college student might want a shirt from a specific store or shoes that reflect his personality and make him feel good about how he looks.

Distinguishing Needs from Wants

The distinction between needs and wants is important and not always black and white. Marketers focus on providing products that fulfill customers' wants, which in turn satisfy their underlying needs. For example, people need transportation to go to work, or to attend school, or to pick up their children. Consumers can meet their *need* for transportation in many ways—by driving a car, taking a bus, or utilizing some other form of mass transit—but marketers can focus on fulfilling a customer's *want* to transport himself or herself in a luxury car or four-wheel-drive vehicle. There are lots of ways to get to work, but a luxury car marketer bets on the fact that you want to get there

Customers who purchase online from Amazon exchange information like their e-mail addresses and mobile phone numbers, which allows marketers to target them for a future exchange when new products are released.

sitting on heated seats while listening to satellite radio. The better a firm understands the difference between customers' needs and wants, the more effectively it can target its message and convince customers to buy its good or service, for the simple reason that the firm's offering will meet its customers' needs and wants better than any competing good or service.

The Ethical Implications of Needs versus Wants

Evaluating customer needs and wants must be done through an ethical framework to avoid potential problems for the firm and society as a whole. The global economic recession that began in December 2007 was, in part, the result of a housing crisis in which the U.S. experienced the largest increase in home foreclosures and drop in home prices in over half a century.[5] The housing crisis was triggered by marketers who took consumers' basic *need* for a house and encouraged their *want* to buy a house that was more than they could afford. It appeared at the time to be a win-win proposition—consumers got the house of their dreams, though perhaps not the income to support it, and the firms that sold, financed, and securitized real estate made hefty profits for years. Ultimately however, this strategy led to billions of dollars in financial losses and millions of job losses. Though marketers were using several of the sound marketing approaches we will discuss throughout this book, the problem stemmed from the fact that many were doing so in an unethical manner. Later in this chapter, you will read about an ethical decision-making framework that you can use as you develop your marketing knowledge. First, we'll discuss the four basic elements that make up the *marketing mix*, a concept that provides a foundation for much of modern marketing.

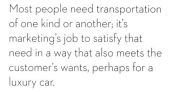

Most people need transportation of one kind or another; it's marketing's job to satisfy that need in a way that also meets the customer's wants, perhaps for a luxury car.

THE MARKETING MIX: THE FOUR Ps

LO 1-4

Explain each of the four elements in the marketing mix.

One thing most business graduates remember from their first marketing class is the four Ps: product, price, place (distribution), and promotion, or more formally, the *marketing mix.* The marketing mix represents everything that a firm can do to influence demand for its good, service, or idea. The four Ps of the marketing mix provide marketers with the tools to increase customer awareness, sales, and

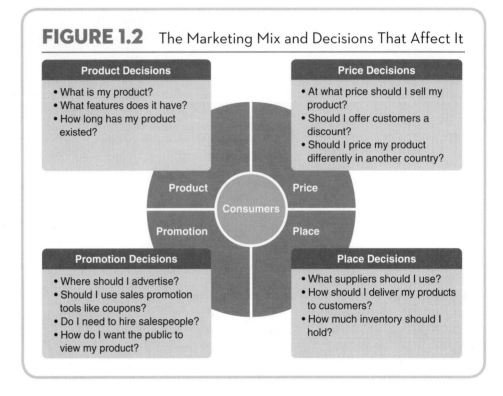

FIGURE 1.2   The Marketing Mix and Decisions That Affect It

Product Decisions
- What is my product?
- What features does it have?
- How long has my product existed?

Price Decisions
- At what price should I sell my product?
- Should I offer customers a discount?
- Should I price my product differently in another country?

Product

Price

Consumers

Promotion

Place

Promotion Decisions
- Where should I advertise?
- Should I use sales promotion tools like coupons?
- Do I need to hire salespeople?
- How do I want the public to view my product?

Place Decisions
- What suppliers should I use?
- How should I deliver my products to customers?
- How much inventory should I hold?

marketing mix

A combination of activities that represent everything a firm can do to influence demand for its good, service, or idea; often referred to as the four Ps of marketing.

profitability. Successful marketing managers can make strategic decisions focusing on a specific element of the marketing mix, such as discounting prices or changing the product's packaging, to gain advantages over competitors and achieve long-term success. Figure 1.2 highlights some of the strategic decisions that can affect each of the marketing mix elements. To develop such strategies, you must first understand each element in more detail.

Product

The discussion of marketing mix typically begins with the product because, without it, a firm has few, if any, decisions to make when it comes to price, place, or promotion. *Product* is a specific combination of goods, services, or ideas that a firm offers to consumers. Consider a good like the Chevrolet Corvette. The Corvette product consists of an engine, tires, seats, transmission, and other parts. Beyond this, a new Corvette comes with a warranty and service guarantee that, while not a physical attribute like an engine, make up part of the car's basic product offering. In addition, the design of the car, the Chevrolet name, and features like satellite radio or the OnStar emergency, security, and navigation system are all part of the product offering. Finally, consumers buy cars not just for the benefit of getting from place to place but also for what cars represent, for example, status, freedom, and youth. All of these tangible and intangible characteristics are components of the Corvette product.

In addition to goods, such as automobiles, products can also take the form of services, such as those provided by an attorney or electrician, or ideas, like those offered by a consultant. We will discuss each of these product types in greater detail in the "Developing Your Product" chapter.

Price

Price is the amount of something—money, time, or effort—that a buyer exchanges with a seller to obtain a product. Setting a price is one of the most important strategic decisions a firm faces because it relates to the value consumers place on the product. How many firms can you think of that are impacted by what price they charge for their products? Your list could include nearly every firm you know! Pricing's power is a result of the signal it can send about product quality. If we put three jars of peanut butter in front of you with no labels except tags listing prices of $1, $5, and $10, which jar would you say is of the highest quality? Even without tasting the product, you might say the $10 jar, simply because of the higher price.

In addition, pricing is typically the easiest marketing mix element to change, making it a powerful tool for firms looking to quickly adjust their market share or revenue. Revenue is a function of the price of a product multiplied by the number of units sold. If the firm sets the price too high, it will sell fewer units, thus reducing revenue. If the firm sets the price too low, it may sell more units, but could still see a reduction in overall revenue if the money earned from the additional units sold isn't enough to offset the lower price. Suppose you sell someone an NFL football game ticket for $50, but find out later that the buyer would gladly have paid $100. Yes, you sold the ticket, but you also lost $50 of potential revenue. We will discuss pricing and how pricing strategy is changing in more detail in the chapter "Pricing for Profit and Customer Value."

New technology like smartphone barcode scanners makes pricing a complicated and influential component of the marketing mix because consumers can quickly compare prices from firm to firm and from store to store.

As you read, keep an eye out for tie-back features in which the executive profiled at the start of the chapter comments on how the chapter concepts relate to his or her professional experience.

Place

Place is one of the most remarkable parts of marketing. Consider this: You can travel to some of the most remote towns in the world and find McDonald's products close by. This is possible because McDonald's focuses heavily on the place element of its marketing mix. *Place* includes the activities a firm undertakes to make its product available to potential consumers. Companies must be able to distribute products to customers where they can buy and consume them without difficulty. Even if you have the right product at the right price, if customers cannot easily purchase the product, they will likely find a substitute. As an example, let's say that a consumer in Oklahoma City, Oklahoma, loves Minute Maid Heart Wise Orange Juice, but, due to distribution problems, the closest place he can buy it is Dallas, Texas. Chances are the consumer in Oklahoma City will begin drinking Tropicana or some other type of orange juice that's available closer to home. Minute Maid has just lost business because it couldn't deliver its product to its customer. Place decisions relate to locations, transportation, logistics, and managing the supply chain.

Promotion

The promotion element of the marketing mix is what most people think of when asked what marketing is. *Promotion* is all the activities that communicate

EXECUTIVE PERSPECTIVE

Steve DeVore
Senior Vice President and General Manager
Twin Oaks Integrated Marketing

Which marketing mix element is most important in your role?

All of the marketing mix elements are important to what we do, but promotion is probably the most critical. Our focus is shopper marketing, which is one of those things that, if you asked 10 people what it was, you would get 10 different responses. The best way I can describe it is that we're part ad agency, part retail-strategy consultant. Some have described shopper marketing as in-store marketing, where you see sales promotions like signage or an in-store display that encourages you to buy a certain kind of toothpaste at the store. I think it's something much more strategic than that. It's creating relationships with customers before, during, and after they visit the marketplace (brick-and-mortar or online), ultimately turning one-time customers into repeat customers.

the value of a product and persuade customers to buy it. Promotion includes advertising, public relations, personal selling, and sales promotion. If you've ever seen television commercials for car insurance, restaurants, resorts, or thousands of other products; talked with a salesperson; or used a coupon (a form of sales promotion) to purchase some product, you've been on the receiving end of a promotional activity. As is the case with every element of the marketing mix, successful promotion involves the firm's ability to integrate these activities in a way that maximizes the value of each. You have probably heard the saying "the whole is greater than the sum of its parts," perhaps said about a successful sports team. It means that the players might be good by themselves but great when they work together as a team. The same can be said of marketing—a successful firm's whole promotional strategy is better than the sum of its parts. It effectively integrates advertising, public relations, personal selling, and sales promotion to communicate a product's value to potential customers.

An integrated approach will always be important to the success of a promotional strategy, but in recent years, the way a firm executes its promotional activities has evolved. Today, firms of all sizes and from all industries can communicate quickly and directly with their customers using a variety of online and digital tools, such as smartphone apps and social media. The term social media refers to a group of Internet-based applications that allow the creation and exchange of user-generated content. Firms that use social media for promotion try to create content that attracts attention and encourages readers to share the content with their social networks. In this way, a corporate message spreads from user to user and, presumably, resonates with consumers because it appears to come from a trusted, third-party source as opposed to the company itself. Social media communication is driven by word of mouth, meaning it results in free media rather than paid media. It has also become easily accessible to anyone with Internet access. As a result, social media serve as a relatively inexpensive platform for smaller firms and nonprofit organizations to implement promotional strategies.[6]

Icons throughout the chapter highlight social media-related content.

social media

A group of Internet-based applications that allow the creation and exchange of user-generated content.

---

 connect |MARKETING

Interactive Assignment 1-1
Social Media in Action

The motion picture industry is increasingly using social media to market movies to audiences. Marketers for the 2012 movie *Ted* created a complete social media profile for the foul-mouthed stuffed animal that starred in the movie. Fans could follow the teddy bear's thoughts on Twitter @WhatTedSaid or read his rants on a variety of subjects on his blog titled "Ted's Fuzzy Thoughts." By the time the movie was released @WhatTedSaid had over 200,000 followers and *Ted* surprised movie insiders with a first weekend box office take of $54 million, with much of the credit given to the innovative social media marketing campaign surrounding the movie.

The most influential movie-going audience, 18–29 year olds, are also the heaviest users of social media. Facebook campaigns for movies like *Paranormal Activity 4* and Twitter campaigns for *Super 8* serve as examples of how social media can spread excitement among 18–29 year olds and increase the success and profitability of these movies. Today, movie marketers use all social media tools at their disposal to reach their audience and drive demand for their product.

Social Media in Action features discuss how companies use social media to market their products. The interactive assignment that accompanies the feature, which is available in McGraw-Hill *Connect*, asks you to make decisions about the best use of social media in a specific marketing scenario.

The Social Media in Action *Connect* exercise in Chapter 1 will let you choose how best to use social media to successfully market a new movie about to be released. By understanding the power of social media marketing, you will be able to apply these strategies to promote and create buzz for your organization in the years ahead.

Source: See Rachel Dodes, "Twitter Goes to the Movies," *The Wall Street Journal,* August 3, 2012, http://online.wsj.com/article/SB10000872396390443343704577553 270169103822.html.

TRENDS AFFECTING MARKETING

The social media trend will increasingly influence how marketers promote their products to customers, but it isn't the only trend affecting modern marketing. Firms today must take a broader focus than they have in the past. While marketers want to expand their reach to international consumers, they face new challenges resulting from the global competition. Meanwhile, more and more consumers seek out firms that emphasize social responsibility and ethical practices. In the sections that follow, we'll discuss globalization, corporate social responsibility, and ethics. In each chapter of this product, you will see how these trends affect core marketing principles, including marketing planning, marketing research, and market segmentation.

LO 1-5

Discuss the importance of globalization in the field of marketing.

Global Marketing

Modern marketers must not only create, communicate, and deliver value but also do so in a truly global marketplace. Global forces impact everything thing we do in marketing, from pricing to product development to supply chain management. The earthquake and tsunami that struck Japan in 2011 disrupted supply chains for products around the world, causing delays in product development and delivery schedules.[7] Much of the growth in U.S. firms ranging from McDonald's to General Motors comes from their expansion into international markets.

Events of the past decade have clearly illustrated how connected the global economy is. When the United States entered a significant recession starting in December 2007, manufacturing at Chinese plants of products targeted to American consumers declined significantly, increasing unemployment and slowing growth in China.[8] As the European Union dealt with a continent-wide banking crisis, American firms saw their stock prices drop as investors feared possible exposure to the problems in Europe. More than at any time in history, businesses today are impacted by developments across the globe. Consider these facts:

Globalization affects almost every aspect of marketing. Icons within each chapter highlight discussions of the concepts in a global context.

- One in every nine jobs in the United States is directly supported by exports.[9]
- In 2012, total U.S. exports were worth more than $2 trillion.[10]
- The United States is the world's leading exporter of beef, wheat, corn, and copyrighted material.[11]
- Exports account for 14 percent of the total U.S. economy.[12]

The Interconnected World The idea of *globalization,* the increasingly interconnected nature of the world economy, evokes different reactions from different people. International trade agreements, such as the North American Free Trade Agreement (NAFTA) that relaxed trade restrictions between the U.S., Canada, and Mexico, can be viewed both positively and negatively depending on an individual's circumstances. For U.S. farmers who have been able to ship and sell their produce to Canada and Mexico, NAFTA has given them the opportunity to expand their business and increase profits. Canada and Mexico have accounted for 37 percent of the total growth of U.S. agricultural exports since 1993.[13] The share of total U.S. agricultural exports destined for Canada or Mexico grew from 22 percent at the time NAFTA was passed in 1993 to over 30 percent less than 15 years later. However, in the view of employees from some manufacturing firms, NAFTA has made it easier for companies to move jobs to lower wage areas on the continent, endangering local job prospects and threatening the existence of entire communities. The importance of globalization grows with each passing year, and marketers must develop a global vision by proactively recognizing and responding to international marketing opportunities.

Marketing on a Global Scale

Less than 5 percent of the world's population lives in the United States, which leads marketers to seek ways to promote and sell their products to the billions of potential consumers living outside the U.S. Global marketing is a marketing strategy that consciously addresses customers, markets, and competition throughout the world.[14] Coca-Cola is one of the most globally active companies. It sells over 3,500 different beverages in different places throughout the world,[15] and over 80 percent of firm sales come from international markets.[16] Coca-Cola's marketers have developed products to meet the unique tastes of international customers. The firm actively promotes its brand—the name, term, symbol, design, or any combination of

global marketing

A marketing strategy that consciously addresses customers, markets, and competition throughout the world.

brand

The name, term, symbol, design, or any combination of these that identifies and differentiates a firm's products.

Coca-Cola has demonstrated a commitment to using each of the four Ps—product, price, place, and promotion—to drive global success.

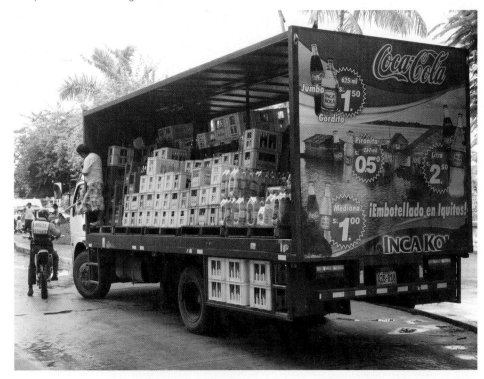

these that identifies and differentiates a firm's products—through advertising and social media and makes pricing decisions based on economic and competitive factors in each region of the world in which it does business. Coca-Cola is also at the cutting edge of delivering its products to places where global customers can buy them, whether that means moving bottling operations to Turkey or coordinating deliveries to remote places in Africa.

As the influence of firms like Coca-Cola spreads around the world, they must increasingly focus on their responsibility to conduct themselves as good corporate citizens and behave ethically in their dealings with those affected by the company's actions at home and abroad.

Corporate Social Responsibility

More and more, communities, shareholders, and other stakeholders demand that firms take a proactive stance on social responsibility. Corporate social responsibility (CSR) refers to an organization's obligation to maximize its positive impact and minimize its negative impact on society. Stakeholder responsibility focuses specifically on the obligations an organization has to those who can affect whether or not it achieves its objectives. For example, a company that makes toys has a responsibility to its shareholders to return a profit and also a responsibility to customers to sell products that are safe for their children. Firms have responsibilities to a variety of internal and external stakeholder groups, as identified in Figure 1.3. Internal stakeholders include employees, managers, and owners. External stakeholders include customers, suppliers, creditors, shareholders, governments, and society as a whole. Marketers make decisions that impact these stakeholders almost every day.

Corporate social responsibility is expanding to include a wide range of initiatives, such as creating corporate charitable foundations, supporting minority activities, and demanding responsible business practices throughout the organization. The number of firms that report corporate social responsibility information has increased dramatically in the past decade. In 2002, only about a dozen Fortune 500 firms issued a CSR report. Today, over 300 Fortune 500 firms issue a CSR report annually.[17]

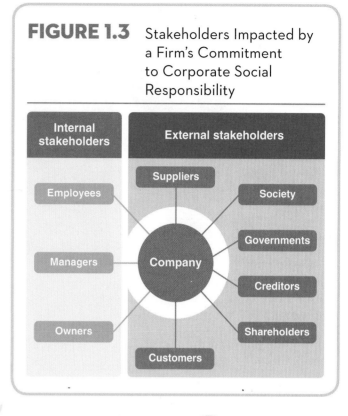

FIGURE 1.3   Stakeholders Impacted by a Firm's Commitment to Corporate Social Responsibility

LO 1-6

Evaluate the potential benefits of corporate social responsibility.

corporate social responsibility (CSR)

An organization's obligation to maximize its positive impact and minimize its negative impact on society.

stakeholder responsibility

The obligations an organization has to those who can affect whether or not it achieves its objectives.

In addition to the Social Media in Action feature, several additional Interactive Assignments, available in McGraw-Hill *Connect*, provide you with an opportunity to apply the concepts you've just learned to a real-world scenario.

---

connect | MARKETING   **Interactive Assignment 1-2**

Please complete the *Connect* exercise in Chapter 1 focused on corporate social responsibility. By identifying which stakeholder groups will be impacted by the decisions that a firm makes, you willl better understand the consequences of each marketing decision.

Firms like Disney and Nestlé that consistently issue CSR reports and publicize CSR initiatives rank among the most admired companies in the world.[18]

LO 1-7

Demonstrate the relationship between ethical business practices and marketplace success.

ethics
Moral standards expected by a society.

Ethics in Marketing

Like globalization and corporate social responsibility, ethical decision making should be a key component of a successful marketing approach. Ethics are moral standards expected by a society. Marketers should clearly understand the norms and values expected of them and act in a way that reflects their company, their profession, and themselves in a positive, ethical light. The American Marketing Association has published a thorough Code of Ethics, which marketers should read and adhere to. We encourage you to read the AMA Code of Ethics in Figure 1.4 and use it as a guide as you develop your marketing knowledge throughout this text.

The Impact of Ethics on Business   The consequences of not adhering to an ethical code can be serious. Ignoring ethical considerations has destroyed some of the largest companies in the world over the past 15 years, including Enron (No. 18 on the Fortune 500 list of the world's largest corporations in 2000), telecommunications giant WorldCom, Arthur Andersen (the largest accounting firm in the United States in 2000), and AIG (the largest insurance company in the world in 2008).[19] Each of you, as a college graduate, will face a more challenging job market, partly because of unethical behavior by firms. For example, Arthur Andersen was a leading recruiter of college graduates throughout the 1990s, until a series of unethical decisions by a limited number of employees led to its demise. This year, Arthur Andersen, WorldCom, Enron, Bear Stearns, and a host of other large firms that fell victim to ethical lapses will hire no college graduates. As you can see, unethical marketing practices harm not only customers but also society as a whole.

Making ethical decisions not only makes good business sense, it can also generate profits, even during a recession. Figure 1.5 illustrates the relationship between ethical business practices and marketplace success. The graph compares the percentage returns of the WME Index, which includes all publicly traded World's Most Ethical Company honorees, to the S&P 500 index, one of the most commonly used benchmarks of U.S. stock performance. As you can see, firms that were identified as ethical were more profitable on the whole than the mix of companies included in the S&P 500 index. This held true even in 2008, during the worst of the U.S. recession.

FIGURE 1.4   American Marketing Association Code of Ethics

PREAMBLE

The American Marketing Association commits itself to promoting the highest standard of professional ethical norms and values for its members (practitioners, academics and students). Norms are established standards of conduct that are expected and maintained by society and/or professional organizations. Values represent the collective conception of what communities find desirable, important and morally proper. Values also serve as the criteria for evaluating our own personal actions and the actions of others. As marketers, we recognize that we not only serve our organizations but also act as stewards of society in creating, facilitating and executing the transactions that are part of the greater economy. In this role, marketers are expected to embrace the highest professional ethical norms and the ethical values implied by our responsibility toward multiple stakeholders (e.g., customers, employees, investors, peers, channel members, regulators and the host community).

ETHICAL NORMS

As Marketers, we must:

1. **Do no harm.** This means consciously avoiding harmful actions or omissions by embodying high ethical standards and adhering to all applicable laws and regulations in the choices we make.
2. **Foster trust in the marketing system.** This means striving for good faith and fair dealing so as to contribute toward the efficacy of the exchange process as well as avoiding deception in product design, pricing, communication, and delivery of distribution.
3. **Embrace ethical values.** This means building relationships and enhancing consumer confidence in the integrity of marketing by affirming these core values: honesty, responsibility, fairness, respect, transparency and citizenship.

ETHICAL VALUES

Honesty—to be forthright in dealings with customers and stakeholders. To this end, we will:

- Strive to be truthful in all situations and at all times.
- Offer products of value that do what we claim in our communications.
- Stand behind our products if they fail to deliver their claimed benefits.
- Honor our explicit and implicit commitments and promises.

Responsibility—to accept the consequences of our marketing decisions and strategies. To this end, we will:

- Strive to serve the needs of customers.
- Avoid using coercion with all stakeholders.
- Acknowledge the social obligations to stakeholders that come with increased marketing and economic power.
- Recognize our special commitments to vulnerable market segments such as children, seniors, the economically impoverished, market illiterates and others who may be substantially disadvantaged.
- Consider environmental stewardship in our decision-making.

Fairness—to balance justly the needs of the buyer with the interests of the seller. To this end, we will:

- Represent products in a clear way in selling, advertising and other forms of communication; this includes the avoidance of false, misleading and deceptive promotion.
- Reject manipulations and sales tactics that harm customer trust.
- Refuse to engage in price fixing, predatory pricing, price gouging or "bait-and-switch" tactics.
- Avoid knowing participation in conflicts of interest.
- Seek to protect the private information of customers, employees and partners.

Respect—to acknowledge the basic human dignity of all stakeholders. To this end, we will:

- Value individual differences and avoid stereotyping customers or depicting demographic groups (e.g., gender, race, sexual orientation) in a negative or dehumanizing way.
- Listen to the needs of customers and make all reasonable efforts to monitor and improve their satisfaction on an ongoing basis.
- Make every effort to understand and respectfully treat buyers, suppliers, intermediaries and distributors from all cultures.
- Acknowledge the contributions of others, such as consultants, employees and coworkers, to marketing endeavors.
- Treat everyone, including our competitors, as we would wish to be treated.

Transparency—to create a spirit of openness in marketing operations. To this end, we will:

- Strive to communicate clearly with all constituencies.
- Accept constructive criticism from customers and other stakeholders.
- Explain and take appropriate action regarding significant product or service risks, component substitutions or other foreseeable eventualities that could affect customers or their perception of the purchase decision.
- Disclose list prices and terms of financing as well as available price deals and adjustments.

Citizenship—to fulfill the economic, legal, philanthropic and societal responsibilities that serve stakeholders. To this end, we will:

- Strive to protect the ecological environment in the execution of marketing campaigns.
- Give back to the community through volunteerism and charitable donations.
- Contribute to the overall betterment of marketing and its reputation.
- Urge supply chain members to ensure that trade is fair for all participants, including producers in developing countries.

IMPLEMENTATION

We expect AMA members to be courageous and proactive in leading and/or aiding their organizations in the fulfillment of the explicit and implicit promises made to those stakeholders. We recognize that every industry sector and marketing sub-discipline (e.g., marketing research, e-commerce, Internet selling, direct marketing, and advertising) has its own specific ethical issues that require policies and commentary. An array of such codes can be accessed through links on the AMA Web site. Consistent with the principle of subsidiarity (solving issues at the level where the expertise resides), we encourage all such groups to develop and/or refine their industry and discipline-specific codes of ethics to supplement these guiding ethical norms and values.

Source: American Marketing Association, "Statement of Ethics," n.d., http://www.marketingpower.com/aboutama/pages/statement%20of%20ethics.aspx.

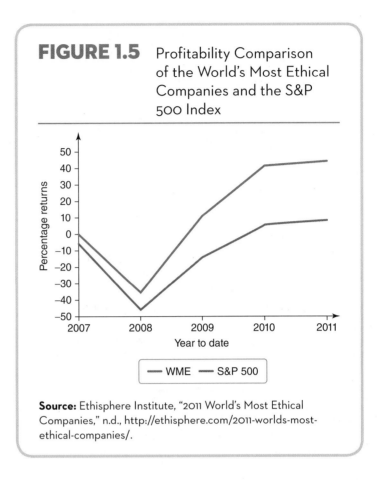

FIGURE 1.5 Profitability Comparison of the World's Most Ethical Companies and the S&P 500 Index

Source: Ethisphere Institute, "2011 World's Most Ethical Companies," n.d., http://ethisphere.com/2011-worlds-most-ethical-companies/.

Ethical Decision-Making Framework Despite the positive impact ethical decision making can have on a firm, the ethical choice is not always clear. Figure 1.6 illustrates an ethical decision-making framework that you can use in your future career and in almost any marketing challenge you will encounter, in this class and beyond.[20] You can apply this systematic framework to the ethical problems discussed throughout this course.

1. **Determine the facts in an unbiased manner.** First, determine the factual elements of a specific problem without letting any potential bias influence the decision. We are all products of our environment, and each of us brings our background, history, and experiences to any ethical problem. These fundamental factors can influence how we review and interpret the facts at hand if we don't make a conscious effort to determine the relevant information in an unbiased way.

2. **Identify the ethical issue at hand.** It's possible to avoid ethical problems if the ethical issue is clearly identified. The rest of the ethical decision-making framework will be valuable only if the issue itself is clearly understood.

3. **Identify the stakeholders impacted by the decision.** Remember, stakeholders can be both external and internal and include the firm's employees, both current and retired; customers; suppliers; shareholders; and the community in which the firm operates. Identify and consider each group as part of the ethical decision-making framework.

4. **Consider all available alternatives.** After the relevant stakeholders have been identified, all parties should brainstorm alternatives. Different groups

often view issues through different perspectives, and brainstorming can lead to creative and useful solutions.

5. **Consider how the decision will affect the stakeholders.** Managers sometimes refer to this step as "seeing through a problem to the other side." This means that we should consider ahead of time how the decision will affect all stakeholders. For example, mortgage companies that engaged in subprime lending in the years leading up to 2008 should have considered how lax lending standards might affect stakeholders over the long term rather than waiting until foreclosures and unemployment increased during the recession.

6. **Discuss the pending decision with the stakeholders.** Seek feedback on potential decisions from stakeholders. It is often impossible to fully appreciate all of the dynamics of an ethical decision without getting input from those who will be affected. Many business problems can be avoided if a thoughtful discussion occurs when the decision is still pending.

7. **Make the decision.** Once the issue has been discussed with the relevant parties, make a final decision based on the stated criteria. Making decisions that impact others can be a stressful and challenging task, but using this decision-making framework can ensure thoroughness in arriving at the decision.

8. **Monitor and assess the quality of the decision.** The economy, regulatory environment, and consumer opinions are always changing and developing. A generation or two ago, smoking cigarettes on planes and in office buildings was considered perfectly ethical. Today, because we have more information about the dangers of second-hand smoke, laws prevent people from smoking in many public places. Firms will face many ethical challenges in the years ahead—online privacy regulations, environmental concerns, sustainability, and childhood obesity, to name a few. It will be incumbent upon all business professionals, including marketers, to monitor and assess whether the decisions they've made still represent the right and ethical choice for the firm, their consumers, and society as a whole.

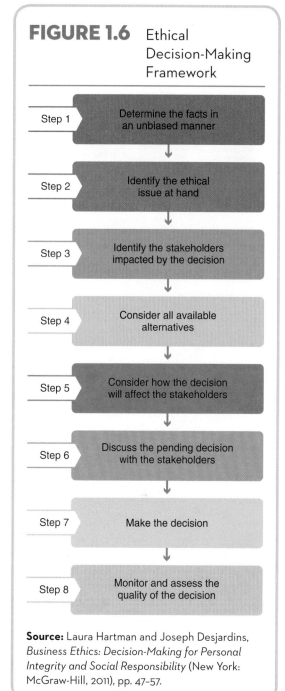

FIGURE 1.6   Ethical Decision-Making Framework

Step 1 — Determine the facts in an unbiased manner

Step 2 — Identify the ethical issue at hand

Step 3 — Identify the stakeholders impacted by the decision

Step 4 — Consider all available alternatives

Step 5 — Consider how the decision will affect the stakeholders

Step 6 — Discuss the pending decision with the stakeholders

Step 7 — Make the decision

Step 8 — Monitor and assess the quality of the decision

Source: Laura Hartman and Joseph Desjardins, *Business Ethics: Decision-Making for Personal Integrity and Social Responsibility* (New York: McGraw-Hill, 2011), pp. 47–57.

Marketers may confront decisions that will boost short-term sales at the expense of the long-term reputation of the company. Employees may have to choose between the short-term benefit of a commission and the potential long-term damage to their personal brand if they don't adhere to ethical standards. The list that follows contains some common ethical questions that marketers may face within each element of the marketing mix during their career. As you read each item, think about how you might respond, using the ethical decision-making framework as a guide.

Product
- What default privacy settings should be built into a website?
- What safety risks, especially for children and the elderly, might a product pose?
- Should environmentally friendly packaging be used even if it costs more?

EXECUTIVE PERSPECTIVE

Steve DeVore
Senior Vice President and General Manager
Twin Oaks Integrated Marketing

Do you use an ethical framework when making decisions?

Absolutely I do. Ethical principles are at the heart of everything we do as a company. I use a framework because it takes the emotion out of decisions. We want to develop relationships with all of our stakeholders, and relationships are not possible if there isn't a foundation of trust and ethical behavior.

Place
- Should jobs be outsourced to other members of the supply chain?
- Are the relationships between wholesalers and retailers inappropriate?
- What opportunities for personal gain might tempt a firm's suppliers?

Pricing
- Should the firm charge customers different prices based on their ability to pay?
- Should the firm increase prices due to a lack of local competition?
- Should the firm lower prices on soft drinks and fast food to attract a greater customer following, even if those products may present health risks?

Promotion
- Does the advertising message represent the product's benefits honestly?
- Does the promotional strategy incorporate violence, sex, or profanity that may be inappropriate for some members of society?
- Does the advertising message attack competing products rather than highlight the benefits of the firm's product?

---

connect™ |MARKETING Interactive Assignment 1-3

Please complete the *Connect* exercise for Chapter 1 that focuses on ethics. Applying the ethical decision-making framework to an actual scenario will provide insight into how to evaluate ethical challenges and the potential risks involved when an ethical approach is not selected.

LO 1-8

Analyze the functions of marketing beyond the for-profit firm.

MARKETING FOR NONPROFIT ORGANIZATIONS

So far, in this chapter, we've focused on for-profit firms; however, nonprofit organizations are a growing part of the U.S. economy. Nonprofit organizations employ about one in 10 American workers or 13.5 million people,[21] and they continued to employ and even hire workers during the recession that began in late 2007. A Johns Hopkins University study found that, between 2000 and 2010, the nonprofit sector grew at an average annual rate of 2.1 percent. During the same time period, for-profit jobs were declining by 0.6 percent a year.

As with for-profit firms, marketing efforts are an essential part of the success of nonprofit organizations. Despite being able to hire when for-profit firms could not, the economic turmoil of the recession left many nonprofits facing increased competition for support, membership, and donations. Successful marketing helps nonprofit organizations, including hospitals, charities, universities, zoos, and churches, attract membership and much-needed funds.

Lance Gooch
Account Manager

Memphis Grizzlies
http://www.nba.com/grizzlies

The Memphis Grizzlies are a professional basketball team in the National Basketball Association (NBA).

Lance Gooch

Account Manager
Memphis Grizzlies

Each chapter contains a profile of a recent (within five years) business graduate that focuses on how to market oneself. These professionals describe how developing their personal brand has helped advance their careers.

Describe your job. I sell and organize group outings and events to Grizzlies games for businesses, schools, church groups, and communities. I have worked with companies to sponsor a company night at the game for which all of the employees can buy discounted tickets. I have also worked with schools, arranging for students to come to our arena and listen to career guidance from speakers who work in sports before attending a game. It is a great job that requires me to develop relationships with people from many types of organizations.

Describe how you got the job that you have. It was not until my sophomore year in college that I realized I wanted to work in the sports business. I went to my advisor, who pointed me to the assistant athletic director of marketing at my university's athletic department. Because I was still three semesters away from having enough credit hours to start an internship with the athletic department, I decided to volunteer my time those three semesters to get my foot in the door. I did not receive one dime or one credit hour while doing so (though I did receive a few free hot dogs while working the games!). After my third semester of volunteering, I finally had the credit hours to qualify for the internship. While finishing my last year of college, I

formed a great relationship with a professor who just happened to be a huge sports fan and a season ticket holder and group leader for the Memphis Grizzlies. After learning through him that there was a job opening with the Grizzlies, I applied and ended up getting the job.

What has been the most important thing in making you successful at your job? Caring about my clients and actually taking the time to listen (which, being a client to other businesses, I've noticed is becoming a lost art). I try to treat every client as more of a friend than an actual client. One thing I've learned is, when you make clients your friends, they will sing your praises to their own friends and peers, which will lead to a lot of referral sales.

What advice would you give soon-to-be graduates? Whatever you want to do in life, work hard to achieve it. It is extremely easy for a boss to recognize someone who is truly driven and wants to work hard versus someone who is complacent. The person who hired me to work for the Memphis Grizzlies did so partly because of the dedication I showed through my volunteer work. A negative stereotype associated with my generation is that we are impatient and want things immediately, but if you show that you are willing to take time and work at something, you will be a rarity in the eyes of potential employers.

What do you consider your personal brand to be? My personal brand is leadership. This applies to how I am seen both internally and externally. Even though I was hired on as the youngest of 16 account executives with the Grizzlies, I immediately tried to lead by motivating and encouraging my coworkers. Simply telling someone they did a good job, telling a joke, or helping out a colleague in a tough situation can go a long way toward not only brightening the mood in the office but to bettering the organization in multiple ways. There are also ways of applying leadership externally. For example, I find it's better to talk less and do more. Leadership is a great technique to develop because it can be so rewarding, both at your job and in your daily life.

As part of its "Chili's More Hope Campaign for St. Jude," Chili's invites restaurant patrons to make individual donations to St. Jude Children's Research Hospital and donates its net profits from one day of business to the hospital.

For example, St. Jude Children's Research Hospital in Memphis, Tennessee, focuses much of its marketing efforts on raising money to treat children with cancer. St. Jude partners with more than 70 corporate supporters, such as Chili's and Target, to raise money for its research.[22] Target is a major partner in St. Jude's annual "Thanks and Giving" campaign, which is focused on increasing awareness of the hospital's work and encouraging individual consumer donations. Such marketing efforts allow St. Jude to raise the $1.8 million per day it takes to fund one of the leading children's research hospitals in the world, a place where children and parents are never asked to pay for care.[23] As you continue through this course, you'll see how the marketing principles that apply to for-profit firms also impact nonprofit firms.

MARKETING YOURSELF

Some of you reading this book will become marketing majors and take courses in consumer behavior, professional selling, marketing research, and advertising. Some of you will major in another subject. Either way, your ability to use the principles of this book to market yourself will be critical to your success after you leave college. Don't look at the information this book provides as a collection of random concepts that you can forget about once your final exam is taken. Instead, think about how it will help you position yourself relative to others competing for the same job. As you prepare your resume, think about how to communicate your value so that you get an interview over the other hundreds of candidates.

The era of mass marketing has passed. So also has the day when simply putting your name and college degree on a resume guaranteed you a great job for life. Some of you will work for firms looking to increase profits, and your job will be to successfully market the firm's goods and services through a minefield of competitors, global economic uncertainty, and new advertising media. Some of you will work for nonprofit companies in which you will have to successfully market your organization to prospective donors, possibly in an environment in which people fear for their jobs and economic future, and charitable organizations compete for a shrinking pool of dollars. Ultimately, wherever your career leads you, you will need to market yourself effectively to reach the professional goals you have set. This book will arm you with the marketing knowledge to answer challenging questions in the future, perhaps most relevantly, Why should I hire *you?*

---

connect **Interactive Assignment 1-4**

|MARKETING Please complete the *Connect* exercise for Chapter 1 that focuses on careers in marketing. Match the personal and job characteristics to specific marketing careers to better understand how your passion may be best served through a career in marketing.

SUMMARY

LO 1-1 Define marketing and describe a marketer's role in creating, communicating, and delivering value.

Marketing is an organizational function and set of processes for creating, communicating, and delivering value to customers and for managing customer relationships in ways that benefit the organization and its stakeholders. To create value, the new good or service must satisfy a perceived marketplace demand. Once a valuable good or service has been created, it is the responsibility of the marketer to communicate this value to potential customers. A company's supply chain is critical in delivering value. Members of the supply chain can include suppliers, manufacturers, wholesalers, distributors, retailers, transportation companies, and other groups, depending on the specific industry.

LO 1-2 Differentiate among the various eras in the history of marketing.

Prior to the 1920s, most firms were production oriented and believed that quality products would simply sell themselves. Beginning in the mid-1920s, many firms shifted to a sales orientation, where the task of personal selling and advertising was to persuade consumers to buy new products and more of existing products. After two decades of economic depression and world war, the economy entered an era of expansion, in which the demand for goods and services increased significantly. The marketing concept was developed during this period and reflects a company-wide consumer orientation with a focus on establishing, maintaining, and growing relationships with customers.

LO 1-3 Distinguish between consumer needs and consumer wants.

Perhaps the most basic concept underlying marketing is that of needs versus wants. Human needs are states of felt deprivation. They include the need for food, clothing, shelter, transportation, and safety. Wants are the form that human needs take as they are shaped by personality, culture, and buying situation. The better a firm understands the difference between customers' needs and wants, the more effectively it can target its message and convince customers to buy its good or service.

LO 1-4 Explain each of the four elements in the marketing mix.

The marketing mix, made up of the four Ps—product, price, place, and promotion—represents everything that a firm can do to influence demand for its good or service. Product is the specific combination of goods or services that a firm offers to consumers. Price is the amount of something that a buyer must exchange with a seller to obtain a product. Place includes the activities that make the product available to potential consumers. Promotion is all the activities that communicate the value of the product and persuade customers to buy it, including advertising, public relations, personal selling, and sales promotion.

LO 1-5 Discuss the importance of globalization in the field of marketing.

Global marketing is a marketing strategy that consciously addresses customers, markets, and competition throughout the world. Global forces impact everything we do in marketing, from pricing to supply chain management to product development. The importance of globalization grows with each passing year, and marketers must develop a global vision by proactively recognizing and responding to international marketing opportunities.

LO 1-6 Evaluate the potential benefits of corporate social responsibility.

Corporate social responsibility refers to an organization's obligation to maximize its positive impact and minimize its negative impact on society. Stakeholder responsibility focuses specifically on the obligations an organization has to those who can affect achievement of its objectives. Marketers make decisions impacting stakeholders and relating to social responsibility almost every day.

LO 1-7 Demonstrate the relationship between ethical business practices and marketplace success.

Ethics are moral standards expected by a society. Unethical marketing practices can harm both customers and society as a whole. Marketers are sometimes faced with decisions that will boost short-term sales at the expense of the long-term reputation of the company. Using an ethical decision-making framework to make decisions is important because the right choice will not always be clear.

 LO 1-8 Analyze the functions of marketing beyond the for-profit firm.

Nonprofit organizations rely on marketing to raise money and support, particularly in economically difficult times. Though nonprofit marketing faces unique challenges, many marketing principles concepts apply to both for-profit and nonprofit firms. Whether you eventually work in a firm concerned with maximizing profit or a nonprofit organization focused on awareness and fundraising, ultimately, you will need to be able to market yourself effectively to reach the professional goals you have set.

KEY TERMS

brand (p. 14)
corporate social responsibility
    (CSR) (p. 15)
customer value (p. 5)
ethics (p. 16)
exchange (p. 8)
global marketing (p. 14)

logistics (p. 6)
marketing (p. 4)
marketing concept (p. 7)
marketing mix (p. 10)
needs (p. 8)
production orientation (p. 6)
relationship marketing (p. 7)

sales orientation (p. 7)
social media (p. 12)
stakeholder responsibility (p. 15)
supply chain (p. 6)
wants (p. 8)

A Marketing Plan Exercise in each chapter helps you learn the elements of the marketing plan in the context of marketing the most important product or brand of your life: yourself.

MARKETING PLAN EXERCISE

As a professional in any field, it is important to have a comprehensive understanding of what a marketing plan is and why it is there. A marketing plan is an action-oriented document or playbook that guides the analysis, implementation, and control of all marketing activities. Throughout the course of this book, you will develop a professional marketing plan. The twist is that your marketing plan will focus on how to market yourself to achieve your career goals.

Many businesses fail to execute on their marketing plans because they did not spend adequate time clearly identifying what they wanted or expected to do. As a first step in developing your personal marketing plan, you will need to identify the specific objectives that you want to achieve. In developing these objectives, you should ask yourself several questions, such as

- Do I want to attend graduate school? If so, where and what program?
- Where do I want to work?

- Where do I want to live?
- What kind of life do I want to have?
- How much will I need to earn to have that life?

These types of questions will help you focus on what specific things you need to do to achieve your goals. As with a firm putting together a corporate marketing plan, the more clearly you define your objectives, the more likely you are to realize them.

Your Task: Clearly state three to five specific objectives for your future and include a brief one to two sentence description of each objective.

DISCUSSION QUESTIONS

1. Identify a firm that you think effectively markets its goods, services, or ideas and describe how the firm creates, communicates, and delivers value.
2. Reflect on the evolution of marketing over the past century and describe three major changes that you

think will impact the field of marketing over the next decade.
3. Ask five people you know to list their needs and wants. Are their lists accurate reflections of the definition of each? Are there any differences due to age or gender?

4. Illustrate each step of the ethical decision-making framework by examining whether the state you live in should use a lottery to help pay for part of your college tuition. What are the ethical issues? Who are the relevant stakeholders? How are those stakeholders affected by potential outcomes? What decision would you make?

5. Describe three examples of promotion that caught your attention in your hometown. Why do you think each worked so well?

The Social Media Application asks you to analyze the social media activities of the organizations with which you are most familiar, including your school, your favorite restaurant, or the company you'd like to work for after obtaining your degree.

SOCIAL MEDIA APPLICATION

Choose three products that you currently use, for example, clothes that you wear, restaurants where you eat, or the car that you drive. Analyze the social media presence of these products using the following questions and activities as a guide:

1. What is being done to market each product on social media?
2. What are people saying about each product on social media?

3. Give each of the three products a grade (A-F) based on how effective you feel its social media presence is.
4. Describe why you gave each the grade that you did, and make recommendations for how the product's firm could improve its social media marketing activities (e.g., modifying content or utilizing a different social media platform).

Ethical Challenges in each chapter ask you to consider how ethical issues permeate every marketing decision.

ETHICAL CHALLENGE

As more state governments dealt with budget deficits following the recession in 2007 and beyond, one strategy to increase revenues focused on state lotteries. The state of Arizona used marketing strategies to promote its state lottery, including holding focus groups, introducing new products and games, and increasing its advertising and social media budget by almost 50 percent. The marketing efforts paid off as Arizona saw lottery ticket sales increase by 14 percent between 2009 and 2010. Other states, including New York, implemented similar strategies and by 2011 lottery ticket sales in the U.S. had risen to $56 billion.

While these successful marketing efforts provided the states with much-needed revenue to fund programs, including higher education, some have ethical concerns about relying on lotteries for funding. When Minnesota followed others in offering online lottery subscriptions, Assistant Senate Majority Leader David Hann called the move to encourage gambling "reprehensible."

The choice between increasing revenues and the potential dangers of increased gambling by citizens provides an ethical challenge for marketers. Use the ethical decision-making framework to answer the following questions:

1. What are the major ethical issues surrounding Arizona's decision to more aggressively market its state lottery to increase revenues? Who are the affected stakeholders? How will those stakeholders be affected?
2. If you were helping the state of Arizona to market its lottery, what would you recommend?
3. Which element of the marketing mix (promotion, price, place, or product) do you think is most valuable in promoting state lotteries? Which element do you think presents the greatest potential ethical risk when marketing state lotteries?

Source: See Amanda J. Crawford, "Lottery Sales Rise to Record as Cash-Hungry States Search for More Revenue," *Bloomberg Businessweek*, November 29, 2011, http://www.bloomberg.com/news/2011-11-30/lottery-sales-rise-to-records-as-states-wager-for-more-revenue.html.

Video Cases with each chapter, available in McGraw-Hill *Connect,* often feature the executive you've learned about throughout the chapter.

VIDEO CASE

Please go to *Connect* to access the video case featuring Steve DeVore that accompanies this chapter.

CAREER TIPS

Marketing Your Future

Career Tips, often written by the executive featured at the start of the chapter, help you think about how to market yourself and develop your own personal brand.

You have read in this chapter about the importance of marketing yourself. As you get closer to finishing your degree, two major elements of this include developing a resume that will catch the attention of potential employers and giving an effective interview. Steve DeVore, who was featured in the Executive Perspective at the beginning of the chapter and who has hired large numbers of new college graduates, offers the following 10 marketing tips for landing the job of your dreams.

STEP 1. Realize what a resume is and isn't.

a. A majority of new hires come from referrals, not incoming resumes.
b. Like a marketing plan, a resume's objective is to generate interest (not follow a formula).
c. Your resume immediately gives employers a sense of who you are.
d. If your resume looks and feels like all of the others, it will stay with the others in the pile.

STEP 2. Break all the rules … in a smart way.

a. Great resume building is about creativity, not conventional thinking.
b. Don't think of your resume as a list of accomplishments; think of it as a story.

STEP 3. Customize your approach.

a. Don't approach different companies with a copy-and-paste mentality.
b. Consider what skills each company values most and highlight them appropriately.

STEP 4. Be concise, but be meaningful.

a. Don't go into too much depth about your previous experience. For example, make the description of the company and your role at the company each one sentence. You can use some of the saved space to tell three things you accomplished at each company or job.
b. When you are beginning your career, what you learned is more important than where you learned it. Consider adding a box to your resume that lists the knowledge you've gained through volunteering, internships, and group memberships.

STEP 5. Make your resume visually appealing. (Consider adding color, for example.)

STEP 6. Know what you want.

a. Don't be indifferent.
b. Make the interviewer feel your passion.
c. Have a career goal that exceeds what you are interviewing for.

STEP 7. Go beyond Google.

a. Be resourceful. Find out something unique about the company you are applying to and what they do.
b. Just like your resume, your content and responses to application and interview questions should be tailored to fit.

STEP 8. Understand as much as you can about the people interviewing you.

a. Ask whom you will be meeting with and what their roles are.
b. Leverage social media tools to find out more.

STEP 9. Be prepared with unobvious answers.

a. Have a compelling answer about what the company does.
b. Go beyond the surface. Be prepared with answers that not every candidate will give.

STEP 10. Know what equity you want to leave behind.

a. Prepare so that your responses are sharp and differentiated.
b. Find your balance between humility and confidence.
c. Chemistry and cultural fit is as important as talent.

CHAPTER NOTES

1. Ravi Sawhney and Deepa Prahalad, "The Role of Design in Business," *Bloomberg Businessweek,* February 1, 2010, http://www.businessweek.com/stories/2010-02-01/the-role-of-design-in-businessbusinessweek-business-news-stock-market-and-financial-advice.

2. John T. Mentzer (ed.), *Supply Chain Management* (Thousand Oaks, CA: Sage Publications, 2001), p. 14.

3. Leonard L. Berry, "Relationship Marketing of Services— Perspectives from 1983 and 2000," *Journal of Relationship Marketing* 1, no. 1 (2002), http://www.uni-kl.de/icrm/jrm/pages/jrm_01.pdf#page=62.

4. Sam Schechner, "Cord-Cutting Avoids Biggest Cities," *The Wall Street Journal,* November 22, 2010, http://online.wsj.com/article/SB10001424052748703567304575628831283366798.html.

5. Peter Coy, "The Great Recession: An Affair to Remember," *Bloomberg Businessweek,* October 11, 2012, http://www.businessweek.com/articles/2012-10-11/the-great-recession-an-affair-to-remember.

6. Mikaela Louve, "Social Media Marketing: Not a Magic Bean, but a Very Inexpensive One," *Technorati,* September 20, 2011, http://technorati.com/business/small-business/article/social-media-marketing-not-a-magic/page-2/.

7. Miyoung Kim and Clare Jim, "Japan Quake Tests Supply Chain from Chips to Ships," *Reuters,* March 14, 2011, http://www.reuters.com/article/2011/03/14/us-japan-quake-supplychain-idUSTRE72D1FQ20110314.

8. Barry Peterson, "China Feeling Impact of U.S. Recession," CBS News, July 9, 2009, http://www.cbsnews.com/8301-18563_162-5059809.html.

9. John Tschetter, "Exports Support American Jobs," U.S. Department of Commerce, International Trade Administration, n.d., http://trade.gov/publications/pdfs/exports-support-american-jobs.pdf.

10. U.S. Department of Commerce, International Trade Administration, "U.S. Export Fact Sheet," February 10, 2012, http://trade.gov/press/press-releases/2012/export-factsheet-february2012-021012.pdf.

11. Jack Farchy, "Food Crisis Fears as U.S. Corn Soars," *Financial Times,* June 13, 2012, http://www.ft.com/cms/s/0/ad1ec426-cd07-11e1-92c1-00144feabdc0.html#axzz2GBoT3Zhk.

12. Matthew Phillips, "How Europe's Contagion May Hit the U.S. Economy," *Bloomberg Businessweek,* June 7, 2012, http://www.businessweek.com/articles/2012-06-07/how-europes-contagion-may-hit-the-u-dot-s-dot-economy.

13. Office of the United States Trade Representative, "NAFTA Facts," n.d., http://www.ustr.gov/sites/default/files/NAFTA-Myth-versus-Fact.pdf.

14. American Marketing Association, "AMA Dictionary," n.d., http://www.marketingpower.com/_layouts/Dictionary.aspx?dLetter=G.

15. Coca-Cola, "Coca-Cola Beverages and Products," n.d., http://www.worldofcoca-cola.com/coca-colaproducts.htm.

16. William J. Holstein, "How Coca-Cola Manages 90 Different Brands," *Strategy + Business,* November 7, 2011, http://www.strategy-business.com/article/00093?gko=f3ca6.

17. Knowledge@Wharton, "Why Companies Can No Longer Afford to Ignore Their Social Responsibilities," *Time,* May 28, 2012, http://business.time.com/2012/05/28/why-companies-can-no-longer-afford-to-ignore-their-social-responsibilities/.

18. *CNNMoney,* "World's Most Admired Companies," March 21, 2011, http://money.cnn.com/magazines/fortune/mostadmired/2011/full_list/.

19. *CNNMoney,* "Fortune 500 2012," n.d., http://money.cnn.com/magazines/fortune/fortune500/.

20. Laura P. Hartman and Joseph Desjardins, *Business Ethics: Decision Making for Personal Integrity & Social Responsibility,* 2nd ed. (New York: McGraw-Hill, 2010).

21. Paul Schmitz, "Look to Nonprofit Sector to Create Jobs," CNN, October 19, 2012, http://www.cnn.com/2012/10/19/opinion/schmitz-nonprofit-jobs.

22. St. Jude Children's Research Hospital, "St. Jude Receives Halo Award," June 8, 2008, http://www.stjude.org/stjude/v/index.jsp?vgnextoid=8a7374995d1aa110VgnVCM1000001e0215acRCRD.

23. St. Jude Children's Research Hospital, "Fundraising," n.d., http://www.stjude.org/stjude/v/index.jsp?vgnextoid=0ea8fa3186e70110VgnVCM1000001e0215acRCRD&vgnextchannel=fc4c13c016118010VgnVCM1000000e2015acRCRD.

Chapter 2

STRATEGIC PLANNING FOR A SUCCESSFUL FUTURE

LEARNING OBJECTIVES

After reading this chapter, you should be able to

LO 2-1 Discuss the importance of strategic planning for marketing.

LO 2-2 Outline the five main components of the marketing plan.

LO 2-3 Analyze the characteristics of an effective mission statement.

LO 2-4 Explain the elements of a situation analysis.

LO 2-5 Illustrate the major strategic directions a firm might take.

LO 2-6 Discuss the strategic decisions involved in reaching international consumers.

LO 2-7 Discuss the importance of strategic planning for nonprofit firms.

EXECUTIVE PERSPECTIVE

Michael Friloux
Senior Vice President of Business Development
Citynet

Michael Friloux had a plan. He chose computer science as his major in college and intended to pursue a technical career in software development and software engineering. But Friloux quickly discovered that planning is a dynamic process and that meeting his objective of finding a job meant modifying his plans. After college, Friloux accepted a job with a communications firm, which allowed him to combine his technical skills with the marketing knowledge he had acquired during college. Over the course of his career as a product developer, sales engineer, and vice president of marketing and network planning, Friloux sharpened his ability to develop and implement strategic marketing plans. Today, as a senior vice president of business development, his responsibilities include determining Citynet's strategic direction.

What has been the most important thing in making you successful at your job?

I would say the most important thing is my ability to work well with people combined with a strong work ethic and personal integrity. The most difficult part of operating any business lies in the ability to communicate well with people. I try to embrace the uniqueness within people and empower them with situations and opportunities that challenge them and allow them to grow. It's important for managers to surround themselves with people who will challenge their thinking. Managers who need people around to agree with everything they say might not be in the right job.

What advice would you give soon-to-be graduates?

Take responsibility for marketing yourself and your career. Remember that it's easier to blame others for your disappointments than to take responsibility for yourself. If you can learn to take 100 percent responsibility for yourself, you will be empowered to make the decisions you need to make throughout your career. Beyond personal responsibility, it is very important to understand that your professional education is only beginning, not ending, with your college degree. Learn to be a life-long student and

recognize that knowledge is power. To be successful, you will also need social skills, integrity, a good work ethic, and determination. People with strong social skills universally outperform their peers, even if their peers have superior technical abilities. You could be the best engineer, accountant, lawyer, or marketer in the world, but if people don't like working with you, they won't.

How is marketing relevant to your role at Citynet?

Developing marketing strategy and implementing our organization's marketing plan is something I focus on every day. I am always looking at the marketplace to see what opportunities we might have to meet customer demands better or more cheaply than our competitors. I use all of the marketing mix elements in my role, and I make decisions on price points, product development, advertising, and distribution questions almost every week of the year.

What do you consider your personal brand to be?

This is a very important question that everyone should consider carefully. I have always felt that, regardless of your place of employment, you are, in essence, always working for yourself. Your reputation is your brand. It takes years to build one but only minutes to tear one down. I would say my personal brand is a combination of honesty, integrity, openness, and achievement.

Michael Friloux
Senior Vice President of Business Development

Citynet
http://citynet.com/

Citynet is a regional telecommunications company headquartered in West Virginia.

This chapter explores the importance of strategic planning in marketing. Executing a thoughtful strategic marketing plan is the most likely path to sustainable business success. The chapter examines the role of a mission statement, situation analysis, marketing strategy, global marketing strategy, and other elements of an effective marketing plan. As you read through the chapter, consider the following key questions:

1. Why is strategic planning important for marketing?
2. What elements should a marketing plan include?
3. How do I evaluate the effectiveness of a firm's mission statement?
4. What tools can I use to analyze my firm's situation externally and internally?

5. What strategic directions can a firm take?
6. How does globalization affect marketing strategy?
7. Why is strategic planning critical for nonprofit organizations?

LO 2-1

Discuss the importance of strategic planning for marketing.

THE IMPORTANCE OF STRATEGIC PLANNING

Imagine starting college and just randomly taking classes because they are interesting, easy, or you have friends enrolled in a particular section. You could be a full-time student each semester, get good grades, and at the end of four years what would you have? Not much of anything except student loan debt. Most of you have a checklist of courses you must complete to graduate in your selected field. Selecting your

Strategic planning is essential to meeting both professional and personal objectives. In the same way that a strategic plan will help you accomplish your goal of earning a college degree, a firm's strategic plan helps guide it to success.

major as a freshman or sophomore and determining when you will take the required courses is a strategic plan you set for yourself. Without the specific objectives of your degree program and a strategy for balancing your classes with the personal and professional demands on your time, you likely will not succeed in achieving your desired result: a college diploma.

Whether you are marketing yourself or some other product, strategic planning can greatly increase the likelihood of success. Strategic planning is the process of thoughtfully defining a firm's objectives and developing a method for achieving those objectives. Firms must continually undertake the task of strategic planning. Shifting conditions, including changing customer needs and competitive threats, ensure that what worked in the past will not always work in the future, thus requiring firms to modify their strategy. Strategic planning helps to ensure that marketers will select and execute the right marketing mix strategies to maximize success. The primary strategic planning tool for directing and coordinating the marketing effort is the marketing plan.

THE MARKETING PLAN

A marketing plan is part of an organization's overall strategic plan, which typically captures other strategic areas such as human resources, operations, equity structure, and a host of other non-marketing items. The marketing plan is an action-oriented document or playbook that guides the analysis, implementation, and control of the firm's marketing strategy. Creating a marketing plan requires the input, guidance, and review of employees throughout the various departments of a firm, not just the marketing department, so it is important that every future business professional understand the plan's components.

The specific format of the marketing plan differs from organization to organization, but most plans include an executive summary, situation analysis, marketing strategy, financials section, and controls section. These five components communicate what the organization desires to accomplish and how it plans to achieve its goals. Figure 2.1 illustrates the five components and gives a brief description of each. Each of the components should be grounded in the firm's overall mission, which is ideally defined in a clear and succinct mission statement. We'll discuss the characteristics of an effective mission statement in the section that follows before turning to a more in-depth discussion of each of the marketing plan components.

MISSION STATEMENT

The first step in creating a quality marketing plan is to develop an effective mission statement. A mission statement is a concise affirmation of the firm's long-term purpose. An effective mission statement provides employees with a shared sense of ambition, direction, and opportunity. A firm should begin the process of developing a mission statement by considering the following classic questions posed by Peter Drucker, who is considered the father of modern management:[1]

- What is our business?
- Who is our customer?

EXECUTIVE PERSPECTIVE

Michael Friloux
Senior Vice President of Business Development
Citynet

What do you think the role of strategic planning is in an organization?

What is the difference between strategy and vision? How many people in business are truly visionary? I'm afraid the answer is not many. Strategic plans that are not carefully thought out fail a majority of the time and can, in fact, be fatal to a given business enterprise. Only by understanding and weighing the capabilities of a business enterprise can one hope to extrapolate a strategic plan that is both credible and achievable. It is very analogous to baking a cake—you need to get the ingredients right, but you also need to execute the baking to achieve the desired result. A recipe by itself isn't of much value; it's the baking that matters most.

LO 2-2
Outline the five main components of the marketing plan.

strategic planning
The process of thoughtfully defining a firm's objectives and developing a method for achieving those objectives.

marketing plan
An action-oriented document or playbook that guides the analysis, implementation, and control of the firm's marketing strategy.

LO 2-3
Analyze the characteristics of an effective mission statement.

mission statement
A concise affirmation of the firm's long-term purpose.

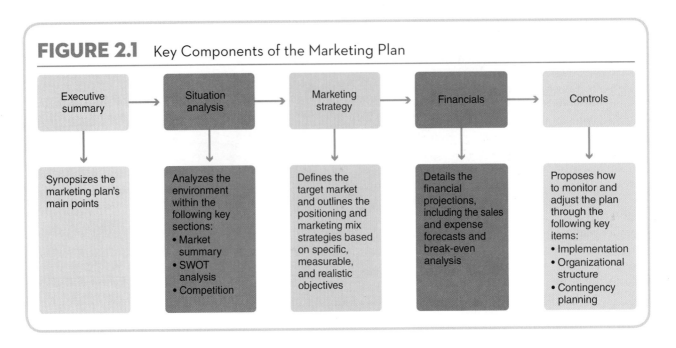

FIGURE 2.1   Key Components of the Marketing Plan

Executive summary	Situation analysis	Marketing strategy	Financials	Controls

| Synopsizes the marketing plan's main points | Analyzes the environment within the following key sections:
• Market summary
• SWOT analysis
• Competition | Defines the target market and outlines the positioning and marketing mix strategies based on specific, measurable, and realistic objectives | Details the financial projections, including the sales and expense forecasts and break-even analysis | Proposes how to monitor and adjust the plan through the following key items:
• Implementation
• Organizational structure
• Contingency planning |

- What is our value to the customer?
- What will our business be?
- What should our business be?

These basic questions are often the most challenging and important that a firm will ever have to answer. From there, the firm should focus on instilling the three primary characteristics of a good mission statement.

1. *The mission statement should focus on a limited number of goals.* Companies whose mission statements contain 10 or more goals are typically focusing too much on small, less meaningful objectives, rather than creating a broader statement that provides purpose and direction to the entire organization.

2. *The mission statement should be customer oriented and focused on satisfying basic customer needs and wants.* Advanced technological products of just a generation ago, such as the VCR or Polaroid camera, are outdated technologies today. Still, consumers' desire to watch movies in their home and to take and share pictures with friends and family is stronger than ever. Apple has been one of the most successful companies of the past decade because it has designed innovative new products like the iPod, iPhone, and iPad. Since it is quite possible that consumers 20 years from now will think of these products the same way you think about VCRs and Atari game systems today, Apple's mission statement should reflect the firm's customer orientation and focus on meeting customer needs.

3. *Mission statements should capture a shared purpose and provide motivation for the employees of the firm.* They should emphasize the firm's strengths, as Google's does: "Google's mission is to organize the world's information and make it universally accessible and useful."[2]

The following mission statements of other leading companies illustrate these three characteristics:

Amazon: We seek to be Earth's most customer-centric company for four primary customer sets: consumers, sellers, enterprises, and content creators.[3]

Citigroup: Citi works tirelessly to serve individuals, communities, institutions and nations. With 200 years of experience meeting the world's toughest

Ice cream company Ben & Jerry's mission statement includes three parts, an economic mission, a product mission, and a social mission, each of which guides the company as it strives to be both profitable and sustainable.

challenges and seizing its greatest opportunities, we strive to create the best outcomes for our clients and customers with financial solutions that are simple, creative and responsible. An institution connecting over 1,000 cities, 160 countries and millions of people, we are your global bank; we are Citi.[4]

CarMax: To provide our customers great quality cars at great prices with exceptional customer service.[5]

Xerox: Through the world's leading technology and services in business process and document management, we're at the heart of enterprises small to large, giving our clients the freedom to focus on what matters most: their real business.[6]

Microsoft: Microsoft's mission is to help people and businesses throughout the world realize their full potential.[7]

Ford: An exciting viable Ford delivering profitable growth for all.[8]

A firm's mission statement drives many of the other decisions it makes, including how best to market its goods and services to consumers. A sound mission statement provides a basis for developing the marketing plan and, as the firm continues to modify its marketing plan to fit changing times, the mission statement provides a standard to ensure that the business never strays too far from its core goals and values. Once the firm has established its mission statement, it can begin to develop the five main components of its marketing plan.

EXECUTIVE SUMMARY

Once you have graduated and begun your career, you will likely come into contact with senior level executives at your firm in casual places, such as the break room or elevator. When they ask what you are working on, you won't have 20 minutes to discuss yourself and your projects. More likely, you will have time for only a short *elevator pitch,* which is a one- to two-minute opportunity to market yourself and share the main points of the work you are doing. The executive summary serves as the elevator pitch for the marketing plan. It provides a one- to two-page synopsis of the marketing plan's main points. In the same way that you should put great effort into making sure that every second of your elevator pitch counts, every line of an executive summary should convey the most valuable information of the marketing plan. Depending on your organization's size and objectives, the marketing plan you create may be viewed by dozens or even hundreds of people. Some will take the time to read each line, but most are looking for a way to quickly understand the basic ideas and strategies behind your plan. The executive summary provides this resource. While the executive summary is listed first, firms should complete this part of the marketing plan last.

SITUATION ANALYSIS

LO 2-4
Explain the elements of a situation analysis.

situation analysis
The systematic collection of data to identify the trends, conditions, and competitive forces that have the potential to influence the performance of the firm and the choice of appropriate strategies.

market
The group of consumers or organizations that is interested in and able to buy a particular product.

market summary
A description of the current state of the market.

The situation analysis section is often considered the foundation of a marketing plan because organizations must clearly understand their current situation to make strategic decisions about how to best move forward. A situation analysis is the systematic collection of data to identify the trends, conditions, and competitive forces that have the potential to influence the performance of the firm and the choice of appropriate strategies. The situation analysis comprises three subsections: market summary, SWOT analysis, and competition.

Market Summary

The market summary sets the stage for the situation analysis section by focusing on the market to which the firm will sell its products. A market is the group of consumers or organizations that is interested in and able to buy a particular product. The market summary describes the current state of the market. For example, a market summary for McDonald's might look at the size of the fast food market in the United States and how rapidly its numbers are growing or declining. A quality market summary should provide a perspective on important marketplace trends. For example, the residential home phone market is a multibillion-dollar-a-year industry. However, a market summary for this service should also point out that the number of traditional landline customers for AT&T, Verizon, and other carriers shrinks every year as more people decide to use only a cell phone. Understanding where a market is and where it might be going gives organizations a much better view of what resources to invest where, and what a firm can achieve through a specific marketing plan. The market summary would also consider the growth opportunities internationally and potential sales through international expansion.

BCG Matrix   One of the most popular analysis tools to describe the current market is The Boston Consulting Group (BCG) matrix. The tool is a two-by-two matrix that graphically describes the strength and attractiveness of a market. Figure 2.2 illustrates The BCG matrix. The vertical axis measures market growth while the horizontal axis measures relative market share, which is defined as the sales volume of a product divided by the sales volume of the largest competitor. The BCG matrix combines the two elements of market growth and relative market share to produce four unique

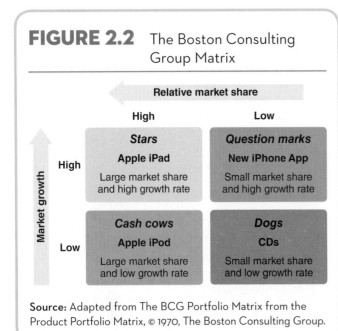

FIGURE 2.2   The Boston Consulting Group Matrix

Source: Adapted from The BCG Portfolio Matrix from the Product Portfolio Matrix, © 1970, The Boston Consulting Group.

product categories—stars, cash cows, question marks, and dogs—each of which requires a different marketing strategy.

- *Star* products combine large market share with a high growth rate. Apple's iPad falls under this category. Firms with star products generally have to invest heavily in marketing to communicate and deliver value as the industry continues to grow. Marketing efforts around star products focus on maintaining the product's market position as a leader in a growing industry for as long as possible.
- *Cash cows* are products that have a large market share in an industry with low growth rates. An example of a cash cow product is the Apple iPod. The market growth rate for MP3 type players has slowed in recent years, but the iPod still retains a large share of the market. As a result, Apple marketers may decide to allocate only enough marketing resources (e.g., television commercials, special pricing discounts) to keep sales strong without increasing costs or negatively affecting profits.
- *Question marks* have small market share in a high-growth industry. Products in this quadrant are typically new to the market and require significant marketing investment in promotion, product management, and distribution. A new iPhone application would be a question mark product. Marketers for the new app must move quickly and creatively to reach Apple product users before competitors develop comparable apps. Question marks have an uncertain future and marketers must monitor the product's position in the matrix to determine whether or not they should continue allocating resources to it.
- *Dogs* are products that have small market share in industries with low growth rates. Products that fall into this category typically should be discontinued so the firm can reallocate marketing resources to products with more profit potential. An example of a dog product might be compact discs, an industry in which no firm has large market share and the growth rate is declining.

As part of the market summary, The BCG matrix allows a company to determine where its product will fall in the marketplace and serves as a starting point for developing marketing strategies to address that market position.

SWOT Analysis

The evaluation of a firm's **s**trengths, **w**eaknesses, **o**pportunities, and **t**hreats is called a SWOT analysis. A SWOT analysis can be a valuable tool in the development of a marketing plan, but only if it's executed well. Perhaps the most common mistake a firm makes when conducting a SWOT analysis is failing to separate internal issues from external issues. Consider how a firm like McDonald's might conduct a SWOT analysis (see Table 2.1).

Internal Considerations The strengths and the weaknesses aspects of the analysis focus on McDonald's internal characteristics. Strengths are internal capabilities that help the company achieve its objectives. McDonald's strengths include its strong brand recognition with consumers of all ages and backgrounds; a system that ties individual store owners' profits to company profits; and the fact that it's a profitable company, which gives it the financial strength to consistently develop new products, further promote its brand, and make strategic acquisitions when opportunities present themselves.

Weaknesses are internal limitations that may prevent or disrupt the firm's ability to meet its stated

SWOT analysis

An evaluation of a firm's **s**trengths, **w**eaknesses, **o**pportunities, and **t**hreats.

strengths

Internal capabilities that help the company achieve its objectives.

weaknesses

Internal limitations that may prevent or disrupt the firm's ability to meet its stated objectives.

Companies like McDonald's often complete a SWOT analysis to identify and evaluate their strengths, weaknesses, opportunities, and threats.

TABLE 2.1   Example SWOT Analysis for McDonald's

Internal Considerations

Strengths

- Brand recognition
- Effective supply chain strategy
- Rigorous food safety standards
- Affordable prices and high-quality products
- Decentralized yet connected system
- Innovative excellence program
- Promotes ethical conduct
- Profitable

Weaknesses

- Inflexible to changes in market trends
- Difficult to find and retain employees
- Drive to achieve shareholder value may conflict with corporate social responsibility
- Promotes unhealthy food

External Considerations

Opportunities

- International expansion
- Positive environmental commitments
- Declining economy could increase demand for lower priced restaurants
- Corporate social responsibility committee
- Honest and real brand image

Threats

- Weak economy could lead to fewer people dining out
- Consumer trend to choose perceived healthier restaurants
- Health concerns surrounding beef, poultry, and fish in some markets
- Potential labor exploitation in some countries
- Contributes to global warming

objectives. One major weakness for a firm like McDonald's is the challenge of finding and retaining quality employees. Another weakness is the perception that McDonald's drives profits by selling unhealthy foods to consumers, especially children. Marketers must be honest with themselves when identifying weaknesses because developing strategies to overcome them begins with recognizing them as problems.

External Considerations

opportunities

External factors that the firm may be able to capitalize on to meet or exceed its stated objectives.

threats

Current and potential external factors that may challenge the firm's short- and long-term performance.

External Considerations   The opportunities and threats aspects of the SWOT analysis focus on the external environment. Opportunities are external factors that the firm may be able to capitalize on to meet or exceed its stated objectives. Opportunities for McDonald's in the years ahead include increased international expansion. McDonald's currently serves approximately 68 million customers each day in 119 countries.[9] International growth, especially in Europe and Asia, has exceeded earnings growth at domestic McDonald's restaurants in recent years.[10]

Threats are current and potential external factors that may challenge the firm's short- and long-term performance. McDonald's faces a number of potential external threats, including a declining global economy and the domestic consumer trend of eating healthier and consuming less fast food.

External factors can be both opportunities and threats. For example, the sluggish economy following the global recession that began in December 2007 has made it harder for many firms to expand their businesses, secure loans, and hire new employees. Restaurants as an industry have faced additional challenges as consumers attempt to reduce the amount of money they spend on luxuries like going out to eat. This reality threatens McDonald's as well. However, the slow economy has also prompted consumers to look for cheaper food alternatives, and, as the world's leading choice for discounted dining, McDonald's has an opportunity to take advantage of this trend. Firms must understand and analyze environmental factors—both internal and external—to develop a quality marketing plan.

---

conNect | Interactive Assignment 2-1
|MARKETING|

Please complete the *Connect* exercise for Chapter 2 that focuses on conducting a SWOT analysis. By identifying which elements of a fictional company's situation analysis fall into each category, you will understand the key differences among each of the four SWOT components.

Competition

Many firms struggle to successfully compile the competition section of the market summary. The section should begin by clearly stating the organization's direct competitors. Continuing with our McDonald's example, direct competitors would include Burger King and Wendy's. The section should briefly describe how Burger King and Wendy's position their products relative to McDonald's. It should also indicate where McDonald's is most vulnerable to Burger King and Wendy's on important customer metrics such as taste, value, pricing, convenience, and customer satisfaction.

While most marketing plans examine direct competitors thoroughly, indirect competitors typically receive far less attention or are overlooked entirely. Indirect competitors can take market share away from a firm as macro trends or consumer preferences change. McDonald's must worry not only about other burger chains but also about the consumer trend of eating healthier, which has translated into massive expansion for chains like Subway. In 2011, Subway surpassed McDonald's as the largest restaurant chain in the world, with almost 34,000 stores worldwide compared to less than 33,000 for McDonald's.[11] Consumers choosing to eat at home rather than purchase fast food in a slow economy also compete indirectly with McDonald's. A good study of the competition provides a thoughtful analysis of both the direct and indirect competitors.

When completing a situation analysis, it's just as important for a firm like McDonald's to analyze indirect competitors, such as Subway, as it is to analyze direct competitors, such as Burger King.

MARKETING STRATEGY

Once the situation analysis is complete, marketers focus on defining their marketing strategy. A strategy is the set of actions taken to accomplish organizational objectives. A successful marketing strategy can lead to higher profits, stronger brands, larger market share, and a number of other desired outcomes for stakeholders of the organization. The marketing strategy component of the marketing plan lists the actions the firm must take to accomplish the marketing objectives it established in its mission statement and strategic planning process. The effectiveness of the marketing strategy depends in part on the clarity of the short- and medium-term objectives the firm has defined. Quality marketing objectives have three basic characteristics:

1. *Specific.* Objectives are not of any value if they are not specific. If Google identified an objective to increase ad revenues, how would it formulate a strategy around that? Would it be happy with $1 of revenue growth over the

LO 2-5

Illustrate the major strategic directions a firm might take.

strategy

The set of actions taken to accomplish organizational objectives.

next 10 years? Would it develop its marketing strategy accordingly? Vague marketing objectives lead to a lack of focus and accountability.

2. *Measurable.* Objectives must be measurable so that marketers know if their strategies are working. A common phrase said in marketing offices around the globe is, "If it can't be measured, it can't be managed." Firms want to see a specific return on their marketing investment. Marketers aren't often fired for having a bad idea (we all have bad ideas), but they can face negative consequences if they keep making the same mistake over and over again because, due to a lack of measurable metrics, they don't realize their strategy isn't working.

3. *Realistic.* Objectives need to be realistic so that marketers do not demotivate their organizations with unattainable goals. Imagine if your professor said that, to get an A in this marketing course, you had to score 100 percent. You might be demotivated to try your best and decide that a B in marketing is good enough. Objectives also should be realistic to show those reading the marketing plan that it is a serious, thoughtful document. A professional sports organization that sets an objective to increase ticket revenue by 300 percent, even though its team continues to lose to competitors, could lead someone reading the document to doubt the reliability of all the other parts of the marketing plan, too.

Based on these criteria, McDonald's marketers might set an objective to sell 5 percent more premium coffee or 3 percent more chicken nuggets in existing U.S. stores. Either of these hypothetical objectives would be specific, measurable, and realistic. Before McDonald's can establish strategies to meet either objective, it must clearly identify which customers are most likely to buy premium coffee or chicken nuggets and decide how best to position each product in the minds of those customers.

Target Markets and Positioning

target market

The group of customers toward which an organization has decided to direct its marketing efforts.

multinational company

A firm that operates in two or more countries.

positioning

The activities a firm undertakes to create a certain perception of its product in the eyes of the target market.

Developing specific, measurable, and realistic marketing objectives provides a good basis for companies as they seek to identify a target market and correctly position their product for that market. A target market is the group of customers toward which an organization has decided to direct its marketing efforts. Small firms may have only one target market. Large organizations might enter multiple target markets. A firm with multiple target markets that operates in two or more countries is called a multinational company. McDonald's has historically targeted adults, teenagers, and families with small children looking for a quality meal that is quick and inexpensive. In recent years, McDonald's has targeted gourmet coffee drinkers in an effort to win them away from companies like Starbucks. Regardless of size, firms tend to enter multiple markets by first serving one group and then expanding based on success with that group.

Success within the target market depends, to some degree, on how the firm positions its product. Positioning refers to the activities a firm undertakes to create a certain perception of its product in the eyes of the target market. The firm has total control over this element of its marketing efforts, and the concept is critical to how it develops the rest of its marketing strategy. To position its product, firms

EXECUTIVE PERSPECTIVE

Michael Friloux
Senior Vice President of Business Development
Citynet

Why is it important to clearly identify a firm's target markets?

The biggest mistake I have seen companies make is trying to be all things to all people because they don't know who their target market is. Part of being a successful marketing executive is knowing why customers buy your products and then having the discipline to focus only on the target markets that are most valuable to the firm. Too many companies spread themselves too thin trying to promote products that their target market does not care about.

must take into consideration issues such as the competition, the needs and wants of the target market, and the element of mystique or drama that the good or service naturally has. When McDonald's entered the gourmet coffee market, it had to overcome the perception that it was simply a place to get Big Macs and Happy Meals. McDonald's marketers launched an advertising campaign called "Unsnobby Coffee," put espresso machines in thousands of its stores, and aggressively positioned itself as a place for consumers to get great coffee for a lower price than Starbucks.

Another example of successful positioning is the Ford Fusion Hybrid. Ford marketers positioned the Fusion as a more stylish, youthful hybrid car compared to competitors like the Toyota Camry Hybrid. The Fusion's Aston Martin–like design helped build excitement among younger buyers, including many who had never purchased a Ford before. The improved positioning helped the Ford Fusion set record hybrid sales numbers for the company and introduced the Ford brand to a new generation of car buyers.

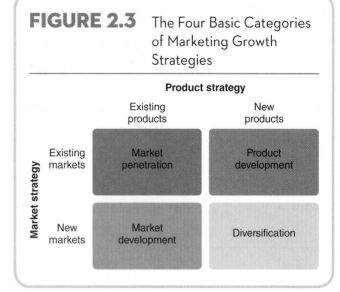

FIGURE 2.3 The Four Basic Categories of Marketing Growth Strategies

| | | **Product strategy** | |
		Existing products	New products
Market strategy	Existing markets	Market penetration	Product development
	New markets	Market development	Diversification

Strategic Directions

A company's marketing strategy can follow various paths based on the product and industry, but most seek to move the product in one of the four directions illustrated in Figure 2.3: market penetration, product development, market development, and diversification.[12] Each of these categories represents the intersection of a strategy related to products and another related to markets. We'll discuss each in more depth in the sections that follow.

Market Penetration
Market penetration strategies emphasize selling more of existing goods and services to existing customers. This type of growth strategy often involves encouraging current customers to buy more each time they patronize a store or to buy from the store on a more frequent basis. For example, marketers at Pizza Hut try to get existing consumers to buy one more pizza each month or add an order of breadsticks to their normal pizza order. They have found success offering the "Big Dinner Box," which includes two medium pizzas and two side items. The product introduced consumers to side dishes, such as wings, pasta, or breadsticks, that they might not have thought to buy from Pizza Hut. For such a market penetration strategy to succeed, firms often must increase advertising expenses, develop new distribution frameworks, or enhance their social media offerings.

Product Development
Product development strategies involve creating new goods and services for existing markets. Dr Pepper used a product development strategy when it introduced Dr Pepper Ten, a 10-calorie soft drink, using a male-targeted marketing campaign with the slogan, "It's not for women." While Diet Dr Pepper's marketing was female-friendly, the Dr Pepper Ten campaign focused

market penetration
A marketing strategy that emphasizes selling more of existing goods and services to existing customers.

product development
A marketing strategy that involves creating new goods and services for existing markets.

The product development strategy behind Dr Pepper Ten was designed to appeal to men who were concerned about calories but felt that Diet Dr Pepper was a female-oriented product.

International expansion is an increasingly necessary part of a successful market development strategy for small firms as well as large retailers like Walmart.

on male consumers who enjoyed Dr Pepper, but were interested in drinking a beverage with fewer calories.[13] Dr Pepper believed that men were generally unhappy with the taste and image of diet drinks and marketed Dr Pepper Ten as a better-tasting, manlier product in an effort to reach its target market in a new way. A new product can also be an improved product or one with a new feature or innovation. Apple has successfully developed multiple new iPhone products with additional features and functionality for its consumers and each has been welcomed by long lines and strong initial sales.

market development

A marketing strategy that focuses on selling existing goods and services to new customers.

diversification

A marketing strategy that seeks to attract new customers by offering new products that are unrelated to the existing products produced by the organization.

Market Development   Market development strategies focus on selling existing goods and services to new customers. The targeted new customers could be of a different gender, age group, or country. Globalization is an increasingly critical strategy for virtually any company or industry. The vast majority of the 100 largest American-based companies are rapidly increasing their international presence and aggressively implementing market development strategies throughout the world. Arkansas-based retail giant Walmart has recently seen its international division grow to account for over 25 percent of total company revenue.[14] In 2012, Walmart International operated in 27 countries, including China, India, Brazil, and Mexico, where it had over 2,200 stores.[15] A company seeking to expand into foreign markets must have a clear strategy for implementation that maximizes its chances for success. Later in the chapter, we'll discuss the various strategies firms can use to enter international markets.

Diversification   Diversification strategies seek to attract new customers by offering new products that are unrelated to the existing products produced by the organization. Disney has diversified significantly over the past few decades, moving from a company that produced animated movies and ran theme parks to an international family entertainment and media enterprise that owns television channels like ABC and ESPN as well as independent production companies like Lucasfilm and sells vacation properties, books, apparel, and international

consumer products. Having developed a positive reputation over many years, the company is poised to further diversify its operations and products to hedge against decreasing sales in some products due to economic conditions.

---

connect | MARKETING   Interactive Assignment 2-2

Please complete the *Connect* exercise for Chapter 2 that focuses on the four strategic directions a firm can take. By identifying which company used each particular strategy, you will understand how all of the strategies may impact your future employer.

Marketing Mix

The final aspect of the marketing strategy section of the marketing plan focuses on determining how each element of the marketing mix will support the chosen strategy.

Product The product section of the marketing plan comprises a detailed description of the product being offered, not only the good or service itself, but also any related services like warranties and guarantees that accompany the good or service. The product description should clearly state what value the product holds for the customer and should build on the competition section to explain what competitive advantage the firm's product offers. A product possesses a competitive advantage when it enjoys a superior position over competing products because consumers believe it has more value than other products in its category. By focusing on the complete product rather than solely on the good or service itself, the firm can differentiate itself from its competitors and satisfy the unmet needs and wants of potential customers. For example, McDonald's provides food and beverage products, but so do many other restaurant chains. McDonald's competitive advantage relates to its ability to provide these items in a fast, low-cost way in a clean restaurant. Thinking of the product as a combination of goods, services, and ideas allows the firm to think beyond hamburgers and chicken nuggets to consider what the consumer is actually buying. For a family stopping at McDonald's on a vacation, it may be the free wireless Internet access or the clean restrooms. The marketing plan should clearly address how the firm communicates what its product is and what value the product holds for the consumer.

competitive advantage

The superior position a product enjoys over competing products if consumers believe it has more value than other products in its category.

Promotion The promotion section of the marketing plan details how the organization will communicate the value of its product. This section builds on the strengths of the product section and references the specific promotional tools—advertising, sales promotion, personal selling, or public relations—the organization will use to reach its target market. For example, McDonald's might decide to increase spending on television advertising to promote its Fish McBites during Lent, when many religious consumers stop eating meat on Fridays. McDonald's could also use part of its approximately $2 billion annual advertising budget to promote the quality of its food on radio, in newspapers, and across social media in an effort to encourage a more selective group of consumers to dine more often.[16]

Distribution Distribution strategies fall within the *place* marketing mix element. The distribution section of the marketing plan describes how the firm will deliver value to its customers. McDonald's has a number of distribution decisions to make. How will it get products to more than 30,000 stores in a fresh and safe

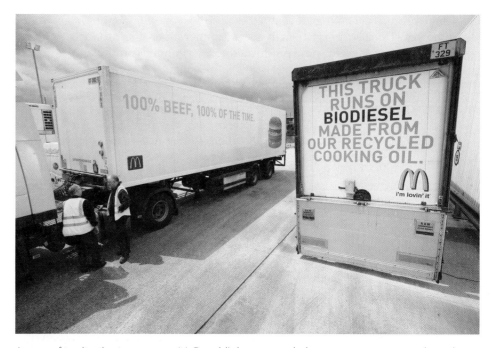

As part of its distribution strategy, McDonald's has responded to customer concerns about the environment by using trucks in the United Kingdom and France powered by biodiesel made from recycled cooking oil. The trucks play a dual role in that they also promote the practice.

manner? What time of day should it make certain items like breakfast food available? Should it partner with gas stations and travel centers to offer its products at facilities beyond McDonald's restaurants? The distribution section should outline all the different companies, people, and technologies that will be involved in the process of delivering the product to customers.

Pricing   The pricing section of the marketing plan specifies how much money customers must pay for the product and describes why that price was selected. For example, McDonald's increased menu prices by 1 percent in March of 2011 because of an increase in the price of commodities like hamburger meat and buns. However, commodity prices rose several percentage points more than 1 percent. McDonald's didn't increase its prices by the same amount because McDonald's marketers understood that consumers remained concerned about overspending in a weak economy.[17] McDonald's marketers believed that keeping price increases small was essential to keeping customer volume up. This type of information should be reflected in the pricing section of the marketing plan.

FINANCIALS

The overall profitability of both the product and the firm can be found in the financial section of the marketing plan. Financial projections provide those reading the plan with a bottom-line estimate of the organization's profitability. Financial projections can include numerous items, but all should contain a sales forecast (or fundraising projections for a nonprofit), an expense forecast, and a break-even analysis.

financial projections
A bottom-line estimate of the organization's profitability.

- *Sales forecast.* Many departments rely on a sales forecast, which projects how many units of a product the company expects to sell during a specific time period.
- *Expense forecast.* The expense forecast is an estimate of the costs the company will incur to create, communicate, and deliver the product. Without

an expense forecast, marketers will have a very difficult time allocating resources and predicting when the product will become profitable.

- *Break-even analysis.* Break-even analysis combines the data provided in the sales and expense forecasts to estimate how much the company needs to sell to cover its expenses.

We will discuss financial projections in more depth in later chapters.

CONTROLS

The final section in most marketing plans outlines the controls the firm will put in place to monitor and adjust the plan as the firm executes on the strategy laid out in it. The controls section should include the following three items:

1. *Implementation.* The implementation section provides a detailed account of how the specific actions of the marketing plan will be carried out and who will be responsible for carrying them out. No matter how good the marketing plan is, it is of no value unless the company implements it successfully. Each step of the implementation of a marketing plan, such as buying advertising on a specific television channel or utilizing a new Twitter hashtag, should tie back to the marketing strategy and the specific objectives laid out in the mission statement and during the strategic planning process. Marketers should carefully monitor each marketing strategy and expect to make adjustments depending on results or as market conditions change over time.

2. *Organizational structure.* An outline of the organizational structure helps hold specific departments and individuals responsible for the parts of the marketing plan that fall under their control. When elements of the marketing strategy are not implemented correctly, it's often because the plan does not clearly indicate who is responsible for carrying out each activity. By clearly outlining who is accountable for which tasks, the marketing plan can help to clarify ownership and drive positive results.

3. *Contingency planning.* Contingency planning defines the actions the company will take if the initial marketing strategy does not achieve results. Coca-Cola famously changed direction after its New Coke product failed to meet company objectives. The firm reintroduced the old Coke formula as Coca-Cola Classic and began to add profits and market share again. Contingency planning is also important as you market yourself throughout your career. Even after completing this course, graduating from college, and gaining more work experience, there will be numerous times in your professional career when strategies you've developed don't work out as planned. To prepare for such eventualities, it will be important for you to consider how you will monitor your progress and change course, if necessary.

Mc Graw Hill cor∩ect™ |MARKETING   ## Interactive Assignment 2-3
Social Media in Action

S Social Media

Procter and Gamble (P&G) was looking for a way to reverse flat or declining sales of its Pepto-Bismol product in 2010. Marketing research suggested that Pepto-Bismol was most commonly discussed on social media during Saturday and Sunday mornings, likely due to the fun consumers were having late on Friday and Saturday nights. To attract consumers to the brand, P&G marketers increased the role of social media in their marketing plan with a Facebook campaign for Pepto focused on the upbeat slogan "Celebrate Life"—a campaign that targeted users when they were most likely to be engaged by the message. The strategy paid off as Pepto-Bismol's market share increased by 11 percent in the 12 months following the introduction of the new strategy.

Such success has prompted P&G to incorporate additional advertising on social media sites into its marketing plan for a variety of products, including Cover Girl makeup and Crest toothpaste. Examples range from a blog called "My Fire Hydrant" that stars a Bichon Frise lap dog to promote Iams pet food to a Facebook page for Secret deodorant aimed at teenage girls and featuring a cast member from the popular television show "Glee." Such strategies have allowed P&G marketers to reach a new group of consumers and build deeper relationships with current customers.

The Social Media in Action *Connect* exercise for Chapter 2 will give you a chance to decide how social media strategies fit into a marketing plan. By understanding the role social media can play in achieving your objectives, you will be able to apply these strategies to successfully implement a marketing plan for your organization in the years ahead.

Source: See Lauren Coleman-Lochner, "Social Networking Takes Center Stage at P&G," *Bloomberg Businessweek*, March 29, 2012, http://www.businessweek.com/articles/2012-03-29/social-networking-takes-center-stage-at-p-and-g.

LO 2-6

Discuss the strategic decisions involved in reaching international consumers.

MARKETING STRATEGY IN A GLOBAL CONTEXT

The marketing plan elements we've discussed up to this point assume the firm's activities will be directed only to the domestic market. However, the new reality of globalization means a firm's strategic planning process must include a discussion about what, if any, international presence the firm wants to pursue. One of the most critical strategic decisions involves how to enter foreign markets. As part of developing a marketing plan that involves global marketing, the firm must choose from among the following five major strategic options for entering the international marketplace: exporting, licensing, franchising, joint venture, or direct ownership. These options are illustrated in Figure 2.4, and each offers a unique mix of risk and reward, which we will discuss in more depth in the sections that follow.

Exporting

exporting

Selling domestically produced products to foreign markets.

Typically, the least risky option for entering international markets is exporting. Exporting is selling domestically produced products to foreign markets. Increasingly, firms of all sizes export their products to other countries. Large firms like Cargill (producer of food, agricultural, financial, and industrial goods and services) and ExxonMobil (oil and gas company), two of the largest domestic

---

FIGURE 2.4   International Market Entry Strategies

Low risk, lower potential return → Exporting → Licensing → Franchising → Joint venture → Direct ownership → High risk, higher potential return

exporters, ship tens of thousands of products annually in support of their various business units. But exporting is not just popular among the companies that make up the Fortune 500. Small companies, like those that many of you will work for after college, account for 96 percent of all U.S. exporters.[18] Social media tools allow small businesses to engage customers around the world in a way that was not possible a decade ago. Logistics firms like FedEx and UPS also help to increase export opportunities by providing small businesses with a quick, efficient way to deliver products almost anywhere in the world. These tools provide almost any small business in the U.S. with the opportunity to become an exporter.

Licensing

Licensing offers marketers the advantages of expanding the reach of their products quickly in a low cost way. Licensing is a legal process in which one firm pays to use or distribute another firm's resources, including products, trademarks, patents, intellectual property, or other proprietary knowledge. Such arrangements occur in the domestic market as well, but in a global context, the domestic licensor allows a foreign company to use its resources. With growing attendance and television ratings in recent years and mounting interest from overseas markets, Major League Baseball (MLB) continues to enjoy strong licensing revenues. MLB licensees operate Clubhouse stores in Puerto Rico and sell MLB-licensed apparel at Harrods department store in London.[19] Revenue from MLB international licensing doubled between 2007 and 2012.[20]

The use of licensing to enter international markets has increased significantly in recent years due to several factors, including more regulation, rising research and development (R&D) costs, and shortened product life cycles. Licensing helps to overcome some of these barriers since the licensee is typically locally owned and brings unique insight about its local consumers. Despite its growing popularity, licensing is typically a riskier option than exporting. Major risks include (1) that the licensor may be inadvertently creating a future competitor in the form of the licensee, (2) that the licensor shares information and the right to use its proprietary technology with the licensee, and (3) that the licensee could potentially misuse trademarks.

Franchising

You already may be familiar with franchising at U.S. companies like McDonald's. Franchising is a contractual arrangement in which the franchisor (McDonald's) provides a franchisee (local owner operator) the right to use its name and marketing and operational support in exchange for a fee and, typically, a share of the profits. International franchise agreements are the same as domestic agreements with the obvious exception that they must meet the commercial laws of the country in which the franchise exists. Franchising is an attractive method of entering foreign markets because franchisees assume the majority of the capital costs and human resource issues. The franchisor provides knowledge and information about running the business, which increases the likelihood of success.

licensing
A legal process in which one firm pays to use or distribute another firm's resources, including products, trademarks, patents, intellectual property, or other proprietary knowledge.

franchising
A contractual arrangement in which the franchisor provides a franchisee the right to use its name and marketing and operational support in exchange for a fee and, typically, a share of the profits.

Major League Baseball has expanded its licensing programs in international markets to include apparel, toys and video games, sporting goods, trading cards, and memorabilia.

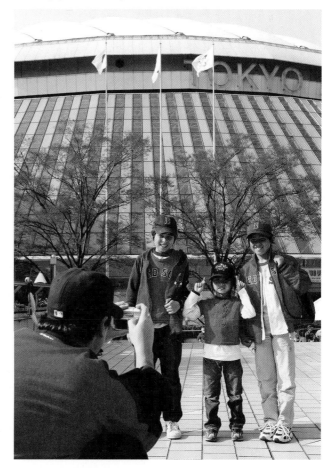

The disadvantages of franchising include the risks of granting your name to a franchisee in a faraway place where direct oversight is difficult. If a McDonald's in South America was involved in a negative public event, it could damage the McDonald's name throughout the world. Franchisors also run the risk of providing such detailed information that a franchisee could potentially have a competitive advantage if they chose to open a competing business.

Joint Venture

joint venture

An arrangement in which a domestic firm partners with a foreign company to create a new entity, thus allowing the domestic firm to enter the foreign company's market.

A riskier option than exporting, licensing, or franchising is a joint venture. In a joint venture, a domestic firm partners with a foreign company to create a new entity, thus allowing the domestic firm to enter the foreign company's market. The local partner shares equity in the new entity and provides the foreign entrant with valuable information about local consumers, suppliers, and the regulatory environment. Joint ventures work best when the partners' strategic goals align, their competitive goals diverge, and they are able to learn from one another without infringing on each other's proprietary skills. For example, Texas-based Exxon-Mobil launched a joint venture with Russian company Rosneft to develop offshore oil fields in the Russian arctic.[21] This joint venture allowed Exxon to benefit from Rosneft's extensive knowledge and infrastructure in Russia, while Rosneft benefited from Exxon's technology and access to several North American drilling projects in which they would now be partners.

Joint ventures come with inherent risk. Domestic and international firms often operate differently, which can lead to culture clashes. Joint ventures also can result in mistrust over proprietary knowledge, conflict over new investments, and disagreements about how to share revenue and profits. AT&T entered into a joint venture with Phillips NV, an Amsterdam-based electronics company, to produce telecommunications equipment in Europe. The venture was ultimately unsuccessful due to Phillips NV's inability to help AT&T penetrate the French telecom market.[22]

Direct Ownership

direct ownership

A method of entering an international market in which a domestic firm actively manages a foreign company or overseas facilities.

The riskiest method of entering an international market is direct ownership, which requires a domestic firm to actively manage a foreign company or overseas facilities. Direct ownership is a good strategic option when the firm sees substantial sales potential in the international market, very little political risk, and similarities between the foreign and domestic cultures.

Still, maintaining 100 percent ownership of offices, plants, and facilities in a foreign country exposes the firm to significant risks. Direct ownership requires far more resources and commitment than any of the other options, and it can be difficult to manage local resources from afar. However, direct ownership provides the firm with more control over its intellectual property, advertising, pricing, and product distribution.

Marketers should diligently and thoroughly analyze the risks and rewards of each type of foreign entry as they develop their marketing plan. Regardless of which method a company ultimately pursues, as with all other strategic decisions, the strategy for entering international markets must align with the firm's objectives as defined in its mission statement and strategic planning process.

---

connect |MARKETING **Interactive Assignment 2-4**

Please complete the *Connect* exercise for Chapter 2 that focuses on the approaches to entering an international market. By identifying an example of each strategy and its risk level, you will understand the potential risks and rewards of marketing your products globally.

Erin Blankenship
Development Coordinator

Harmony Health Clinic
http://www.harmonyclinicar.org/

Harmony Health Clinic (HHC) is a free medical, dental, and pharmaceutical clinic for uninsured and low-income residents near Little Rock, Arkansas.

Erin Blankenship

Development Coordinator
Harmony Health Clinic

Describe your job. My position as development coordinator involves creating sustainability through successful events and loyal donors and developing capacity building processes. Throughout the year, my duties consist of increasing donor support, coordinating fundraising and special events, developing newsletters and monthly mailings, updating social media sites, and providing administrative support to the director.

Describe how you got the job that you have. Finding a job right out of college was no easy task. I secured this job through a series of networking opportunities. Asking my current supervisors, professors, and fellow church members for contacts or information regarding the nonprofit world proved to be very effective. Before I knew it, I was e-mailing people I'd never met asking for assistance. One day, I received a call from Harmony's executive director saying he had received my resume from the director of another nonprofit. The executive director's name was not even familiar to me—the job had found me.

What has been the most important thing in making you successful at your job?

1. Flexibility and self-motivation. Small nonprofits are typically understaffed. Therefore, there is ample amount of responsibility to go around but not much time for a director to micromanage. Every day looks different,

and daily tasks do not always fit into one's job description. This might sound frustrating, but for those who desire a constantly changing work environment, it could be a perfect fit.

2. Not being afraid to ask. New graduates with little experience aren't expected to know it all yet, but they are expected to ask and search for the answer.

3. Ability to be creative with minimal resources. On more than one occasion I was asked to plan an event with a *very* small budget for décor, advertisement, and venue rental. These scenarios require extra effort but have proven to be the most rewarding.

What advice would you give soon-to-be graduates?

- Start looking for jobs early. It can take months to get the right interviews, but adopting the mindset early can help you avoid the shock of the real world after graduation.
- Network, network, network. Even if you are shy, even if it's awkward. No one knows who you are and what you are passionate about unless *you* tell them.

What do you consider your personal brand to be? I'm a personable and passionate advocate. I use creativity and whatever resources are available to me to develop stronger communities and improve the lives of poverty-stricken neighbors.

STRATEGIC PLANNING FOR NONPROFIT ORGANIZATIONS

Marketing plans are an unfamiliar concept for many nonprofits. However, just like in for-profit firms, strategic planning is an essential part of effective marketing at nonprofit organizations. Though some aspects of a nonprofit marketing plan may differ from that of a for-profit firm, the main components and overall structure remain the same.

One of the largest nonprofits in the world is United Way. United Way's mission is to "improve lives by mobilizing the caring power of communities around the world to advance the common good."[23] United Way works with countless partner agencies to help with childhood nutrition, domestic abuse shelters, economic development, and dozens of other important causes. United Way is divided into various state and regional organizations, each with its own marketing plan based on the overall mission of the organization. For example, United Way of Southeast Alaska used the following mission statement in a recent marketing plan. Notice how the mission statement answers the basic questions we discussed earlier in the chapter:

> United Way of Southeast Alaska works to improve lives by organizing the caring power of our communities in Southeast Alaska. We are a volunteer-driven, grass-roots organization that creates lasting change by bringing people and resources together to address local and regional issues. We link donors and volunteers to the issues they care about and form strategic partnerships to achieve community impact. Working with our 33 partner agencies, United Way helps children and youth succeed, supports the elderly and people with special needs, promotes wellness and self-sufficiency, and meets the basic needs of people in crisis.[24]

For the United Way of Southeast Alaska to achieve its mission it must develop quality marketing objectives, just as a for-profit firm would. These objectives could relate to fundraising, volunteers, or awareness. Establishing specific, measurable, and realistic objectives is especially valuable for nonprofits because of their limited resources and their larger goal of providing the maximum amount of services to their constituents in need. Quality marketing objectives that the United Way of Southeast Alaska might use include the following:

- Create consistent brand identity that is recognized by over 70 percent of current and potential donors through all of United Way of Southeast Alaska's communications.
- Increase the number of volunteers by 7 percent through Day of Caring, campaign activities, and the Volunteer Action Center.
- Broaden the base of donors by 10 percent through leadership, corporate, workplace, and in-kind giving.
- Increase the private campaign total by $50,000 through implementing effective marketing strategies and building positive relationships.
- Increase grant awards 12 percent by presenting a clear message about the United Way of Southeast Alaska.

United Way of Southeast Alaska should also outline specific marketing strategies designed to help it spread its message and successfully increase fundraising.

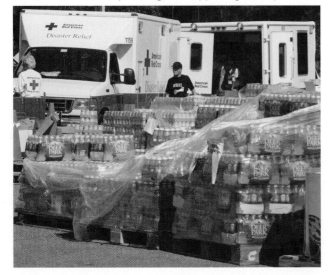

Nonprofit organizations like the American Red Cross rely on strategic planning to ensure that they've allocated resources appropriately to fund their various services, including disaster relief, health and safety training, and supporting military families.

Communication Strategies

Messages will be delivered in a variety of formats both direct and indirect.

Direct messaging will include:
- Brochures/pledge forms
- Annual report
- Quarterly e-mail newsletter to donors
- Monthly e-mail newsletter to campaign representatives
- Campaign representative kits
- One-page information sheet for workplaces on as-needed basis during campaign
- Face-to-face presentations
- Phone conversations, both planned and impromptu
- All donor events

Indirect messaging will include:
- Advertising
- Op-ed columns
- Press releases
- Public service announcements
- Placed news stories
- Public presentations
- Website[25]

Nonprofit marketers should pay especially close attention to the implementation and accountability sections of the marketing plan, as most work on a very tight marketing budget, making every dollar spent a critical investment. Whatever their mission, nonprofit organizations must think strategically about their marketing plan to ensure success. Whether they are churches looking to expand their ministry or university foundations looking to raise money for student scholarships, nonprofits must use effective marketing strategies to compete for donor support.

SUMMARY

 LO 2-1 Discuss the importance of strategic planning for marketing.

Strategic planning helps to ensure that marketers will select and execute the right marketing mix strategies to maximize success. Strategic planning is the process of thoughtfully defining a firm's objectives and developing a method for achieving those objectives. The primary strategic tool for directing and coordinating the marketing effort is the marketing plan.

 LO 2-2 Outline the five main components of the marketing plan.

A marketing plan should be an action-oriented document or playbook that guides the analysis, implementation, and control of the firm's marketing strategy. A typical marketing plan includes an executive summary, a situation analysis, the marketing strategy, financials, and controls.

 LO 2-3 Analyze the characteristics of an effective mission statement.

A quality mission statement provides employees with a shared sense of purpose, direction, and opportunity. Effective mission statements share three key characteristics: (1) they focus on a limited number of goals, (2) they are market oriented and focused on satisfying basic customer needs and wants, and (3) they should capture a shared purpose and provide motivation for the employees of the firm.

LO 2-4 Explain the elements of a situation analysis.

A situation analysis contains the market summary, SWOT analysis, and competition analysis. The evaluation of a firm's strengths, weaknesses, opportunities, and threats is called a SWOT analysis, which is especially important. Strengths are internal capabilities that help the company achieve its objectives. Weaknesses are internal limitations that may potentially prevent or disrupt the firm's ability to meet its stated objectives and goals. Opportunities are external factors that the firm may be able to capitalize on to meet or exceed its stated objectives. Threats are current and potential external factors that may challenge the firm's short- and long-term performance.

 LO 2-5 Illustrate the major strategic directions a firm might take.

While there are a variety of marketing strategies across industries, most fall under four basic categories. Market penetration strategies emphasize selling more of existing goods and services to existing customers. Product development strategies involve creating new products or services for existing markets. Market development strategies involve selling existing products or services to new customers. Finally, diversification strategies seek to attract new customers by offering new products that are unrelated to the existing products produced by the organization.

 LO 2-6 Discuss the strategic decisions involved in reaching international consumers.

Once a company has developed a marketing plan that involves global marketing, it can enter the global marketplace using one of five major approaches: exporting, licensing, franchising, joint venture, and direct ownership. Exporting is selling domestically produced products to foreign markets and is typically the least risky option for entering international markets. Licensing is a legal process in which one firm pays to use or distribute another firm's resources. Franchising is a contractual arrangement in which the franchisor provides a franchisee the right to use its name and marketing and operational support in exchange for a fee and, typically, a share of the profits. In a joint venture, a domestic firm partners with a foreign company to create a new entity. Typically the riskiest method of entering an international market is direct ownership, which requires a domestic firm to actively manage a foreign company or overseas facilities.

 LO 2-7 Discuss the importance of strategic planning for nonprofit firms.

Marketing plans are an unfamiliar concept for many nonprofits. However, just like for-profit firms, nonprofit organizations require effective marketing plans to achieve their objectives. Whether they are churches looking to expand their ministry or university foundations looking to raise money for student scholarships, nonprofit organizations must use effective marketing strategies to compete for donor support.

KEY TERMS

competitive advantage (p. 41)
direct ownership (p. 46)
diversification (p. 40)
exporting (p. 44)
financial projections (p. 42)
franchising (p. 45)
joint venture (p. 46)
licensing (p. 45)
market (p. 34)

market development (p. 40)
market penetration (p. 39)
market summary (p. 34)
marketing plan (p. 31)
mission statement (p. 31)
multinational company (p. 38)
opportunities (p. 36)
positioning (p. 38)
product development (p. 39)

situation analysis (p. 34)
strategic planning (p. 31)
strategy (p. 37)
strengths (p. 35)
SWOT analysis (p. 35)
target market (p. 38)
threats (p. 36)
weaknesses (p. 35)

MARKETING PLAN EXERCISE

In this chapter we discussed the elements and importance of the situation analysis. The next step in developing a full marketing plan for yourself is to conduct a SWOT analysis on yourself that ties back to the objectives you developed at the end of Chapter 1. Be sure to think through each element honestly and assess where you are today. This will help you focus on what you need to accomplish over the rest of your college career.

Strengths. If you ask a group of your friends what their strengths are, they can likely answer you very quickly. Most people have taken the time to

discover their strengths (maybe they're an effective public speaker, pay a great deal of attention to detail, or work well with others) and had those strengths reinforced by those around them over the course of their life. To effectively complete this part of your personal SWOT analysis, list the three to five strengths that you possess that will most impact your ability to achieve the objectives you identified in Chapter 1.

Weaknesses. While most people are very honest about their strengths, they are typically far less likely to be aware of or to acknowledge their weaknesses. Corporate recruiters often tell humorous stories about the responses they receive when asking new college graduates about their biggest weaknesses. Answers range from "I care too much," or "I am too smart for my group members," to "I am too attractive to have many friends." Any of these responses can negatively impact your ability to impress a prospective employer. Give serious consideration to your personal weaknesses, and then list three to five weaknesses that will impact your ability to achieve your objectives. By properly identifying your weaknesses, you can begin to plan strategically how to overcome them or, at the very least, minimize their influence on your career objectives.

Opportunities. As the global economy changes and you enter a job market very different from the one faced by previous generations, it is important to honestly assess your opportunities. Ask yourself questions like, What jobs in my major are most in demand? What internship openings are there and how might those put me in a better position to find my dream job? If your goal is to attend graduate school, what kinds of scholarships, assistantships, or enrollment opportunities are out there for you? Be sure to identify three to five external opportunities that exist to potentially benefit you in your professional development.

Threats. As demonstrated by the economic crisis that began in December 2007, assessing threats is an essential part of developing a strategic plan for your professional future. If the economy goes into a recession at the same time you are planning to graduate, your earnings growth could be reduced for years to come. By examining what potential threats could impact your professional development and creating contingency plans, you will be in a better position to succeed in your pursuit of a job. Describe three to five threats that could impact your ability to achieve your objectives.

Your Task: Describe three to five strengths, weaknesses, opportunities, and threats that could affect your professional development. For each weakness and threat you identify, include a brief one- to two-sentence description of how you might overcome the challenge associated with it.

DISCUSSION QUESTIONS

1. Find mission statements from five Fortune 500 companies, then rank them from best (1) to worst (5) and discuss why you ranked them in that order. Which mission statements did you really like? How would you modify the mission statement you ranked last to make it better?

2. Conduct a SWOT analysis for your college or university. List three to five strengths, weaknesses, opportunities, and threats for your school.

3. Select a marketing strategy implemented by a large firm or nonprofit organization that you think was effective. Describe why you liked the strategy. Identify which of the strategic directions discussed in this chapter best reflects the strategy you chose.

4. Select two businesses you frequent (e.g., restaurants, clothing stores, grocery stores, etc.). Who is their target market? Then identify at least two competitors (either direct or indirect) for each business. Describe how the two businesses you selected position themselves in the market relative to their competitors. Which one of the two businesses does a better job positioning its products to its target market? Explain your answer.

5. Is marketing your products globally always a good decision? Discuss your answer and provide examples of firms that have both succeeded and failed in international markets.

SOCIAL MEDIA APPLICATION

Analyze the social media presence of your college or university using the following questions and activities as a guide:

1. In your opinion, is your institution doing a good job marketing the school through social media?

2. What grade would you give your school's efforts and why?

3. Provide at least two specific recommendations for how your school could improve its social media marketing presence. In addition, provide an example of a university that is doing a better job of marketing through social media than your school and describe what it does.

ETHICAL CHALLENGE

Bank of America announced in 2011 that it was considering introducing a $5 fee for some debit card users. Bank of America introduced several types of accounts that year that require users to pay fees unless they keep minimum balances in the accounts, make regular deposits, or use credit cards. As a shareholder, these fees provide Bank of America with the opportunity to recover some of the profits that were lost when higher swipe fees for debit cards were capped. Without these fees, it is possible that Bank of America's revenues, profits, and stock prices could decline.

However, these debit card fees have a disproportionally negative impact on low-income customers. Customers who do not have much money in their account may not meet the minimum balance requirements and are impacted to a larger degree by the monthly charge that could equal $60 per year. Driving revenue that benefits shareholders and employees at the possible expense of banking's most

vulnerable customers presents marketers with an ethical dilemma. Please use the ethical decision-making framework to answer the following questions:

1. What are the major ethical issues surrounding Bank of America's decision? Who are the affected stakeholders? How will those stakeholders be affected?
2. If you were a competitor of Bank of America, what would your marketing strategy be for dealing with the new Bank of America fee?
3. How is Bank of America positioned in the marketplace? Does this fee reinforce the image it is seeking to create?

Source: See Hugh Son, "BofA Plans $5 Monthly Fee for Some Debit-Cards," *Bloomberg Businessweek*, September 29, 2011, http://www.bloomberg.com/news/2011-09-29/bofa-to-charge-5-monthly-fee-to-customers-using-debit-cards-for-purchases.html.

VIDEO CASE

Please go to *Connect* to access the video case featuring Ford Motor Company that accompanies this chapter.

CAREER TIPS

Marketing Your Future

You have read in this chapter about the importance of planning for your career and future. As you strategically plan for your career, Michael Friloux, who was featured in the Executive Perspective at the beginning of the chapter, encourages you to spend time considering two things that many college graduates don't fully appreciate: the power of questions and the importance of people skills.

THE POWER OF QUESTIONS

I have found that certain habits influence the opportunities and careers of individuals, some more so than others. I would venture to say that the most influential habit to adopt is what I call the power of questions. I have seen many employees, interviewees, colleagues, and superiors

shy away from asking questions for fear of sounding dumb, looking ridiculous, or giving the appearance of weakness. In practice, I have found the exact opposite to be true. Individuals who seek out information and clarity by asking lots of questions, no matter how basic or mundane, not only perform their jobs better, but can also empower those around them, thus indirectly freeing the flow and quality of communications. Many times people perform tasks incorrectly because they failed to ask the right questions. This is harmful not only to the individual but also to the business enterprise. My advice would be to develop the habit of asking questions, to always listen attentively, and to continually seek to improve the quality of the questions you ask. When in doubt, always ask the question. You'll be glad you did.

THE IMPORTANCE OF PEOPLE SKILLS

Take a minute to inventory all of the most successful people you know. My guess is they all have one trait in common: superior people skills. Many people, myself included, begin their careers with the belief that they will create the most value for themselves by being the best at what they do. However, highly focused individuals who overlook the importance of building relationships inhibit their ability to grow and prosper in their careers. You could be the best marketer, engineer, teacher, or chemist (fill in the blank) known to man, but if people don't like you or, for whatever reason, can't relate to you, they aren't going to want to work with you either. Conversely, if you have average technical skills but possess superior people skills, all sorts of opportunities, including promotions, will open up to you. Of course, you should always seek to be the best at whatever trade or course you choose, but recognize that it's equally important to cultivate positive and productive interactions with everyone you work with.

CHAPTER NOTES

1. Peter Drucker, *Management: Tasks, Responsibilities, Practices* (New York: Truman Talley Books, 1986), pp. 58–69.
2. Google, "Company," n.d., http://www.google.com/about/company/.
3. Amazon, "Amazon Investor Relations," n.d., http://phx.corporate-ir.net/phoenix.zhtml?c=97664&p=irol-irhome.
4. Citi, "Our Mission: Enabling Progress," n.d., http://www.citigroup.com/citi/about/mission_principles.html.
5. CarMax, "AboutCarMax," n.d. http://www.carmax.com/enus/company-info/about-us.html.
6. Xerox, "Xerox at a Glance," n.d., http://www.xerox.com/about-xerox/company-facts/enus.html.
7. Microsoft, "Mission," n.d., https://www.microsoft.com/enable/microsoft/mission.aspx. Used with permission from Microsoft.
8. Ford, "Our Company," n.d., http://corporate.ford.com/our-company/our-company-news-detail/one-ford.
9. McDonald's, "Our Story," n.d., http://www.mcdonalds.com/us/en/our_story.html.
10. Dan Burrows, "McDonald's Stock Hits Record High on Global Growth," *Moneywatch*, October 21, 2011, http://www.cbsnews.com/8301-505123_162-49043138/mcdonalds-stock-hits-record-high-on-global-growth/.
11. NewsCore, "Subway Overtakes McDonald's as Largest Fast Food Chain," Fox News, March 7, 2011, http://www.foxnews.com/leisure/2011/03/07/subway-overtakes-mcdonalds-largest-fast-food-chain/.
12. H. Igor Ansoff, "Strategies for Diversification," *Harvard Business Review* 35, no. 5 (September–October 1957), pp. 113–124.
13. Mae Anderson, "Dr Pepper's New Brand Is a Manly Man's Soda," *Associated Press*, October 10, 2011, http://www.msnbc.msn.com/id/44849414/ns/business-us_business/t/dr-peppers-new-brand-manly-mans-soda/.
14. Anne D'Innocenzio, "Wal-Mart 2Q Profit Boosted by Global Growth, Cost Cutting," *USA Today*, August 17, 2010, http://usatoday30.usatoday.com/money/companies/earnings/2010-08-17-walmart_N.htm.
15. Walmart, "Our Story," n.d., http://corporate.walmart.com/our-story/.
16. Keith O'Brien, "How McDonald's Came Back Bigger than Ever," *The New York Times*, May 4, 2012, http://www.nytimes.com/2012/05/06/magazine/how-mcdonalds-came-back-bigger-than-ever.html?pagewanted=all&_r=0.
17. Convenience Store News, "McDonald's Reveals Pricing Strategy," *CSNews Foodservice*, April 22, 2011, http://foodservice.csnews.com/top-story-mcdonald_s_reveals_pricing_strategy_-838.html.
18. U.S. Small Business Administration, "Export Business Planner for Your Small Business," n.d., http://www.sba.gov/sites/default/files/SBA%20Export%20Business%20Planner.pdf.
19. Major League Baseball International, "Licensing and Sponsorship," n.d., http://www.mlbinternational.com/?p=articles&art_cat_id=66.
20. Eric Fisher, Don Muret, and John Ourand, "Names in the Game," *Street & Smith's SportsBusiness Journal*, April 2, 2012, http://www.sportsbusinessdaily.com/Journal/Issues/2012/04/02/In-Depth/Names-in-baseball.aspx.
21. Vladamir Soldatkin and Melissa Akin, "Rosneft wins American Access in Exxon Deal," *Reuters*, April 13, 2012, http://www.reuters.com/article/2012/04/13/us-exxon-rosneft-idUSBRE83C0SY20120413.
22. Aimin Yan and Yadong Luo, *International Joint Ventures: Theory and Practice* (Armonk, NY: M.E. Sharpe, 2001).
23. United Way, "Vision, Mission, and Goals," n.d., http://www.unitedway.org/pages/mission-and-goals/.
24. United Way of Southeast Alaska, "United Way of Alaska 2006 Marketing Plan," May 19, 2006, http://www.rasmuson.org/_attachments/sampleplan1.pdf.
25. Ibid.

APPENDIX 2A   SAMPLE MARKETING PLAN

Cuisine Masters Restaurant Supply

The executive summary provides a one- to two-page synopsis of the marketing plan's main points. While the executive summary is listed first, firms typically complete it last. Every line of an executive summary should convey the most valuable information of the marketing plan.

EXECUTIVE SUMMARY

Cuisine Masters Restaurant Supply, Inc. (CMRS), is offering the Automated Salad Maker (ASM), which is a technologically advanced salad maker that can supply any type of salad within seconds of order entry. The capacity of the Automated Salad Maker will be to produce 60 to 120 salads per hour, depending upon size and ingredients used. This salad maker is a one-of-a-kind piece of equipment with no direct competition; however, CMRS has existing competition within the southeastern and south-central portions of the United States for other restaurant supply products. The targeted market segment will be restaurants that provide house and custom salads to consumers in a high-volume, sit-down style setting in the southeastern and south-central United States. Total market size consists of both chain and privately owned restaurants. The ASM will reduce labor needs and costs for the establishment while producing quality controlled salads in a quick, efficient manner.

The primary marketing objective is to reach a 3 percent share of the market within the first year with volume unit sales of 184 units. Additionally, a 5 percent share of the market will be met in the second year with volume unit sales of 306 units. The final goal is to reach a 10 percent share of the market in the fifth year with volume unit sales of 613 units.

SITUATION ANALYSIS

Cuisine Masters Restaurant Supply, Inc., was founded in 2012 by three entrepreneurs to satisfy the needs of restaurants across the southeastern and south-central United States. Our vision is to supply technologically advanced restaurant equipment to high-volume, sit-down restaurants so they can reduce kitchen support staff while still providing high-quality meals and services to their customers. The business is set up as a limited liability corporation and has distribution rights to several innovative product lines. We offer research and development (R&D) and engineering services to several manufacturing firms and create these strategic alliances based on market trend and market demand needs. We own the patents and intellectual capital for most of these products.

CMRS competes against several large restaurant supply businesses in our area. To successfully compete in our chosen markets, we employ four salespeople to cover the target regions and one additional salesperson for corporate chain accounts. We also partner with manufacturing facilities that are strategically sourced based on engineering and cost support. We employ several full-time R&D engineers to create new, innovative product lines.

Market Summary

Overall restaurant industry sales are expected to post positive growth and reach $604 billion in 2014, which would stop a three-year trend of decreasing sales. The final expectation for 2014 is sales growth of 3.6 percent over and above 2013 sales. There are currently 960,000 restaurant locations that employ 12.8 million people in the United States. Sales at full-service restaurants are projected to reach $194.6 billion in 2014, an increase of 3.1 percent over 2013. The south-Atlantic area of the country is expected to post the strongest restaurant sales growth at 3.9 percent, totaling $93.9 billion among its eight states, which include Delaware, Florida, Georgia, Maryland, North Carolina, South Carolina, Virginia, and West Virginia.

CMRS's target market for the Automated Salad Maker consists of three of the six primary restaurant sectors: family dining, casual dining, and upscale or fine dining. The geographical segmentation for these three sectors is broken down into two service and sales territories: the southeastern United States and

---

The situation analysis identifies the trends, conditions, and competitive forces that have the potential to influence the performance of the firm and the choice of appropriate strategies. In many ways, this section serves as the foundation of the marketing plan. The situation analysis typically comprises three areas: market summary, SWOT analysis, and competition.

The market summary describes the current state of the market, including how large the market is and how quickly it's growing or declining. The market summary also provides a perspective on important marketplace trends.

the south-central United States. The three sectors that CMRS will avoid are fast food, high-end fast food, and specialty beverage shops.

The target market is made up of restaurants that provide house and custom salads to consumers in a high-volume, sit-down style setting. Total market size consists of both chain and privately owned restaurants. To gain market share in this expansive market, we will specifically target nationally branded chain restaurants such as Applebee's, Chili's, Cracker Barrel, Denny's, IHOP, Panera Bread, and Ruby Tuesday. The southeastern U.S. market offers 4,127 chain restaurants and the south-central U.S. market offers 2,098 chain restaurants.

The potential market sales size for the Automated Salad Maker in the southeastern territory is $14,444,500, which is based on 4,127 chain restaurants multiplied by the $3,500 price per automated salad maker. The potential market sales size for the Automated Salad Maker in the south-central territory is $7,343,000, which is based on 2,098 chain restaurants multiplied by $3,500 per automated salad maker. Together, the annual sales potential for the Automated Salad Maker product line is $21.7 million.

Strengths, Weaknesses, Opportunities, and Threats (SWOT) Analysis

Strengths CMRS can build on three important strengths:

1. **Owns patents and intellectual capital for products**—We own the patents and intellectual capital for our products so that they cannot be imitated.
2. **Excellent quality product**—We take great pride in providing a high-quality and durable product, free of defects.
3. **Excellent management team**—The entrepreneurs that own CMRS are three young and highly talented managers with new ideas and determination.

Weaknesses CMRS has three main weaknesses:

1. **Lack of recognition with consumers because CMRS is a startup organization**—We have no established brand or image whereas other manufacturers do. We will address this with aggressive marketing.
2. **The need to take on debt to get the business off the ground**—We have access to a limited amount of cash. Initial financing will not be difficult due to solid credit and the low inventory depreciation rate, but ongoing financing will be more difficult to obtain. It is not the receivable days that will wreak havoc on the cash plan because sales are 100 percent cash; it is the operating and marketing expenses.
3. **CMRS's new and innovative products do not have a lot of visibility in the U.S. yet**—Our products are relatively new to the market and are still unnoticed by many valuable customers.

The SWOT analysis evaluates a firm's strengths, weaknesses, opportunities, and threats. The strengths and the weaknesses aspects of the analysis focus on the firm's internal characteristics, while the opportunities and threats sections focus on the external factors a firm must consider.

Opportunities CMRS can take advantage of three major market opportunities:

1. **No focused, well-marketed competition**—The market for new and innovative restaurant equipment is not very strong or well established. This gives us the opportunity to develop the market and establish ourselves as the market "original."
2. **The cost of Internet and other direct marketing opportunities has decreased in recent years**—The cost of selling via e-commerce and through mail order has decreased tremendously in recent years. Internet domain names (www.yourname.com) cost $35 a year, and e-commerce servers may be set up for only $30 a month. Certain high-circulation catalog companies will develop custom catalogs for vendors and mail them for a fixed fee. This is incredibly cost effective for companies that do not have relationships with printers, graphic artists, and the like. Both direct mail and Internet sales are a growing segment of our business.
3. **Participation in a growing market with a significant percentage of the target market still not aware that CMRS and its products exist**—We are a relatively new company with many opportunities to market ourselves and gain business as we build name recognition.

Threats CMRS faces two main threats:

1. **High capital costs**—The high cost of capital limits us from investing money in other activities, such as marketing, that would enable the business to gain a larger customer base.
2. **Future/potential competition from national companies**—Established companies will soon begin to imitate our products and produce replicas.

Competition

Competition within the restaurant supply industry has been negatively affected since 2007 with the economic downturn and the lack of extra income for nonessential spending. Fortunately, this situation is beginning to improve. The geographic region that CMRS will focus on is served by local, national, and even international suppliers; however, local suppliers can be more reactive to individual customer needs. The key competitors include local suppliers that provide quality customer service, training, and maintenance. Key local competitors are

> **Burr Ridge Fixture and Sales Company Inc.**—Located in Burr Ridge, Illinois, and serving the midwestern United States, which includes Illinois, Michigan, Iowa, Missouri, and Wisconsin. Burr Ridge Fixture and Sales Company has 70 years of experience and provides over 9,000 in-stock items and products from over 10,000 manufacturers. It provides next-day shipping for virtually all items in-stock.

The competition section should address both the direct and indirect competition the firm will face. It should include a brief summary of the most relevant competitors and highlight any major differences between what they offer and what the firm will offer.

Hall Brothers Restaurant Equipment—Located in Moore, Oklahoma, and serving Oklahoma and Southern Kansas, Hall Brothers has over 25 years of experience and provides quality restaurant equipment, as well as delivery, installation, and service.

Marcy's Restaurant Supply—Located in both San Diego and Anaheim, California, and serving over 20 states, Marcy's Restaurant Supply has almost 30 years of experience and provides quality restaurant equipment to over 5,000 customers. Marcy's offers goods and services to enable customers to solve business problems and create cost-effective solutions for their business.

Irwin Restaurant Supply—Located in Oxford, Alabama, and Memphis, Tennessee, Irwin serves these states and provides service for nationwide customers. Irwin Restaurant Supply provides sales and delivery of quality restaurant equipment; however, it does not provide service and installation.

In our effort to supply national chain restaurants, national suppliers will be relevant competition. Key national suppliers include

Southern Restaurant Products—Located in Little Rock, Arkansas, Southern Restaurant Products has been a national supplier of restaurant products for over 20 years. Southern has over 250,000 customers and offers more than 450,000 items from over 1,000 quality brands. It offers e-commerce and technical support services.

The Pilgrim Company—Headquartered in Lancaster, Pennsylvania, Pilgrim has been in business since 1902 and bills itself as "America's leading supplier and distributor of food service supplies and equipment." Pilgrim has distribution centers in Ohio, Pennsylvania, Texas, Florida, and Arizona to make 48-hour delivery possible for its customers.

Competition will be strong; however, CMRS can achieve success in the restaurant supply industry with high-quality equipment offerings and by controlling the patents for innovative equipment, such as the Automated Salad Maker. By offering products that streamline restaurant activities, CMRS will help restaurants achieve greater customer satisfaction and save money.

MARKETING STRATEGY

CMRS's primary marketing strategy will be an extensive promotion to create knowledge and demand in an untapped market. Our primary consumers are chain restaurants, but we are also targeting family dining, casual dining, and upscale or fine dining. CMRS is able to address many different segments of

A mission statement is a concise affirmation of the firm's long-term purpose. Creating an effective mission statement is the first step in developing a quality marketing plan. Once a mission statement is in place, the firm will have an easier time establishing quality objectives for the short and medium terms.

the market because, although each segment is different, CMRS's product is useful to all of the different segments.

Objectives

Mission Statement The vision of Cuisine Masters Restaurant Supply, Inc., is to supply technologically advanced restaurant equipment to high-volume, sit-down restaurants to allow them to reduce kitchen support staff while still providing high-quality meals and services to their customers.

We have set modest but practical and attainable goals for the first, second, and fifth years of market entry. These sales goals are based off historical sales levels achieved for similar product offerings and similar new product launches:

- **First-Year Unit Sales Objective**—We are aiming for a 3 percent share of the salad makers market through volume unit sales of 184 individual units.
- **Second-Year Unit Sales Objective**—Our second-year objective is to capture a 5 percent share of the salad makers market through volume unit sales of 306 individual units.
- **Fifth-Year Unit Sales Objective**—Our fifth-year objective is to achieve 10 percent share of the market through volume unit sales of 613 individual units. We plan to reach this goal by expanding our business and offering additional products for the kitchen.

Target Markets

CMRS is focusing on a positioning strategy of product differentiation. Our primary targets are privately owned and chain restaurants in three different restaurant sectors: family dining, casual dining, and upscale or fine dining. The restaurants in these target markets produce high-volume, high-quality food and offer standardized service across all their locations. The restaurant industry grew by 3 percent in 2013 and is expected to grow by 3.6 percent in 2014. With these expected growth rates, the competition between restaurants should escalate, driving the need for highly specialized restaurant equipment. This equipment will not only help reduce operating costs but should also help produce excellent quality food and improve service times to the customer.

CMRS is specifically targeting chain restaurants because these restaurants are expanding more quickly than privately owned restaurants and they use standardized food preparation products in each individual location. We can increase market share quickly by focusing on these major chain restaurants. Geographical segmentation has produced two territories—the southeastern and south-central regions of the U.S., which now encompass more than 6,000 restaurants. As the business expands, CMRS will seek to reach other markets in the United States.

Quality objectives must be specific, measurable, and realistic. They state the goal or intention of the firm over a certain period of time, usually 1–5 years. The remaining sections of the marketing strategy should be designed to help the firm meet these objectives.

The target markets and positioning sections give a detailed description of the groups of customers toward which the firm has decided to direct its marketing efforts and define how the firm would like customers to perceive the product.

Positioning

CMRS will position the Automated Salad Maker to our target markets as a high-tech, high-quality, high-performance, and innovative piece of equipment that can be integrated into any kitchen to reduce cost while improving service time and food quality to the customer. The selling points we will leverage are greater customer satisfaction due to improved food delivery times and expanded menu choices, increased menu flexibility as a result of computerized salad recipes, five-year parts and labor coverage from highly trained technical representatives located in each sales territory, and on-site training for all restaurant personnel to coincide with the delivery of each Automated Salad Maker.

Marketing Mix

Product CMRS's newest product is the Automated Salad Maker, which is a technologically advanced salad maker that can supply any type of salad within seconds of order entry. The piece of equipment is a little larger than a large bread-making oven and measures 44" wide $\times$ 55.5" deep $\times$ 92" high. It has 15 different styles of stainless steel cutting instruments that are paired with a patented array of size, shape, color, and chemical analyzers. The analyzers allow it to choose from a refrigerated supply of vegetables and other toppings to create either a custom ordered or traditional house salad derived from recipes programmed by the individual restaurant. Its standard features include bins for plate storage and products, dressings and oils, and wireless capability between the automated salad maker and the wait staff's handheld order pads. It also comes fully equipped with a self-cleaning function that can be run nightly to sterilize and fully clean the equipment to governmental standards.

The product element of the marketing mix section comprises a detailed description of the product being offered, not only the good or service itself, but also any related services like warranties and guarantees that accompany the product (as CMRS does with its Automated Salad Maker and training and extended warranty service products). This section should build on the competition section to explain what competitive advantage the firm's product offers.

The sales potential for the Automated Salad Maker product line is $21.7 million based on the potential market size (south-central territory of 2,098 and southeastern territory of 4,127 restaurants) and a sales price of $3,500. The initial goal for CMRS is to achieve a 10 percent share of the target market within five years. Additional products that can be packaged and sold with each Automated Salad Maker include products from the categories of refrigeration, furniture, concessions, food preparation, shelving and carts, dishwashing and sanitation, cooking equipment, and dining room service products. A wide selection of products that range from manual operation to technologically advanced options are offered in each category and provide cost-reducing, service-enhancing options to our end customers.

CMRS is also going to market a service product as part of this offering. CMRS will offer training packages in which members of our team will go to a customer site and demonstrate the best practices for using the product to management and employees. In addition, we will be selling an extended warranty package, which specifies that our expert technicians will continue

The promotion section should outline the key strategies for communicating the value of the product to targeted customers. It will likely include a discussion of one or more of the following promotional tools: personal selling, advertising, sales promotion, or public relations.

to provide on-site repairs and maintenance for as long as the customer pays for the service. Our technical service support will be the best trained and most customer friendly team in the industry.

Promotion An internally trained sales force will make cold calls to all potential customers and franchises operating in each of our three targeted restaurant markets. The salespeople will each be equipped with a full web-based application running off a tablet device that will showcase CMRS's full line of innovative equipment. These tablets will be used to offer each customer a tailored presentation that is created based off information gathered from industry statistics related to that customer's operating market (demographics, price points, traffic analysis, and restaurant capacity). These presentations will showcase the Automated Salad Maker and all other peripheral equipment that could reduce cost and improve delivery to the restaurant's end customer in the targeted market segment. Salespeople will also have an annual budget that will allow them to attend and present at trade shows specifically tailored to our market segments.

Distribution CMRS operates as the supplier and will distribute products by direct sales to create a variety of purchase options for the customer. The purchasing options will include the following:

- Sales representatives are assigned to cover the south-central and south-eastern portions of the United States; two will operate in each region and one additional sales representative will be assigned to the corporate chain accounts. Sales representatives will make cold calls to local and chain restaurants within their service area. They will provide individualized customer service throughout the entire process, from the initial sales call, to the setup, to the installation and training for the purchased item.
- Web purchases are available for standard stock items. Purchases of specialized items that require installation and training may be initiated online but will require contact with a salesperson before the purchase is final.
- Chain restaurant sales may require sales and services to be provided outside the targeted supply area due to the purchasing requirements of the franchise. These needs will be met as if in the targeted supply area.
- Catalogs will include all products while featuring the Automated Salad Maker and other innovative products for which we retain the patents. Purchase requests may be sent via phone, fax, or e-mail and will be processed through the assigned sales representative to ensure that appropriate customer service is available.

Delivery of the products will depend on the items purchased. Smaller, non-specialized items will be shipped via UPS or FedEx, while larger orders

The distribution section explains in detail how a firm plans to make its products available to targeted consumers. It should summarize the various distribution methods, including the key transportation partners that will be used (e.g., FedEx or UPS).

The pricing section details the specific price points of the product for both the goods and services that make up the product offering. In addition, it should address general strategies for price development over time.

will require scheduled deliveries by hired freight companies. Future delivery plans may include an in-house freight delivery system.

Pricing The Automated Salad Maker will be offered for the initial price of $3,500 per unit, with a five-year warranty that includes free maintenance and repairs. CMRS will work to hold this price constant every year as we make manufacturing and engineering improvements to drive down production costs and improve production efficiencies.

For the service aspects of our plan, we will charge $1,000 per one day of training at a customer site plus expenses. If a customer buys 10 or more units within a six-month time period, they are entitled to one free day of training, with the only charge being the expenses of our trainer getting to the customer location. The extended service warranty will be priced at $395 per year and begins after the initial five-year warranty expires. The extended service warranty provides continued basic service, maintenance, and repair for as long as the customer pays for the service.

FINANCIALS

Total first-year sales revenue for the Automated Salad Maker is forecasted to reach $644,000. This represents 3 percent of the market at a sales level of 184 individual units. The Automated Salad Maker's product line revenues and associated costs are shown in Table 1. Based on the first year's forecast costs, this product line is forecasted to lose $69,000 in its first year of sales.

TABLE 1 Sales and Expense Forecast

	Cuisine Masters Restaurant Supply Forecast Income Statement (In thousands) Automated Salad Maker				
	2018	2017	2016	2015	2014
Sales	$2,146	$1,608	$1,340	$1,071	$644
Cost of Goods Sold	1,073	804	670	536	322
Gross Profit	$1,073	$804	$670	$536	$322
Warranty & Training	215	161	134	107	64
Production & Engineering Fees	107	80	67	54	32
Marketing Expenses	64	48	40	32	19
Selling, General and Administrative Expenses	275	275	275	275	275
EBIT	$412	$240	$154	$68	$(69)
EBIT%	19.2%	14.9%	11.5%	6.3%	(10.7)%

Break-even sales in the first year of production are shown in Table 2. Break-even sales in units for the first year are 240 units, based on monthly sales of 20 units at a sales price of $3,500 per unit.

TABLE 2 Break-Even Analysis

	2014
Monthly Units Breakeven	20
Monthly Sales Breakeven	$70,000
Assumptions	
Average Per-Unit Revenue	$3,500
Average Per-Unit Variable Cost	$1,400
Estimated Monthly Fixed Cost	$41,432

The marketing expenses are forecasted to be 3 percent of product line revenue and are shown in Table 3. The individual expense line items are forecasted as an estimated percentage of total spending based on historical spending patterns for other product lines. The marketing manager is responsible for tracking and managing the marketing expense budget.

TABLE 3 Marketing Expense Budget

	Cuisine Masters Restaurant Supply Forecast Marketing Expense Automated Salad Maker				
	2018	**2017**	**2016**	**2015**	**2014**
	$64,365	$48,248	$40,189	$32,130	$19,320
Advertisements	$25,746	$19,299	$16,076	$12,852	$7,728
Website Charges	16,091	12,062	10,047	8,033	4,830
Printed Material	12,873	9,650	8,038	6,426	3,864
Entertainment	9,655	7,237	6,028	4,820	2,898
Total Expenses	$64,365	$48,248	$40,189	$32,130	$19,320

CONTROLS

The purpose of CMRS's marketing plan is to enable senior management to guide the organization in the correct and most profitable way. The following areas will be monitored continuously to help maintain efficiency and gauge performance:

- Revenue: monthly and annually
- Expenses: monthly and annually

Financial projections provide a bottom-line estimate of the organization's profitability. Financial projections can include numerous items, but all should contain a sales forecast (or fundraising projections for a nonprofit), an expense forecast, and a break-even analysis.

The controls section is the final section in most marketing plans. It outlines the systems that will be put in place to monitor and adjust the plan as the firm executes on the marketing strategy. The control section should discuss implementation, organizational structure, and contingency planning. The implementation section should provide a detailed list of specific items that must be executed to achieve the objectives set by the firm. This section should act as a playbook for the firm's activities for the first six months after the product launch. The organizational structure section should clarify who is accountable for the marketing activities for the specific project. Finally, the contingency planning section should outline potential threats that might derail the success of the marketing plan.

- Customer satisfaction: continuous
- New product development: continuous

Implementation

CMRS will use our interactive sales representatives to track customer response to all equipment purchased and to determine additional needs of the customer. Additionally, tight quality control measures are in place to ensure products delivered to customers are of high quality and defect free. Sales representatives oversee the installation and training needed for major equipment, providing on-site assistance to avoid potential issues with purchases. Sales numbers will be monitored monthly to ensure we are on track to reach our objectives. Owners will meet with the sales representatives monthly to discuss any issues with sales and the success of the marketing plan. If any issues are found, immediate action will be taken to improve the situation.

In order to have a successful product launch and to begin realizing targeted first year sales of 184 units, we have created a series of actions and programs that will be implemented in sequential, campaign order:

1. December 2013—Product literature is printed and distributed. This includes electronic distribution from our internal website and print brochures for direct mailings and face-to-face sales calls.
2. December 2013—Salespeople are provided computer tablets with product applications and marketing campaign literature.
3. December 2013—Salespeople are given sales routes and first product meetings are scheduled and completed with top 20 targeted customers.
4. January 2014—Invite representatives from targeted top five restaurant chains to tour the Automated Salad Maker's production facility and to discuss new opportunities.
5. February 2014—Chosen company representatives attend and present at the Southeastern Restaurant Supply Conference and Trade Show to provide information and demonstration of CMRS's products. This is a shared action item across all product lines with cost support to come from the general marketing fund. All new company products will be displayed at the CMRS booth.
6. March 2014—Advertise in two trade magazines: *Chain Leader* and *Restaurant Report.*
7. April 2014—Host internal sales conference to provide salespeople with Quarter 1, 2014, statistics, solicit feedback on the level of success of the marketing plan, and make adjustments to the plan accordingly.

Organizational Structure

CMRS owners work as a team to manage the marketing activities of the company. Initial plans are discussed and decisions are approved before implementation, which is the responsibility of the vice president of marketing. A catalog publication firm will be hired to provide customized catalogs for the different target segments, and a consultant will be retained to build a website for customer communication and purchasing.

Contingency Planning

Difficulties and Risks

- Problems generating visibility.
- An entry into the market that adopts similar products.

Worst Case Risks May Include

- Determining that the business cannot support itself on an ongoing basis.
- Having to liquidate equipment to cover liabilities.

Chapter 3

ANALYZING YOUR ENVIRONMENT

LEARNING OBJECTIVES

After reading this chapter, you should be able to

LO 3-1 Differentiate between direct and indirect competition.

LO 3-2 Summarize the major external factors that influence the marketing environment.

LO 3-3 Extend the analysis of the marketing environment beyond the borders of the United States.

LO 3-4 Identify the major trade agreements, monetary unions, and organizations that impact the global marketing environment.

LO 3-5 Describe the emerging factors influencing the nonprofit marketing environment.

EXECUTIVE PERSPECTIVE

Erin Brewer
Managing Partner
RedPin Bowling Lounge and The Basement Modern Diner

As a small business owner, Erin Brewer has become an expert at analyzing the world around her and making decisions based on that analysis. After obtaining a bachelor's degree in anthropology and a master's in human relations, Brewer spent 10 years working in the nonprofit sector for various organizations, including United Way. Through her nonprofit work, she gained experience in fundraising, communications, and event planning, among other things. When she decided to explore launching a small business, Brewer analyzed the external factors that would impact her company. She developed a business and marketing plan that fit into the hip locale her firm now occupies and promoted the local culture through the menu. Today, RedPin Bowling Lounge and The Basement Modern Diner is one of the most popular spots in downtown Oklahoma City.

What has been the most important thing in making you successful at your job?

The most important thing that has made me successful in my work is my desire to learn all I can. I'll be the first to admit that I always have more to learn. I'm a careful student of the people around me, an organization's history and goals, the work others are doing (even if it doesn't directly apply to my job), and emerging trends both in and around my work. Knowing more than I need to know gives me an edge over those around me. It also puts me in a position to work quickly and efficiently, solve problems effectively, and negotiate well.

What advice would you give soon-to-be graduates?

First, if a good job that offers you a nice salary comes along, take it! Don't be afraid to apply for a position that interests you even if your experience doesn't exactly match the preferred criteria. Make sure that your resume is tailored to each potential job. Once you start working, learn everything you can from the moment you begin. Keep in mind that learning includes things about your specific role as well as things about office environments and the environment beyond your office. If you love your job, find ways to earn promotions. If you hate your job, keep learning while you look for something else. Be comforted by the fact that most of us don't really know what we want to be when we grow up. Whether you know or not, be prepared for change! Set personal goals but be comfortable with alterations to your plan. It's okay to change course. Most importantly, enjoy what you do.

How is marketing relevant to your role at RedPin?

If a small business like ours does not excel at marketing, we will not be in business very long. There are lots of food and entertainment options in Oklahoma City, and we can only succeed if we develop great products that people enjoy, promote those products in a way that gets people in the door, and provide great customer service that makes people want to come back. We have developed unique marketing strategies depending on what is going on around us, including seasonal promotions around holidays and special pricing at targeted times of the day, that have helped us succeed even as external factors such as the economy have changed.

What do you consider your personal brand to be?

I strive to enjoy the moment, make decisions that leave me without regret, treat others with courtesy and respect, learn something every day, and be comfortable in my own skin. I love asking and trying to answer tough questions! I'm getting more and more comfortable not knowing all the answers. I believe people, me included, can change if they choose. I have a running list of things to improve within myself. I proudly own my own history with all the failures, successes, decisions, friends, and experiences that have shaped me. In short, I'm trying to be the best me I can be.

Erin Brewer
Managing Partner

RedPin Bowling Lounge and The Basement Modern Diner
http://www.bowlredpin.com/

RedPin is a combination restaurant, bowling alley, and bar in Oklahoma City. It boasts 10 bowling lanes; a full-service bar; space for private parties; a menu of local, made-from-scratch fare; and a large canal-front patio.

FORECAST

This chapter explores the importance of analyzing the external environment when making marketing decisions. Whether you work for a Fortune 500 company looking to expand internationally or a nonprofit organization seeking funds to help at-risk teens, you must understand what is going on outside the firm. Listening to changing customer demands and monitoring your environment allow you and the firm to identify potential growth opportunities. As you read through the chapter, consider the following key questions:

1. What is the difference between direct and indirect competition?
2. How do external factors impact my marketing environment?
3. Why is it important to consider the global marketing environment?
4. Why do international entities like the European Union matter to marketers?
5. What additional factors impact the nonprofit marketing environment?

LO 3-1

Differentiate between direct and indirect competition.

COMPETITIVE ENVIRONMENT

SiriusXM was launched a little more than a decade ago. It is the largest satellite radio provider in North America, offering hundreds of channels of commercial-free music, sports, and talk. Today over 20 million subscribers pay a monthly fee for the service. Companies like SiriusXM compete in a dynamic and changing environment. To be successful, SiriusXM's marketers must understand that environment, including the competition and the domestic and international factors that impact the company.

direct competition

A situation in which products that perform the same function compete against one another other.

substitute products

Goods and services that perform very similar functions and can be used in place of one another.

Marketing professionals at SiriusXM and every organization must recognize the challenges both direct and indirect competition present and develop strategies to protect and expand their organization in light of those challenges.

Direct Competition

As companies plan for the future, they must identify and evaluate the competitive environment they face. The competitive environment includes the direct competitors and indirect competitors seeking to acquire market share and profits. The most commonly discussed form of competition is direct competition (also called *category competition* or *brand competition*), in which products that perform the same function compete against one another. For example, Wendy's competes directly with hamburger chains McDonald's and Burger King for customers and market share. In 2012, Wendy's passed Burger King in sales volume for the first time to become the second largest U.S. hamburger chain behind McDonald's. Between 2006 and 2011, domestic sales at Wendy's increased by 9 percent because of successful promotions such as the "My 99¢" value menu and Dave's Hot-n-Juicy Burger. Burger King's sales were flat during that same period.[1] However, gains at Wendy's were dwarfed by its other major direct competitor—McDonald's. During the same period, sales at McDonald's increased 26 percent, and the firm's total U.S. sales volume rose to $34.2 billion, nearly twice that of Burger King and Wendy's combined.

The direct competition for SiriusXM includes traditional radio stations and Internet radio services like Pandora that stream across broadband connections. Traditional and Internet radio are examples of substitute products. Substitute products are goods and services that perform very similar functions and can be used in place of one another. For SiriusXM to succeed, it must differentiate its product from substitutes in ways that add value to the customer's listening experience. SiriusXM does this by forgoing commercials and offering specific content that is not available on any substitute product.

Indirect Competition

In addition to the direct competition companies like SiriusXM face, they also face indirect competition. Indirect competition occurs when products provide alternate solutions to the same market. For SiriusXM, indirect competition would include products such as Apple's iPod, which allows consumers to download their favorite music, audiobooks, and podcasts to listen to in their home or car. Indirect competition also impacts the fast food industry. Despite passing Burger King and ascending to the No. 2 position among U.S. hamburger chains, Wendy's overall growth was relatively small due to increased indirect competition. As U.S. consumers looked for healthier dining choices, Subway jumped both Wendy's and Burger King to become the second largest restaurant chain in the United States, with approximately $11.4 billion in sales.[2] While Wendy's products were able to make gains relative to Burger King's Whopper, they lost ground to healthier sandwiches and Subway's cleverly marketed "$5 Footlong" campaign.

The beverage category offers another example of the impact of indirect competition. Direct competitors Coca-Cola and Pepsi have battled over soft-drink market share for decades. However, as consumers seek healthier drinks, soft-drink sales have begun to decline. Coca-Cola and Pepsi have seen indirect competitors selling juices, teas, energy drinks, and different types of water gain market share. Consumers have given increasing market share to products like Arizona brand iced tea and Nestlé's Pure Life bottled water. Faced with this marketing trend, Coca-Cola and Pepsi have aggressively expanded their offerings by acquiring brands (e.g., Coca-Cola with Dasani and Pepsi with Gatorade and Tropicana) in these emerging drink categories.

The shift in consumers' desire to eat, drink, and live healthier is one of several external factors that impact the marketing environment. To be successful, a firm must understand and adjust to the external environment, both domestic and international, in which it operates. In the next section, we'll discuss the major external factors firms should consider.

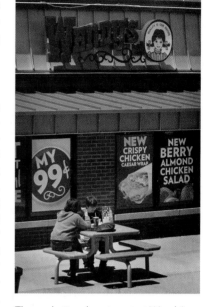

The marketing department at Wendy's closely monitors the products and advertising of its direct competitors, looking for opportunities to better serve customers of fast food hamburger chains.

indirect competition

A process in which products provide alternative solutions to the same market.

LO 3-2

Summarize the major external factors that influence the marketing environment.

EXTERNAL MARKETING ENVIRONMENT

Firms that closely monitor indirect competition can take steps to reduce its impact by expanding their offerings, as Coca-Cola did in response to competition from firms promoting healthy alternatives to soft drinks.

Marketing does not occur in a vacuum. Unforeseen developments external to the firm can directly impact the success of its marketing strategy. For this reason, marketing professionals continually scan and analyze the external environment. Environmental scanning involves monitoring developments outside of the firm's control with the goal of detecting and responding to threats and opportunities. Historically, environmental scanning at U.S. companies focused almost exclusively on the domestic environment. American car industry giants Ford, General Motors, and Chrysler spent much of the twentieth century concerned mostly with competition from each other. However, as the world's economies have become increasingly interconnected, firms

FIGURE 3.1 The External Factors Affecting the Marketing Environment

environmental scanning

The act of monitoring developments outside of the firm's control with the goal of detecting and responding to threats and opportunities.

gross domestic product (GDP)

A measure of the market value of all officially recognized final goods and services produced within a country in a given period.

recession

A period of time during which overall gross domestic product (GDP) declines for two or more consecutive quarters.

have expanded their scanning activities to include the environment beyond U.S. borders. Today international car manufacturers such as Honda impact General Motors just as much as Ford.

In subsequent sections, we'll discuss the six major external factors that influence the firm's marketing environment—economic, demographic, sociocultural, political, legal, and technological—shown in Figure 3.1. Though all of these factors occur on both a domestic and global scale, we'll first focus on how they occur in the domestic environment before expanding our discussion to include the global environment as well.

Economic

Economic factors influence almost every marketing decision a firm makes. Economic conditions impact consumers' willingness and ability to buy products. Consequently, firms must create, communicate, and deliver value in a way that's appropriate for the current economic climate. To break it down further, four economic elements influence marketers: gross domestic product (GDP), income distribution, inflation, and consumer confidence.

Gross Domestic Product Gross domestic product, while not the only economic measure firms should pay attention to, paints a simple picture of the economic health of a nation. Gross domestic product (GDP) refers to the market value of all officially recognized final goods and services produced within a country in a given period. GDP per capita is often considered an indicator of a country's standard of living.[3] For example, the GDP per capita in the U.S. was $48,112 in 2011 compared with $10,047 in Mexico and $5,445 in China.[4] Meanwhile, overall GDP is the most common gauge of the overall expansion or contraction of an economy. A recession occurs when overall GDP declines for two or more consecutive quarters. The U.S. recession that began in December 2007 was characterized as such because GDP declined in both 2008 and 2009.[5] Recessions can have a powerful negative effect on marketing. They typically involve layoffs, increased unemployment, and reduced consumer confidence. These factors influence consumers' ability and willingness to buy products and contribute to nonprofit organizations.

The United States has the largest gross domestic product in the world for a single country, with more than $14 trillion in 2011.[6] However, in recent years, China, India, and other developing nations have seen the highest GDP growth rates. While the U.S. grew 3.0 percent in 2011, China's economy grew more than three times faster, at 9.3 percent.[7] Higher GDP growth often drives lower unemployment rates, higher consumer confidence, and increased wealth across most income levels. All of this leaves customers with more money to spend. However, lower GDP growth can also open up opportunities for marketers who anticipate the trend and modify their marketing mix strategy accordingly.

Income Distribution How income is distributed across the U.S. population has shifted over the past several decades. This shift has forced marketers to develop new strategies to satisfy consumers at different ends of the spectrum. In 2011, the top 5 percent of the U.S. population earned almost 25 percent of the country's adjusted gross income. Meanwhile, the bottom 40 percent of earners earned approximately 10 percent of the country's income.[8] Figure 3.2 illustrates

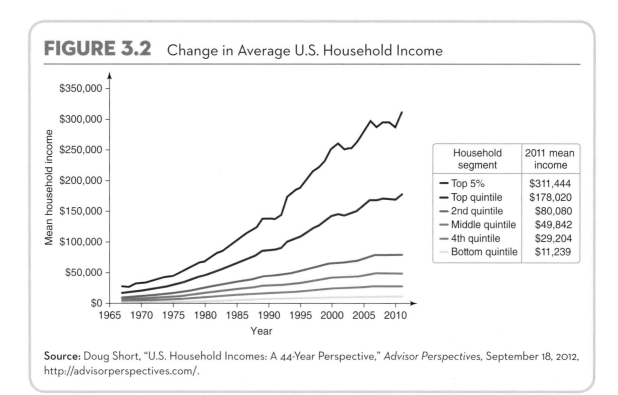

FIGURE 3.2   Change in Average U.S. Household Income

Household segment	2011 mean income
— Top 5%	$311,444
— Top quintile	$178,020
— 2nd quintile	$80,080
— Middle quintile	$49,842
— 4th quintile	$29,204
Bottom quintile	$11,239

Source: Doug Short, "U.S. Household Incomes: A 44-Year Perspective," *Advisor Perspectives*, September 18, 2012, http://advisorperspectives.com/.

the change in mean household income in the U.S. for various household segments over the past few decades in current dollar values. As the figure shows, though income for all household segments increased, income for the highest wage earners grew at a much quicker pace than it did for households in the bottom quintile.

Shifting income distribution offers marketers new opportunities to satisfy consumer needs and wants at both higher and lower income levels. Many companies, such as Dollar General, have thrived targeting consumers with modest incomes. Dollar General's marketing strategy includes offering low-income families quality food, health, and beauty products at reduced prices. This approach has turned the

Though they pursued markedly different strategies, both Louis Vuitton and Dollar General had success marketing to a U.S. population characterized by shifting income distribution.

company into a retailing bright spot over the past decade. While other firms struggled during the recession that began in December 2007, Dollar General opened new stores. Beyond this, it gained customers who have stayed loyal even as the economy began to rebound.[9]

On the other end of the spectrum, luxury brand Louis Vuitton has had tremendous success catering to high-income consumers. The company, which makes shoes, watches, accessories, and other premium items, has been one of the most successful luxury brands for years and has consistently increased its brand value. During the most recent recession, Louis Vuitton's marketing strategy involved raising prices and heightening its focus on quality. The result was additional sales to the firm's wealthiest clients and thus higher profits.[10]

Inflation You may have heard older friends and relatives talk about how, in the good old days, a gallon of milk cost less than $2. The fact that the same gallon of milk costs over $4 today is the result of inflation. Inflation is an increase in the general level of prices of products in an economy over a period of time. When the general price level rises, each unit of currency (e.g., each U.S. dollar) buys fewer goods and services. Consequently, inflation also reflects erosion in the purchasing power of money. Purchasing power is the amount of goods and services that can be purchased for a specific amount of money. For example, if the price of gasoline goes up 10 percent this year, the amount of gasoline you can purchase for $20 decreases by that same 10 percent. Two decades ago, $20 might have filled up your tank as average gas prices in the late 1990s were below $1.50 per gallon.[11]

Inflation can impact marketing significantly if prices rise faster than consumer incomes. In the last decade, American consumers have seen significant increases in the cost of gasoline and food. During the same period they've experienced a comparable decrease in the amount left to spend on all other goods and services. Each of you may be experiencing the impact of inflation as you read these words. College tuition and fees have increased 440 percent since 1980. Meanwhile the average family's income has risen less than 150 percent.[12] Because the cost of college has outpaced average family income, more students have been forced to take out additional student loans and families must spend a greater percentage of their household budgets to send children to college. Consequently, university marketing professionals are increasingly tasked with providing evidence of the value of higher education to current and future students. Their strategy includes increasing career service staffs, offering more integrated course programs, and spending more time educating people about the financial benefits of a college degree.

Consumer Confidence Consumer spending accounts for more than two-thirds of U.S. economic activity. The amount consumers spend is often based on their confidence in the stability of their future income. As a result, consumer confidence can provide an effective measure of the health of the economy. Consumer confidence measures how optimistic consumers are about the overall state of the economy and their own personal finances. Consumers purchase more when consumer confidence is high because they feel more secure in their jobs. If the economy contracts and people lose jobs, consumer confidence decreases, leading to more saving

inflation
An increase in the general level of prices of products in an economy over a period of time.

purchasing power
A measure of the amount of goods and services that can be purchased for a specific amount of money.

consumer confidence
A measure of how optimistic consumers are about the overall state of the economy and their own personal finances.

EXECUTIVE PERSPECTIVE

Erin Brewer
Managing Partner
RedPin Bowling Lounge and The Basement Modern Diner

Why does consumer confidence matter to your business?

If people do not feel good about the economy or their job, they are not going to choose to spend money eating out at a place like RedPin. Whatever our marketing strategy, how consumers feel about their personal economic fortunes has a lot to do with their decision to come to our establishment, to bring friends, and to encourage others to visit us as well.

and less spending. The effects of this could be seen in the U.S. during the most recent recession. Figure 3.3 illustrates the changes in consumer confidence over the past several decades and the subsequent change in real consumer spending. The green line reflects consumer confidence while the red line illustrates the change in real consumer spending over the same time period. As you can see, these measures often trend together, though there isn't an exact correlation between the two.

Marketers who can find strategic ways to help consumers feel confident about their purchases can improve performance during challenging times. For example, in 2009, Hyundai recognized that U.S. consumers were not confident in buying a new car as a consequence of their fear of losing their jobs. In response, Hyundai launched the Buyer Assurance program. The program allowed Hyundai buyers to return their car within 12 months, no questions asked, if they lost their job.[13] Hyundai identified and tapped into basic and powerful consumer fears to develop a strategy that sought to calm those fears and helped consumers feel more confident in purchasing.

FIGURE 3.3 Relationship between Consumer Confidence and Real Consumer Spending

Note: Shaded areas indicate U.S. recessions.

Source: Federal Reserve Bank of St. Louis, "FRED Graph," n.d., http://research.stlouisfed.org/fred2/graph/?utm_source=research&utm_medium=website&utm_campaign=data-tools.

Hyundai's Buyer Assurance program, which focused on addressing low consumer confidence due to a weak economy, allowed the car company to increase domestic sales, profits, and market share during an economic recession.

In response to a specific economic environment, Subway took its existing goods and services and adjusted the marketing mix so that the product resonated in a new way with customers.

demographics
The characteristics of human populations that can be used to identify consumer markets.

baby boomers
The generation born between 1946 and 1964.

disposable income
The amount of spending money available to households after paying taxes.

Marketers cannot dictate the state of the economic environment, but they must develop marketing strategies to put their firm in the best possible position for success, regardless of economic factors. From 2008 to 2010, with consumer confidence low due to the recession, Subway was looking for a value offering to compete against other restaurant chains that were expanding their low-price menus. A local Subway franchise in Miami first offered footlong sandwiches for only $5 on the weekends.[14] When the stores offering the promotion had lines out the doors, Subway knew it had a winning marketing strategy. Subway worked with its ad agency to develop the now famous "$5 Footlong" jingle, and the popularity of the item soared. More customers upgraded their orders from 6-inch subs to footlongs; others bought a footlong sandwich, ate half, and saved the rest for lunch the next day. The $5 footlong helped Subway expand domestic sales by 17 percent, at a time when virtually all other restaurant chains were watching sales decrease.[15] Just three years after the introduction of the $5 footlong, Subway surpassed McDonald's; it now operates the most locations of any restaurant chain in the world.[16]

Demographic

While economic factors provide a macro framework for understanding consumer purchase patterns, marketers are equally concerned with identifying consumers' demographic characteristics. Demographics are the characteristics of human populations that can be used to identify consumer markets. They include things such as age, gender, ethnicity, and education level, all of which influence the products consumers buy. Typical demographic information is readily available from the U.S. Census Bureau and research firms such as Nielsen. Access to demographic information is essential to identifying and characterizing a firm's target markets.

Age Do you consume information in the same way as your parents? Do you consume information the same way you did five years ago? The likely answer to both of these questions is no. Age plays an important role in how consumers process information. This in turn affects what marketing strategy firms should use to reach them.

Each year, the average age of the population of the United States rises, and seniors are the fastest growing demographic group. As illustrated in Figure 3.4, the percentage of Americans aged 65 and older is expected to almost double over the next 50 years. There are 76 million baby boomers—the generation of children born between 1946 and 1964—retiring at a rate of 10,000 per day.[17] Members of this generation typically possess two things that marketing professionals seek: disposable income, which is the amount of spending money available to households after paying taxes (baby boomers represent the wealthiest generation in U.S. history), and the free time to spend it. Rapidly retiring baby boomers make up only a quarter of the U.S. population but account for 50 percent of all domestic consumer spending.[18] In an effort to reach this demographic, firms are making changes to encourage older Americans to shop at their stores. Paint retailer Sherwin Williams has redesigned its 3,400 stores to make them more comfortable for older shoppers by adding more lighting and seating. Pharmacy CVS Caremark has retrofitted its stores to appeal to older shoppers by lowering shelves and adding carpeting to reduce slipping.[19] However, the news is not all positive for marketers looking to target older Americans. Seniors are more likely to complain and often require more special attention and resources than their younger counterparts.

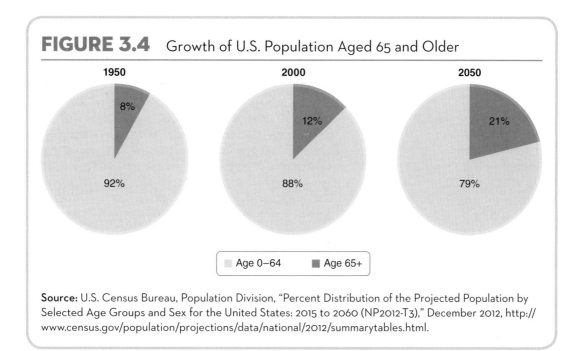

FIGURE 3.4   Growth of U.S. Population Aged 65 and Older

| 1950 | 2000 | 2050 |

Age 0–64   Age 65+

Source: U.S. Census Bureau, Population Division, "Percent Distribution of the Projected Population by Selected Age Groups and Sex for the United States: 2015 to 2060 (NP2012-T3)," December 2012, http://www.census.gov/population/projections/data/national/2012/summarytables.html.

Many of you reading this belong to a generational cohort known as millennials, or *generation Y,* those born between 1978 and the late twentieth century. Millennials comprise over 75 million members in the United States.[20] They are the second largest generational group behind the baby boomers. Millennials generally have the greatest familiarity with and most use for digital communication, social media, and other forms of technology. Marketers trying to reach this large consumer group increasingly deliver their messages using channels, like the Internet, that are most likely to be used by this market. For example, Gap targeted millennials by promoting the brand on the Internet and participating in design collaborations with fashion blogs that are popular with younger consumers.[21]

millennials

The generation born between 1978 and the late twentieth century.

 connect
|MARKETING

Interactive Assignment 3-1
Social Media in Action

Social media have become powerful tools for small business marketers looking to compete with larger firms. Jill Nelson is the founder of Oregon-based Ruby Receptionists, which provides virtual receptionists for other small businesses. She believes that social media level the playing field with bigger competitors. One of Nelson's biggest target markets is attorneys needing a virtual receptionist. When she hears via social media that an attorney has won a big case, her firm makes sure to congratulate them. This strategy allows Ruby Receptionists to provide a personal touch that large firms may not offer.

As beneficial as social media can be, firms must still use such tools strategically. Small business owners should focus on developing social media marketing strategies for specific sites and platforms. Those who start using multiple social media marketing tools all at once may lose focus or become discouraged because of the lack of immediate results. An emerging number of firms such as Ghost Tweeting are completely devoted to helping small businesses understand how to use social media and guiding the implementation of social media marketing strategies that drive new revenues and increase profits.

The Social Media in Action *Connect* exercise in Chapter 3 will let you develop different social media marketing strategies for a small local restaurant. By understanding how social media can help small businesses, you will be able to apply these strategies in the service of a small business you might work for or own in the years ahead.

Source: See Christine Dugas, "Small Businesses Get Personal with Social Media," *USA Today*, November 12, 2012, http://www.usatoday.com/story/money/business/2012/11/11/small-business-use-social-media/1692851/.

Gender One of the most important changes in the United States in recent decades has been the roles, attitudes, and buying habits of men and women in the marketplace. Historically, female consumers were targeted for a much less diverse set of goods and services than men. Today women take on the role of decision maker across a large and expanding variety of products. Female consumers now account for 85 percent of all consumer purchases in the United States, including everything from cars to groceries to health care.[22] Seventy-five percent of women identify themselves as the primary shopper in their household.[23]

Female control over the majority of consumer spending makes them a target for marketers across products. Women are responsible for more than half of the new car purchases in the U.S. Marketers at Toyota targeted their promotional activities for the Sienna minivan toward female buyers with a marketing campaign entitled "Swagger Wagon." The campaign appealed emotionally to female consumers who did not want parenthood to take away from their ability to drive a cool car. Delivered via television and over two dozen YouTube videos, the ads featured a woman and her family describing how the Sienna fit their lifestyle rather than a laundry list of features. "Swagger Wagon" generated over 5 million YouTube hits and was named one of the top marketing campaigns of the year.[24]

Education During the height of the recession that began in December 2007, the unemployment rate for college-educated workers was approximately half that of the nation as a whole.[25] As shown in Figure 3.5, historically, highly educated consumers are more likely to be employed. Though the trend in the unemployment rate for college-educated consumers mirrors the trend for the rest of the population, their overall unemployment numbers remain low in comparison. Educated consumers are also likely to earn significantly more money throughout the course of their lifetime and comprehend an advertiser's message more readily, making them prime targets for marketing strategies.

The U.S. is pushing to lead the world in college graduation rates by 2020.[26] As a result, the number of professional workers with college degrees is expected to increase significantly in the coming years. This increase in the average education level of the country will give marketers new opportunities. Some are already reaching out to this growing demographic. Knowing that highly educated consumers tend to be environmentally conscious and value technological features, Ford introduced the C-Max hybrid, emphasizing its fuel efficiency and advanced features.[27] In addition, products like Barnes and

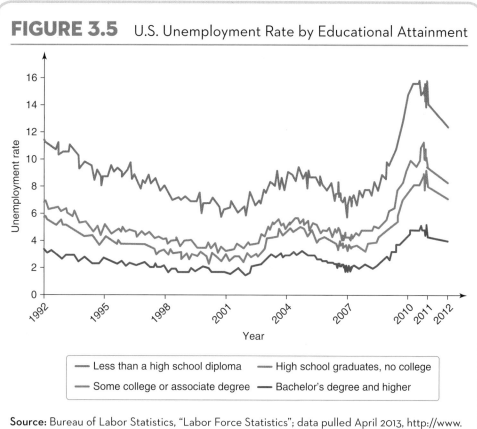

FIGURE 3.5 U.S. Unemployment Rate by Educational Attainment

Legend:
— Less than a high school diploma   — High school graduates, no college
— Some college or associate degree   — Bachelor's degree and higher

Source: Bureau of Labor Statistics, "Labor Force Statistics"; data pulled April 2013, http://www.bls.gov/webapps/legacy/cpsatab4.htm.

Noble's Nook and Apple's iPad target educated consumers seeking to read more digital content on the go.

Ethnicity The ethnic composition of the U.S. population is changing rapidly. Projections indicate that by 2050 the Hispanic population in the United States will almost double to more than 127 million, representing 29 percent of the entire U.S. population.[28] The African American population in the U.S. grew over 12 percent between 2000 and 2010 and now makes up over 13 percent of the total U.S. population.[29] Asian Americans represent approximately 5 percent of the U.S. population but have the highest average family income of all ethnic groups, thereby increasing their purchasing power and importance to marketers.[30] Figure 3.6 illustrates how the ethnic breakdown of the United States has changed over the past two decades and what changes are projected for the decades ahead.

The United States is moving rapidly toward greater multiculturalism. Ethnic minorities' purchasing power is projected to reach $2 trillion by 2015.[31] Marketers already have taken basic steps, such as advertising in multiple languages, to reach out to different ethnic groups. Food company General Mills's research showed that Hispanic consumers prefer to buy the brands of goods and services they see advertised on television. The company significantly increased the number of ads it ran on Spanish language media and saw sales of popular General Mills products like Progresso soup and Honey Nut cheerios soar.[32] As the ethnic makeup of the U.S. continues to change, marketing professionals will need to keep studying different ethnic groups and their buying behavior.

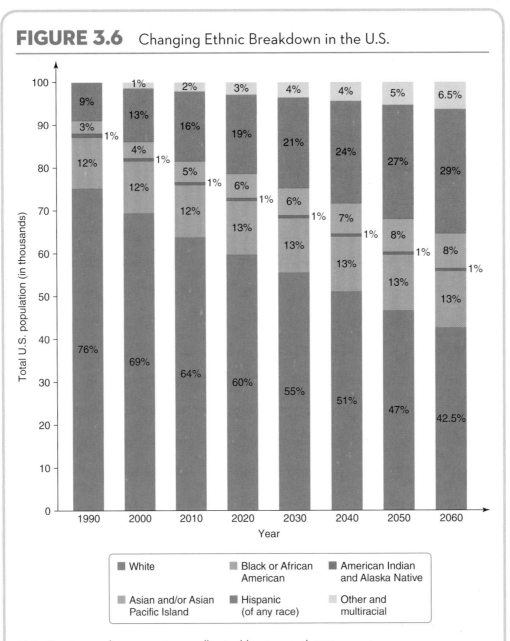

FIGURE 3.6 Changing Ethnic Breakdown in the U.S.

Note: Due to rounding, percentages will not add up to exactly 100 percent.

Sources: United States Census Bureau, "United States Census 1990," http://www.census.gov/prod/cen1990/cp1/cp-1-1.pdf; Karen R. Humes, Nicholas A. Jones, and Roberto R. Ramirez, "Overview of Race and Hispanic Origin: 2010," http://www.census.gov/prod/cen2010/briefs/c2010br-02.pdf; and United States Census Bureau, "2012 National Population Projections: Summary Tables," http://www.census.gov/population/projections/data/national/2012/summarytables.html.

Sociocultural

The society and culture we live in helps to shape our beliefs, values, and norms, which, in turn, define our tastes and purchasing habits. Sociocultural refers to the combination of social and cultural factors that affect individual development. One of the biggest sociocultural changes in the United States over the past half century has been the shift from a nation of primarily one-income families, where

sociocultural

The combination of social and cultural factors that affect individual development.

one spouse stayed home to raise children, to one in which two-income families and single-parent households predominate. In fact, in 2010, only 21 percent of American households were composed of a married couple with children.[33] Only 16 percent consisted of working fathers and stay-at-home moms.[34] This change has led to a "money rich, time poor" society, that is, a nation with money to spend but little time to spend it.

The new sociocultural reality of busier families has created opportunities for firms to offer new kinds of value. Banks, for example, have expanded their offerings to include later evening hours and more services through ATM machines. They've also launched additional online banking options that give busy consumers more opportunities to use the bank's services. Other sociocultural changes in the U.S.—the increasing number of single adults, rising concerns about protecting consumer privacy, and the growth in environmentally conscious consumers—provide firms with many reasons to market products in new and better ways. For example, in response to the increase in consumer demand for environmentally friendly goods and services, car manufacturers have increased their hybrid and electric car offerings and marketers of personal care products have introduced a wider selection of natural and organic items.

Oscar Mayer's Lunchables, which typically include crackers, cheese, and meat slices, appeal to busier families looking for a convenient way to prepare their children's lunch.

Political

The political climate in the United States can change the direction of government policy quickly and impact how marketers position their products. For example, video game marketers were very concerned about legislation that was passed in California in 2005 banning the sale or rental of violent video games to anyone under the age of 18.[35] Since many of the consumers of these popular games are teenagers, such a ban would have forced marketers to reconsider their target market and positioning strategies as they sought to make up sales in other demographic segments. Critics called the ban censorship and immediately began appealing the ruling. The law was eventually overturned by the U.S. Supreme Court. Still, California and many other states continue to deal with political pressure to reduce youth violence.

Firms must understand how the changing political climate affects them and develop marketing strategies that will allow them to succeed under various conditions. However, firms need not be completely passive when it comes to the political decisions that affect their business. It's becoming increasingly possible for firms to impact politics. For example, the past two decades have seen a dramatic increase in the number and influence of political action committees (PACs). PACs have raised money to help elect individuals who regard their organization positively or to promote a particular issue related to their industry. PACs lobby government officials to focus more closely on a particular issue, including some that impact marketing, such as restrictions on certain types of advertising or protecting consumers' rights. For example, in 2013, California, Vermont, New York, and other states passed laws banning tanning salons from serving minors, even with their parents' permission.[36] The American Suntanning Association, a group of 1,400 U.S. tanning salons, began lobbying the federal and state governments for fewer restrictions on tanning. If the group is successful, it could enhance marketers' ability to generate revenue from younger consumers and change the legal environment within the tanning industry.

Legal

The legal system represents another component of the external environment that affects how firms market their products. The legal environment within the U.S. continues to change, forcing marketing professionals to refine their strategies.

TABLE 3.1 U.S. Laws That Affect Marketers

Legislation	Importance to Marketing
Sherman Antitrust Act (1890)	Combats anticompetitive practices, reduces market domination by individual corporations, and preserves unfettered competition as the rule of trade.
Robinson-Patman Act (1936)	Prohibits firms from selling the same product at different prices in interstate commerce unless based on a cost difference or if the goods are not of similar quality.
Wheeler-Lea Amendment (1938)	Authorizes the Federal Trade Commission to restrict unfair or deceptive acts; also called the Advertising Act. Broadened the Federal Trade Commission 's powers to include protection of consumers from false advertising practices.
Fair Packaging and Labeling Act (1966)	Applies to labels on many consumer products. It requires the label to state the identity of the product; the name and place of business of the manufacturer, packer, or distributor; and the net quantity of contents.
Telephone Consumer Protection Act (1991)	Limits commercial solicitation calls to between 8 a.m. and 9 p.m., and forces telemarketers to maintain a do-not-call list and honor any request to not be called again.
Credit Card Accountability, Responsibility, and Disclosure Act (2009)	Protects consumer rights and abolishes deceptive lending practices.

Table 3.1 highlights some of the U.S. laws that are most important to understanding the marketing environment.

Federal, state, and local governments enact regulations for two main purposes:

1. To ensure businesses compete fairly with each other. For example, the Sherman Antitrust Act (1890) was passed to eliminate monopolies and guarantee competition. The Robinson-Patman Act (1936) refined prohibitions on selling the same product at different prices. The Wheeler-Lea Act (1938) made deceptive and misleading advertising illegal. These laws are among those enforced by the Federal Trade Commission (FTC), which serves as the consumer protection agency for the United States. The FTC collects complaints about organizations that violate regulations, which can lead to investigations and prosecutions.

2. To ensure businesses don't take advantage of consumers. For example, the Fair Packaging and Labeling Act (1966) guarantees that product packages are labeled correctly. The Telephone Consumer Protection Act of 1991 has reduced the use of telemarketing, which is when a firm sells products directly to consumers over the telephone. The act allows consumers to limit the number of telemarketing calls they receive and opt out of being called by some companies.[37] Banks and other financial institutions were required to change how they dealt with consumers following passage of the Credit Card Accountability, Responsibility, and Disclosure (CARD) Act of 2009. The law banned unfair credit card rate increases and required that disclosures regarding minimum payments and interest rates be made in plain English to better protect younger consumers.[38]

Federal Trade Commission (FTC)

The consumer protection agency for the United States.

Technology

Of all the external factors, rapidly evolving technology arguably represents one of the most significant challenges, as well as one of the most significant opportunities, for marketing professionals. Technology influences how consumers satisfy their needs and wants, the basic concept underlying all marketing activities. For example, if you had been at college in the early 1990s and heard a song on the radio you wanted to buy, you had a couple of options. You could buy the song as a single on compact disc (CD) for $3 to $5 or buy the artist's entire album on CD for $15 to $20, even though the album was filled with nine other songs you could care less about. Apple's iPod and iTunes Store changed the market by allowing consumers to purchase only the specific songs they liked for a mere $0.99. This technological advancement changed the way consumers purchased music forever.

In addition to affecting how consumers use products, technology changes the way firms promote their products. In recent years, a growing number of consumers have abandoned the traditional landline telephone in favor of cell phones. This technology-driven change gives marketers new ways to reach consumers. Applications that track consumer locations, electronic coupons such as those provided by Groupon, and high quality smartphones make it possible for marketers to know where a customer is and to communicate directly to him or her with an offer for that moment and location. Imagine walking through downtown Chicago around dinner time and receiving an electronic coupon for a deep dish pizza restaurant less than a block from where you are. In fact, we don't have to imagine such a scenario. These tools are available today, and they illustrate how technology can change the way firms market to consumers.

Walt Disney World Resort is using technology to provide a more hassle-free experience at its theme parks. In 2013, Disney introduced MagicBands, which are wristbands enabled with a radio-frequency identification device (RFID) chip. MagicBands function as a room key and park entry pass for guests at Disney's parks.[39] The MagicBand can also be linked to a Walt Disney World Resort hotel guest's hotel bill, making purchases within the parks easier and quicker. Beyond

New technology, such as Disney's MagicBands, not only delivers convenience to consumers but also provides marketers with valuable information about a customer's purchasing patterns and habits.

the added value of improving the guest experience, MagicBands also provide marketers with useful information. By tracking consumers' ride and purchasing patterns, Disney can design attractions to best meet customer needs and wants.

connect Interactive Assignment 3-2

|MARKETING Please complete the *Connect* exercise in Chapter 3 that focuses on the external factors that impact marketers. By identifying how external factors impact large organizations, you will understand how forces outside the marketing department's control can impact decisions the firm must make.

LO 3-3

Extend the analysis of the marketing environment beyond the borders of the United States.

GLOBAL MARKETING ENVIRONMENT

Recent estimates put the world's population at over 7 billion people. Experts predict that it will grow to almost 10 billion people by the year 2050.[40] For some firms, analyzing external factors as they occur in the United States is sufficient. Increasingly, however, even small businesses and firms that sell primarily to U.S. customers are affected by global trends, events, and competitors. The process of environmental scanning must take those into account as well.

In theory, the key external factors that impact a firm in the international space don't differ substantially from those in the domestic space. Consumers' age, education level, and gender still matter. The political and legal systems within a given country often dictate how easy it will be to sell and distribute products there. And a country's level of technological advancement has important implications for how the firm promotes its product to the local population. In practice, though, environmental scanning on a global scale often has added layers of complexity. In this section, we'll discuss some of the factors that marketers should be aware of when analyzing the global marketing environment.

Currency Fluctuation

currency exchange rate

The price of one country's currency in terms of another country's currency.

Currency fluctuation refers to how the value of one country's currency changes in relation to the value of other currencies. Currency fluctuation can impact how firms market products internationally either positively or negatively, depending on one's perspective. Consider, for example, the currency exchange rate between the U.S. dollar ($) and the European Union's currency, the euro (€). The currency exchange rate is the price of one country's currency in terms of another country's currency. On January 31, 2012, €1 was worth $1.29. One year later, the same €1 was worth $1.33.[41] As the value of the euro appreciated relative to the dollar, it reduced the spending power of American consumers seeking to buy European products. In contrast, as the dollar depreciated, American goods and services became more affordable to European consumers.

The world's largest country in terms of population, China, has been criticized for undervaluing its currency, that is, pricing it lower than it is actually worth. Many nations believe this gives China an advantage in selling exports because it can price its products cheaper than other countries' products. However, recent growth in the value of the yuan relative to the dollar has increased the purchasing power of Chinese consumers.[42] U.S. marketers ranging from Coca-Cola to General Motors are stepping up advertising and distribution efforts in an attempt to entice Chinese consumers to buy more of their products, which now cost less due to the stronger yuan-to-dollar exchange rate.

Currency fluctuations can provide marketing opportunities whether a currency is appreciating or depreciating. For example, an increase in the value of the euro relative to the dollar may encourage more European families to travel to Walt

Disney World in Orlando, Florida, because they could do so cheaply. Disney marketers could target these families with advertisements promoting the idea that there has never been a better time to go to a theme park in the U.S.

Income Distribution

A country's income distribution often provides the most reliable picture of its purchasing power. Marketers are particularly attracted to countries with a growing middle class, since a nation's purchasing capability tends to increase as the proportion of middle-income households increases. For example, income growth in developing nations in Asia and Latin America is likely to stimulate world trade as more of their residents move into the middle class. Figure 3.7 illustrates how the percentage of middle-class consumption in key Asian countries is projected to change in comparison to the U.S. over the next few decades. As you can see, the percentage of middle-class consumption in India may outstrip that of the U.S. by the year

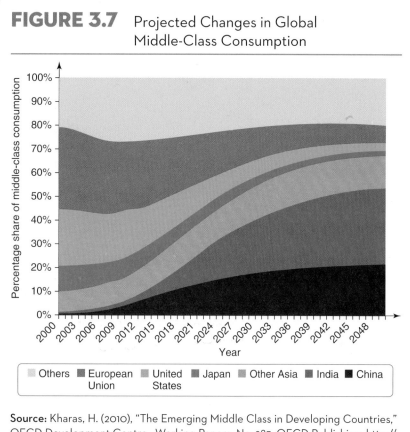

FIGURE 3.7 Projected Changes in Global Middle-Class Consumption

Source: Kharas, H. (2010), "The Emerging Middle Class in Developing Countries," OECD Development Centre, Working Papers, No. 285, OECD Publishing. http://dx.doi.org/10.1787/5kmmp8lncrns-en.

2050. Even countries that don't have a rapidly increasing middle class may have higher purchasing power than may be apparent from initial statistics due to government subsidies for food, transportation, or health care.

Continuously scanning the global economic environment is an important aspect of doing business in international markets. In addition, marketing professionals must possess a working knowledge of the major trade agreements and organizations that could govern their firm's interaction with those markets. Whether you work for a firm such as Bank of America that is planning to expand in China or a small rice farm hoping to sell more products to European countries, you will need a basic understanding of each of these agreements and organizations to successfully navigate the global marketplace.

Major Trade Agreements and Organizations

International trade agreements, monetary unions, and organizations can impact substantially the environment in which a firm operates. They can affect how easy it is for firms to enter a foreign market, what the currency exchange rate is between countries, and even what competition firms will encounter in the domestic market. Trade agreements and monetary unions facilitate the exchange of money and products across borders. International organizations provide regulatory oversight to economic activity. We'll discuss the key entities you should be aware of in the sections that follow.

LO 3-4

Identify the major trade agreements, monetary unions, and organizations that impact the global marketing environment.

North American Free Trade Agreement Perhaps the most familiar U.S. trade agreement is the North American Free Trade Agreement (NAFTA). As Figure 3.8 shows, the U.S. exports more products to Canada and Mexico than to

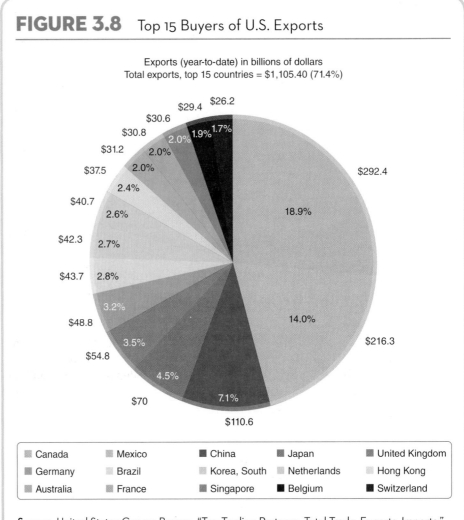

FIGURE 3.8   Top 15 Buyers of U.S. Exports

Exports (year-to-date) in billions of dollars
Total exports, top 15 countries = $1,105.40 (71.4%)

$26.2
$29.4
$30.6
$30.8
$31.2
$37.5
$40.7
$42.3
$43.7
$48.8
$54.8
$70
$110.6
$216.3
$292.4

1.7%
1.9%
2.0%
2.0%
2.0%
2.4%
2.6%
2.7%
2.8%
3.2%
3.5%
4.5%
7.1%
14.0%
18.9%

Canada	Mexico	China	Japan	United Kingdom
Germany	Brazil	Korea, South	Netherlands	Hong Kong
Australia	France	Singapore	Belgium	Switzerland

Source: United States Census Bureau, "Top Trading Partners—Total Trade, Exports, Imports," December 2012, http://www.census.gov/foreign-trade/statistics/highlights/top/top1212yr.html.

North American Free Trade Agreement (NAFTA)

An international agreement that established a free trade zone among the United States, Canada, and Mexico.

tariffs

Taxes on imports and exports between countries.

any other individual country. This is largely because NAFTA has made exchange among the three countries so easy.

The North American Free Trade Agreement (NAFTA) established a free trade zone among the United States, Canada, and Mexico. Its goal was to eliminate barriers to trade and investment among the three countries. One of the key barriers to trade in the region was tariffs, which are taxes on imports and exports between countries. NAFTA's implementation on January 1, 1994, brought the immediate elimination of tariffs on more than one-half of U.S. imports from Mexico and more than one-third of U.S. exports to Mexico. Within 10 years of implementation, all U.S.–Mexico tariffs were eliminated, except for some on U.S. agricultural exports to Mexico that were to be phased out within 15 years. Most U.S.–Canada trade was already free of tariffs. NAFTA also seeks to eliminate nontariff trade barriers such as embargoes or sanctions. As a result, trade among the three countries has nearly tripled from $288 billion in 1993 to $1 trillion in 2011.[43]

Dominican Republic–Central America Free Trade Agreement
A decade after NAFTA was implemented, the U.S. entered discussions about a

new agreement with the Central American countries of Costa Rica, El Salvador, Guatemala, Honduras, and Nicaragua called the Central America Free Trade Agreement (CAFTA). In 2004, the Dominican Republic joined the negotiations, and the agreement was renamed Dominican Republic–Central America Free Trade Agreement. Like NAFTA, the Dominican Republic–Central America Free Trade Agreement (DR-CAFTA) focuses on eliminating tariffs, reducing nontariff barriers, and facilitating investment among the member states. With the addition of the Dominican Republic, the trade group's largest economy, the region covered by DR-CAFTA is the second-largest Latin American export market for U.S. producers behind Mexico. It buys $15 billion worth of goods from the U.S. a year.[44] Trade between the U.S. and countries covered under this agreement amounts to about $32 billion annually.

European Union

Agreements like DR-CAFTA are designed to ease trade between nations. Entities like the European Union go further, integrating countries to a much larger degree. The European Union (EU) was formed to create a single European market by reducing barriers to the free trade of goods, services, and finances among member countries. It is an economic, political, and monetary union of 27 European nations. In 2010, the EU generated an estimated 26 percent share of the global gross domestic product, making it the largest economy in the world.[45] It is the largest exporter, the largest importer, and the biggest trading partner for several large countries, including China, India, and the United States. However, EU nations such as Greece, Spain, Portugal, and Italy have faced significant economic challenges in recent years. These challenges have negatively impacted their domestic markets as well as U.S. marketers' ability to sell their products to consumers in those countries.

World Trade Organization

The World Trade Organization was officially formed on January 1, 1995, under the Marrakech Agreement. It is the only international organization dealing with the rules of trade between nations. The World Trade Organization (WTO) regulates trade among participating countries and helps importers and exporters conduct their business. In addition, the WTO provides a framework for negotiating and formalizing trade agreements and a dispute resolution process aimed at enforcing participants' adherence to WTO agreements. The WTO, headquartered in Geneva, Switzerland, has 153 members, representing more than 97 percent of the world's population, and 30 observer nations, most of which are seeking membership.

International Monetary Fund

Soon after the end of World War II, 29 countries signed an agreement to form the International Monetary Fund, headquartered in Washington, D.C. The International Monetary Fund (IMF) "works to foster international monetary cooperation, secure financial stability, facilitate international trade, promote high employment and sustainable economic growth, and reduce poverty around the world. Created in 1945, the IMF is governed by and accountable to the 188 countries that make up its near-global membership."[46] It was formed to promote international economic cooperation, trade, employment, and currency exchange rate stability, including by making resources available to member countries to help them manage their debts.

Each country contributed to a pool which could be borrowed from, on a temporary basis, by countries with debt obligations they couldn't meet. The IMF was particularly important when it was first created because it helped stabilize the world's economic system following World War II. To this day, the IMF works to improve the economies of its member countries.

Dominican Republic–Central America Free Trade Agreement (DR-CAFTA)

An international agreement that eliminated tariffs, reduced nontariff barriers, and facilitated investment among the United States, Costa Rica, El Salvador, Guatemala, Honduras, Nicaragua, and the Dominican Republic.

European Union (EU)

An economic, political, and monetary union among 27 European nations that created a single European market by reducing barriers to the free trade of goods, services, and finances.

World Trade Organization (WTO)

An international organization that regulates trade among participating countries and helps importers and exporters conduct their business.

International Monetary Fund (IMF)

An international organization that works to foster international monetary cooperation, secure financial stability, facilitate international trade, promote high employment and sustainable economic growth, and reduce poverty around the world.

Interactive Assignment 3-3

Please complete the *Connect* exercise for Chapter 3 that focuses on international trade agreements. By identifying the major aspects of critical trade agreements, you will understand the global marketing environment and be prepared to develop effective global marketing strategies.

Technology

Once marketers understand the economic factors and trade agreements and organizations that impact their global activities, they must look more specifically into how best to reach their international audience. Today, technology enables even small businesses to reach consumers across the globe. Websites act as a front door to billions of potential consumers, and social media help companies develop relationships with customers anywhere for very little cost. Tools such as Google Translate allow customers to view websites in their own language, making it easier to promote products in different countries. In addition, global shipping firms like FedEx and UPS enable small manufacturers to ship their products to customers around the world and have those shipments tracked by both the buyer and the seller online. Understanding how technology impacts the global marketing environment benefits marketers as they attempt to meet the needs and wants of consumers in international markets.

Cultural Fit

One of the biggest mistakes domestic firms make when they attempt to take their business global is to believe that foreign consumers want exactly the same products that are sold in the United States and want them marketed in the same way. Burger King was widely criticized when it created an in-store ad for some European stores that showed a Hindu goddess atop a ham sandwich with the caption, "A snack that is sacred".[47] Many of the nearly 1 billion Hindus throughout the world, most of whom are vegetarian, were offended and protested the use of the ad. Burger King eventually pulled it. The negative attention and the potential long-term damage to Burger King's goal of expanding its market illustrate the importance of understanding cultural fit.

consumer ethnocentrism

A belief by residents of a country that it is inappropriate or immoral to purchase foreign-made goods and services.

A growing concern for firms with overseas operations is consumer ethnocentrism. Consumer ethnocentrism refers to a belief by residents of a country that it is inappropriate or immoral to purchase foreign-made goods and services.[48] This belief is on the rise in many developed nations, including the United States, France, Germany, and China. Consumer ethnocentrism is rarely grounded in fact, making the marketer's job even more difficult. For example, in 2003, following France's refusal to join the United States military operation in Iraq, many U.S. consumers refused to eat french fries, even though there was nothing French about the product. Proactive marketers across the country looked for a clever way to resolve the issue and, for a brief time, renamed their product "freedom fries."

Analyzing cultural fit and overcoming consumer ethnocentrism are essential aspects of environmental scanning on a global scale that help firms create value for international consumers.

Consumer ethnocentrism sometimes presents a challenge to marketers with international operations. Promoting a product in a different way can overcome such challenges.

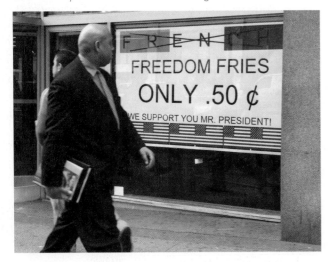

Halsey Ward

Sponsorship and Sales Executive
Australian National Basketball League

Describe your job. I work for the New Zealand franchise of the ANBL, the SKYCITY Breakers. Relative to the NBA and other American professional sporting leagues, the ANBL and its franchises are young entities. We are still developing our brand and fighting for market share in a sports market that is saturated with avid rugby fans. In my current role, I am largely responsible for the management and development of our corporate sponsorship accounts. However, I'm also loosely in charge of all game-day events for our corporate accounts, hospitality clients, and any sizeable group that may be in attendance.

Describe how you got the job that you have. I have always had a passion for sports and the culture that comes with being in a competitive atmosphere. I also wanted to pursue a career abroad and garner international experience. My goal was always to work for an international sports league. Having a focused, detailed goal is what ultimately helped me get a job with the SKYCITY Breakers.

What has been the most important thing in making you successful at your job? Confidence. It's easy to feel insecure and inept when you start a job. Fear of the unknown is inevitable. I've found that if you meet that fear with confidence and diligence the job becomes less intimidating and the task at hand becomes more familiar.

Believing that I can do the job and do it well have been key to finding success in my career.

What advice would you give soon-to-be graduates? As a shooter in college, my coach used to tell me, "You miss all the shots you never take! Shoot till you miss, then shoot till you make!" I definitely missed more shots than I made, but I never stopped shooting. The same applies to finding a job and succeeding at the job. Once you have your goal in mind, never let all the no's keep you from going after that one crucial yes.

What has been most challenging about working internationally? There are definitely challenges to learning a new culture and trying to figure out how consumers in New Zealand prioritize sports compared to U.S. consumers. However, most of the marketing skills I learned translate very well. I use all of the four Ps every day to drive sales, promote our events, and deliver value to customers.

What do you consider your personal brand to be? There is one word that comes to mind: Compete. When I'm competing, it doesn't feel like a job, it feels like a game. In branding myself to future employers, I know that my competitive edge is what separates me from other candidates. Competition makes things fun, keeps those around me on their toes, and ensures that I'm always putting my best foot forward.

connect
|MARKETING

Interactive Assignment 3-4

Please complete the *Connect* exercise in Chapter 3 that focuses on how cultural fit affects the global marketing environment. By understanding which domestic firms and products are more likely to fit with the culture in specific foreign countries, you will be able to develop a more effective global marketing strategy.

LO 3-5
Describe the emerging factors influencing the nonprofit marketing environment.

NONPROFIT MARKETING ENVIRONMENT

Environmental scanning for a nonprofit organization presents challenges that for-profit businesses do not face. Those who donate money to a nonprofit do not walk away with a tangible product or benefit directly from any service. Instead, nonprofit marketers must convince donors to support the mission of the organization without receiving any direct benefit. Nonprofits primarily rely on three sources of funding—grants, special events, and individual donations. Marketing generally plays an important role in securing each.

The competitive environment for nonprofit funding has increased dramatically in recent years. In 1995, there were only 600,000 nonprofits in the U.S. Today, that number is over 1.8 million and growing rapidly.[49] Not only has the number of nonprofit organizations increased by more than 300 percent, the total donations those organizations have had to divvy up dipped from 2007 to 2009 as the recession worsened. Figure 3.9 illustrates how total giving to nonprofit organizations changed during the height of the recession. For nonprofit marketers to be successful in this type of competitive environment, they must understand the external environment in which they operate.

Nonprofit marketers are impacted by many of the same external factors discussed earlier in the chapter, including economic, legal, political, and technological factors. However, due to their mission and chronic lack of funds, the impact can be quite different.

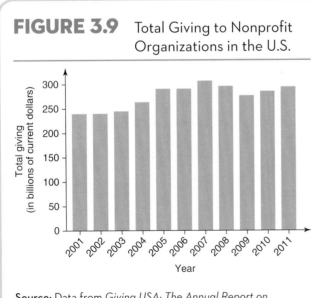

FIGURE 3.9 Total Giving to Nonprofit Organizations in the U.S.

Source: Data from *Giving USA: The Annual Report on Philanthropy for the Year 2011 (2012)*. Chicago: Giving USA Foundation.

Economic

During the recession that began in December of 2007, Americans reduced their overall charitable giving by over 20 percent from levels prior to the recession.[50] The decline was far sharper than in previous economic recessions. One strategy nonprofit marketers have used to combat the new reality is developing new ways to recognize existing donors for their contributions. For example, a hospital might display a digital recognition system in its front lobby listing donors of all sizes. These new methods foster pride and enthusiasm in donors about how their efforts improve the lives of others.

Political

In addition to its economic impact, the recession led to political pressure to reduce federal, state, and municipal budgets. This, in turn, has forced many nonprofit organizations to fund basic programs in innovative ways. Public universities, which receive a substantial portion of their funding from their respective state legislatures, have been hit especially hard. Figure 3.10 highlights the decrease in state funding as a percentage of total projected revenues at Temple University. This trend is consistent across many public universities throughout the United States.

In order to increase student financial aid and faculty retention, universities must raise more money from alumni and other supporters. The marketing department at the University of Colorado had success by increasing the profile of planned gifts on campus. These bequests, which are given to the nonprofit upon the death of the donor, became a major part of the University of Colorado's increased fundraising success. The university developed new packets of information for planned giving and promoted the program at all types of university events. They also delivered value to donors that did not require them to sacrifice financially during their life but helped them leave a legacy at the university they loved. In the first year after the marketing program began, the University of Colorado saw a 700 percent increase in bequests that will help students and the university for generations to come.[51]

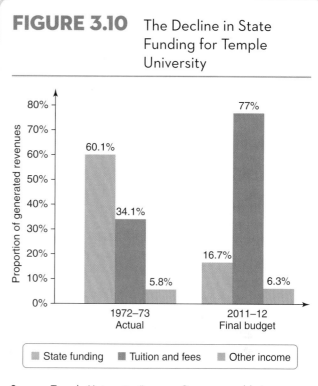

FIGURE 3.10   The Decline in State Funding for Temple University

Source: Temple University, "2012-13 Commonwealth Appropriation Budget Request," February 22, 2012, http://temple.edu/sites/temple/files/uploads/documents/Attachment_9-2012-Table_5-Generated_Revenue.pdf.

Legal

In addition to the economic factors that have challenged nonprofit firms, several new laws and regulations have had an impact as well. The benefit nonprofit marketers offer to potential donors typically includes some combination of information about how the donation will be used, how the donor will be recognized, and the tax incentives (e.g., the tax deductibility of charitable gifts) that will accompany the donation. Legal changes to the tax incentive element can alter the way marketing professionals communicate the organization's value to potential donors. For example, the state of New York proposed a law that restricts the amount of charitable contributions that very wealthy people can deduct from their taxes.[52] Wealthy contributors, those making over $10 million per year, are the largest donors to numerous charities throughout the state of New York. Nonprofit marketing professionals worry that this change in the tax law will act as a disincentive, further challenging fundraising efforts in a difficult economy. In addition, they fear that, without tax incentives, charitable giving may decline in the years ahead. Such legal changes have made it increasingly necessary for nonprofit firms to develop programs that generate more first-time contributors to make up for potential reductions from high-income donors.

Technology

Many nonprofit organizations utilize new technology to increase awareness and enhance relationships with donors. The rise of social media has changed the landscape in important ways. Nonprofit organizations such as Greenpeace, Amnesty International, and the Sierra Club have benefited from the appeal of social media. Social media sites let them engage interested parties through more personal

Many nonprofit organizations, such as Big Brothers Big Sisters, use social media to deepen engagement with stakeholders as part of their marketing strategy.

connections than more mainstream platforms. Social media give nonprofit organizations substantial advantages when it comes to organizing activists, conducting charity campaigns, or simply influencing communities and stakeholders. Big Brothers Big Sisters of America used social media to deepen engagement among new members; promote collaboration to generate new ideas; and increase loyalty, interest, and volunteer retention. In 2013, the organization used Facebook to reunite program participants with their big brother or big sister from childhood. The project was successful in re-engaging many individuals who had been impacted by the organization and retaining them as volunteers in the future.

SUMMARY

LO 3-1 Differentiate between direct and indirect competition.

The competitive environment includes the direct competitors a firm faces and the indirect competitors seeking to take market share and profits. The most commonly discussed form of competition is direct competition. Direct competition occurs when products performing the same function compete against each other. Indirect competition occurs when products provide an alternative solution to the same market.

LO 3-2 Summarize the major external factors that influence the marketing environment.

There are six major external factors that influence the marketing environment: economic, demographic, sociocultural, political, legal, and technological. Economic factors like GDP, consumer confidence, and income distribution influence almost every marketing decision a firm makes. Demographics, including age, gender, education level, and ethnicity, indicate the characteristics of human populations and groups that are used to identify consumer markets. Federal, state, and local governments enact regulations to promote two key objectives: that businesses compete fairly with each other and that they don't take advantage of consumers. Legal changes, such as new laws that protect consumers against unfair practices related to credit cards, continue to refine the way marketers promote their goods and services. Technological change affects how consumers use products and the way firms promote their products.

LO 3-3 Extend the analysis of the marketing environment beyond the borders of the United States.

The currency exchange rate, which is the price of one country's currency in terms of another country's currency, affects how firms market products internationally. A country's income distribution often gives the most reliable picture of a country's purchasing power. Marketers are particularly attracted to countries with a growing middle class because a nation's purchasing capability tends to increase as the proportion of middle-income households increases. In addition, marketers must understand how technology can facilitate communicating and delivering value to consumers around the world and how the firm's goods and services fit with different cultures.

LO 3-4 Identify the major trade agreements, monetary unions, and organizations that impact the global marketing environment.

The North American Free Trade Agreement (NAFTA) established a free trade zone among the United States, Canada, and Mexico. The Dominican Republic–Central America Free Trade Agreement (DR-CAFTA) is a free trade agreement among the U.S., Costa Rica, El Salvador, Guatemala, Honduras, Nicaragua, and the Dominican Republic. The European Union (EU) was formed to create a single European market by reducing barriers to the free trade of products, services, and finances among member countries. The World Trade Organization (WTO) was created to supervise international trade. The International Monetary Fund (IMF) is an intergovernmental organization that promotes international economic cooperation.

LO 3-5 Describe the emerging factors influencing the nonprofit marketing environment.

The competitive environment for nonprofit funding has increased dramatically in recent years. In 1995, there were only 600,000 nonprofits in the U.S. Today that number is over 1.8 million and growing rapidly. For nonprofit marketers to be successful in this type of competitive environment, they must understand the external environment in which their organization operates. Changes to external economic, political, legal, and technological factors can impact nonprofit marketers' strategies, restrictions, and resources.

KEY TERMS

baby boomers (p. 74)
consumer confidence (p. 72)
consumer ethnocentrism (p. 86)
currency exchange rate (p. 82)
demographics (p. 74)
direct competition (p. 68)
disposable income (p. 74)
Dominican Republic–Central America Free Trade Agreement (DR-CAFTA) (p. 85)

environmental scanning (p. 70)
European Union (EU) (p. 85)
Federal Trade Commission (FTC) (p. 80)
gross domestic product (GDP) (p. 70)
indirect competition (p. 69)
inflation (p. 72)
International Monetary Fund (IMF) (p. 85)
millennials (p. 75)

North American Free Trade Agreement (NAFTA) (p. 84)
purchasing power (p. 72)
recession (p. 70)
sociocultural (p. 78)
substitute products (p. 68)
tariffs (p. 84)
World Trade Organization (WTO) (p. 85)

MARKETING PLAN EXERCISE

In this chapter we discussed the importance of analyzing the marketing environment. In the next section of the marketing plan exercise, you will analyze the environment you will be entering upon graduation. Your assignment is to prepare a market summary for the job or graduate school program you discussed as your objective in Chapter 1. If your objective is a specific job or career, you need to answer questions like

- What is the average salary?
- What are the companies that are best positioned to offer the kind of job you want?
- Are there jobs in this field located where you want to live?
- What is the total size and growth rate of the industry you are planning to enter?
- What is the current unemployment rate in that field and what percentage of jobs are filled by new college graduates?

If your objective is graduate school, you need to answer questions like

- What schools offer this program?
- What are those schools' admission statistics (percentage accepted, tuition and fees, financial aid available, etc.)?
- What are the average Grade Point Average (GPA) and entrance exam (LSAT, GMAT, MCAT, etc.) scores?
- What is the average starting salary for graduates of these programs?

It is important to conduct an honest environmental assessment. Students sometimes have unrealistic expectations of what their first job out of school or a graduate program may be like. The better you understand the environment you are entering, the better you will be able to market yourself and your skills to succeed in it.

Your Task: Write at least a two-paragraph marketing summary describing the environment you will face after graduation.

DISCUSSION QUESTIONS

1. Consider your current university or college and develop a list of the direct and indirect competitors it will face in the next decade.
2. Assume you are going to open a new pizza restaurant in the town in which you live. What external factors will impact your business decisions? What types of technology would you use to market your pizza business and how would you use them?
3. Assume you work in marketing for Dr Pepper and you are looking to expand the brand internationally. Your final three choices are Mexico, Australia,

and India. Using the global environmental factors discussed in this chapter—currency fluctuations, income distribution, cultural fit, and technology—rank the countries based on which would provide the best opportunity for Dr Pepper's expansion. Explain your ranking for each country.

4. Choose a firm that you are familiar with that is located in the same state as your university. Next, decide if the North American Free Trade Agreement (NAFTA) has been good or bad for that business. Explain your answer. Has NAFTA been good or bad for all of that firm's stakeholders (investors, employees, communities, etc.) or has it been good for some and bad for others? Explain your answer.

5. Choose a nonprofit organization that you think markets itself effectively. Why did you pick that organization? What external factors do you think the organization should be most concerned about?

SOCIAL MEDIA APPLICATION

Choose a charity that you support. It could be anything from the Salvation Army to the United Way to your local church. Analyze the charity's efforts to market itself through social media using the following questions and activities as a guide:

1. What is the charity doing to market itself through social media?
2. What grade would you give the organization on its social media efforts and why?

3. Provide at least two recommendations for how the charity could improve its social media marketing activities. In addition, provide an example of a charity that you think is doing a great job marketing itself using social media and describe what it does.

ETHICAL CHALLENGE

The economic environment has changed in the past decade due to stock market losses, rising health care costs, and declining property values. As a result, many seniors were forced to look for new ways to generate income after their working careers ended. One of the primary beneficiaries of this shift was firms marketing reverse mortgages.

Reverse mortgages allow older homeowners to tap into the equity of their home and receive payments against its value. Typically, when the homeowners die, their heirs must repay the loan, including interest and fees. For the past two decades, the vast majority of reverse mortgages have been offered under the federally insured Home Equity Conversion Mortgages program, which applies to people aged 62 and older.[53] Market factors, including the rising number of seniors in the U.S., have led to an increase in advertisements promoting the benefits of these programs. The loans have become more attractive to lenders as traditional real estate sales have struggled in the years since the collapse of the housing market in 2007.

Like many other industries, the reverse mortgage business contains two sides of an ethical dilemma. On one side are those marketers who are increasing profits by helping seniors access the equity in their home; on the other are those who are potentially taking advantage of desperate seniors who may not fully understand what a reverse mortgage is. Please use the ethical decision-making framework to answer the following questions:

1. Which parties are impacted by reverse mortgages marketing strategies?
2. If you are a bank hoping to increase profits, would you try to expand your marketing of reverse mortgages to seniors?
3. If you are a marketing manager at a bank that has made the strategic decision to grow its reverse mortgage business, how would you go about promoting the product?

VIDEO CASE

Please go to *Connect* to access the video case featuring Erin Brewer that accompanies this chapter.

CAREER TIPS
Marketing Your Future

You have read in this chapter about the marketing environment and how external factors influence that environment for both for-profit and nonprofit organizations. As you think about your future, you may be considering a career in the nonprofit sector. Erin Brewer, who was featured in the Executive Perspective at the beginning of the chapter, spent a decade working for various nonprofit organizations and has some tips for securing a nonprofit position.

- **Gain experience.** Before you start interviewing for full-time positions, get some experience in charity work as a volunteer or an intern. The vast majority of nonprofits utilize both, so plenty of opportunities are available. A combination of volunteerism and internships provides the biggest advantage to a job seeker. It shows the hiring nonprofit that you're passionate about helping and that you know how similar organizations function. Some people begin their careers in the nonprofit world to gain significant hands-on experience

before making the leap to the corporate world. Others go the reverse route, getting their feet wet on the corporate side, and then taking on positions of greater responsibility in the charitable realm. The same principles of marketing apply to both sides of the spectrum and the smart professional can readily adapt.

- **Craft an effective resume.** Communicating who you are on a single piece of paper is a daunting task! Make sure that your resume conveys the right things about you. Be succinct, be compelling, be professional, and show a bit of personality. Highlight your unique accomplishments rather than simply listing your responsibilities, tailor your resume for each job you apply for, and always run spell check.

- **Put your intangibles to work.** Let your charm, gift for the spoken word, and passion for service shine. Once you have secured an interview, be prepared. Anticipate questions you may be asked and prepare a brief description of yourself and your goals. Be ready to ask some questions of your own. (To this day, I won't hire a candidate that doesn't ask a question.) Use your marketing coursework to your advantage by "spinning" your experience to suit the position you hope to attain. Be polite, be punctual, be honest, and most importantly, be yourself. And always send a thank you note.

CHAPTER NOTES

1. Candice Choi, "Wendy's Takes No. 2 Spot from Burger King," *Bloomberg Businessweek*, March 19, 2012, http://www.businessweek.com/ap/2012-03/D9TJLUH00.htm.
2. Tiffany Hsu, "Wendy's Dethrones Burger King, but Five Guys Grows Fastest," *Los Angeles Times*, March 19, 2012, http://www.sltrib.com/sltrib/money/53750045-79/sales-burger-king-wendy.html.csp.
3. Tim Callen, "Gross Domestic Product: An Economy's All," March 28, 2012, http://www.imf.org/external/pubs/ft/fandd/basics/gdp.htm.
4. The World Bank, "GDP Growth," n.d., http://data.worldbank.org/indicator/NY.GDP.MKTP.KD.ZG.
5. Ibid.
6. Ibid.
7. Ibid.
8. Kevin McCormally, "Where Do You Rank as a Taxpayer?" *Kiplinger*, December 12, 2012, http://www.kiplinger.com/features/archives/how-your-income-stacks-up.html.
9. Gene Marchial, "Discount Retailer Dollar General Taking Away Market Share from No. 1 Wal-Mart," *Forbes*, December 29, 2011, http://www.forbes.com/sites/genemarcial/2011/12/29/discount-retailer-dollar-general-taking-away-market-share-from-no-1-wal-mart/.
10. "The Substance of Style," *The Economist*, September 17, 2009, http://www.economist.com/node/14447276.
11. William Browning, "U.S. Gas Price History: From 25 Cents to Nearly $5 a Gallon," *Yahoo! News*, April 25, 2011, http://news.yahoo.com/u-gas-price-history-25-cents-nearly-5-170400039.html.
12. Louis Lataif, "Universities on the Brink," *Forbes*, February 1, 2011, http://www.forbes.com/2011/02/01/college-education-bubble-opinions-contributors-louis-lataif.html.
13. Stephanie Startz, "Hyundai Formula: Inconspicuous Luxury Plus Empathy," *BrandChannel*, September 22, 2009, http://www.brandchannel.com/home/post/2009/09/22/Hyundai-Formula-Inconspicuous-Luxury-Plus-Empathy.aspx#.
14. Mathew Boyle, "The Accidental Hero," *Bloomberg Businessweek*, November 5, 2009, http://www.businessweek.com/magazine/content/09_46/b4155058815908.htm.
15. Ibid.
16. Julianne Pepitone, "Subway Beats McDonald's to Become Top Restaurant Chain," *CNNMoney*, March 8, 2011, http://money.cnn.com/2011/03/07/news/companies/subway_mcdonalds/index.htm.
17. *Public Agenda*, "Social Security," n.d., http://www.publicagenda.org/articles/social-security.

18. *Immersion Active,* "50+ Facts and Fiction," n.d., http://www.immersionactive.com/resources/50-plus-facts-and-fiction/.

19. Ellen Byron, "From Diapers to 'Depends': Marketers Discreetly Retool for Aging Boomers," *The Wall Street Journal,* February 5, 2011, http://online.wsj.com/article/SB10001424052748704013604576104394209062996.html.

20. Danielle Sacks, "Scenes from the Culture Clash," *Fast Company,* January 1, 2006, http://www.fastcompany.com/54444/scenes-culture-clash.

21. Matt Townsend, "Young Consumers Pinch Their Pennies," *Bloomberg Businessweek,* March 22, 2012, http://www.businessweek.com/articles/2012-03-22/young-consumers-pinch-their-pennies.

22. Ekaterina Walter, "The Top 30 Stats You Need to Know When Marketing to Women," *The Next Web,* January 24, 2012, http://thenextweb.com/socialmedia/2012/01/24/the-top-30-stats-you-need-to-know-when-marketing-to-women/.

23. Ibid.

24. Greg Bardsley, "This Year's Top 4 Integrated Campaigns," *iMedia Connection,* September 2, 2010, http://www.imedia-connection.com/content/27503.asp.

25. Derek Thompson, "A Case for College: The Unemployment Rate for Bachelor's-Degree Holders Is 3.7%," *The Atlantic,* February 1, 2013, http://www.theatlantic.com/business/archive/2013/02/a-case-for-college-the-unemployment-rate-for-bachelors-degree-holders-is-37-percent/272779/.

26. Tamar Lewin, "Once a Leader, U.S. Lags in College Degrees," *The New York Times,* July 23, 2010, http://www.nytimes.com/2010/07/23/education/23college.html?_r=0.

27. Joseph B. White, "Hitching the New Small Wagon to Better Fuel Efficiency," *The Wall Street Journal,* December 24, 2012, http://online.wsj.com/article/SB10001424127887324907204578187560383059762.html.

28. Haya El Nasser, "U.S. Hispanic Population to Triple by 2050," *USA Today,* February 12, 2008, http://usatoday30.usatoday.com/news/nation/2008-02-11-population-study_N.htm.

29. Sonya Rastogi, Tallese D. Johnson, Elizabeth M. Hoeffel, and Malcolm P. Drewery, Jr., "The Black Population: 2010," United States Census Bureau, September 2011, http://www.census.gov/prod/cen2010/briefs/c2010br-06.pdf.

30. Pew Research, "The Rise of Asian Americans," *Social & Demographic Trends,* June 19, 2012, http://www.pewsocialtrends.org/2012/06/19/the-rise-of-asian-americans/.

31. Sam Fahmy, "Despite Recession, Hispanic and Asian Buying Power Expected to Surge in U.S., According to Annual UGA Selig Center Multicultural Economy Study," *News at the Terry College of Business,* November 4, 2010, http://www.terry.uga.edu/news/releases/2010/minority-buying-power-report.html.

32. Adweek, "Are You Winning with Hispanics?" April 27, 2011, http://www.adweek.com/sa-article/are-you-winning-hispanics-131093.

33. U.S. Census Bureau, "U.S. Census Bureau Reports Men and Women Wait Longer to Marry," November 10, 2010, http://www.census.gov/newsroom/releases/archives/families_households/cb10-174.html.

34. Alex Williams, "Just Wait until Your Mother Gets Home," *The New York Times,* August 10, 2012, http://www.nytimes.com/2012/08/12/fashion/dads-are-taking-over-as-full-time-parents.html?pagewanted=all.

35. Bill Mears, "California Ban on Sale of 'Violent' Video Games to Children Rejected," *CNN U.S.,* June 27, 2011, http://www.cnn.com/2011/US/06/27/scotus.video.games/index.html.

36. John Tozzi, "The Tanning Industry Is Tired of Getting Burned," *Bloomberg Businessweek,* January 3, 2013, http://www.businessweek.com/articles/2013-01-03/the-tanning-industry-fights-teen-bans.

37. Federal Communications Commission, "Unwanted Telephone Marketing Calls," n.d., http://www.fcc.gov/guides/unwanted-telephone-marketing-calls.

38. Ron Lieber, "Consumers Are Dealt a New Hand in Credit Cards," *The New York Times,* May 19, 2009, http://www.nytimes.com/2009/05/20/your-money/20money.html.

39. Ben Weitzenkorn, "Disney World to Track Visitors with Wireless Wristbands," NBC News, January 8, 2013, http://www.nbcnews.com/travel/travelkit/disney-world-track-visitors-wireless-wristbands-1B7874882.

40. Justin Gillis and Celia Dugger, "U.N. Forecasts 10.1 Billion People by Century's End," *The New York Times,* May 3, 2011, http://www.nytimes.com/2011/05/04/world/04population.html?_r=0.

41. X-Rates, "US Dollar per 1 Euro Monthly Average," n.d., http://www.x-rates.com/average/?from=EUR&to=USD&amount=1&year=2012.

42. Jason Dean, "Multinationals May Gain from the Yuan," *The Wall Street Journal,* June 21, 2010, http://online.wsj.com/article/SB10001424052748704638504575318740664651482.html.

43. NAFTA Free Trade Commission, "Joint Statement," April 3, 2012, http://www.international.gc.ca/trade-agreements-accords-commerciaux/agr-acc/nafta-alena/js-washington-dc.aspx?lang=eng.

44. Office of the United States Trade Representative, "Dominican Republic Joins Five Central American Countries in Historic FTA with U.S.," August 2004, http://www.ustr.gov/about-us/press-office/press-releases/archives/2004/august/dominican-republic-joins-five-central-amer.

45. United States Department of Agriculture, "Overview," n.d., http://www.ers.usda.gov/data-products/international-macroeconomic-data-set.aspx.

46. International Monetary Fund, "The IMF at a Glance," August 22, 2012, http://www.imf.org/external/np/exr/facts/glance.htm.

47. ABC News, "Burger King Ad Outrages Hindus," July 7, 2009, http://abclocal.go.com/kgo/story?section=news/national_world&id=6904129.

48. Terence A. Shimp and Subhash Sharma, "Consumer Ethnocentrism: Construction and Validation of the CETSCALE," *Journal of Marketing Research,* 24 (August 1987), pp. 280–289.

49. William Bills, "Called Only to Make a Difference," *Smart Talkers,* July 25, 2012, http://gumchurch.wordpress.com/2012/07/25/called-only-to-make-a-difference/.

50. Holly Hall, "Americans Gave a Lot Less in the Recession than Experts Predicted," *The Chronicle of Philanthropy,* April 22, 2011, http://philanthropy.com/article/Americans-Gave-a-Lot-Less-in/127244/.

51. Kristen L. Dugdale, "University of Colorado Foundation," *Crescendo,* n.d., http://cals.giftlegacy.com/egifts.jsp.

52. Grant Williams, "Nonprofit Groups Try to Block New York Charitable-Deduction Limit," *The Chronicle of Philanthropy,* June 29, 2010, http://philanthropy.com/article/Nonprofit-Groups-Try-to-Block/66085/.

53. David Bogoslaw, "Boomers' Shrunken 401(k)s Spark Interest in Reverse Mortgages," *Bloomberg Businessweek,* October 7, 2010, http://www.businessweek.com/investor/content/oct2010/pi2010107_409429.htm.

PART TWO
Understanding Your Customer

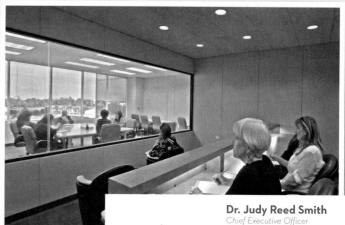

Dr. Judy Reed Smith
Chief Executive Officer

ATLANTIC ▪ ACM

ATLANTIC-ACM
http://www.atlantic-acm.com/

ATLANTIC-ACM delivers quantitative and qualitative research—including market sizing, forecasting, segmentation, customer satisfaction measurement, and competitive benchmarking—to executives.

Tracey Rogers
Vice President and General Manager

KAIT-TV
http://www.kait8.com/

KAIT-TV is a Raycom-owned ABC television affiliate located in the southern United States.

PEG
Bandwidth

Tom Payne
Director of Access Planning

PEG Bandwidth
http://pegbandwidth.com/

PEG Bandwidth focuses on customizing solutions for wireless carriers through broad partnerships with numerous telecommunications firms.

Cornelius Lovelace
Executive Director

Fitness Bootcamp Unlimited
http://www.fitnessbootcampunlimited.com/

Fitness Bootcamp Unlimited is a small health club with multiple locations in the southern United States that focuses on helping people lead healthier lives.

Chapter 4

MARKETING RESEARCH

LEARNING OBJECTIVES

After reading this chapter, you should be able to

LO 4-1 Explain the importance of marketing research to firms and individuals.

LO 4-2 Organize the five steps of the marketing research process.

LO 4-3 Describe the various types of marketing information systems and where they get information from.

LO 4-4 Explain why competitive intelligence is an important form of marketing research.

LO 4-5 Explain the importance of sales forecasting and compare the three basic types of forecasting techniques.

LO 4-6 Explain the importance of research to firms marketing products globally.

LO 4-7 Discuss the main ethical issues in conducting marketing research.

EXECUTIVE PERSPECTIVE

Dr. Judy Reed Smith
Chief Executive Officer
ATLANTIC-ACM

A passion for research made an entrepreneur of Dr. Judy Reed Smith, but it didn't happen overnight. During college, her interest in research led her to pursue a degree in biology. She spent 10 years as a biology teacher before changing course to rediscover her roots in research. After earning a graduate degree and working for several established marketing research firms, she decided to use the personal marketing skills she had developed to start her own company, ATLANTIC-ACM. Today, her firm delivers quantitative and qualitative research documents and advisories that provide executives with strategies for increasing revenues, shoring up existing customer bases, penetrating new markets, and navigating changes in market dynamics.

What has been the most important thing in making you successful at your job?

The clients we work with are worthy of deep respect. I greatly enjoy my clients as well as the challenges they offer to us. I think this, plus hard work, honesty, hiring people who are brighter than I am and intelligent in different ways, and a general consideration for others, make our firm successful. This sounds pretty ordinary, but we are always amazed at how many of our competitors don't make such things a priority.

What advice would you give soon-to-be graduates?

Choosing a job: Choose your first job not because it pays the most but because you will learn the most from it. One of my professors said, "Remember that you only need one job you like so don't try to collect many offers just to impress your friends." Do some homework to figure out which industries are likely to expand over the coming years, as growth brings opportunity for responsibility.

Doing the job: Once you get a job, listen, read, and spend time out of the office learning about your industry. Save party evenings for weekends so you are awake and sharp in the office. Invest your energy in whatever else will speed your learning and help you earn respect and responsibility.

The long-term view: It will likely take some years of working to know what type of work fits your style and skills and really satisfies you. Once you feel you know, follow that path, even if it isn't the most lucrative or prestigious. In the long run, you will be richer and more fulfilled than those who mindlessly chase the dollar.

How is marketing relevant to your role at ATLANTIC-ACM?

Helping companies make better marketing decisions is at the heart of what we do at our company. Our marketing research helps guide our clients as to what products they should develop, what pricing strategies they should use, and how customers feel about the services provided by that firm. Marketing has helped me to create a successful small business by meeting the needs of our customers.

What do you consider your personal brand to be?

I aim to be respected for always going the extra mile and for being able to listen and really understand what a client needs. I try to work with integrity and honesty, and to connect to friends, colleagues, and clients for the long term.

ATLANTIC · ACM

Dr. Judy Reed Smith
Chief Executive Officer

ATLANTIC-ACM
http://www.atlantic-acm.com/

ATLANTIC-ACM delivers quantitative and qualitative research—including market sizing, forecasting, segmentation, customer satisfaction measurement, and competitive benchmarking—to executives.

FORECAST

This chapter explores the importance of marketing research to individuals and firms. Good information leads to good decisions. Without accurate information, you may find yourself delivering and promoting products customers don't want at prices they're unwilling to pay. The chapter outlines the steps in a properly conducted research project, discusses various information systems that aid in marketing research, covers the importance of marketing research, and explains several types of marketing research. As you read through the chapter, consider the following key questions:

1. How does marketing research help organizations achieve their goals?
2. What guidelines can I follow to make sure that the marketing research I do adds value to my organization?
3. How can marketing information systems help me make better decisions?
4. Why should I care what my competitors are doing?

5. How can marketing research like sales forecasting give me a better idea of how much my customers will buy?
6. Who can help my organization obtain better marketing research?
7. How can marketing research help my firm successfully market to a global audience?
8. How can I make sure that my organization's marketing research is done in an ethical way?

LO 4-1

Explain the importance of marketing research to firms and individuals.

MARKETING RESEARCH

BlackBerry (formerly Research in Motion), maker of the BlackBerry smartphone, once led the market in cell phone technology. Over a period of four years, from 2008 to 2012, Apple and Android phones overtook BlackBerry's position, costing the firm $200 million in losses and forcing it to lay off thousands of workers. By the fall of 2012, BlackBerry's stock price had dropped 90 percent from its peak in 2008.[1] Three problems led to the firm's downfall. First, BlackBerry did not anticipate that individual consumers rather than business customers would drive the market in smartphones, so it ignored innovations that benefited consumers. Second, the firm failed to predict the emergence of applications (apps) as opposed to keyboards as the standard for smartphones, which left the company well behind Apple and other smartphone offerings. Third, BlackBerry did not see the emerging trend of consumers using smartphones as entertainment as well as communication devices. Basically, BlackBerry failed to respond to rapid changes in the cell phone market. As a result, it designed and marketed phones that were no longer attractive to consumers. Could BlackBerry have benefited from more knowledge of emerging trends? Most likely. In rapidly changing markets like those driven by technology, yesterday's winner can be today's also-ran if the firm lacks access to accurate data.

Marketing Research as a Navigation Tool

Like ancient mariners who could not venture far from land without fear of getting lost due to their lack of navigation aids, companies get lost trying to navigate markets without the aid of research. Marketing research is the act of collecting, interpreting, and reporting information concerning a clearly defined marketing problem. When done properly, marketing research helps companies understand and satisfy the needs and wants of customers. Marketing research has become more important, and more complicated, as markets continue to become globalized and product life cycles become shorter. In such a climate, companies need accurate information to reduce risk and make good decisions. This quest for information compels companies to spend billions of dollars each year on marketing research.

In response to increasingly globalized markets, multinational companies seeking to compete in the global marketing arena must have a working knowledge of international trends. For example, consumer packaged goods companies

marketing research

The act of collecting, interpreting, and reporting information concerning a clearly defined marketing problem.

Marketing research helped Unilever PLC develop small sachets of deodorant and shampoo to sell to customers in Indonesia who don't want to spend a large proportion of their paycheck on personal care products.

like Unilever PLC have discovered that it's good business to sell to low-income consumers in Indonesia.[2] These consumers earn a fraction of what a worker in Europe or the United States earns, yet they still buy products like food, soap, and shampoo. In fact, low-income Indonesian consumers differ from affluent ones elsewhere mostly with regard to packaging. Indonesian consumers want smaller package sizes so that they don't have to lay out a large percentage of their monthly income on one item. Marketing research has provided multinational companies like Unilever with an opportunity to profit from sales of their products in what, on the surface, would seem like a less-than-attractive market.

In addition to globalization, trends such as quickly changing patterns of consumer behavior also provide an incentive for firms to acquire fresh information through marketing research. Firms can no longer rely only on historical data to determine future marketing strategies. Now, they must generate timely information, interpret it quickly, and take action before the competition does. If they don't, they will be beaten before they can even begin.

The Impact of Marketing Research

Marketing research impacts almost every aspect of a company's business. We can see this impact clearly in terms of the four Ps—product, price, place, and promotion.

1. **Products** need to be developed based on real customer needs and wants, not just the whims of marketing departments. Product developers in research and development departments must have an idea of what customers want before they can create new products, and finance departments must have good information concerning the viability of a product to approve expenditures on new product development.
2. **Pricing** requires analysis of the size of the potential market and the effects of price changes on demand. This information comes from demand analysis, a type of research used to estimate how much customer demand there is for a particular product and understand the factors driving that demand.[3]

demand analysis

A type of research used to estimate how much customer demand there is for a particular product and understand the factors driving that demand.

After previous phones sold poorly, BlackBerry conducted marketing research to develop the BlackBerry 10, which was released with no physical keyboard and a unique user interface to support multitasking, something consumers wanted in a smartphone.

sales forecasting

A form of research that estimates how much of a product will sell over a given period of time.

advertising effectiveness studies

A type of research that measures how well an advertising campaign meets marketing objectives.

sales tracking

A type of research that follows changes in sales during and after promotional programs to see how the marketing efforts affected the company's sales.

3. Decisions regarding the **place** or distribution function must be made using sales forecasting, which is a form of research that estimates how much of a product will sell over a given period of time. Using this research, firms know how much product to hold in inventory at various points in the distribution network. We will discuss sales forecasting in more depth later in the chapter.

4. **Promotional** activities such as advertising must be evaluated based on their effectiveness. Firms use advertising effectiveness studies and sales tracking to gauge how well advertising and promotional campaigns are working. Advertising effectiveness studies measure how well an advertising campaign meets marketing objectives like increasing market share, generating consumer awareness of a product, or creating a favorable impression of the company's products.[4] Sales tracking follows changes in sales during and after promotional programs to see how the marketing efforts affected the company's sales. Marketing professionals use the results of this research to adjust where and how they apply promotional efforts.

In addition to its impact on firms, marketing research matters to consumers like you. Consumers rely on companies to develop and market the products they need and want. For example, after sales and profits sagged, BlackBerry researched what customers wanted from a smartphone in terms of function, user interface, and applications. They redesigned their smartphones accordingly. Without marketing research, companies would mostly be guessing at what consumers want, often missing badly, as in the case of previous BlackBerry phones.

Marketing researchers use a variety of techniques and gather data from an assortment of sources to provide the goods and services truly desired by people. Regardless of the technique employed, firms follow five basic steps when they engage in the marketing research process. We'll discuss these five steps in depth in the next section.

LO 4-2

Organize the five steps of the marketing research process.

THE MARKETING RESEARCH PROCESS

The marketing research process is a well-defined set of steps that, if followed, should yield invaluable information concerning a firm's market. A systematic approach to marketing research follows a five-step process: (1) problem definition, (2) plan development, (3) data collection, (4) data analysis, and (5) taking action. Figure 4.1 shows this process for a hypothetical product sold by beverage company Fuze, which produces several popular tea and juice drinks. Although Figure 4.1 shows the process as a linear progression, sometimes marketers skip steps if they get an early solution to the problem, or go back to an earlier step to gather additional information or reanalyze data as needed.

Step 1: Problem Definition

Problem definition is the first step in the marketing research process. Often firms know that they have a problem but cannot precisely pinpoint or clearly define the problem. Clarifying the exact nature of the problem prevents the firm from wasting time, money, and human resources chasing the wrong data and coming up with the wrong solutions. To begin, a firm should set specific research objectives. As with overall marketing objectives, research objectives should be specific and measurable. They represent what the firm seeks to gain by conducting the research.

To illustrate using our Fuze example, let's assume that one of the beverages Fuze produces has seen its profits slip over the past year. In this case, Fuze's defined problem would be *to determine why the beverage business has lost profitability over the past year*. To begin, the company might perform a situation analysis. The situation analysis could include the composition of the target market, specifics of the marketing mix currently in use, economic factors such as employment and inflation, and the state of the competition. For example, if the beverage market itself is becoming less profitable, the firm may not need to continue to research why the company's profits have slipped. In that case, Fuze would go back and redefine the problem. If, however, the situation analysis reveals that other companies are still profitable, Fuze should seek possible root causes of the problem.

Let's assume Fuze determines that consumers like the product, but the company's promotional efforts are not producing results. Consequently, Fuze is losing market share. From there, Fuze sets its research objective: to determine what exactly about the promotional campaign is causing the company to lose market share. With this objective in hand, the Fuze marketers can write a formal proposal to senior management outlining the research and seeking approval to develop a plan for the project.

Step 2: Plan Development

Plan development, sometimes called *research design*, involves identifying what data sources will be utilized, what specific type of research will be used, and what sampling methods will be employed. The first aspect of designing the research plan involves hypothesis development. A hypothesis is an educated guess based on previous knowledge or research about the cause of the problem under investigation. In our beverage example, Fuze may develop a hypothesis that the target market has not been sufficiently exposed to the promotional campaign.

Data Sources To test its hypothesis, Fuze must collect data. First, it must determine whether it should seek primary or secondary data. Primary data are collected *specifically* for the research problem at hand. In the case of Fuze's product, such data might include how many people in the target market have been exposed to a particular advertisement, or how they've reacted to the advertisement. Secondary data are collected for purposes other than answering the firm's research questions. Often the company itself has collected this data from its day-to-day operations and can access it directly. Other times, it must go to another source. For example, if Fuze wanted to know the size of its target market, it could go to the United

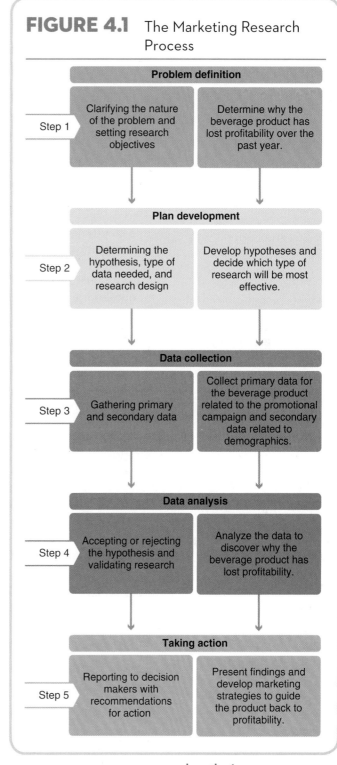

FIGURE 4.1 The Marketing Research Process

hypothesis
An educated guess based on previous knowledge or research about the cause of the problem under investigation.

primary data
Data collected specifically for the research problem at hand.

States Census Bureau's website (www.census.gov) to find out how many people belong to a particular demographic group, or how many people from a demographic group live in a certain geographic area. While primary data are more expensive to collect than secondary data, firms generally find primary data more valuable because they are collected to answer a specific research question. In the case of Fuze, the nature of the research objective would likely lead the firm to seek primary data. Secondary data may not shed light on the connection between the firm's promotional activities and the product's falling market share. Table 4.1 outlines the differences between primary and secondary data.

Types of Research   Next, Fuze marketers must decide what type of research they should use to collect the data. The firm can choose from among the following three basic types of research:

1. Exploratory research seeks to discover new insights that will help the firm better understand the problem or consumer thoughts, needs, and behavior. Exploratory research usually involves some type of face-to-face interaction between the person or persons collecting the data and the person or persons providing the data. For example, Fuze could interview people to ask them questions about their beverage buying behaviors to understand how nutritional information affects consumer purchases.

TABLE 4.1   Differences between Primary and Secondary Data

	Primary Data	Secondary Data
Collection Method Examples	Focus groups Surveys Observations Data gathered by equipment (e.g., video) In-depth personal interviews	Literature reviews Online electronic searches Company records Marketing information systems Private research companies Boundary spanners (e.g., salespersons)
Advantages	Pertains only to firm's research May provide insight into why and how consumers make choices	Less expensive (often free) Information typically readily accessible
Disadvantages	More expensive May be difficult to enlist customer participation May take excessive amount of time to collect	Data may not be relevant Data may not be accurate Data may have been altered Data may contain bias
Examples of Use	To understand what motivates consumers To determine the effect of variables (e.g., price) on product choice To gain feedback on company's existing and proposed products	To gather macroeconomic data To gather socioeconomic data To obtain information about competitors To gain insight into international cultures and markets

2. Descriptive research seeks to understand consumer behavior by answering the questions who, what, when, where, and how.[5] Examples of descriptive information include a consumer's attitude toward a product or company; a consumer's plans for purchasing a product; specific ways that consumers behave, such as whether they prefer to shop in person or online; and demographic information like age, gender, and place of residence. To conduct descriptive research, Fuze could conduct an in-store survey that asks consumers how they view the company and its beverage products.

3. Causal research is used to understand the cause-and-effect relationships among variables. Causal research involves manipulating independent variables (the cause or source) to see how they impact a particular dependent variable (the effect or outcome). Fuze could conduct an experiment, for example, that manipulates the packaging of its beverages (the independent variable) to see how different package styles affect sales (the dependent variable).

Fuze marketers will establish data collection procedures, which we will discuss in the next section, based on the type of research the company decides is most appropriate to achieve the research objective or objectives. Companies need not limit themselves to one type of research. For example, Fuze may use exploratory methods to get a deeper understanding of what motivates people to buy a beverage product and causal techniques to analyze how changes to the product or price will affect sales.

Sampling Methods

It would be impossible—from both a budget and time perspective—for marketing professionals to obtain feedback from all the members of its target market. Instead, they must rely on sampling. Sampling is the process of selecting a subset of the population that is representative of the population as a whole. How researchers conduct sampling is critical to the validity of the research findings. If the firm uses secondary data, the marketer must make sure that the population from which the data are taken relates to the research objective. For example, if Fuze uses archived data that the firm compiled itself, it must ensure that the data represent consumers from its target market. Irrelevant data from another target market may lead to inaccurate conclusions. If the firm requires primary data, it can select a sample from which it can generalize findings. A sample is a representative subset of the larger population (in this case, beverage drinkers). Sampling can be broken down into two basic types: probability and nonprobability.

Probability sampling ensures that every person in the target population has a chance of being selected, and the probability of each person being selected is known. To conduct probability sampling, Fuze would need to structure its study so that it could calculate each beverage drinker's probability of being included in the sample. The most common example of probability sampling is simple random sampling. In simple random sampling, everyone in the target population has an *equal* chance of being selected. Implementing a simple random sample typically involves generating a table of random numbers and assigning one number to each potential participant. The researcher then uses the number (or numbers) to select the members of the population to receive a survey. Simple random sampling is the equivalent of drawing names from a hat; every name in the hat has an equal chance of being chosen.

Nonprobability sampling, on the other hand, does not attempt to ensure that every member of the target population has a chance of being selected. Nonprobability sampling contains an element of judgment in which the researcher narrows the target population by some criteria before selecting participants. Examples include quota sampling, in which the firm chooses a certain number of participants based on selection criteria such as demographics (e.g., race, age, or gender), and snowball sampling, in which a firm selects participants based on the referral of other participants who know they have some knowledge of the subject in

descriptive research

A type of research that seeks to understand consumer behavior by answering the questions who, what, when, where, and how.

causal research

A type of research used to understand the cause-and-effect relationships among variables.

sampling

The process of selecting a subset of the population that is representative of the population as a whole.

sample

A representative subset of the larger population.

probability sampling

A type of sampling in which every person in the target population has a chance of being selected, and the probability of each person being selected is known.

simple random sampling

A type of sampling in which everyone in the target population has an equal chance of being selected.

nonprobability sampling

A type of sampling that does not attempt to ensure that every member of the target population has a chance of being selected.

quota sampling

A type of sampling in which a certain number of participants is picked based on selection criteria such as demographics.

snowball sampling

A type of sampling in which a set of participants is selected based on the referral of other participants who know they have some knowledge of the subject in question.

Firms like Trader Joe's can use causal research to analyze the effect of a potential price increase on products such as Charles Shaw brand wine, which was known as "Two-Buck Chuck" during its first 11 years at Trader Joe's stores.

question. While probability sampling enables researchers to generalize findings from a portion of a target population, nonprobability sampling can generate findings that may be more appropriate to the research question.

Step 3: Data Collection

The third step of the marketing research process, data collection, begins with the firm's decision to use secondary or primary data.

Secondary Data Collection Secondary data can come from two sources: internal and external. Internal data are collected by the company and can include things like sales by product, information about individual purchases from loyalty cards, previous research reports, accounting records, and market information from the sales force. Companies often build large internal databases in which to store such data. Much of this information now comes from company websites, such as Amazon's database on individual customer purchases.

External secondary data can come from many sources. Governments compile a lot of data and make it available to the general public. U.S. government agencies like the Economics and Statistics Administration and the Census Bureau provide a great deal of useful secondary data in various publicly available reports. Information on competitors can be found on the U.S. Securities and Exchange Commission website (www.sec.gov). Other sources of secondary data include trade associations, academic journals, business periodicals, and commercial online databases such as LexisNexis. The Internet is a rich source of secondary information. Search engines like Google and Bing help researchers find secondary sources of information. However, it is important to understand that information found on the Internet can be biased, inaccurate, and unsubstantiated. Researchers must always be cautious about using such information and verify its accuracy against known valid sources before using it.

Primary Data Collection Primary data collection may be necessary if secondary information cannot adequately answer the research question. Depending on the research design (exploratory, descriptive, or causal), the company can choose to use one of a variety of primary data collection methods. Primary data collection methods can be either qualitative or quantitative. Figure 4.2 shows the relationships among research objectives and the collection methods and types.

Qualitative research includes exploratory types of research such as focus groups, interviews, and observation.

- Focus groups are conducted by a moderator and involve a small number of people (usually 8–12) who interact with each other in a spontaneous way as they discuss a particular topic or concept. Researchers can hold focus groups either in person (e.g., in a special room in a shopping mall) or in an online format. Fuze could use focus groups to better understand how consumers feel about its product versus other beverages. The interactive nature of this setting lends itself to drawing out opinions and generating insights into a marketing question. However, focus groups are expensive to perform and must be conducted by experienced people who know how to properly direct discussions in a way that elicits useful information from participants.
- In an interview, the researcher works with one participant at a time. During the interview, the researcher asks open-ended questions about how the individual perceives and uses various products or brands. For example, Fuze

focus groups

Data collection tool in which a moderator engages a small group of people as they discuss a particular topic or concept with each other in a spontaneous way.

interview

A data collection tool in which the researcher works with one participant at a time, asking open-ended questions about how the individual perceives and uses various products or brands.

FIGURE 4.2   The Relationships among Research Objectives and Collection Options

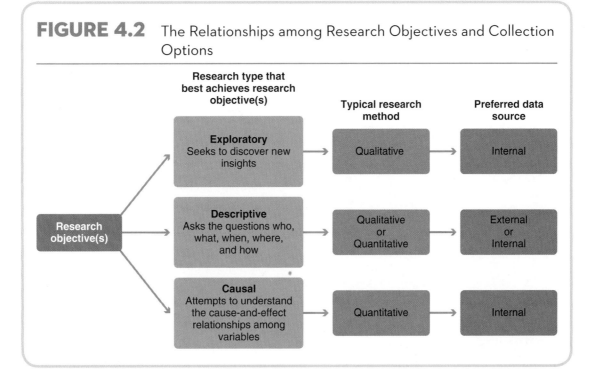

could ask participants what thoughts go through their heads when they see the beverage on the store shelf. Interviews can be useful in figuring out what people think but have the limitation of being very time-consuming.

- Observation involves watching how people behave and recording anything about that behavior that might be relevant to the research objective. For example, Fuze could set up a mock store aisle full of beverages and watch how participants react to various types of packaging or where beverages are positioned in the aisle. Companies often find such information useful, but participants may subconsciously try to please researchers and act as they think researchers expect them to. To combat this tendency, major consumer packaged goods companies like Procter & Gamble, Unilever PLC, and Kimberly-Clark are combining eye-tracking technology with computer simulations of products and store layouts to find out which of their designs get noticed in the first 10 seconds that a customer spends looking at a simulated store shelf.[6] While observation allows researchers to see *how* people behave, it is not useful in determining *why* they behave that way. Firms often use observation in conjunction with other techniques that help researchers identify the motivation behind particular behaviors.

Beyond these traditional qualitative methods, the Internet is giving rise to a new form of qualitative research called *netnography,* which involves observing the behavior of online communities that have been organized around a particular consumer interest. Often the members of such communities are first movers, that is, consumers who take the lead in adopting new products and are dedicated to the product. The researcher enters the online forums to gather data and then uses the community members to verify his or her findings.

Qualitative methods like interviews and focus groups can provide researchers a great deal of insight, but they don't always allow researchers to draw generalized conclusions about the larger consumer population. To collect the necessary data to achieve their research objective, companies often turn to quantitative research. Quantitative research includes surveys, experiments, and mathematical modeling.

- Surveys or questionnaires pose a sequence of questions to respondents. They provide a time-tested method for obtaining answers to who, what, where, why, and how types of questions and can be used to collect a wide variety of data.[7] In addition, they help determine consumer attitudes, intended behavior, and the motivations behind behavior. Surveys often employ multiple-choice questions, making them appropriate for gathering feedback from a large number of participants. They can be administered by mail, at shopping malls, on the telephone, or online. Fuze could use a survey to gather data from a large population about which of the company's promotions consumers have seen and their reactions to those promotions.

- Experiments are procedures undertaken to test a hypothesis. They allow researchers to control the research setting so that they can examine causal relationships between variables. Fuze could undertake an experiment in which researchers change the color of the product's packaging (an independent variable) and observe how often consumers look at the product (the dependent variable) on a simulated store shelf in a laboratory. Researchers perform field experiments in natural settings like stores or malls. While field settings offer an element

observation

A data collection tool that involves watching how people behave and recording anything about that behavior that might be relevant to the research objective.

surveys

A data collection tool that poses a sequence of questions to respondents.

experiments

Procedures undertaken to test a hypothesis.

field experiments

Experiments performed in natural settings like stores or malls.

To circumvent the bias that can sometimes arise through traditional observation studies, some large firms use eye-tracking technology, which creates heatmaps like the one shown here, to determine how long and how often research participants look at packages on a computer screen or in a store.

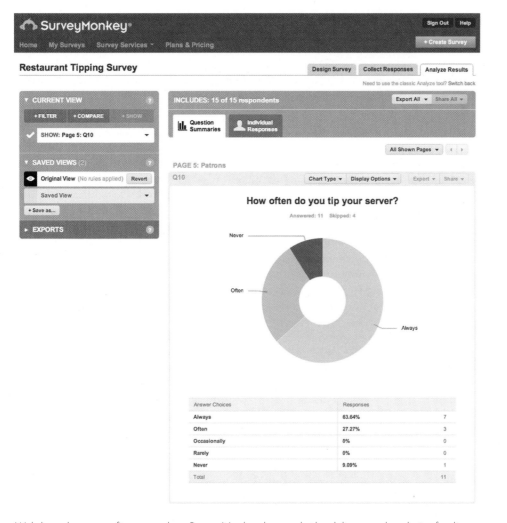

Web-based survey software, such as SurveyMonkey, has made the delivery and analysis of online surveys much easier for researchers.

of realism, they are also more difficult to control, which can lessen the validity of the experiment. Some companies use neuromarketing techniques that measure brain activity when a participant is subjected to a particular stimulant to understand how consumers feel about products, packaging, and advertisements. One neuromarketing study compared the brain scans of participants tasting Pepsi and Coke. In this experiment, taste was the stimulant. Based on the part of the brain activated during the tasting session, the researchers found that participants in the study were buying Coke for reasons related less to their taste preferences and more to their experience with the Coke brand. This type of finding could be used to develop advertisements that relate a product to the type of thought processes that people use to choose products.

- Another type of causal research involves mathematical modeling, in which equations are used to model the relationships between variables. For example, Fuze could use mathematical modeling to investigate the effect on sales if the firm were to increase or decrease the price of the product.

As with secondary data, the Internet can be leveraged as a tool for collecting primary data. We will discuss how the Internet has impacted primary data collection later in the chapter. Once data have been collected, the marketing researcher moves on to the next step: data analysis.

neuromarketing

A technique that measures brain activity when a participant is subjected to a particular stimulant to understand how consumers feel about products, packaging, and advertisements.

mathematical modeling

A type of causal research that involves using equations to model the relationships between variables.

Step 4: Data Analysis

The purpose of data analysis is to convert the data collected in Step 3 into information the firm can use to solve the marketing problem originally identified. Analysis of the data should allow marketers to accept or reject the research hypothesis or hypotheses. If it doesn't, more research might be necessary.

Analyzing Qualitative Data
Data analysis can be challenging, particularly when applied to qualitative data. For example, interviews can be directed in a way that takes participants away from what they were thinking and toward what the researcher wants to hear. Results may be difficult to measure objectively and in ways that help marketers formulate a marketing strategy. Additionally, due to the time-consuming nature of qualitative research, sample sizes can be very small and therefore may not represent the general population of the target market. Poor interpretation presents another challenge to data analysis. Qualitative data, which often involves open-ended questions, can include subtleties that a marketer might miss. For example, if the researcher fails to notice that the participant pauses when trying to recall details of one advertisement but quickly gives accurate descriptions of another advertisement, a significant finding—that the second advertisement may be more effective than the first—would be lost. Alternately, marketers could misunderstand respondents' feedback or allow their own bias to influence their interpretation. One way that researchers check their interpretations is to review their findings with research participants to make sure that they understood what the participant actually meant.

Despite its drawbacks, researchers can gain substantial insight from qualitative research. Qualitative data gathering and analysis can give researchers ideas about the subject that can later be tested through quantitative research. Because there are no predetermined sets of responses (e.g., multiple-choice answers), the participant can open up to the interviewer and cover things that the researcher may not have thought of previously. Also, the researcher can probe the subject in greater detail and with much more flexibility, and therefore may come up with more details concerning consumer motivations and behaviors than quantitative methods can reveal.

Analyzing Quantitative Data
Quantitative methods for collecting and analyzing data can often be done quickly, at low cost, and may help researchers understand cause-and-effect patterns in consumer behaviors. However, as with qualitative data, there are drawbacks. While statistical analysis of quantitative data might give marketing professionals insight into consumer behavior, whether or not the results should be accepted depends on how well the sample represents the general population. This can be determined using statistical software. The representative nature of the statistics may impact whether or not the marketing team ultimately accepts the original hypothesis. For example, Fuze would need to confirm that the results of a survey related to the firm's promotional materials represent the behaviors and attitudes of the overall beverage market, with no bias toward one group of consumers through sampling errors.

validity

The extent to which data measure what the researcher intended to measure.

Data analysis can involve other issues. Validity concerns how well the data measure what the researcher intended to measure. Often validity is called into question because of poorly worded questions that can be interpreted by the participant in several ways. To prevent this, researchers often pretest the questions before using them to evaluate how well people filling out the survey understand them. In addition, quantitative data suffers from issues related to participation. Surveys often have low response rates, and it can be difficult to determine why some people have not responded to a survey. Respondents who select to participate may exhibit a bias stemming from their willingness to provide feedback.

TABLE 4.2   Advantages and Disadvantages of Qualitative and Quantitative Research

Research Method Type	Advantages	Disadvantages
Qualitative	Uncovers details concerning the motivations behind behaviors	Results may be difficult to measure objectively
	Is not limited to a predetermined set of responses	Research can take longer than quantitative methods
	Can be a good way to start research into a marketing problem	Potential for researcher bias
	Can be very flexible in approach	Individual participants may not represent general target market
	Can be used to generate marketing ideas	Small sample size
Quantitative	Results may be generalizable to a larger population	May be limited by researchers' questions
	Some methods can be conducted quickly and inexpensively	Response rates can be very low
	Analysis of data can be faster than in qualitative research	Difficult to determine nonresponse bias
	Can conduct causal studies that indicate why behaviors occur	Possible respondent self-selection bias
	Can be cost effective	Participant resistance to giving sensitive information
	Often convenient for respondent	

Other problems with quantitative methods include the restrictive nature of surveys that do not give respondents an opportunity to explain or further elaborate on their answers. For these reasons, marketing professionals must understand the potential pitfalls of a research project and work together with the researcher to avoid as many as possible. Table 4.2 lists some of the advantages and disadvantages of qualitative and quantitative research methods.

In our beverage example, Fuze hypothesized that the decrease in profits stemmed from the fact that the target market had not been sufficiently exposed to the promotional campaign. Let's assume this hypothesis was accepted based on data showing that much of the firm's target market had not seen the firm's latest television ad. Once marketers have interpreted the data and feel confident about the findings, they can move to the final step of the process: taking action.

___

connect
|MARKETING

Interactive Assignment 4-1

Please complete the *Connect* exercise for Chapter 4 that focuses on the steps of the marketing research process. By understanding the decisions at each step, you will be able to conduct better marketing research and thus improve the quality of your marketing strategy going forward.

EXECUTIVE PERSPECTIVE

Dr. Judy Reed Smith

Chief Executive Officer
ATLANTIC-ACM

What is the biggest mistake that new professionals make when conducting marketing research?

The biggest mistake that I see new professionals make is to try to analyze data in such a way that it tells them exactly what they want to hear. This is not effective. Quality marketing research helps to answer a question or solve a problem, but too many people try and turn data into their personal yes-man. Numbers can be manipulated, but marketers must honestly analyze the data and listen to what the research is telling them about their customers or products, even if it is not something they want to hear.

Step 5: Taking Action

The culmination of the marketing research process is a formal, written report to decision makers. The report typically includes a summary of the findings and recommended actions to address the problem. Usually, an oral report on the project is presented along with a written one. Both reports should communicate any limitations of the research. Limitations could include a variety of things, including inadequate sample sizes or samples that do not adequately represent the population under study. It is important that marketers honestly discuss the limitations of the research. Such limitations should be considered before the firm makes any final decisions based on the research.

Research report findings should be presented in a clear and understandable manner and include appropriate visual data, such as figures and tables, to support the findings and recommendations. The research report should allow the marketing manager to solve the marketing problem. For example, let's say that the results of Fuze's research indicate that its consumers spend their time on the Internet watching videos and streaming shows and movies rather than watching cable TV. This finding might prompt the marketing department to develop a new promotional campaign that includes YouTube videos and ads on services like Hulu, potentially increasing market share and profitability.

As we've seen, information about what consumers need and want and what motivates their buying behaviors is available, but it must be collected and analyzed effectively. In the next section we will discuss how technology can help firms complete marketing research projects more effectively and efficiently.

LO 4-3
Describe the various types of marketing information systems and where they get information from.

INFORMATION-SYSTEM-ENABLED RESEARCH

Powerful computer software and hardware make marketing research easier to conduct than ever before. In-house systems, such as marketing decision support systems (DSS) and online systems like those that support social media sites allow companies to collect and analyze huge amounts of data. We discuss these types of systems next.

Marketing Information Systems

Research reports based on old or inaccurate information or personal experience that's outdated or not applicable to the current situation can cause a company to make poor marketing decisions. Many managers rely on their "gut" instinct, and it can be difficult for junior managers to persuade senior managers that their judgment is wrong. Timely and accurate facts provide the best counterbalance to such situations.

A marketing information system (MIS) is computer software that helps companies continuously capture information and store it in a way that makes it accessible to researchers and decision makers so they have a good foundation for

marketing information system (MIS)

Computer software that helps companies continuously capture information and store it in a way that makes it accessible to researchers and decision makers.

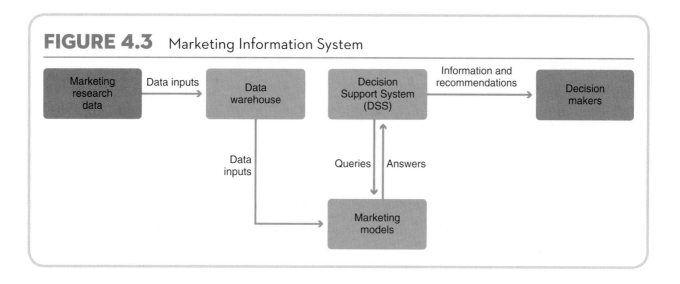

FIGURE 4.3   Marketing Information System

planning. Figure 4.3 shows how an MIS is configured. An MIS consists of a data warehouse that stores information and a decision support system. A decision support system (DSS) is a computer program that enables access and use of the information stored in the data warehouse. Database management software within the DSS allows analysts to sort and access data from the database. A DSS can process internal information that the company collects (e.g., sales data) as well as external information that's entered into the database (e.g., competitor information). Within the DSS, a marketing model may be set up to manipulate variables to predict the outcome of changes in the marketing mix. For example, a marketing model can be constructed to calculate the impact of price changes on sales and profits. A DSS also allows managers to manipulate data and organize it in a useful way, look for trends in sales, identify problems with elements of the marketing mix, and provide quick feedback to managers concerning proposed marketing plans. Additionally, data mining techniques can be applied to find patterns in the data that would otherwise be inaccessible. Data mining is a process that involves the computerized search for meaningful trends in a large amount of data.[8] SAS Enterprise Miner, Rapid Miner, Data Mining Technologies Inc., Oracle Data Mining, and Statistical Data Miner are examples of software that companies use to discover patterns in large data sets that can be used in various marketing functions such as promotions and customer segmentation.

Though an MIS can give a firm an advantage over its competitors, there is a potential downside to collecting and storing information about customers—it can be stolen. In China, approximately 70 percent of companies are at risk for data leakage as computer hackers realize the benefits of obtaining personal information to sell to companies that develop lists of potential customers for their own use. Hackers can break into the files of a company's customers even if the files are being maintained in-house. Companies therefore have to stay ahead of hackers and protect their data from those who seek to steal it.

decision support system (DSS)
A computer program that enables access and use of the information stored in the data warehouse.

data mining
A process that involves the computerized search for meaningful trends in a large amount of data.

connect |MARKETING **Interactive Assignment 4-2**

Please complete the *Connect* exercise for Chapter 4 that focuses on data mining strategies and how they can help marketers make decisions. By knowing how to use consumer data more strategically, you will understand how to develop and promote products that best meet your customers' needs.

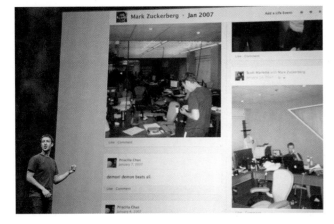

Facebook's Timeline was, in part, designed by online focus group feedback about the application's interface. The feedback resulted in changes, such as a line down the middle of the screen that shows different points in time, that make the product easier to use.

Internet-Enabled Research

The Internet has become a major tool for collecting primary data. The Internet now enables both qualitative and quantitative methodologies that are considered valid ways to conduct research. In many cases, Internet-enabled research is more effective than traditional methods. For example, delivering surveys via the Internet provides additional control because respondents can only select the responses available on the screen. They can no longer alter the survey as they could with traditional paper surveys. Also, respondents must answer the questions in the order presented and cannot move on without answering them, which often leads to a more complete set of answers. Finally, participants seem more willing to take online surveys than traditional paper ones, perhaps due to the convenience offered by this type of presentation.[9]

Focus groups can also be conducted via the Internet. Respondents can log in to a website at a predetermined time and type answers to questions posed by a moderator. The format is often like a private chat room in which participants can see each of the questions and the responses to those questions. For example, Del Monte used an online focus group to find out what members of a dog lovers community wanted to feed their pets in the morning.[10] A transcript of these sessions provided a basis for researchers to do analysis and ultimately helped Del Monte develop bacon-flavored breakfast bites with an extra dose of vitamins, which were well received in the marketplace. Companies like Del Monte can obtain participants for online focus groups and panel discussions from panel providers that match a list of willing respondents—those who have answered a series of questions about themselves—with the research needs of the company conducting marketing research. In this way, members of target groups can be easily identified and recruited for research.[11]

Social media provide additional sources of information for marketing researchers. The explosive growth of social media sites has given rise to many opportunities for marketing researchers to get information free of charge. Millions of people use one or more forms of social media daily, which means the potential for capturing information from these sites is tremendous. Social media users on sites like Facebook often share information concerning their purchases or intended purchases as well as personal information about themselves that can be useful to researchers. Blogs, podcasts, message boards, and opinion and review sites all allow people to post valuable commentaries on a variety of subjects. Several companies have developed software to track popular topics on blog sites and obtain opinions of goods and services and other data, such as consumer trends, that researchers can analyze. As with an MIS, Internet-enabled research presents ethical challenges to marketing professionals seeking consumer information. We will discuss the ethical issues surrounding consumer privacy later in this chapter.

 Interactive Assignment 4-3

Social Media in Action

Social media are changing the way organizations conduct marketing research. For example, Dr Pepper uses marketing insights from over 8 million Facebook fans to figure out which marketing messages might work best. Dr Pepper sends out multiple messages each day and then tracks and monitors fan reactions. Social media allow Dr Pepper to measure how many times a message is viewed, how many times it is shared with other users, and what people are saying about it. One of the insights the company captured from this research is that loyal Dr Pepper customers like "edgy" one-line messages such as, "If liking you is wrong, we don't want to be right." These types of messages were more likely to be passed along to other users.

Other firms, including language learning company Rosetta Stone, use social media's research and targeting capabilities to find new markets for their products. Social media marketing research suggested that some consumers want to learn a new language for the mental challenge rather than for reasons such as their job or an upcoming trip. Based on this marketing research, Rosetta Stone targeted social media ads to people interested in mental fitness. The marketing campaign based on social media research was well received, performing better than previous campaigns.

The Social Media in Action *Connect* exercise in Chapter 4 will let you decide how to utilize social media to improve marketing research and then how to develop strategies from those findings. By understanding the role social media can play in helping your organization gain insights from consumers, you will be able to apply these strategies to successfully target current and potential customers.

Source: See Geoffrey A. Fowler, "Are You Talking to Me?" *The Wall Street Journal*, June 18, 2012, http://online.wsj.com/article/SB10001424052748704116404576263083970961862.html.

competitive intelligence
Involves systematically gathering data about what strategies direct and indirect competitors are pursuing in terms of new product development and the marketing mix.

LO 4-4
Explain why competitive intelligence is an important form of marketing research.

Social media sites like Glassdoor, Monster, and Indeed, which give employees an opportunity to rate and review the companies they work for, allow firms to collect information about their competitors in new ways.

COMPETITIVE INTELLIGENCE

Until now, we have focused on research related to the firm itself. But another important component of marketing research involves gathering data about what competitors are doing in the marketplace. Competitive intelligence involves systematically gathering data about what strategies direct and indirect competitors are pursuing in terms of new product development and the marketing mix. Such information can provide a firm with foreknowledge of a competitor's upcoming promotions or products, allowing it to respond in a way that blunts the effects of the competitor's actions. For example, beverage company Fuze would find it helpful to know that a rival company was planning a price reduction in the near future. The knowledge could be used to counter the price decrease with a promotional campaign that meets or beats the new prices offered by the competition, thereby heading off any increase in the competitor's market share.

A company can obtain information about another company's activities and plans in a number of ways, including conferences, trade shows, social media sites, competitors' suppliers, distributors, retailers, and the competitor's customers. Competitor websites and the websites of government agencies such as the Securities and Exchange Commission (SEC) and the U.S. Patent and Trademark Office may contain financial and new

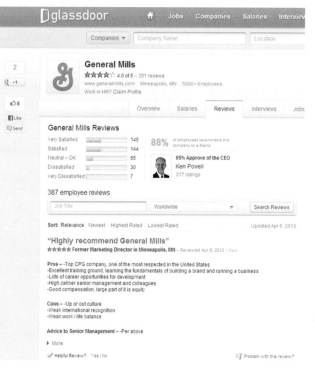

EXECUTIVE PERSPECTIVE

Dr. Judy Reed Smith
Chief Executive Officer
ATLANTIC-ACM

What new strategies for gathering competitive intelligence are emerging?

Technology has made gathering competitive intelligence much easier than it once was. Social media are powerful tools for gathering information about what competitors are doing. The Internet allows you to see pricing in different parts of the country as well as read both positive and negative customer reviews. Today, researchers for even very small businesses can find out a great deal about their competitors and why customers like or dislike them. These research insights can be very helpful in designing products, promotions, and pricing to win these customers over and increase market share.

product information about competitors. Firms also can obtain information for a fee from a number of companies that collect data and make it accessible, such as ATLANTIC-ACM, which is highlighted in this chapter's Executive Perspective feature.

There are also unethical ways of obtaining competitive intelligence. Bribing competitor employees for information and hiring people to tap phone lines or place surveillance cameras on the premises of rival companies are both examples of unethical and illegal ways of getting competitive information. Firms should scrupulously avoid these activities for legal reasons as well as for the damage they can do to a company's image and reputation. We will talk more about the ethical implications of marketing research later in the chapter. First, we discuss another vital component of marketing research: sales forecasting.

SALES FORECASTING

As noted earlier in the chapter, sales forecasting plays an important role in managing the place aspect of the four Ps. The logistics department uses sales forecasts to ensure the firm has enough transportation, warehousing, and distribution capacity to store and move materials and finished products. However, sales forecasting goes beyond logistics. Marketing needs sales forecasts to establish the marketing mix, including pricing and promotional activities, for new and existing products. Finance needs sales forecasts to project cost and profits and to determine how much money will be needed to support the firm's operations. Production planning and purchasing need forecasts to plan how much of and when a product should be made and to procure the necessary materials to support production.[12]

Sales forecasting is based on research that estimates how much of a product will sell over a given period of time. It is similar to other forms of marketing research in that collecting the right data and analyzing it appropriately are instrumental to using it effectively. A firm can use a number of different techniques to develop a sales forecast. We can classify these into three general categories: time series, regression, and judgmental.[13]

Time Series Techniques

Sales forecasting techniques can be either quantitative or qualitative. Time series techniques, which are quantitative in nature, seek to establish the level, trend, and seasonality of a product's sales. Level is what sales would be without the influence of a trend or seasonality. An established brand that is not influenced by seasonality will likely have level sales. Trend is a pattern characterized by increasing or decreasing sales. New products typically trend upward while older products often trend downward. Figure 4.4 illustrates the current trend in refrigerator sales. As you can see, sales are trending upward. Seasonality is a regularly repeating pattern of sales centered on a particular period of the year. The sales of lawn sprinkler systems would indicate distinct seasonality since people in colder climates do not water their lawns in the winter. Figure 4.5 indicates the seasonality of bicycle sales. Quarters 2 and 4 show strong sales compared to the other two quarters due

---

LO 4-5

Explain the importance of sales forecasting and compare the three basic types of forecasting techniques.

time series techniques

A forecasting method that seeks to establish the level, trend, and seasonality of a product's sales.

level

What sales would be without the influence of a trend or seasonality.

trend

A pattern characterized by increasing or decreasing sales.

seasonality

A regularly repeating pattern of sales centered on a particular period of the year.

to summer and Christmas sales. Time series techniques also seek to determine the amount of random fluctuation in sales data caused by factors like special promotional activities.

Regression Techniques

Like time series techniques, regression is quantitative in nature. Regression attempts to draw relationships between the sales of a product and some other variable or variables that may be affecting those sales. It helps firms isolate variables that influence or are influenced by sales. These variables could be within the firm's control, such as price changes or advertising campaigns, or outside its control, such as economic conditions and the actions of competitors. Using regression, firms can analyze these factors to predict future sales.

Judgmental Techniques

In contrast to the other two forecasting methods, judgmental techniques are qualitative. Judgmental forecasting involves asking experienced company personnel such as salespersons, marketers, and senior managers to give their best estimate of future sales. This is particularly effective if little or no historical sales data exist, such as with new-to-the-market or new-to-the-company products. While judgmental forecasting can be valuable in certain situations, it can be influenced by personal bias or cultural bias, such as a company-wide emphasis on projecting high sales. Marketers must carefully screen this type of qualitative forecasting for such influence.[14,15]

Sales forecasting is a crucial form of marketing research. Unfortunately, sales forecasts often can be wildly inaccurate due to the many unknown variables involved. And when the sales forecast is inaccurate, much can go wrong, including lost sales and customers, excess and obsolete inventory, wasted money, and general frustration within all areas of the company. To counter this, firms should invest in forecasting systems, develop a culture that strives toward forecasting excellence, drive elements of personal and cultural bias out of the data, and establish a forecasting process that is followed by all individuals.

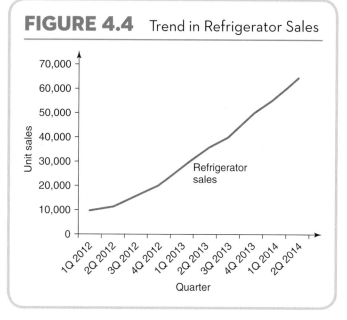

FIGURE 4.4   Trend in Refrigerator Sales

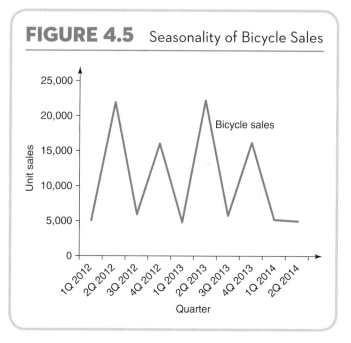

FIGURE 4.5   Seasonality of Bicycle Sales

regression

A forecasting method that attempts to draw relationships between the sales of a product and some other variable or variables that may be affecting those sales.

judgmental forecasting

A method that involves asking experienced company personnel such as salespersons, marketers, and senior managers to give their best estimate of future sales.

---

connect | MARKETING   **Interactive Assignment 4-4**

Please complete the *Connect* exercise for Chapter 4 that focuses on analyzing research data to determine trends and seasonality. By understanding market trends and seasonality, you will be able to effectively manage inventory, set prices, and advertise your products.

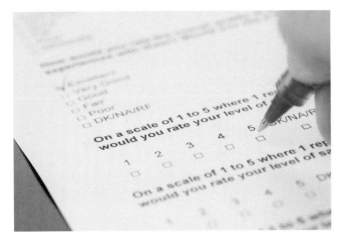

Standardized marketing research firms like Nielsen consistently study consumer trends, including global consumer confidence, the effectiveness of advertising through social media, and mobile device usage, across the country and around the world.

customized research firms
Research providers that offer services designed specifically for their customers.

standardized research firms
Research providers that use common research designs that may apply to the research needs of many firms.

THE MARKETING RESEARCH INDUSTRY

Most companies do not have the resources to fund a marketing research department. Even companies that do have a research department may need help conducting complex research projects. Marketing research providers like ATLANTIC-ACM can benefit companies in many ways. To start, they are likely to be unbiased in their research procedures and recommendations, unlike in-house research departments, which can be influenced by company politics.[16] Also, unlike the companies they work for, marketing research is the core competency of these providers. Firms can hire them to conduct the full range of research activities, including plan development, data collection, data analysis, and report preparation and presentation. Though marketing research providers charge a fee for their services, there are considerable overhead costs associated with operating an internal research department that only companies large enough to require many marketing research projects can justify financially.

Customized Research Firms

Marketing research providers can be customized or standardized.[17] Customized research firms offer services designed specifically for their customers. They sometimes specialize in one area of research, such as focus groups, but some conduct research in many areas. SNG Corporation, for example, provides research in corporate image studies that measure how people feel about a company as a whole, new product development research, and customer satisfaction surveys. It uses both qualitative methods in the form of focus groups and interviews and quantitative methods in the form of mail- and web-based surveys.

Standardized Research Firms

Though customized research providers can provide the exact data a company requires, they can also be prohibitively expensive, particularly for small firms. Standardized research firms, in contrast to customized providers, use common research designs that may apply to the research needs of many firms, which can reduce the cost of the research. Nielsen, well known for tracking television show consumption patterns, is an example of this type of research firm. It covers markets in more than 100 countries and services many different types of companies in a variety of businesses, including television, radio, retail, and sports. Marketing research providers can be especially helpful to firms that need to know more about markets in foreign countries. Companies that hire research firms with expertise in specific countries or regions are likely to get information that is in tune with the cultural and economic conditions unique to foreign markets.

LO 4-6

Explain the importance of research to firms marketing products globally.

GLOBAL MARKETING RESEARCH

Global marketing research presents a number of different challenges compared to domestic research. While domestic marketing research deals with similar markets, international markets present a much more diverse set of marketing factors. Political, legal, sociocultural, and technological factors influence whether a company can successfully market products in a particular country. Multiply those factors by the almost 200 countries in the world and you can begin to understand the complexity and potential for error involved in global marketing research. Ignorance of customer needs and wants in other regions often prevents firms from marketing products globally. As Frans van Houten, chief executive officer of the Dutch health and well-being company Royal Philips Electronics, says: "In a very diverse world with customers in China, Brazil, and in the U.S., we cannot generalize that they [customers] have the same needs. Innovation is only really meaningful when it is relevant to the local market."[18]

Consider China, the most populous country on the planet. The rise of China as an economic powerhouse makes companies want to sell their products there. But Chinese consumer culture is unique to that country. Chinese consumers are very conscientious about saving money, extremely price sensitive, and do not like to pay by credit card.[19] However, the Chinese still want luxury products. They are willing to pay more for products consumed in public than those consumed in private. Consequently, they seek luxury items more as status symbols than for their intrinsic value. While they want to remain understated in their choices, Chinese consumers also want to stand out. Western companies that have not conducted research into the consumer culture in China would have a difficult time marketing products there because the culture differs considerably from that of the United States or Europe.

Global marketing research can be conducted by the firm itself, but not all firms are familiar with international data sources and may not be equipped to use them even if they are aware of them. The absence of good secondary data in foreign countries increases the difficulties facing global marketing researchers.[20] A good way for a company to learn about consumer behavior in other regions is to use local marketing research companies, where available. These firms recognize

In response to marketing research indicating that Chinese customers value space in which to meet with friends and colleagues, Starbucks plans to build large stores with multiple couches in China instead of the kiosk-sized stores popular in the United States.

Ashlyn Kohler
Marketing Director
Gearhead Outfitters

Ashlyn Kohler
Marketing Director
Gearhead Outfitters
www.gearheadoutfitters.com/

Gearhead Outfitters is a family-owned and -operated business that specializes in outdoor lifestyle clothing and footwear.

Describe your job. I manage and coordinate all marketing, advertising, and promotional activities for the company. I put a special emphasis on conducting marketing research to determine market requirements for existing and future products.

Describe how you got the job that you have. I heard about the position at Gearhead from a friend. I had recently graduated from college and was looking for a new opportunity. My friend recommended me to the owner of the company, and I met with the general manager about a week later. This was evidence to me of how important it is to network while in school and to build professional relationships.

What has been the most important thing in making you successful at your job? Being successful means having drive and ambition. Our employees take strength finding tests so that our team knows what everyone's contribution can be. My strengths included futuristic thinking and positivity. I think both of these strengths have played such an important role in my success at Gearhead. I strongly believe in having goals and always striving to reach them. Gearhead is a growing company and my futuristic strength helps in envisioning where Gearhead can go and helping us get there. Positivity has also contributed to my success because it's important to be a team player and to go above what you're

expected to do. When you love your job, it's easy to be positive and really contribute to your team's success.

What advice would you give soon-to-be graduates? Build professional relationships and take advantage of every opportunity. Networking is one of the best things a college student can do to prepare for conquering the job market. The competition for jobs is intense. By networking and building professional relationships, you can learn firsthand what employers are looking for. Envision your dream job, think of people who hold those positions and do some research, find out how they got to where they are and create your own plan. College students have so many opportunities for internships and volunteer work. Build your resume while in school and take advantage of learning as much as you can. What you learn in class is very different than what you will learn in the workplace. Both experiences will help prepare you for a successful career.

What do you consider your personal brand to be? A young professional who believes in ambition and dedication. A dreamer who wants to be part of something bigger than myself. A leader who thrives on personal relationships and encouraging others. A representative of a wonderful company who hopes to exceed the expectations of our stakeholders and help those in our communities live better, richer, and healthier lives.

potential problems with collecting primary data, such as higher costs, potential language barriers, and the lack of a technical infrastructure (e.g., working phone numbers or valid e-mail addresses) to reach respondents. Such companies are familiar with the local population and language. This knowledge can help eliminate many of the mistakes a company might make as it seeks to enter foreign markets. Local marketing research companies can also assist in collecting secondary data from sources that may be unfamiliar to a foreign company.

Whether a company conducts its own research or hires an international research firm to do it, the tasks remain the same:

1. Analyze the global market to understand things like the fastest growing markets overall, the largest markets for the firm's products, trends in the various global markets that relate to the firm's products, and any restrictions on the importing of the firm's products such as quotas or tariffs.[21] This type of information may be obtained through secondary sources, such as trade reports and websites, specific to the country being researched.
2. Acquire specific information about the products the firm wants to sell globally, including the names of the competitors, what market share they hold, what promotional activities they engage in, and at what prices they sell their products. Additionally, potential market share and sales of products at particular price points should be estimated to ensure that the venture will be a profitable one.

Once the firm obtains the above information, it can develop a marketing mix designed to penetrate the target country's market.

Companies can ill afford to pass up marketing their product globally. However, without accurate research information, they very well might underperform or fail outright in their attempt. This is why global marketing research is so important to companies that want to enter international markets.

MARKETING RESEARCH ETHICS

LO 4-7

Discuss the main ethical issues in conducting marketing research.

Whether conducting research for a domestic or international market, firms must always consider the ethical implications of gathering data on customers and competitors. Such considerations have become even more essential in a world of rapidly changing technology.

Privacy in a Digital Age

The increasingly powerful computer capabilities available to companies allow for the collection, storage, and analysis of data from millions of consumers. Online platforms like Twitter that are used by millions of consumers present firms with almost unlimited access to personal data. But companies must be careful not to go too far in collecting information of a sensitive nature. There is enough concern in the marketing industry about consumer privacy that many companies now have chief privacy officers who serve as watchdogs, guarding against unethical practices in their company's collection of consumer data.

At issue is the willful intrusion on the privacy of individuals. Consider mobile ad network companies that use unique identifiers embedded in smartphones to collect information about consumer preferences as they move from one app to another. To do this, such companies have worked around efforts by Apple to protect the privacy of iPhone and iPad users. The companies say they need personal data from users or they will lose millions of dollars of revenue from the firms that hire them, such as Mazda and Nike. While Mazda and Nike don't participate in the actual tracking of data, they could potentially use what's collected to target

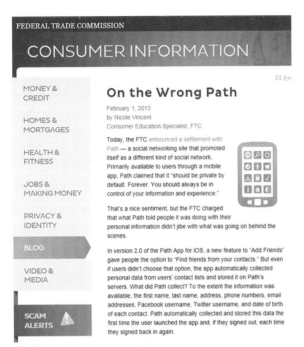

CONSUMER INFORMATION

MONEY & CREDIT

HOMES & MORTGAGES

HEALTH & FITNESS

JOBS & MAKING MONEY

PRIVACY & IDENTITY

BLOG

VIDEO & MEDIA

SCAM ALERTS

✉ Em

On the Wrong Path

February 1, 2013
by Nicole Vincent
Consumer Education Specialist, FTC

Today, the FTC announced a settlement with Path — a social networking site that promoted itself as a different kind of social network. Primarily available to users through a mobile app, Path claimed that it "should be private by default. Forever. You should always be in control of your information and experience."

That's a nice sentiment, but the FTC charged that what Path told people it was doing with their personal information didn't jibe with what was going on behind the scenes.

In version 2.0 of the Path App for iOS, a new feature to "Add Friends" gave people the option to "Find friends from your contacts." But even if users didn't choose that option, the app automatically collected personal data from users' contact lists and stored it on Path's servers. What did Path collect? To the extent the information was available, the first name, last name, address, phone numbers, email addresses, Facebook username, Twitter username, and date of birth of each contact. Path automatically collected and stored this data the first time the user launched the app and, if they signed out, each time they signed back in again.

Path, the developer of a smartphone app that allows users to chat and share videos, photos, locations, and music with family and friends, settled Federal Trade Commission charges that it violated privacy protections by collecting personal information from users of the app without their permission.[23]

customers based on geographic or demographic profiles. Meanwhile the Federal Trade Commission (FTC) is evaluating mobile tracking technology as part of its ongoing mission to protect consumer privacy.[22] It is trying to determine how far a company can go in tracking personal information before it invades customer privacy and becomes unethical.

Using Data Appropriately

Another ethical issue in marketing research is the misuse of research methods and findings. Marketing research firms may be compelled by their clients to return findings favorable to the client or to arrive at a conclusion predetermined by the client. Or marketing research firms may have employees who report false data, do not follow the directions for conducting the research, or claim credit for surveys that never were conducted.[24] Organizations like the American Marketing Association, the Marketing Research Association, the International Chamber of Commerce (ICC), and ESOMAR, concerned with the reliability of research results, have established ethical standards for conducting research. Table 4.3 lists the key components of the ICC/ESOMAR standards. Such standards are important to the industry because they help gain the trust of consumers. Without that trust, individuals will be less likely to participate in marketing research. Clearly, it is in the best interest of companies to conduct marketing research in the most ethical manner possible. If they don't, consumers may refuse to participate in research studies, provide personal information either online or face-to-face, visit company websites, or order products online. Additionally, ethical behavior on the part of companies will make it unnecessary for the government to increase regulation of marketing research practices.

TABLE 4.3   Key Fundamentals of the ICC/ESOMAR International Code on Market and Social Research

1. Market researchers shall conform to all relevant national and international laws.
2. Market researchers shall behave ethically and shall not do anything which might damage the reputation of market research.
3. Market researchers shall take special care when carrying out research among children and young people.
4. Users' cooperation is voluntary and must be based on adequate, and not misleading, information about the general purpose and nature of the project when their agreement to participate is being obtained and all such statements shall be honored.
5. The rights of users as private individuals shall be respected by market researchers and they shall not be harmed or adversely affected as the direct result of cooperating in a market research project.
6. Market researchers shall never allow personal data they collect in a market research project to be used for any purpose other than market research.
7. Market researchers shall ensure that projects and activities are designed, carried out, reported and documented accurately, transparently and objectively.
8. Market researchers shall conform to the accepted principles of fair competition.

Source: ICC and ESOMAR. This Code was drafted in English and the English text is the definitive version. As the Code and ESOMAR guidelines are updated on a regular basis, please refer to www.esomar.org for the latest English text.

TRENDS IN MARKETING RESEARCH

Marketing research is clearly important to both companies and individuals. When conducted properly, companies can identify the kinds of goods and services people need and want. This knowledge allows companies to develop and market products effectively and profitably. It also benefits consumers because the types of goods and services they want are available in the marketplace. Marketing research is evolving and some trends are emerging in this field.[25] One is an increased reliance on secondary data because of its availability, particularly on the Internet, and the cost effective ways it can be obtained. Another trend is toward the use of technology such as marketing information systems to gather, organize, and analyze information from both in-house and Internet sources. A third trend is toward the use of international marketing research to better understand market opportunities outside a company's home country. As technology and computing power continue to grow, there will be many changes in the future that will give companies even more capability for understanding the marketplace and fulfilling their customers' requirements.

SUMMARY

LO 4-1 Explain the importance of marketing research to firms and individuals.

Marketing research involves defining a marketing problem, designing ways to collect information concerning that problem, implementing a data collection plan, interpreting the data collected, and reporting results of that interpretation to help companies understand and satisfy the needs and wants of customers. This task has become more important, and more complicated, as markets continue to become globalized, product life cycles continue to become shorter, and markets continue to change rapidly. In addition to its impact on businesses, marketing is important to consumers as well. Consumers rely on companies to develop and market goods and services that they need and want.

LO 4-2 Organize the five steps of the marketing research process.

The marketing research process is a well-defined set of five steps that, if followed, should yield invaluable information concerning a firm's market and its competition. The five steps include: (1) problem definition, (2) plan development, (3) data collection, (4) data analysis, and (5) taking action. During problem definition, the firm clarifies the exact nature of the problem. Plan development involves identifying what data sources will be utilized, what specific research approach will be used, and what sampling methods will be employed. The third step, data collection, begins with the firm's decision to use secondary or primary data. Secondary data may already reside in the company's management information system or may be obtained from outside

sources like the Internet. Primary data can be collected by various quantitative and qualitative techniques, including focus groups, interviews, observation, surveys, experiments, and mathematical modeling. Data analysis is the process of converting collected data into information that will be useful to marketers. The culmination of the research is a formal, written report to decision makers that includes an executive summary, research objectives, methods used, findings, and recommendations about how the firm should take action.

LO 4-3 Describe the various types of marketing information systems and where they get information from.

Effective marketing requires knowledge about current trends in the marketplace and information about what individual consumers are buying or are interested in buying. In-house systems, such as decision support systems (DSS) and online systems that support social media sites, allow companies to collect and analyze huge amounts of data. From there, recommendations for marketing actions can be made. Marketing information systems (MIS) can help companies continuously capture information and store it so that researchers and decision makers can access it easily. The Internet enables researchers to conduct a variety of research, such as surveys, focus groups, and social media website monitoring.

LO 4-4 Explain why competitive intelligence is an important form of marketing research.

Competitive intelligence involves systematically gathering information about what direct and indirect competitors are doing in terms of new product development and their marketing mix. Such information can give a firm foreknowledge of a competitor's upcoming promotions or products, so that it can respond in a way that blunts the effects of the competitor's actions.

 LO 4-5 Explain the importance of sales forecasting and compare the three basic types of forecasting techniques.

Sales forecasting is a type of research that estimates how much of a product will sell over a period of time. Sales forecasts are important to a number of departments in a business, including marketing, finance, production, and logistics. A firm may use a number of different techniques to come up with a sales forecast. These can be placed into three general categories: time series, regression, and judgmental. Time series techniques seek to establish the level, trend, and seasonality of a product's sales. Regression attempts to draw relationships between the sales of a good or service and some other variable or variables that may be affecting those sales. Judgmental forecasting is a qualitative technique that relies on the experience of company personnel such as salespersons, marketers, and senior managers and their best estimate of sales.

 LO 4-6 Explain the importance of research to firms marketing products globally.

Global marketing research presents a number of different challenges compared to domestic research. One is the unfamiliar nature of foreign markets. A good way for a company to learn about consumer behavior in other regions is to use local marketing research companies, where available. Political, legal, sociocultural, and technological factors influence whether a company's products can be successfully marketed in a particular country.

 LO 4-7 Discuss the main ethical issues in conducting marketing research.

The increasingly powerful computer capabilities available to companies allow for the collection, storage, and analysis of data from millions of consumers. But companies must be careful not to go too far in collecting information of a sensitive nature. Another ethical issue in marketing research is the misuse of research methods and findings. Marketing research firms may be compelled by their clients to return findings favorable to the client or to arrive at a conclusion predetermined by the client. Marketing organizations like the American Marketing Association, the Marketing Research Association, and ESOMAR are concerned with the reliability of research results and have set up ethical standards for conducting research.

KEY TERMS

advertising effectiveness studies (p. 100)
causal research (p. 103)
competitive intelligence (p. 113)
customized research firms (p. 116)
data mining (p. 111)
decision support system (DSS) (p. 111)
demand analysis (p. 99)
descriptive research (p. 103)
experiments (p. 106)
exploratory research (p. 102)
field experiments (p. 106)
focus groups (p. 105)
hypothesis (p. 101)

interview (p. 105)
judgmental forecasting (p. 115)
level (p. 114)
marketing information system (MIS) (p. 110)
marketing research (p. 98)
mathematical modeling (p. 107)
neuromarketing (p. 107)
nonprobability sampling (p. 103)
observation (p. 106)
primary data (p. 101)
probability sampling (p. 103)
quota sampling (p. 103)
regression (p. 115)

sales forecasting (p. 100)
sales tracking (p. 100)
sample (p. 103)
sampling (p. 103)
seasonality (p. 114)
secondary data (p. 102)
simple random sampling (p. 103)
snowball sampling (p. 103)
standardized research firms (p. 116)
surveys (p. 106)
time series techniques (p. 114)
trend (p. 114)
validity (p. 108)

MARKETING PLAN EXERCISE

In this chapter we focused on the importance of marketing research. The next step in developing your personal marketing plan is to conduct some research of your own to better understand the competition you will face for your dream job or graduate school program. Your assignment is to research online the job or graduate school program you discussed as your objective in Chapter 1. Try to figure out how competitive the applicant pool is. Check with someone at the firm's human resource department or contact the graduate school's admissions office to find out the average number of applicants for each open slot. Often, you can find summary statistics on the average work experience or GPA that is common among newcomers, which will give you an idea of where you stand relative to your competition.

For those of you targeting graduate school, you should conduct extensive research on the GPA and entrance exam (GMAT, LSAT, GRE, etc.) requirements for the programs you are targeting. The Internet and publications such as *U.S. News and World Report* provide a wealth of data on all types of graduate school programs. You should see how your GPA and entrance exam scores compare to the averages at your targeted schools. In the same way that firms want to know what their competition is

doing to better understand their potential for success, so should you.

Your Task: Prepare a one- to two-paragraph research report that summarizes your findings and describes the actions you will take based on your research. Your report should include the following information:

1. If focusing on a specific job, list the average number of applicants, the starting pay, and where these types of job openings are most commonly found.
2. If your focus is on graduate school, list what the average GPA and entrance exam score is for the program as well as the acceptance rate for that program.
3. Make an honest assessment of the likelihood that you will get your desired job or be accepted to the graduate program. Based on this assessment, what is the one area that you need to improve upon to increase your chances of achieving your goal?

DISCUSSION QUESTIONS

1. What are the ways that marketing research enables companies to meet their objectives? Explain the reasoning behind your answer.
2. Your company is considering re-launching its most profitable line of products: shampoo and conditioner. The manager wants to ensure that the new package will be one that consumers are drawn to. What research method do you think would be best for determining how to design the new package? Explain why you selected that method.
3. Go to your Facebook page or that of a friend. What information is available on the page that might be useful to marketing researchers? Do you feel that using that information for marketing research purposes would be an invasion of privacy? Explain your answer.

4. You are the head of marketing research at a major retailer. You have been asked to conduct research about your competitors' products, including prices and features. What are some of the ways you could access that type of information?
5. What are the main benefits of an accurate sales forecast to an organization? What are some of the adverse effects of a poor sales forecast on an organization?
6. List at least six types of information a company would need to know about an international market before the company can successfully sell its products in that market. How might an organization get that type of information? From where would it be obtained?

SOCIAL MEDIA APPLICATION

S Social Media Pick an organization that you are familiar with and then go out and visit that organization's social media presence. Analyze the organization's efforts to market itself through social media using the following questions and activities as a guide. Be sure to support each of your answers with specific quotes, pictures, or comments from social media users.

1. Based on what you read on the organization's various social media platforms, what information about the company can you find?

2. Who are the most frequent types of customers for the organization?
3. Which of the organization's products are well received and which ones have a more negative perception?
4. Should you visit a competitor's social media sites and, if so, what should you be looking for?

ETHICAL CHALLENGE

Social media are increasingly used as a source of data for marketing research. Marketing researchers can find comments about goods and services as well as personal information. Imagine that you are the vice president of marketing for a large consumer electronics company, and the head of your marketing research department has just given a presentation on how to mine data on the Internet by electronically searching social network sites for key words and phrases. The manager of the video games division was at the presentation and is very keen to gather data on pre-teen boys between 10 and 12 years old concerning their use of violent video games. She wants to have the research department gather data on as many pre-teen boys as possible to determine who they are, where they live, who else is in their family, who their friends are, and what types of games they are interested in playing. She is asking for your permission and funding to undertake this type of research. Please use the ethical decision-making framework to answer the following questions:

1. First, research the ICC/ESOMAR Standards for Marketing Research by going on its website (www. esomar.com), downloading its "Notes on How to Apply ICC/ESOMAR Code," and reading the code. Next, using the notes, identify at least three potential ethical problems with the manager's proposal. Explain why you think they may be an issue.
2. What might your company do to work around any ethical issues you identified?
3. Would you approve this proposal or not? Explain your answer.

VIDEO CASE

Please go to *Connect* to access the video case featuring Experian that accompanies this chapter.

CAREER TIPS

Marketing Your Future

You have read in this chapter about the importance of marketing research. Marketing research is one of the fastest growing areas in marketing and can be an exciting, fulfilling, and financially rewarding direction to go with your career. As you consider your future, Judy Reed Smith, who was featured in the Executive Perspective at the beginning of the chapter, has highlighted some things that can help you get a marketing research job and then build a career in this industry.

1. While you are in college, challenge yourself with statistics classes, database information, and possibly some computer programming. Continued technological change will give firms access to more and more data in coming years that will need deeper analysis and broader data organization capabilities.

2. Read to keep up with trends in your industry. The world is changing faster, so learn to skim for ideas. Find the most valuable things to read to enhance your knowledge and maximize your value.

3. Before your job interview, learn all you can about the company and its competitors. Go online for a few hours of skimming for knowledge they have so you can explain how you can contribute to the organization's mission and demonstrate your interest in their world. You will not get a marketing research job if it is not clear that you have done significant marketing research on the company you are interviewing with.

4. My most valuable employees keep everyone up to date with new happenings in the industries in which we work. Talk to people, stay engaged, pay attention to what is happening in the industry around you. The one who knows what merger is happening by 8 a.m. and tells us all is greatly appreciated.

5. To keep up your knowledge, subscribe to the best daily print and digital information sources from your industry and skim them in the morning or in the evening after work. Make a point of gaining additional knowledge on your own.

CHAPTER NOTES

1. Will Connors, "RIM's Sales Drop 31% ahead of New Phone," *The Wall Street Journal*, September 28, 2012, http://online.wsj.com/article/SB10000872396390443507204578022713078333152.html.
2. Matthew Boyle, "In Emerging Markets, Unilever Finds Passport to Profits," *Bloomberg Businessweek*, January 3, 2013, http://www.businessweek.com/articles/2013-01-03/in-emerging-markets-unilever-finds-a-passport-to-profit.
3. Joseph R. Hair, Jr., Robert P. Bush, and David J. Ortinau, *Marketing Research in a Digital Information Environment*, 4th ed. (New York: McGraw-Hill/Irwin, 2009).
4. Ibid.
5. Joseph R. Hair, Jr., Mary F. Wolfinbarger, David J. Ortinau, and Robert P. Bush, *Essentials of Marketing Research*, 2nd ed. (New York: McGraw-Hill/Irwin, 2010).
6. Emily Glazer, "The Eyes Have it: Marketers Now Track Shoppers' Retinas," *The Wall Street Journal*, July 12, 2012, http://online.wsj.com/article/SB10001424052702303644004577520760230459438.html.
7. Hair, Jr., Wolfinbarger, Ortinau, and Bush, *Essentials of Marketing Research*.
8. Gordon S. Linoff and Michael J. Barry, *Data Mining Techniques: For Marketing, Sales, and Customer Relationships*, 3rd ed. (Indianapolis, IN: Wiley, 2011).
9. Hair, Jr., Bush, and Ortinau, *Marketing Research in a Digital Information Environment*.
10. Emily Steel, "The New Focus Groups: Online Networks," *The Wall Street Journal*, January 14, 2008, http://online.wsj.com/article/SB120027230906987357.html.
11. Ibid.
12. John T. Mentzer and Carol C. Bienstock, *Sales Forecasting Management* (Thousand Oaks, CA: Sage Publications, 1998).
13. John T. Mentzer and Mark A. Moon, *Sales Forecasting Management*, 2nd ed. (Thousand Oaks, CA: Sage Publications, 2005).
14. John E. Mello, "The Impact of Sales Forecast Game Playing on Supply Chains," *Foresight: The International Journal of Applied Forecasting* 13, no. 1 (2009).
15. John E. Mello, "The Impacts of Corporate Culture on Sales Forecasting," *Foresight: The International Journal of Applied Forecasting* 2, no. 2 (2005).
16. Hair, Jr., Bush, and Ortinau, *Marketing Research in a Digital Information Environment*.
17. Hair, Jr., Wolfinbarger, Ortinau, and Bush, *Essentials of Marketing Research*.
18. Kate Linebaugh, "For Philips, Matching the Product to the Market," *The Wall Street Journal*, May 30, 2012, http://online.wsj.com/article/SB10001424052702303395604577434171435274122.html.
19. Tom Doctoroff, "What the Chinese Want," *The Wall Street Journal*, May 18, 2012, http://online.wsj.com/article/SB10001424052702303360504577408493723814210.html.
20. Hair, Jr., Wolfinbarger, Ortinau, and Bush, *Essentials of Marketing Research*.
21. Ibid.
22. Richard Lardner, "Government Investigating Makers of Cell Phone Apps," *Bloomberg Businessweek*, December 10, 2012, http://www.businessweek.com/ap/2012-12-10/government-investigating-makers-of-cellphone-apps.
23. Jessica Guynn, "Mobile Social Networking App Path Settles with FTC for $800,000," *Los Angeles Times*, February 1, 2013, http://articles.latimes.com/2013/feb/01/business/la-fi-tn-ftc-path-settlement-20130201.
24. Hair, Jr., Wolfinbarger, Ortinau, and Bush, *Essentials of Marketing Research*.
25. Ibid.

Chapter 5

KNOWING YOUR CUSTOMER: CONSUMER AND BUSINESS

LEARNING OBJECTIVES

After reading this chapter, you should be able to

LO 5-1 Explain the consumer decision-making process.

LO 5-2 Describe how situational influences impact consumer behavior.

LO 5-3 Describe the psychological processes that influence consumer behavior.

LO 5-4 Summarize the relationship between involvement and consumer decisions.

LO 5-5 Compare business-to-business marketing to business-to-consumer marketing.

LO 5-6 Compare the different buying situations in business-to-business marketing.

EXECUTIVE PERSPECTIVE

Tracey Rogers
Vice President and General Manager
KAIT-TV

Knowing her customer has always been part of Tracey Rogers's business. After graduating with a degree in journalism, Rogers spent her early career working in television newsrooms across the United States. As she progressed from an assignment editor to a news director, understanding what mattered to her viewers was an essential component in developing a news program to meet their needs. In her current role at KAIT, Rogers's focus has expanded to include relationship development with other organizations. As vice president and general manager, she engages in critical marketing functions such as selling advertisements on the station and helping organizations in the viewing area reach their potential consumers. To be successful, Rogers must understand not only the viewers who ultimately see the ads but also the organizations she's selling the ad time to.

What has been the most important thing in making you successful at your job?

I have been a student of what makes people tick. I have a diverse team, and I need to make sure that I am managing in a way that provides the maximum motivation for each of them. In order to have a successful team, I must surround myself with people who are positive minded, can deliver what they promise, and want to win.

What advice would you give soon-to-be graduates?

Master and exceed customer service expectations no matter whom you are serving, your client or your coworker. If you want customers to come back, you have to provide excellent customer service every time. Customers will be loyal and even willing to pay more if they feel they are getting world-class service. If you can't master and exceed your customer's or your employer's expectations, they will find someone else who will.

How is marketing relevant to your role at KAIT?

Marketing is one of the most important parts of my job. At a television station, we have to be good marketers to be successful, but we also have to help our customers be good marketers. We may have a client who just opened a new salon in town and needs our television and digital platforms to let potential customers know the salon exists. We want to develop marketing solutions that provide that salon with the most benefit for the price so that they can do well. If our customers' marketing efforts succeed, that usually means that we are succeeding as well.

What do you consider your personal brand to be?

I am passionate and conscientious about everything I do down to the tiniest detail and serve my customers with care. I believe that I am better at what I do because of the passion I have for my job, my company, and my team.

Tracey Rogers
Vice President and General Manager

KAIT-TV
http://www.kait8.com/

KAIT-TV is a Raycom-owned ABC television affiliate located in the southern United States.

This chapter explores the importance of knowing your customers, both individual consumers and other businesses, and how they make decisions. If you understand why the people and firms buying your product behave the way they do, you will be able to develop effective marketing strategies that appeal specifically to them. This chapter outlines the consumer decision-making process, describes how situational and psychological factors influence consumers, and discusses the differences between marketing to individual consumers and marketing to other firms. As you read through the chapter, consider the following key questions:

1. How do I make decisions about what to purchase?
2. What things in my life influence my purchase decisions?
3. How does my attitude and personality impact what I buy?
4. Does the price of a product change my decision-making process?

5. How should I market my product differently if my customer is another business rather than an individual consumer?
6. What type of buying situation might I find myself in when marketing to another business?

LO 5-1

Explain the consumer decision-making process.

consumer behavior

The way in which individuals and organizations make decisions to spend their available resources, such as time or money.

THE CONSUMER DECISION-MAKING PROCESS

Each of you reading this book is a consumer. Each of you makes numerous consumer decisions every day, ranging from where you buy lunch, to what cell phone plan you use, to what radio station you listen to. For marketers to understand how to best appeal to you, they must first clearly understand the process you go through when making decisions. Consumer behavior is the way in which individuals and organizations make decisions to spend their available resources, such as time or money. This chapter includes a discussion of consumer behavior as it relates to two major types of marketing: business-to-consumer and business-to-business. We will begin by focusing on the role of consumer behavior in business-to-consumer marketing (B2C), which involves selling goods and services to end-user customers. Examples of B2C businesses include restaurants, car dealerships, and barber shops, each of which market to individual consumers like you who might use their products.

Whether you are deciding where to eat or what cell phone plan to purchase, most consumers targeted by B2C marketers go through a common decision-making process. The process has five stages, which are shown in Figure 5.1 and described in the following sections.

Step 1: Problem Recognition

The buying process begins when consumers recognize they have a need to satisfy. This is called the problem recognition stage. Imagine leaving class to find that high winds had blown one of the oldest trees on campus directly onto your car. You need your car to get to school, work, and social events with your friends and family. Because your current car is destroyed, you would immediately recognize that you need a new type of transportation. In this case, due to a lack of public transportation and the distance you must travel to meet your day-to-day obligations, you need to purchase a new car.

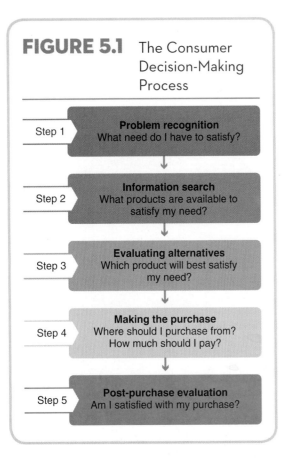

FIGURE 5.1 The Consumer Decision-Making Process

Step 1 — **Problem recognition**
What need do I have to satisfy?

Step 2 — **Information search**
What products are available to satisfy my need?

Step 3 — **Evaluating alternatives**
Which product will best satisfy my need?

Step 4 — **Making the purchase**
Where should I purchase from? How much should I pay?

Step 5 — **Post-purchase evaluation**
Am I satisfied with my purchase?

From a marketing perspective, it's important to keep in mind the following two important issues related to problem recognition:

1. Marketers must understand all aspects of consumers' problems, even those that are less obvious, to create products that improve or enhance consumers' lives. For example, if marketing professionals don't know what problem, beyond the need for transportation, you want to solve by purchasing a new car, they are not likely to develop strategies that will resonate with you. Are you looking for added prestige or do you want to spend less money on monthly payments? Marketers also must recognize that consumers might be buying the same car to solve very different problems.

2. Marketers must remember that if the consumer is not aware of a problem or does not recognize a need, he or she is unlikely to engage in any of the subsequent steps of the buying process. Marketing professionals working in the political world confront this challenge each election cycle. Incumbent politicians of both major political parties running for the United States Congress are re-elected at an average rate of over 90 percent.[1] If voters, the consumers in this example, do not recognize a problem with their current elected official, they most likely will vote to keep that person in office. Before political marketers can promote an alternative candidate, they must make sure that a sufficient number of voters consider the incumbent a problem and are open to potential alternatives.

Step 2: Information Search

Once consumers recognize a problem, they seek information that will help them make the best possible decision about whether or not to purchase a product to address the problem. Consumers will expend effort searching for information based on how important they consider the purchase. Larger purchases, like buying a house or a new car, often require a great deal of information gathering. Smaller purchases, such as a gift for a new boyfriend or new car speakers, may also involve extensive information searches because of their importance to the consumer. Information searches fall into two main categories: external and internal.

External Information Search When consumers seek information beyond their personal knowledge and experience to support them in their buying decision, they are engaging in an external information search. Marketers can help consumers fill in their knowledge gaps through advertisements and product websites. The Internet has become an increasingly powerful tool because it provides consumers with on-demand product information in a format that offers them as much or as little detail as they prefer.

Many firms use social media to empower consumers' external information search. For example, Ford uses Facebook, Twitter, YouTube, Flickr, and Scribd to communicate information and deepen relationships with customers. Ford combined paid advertising and content on Facebook by placing a sponsored video about the Ford Mustang on the Facebook logout page. Over 1 million people viewed the video in just one

business-to-consumer marketing (B2C)
Selling goods and services to end-user customers.

problem recognition
The stage of the buying process in which consumers recognize they have a need to satisfy.

external information search
When consumers seek information beyond their personal knowledge and experience to support them in their buying decision.

Ford has found Facebook to be particularly effective in delivering exactly the external information that potential consumers want with a message that is fine-tuned for specific languages, regions, and countries.

day, allowing Ford to provide external information about the Mustang to a large audience of consumers.[2]

The consumer's friends and family serve as perhaps the most important sources of external information. Think about the example of buying a new car and what those in your life might say about different brands or types of vehicles. You might be impressed by the salespeople and commercials for a certain type of car, but if your parents or friends tell you about a bad experience they had with it, their opinions probably carry more weight. The power of these personal external information sources highlights why marketers must establish good relationships with all customers. It's impossible to predict how one consumer's experience might influence the buying decision and information of another potential customer.

Interactive Assignment 5-1
Social Media in Action

A recent evolution in marketing involves organizations running online ads that promote their social media presence rather than their products. Consumers who click on the online ads can view firm-created YouTube videos, actual Facebook wall posts, and the company's Twitter page. This type of engagement increased the average amount of time consumers spent interacting with the ad over 250 percent, with an even larger increase in the number of consumers who clicked the Learn More button attached to the ad.

Ritz crackers used social media to highlight a sweepstakes attached to the television show *Glee* in which winners were flown to California to meet the show's cast. Marketers at Ritz partnered with website management firm Kontera to highlight certain keywords related to the show, such as the names of characters, on the websites the company manages. When a reader hovered over the highlighted words, an ad appeared that promoted the sweepstakes and showed consumer posts related to the sweepstakes on the Ritz Facebook page. The promotion helped to engage fans of *Glee* and, since it required them to sign up as followers of Ritz to compete in the sweepstakes, increased the connection between the brand and potential consumers.

The Social Media in Action *Connect* exercise in Chapter 5 will let you develop social media strategies to maximize the engagement between your brand and the consumer. As social media become an important influence on consumer behavior, it's important to consider ways to maximize their full marketing potential.

Source: See Andrew Adam Newman, "Brands Now Direct Their Followers to Social Media," *The New York Times*, August 3, 2011, http://www.nytimes.com/2011/08/04/business/media/promoting-products-using-social-media-advertising.html?_r=0.

Internal Information Search Not all purchases require consumers to search for information externally. For frequently purchased items such as shampoo or toothpaste, internal information often provides a sufficient basis for making a decision. In an internal information search, consumers use their past experiences with items from the same brand or product class as sources of information. You can easily remember your favorite soft drink or vacation destination, which will likely influence what you drink with lunch today or where you go for spring break next year.

internal information search

When consumers use their past experiences with items from the same brand or product class as sources of information.

In our car example, your past experience with automobiles plays a significant role in your new car purchase. If you have had a great experience driving a Ford Escape or Toyota Camry, for example, you may decide to buy a newer model of that same car. Alternatively, if you have had a bad experience with a specific car, brand, or dealership, you may quickly eliminate those automobiles from contention.

Step 3: Evaluating Alternatives

Once consumers have acquired information, they can use it to evaluate different alternatives, typically with a focus on identifying the benefits associated with each product. Consumers' evaluative criteria consist of attributes that they consider important about a certain product. For example, you would probably consider certain characteristics of a car, such as the price, warranty, safety features, or fuel economy, more important than others when evaluating which one to buy. Car marketers work very hard to convince you that the benefits of their car, truck, or SUV reflect the criteria that matter to you.

Subaru has made safety a key selling feature of its various models, including the Outback and the Tribeca.

evaluative criteria
The attributes a consumer considers important about a certain product.

Marketing professionals must not only emphasize the benefits of their good or service but also use strategies to ensure potential buyers view those benefits as important. A company marketing an extremely fuel efficient car might explain that you can use the several thousand dollars a year you will save on gas to pay off credit card debt or fund a family vacation. In contrast, a company marketing a giant SUV with poor fuel efficiency might tell you about the vehicle's safety features and how it can protect your family, or the flexibility it will give you to take more family members on trips.

You should also keep in mind the importance of this stage of the decision-making process as you interview for potential jobs. Employers are likely to evaluate you against other job applicants on various attributes, such as college major, GPA, work experience, skill sets, and potential for development within the organization. Your resume and interview need to market the idea that the benefits you would bring to the organization reflect the criteria that matter to the prospective employer. For example, if your GPA is low relative to others, highlight your work experience or leadership in student organizations and emphasize that the employer needs someone with a proven track record of delivering results and leading others. If your work experience is limited, highlight other benefits you bring. You might stress the idea that your high GPA shows discipline, focus, and high intellectual ability that will help you bring fresh innovative ideas to your role with the company. Your ability to match your best attributes to the attributes most important to the hiring firm will directly benefit your search for a fulfilling career.

Step 4: Making the Purchase

After evaluating the alternatives, a customer will most likely buy a product. Usually the marketer has little control over this part of the consumer decision-making process. Still, consumers have several decisions to make at this point. For example, once you have decided on the car you want, you have to decide where to buy it. Price, sales team, and past experience with a specific dealership can directly impact this decision as can financing terms such as lower interest rates. If you decide to lease a car rather than buy one, you would make that decision during this step.

An effective marketing strategy should seek to encourage ritual consumption. Ritual consumption refers to patterns of consumption that are repeated with regularity. These patterns can be as simple as buying the same soft drink or

ritual consumption
Patterns of consumption that are repeated with regularity.

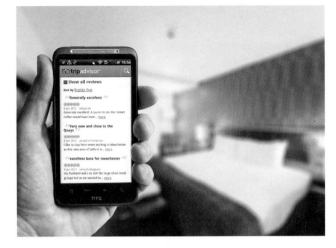

When buying a new car, booking a hotel room, or choosing a restaurant, consumers increasingly use sites like Yelp and TripAdvisor to read other consumers' evaluations prior to making a purchase.

cognitive dissonance
The mental conflict that people undergo when they acquire new information that contradicts their beliefs or assumptions.

stopping at the same place for breakfast every morning. These types of repeat purchases often provide firms with higher profits and a steady stream of customer sales.

Step 5: Post-Purchase Evaluation

Consumers' post-purchase evaluation is critical because their feelings about the purchase will likely impact whether or not they become repeat buyers of that particular good or service. As a consumer, you likely have experienced cognitive dissonance, which is the mental conflict that people undergo when they acquire new information that contradicts their beliefs or assumptions.[3] Cognitive dissonance is sometimes referred to as buyer's regret and often arises when consumers begin to wonder if they made the right purchase decision.

Cognitive dissonance after making a purchase can arise for numerous reasons. Perhaps you discover that the car you just bought doesn't get as good gas mileage on the highway as you'd expected, or you find out a member of your extended family bought the same car for a lower price, or you hear a friend talking about how much she enjoys another make of car. Marketers do various things to reduce the level of dissonance felt by the consumer. For example, a car company might offer an extended warranty or a toll-free number for you to call with any issues about your new car. They may also enhance your early experience with your new car by offering free trials of popular features like the OnStar system or SiriusXM satellite radio. These additional free features typically extend through the first 6 to 12 months after your new car purchase, the time during which consumers are most likely to experience cognitive dissonance. By making consumers feel better about their car purchase, marketers increase the likelihood that those consumers will provide positive external information about the car to other people and ultimately consider returning for their next car purchase. Post-purchase evaluation is even more important to marketers today because of the power of customer reviews available on the Internet. Such reviews can become critical factors in the firm's ability to win over new customers.

Though the decision-making process provides marketers with a framework for understanding how consumers decide to purchase a product, consumers don't always follow the orderly stages discussed. Marketers should not assume that because their strategy succeeds at one stage of the consumer decision-making process it will succeed at the next. For example, a car company might do an excellent job of providing external information to help interest you in its car but still not receive your business because of your inability to secure financing or the objections of your family members. Numerous situational influences like these, discussed in more depth in the next section, can occur at various points in the decision-making process and change the customer's path.

connect | MARKETING ## Interactive Assignment 5-2

Please complete the *Connect* exercise for Chapter 5 that focuses on the consumer decision-making process. By understanding the dynamics of each stage, you should gain insight into how marketers can impact consumer decisions and help their organizations succeed.

SITUATIONAL INFLUENCES AND THE CONSUMER

LO 5-2
Describe how situational influences impact consumer behavior.

Numerous factors affect the consumer decision-making process at every stage and an effective marketing strategy must take these factors into account. We can break these factors down broadly into situational and psychological influences. We'll begin by discussing situational influences, which include factors like time and social surroundings that serve as an interface between the consumers and their decision-making process.[4]

situational influences
Factors like time and social surroundings that serve as an interface between the consumers and their decision-making process.

Time

Consumers value their time greatly and time considerations often affect what consumers buy. Most consumers feel more pressure on their time today than they did a generation or two ago. Companies throughout the world understand consumers' time pressures and design goods and services to accommodate them better. For example, many of the most successful banks have expanded their hours to offer a full slate of financial services to people whose time commitments prevent them from banking during traditional daytime hours.

Time can also impact what a consumer ultimately pays for a good or service. Consumers are often willing to pay more for products if the placement of those products saves them time. For example, though a consumer may realize that soft drinks, potato chips, or bread are significantly more expensive at a local gas station than at a supermarket, he or she may be willing to pay a premium for the time savings of parking close, shopping in a smaller store, and checking out more quickly. By placing products in a more convenient location, marketers can often increase their profits on individual items while still providing great value to their customers.

Social Factors

Social factors develop from a consumer's relationships with others and can significantly impact his or her behavior. Social factors that impact the consumer decision-making process include family influences, reference groups, and opinion leaders.

Family Influences
Family members are one of the greatest influences on consumer behavior. The level of influence can vary across families and can evolve as a family ages and new members join the family through marriage or birth. The composition of families has changed greatly in recent decades to include more single parents and same-sex households, which can impact consumer decisions in different ways important to marketers. Family influences are particularly important in some cultures. Family is of primary importance in the Hispanic culture and should be a central theme when developing targeted messages for the Hispanic population in the United States and throughout the world.

Children's Influence on Family Purchases
Children often greatly influence a household's purchase decisions, particularly in the realm of grocery shopping and dining out. Marketers at McDonald's, Sonic, and Burger King spend a significant amount of money advertising to young consumers and giving away toys and books with their kids' meals. McDonald's has dedicated an entire website, www.happymeal.com, to marketing to kids through fun games and technology. These successful promotions aimed at children can enhance restaurant traffic and revenues. However, marketing food to children has become a controversial topic

FIGURE 5.2   Stages of the Family Life Cycle

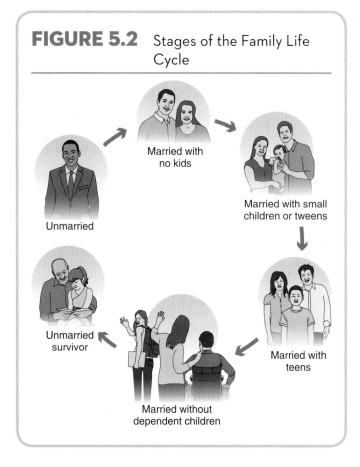

for firms. You can examine the growing concern over the relationship between marketing food to kids and childhood obesity in the Ethical Challenge at the end of this chapter.

The Family Life Cycle Few situational factors have a more significant impact on consumer behavior than the family life cycle. The family life cycle describes the distinct family-related phases that an individual progresses through over the course of his or her life. Figure 5.2 illustrates six stages that an individual might go through as part of his or her family life cycle: (1) unmarried, (2) married with no kids, (3) married with small children or tweens, (4) married with teens, (5) married without dependent children, and (6) unmarried survivor. Each stage impacts consumer behavior, and thus a firm's marketing strategy to that consumer, differently. Imagine two 30-year-old best friends. Both grew up in the same town, went to the same university, graduated with the same degree, attend the same church, and now live next door to each other. Based on those similarities, a marketer might mistakenly assume that their purchase behaviors are very similar. However, one is an unmarried pharmaceutical executive who travels 200 days a year for business. The other is a married, stay-at-home mom with two small children. Despite their similarities, family life cycle differences place these two individuals into very different groups for marketers. The products they buy and the marketing strategies most likely to appeal to them are very different.

Consider where you are in the family life cycle and how that impacts your buying behavior. You may be single and working part time while attending college. You might not own a house, be investing for retirement, or have a need for much life insurance. However, in the years ahead these things are likely to change, and marketers want to develop products that can meet your demands as you progress through your life. Companies like State Farm Insurance actively promote their ability to service consumers throughout the entire family life cycle with products that help customers insure their first car, secure their family with life insurance, and invest in products for retirement.

In addition to family, consumers typically belong to or come into contact with various other social groups—schools, workplaces, churches, and volunteer groups—that can influence their purchase decisions.

family life cycle

The distinct family-related phases that an individual progresses through over the course of his or her life.

reference group

A collection of people to whom a consumer compares himself or herself.

Reference Groups   Reference groups can provide consumers with a new perspective on how to live their lives. When, as a new college graduate, you take your first job, how will you know what to wear on your first day at work? Most companies don't have a formal dress code; rather you might recall what you saw people around the office wearing when you interviewed or ask your new coworkers what they wear to work. In such a case, your coworkers serve as your reference group. A reference group is made up of the people to whom a consumer compares himself or herself. Marketers should understand that the more public the purchase decision, the more impact reference groups are likely to have. For example, reference groups tend to significantly influence a consumer's clothing purchases.

State Farm marketers hope that if they provide consistently great service they can develop loyal customers for life.

Firms typically focus on the following three consumer reference groups when developing a marketing strategy:

1. A membership reference group is the group to which a consumer actually belongs. Membership groups could include school clubs, fraternities and sororities, and the workplace. Marketers who understand the influence other members of these groups have on consumers can target products that would be ideal for the group members. For example, a local bank might market itself as the official bank of your university and offer free checks for students or a debit card featuring the school's logo. Purchasing such products might be seen by new students as a way to better assimilate to their new reference group.

2. An aspirational reference group refers to the individuals a consumer would like to emulate. For example, professional athletes represent an ideal for many people. Subway made use of this reference group in its marketing campaign in the weeks leading up to the 2012 Summer Olympics in London. Subway commercials showed athletes, such as swimmer Michael Phelps, talking about Subway products as an important part of their training regimen.

3. Dissociative reference groups include people that the individual would *not* like to be like. Teenagers and young adults provide perhaps the most notable example of this by actively seeking to dissociate themselves from groups they view as "uncool" or something their parents might be interested in. But dissociative reference groups can play a role in marketing to all consumers. DIRECTV has run a series of marketing campaigns to encourage consumers not to be like those who have traditional cable television. Marketers for mouthwash and certain types of chewing gum encourage consumers to use their product as a way to avoid being associated with those who have bad breath.

Family influences and reference groups, while typically the most influential, aren't the only social factors that impact a consumer's decision to purchase goods and services. Opinion leaders—in the form of celebrities or even very vocal bloggers and other contributors to social media—can also influence the decision-making process.

Opinion Leaders Individuals who exert an unequal amount of influence on the decisions of others because they are considered knowledgeable about particular products are called opinion leaders.[5] Opinion leadership ranges from Michael Jordan endorsing a pair of Nike shoes to Rachael Ray promoting a specific type of cooking utensil. Opinion leaders are not just celebrities; social media

membership reference group
The group to which a consumer actually belongs.

aspirational reference group
The individuals a consumer would like to emulate.

dissociative reference groups
The people that the individual would *not* like to be like.

opinion leaders
Individuals who exert an unequal amount of influence on the decisions of others because they are considered knowledgeable about particular products.

EXECUTIVE PERSPECTIVE

Tracey Rogers
Vice President and General Manager
KAIT-TV

Is using opinion leaders an effective way to market to consumers?

I would say absolutely yes. I have seen firsthand the positive impact opinion leaders, including athletes, actors, former elected officials, or simply well-respected people in the community, have had on advertising. These types of opinion leaders seem to resonate with a wider audience, and, if matched well with the product being advertised, can make viewers more likely to consider or buy a specific product. The key step is making sure the opinion leader fits the audience that you want to sell the product to.

allow small numbers of consumers to influence the consumer decisions of a much larger group. For example, Ree Drummond, known as The Pioneer Woman, blogs about her life on a cattle ranch with her husband and four children. She was ranked as one of the 10 most popular female bloggers in the United States and influences her readers' buying decisions on a variety of topics, including food purchases and preparation.[6] More marketers are trying to tap into the power of these social media opinion leaders through perks and other benefits. For example, credit card companies offer special rewards to customers that have the potential to influence others; airlines give these same types of opinion leaders free flights in an effort to encourage them to use their influence on behalf of the company's products.[7]

Personal Factors

While social factors can significantly impact a consumer's buying decision, consumers also make decisions based on personal factors. A consumer's personality, lifestyle, and values directly impact his or her behavior and firms should understand how so they can tailor their marketing strategy accordingly.

personality

The set of distinctive characteristics that lead an individual to respond in a consistent way to certain situations.

Personality A consumer's personality might include traits that make them confident, personable, deferential, adaptable, or dominant. Personality is the set of distinctive characteristics that lead an individual to respond in a consistent way to certain situations. Personality strongly influences a consumer's decision to purchase products. For example, driving a Toyota Prius might demonstrate a consumer's passion for the environment, whereas buying a Ford F-150 truck might represent an individual's commitment to hard work. Toyota marketed the 2010 Prius with the slogan "Harmony between man, nature and machine."[8] The Prius marketing campaign combined beautiful images of the environment with technology features, such as solar panels on the roof of the car, that were designed to appeal to the target consumer's personality. Marketing professionals should strive to identify personality traits that distinguish large groups of people from each other and then design strategies that best appeal to those consumers.

lifestyle

A person's typical way of life as expressed by his or her activities, interests, and opinions.

Lifestyle Lifestyle characteristics are often easier for a firm to understand and measure than personality traits because it is relatively easy to observe how consumers express themselves in social and cultural settings. Lifestyle is a person's typical way of life as expressed by his or her activities, interests, and opinions. Marketers can potentially reach their targeted consumers by sponsoring events those consumers are passionate about or advertising on social media. EA Sports, the maker of numerous popular video games, used a lifestyle marketing campaign to support its EA Sports College Football game. The "EA Sports Campus Challenge Tour," at which college students could play each other in the firm's college football video game for prizes, visited 25 university campuses during eight weeks of the 2012 college football season. EA Sports's lifestyle marketing campaign was able to engage college students who enjoy video games in a unique way.

Lifestyle marketing campaigns, like the one initiated by video game maker EA Sports that specifically targeted college football fans, allow companies to reach consumers through the activities that most interest them.

Values Think about how your personal value system influences how you live your life. It is likely that your value system also corresponds to your buying behavior for many goods and services. Values reflect a consumer's belief that a specific behavior is socially or personally preferable to another behavior. Personal values, which include everything from a consumer's religious beliefs to a belief in self-responsibility, can impact the decision-making process. For example, a consumer who values self-responsibility might have been attracted to Ford's 2009 marketing message emphasizing that Ford was the only major U.S. automaker that didn't need a taxpayer-funded bailout.

Increasingly, many consumers look for goods and services that embrace sustainability, that is, products that are produced in a responsible way. This trend in consumer behavior is especially relevant in emerging economies. Almost two-thirds of consumers in these economies consider the social and environmental impact of their purchases, which is double the percentage of consumers in developed economies like the United States.[9] Factors related to another major trend, globalization, also impact consumer behavior. We'll discuss these factors in the next section.

Global Factors

Marketers should be aware of how unique factors in different nations throughout the world can influence consumer behavior. For example, the image global

Clothing company Patagonia's ad telling people not to buy its apparel was a counter-intuitive attempt to appeal to consumers' concerns about environmental responsibility and sustainability.

country-of-origin effects

The beliefs and associations people have about a country.

consumers have of the U.S. can lead to country-of-origin effects. Country-of-origin effects are the beliefs and associations people have about a country. They can reflect an overall positive or negative feeling about that country or be specific to certain products. Germany, for example, has a reputation for manufacturing high-quality cars. The more favorable the country-of-origin image, the more marketers should emphasize the country in their advertisements. Marketers at German-owned BMW have focused on the German precision of their automobiles to appeal to consumers in other countries.

Marketers should also be aware of how consumer behavior differs in international markets. For example, the needs or interests of a consumer's family impacts consumer behavior in China more than consumer behavior in the U.S. and Europe.[10] The behavior of young Chinese consumers appears to be increasingly driven by a spirit of individualism, or "what fits me," rather than a desire to make a social statement, an attitude more common with young U.S. consumers.[11] As more firms market to international consumers, they must be aware of the unique pattern of consumer behavior around the world.

LO 5-3

Describe the psychological processes that influence consumer behavior.

psychological processes

The underlying psychological mechanisms that can influence consumer behavior.

PSYCHOLOGICAL PROCESSES AND THE CONSUMER

For consumers to make purchase decisions, they must engage in certain psychological processes, such as attitude, learning, and motivation. Psychological processes are the underlying psychological mechanisms that can influence consumer behavior. These processes, combined with situational and personal influences, ultimately result in consumer decisions and purchases. Through the course of the decision-making process, consumers develop attitudes about a product's meaning to their lives, acquire knowledge about the product, and must be motivated to purchase the product.[12] Marketers need to understand each of these psychological processes as they develop strategies to reach consumers.

Attitude

attitude

A person's overall evaluation of an object involving general feelings of like or dislike.

Attitudes reflect a person's view of something, such as a product, nonprofit organization, or political candidate. Attitude is a person's overall evaluation of an object involving general feelings of like or dislike. It can significantly affect consumer behavior. For example, as firms offer more of their goods and services online, customers are understandably worried about how the data they provide when they purchase online products will be used and protected. Consumer attitudes toward privacy affect all marketers who collect and use online data. Research shows that a sizeable proportion of consumers prefer to closely control their online privacy. Events like the 2011 Sony PlayStation privacy breach, in which an unauthorized user stole names, addresses, and other information from 77 million users, only heighten consumers' privacy concerns.[13]

Attitude affects marketing strategy. Firms marketing online must understand and comply with privacy laws and implement the right messaging and policies to demonstrate that they take consumers' attitudes about privacy seriously. Attitudes are both an obstacle and an advantage to a marketer. Choosing to discount or ignore consumers' attitudes toward a particular good or service when developing a marketing strategy guarantees the campaign will enjoy only limited success. In contrast, perceptive marketers leverage their understanding of attitudes to predict the behavior of consumers and develop a marketing strategy that reflects that behavior.

Learning

Consumer learning may or may not result from things marketers do; however, almost all consumer behavior is learned. Learning refers to the modification of behavior that occurs over time due to experiences and other external stimuli.[14] Marketers can influence consumer learning, and, by doing so, impact consumer decisions and strengthen consumer relationships, but they must first understand the basic learning process. Learning typically begins with a stimulus that encourages consumers to act to reduce a need or want, followed by a response, which attempts to satisfy that need or want. Marketers can provide cues through things like advertisements that encourage a consumer to satisfy a need or want using the firm's good or service. The specific response a consumer chooses depends on many of the factors we've already discussed. Reinforcement of the learning process occurs when the response, eating a hamburger, for example, reduces the need, in this case, for food. Consistent reinforcement that a particular hamburger satisfies the consumer's need can lead the consumer to develop a habit of making the same purchase decision over and over again without much thought. Think about the drink you order at a restaurant or after you work out. Is it always the same? How much thought do you give to this decision? Marketers who satisfy their consumers are likely to have higher numbers of repeat consumers, leading to increased profitability.

Marketers can capitalize on consumer learning by designing marketing strategies that promote reinforcement. Bounty has promoted its paper towels using the slogan "the quicker picker upper" for more than 40 years. Through repetition in promotion, the company hopes to influence consumer learning by associating the Bounty product with the idea of cleaning up spills quickly. The strategy has worked; Bounty remains the market share leader in paper towels and continues to grow in sales volume even as other paper towel brands have faced years of declines.[15]

Motivation

A third psychological process that affects consumer behavior is motivation. Motivation is the inward drive we have to get what we need or want. Marketers spend billions of dollars on research to understand how they can motivate people to buy a full range of consumer products. One of the most well-known models for understanding consumer motivation was developed by Abraham Maslow in the mid-1900s. He theorized that humans have various types of needs, from simple needs like water and sleep to complex needs like love and self-esteem.[16] Maslow's hierarchy of needs model, shown in Figure 5.3, illustrates his belief that people seek to meet their basic needs before fulfilling higher-level needs.

Physiological Needs For the most part, physiological needs, which form the base of Maslow's hierarchy, are the simple requirements for human survival. If these requirements, such as food or shelter, are not met, the human body simply cannot continue to function. A consumer who lacks food, safety, love, and esteem would

learning
The modification of behavior that occurs over time due to experiences and other external stimuli.

motivation
The inward drive we have to get what we need or want.

Bounty has remained the market share leader in paper towels by successfully influencing consumer learning, and thus consumer behavior, partly through promotion repetition.

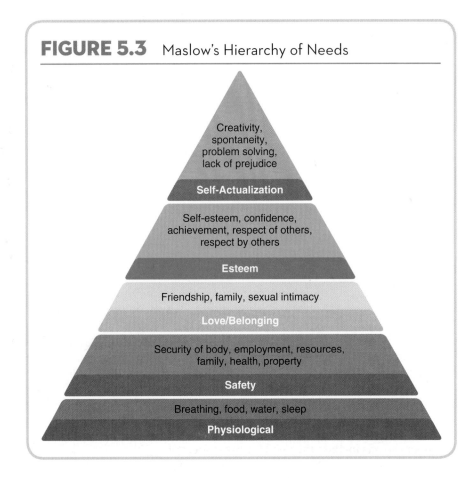

FIGURE 5.3   Maslow's Hierarchy of Needs

consider food his or her greatest need and, according to Maslow, would seek to fulfill that need before any of the others. Marketers of food, bottled water, and medicine are often focused on meeting the physiological needs of their target customers.

Safety Needs   Once their physical needs have been satisfied, consumers' safety needs take precedence and begin to dominate behavior. Safety can take different forms, including physical safety and economic safety. The absence of physical safety—due to war, natural disaster, or family violence, for example—can lead people to experience post-traumatic stress disorder or other emotional conditions. ADT has been very successful in marketing home security systems to a much wider target audience since it began employing television commercials, online marketing, and other tools focused on the ways that ADT's goods and services can make consumers feel safer.

The absence of economic safety—due to economic crisis or lack of job opportunities—leads consumers to want job security, savings accounts, insurance policies, reasonable disability accommodations, and the like. Marketers often look for ways to match a consumer's need for economic safety and security with the goods and services they offer. Aflac has been very successful targeting consumers ages 35–54 with products focused on accident and disability insurance. Popular commercials featuring the Aflac duck emphasize the idea that consumers may need supplemental insurance if they get hurt and have to miss work. Aflac has been able to provide a greater sense of safety to many working consumers and has seen profits grow significantly in recent years as a result.[17]

Love and Belonging   The third level of human needs, after physiological and safety needs are fulfilled, involves love and belonging. Deficiencies with respect to these interpersonal needs can impact an individual's ability to form and maintain emotionally significant relationships with romantic partners, friends, and family. Love has become big business for marketers. The online dating site eHarmony was founded in 2000 and made its mark in the online dating landscape by establishing its brand as the site for the serious relationship seeker, particularly women. The result of creating a product suited to women seeking marriage or serious relationships had two financial benefits for eHarmony. First, it could charge more and thus enjoy higher profits than competitors. Because the perception of finding a soul mate provides more value to the user than just finding a date, eHarmony was able to charge customers a premium of up to $60 per month for matches.[18] Second, eHarmony was able to reach out to female consumers more effectively than other sites. While many dating sites make most of their money on men, eHarmony is more successful with women; almost 60 percent of its paying users are female.[19]

eHarmony, like many other dating sites, has developed a marketing strategy based on the human need for love and belonging.

Esteem   The fourth level in the hierarchy of needs is esteem. Esteem is the need all humans have to be respected by others as well as by themselves. Maslow described two kinds of esteem needs: lower and higher. Lower esteem needs include the need for the respect of others, status, recognition, fame, prestige, and attention. Jewelry stores and luxury car makers like Lexus often target their marketing at consumers with lower esteem needs, or those looking to increase their status or prestige. Lexus commercials often focus on all of the neighbors admiring the new Lexus that has just been purchased.

esteem

The need all humans have to be respected by others as well as by themselves.

Higher esteem needs include the need for self-respect, strength, competence, mastery, self-confidence, independence, and freedom. For example, makers of foreign language education software market their products as a way for consumers to fulfill a lifelong dream of speaking a new language. Their commercials show happy customers who say that learning a new language has helped them excel at their job, increased their mental dexterity, or enhanced their vacations in foreign countries. Rosetta Stone has used this marketing strategy to become the top-selling language learning software company in the world, with over $200 million in annual sales.[20]

Self-Actualization   Maslow describes the top tier of the hierarchy as the aspiration to become everything that one is capable of becoming. Self-actualization pertains to what a consumer's full potential is and the need to realize that potential. This is a broad definition of the need for self-actualization, but when applied to individual consumers, the need is specific. For example, one individual may have a strong desire to become an ideal parent, another may want to become a superior athlete, and another may want to excel at painting, photography, or inventing. Professional basketball player Dwyane Wade looked to target consumers with needs on the high end of the hierarchy by establishing a basketball fantasy camp. The cost for the four-day camp started at $12,500, and the camp was promoted as a way for successful adults to realize their dream of playing basketball against an NBA star.[21]

self-actualization

A consumer's full potential and the need to realize that potential.

Situational factors like time and reference groups and psychological factors like motivation influence the consumer decision-making process, but the nature of the decision also plays a role in how the consumer moves through the process and the emphasis he or she places on each step. In the next section, we'll discuss how the consumer's level of involvement in the buying decision affects the decision-making process.

---

connect | MARKETING Interactive Assignment 5-3

Please complete the *Connect* exercise for Chapter 5 that focuses on Maslow's hierarchy of needs. By understanding the dynamics of each stage, you should gain insight into how marketers can impact consumer decisions and help their organizations be more successful.

LO 5-4

Summarize the relationship between involvement and consumer decisions.

INVOLVEMENT

How consumers make choices is influenced by their level of involvement in the decision process. Involvement is the personal, financial, and social significance of the decision being made.[22] The study of high and low involvement focuses on how consumers choose which alternative to purchase and is important for firms to understand as they develop strategies to sell their products. Figure 5.4 compares the characteristics of high-involvement buying decisions with those of low-involvement buying decisions.

Low-Involvement Buying Decisions

Most likely, you have made an impulse purchase sometime in the past month. Impulse buying is purchasing a product with no planning or forethought. Buying gum in a grocery store checkout line or a new cap that you notice as you walk through a mall are examples of impulse buying. Impulse purchases usually occur with low-involvement products. Low-involvement products are inexpensive products that can be purchased without much forethought and that are purchased with some frequency.

Consumers often do not recognize their desire for a low-involvement product until they are in the store, which influences the strategic decisions for marketing these items. In-store promotion, for example, is a very useful tool for marketing low-involvement products. Unique packaging or special displays help to capture the consumer's attention and quickly explain the product's purpose and benefits. Marketing

involvement

The personal, financial, and social significance of the decision being made.

impulse buying

Purchasing a product with no planning or forethought.

low-involvement products

Inexpensive products that can be purchased without much forethought and that are purchased with some frequency.

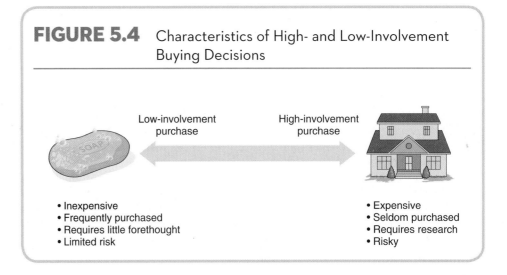

FIGURE 5.4 Characteristics of High- and Low-Involvement Buying Decisions

Low-involvement purchase ⟷ High-involvement purchase

- Inexpensive
- Frequently purchased
- Requires little forethought
- Limited risk

- Expensive
- Seldom purchased
- Requires research
- Risky

strategies for low-involvement products include colorful packaging that highlights discounted DVDs for sale at Target, Kellogg's signage at Walmart stores explaining the relatively low cost of eating breakfast at home versus at a restaurant, or a promotional sign by Sara Lee in a grocery store aisle that focuses on a promotional tie-in between its "soft and smooth bread" and Disney's movie *High School Musical 3: Senior Year.* Tactics like low-tech cardboard displays found at the end of aisles can potentially drive more impulse purchases than temporary price reductions.

High-Involvement Buying Decisions

Perhaps the two most common examples of high-involvement purchases are a car and a house. High-involvement products include more significant purchases that carry a greater risk to consumers if they fail. Companies that market high-involvement products must provide potential consumers with extensive and helpful information as they go through the decision-making process. An informative advertisement can outline to the consumer the major benefits of a specific product purchase. Residential brokerage firm Coldwell Banker provides a wealth of information about the homes it is attempting to sell to help potential buyers understand more not just about the house itself but also about local schools, financing options, and moving services.

Firms must remember that the difference between low-involvement and high-involvement products is not always absolute and depends on the priorities of the individual consumer. A female consumer whose appearance is extremely important to her might view the purchase of shampoo as a high-involvement item and spend considerable time searching for information and evaluating alternatives. If the consumer is pleased with her post-purchase evaluation of the shampoo, she will likely continue to buy it on a regular basis with far less involvement. If marketers can effectively remove doubts about the efficacy of the product, they can transition certain high-involvement products to low-involvement products for satisfied consumers.

high-involvement products
Significant purchases that carry a greater risk to consumers if they fail.

Whether a purchase decision is high or low involvement often depends on the individual consumer. For some, purchasing sunglasses is a low-involvement decision made up of a 15-minute stop at Walmart or Target for a $10 pair. For others, the decision is a high-involvement fashion statement that can involve a large outlay of money and time.

LO 5-5

Compare business-to-business marketing to business-to-consumer marketing.

business-to-business marketing (B2B)

Marketing to organizations that acquire goods and services in the production of other goods and services that are then sold or supplied to others.

BUSINESS-TO-BUSINESS MARKETING

Up to this point, we've focused on the behavior and decision-making process of individual consumers and discussed how understanding them allows firms to market to them successfully. However, firms also sell and market their goods and services to other businesses. Business-to-business marketing (B2B) consists of marketing to organizations that acquire goods and services in the production of other goods and services that are then sold or supplied to others. For example, companies like American Tower build cell phone towers not to sell to individual consumers but rather to help businesses like AT&T and Sprint service consumers like you. An increasing number of college graduates are working for organizations focused on business-to-business marketing, and more dollars now change hands in sales to business buyers than to end consumers. While B2B marketers face many of the same challenges B2C marketers do, they also have to concern themselves with several factors unique to business markets.

Professional Purchasing

An individual consumer can choose to buy ice cream or a new set of golf clubs at any time for any reason, but business sales typically involve professional purchasing managers who are experienced in the policies and procedures necessary to make a large deal. For example, a professional buyer at JCPenney or Dillard's will be responsible for purchasing the shoes and clothes that will eventually be featured in those stores. The B2B purchasing process is often far longer than the consumer decision-making process and requires standardized procedures, such as a request for proposal (RFP) and contract negotiations, that are not typically found in consumer buying.

Derived Demand

The need for business goods is derived from demand for consumer goods. For example, business-to-business telecommunications companies such as Level 3 Communications, headquartered in Broomfield, Colorado, provide fiber-optic bandwidth for wireless companies like AT&T, Verizon Wireless, and Sprint. The demand that AT&T, Verizon, and Sprint have for Level 3 services is derived from the demands of their wireless customers. Derived demand occurs when demand for one product occurs because of demand for a related product. While Level 3 does not provide wireless goods and services to individual consumers, the success of its business depends directly on the buying patterns of individual consumers.

derived demand

When demand for one product occurs because of demand for a related product.

Derived demand also provides an important reason to develop mutually beneficial relationships with business-to-business partners. Imagine a scenario in which you are the only provider of food to your school's cafeteria because of supply chain problems for a competing provider. Since your firm is the school's only option, you have the ability to charge far more than is necessary for your goods, thereby maximizing your profit. However, if you choose to charge the school ever higher prices, it, in turn, will have to pass those cost increases on to students. Once the price of cafeteria dining gets too high, students will simply find other places to eat on or off campus. The student demand for cafeteria meals would decrease, thereby decreasing the school's need for your products since that demand is derived from student demand. Marketers must take a strategic view of business-to-business relationships and understand all of the potential impacts their actions can have on derived demand.

Fewer Buyers

Business marketers typically deal with far fewer buyers than consumer marketers. And usually, each of these customers is larger and more essential to the firm's success than an average consumer because there are fewer business buyers. For example, the potential demand for pizza is almost unlimited in the United States. However, the demand for large-scale pizza ovens is confined to medium and large pizza establishments, many of which belong to Pizza Hut, Little Caesars, and other major national chains. Because there are fewer buyers, B2B marketers feel even more pressure to make sure they offer high quality products to and establish good relationships with their business customers. A bad relationship with an individual pizza consumer might cost the local Pizza Hut $20 per week, whereas a bad relationship with Pizza Hut might cost a pizza oven maker its entire annual profit or even its future.

Large events like the Olympics stimulate derived demand for many things, including construction workers and equipment, as the cities in which they occur, such as Rio de Janeiro, spend billions of dollars building stadiums, hotels, and public transportation to host athletes and visitors.

TYPES OF BUSINESS CUSTOMERS

Business-to-business marketing professionals focus on several major categories of business customers, including government markets, institutional markets, and reseller markets.

Government Markets

Government markets include thousands of federal, state, and local entities that purchase everything from heavy equipment to clear snowy roads to paperclips to keep office records organized. The United States government is one of the world's largest customers, spending hundreds of billions of dollars a year. Marketing goods and services to the U.S. government requires strict adherence to certain policies, procedures, and documentation obligations. Because the public holds the government accountable for its purchases, complex buying procedures are often used to ensure that purchases meet the necessary requirements. Firms must be detail oriented and complete extensive documentation to succeed at marketing to federal agencies and departments, such as the Department of Defense. For example, Mississippi-based Gulf Coast Produce spent considerable time and resources winning a government contract to provide millions of dollars in fruits and vegetables to the military.[23] This complicated and often slow process has made some marketers, especially in small businesses, reluctant to bid on government business. Of the

EXECUTIVE PERSPECTIVE

Tracey Rogers
Vice President and General Manager
KAIT-TV

Why is relationship development so important in B2B marketing?

The simplest answer is that there are fewer buyers out there. Regardless of the size of market you are in, there is a finite number of B2B firms that can be potential customers. We try very hard to make sure that each of our business customers receives great value from its relationship with KAIT. Our sales and marketing team focuses on developing these mutually beneficial relationships because, if we lose a B2B customer, it is hard to replace them.

Boeing, which produces the presidential airplane, Air Force One, in addition to a number of military aircraft, is one of the largest U.S. Defense Department contractors partly because of its ability to meet the complex requirements of selling to a government entity.

20 million small businesses in the U.S., only about 500,000 of them have completed the documentation necessary to be eligible to sell to the government.[24] However, government markets can be highly lucrative for smart marketers and organizations.

In addition to the federal government, there are 50 state governments and approximately 90,000 local governments, all of which must purchase goods and services to survive. The amount spent by local governments increased rapidly in previous decades as the number of services they provided expanded. However, in recent years, budget deficits and cutbacks have made many local governments more conscious of how they spend each dollar and forced them to focus on increasing the value of their purchases.

North American Industry Classification System   While marketing to a government entity is typically a more complex process than marketing to other business customers, a working knowledge of the type of information governments need to make decisions about what to purchase can ease the process for marketers. The North American Industry Classification System (NAICS) is a single industry classification system used by the members of the North American Free Trade Agreement (NAFTA)—the United States, Canada, and Mexico—to generate comparable statistics for businesses and industries across the three countries. NAICS information is one of the most common requirements in completing the documentation to sell to government entities. The NAICS classifications are based on the types of production activities performed. The list divides industrial activity into 20 sectors, from construction and retail to education services. Table 5.1 lists the NAICS sectors that have been identified, along with the two-digit code assigned to each that makes it possible for governments to compare and make purchase decisions across industries.

Organizations in the NAFTA member countries are each given a six-digit code that can help marketers identify whether or not the business fits within their target market. The first two numbers in the code represent the two-digit sector designation from Table 5.1. The third digit reflects the subsector, the fourth digit reflects the industry group, and the fifth digit represents the industry. The first five digits of the NAICS codes are fixed among the members of NAFTA. The sixth digit can vary among NAFTA countries. Figure 5.5 on page 148 shows the NAICS code for a mechanical pulp mill in Canada. In this example, the sixth digit reflects specific data from Canada.

North American Industry Classification System (NAICS)

A single industry classification system used by the members of the North American Free Trade Agreement—the United States, Canada, and Mexico—to generate comparable statistics for businesses and industries across the three countries.

Institutional Markets

Institutional markets represent a wide variety of organizations, including hospitals, schools, churches, and nonprofit organizations. Institutional markets can vary widely in their buying practices. For example, a large megachurch with thousands

TABLE 5.1 NAICS Sectors

Code	NAICS Sectors
11	Agriculture, Forestry, Fishing, and Hunting
21	Mining
22	Utilities
23	Construction
31–33	Manufacturing
42	Wholesale Trade
44–45	Retail Trade
48–49	Transportation and Warehousing
51	Information
52	Finance and Insurance
53	Real Estate and Rental and Leasing
54	Professional, Scientific, and Technical Services
55	Management of Companies and Enterprises
56	Administrative and Support and Waste Management and Remediation Services
61	Educational Services
62	Health Care and Social Assistance
71	Arts, Entertainment, and Recreation
72	Accommodation and Food Services
81	Other Services (except Public Administration)
92	Public Administration

Source: U.S. Census Bureau, "2012 NAICS," November 7, 2011, http://www.census.gov/cgi-bin/sssd/naics/naicsrch?chart=2012.

of members and a multimillion-dollar budget will likely have a buying manager or purchasing agent for firms to work with, whereas marketing to a new church with a very small congregation might simply require speaking with the pastor. These diverse buying situations pose unique challenges for institutional marketers. They must develop flexible, customized solutions that meet the specific needs of, for example, differently sized school districts or hospitals. Educating institutional customers about how specific goods and services can make their organizations more efficient or effective is a firm's best tool for selling products in this type of business market. For example, marketers for a medical technology firm could show a hospital how their customized technology solutions can reduce costs for the hospital while also improving patient care.

Reseller Markets

Resellers include retailers and wholesalers who buy finished goods and resell them for a profit. A retailer, such as a clothing or grocery store, is a firm that sells mainly to end-user consumers like you. There are over 1 million different retailers in the United

resellers
Retailers and wholesalers who buy finished goods and resell them for a profit.

retailer
A firm that sells mainly to end-user consumers.

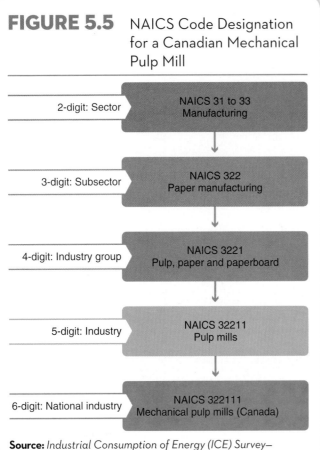

FIGURE 5.5   NAICS Code Designation for a Canadian Mechanical Pulp Mill

2-digit: Sector	NAICS 31 to 33 Manufacturing
3-digit: Subsector	NAICS 322 Paper manufacturing
4-digit: Industry group	NAICS 3221 Pulp, paper and paperboard
5-digit: Industry	NAICS 32211 Pulp mills
6-digit: National industry	NAICS 322111 Mechanical pulp mills (Canada)

Source: *Industrial Consumption of Energy (ICE) Survey— Summary Report of Energy Use in the Canadian Manufacturing Sector, 1995–2005,* http://oee.nrcan.gc.ca/publications/ statistics/ice10/appendixc.cfm, Office of Energy Efficiency, Natural Resources Canada. Reproduced with the permission of the Minister of Public Works and Government Services Canada, 2013.

wholesaling

The sale of goods or merchandise to retailers; industrial, commercial, institutional, or other professional business users; or other wholesalers.

wholesaler

A firm that sells goods to anyone other than an end-user consumer.

new buy

A buying situation in which a business customer is purchasing a product for the very first time.

LO 5-6

Compare the different buying situations in business-to-business marketing.

States. Figure 5.6 on page 150 shows the 10 largest U.S. retailers as determined by total retail sales.

Wholesaling is the sale of goods or merchandise to retailers; industrial, commercial, institutional, or other professional business users; or other wholesalers. In general, a wholesaler is a firm that sells goods to anyone other than an end-user consumer. Wholesalers frequently purchase a large quantity of a good (e.g., hamburger meat) at a low cost and then sell off smaller quantities of the good (e.g., hamburger meat packaged for an individual family) at a higher per-unit price. Traditionally, wholesalers were physically closer to the markets they supplied than the source from which they got the products. However, technology advances in developing nations have increased the number of wholesalers located near manufacturing bases in, among other places, China, Taiwan, and Southeast Asia.

All of these different business markets present unique challenges to firms engaged in B2B marketing. In the next section, we'll discuss the various buying situations that impact how a firm markets its product to the types of business customers we've discussed.

BUYING SITUATIONS

While the types of B2B customers can vary, the buying situations for each are often quite similar. Marketers can classify business-to-business buying situations into three general categories:

1. A new buy involves a business customer purchasing a product for the very first time. For example, let's say that Dell is looking to market its personal computers to a college that has not previously bought from the company. Since the college has little or no experience with Dell, its decision process will likely be extensive, with the college requiring a significant amount of information and negotiation. From a marketing standpoint, Dell's reputation for meeting specifications and providing high-quality service to its current business and college customers could prove to be a critical factor in selling to the college for the first time.

2. A straight rebuy occurs when a business customer signals its satisfaction by agreeing to purchase the same product at the same price. B2B marketers prefer the straight rebuy outcome to any other because straight rebuys normally do not require any additional design modifications or contract negotiations.

   Another major advantage of a straight rebuy is that the customer typically does not look for competing bids from other companies. To revisit our Dell example, in a straight rebuy scenario, Dell should work hard to produce high-quality computers at a competitive price with great service that makes the college feel good about its purchase decision. In addition, Dell marketers might also look for ways to make ordering more personal computers easier, such as simple online or automated reordering systems through which the

Caitlin Winey

Sales Representative
Forest Pharmaceuticals

Describe your job. I travel across my extensive territory to see family practice and specialty doctors and sell them my products. I also leave samples of my medicines so that the patients are able to try the drug, usually for a month, at no cost.

Describe how you got the job that you have. For me, it was all about knowing the right people. My position had been open for six months, and my company just hadn't found the right person to fill the spot. My boss contacted my university's athletic director looking for possible job candidates who were athletes and business majors. Apparently, my company liked to hire athletes because they knew we would be competitive, driven, coachable, and work well as a member of a team. I fit the criteria, so my athletic academic advisor called me, and I contacted my future manager about the job opening. The interview process was lengthy, lasting almost eight weeks. I went through six different interviews, including being flown to the company's headquarters and interviewing with a senior vice president, before officially being offered the job.

What has been the most important thing in making you successful at your job? My positive attitude. This job can be very stressful. Your bosses are always checking your sales numbers. That, together with the reality of being told no multiple times a day, can definitely wear on a person.

Doctors and nurses have very demanding jobs, having to see more patients in less time. Because of this, there isn't always time for them to see me, so I face rejection a lot. There are also doctors who just don't like my products and are not afraid to tell me. I have to remind myself on a daily basis not to take a doctor's distaste for my product personally. By staying positive, I can walk out of an office in which I have been rejected into the next office with a clean slate and try all over again with the same energy and enthusiasm as the first office.

What advice would you give soon-to-be graduates? Network everywhere you go and make a conscious effort to make a good impression on everyone you meet. You never know who could be the key that opens the door for a potential job offer. The best example I have of this is from my days in college. The marketing club at my university brings in local business leaders to speak. Afterward, I would mingle with the speaker, ask questions, get to know them on a personal level. I kept in contact with one in particular and he ended up asking me to interview for a position in his company when I graduated. When I graduated, I had two job offers, one from him, and the other from the pharmaceutical company. I ended up choosing the pharmaceutical job because of the location, but it just proves how important networking is when trying to find a job after college.

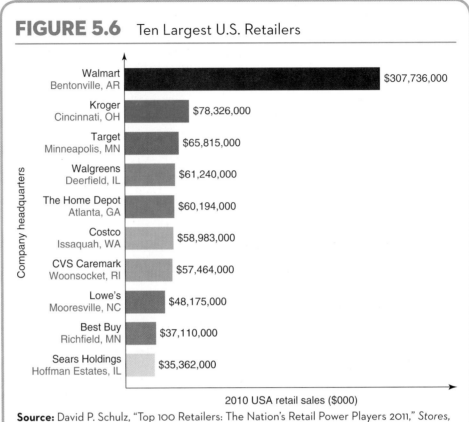

FIGURE 5.6   Ten Largest U.S. Retailers

Company headquarters	2010 USA retail sales ($000)
Walmart — Bentonville, AR	$307,736,000
Kroger — Cincinnati, OH	$78,326,000
Target — Minneapolis, MN	$65,815,000
Walgreens — Deerfield, IL	$61,240,000
The Home Depot — Atlanta, GA	$60,194,000
Costco — Issaquah, WA	$58,983,000
CVS Caremark — Woonsocket, RI	$57,464,000
Lowe's — Mooresville, NC	$48,175,000
Best Buy — Richfield, MN	$37,110,000
Sears Holdings — Hoffman Estates, IL	$35,362,000

Source: David P. Schulz, "Top 100 Retailers: The Nation's Retail Power Players 2011," *Stores*, July 2011, http://www.stores.org/2011/Top-100-Retailers.

straight rebuy

A buying situation in which a business customer signals its satisfaction by agreeing to purchase the same product at the same price.

modified rebuy

A buying situation in which the customer's needs change slightly or they are not completely satisfied with the product they purchased.

With the release of Office 365, Microsoft has made the straight rebuy even easier by offering subscription access to its Office Suite. Instead of paying to place the software on one computer each time the software is upgraded, businesses can pay monthly for a subscription to the software that can be used across multiple computers and get additional perks like web conferencing and document sharing.

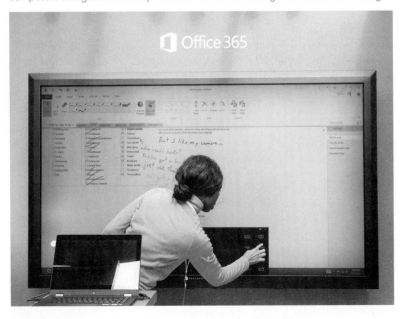

college can quickly order new computers without delays or hassle. Marketers who make it as easy as possible for customers to do business with their firm increase the likelihood that the customers will perceive value and develop loyalty.

3. A modified rebuy occurs when the customer's needs change slightly or they are not completely satisfied with the product they purchased. In our Dell example, the college might want Dell to modify its computers to add additional features, lower its prices, or reduce delivery times to get new products to the school. Modified rebuys provide marketers with both positive and negative feedback. By buying from Dell again, the college signals that it is pleased with at least certain parts of its purchase experience. However, modified rebuys can also be negative if the college asks Dell to reduce its price or modify design

characteristics to a point where the agreement no longer earns Dell a profit.

The ability to walk away from potential modified rebuys provides marketers with an important tool. If Dell agrees to terms that cause the company to lose money, its long-term health as an organization could be in jeopardy. In every decade, we can find examples, from General Motors to Lehman Brothers, of businesses whose revenue continued to increase, while profitability decreased. Apple marketers have become concerned about this in recent years. At the beginning of 2013, Apple's overall earnings report showed an 18 percent revenue increase, but a less than 1 percent increase in profits.[25] In some global markets the results were even more alarming. For example, while Apple reported a 22 percent increase in revenue for the Australia and New Zealand markets, total profits in those markets declined 38 percent for the 2012 fiscal year.[26]

Regardless of what type of business customer B2B marketers are selling to or what type of buying situation they're in, B2B marketing should seek to create, communicate, and deliver value to customers in a way that is ultimately profitable, just as marketers would with individual consumers.

---

 connect | MARKETING   ## Interactive Assignment 5-4

Please complete the *Connect* exercise for Chapter 5 that focuses on the differences between business and consumer markets. By understanding the strategic decisions marketers face in B2C and B2B organizations, you will be able to successfully develop strategies to succeed in either.

SUMMARY

 LO 5-1 Explain the consumer decision-making process.

The consumer decision-making process has five stages: (1) the consumer recognizes there is a need to satisfy or a problem to solve, (2) he or she seeks information in an effort to make the best possible purchase decision, (3) the consumer evaluates the alternatives, (4) the consumer buys a product, and (5) the consumer evaluates his or her purchase. The process does not always occur in the orderly stages discussed, and marketers should not assume that success at one stage of the process guarantees success at the next. Numerous situational influences can occur at various points in the process to change the path taken by any customer.

LO 5-2 Describe how situational influences impact consumer behavior.

Situational factors that influence consumer behavior include time, social

factors, and personal factors. Consumers value their time greatly and timing often affects what consumers buy. The amount of time involved in a purchase can also impact what a consumer is willing to pay. Social factors develop from a consumer's relationships with others and have a significant impact on consumer behavior. These social factors include family influences, reference groups, and opinion leaders. A consumer also makes decisions based on personal factors, such as personality, lifestyle, and values.

 LO 5-3 Describe the psychological processes that influence consumer behavior.

Psychological processes that influence consumer behavior include attitude, learning, and motivation. Attitude is a person's overall evaluation of an object involving general feelings of like or dislike. Learning refers to behavior modifications that result from repeated experiences. Motivation is the inward drive we have to get what we need. One of the most useful models in understanding consumer motivation was developed by Abraham Maslow in the mid-1900s. His hierarchy of needs model theorizes that consumers will seek to meet their lower-level needs (e.g., physiological and safety) before they begin fulfilling higher-level needs (e.g., belonging, esteem, and self-actualization).

 LO 5-4 Summarize the relationship between involvement and consumer decisions.

Involvement is the personal, financial, and social significance of the decision being made. Impulse buying, which is purchasing a product with no planning or forethought, usually occurs with low-involvement products, which are typically inexpensive and can be purchased with little forethought and some frequency. High-involvement products include more significant purchases that carry a greater risk to consumers if they fail. It is also important for marketers to remember that the difference between low-involvement and high-involvement products is not always absolute and depends on the priorities of the individual consumer.

 LO 5-5 Compare business-to-business marketing to business-to-consumer marketing.

Business-to-business marketing consists of marketing to organizations that acquire goods and services in the production of other goods and services that are then sold or supplied to others. While business-to-business marketers face many of the same challenges as marketers to individual consumers, they are impacted by several factors unique to business markets, including professional purchasing, derived demand, and fewer buyers. Several major categories of business customers matter to marketers—government markets, reseller markets, and institutional markets.

 LO 5-6 Compare the different buying situations in business-to-business marketing.

Marketers can classify business-to-business buying situations into three general categories. A new buy involves a business customer purchasing a product for the very first time. A straight rebuy occurs when a business customer signals its satisfaction by agreeing to purchase the same product at the same price. A modified rebuy occurs when the customer's needs change slightly or they are not completely satisfied with the product they purchased.

KEY TERMS

aspirational reference group (p. 135)
attitude (p. 138)
business-to-business marketing
    (B2B) (p. 144)
business-to-consumer marketing
    (B2C) (p. 129)
cognitive dissonance (p. 132)
consumer behavior (p. 128)
country-of-origin effects (p. 138)
derived demand (p. 144)
dissociative reference groups (p. 135)
esteem (p. 141)
evaluative criteria (p. 131)
external information search (p. 129)

family life cycle (p. 134)
high-involvement products (p. 143)
impulse buying (p. 142)
internal information search (p. 130)
involvement (p. 142)
learning (p. 139)
lifestyle (p. 136)
low-involvement products (p. 142)
membership reference group (p. 135)
modified rebuy (p. 150)
motivation (p. 139)
new buy (p. 148)
North American Industry Classification
    System (NAICS) (p. 146)

opinion leaders (p. 135)
personality (p. 136)
problem recognition (p. 129)
psychological processes (p. 138)
reference group (p. 134)
resellers (p. 147)
retailer (p. 147)
ritual consumption (p. 131)
self-actualization (p. 141)
situational influences (p. 133)
straight rebuy (p. 150)
values (p. 137)
wholesaler (p. 148)
wholesaling (p. 148)

MARKETING PLAN EXERCISE

In this chapter we discussed the differences between consumer and business markets. In the next section of the marketing plan exercise, you will evaluate the characteristics of each and decide which may be better for you as a career choice. Your assignment for this chapter is to decide whether you would prefer to have a career in a B2B or a B2C organization. Think through each type of organization carefully and assess which best fits your personality. Finding a good fit will impact your ability to excel and enjoy your career after college. This will help to focus you in your job search whether you are going to work in marketing, finance, human resources, or any other area of the organization. Many professionals end up working in both types of organizations over the course of their careers, and you will likely have many opportunities to move from one to the other in the future. However, the additional focus will help you build a career that can put you ahead of your fellow graduates.

Your Task: Write a one-paragraph summary explaining whether you would prefer to work in a B2C or B2B organization and discuss what organizational characteristics impacted your decision. Conclude your paragraph with the names of three potential employers in the area where you would most want to live that focus on your chosen market.

DISCUSSION QUESTIONS

1. Think of a recent purchase you have made and describe the actions you took at each stage of the consumer decision-making process. Did you skip any of the stages? Which stage do you think should be most important to marketers? Does it depend on what type of product is being marketed?
2. Which of the situational influences described in this chapter influence your buying decisions most? Explain your answer.
3. List two high-involvement purchases you have made in the past year. What made them high involvement to you?
4. Describe how derived demand might impact a college campus bookstore.
5. Pick a company that you or someone in your family has worked for. Then go to the NAICS website at www.census.gov/eos/www/naics/ and figure out the full six-figure NAICS code for that company. What are two other companies with the same code? How can this information be valuable to a small business marketer?

SOCIAL MEDIA APPLICATION

S Social Media

Pick a company that you would like to work for after graduation and assume that you have been asked to interview with them for a job next month. Analyze how social media can help you prepare for your interview using the following questions and activities as a guide:

1. Go onto the firm's social media platforms and find at least two helpful pieces of information that you can use in your interview that cannot be found on the organization's general website.

2. In addition to the organization's social media platforms, do the executives or managers of the firm actively engage through social media? If so, are there useful pieces of information (such as Facebook posts or tweets) that can help give you an advantage over others competing for the same job?
3. What are two things you can do with your own social media presence to better position yourself for the interview?

ETHICAL CHALLENGE

"For parents trying to promote healthy eating habits, online sales pitches are making mealtime no picnic, according to a new study. Researchers from the Center for Digital Democracy and American University released a report detailing how low-nutrient foods are marketed online to kids and teens using everything from avatars in virtual worlds to instant-messaging chat tools, and from web sweepstakes to interactive games. The report's authors suggest that a rise in such marketing on sites where kids are spending larger chunks of time is contributing to childhood obesity and diet-related health problems by encouraging kids to make poor food choices.

Report author Kathryn Montgomery, a communications professor at American University, says that online food marketing has 'stacked the deck' against parents when it comes to getting children and teens to avoid high-sugar, high-fat foods. 'I think we have really set parents up here,' says Montgomery. 'We shouldn't be having debates with our kids in the aisles of grocery stores and every parent I know has had to do that.'

Saundra Ayala, mother of three young children, knows just how difficult it is to fight the brand appeal of fast food and sugary snacks. Thanks to advertisements, her kids and many of their friends see McDonald's as a fantastic place. They know the jingle. They know about the toys in the kids' meals. So, it's not easy trying to explain why she won't let the family eat there more than once a month. 'I think it would be easier as parents to have your kids eat healthy if you weren't bombarded with ads,' says Ayala.

Food advertising is a central part of many of the free, ad-supported online services offered to kids. Part of the reason is that advertisers know food, like toys, is an area where kids have both purchasing power and sway over their parents' decisions, says Montgomery. Kids between ages 4 and 12 spend over $30 billion annually, according to Juliet Schor, co-author of *Born to Buy: The Commercialized Child and the New Consumer Culture.*

Some marketing practices highlighted by the study include the use of social networks to spur young people to add brands as 'friends' and promote them to actual friends in exchange for free stuff. Such practices can turn kids into brand advocates, giving the brand a social status and identity appeal. And that form of marketing is far more influential than a 30-second TV spot, says Montgomery.

Brands are also implanting their logos where kids spend most of their time, such as with items in virtual worlds. Companies are also drawing kids to their heavily branded sites with interactive games, video-editing software, and music competitions. The report cites Kellogg's promotion of its Pop Tarts pastries on Habbo Hotel, an online virtual community aimed at kids and teens. In exchange for answering a poll asking kids 13-and-over to pick the Pop Tart flavor most like them, respondents were entered to receive virtual furniture for their avatars.

The food companies note that the marketing targeting kids is often less aggressive than most marketing targeting adults. There is a law, the Children's Online Privacy Protection Act, that prevents companies from collecting information on kids in order to target ads more directly to them.

Points for Healthy Foods: Many companies cite additional internal practices they have adopted in order to address concerns about marketing to kids. Kraft says it 'reset its approach to youth advertising' several years ago, stopping all advertisements to kids under 6 and advertising only 'better-for-you' products in all media to kids ages 6 to 11.

The company also includes logos on web pages to encourage kids to go offline and do something active, and provides links to kid-friendly government health sites such as mypyramid.gov. Both McDonald's and Kellogg's say they are working on industry self-regulation initiatives. Kellogg's is a member of the Children's Food and Beverage Advertising initiative, which is 'reviewing website activities,' says Jill Saletta, director of communications for Kellogg Company.

And the companies note that their sites often promote healthy foods, too. General Mills's popular site Millsberry.com, a virtual town for kids, encourages kids to create a buddy avatar. The avatar eats food it buys from the grocery store. Healthier items, such as fruits, vegetables, and whole grains give the avatar more health points and a better mood, which helps it perform better in online competitions, says company spokesman Tom Forsythe.

The FTC could decide that more brands have to promote veggies and other healthy foods on their sites, regardless of whether they sell them or not. Or it could leave the industry to regulate itself in hopes that brands, wary of angering parents with ultimate control over pocketbooks, will limit ads for less-healthy alternatives. Either way, Montgomery says something has to be done to limit the ads and the intake of high-calorie, low-nutritional-value food. 'This is such a rising level of concern and the industry knows it too,' says Montgomery."

Source: Catherine Holahan, "Is Online Marketing Making Kids Obese?" *Bloomberg Businessweek,* May 17, 2007, http://www.businessweek.com/stories/2007-05-17/is-online-marketing-making-kids-obese-businessweek-business-news-stock-market-and-financial-advice.

Please use the ethical decision-making framework to complete the following activities:

1. Analyze McDonald's efforts to market Happy Meals that contain free toys to children.
2. Find a company or organization that you think is using online marketing tools to reduce the trend in childhood obesity. List the website and describe what the company is doing to lessen childhood obesity in the United States.
3. Can online marketers promote healthy choices and still be profitable? Explain your reasoning and provide examples for why or why not.

VIDEO CASE

Please go to *Connect* to access the video case featuring Chipotle that accompanies this chapter.

CAREER TIPS

Marketing Your Future

You have read in this chapter about the importance of understanding what drives purchase decisions for both individual consumers and organizations. Whether your passion is working in a B2C or B2B world, media marketing can be a very rewarding career. As you consider your future, Tracey Rogers, who was featured in the Executive Perspective at the beginning of the chapter, offers some tips that have helped her achieve success in the field of media marketing.

- **Love what you do.** If you do not have passion for a job, it is doubtful that the money you get paid will ever be enough to make you happy. I have found consistently that the best people I hire are people who truly want to be here and enjoy what they do. You have your whole lives ahead of you to work, so make sure you pursue something you are passionate about.

- **Know your audience.** When you are on the job hunt, you should know who your target audience is. You are typically trying to impress people who are older than you and established in their careers. They will often expect certain things from you during the interview process, including large things like a demonstration of what you know about the company to small things like whether your attire is suitable. The better you understand what potential employers expect, the better you will be able to position yourself to win the job.

- **Learn every aspect of media marketing.** The more versatile you are, the more attractive you will be as a team member. Look to develop different skills. If you want to work on the more creative aspects of media marketing, a job in sales is often a great way to get your foot in the door.

- **Pay your dues.** Take on all the tasks that are offered and view every one as an opportunity. Too many young professionals want to stay within the box of their job description. In media marketing, there is always a new challenge or emerging technology that offers opportunities for those who are not afraid to take them on. Some of the best moves of my career occurred when I took on challenges that others did not want and made an impact that my managers noticed. Look for ways to expand your job and you can impress more people.

- **Be a cheerleader for those around you.** This is a lost art in most media companies. We have way too many people who want to take all of the credit and deflect the blame to others. As a manager, I can tell you that this act gets old very fast. A positive person who is great at what they do and can also help and support others will increase their odds of being noticed, respected, and promoted to higher levels of the organization.

CHAPTER NOTES

1. Greg Giroux, "Voters Throw Bums In While Holding Congress in Disdain," *Bloomberg*, December 12, 2012, http://www.bloomberg.com/news/2012-12-13/voters-throw-bums-in-while-disdaining-congress-bgov-barometer.html.

2. Dale Buss, "Ford Thinks It Has a Better Idea about How to Handle Facebook," *Forbes*, May 15, 2012, http://www.forbes.com/sites/dalebuss/2012/05/15/ford-thinks-it-has-better-idea-about-how-to-handle-facebook/.

3. James Montier, *Behavioral Finance: Insights into Irrational Minds and Markets* (Hoboken, NJ: Wiley, 2002).

4. R. W. Belk, "Situational Variables and Consumer Behaviour," *Journal of Consumer Research*, December 1975, pp. 157–164.

5. Leisa Reinecke Flynn, Ronald E. Goldsmith, and Jacqueline K. Eastman, "Opinion Leaders and Opinion Seekers: Two New Measurement Scales," *Journal of the Academy of Marketing Science* 24, no. 2 (1996), pp. 137–147.

6. Alicia Purdy, "10 of the Most Popular Women Bloggers in the U.S.," May 18, 2012, http://www.deseretnews.com/top/701/3/Ree-Drummond-10-of-the-most-popular-women-bloggers-in-the-US-.html.

7. Zsolt Katona, "How to Identify Influence Leaders in Social Media," *Bloomberg*, February 26, 2012, http://www.bloomberg.com/news/2012-02-27/how-to-identify-influence-leaders-in-social-media-zsolt-katona.html.

8. John Voelcker, "2010 Toyota Prius Marketing Theme: Harmony between Man, Nature, and Machine," May 11, 2009, http://www.greencarreports.com/news/1020596_2010-toyota-prius-marketing-theme-harmony-between-man-nature-and-machine.

9. Accenture, "Long-Term Growth, Short-Term Differentiation, and Profits from Sustainable Products and Services," http://www.accenture.com/SiteCollectionDocuments/PDF/Accenture-Long-Term-Growth-Short-Term-Differentiation-and-Profits-from-Sustainable-Products-and-Services.pdf.

10. McKinsey and Company, "2010 Annual Chinese Consumer Study," August 2010, https://solutions.mckinsey.com/insightschina/_SiteNote/WWW/GetFile.aspx?uri=/insightschina/default/en-us/aboutus/news/Files/wp2055036759/McKinsey%20Insights%20China%20-%202010%20Annual%20Consumer%20Study%20-%20EN_d81cb1d7-3a47-4d27-953f-ede02b28da7a.pdf.

11. Ibid.

12. Wayne D. Hoyer, Deborah MacInnis, and Rik Pieters, *Consumer Behavior* (Mason, OH: South-Western Cengage, 2012).

13. Lars Paronen, "Sony Admits PlayStation Privacy Breach," *Reuters,* April 26, 2011, http://blogs.reuters.com/mediafile/2011/04/26/tech-wrap-sony-admits-playstation-network-privacy-breach/.

14. Jim Blythe, *Consumer Behaviour* (London: Thomson, 2008).

15. Ellen Byron, "Bounty Puts a New Spin on Spills," *The Wall Street Journal,* February 17, 2009, http://online.wsj.com/article/SB123482144767494581.html.

16. Abraham Maslow, *Motivation and Personality* (New York: Harper, 1954), p. 236.

17. Zachary Tracer, "Aflac Profit Increases 14% to $892 Million on Investments," *Bloomberg,* April 24, 2013, http://www.bloomberg.com/news/2013-04-24/aflac-profit-increases-14-to-892-million-on-investments.html.

18. John Tierney, "A Match Made in the Code," *The New York Times,* February 11, 2013, http://www.nytimes.com/2013/02/12/science/skepticism-as-eharmony-defends-its-matchmaking-algorithm.html?pagewanted=all&_r=0.

19. Lisa Baertlein, "Dating Site eHarmony Has 436 Questions for You," *USA Today,* June 2, 2004, http://usatoday30.usatoday.com/tech/webguide/internetlife/2004-06-02-eharmony_x.htm.

20. Andrew Adam Newman, "An Emphasis on Fun for Language Learners," *The New York Times,* June 19, 2012, http://www.nytimes.com/2012/06/20/business/media/rosetta-stone-ads-emphasize-fun-not-efficiency.html.

21. Ira Winderman, "Dwyane Wade Miami Beach Fantasy Camp Carries $12,500 Tab," *South Florida Sun Sentinel,* May 11, 2011, http://articles.sun-sentinel.com/2011-05-11/sports/sfl-miami-heat-dwyane-wade-s051111_1_fantasy-camp-youth-camps-website.

22. John C. Mowen and Michael Minor, *Consumer Behavior: A Framework* (Upper Saddle River, NJ: Pearson Prentice-Hall, 2001).

23. AP News, "Miss. Producer Distributor Has Military Contract," *Bloomberg Businessweek,* March 29, 2013, http://www.businessweek.com/ap/2013-03-29/miss-dot-produce-distributor-has-military-contract.

24. Sharon McLoone, "Getting Government Contracts," *The New York Times,* October 7, 2009, http://www.nytimes.com/2009/10/08/business/smallbusiness/08contracts.html?_r=0.

25. Adam Santiarano, "Apple Sales Gain Slowest since 2009 as Competition Climbs," *Bloomberg,* January 24, 2013, http://www.bloomberg.com/news/2013-01-23/apple-s-holiday-sales-miss-predictions.html.

26. Josh Taylor, "Apple's Australian Profit Drops despite AU $6B Revenue," January 29, 2013, http://www.zdnet.com/au/apples-australian-profit-drops-despite-au6b-revenue-7000010462/.

Chapter 6

DEVELOPING YOUR PRODUCT

LEARNING OBJECTIVES

After reading this chapter, you should be able to

LO 6-1 Distinguish among the different types of new products and describe the advantages and risks of each.

LO 6-2 Outline the various stages of new-product development.

LO 6-3 Summarize the major risks in new-product development and discuss ways to reduce those risks.

LO 6-4 Summarize the ethical issues in new-product development.

LO 6-5 Describe the consumer adoption process and explain how types of adopters and the characteristics of a new product affect product diffusion.

LO 6-6 Illustrate the product life cycle and describe its stages and aspects.

EXECUTIVE PERSPECTIVE

Tom Payne
Director of Access Planning
PEG Bandwidth

During college, Tom Payne came to realize that he had a talent for solving problems. After obtaining a degree in applied mathematics at West Point, he put those skills to use as an officer in the United States Army. When he returned to civilian life, Payne took a position as a product analyst for a large telecommunications manufacturer and quickly realized that problem solving was also an essential part of product management and development. Today, as director of access planning at PEG Bandwidth, Tom manages a team made up of representatives from various departments that develops product solutions for the firm's customers, including large wireless companies.

What has been the most important thing in making you successful at your job?

A positive attitude. Again and again I have seen very talented people reviewed poorly and passed over for raises because of their attitude. They either felt the company owed them more than was reasonable, or they did not work well with others. Companies are just groups of people joined in a common activity. Like any group of people, they do not respond well to group members who are arrogant, ill-tempered, or depressing. While people I've worked with in the past may say many different things about me, I don't think anyone would ever say I had a bad attitude.

What advice would you give soon-to-be graduates?

There are a couple of areas that I always like to tell new graduates to think about when entering corporate America. The first is flexibility. When your manager comes to you with a problem no one has solved, that is opportunity knocking. Even if you are hired as a product manager, you may be asked to develop and give presentations to key customers for products you don't actually make, or you may have to step in and take charge of a production line or process. We remember heroes, we forget crowds. The last bit of advice I would give is so obvious, but so few really seem to get it: Use your personal network. There are dozens of companies begging your university for good candidates—use these resources. Also open your eyes to what your friends and relatives do

for a living. A personal introduction or reference is better than sending 500 resumes blindly into some "job bank." Family and friends, professors, university recruiters, and private recruiters are how I would rank the best sources for a great job.

How is marketing relevant to your role at PEG?

Marketing is relevant to every job that anyone has in an organization. Marketing is the key driver to increase revenues and profits, without which it is impossible to have a viable business. To be successful at my job, I have to make product decisions daily that help to determine the satisfaction of our customers. I help our sales team develop solutions that provide a valuable service to our customers and generate profits for our company. I have worked for companies of all sizes across different industries; marketing has been very relevant to every job I have ever held.

What do you consider your personal brand to be?

Companies I've worked for have gone bankrupt, been sold, and been relocated. I have changed jobs several times and had many different titles and responsibilities, but I have never had to look for work. My personal brand has made that possible. I think people who know me and have worked with me understand that I bring two things to the job: attitude and character. No one hires me thinking they will get the smartest telecommunications professional in the business; however, they know they will get a guy who will work hard, treat the company's money like his own, and have a positive attitude about whatever job I'm given. Develop and encourage those traits, and people will want to hire you.

Tom Payne
Director of Access Planning

PEG Bandwidth
http://pegbandwidth.com/

PEG Bandwidth focuses on customizing solutions for wireless carriers through broad partnerships with numerous telecommunications firms.

FORECAST

This chapter explores the importance of developing and managing products, whether it's a good, service, or idea. It is essential that you understand the dynamics of introducing and managing a product, including the most important product that you will ever market: yourself. The chapter discusses the different types of new products, outlines the various stages of the new-product development process, and describes how marketing strategy and consumer adoption change during the product life cycle. As you read through the chapter, consider the following key questions:

1. What makes a product new, and how do I adapt my marketing strategy to the various new-product categories?
2. What is the process for developing a new product?
3. What can go wrong when developing new products?

4. What ethical issues might I face as I develop new products?
5. Why does the type of product I am marketing matter to how fast consumers will choose to buy it?
6. How should my marketing strategy change as a product goes through its life cycle?

LO 6-1

Distinguish among the different types of new products and describe the advantages and risks of each.

WHAT IS A NEW PRODUCT?

For thousands of years people could live their entire lives and only rarely see a new product. In modern times it seems we hear about a new product every day. Several things led to this change.

1. *Faster and more economical transportation.* A millennium ago routes were slow and, at each long and dangerous stage of the journey, goods would change hands at dramatically high prices. Today most cargo spans vast distances with only a modest increase in price and in a dramatically shorter period of time. As late as the nineteenth century a traveler never saw information, goods, or people travel faster than the speed of a horse; today it can take as few as 11 days for a product to cross the Pacific Ocean by ship, hours by aircraft, and almost no time at all if it can be digitized.

2. *Mass production.* Books, for example, used to be copied by hand, greatly limiting the number of copies available to prospective readers. Around 1439, Johannes Gutenberg was the first European to use movable type printing, which allowed books to be mass produced and become much more affordable. With few exceptions, most modern products can be mass produced, which makes them available to many customers as well as more affordable.

3. *The advent of electronic communication.* Consumers can now become aware of new products through television advertising, company web pages, social media, and smartphone apps, among other things. This allows news of a product to spread quickly across the globe. It also allows companies to promote their products and create excitement about them even before they reach the market. Consumers now hold more power because they can access information about products easily, including the product's features, functions, and price versus the competition.

product

The specific combination of goods, services, or ideas that a firm offers to its target market.

A product, the specific combination of goods, services, or ideas that a firm offers to its target market, enriches the lives of consumers by providing designs, features, and functions that people need and want. Goods are tangible products, like a car, with physical dimensions. Services are intangible products, such as a tune-up on the car; they cannot be touched, weighed, or measured. Ideas are also intangible and represent formulated thoughts or opinions. The perfect vacation that the state of Michigan promotes through its "Pure Michigan" marketing campaign is an example of an idea. New goods, services, and ideas are critical to a company's survival in today's marketing environment, which places an ever-increasing emphasis on new, improved, and technologically advanced product offerings.

Many companies have fallen by the wayside because they failed to innovate. Atari, for example, dominated the home video game market in the early- to mid-1980s but lost ground to Nintendo and Sony because of their superior technology.[1] Other companies, such as Hewlett-Packard, must introduce thousands of new products each year to remain an industry leader because digital products become obsolete so rapidly and competition is fierce.

A new product is one that is new to a company in any way. If a product is functionally different from existing products in the market or is not marketed in its current form or manner by the company, it can be considered a new product. We categorize new products in the following four ways:

- New-to-the-market products
- New category entries
- Product line extensions
- Revamped products

We'll discuss each of these in more depth in the sections that follow. A company's core competencies and strengths influence its strategy toward developing new products. Firms that have a strong research and development (R&D) department will focus on developing new-to-the-market products to beat the competition, while firms that have a strong brand and company image can take advantage of existing products to extend or revamp their current product lines with similar but somehow differentiating attributes.

New-to-the-Market Products

Inventions that have never been seen before and create a new market are considered new-to-the-market products. They make up the smallest percentage of new products but carry the most potential (and risk) for the company introducing them. They disrupt the market because they provide innovative benefits that offer so much value to customers that they often render existing products obsolete. This represents tremendous upside potential for firms because getting to the market before competitors do often means increased sales, profits, and customer loyalty,

new-to-the-market products

Inventions that have never been seen before and create a new market.

The Lytro camera reflects Lytro's commitment to heavy investment in its core competence—research and development. The camera has a unique design that allows users to take pictures with one hand. It never needs to be focused and is light and compact.

as well as a leadership position in that market. However, new-to-the-market products can be time-consuming and expensive to develop, creating significant risk for a firm. This is particularly important to note because the vast majority of new products fail, leaving the firm with development costs and no offsetting revenue to compensate for expenditures of financial and human resources. Apple's iPad can be classified as a new-to-the-market product. Apple puts significant resources into R&D in hopes of inventing new-to-the-market products that can put it ahead of competitors. Even after the dot-com bubble burst in 2000, while most Silicon Valley companies cut back or stopped spending money, Apple continued to invest heavily in R&D.[2] Some of the results of this emphasis on R&D are the iPod, the iTunes store, Apple stores, and the OS X operating system.

New Category Entries

new category entries

Products that are new to a company but not new to the marketplace.

New category entries help companies compete better in an already-established market or enter a new market. Entering new markets is very important to businesses because it opens up a whole new set of customers and potentially a great deal more revenue and profits. New category entries are products that are new to a company but *not* new to the marketplace. They are less risky than new-to-the-market products because they don't represent something that has never been sold before, and therefore the company can access information on sales trends, competitor products and prices, location of markets, and so on. However, there is still considerable risk in developing this type of product because the company has little to no experience with it. The Chevy Volt represents a new category entry for General Motors (GM). The Volt is an electric vehicle designed to run almost exclusively on battery power. GM designed the car to compete with fuel-efficient models such as the Ford Fusion Hybrid and Toyota's Prius, both of which have done well in the market. However, GM ran into problems when it tried to market the Volt. First, the car is expensive compared to its competitors—$41,000 at the time of its introduction, which was significantly more than the Fusion or Prius and over $8,000 more than the Nissan Leaf.[3] Second, the Chevy Volt battery had a range of only 40 miles while the Nissan Leaf allowed consumers to drive 100 miles at a time on its battery.[4] In 2012, GM was

The Chevy Volt illustrates the risks involved in developing a new category entry. Though General Motors has been producing cars for over a century, it suffered setbacks when it tried to branch out into the electric vehicle product category.

forced to idle the Volt production line due to slow sales, even though buyers were eligible for a $7,500 tax break from the U.S. government.[5]

Product Line Extensions

Product line extensions add new functions, flavors, or other attributes to an existing product line. A product line is a group of related products marketed by the same firm. Product line extensions are products that extend and supplement a company's established product line. Advantages of a product line extension include that the company and brand may be easily recognized; customers may already feel loyalty to the product line; for goods, manufacturing may be easier and more efficient because the firm already produces similar goods; and the new product can be advertised alongside existing products. Product line extensions are common, especially among companies hoping to offset reduced sales on other products due to seasonality or trends. For example, the Vaseline Intensive Care brand added sun care products to its product line in part due to slower sales of body lotions during the summer months. Product line extensions carry some risk due to uncertainty about how well the new products will be accepted by the market, but overall, they carry far less risk than new-to-the-market products or new category entries.

product line
A group of related products marketed by the same firm.

product line extensions
Products that extend and supplement a company's established product line.

Revamped Products

A new product can sometimes take the form of a revamped product that has new packaging, different features, and updated designs and functions.[6] If you have seen a label claiming a product is new and improved, it falls within this category. Legally, a company can only label a product *new* if, according to the Federal Trade Commission (FTC), the product has been changed in a "functionally significant or substantial respect."[7] Also, the company can only advertise a product as new and improved for six months after it hits store shelves.

revamped product
A product that has new packaging, different features, and updated designs and functions.

Reformulations of current products are a common type of revamped product. For example, laundry detergent companies have begun making concentrated liquids under existing brand names that they claim clean as effectively as their regular line of detergents. The packaging uses less plastic, which has environmental as well as cost implications. Companies save money on materials and need less space to store the finished goods, the products weigh less and are therefore cheaper to ship, and consumers send less plastic to a landfill if they choose not to recycle the package.

Some entrepreneurs intentionally invest in revamping old brands or products because far less money has to be spent on product development and marketing compared to new-to-the-market products or new category entries. Astro Pops serves as an example. In 2004, Spangler Candy stopped making the world famous Astro Pops candy. In 2010, Leaf Brands acquired the rights to Astro Pops, but all the original specialized equipment was sold for scrap before the sale. After almost two years of research and development, Leaf Brands redesigned the manufacturing process to bring back Astro Pops the way consumers remember them.

Because firms base revamped products on existing brands, they carry much less risk than new-to-the-market products or new category entries. In addition to leveraging brand recognition and customer loyalty to existing products, firms can advertise the revamped products along with existing ones and capitalize on the network that already exists to sell the products.

---

connect
|MARKETING

Interactive Assignment 6-1

Please complete the *Connect* exercise for Chapter 6 that focuses on identifying new product categories. By better understanding the different types of new products, you will be able to successfully develop strategies for marketing different goods and services.

THE STAGES OF NEW-PRODUCT DEVELOPMENT

Whatever new product type a firm plans to develop, it will likely follow a formal new-product development (NPD) process similar to the one described in the sections that follow. This process, shown in Figure 6.1, consists of seven stages: (1) new-product strategy development, (2) idea generation, (3) idea screening, (4) business analysis, (5) product development, (6) test marketing, and (7) product launch.

Stage 1: New-Product Strategy Development

In the first stage of the NPD process, the firm establishes a new-product strategy to align the development of products with the company's overall marketing strategy. New-product strategy development involves determining the direction a company will take when (not if) it develops a new product. A new-product strategy accomplishes the following:

- Provides general guidelines for the NPD process.
- Specifies how new products will fit into the company's marketing plan.
- Outlines the general characteristics of the types of products the firm will develop.
- Specifies the target markets to be served by new products.

Some companies use a SWOT analysis and environmental scanning to determine where new products may be able to help strengthen the firm's marketing position. A new-product strategy should include an estimate of the profit the company hopes to make and when the firm can expect the product to be profitable. The same methods for strategy development should be used for goods and services alike. As with goods, the strategy for developing a new service should be tied to overall marketing plans. It should also identify the type of service the company plans to develop as well as the specific target markets to be served.

Due to the globalization of markets and the tremendous opportunities for expanding into established and developing regions of the world, a new-product strategy also should consider the potential benefits and risks involved in bringing new products into international markets. Many multinational firms develop new products for international markets. Some of these products are standardized, while others are individualized for specific markets. For example, Hyundai offers cup holders that fit travel coffee mugs in U.S. versions of its automobiles, while cars designed for the Korean market have cup holders only large enough to hold a Dixie cup. As disposable incomes continue to rise throughout the world, companies that once found it difficult, if not impossible, to sell their products in developing countries are seeing markets open up. As a result, including international opportunities in a new-product strategy is critical for many companies.

FIGURE 6.1   Stages of the New-Product Development Process

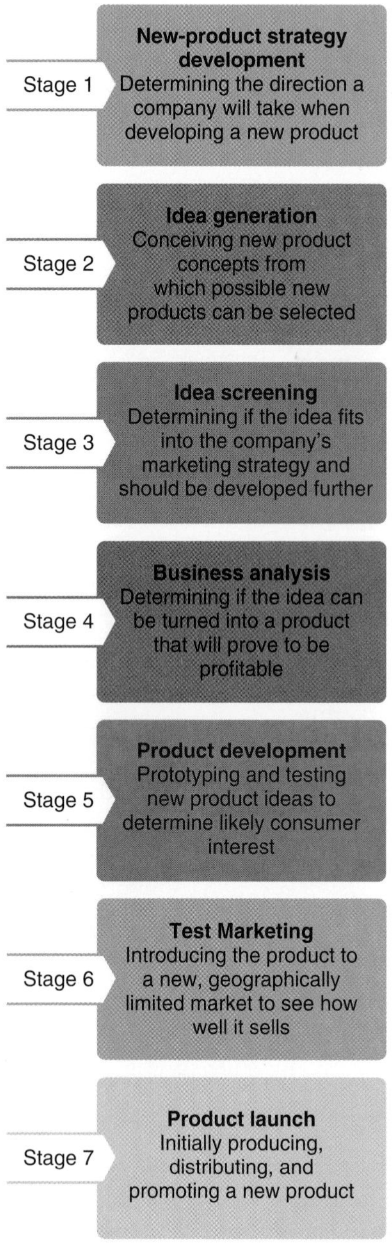

Stage 1
New-product strategy development
Determining the direction a company will take when developing a new product

Stage 2
Idea generation
Conceiving new product concepts from which possible new products can be selected

Stage 3
Idea screening
Determining if the idea fits into the company's marketing strategy and should be developed further

Stage 4
Business analysis
Determining if the idea can be turned into a product that will prove to be profitable

Stage 5
Product development
Prototyping and testing new product ideas to determine likely consumer interest

Stage 6
Test Marketing
Introducing the product to a new, geographically limited market to see how well it sells

Stage 7
Product launch
Initially producing, distributing, and promoting a new product

Stage 2: Idea Generation

Once the firm establishes a new-product strategy, it moves to the second stage of the NPD process, idea generation. Idea generation involves coming up with a set of product concepts from which to identify potentially viable new products. Few of these ideas ever become marketed products. In fact, a firm must generate as many as 100 ideas to find one product that will actually make it to the marketplace.[8]

Internal Idea Generation   Ideas for new products can come from a variety of sources. Some come from company employees. For example, Arthur Fry was an engineer at 3M in its paper products division. He attended a presentation by another engineer, Sheldon Silver, who had developed a weak glue compound. Mr. Fry was not particularly impressed; however, he was a member of his church choir and had a habit of marking the songs to be sung during church service with pieces of paper in his hymnal. The pieces of paper often fell out of the book, leaving Mr. Fry frantically searching for the right hymn. One day, he had an idea: apply Silver's glue to the pieces of paper. The pieces would stick well enough to hold on the book, but they could also be reused for next week's songs. Post-It Notes was born! Smart companies incentivize their employees to suggest new product ideas.

External Idea Generation   Many ideas originate from external sources. Procter & Gamble, for example, gets more than half of its new product ideas from outside the company.[9] Customers can be excellent sources of ideas. Salespeople talk to individual customers as well as business customers like resellers, those closest to the market, on a regular basis; if they ask the right questions, they can acquire feedback on what their customers need and want. Competitors' products also provide an important idea source. Many companies, such as automobile manufacturers, purchase and analyze the new products their competitors offer as a basis for devising similar, but better, alternatives. Similarly, companies developing new ideas for services use existing service offerings from other companies as a basis for creating new services. A number of online dating services, for example, have taken the idea developed by OkCupid of giving singles a "match percentage" to quantify compatibility with prospective dates. Blendr matches singles based on GPS proximity. Research and development departments within a company exist to come up with innovative product ideas for companies, although only a small percentage of new product ideas come from this source. Firms can also outsource their R&D to independent laboratories that provide new product ideas. Outsourcing occurs when a firm procures goods, services, or, in this case, ideas from a third-party supplier rather than from an internal source. Other possible sources of inspiration include suppliers, universities, and independent inventors.

Companies with cultures that value all new product ideas, whatever the source, tend to develop more blockbuster products than companies that are unwilling to search far and wide for sources of innovation. Flexibility can be an asset as well. Sometimes ideas

new-product development (NPD)
The process of conceiving, testing, and launching a new product in the marketplace.

new-product strategy development
The stage of new-product development in which the company determines the direction it will take when it develops a new product.

idea generation
The stage of new-product development in which a set of product concepts is generated from which to identify potentially viable new products.

outsource
To procure goods, services, or ideas from a third-party supplier rather than from an internal source.

Eli Lilly, one of the largest pharmaceutical companies in the world, is among a growing number of industry leaders looking outside the company for new and innovative ideas. Former Lilly executive Jamie Dananberg works with students at Keck Graduate Institute (KGI) as part of a Team Master's Project, a capstone project in which teams of three to six students work with sponsoring companies to solve real problems.

that start out going in one direction can be pivoted, which involves applying an idea in one way, then, if that does not work out, applying it in another way. Pivoting occurs mainly in the mobile and web sectors, where it is possible to quickly and inexpensively develop and change a software product.

Stage 3: Idea Screening

idea screening

The stage of new-product development in which the firm evaluates an idea to determine whether it fits into the new-product strategy.

concept test

A procedure in which marketing professionals ask consumers for their reactions to verbal descriptions and rough visual models of a potential product.

Once one of the sources already described has suggested an idea, the firm evaluates the idea to determine whether it fits into the new-product strategy during the idea screening stage. At this stage, the company often ends up rejecting most new goods and services ideas for one reason or another. Firms may reject products on a number of different bases. Potential issues with product safety may cause a firm to reject an idea for both regulatory compliance and liability reasons. Firms may also want to make sure that the potential product meets their return-on-investment (ROI) requirements. Companies often have a minimum ROI "hurdle" over which a new product must pass to be considered for further development. If the potential revenue generated by the product doesn't meet the minimum requirement, the idea goes no further. It's not unusual to attend product meetings in which the head of the finance department rejects several new product ideas based on such an ROI hurdle.

Idea Screening Questions Beyond ROI requirements, firms should ask (and answer) key questions during the idea screening stage, including the following:

Clorox has established a social media site called *CloroxConnects®* that allows consumers to review and provide feedback on new products, submit ideas of their own, and compete in contests for the best idea to solve company-posed challenges.

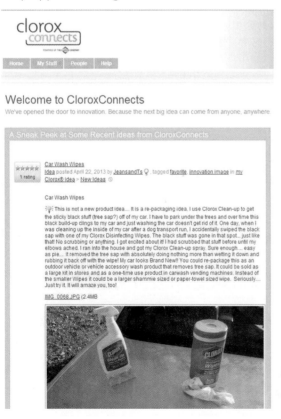

- *Will the product sell?* Companies can often confirm an idea's sales potential through a concept test. In a concept test, marketing professionals ask consumers for their reactions to verbal descriptions and rough visual models of a potential product.
- *Can the product be developed and marketed within the time and budget constraints of the company?* If a lack of resources means the company can't beat the competition to market, the lost sales that may result from being second may render the product less attractive. Additionally, human and financial resources are finite. New ideas must be compared based on the expenditure of these resources. A perfectly good idea may need to be rejected if another new idea that requires the same resources seems more promising.
- *Is the proposed product within the company's ability to produce?* If a new product would require a firm to purchase new equipment, build more space, or establish different processes, the project may be rejected based on the time and uncertainty this could add to the product launch. Again, such considerations often make product line extension and revamped product ideas more attractive than other new product types.

The Role of Social Media in Idea Screening

Organizations increasingly use social media to evaluate potential new products. Social media are especially valuable for small businesses and nonprofit organizations, which typically have less money to spend on the NPD process. Flash Purchase in Charlotte, North Carolina, deployed surveys on various social media platforms to gauge which new product ideas would be of most interest to consumers.[10] Creme Delicious, a dessert boutique in New York City, uploaded pictures of new cake designs to its Facebook page to obtain consumer feedback.[11] Using social media, marketers can engage consumers in helping them screen potential ideas and ensure only those new products that will be best received in the market move ahead in the process.

Stage 4: Business Analysis

Even if a product passes the idea screening step, the firm cannot guarantee that it will be profitable. Though a product may overcome the ROI hurdle, ROI calculations tend to be simple formulations that don't take into account how money changes value over time. Firms must use additional, more complex analysis before they can be reasonably sure that a new product will provide sufficient profitability to make it worthwhile to develop and market. Profitability, measured by subtracting costs (i.e., all the costs to produce and sell the good or service) from revenue (i.e., the price of the good or service multiplied by the number of units sold), can be very difficult to determine, especially if the product is new-to-the-market. To determine profitability, a company must undertake a business analysis, which includes

business analysis
The process of analyzing a new product to determine its profitability.

1. ***Estimating costs.*** Firms must estimate all costs related to the product. To limit costs, firms often try to achieve economies of scale, which allow them to spread the cost of production across a large number of goods thereby reducing the average cost of each. They may also use less expensive components, outsource production and distribution activities to third parties, or find offshore companies that will produce a good or perform a service for less than domestic suppliers. An offshore organization is one that is located or based in a foreign country.

offshore
An organization that is located or based in a foreign country.

2. ***Identifying at what price the product will likely be sold.*** This involves both marketing research and the cost estimates mentioned previously. Marketing research can tell the company what prices customers are willing to pay for the good or service. If customers won't pay a price higher than the cost of developing the product, the company will not make any money.

3. ***Estimating demand for the product.*** This is the tricky part. If the product is similar to ones the company or other companies have marketed already, the company can use an established sales baseline to estimate the sales forecast. When Starbucks came out with its Pike Place Roast coffee, it already had sales data for previous line extensions and therefore could forecast sales of the new flavor. For new-to-the-market products, firms can research the potential size of the market, what customers are willing to pay, market trends, and economic indicators to gauge potential opportunities for, or threats to, future sales of the product.

---

connect **Interactive Assignment 6-2**
|MARKETING   Please complete the *Connect* exercise for Chapter 6 that focuses on business analysis of new products. By better understanding the tools for projecting revenues and costs, marketers will have a more complete picture of the likelihood that a new product will be profitable.

Honda designers develop prototypes, such as the one of a sedan in the photo on the left, at the company's research and design center in Tokyo. They use such prototypes to ensure that Honda can efficiently build the production version of its cars, including the Honda Insight shown in the photo on the right.

Stage 5: Product Development

product development

The stage of new-product development at which a firm determines that the good can be produced or the service can be offered in a way that meets customer needs and generates profits.

prototype

A mockup of a good, often created individually with the materials the firm expects to use in the final product.

Once a firm feels confident that the new product will generate a profit for the company, it enters Stage 5 of the NPD process. In the product development stage, the firm determines that the good can be produced or the service can be offered in a way that meets customer needs and generates profits. For a good, the company may create a prototype based on previous concept testing. A prototype is a mockup of the good, often created individually with the materials the firm expects to use in the final product. Prototype tests ensure that the product will not be a hazard to users or their families, that it can be produced in the company's or supplier's manufacturing facilities, and that it can be manufactured at a cost low enough to generate profits.

If the firm is developing a new service rather than a good, it may use this stage to establish protocols for training employees, identify the types of equipment needed, and determine the staffing required to provide the service. The marketing department should also begin developing a marketing strategy during this stage. Regardless of whether the product is a good or service, the product development stage of the NPD process can be long and costly, which is another reason only a small number of ideas make it this far in the process. Once the firm determines that it can feasibly offer the product, it moves to the next stage of the process: test marketing.

Stage 6: Test Marketing

test marketing

Introducing a new product in its final form to a geographically limited market to see how well the product sells and get reactions from potential users.

A product that makes it past the product development stage is ready to be tested more fully with potential customers. Test marketing involves introducing a new product in its final form (which may be different from the prototype) to a geographically limited market to see how well the product sells and get reactions from potential users. The company selects test markets based on how well they mirror the overall target market in terms of demographics, income levels, lifestyles, and so on. The selection of test markets is critical to ensuring that the results of the test will be representative of the sales the company can expect. An example of an inappropriate test market would be selecting an area that has a very high population of retired persons to test how well a new video game will sell. Some cities are regularly selected for test sites because they reflect the demographics of the nation as a whole, including Albany, Syracuse, and Rochester, New York; Greensboro and Charlotte, North Carolina; Birmingham, Alabama; Nashville, Tennessee; and Eugene, Oregon.

During the test marketing stage, the firm tests not only the product itself but also the marketing strategy related to it. The marketing department may simultaneously try different approaches in different test markets to see which marketing mix approach works best. For example, an airline might offer more leg room in certain sections of the airplane at a higher price in one region while offering no luggage fees for first- and business-class customers in another region to see which service offering generates the most seat upgrades.

simulated test markets

A procedure in which the firm builds a mock shopping experience for participants to observe their response to marketing stimuli.

product launch

Completing all the final preparations for making the fully tested product available to the market.

Risks of Test Marketing
Although test marketing can be valuable, there are downsides. First, the process is expensive. Second, it can be time-consuming. For example, Unilever established a test market for one of its products, a Nordic shampoo called Timotei. The test market was extensive, involving multiple test sites and thousands of samples, and lasted more than a year. After expending a great deal of money and resources the company determined that the product had little chance of making a profit in the U.S. and dropped it from the NPD process. A third risk to test marketing is that firms open themselves up to imitation from competitors, which can diminish the advantages of being first to market.

Economical Test Marketing Options
Some companies use less costly means for test marketing. Simulated test markets, in which the firm builds a mock shopping experience for participants to observe their response to marketing stimuli, can be used to introduce a new product. Simulated test markets often show potential consumers advertisements for the new product and its competitors and ask consumers to choose between the firm's product and competing products. Online test marketing represents another test marketing tool. In an online test market, firms sell consumers sample products that are unavailable in stores through their websites, allowing the firm to keep costs down while still obtaining valuable information. Test marketing can keep firms from potentially wasting money before they know what the consumer reaction to the product will be and allow them to fine-tune their marketing plan as they prepare to launch the product.

Stage 7: Product Launch

Once the firm feels the product is ready for the market, it enters the final stage of the NPD process. The product launch involves completing all the final preparations for making the fully tested product

EXECUTIVE PERSPECTIVE

Tom Payne
Director of Access Planning
PEG Bandwidth

What is the step in the product development process that companies get wrong more than any other?

I would say test marketing, for a couple of reasons. First, test marketing is expensive and companies try to pinch pennies and reduce test marketing times or locations, which is usually a big mistake. As a product manager, you want to be very sure that your product will be successful before you launch it across the country and throughout the world. Too many marketers end up saving a little money by reducing their test market expenses, only to lose significantly more money by rolling out a product that fails in a larger market.

The other reason surrounds processes. It is the responsibility of product managers to make sure the processes are in place for the product during the test marketing phase. They should have clear guidelines for how the product is packaged, billed, priced, and serviced. It should be very clear within the organization which specific people or groups are responsible for every one of these items. Unfortunately, too many companies and product managers lack the attention to detail to get this right which causes more problems down the road.

available to the market. At this stage, the firm may undertake any or all of the following activities:

- Purchasing the materials to make and package the good.
- Hiring employees, such as bank tellers, to provide the service.
- Manufacturing enough of a good to fill the distribution pipelines and to store as inventory for continuing distribution, or building enough capacity to provide a service for the expected level of sales of that service.
- Strategically placing the good in warehouses in preparation for customer orders.
- Preparing internal systems for taking service orders.
- Training new employees on how best to deliver the service.

Firms must carefully plan the product launch to ensure that the product hits the market according to schedule; still, even the best efforts to plan a product launch can be disrupted by unforeseen problems or those beyond the control of the company. Numerous product launches have been delayed because suppliers could not deliver on time, consumer demand was unexpectedly high, or goods couldn't be released due to quality problems, among other things. In 2012, BlackBerry (formerly Research in Motion) announced that its BlackBerry 10 smartphone launch would be delayed by several additional months after two years of development because the company failed to get the final version of the new phones to U.S. carriers on time.[12] Delayed product launches often cost companies a great deal of money in overtime labor and shipping charges.

The launch stage of the NPD process is usually the most expensive stage for new products. To minimize the cost implications and smooth out production levels and marketing activities, some companies release new products to geographic areas in a gradual manner. But firms take a risk by proceeding slowly with product launches. The speed with which a company launches a product, or the product's time to market, can be extremely important, especially when it comes to high-tech products. Being the first company to market a new product can mean the difference between success and failure.

time to market

The speed with which a company launches a product.

Boeing's 787 Dreamliner provides an extreme example of the price of a delayed product launch. The unexpected additional costs of a three-year delay due to design and supply chain problems seriously impacted the company's near-term sales opportunities.[13]

Interactive Assignment 6-3
Social Media in Action

Social media are becoming increasingly powerful tools for new product launches. In just a couple of months, Unilever's Clear shampoo and conditioner went from anonymity to a product line that had consumers across the U.S. talking largely because of social media. Clear's social media–heavy product launch drew hundreds of thousands of consumers into conversation about the new product. Consumers were encouraged to go to the brand's Facebook page and order a free sample of the product. Marketers created a celebrity-driven web mini-series called "Best Night Ever" that featured people using the new product. Twitter hashtags specifically for the product launch helped bridge the conversation across multiple social media platforms and spread positive opinion more quickly.

The Social Media in Action *Connect* exercise in Chapter 6 will let you develop social media strategies to enhance a new product launch. Product launches occur at practically every company, making it important for you to consider ways to utilize all of the available social media tools to make each product launch as successful as possible.

Source: See Doren Bloch, "Top 5 Product Launch Lessons from Clear Hair Care's Big Debut," *Forbes*, July 12, 2012, http://www.forbes.com/sites/yec/2012/07/12/top-5-product-launch-lessons-from-clear-hair-cares-big-debut/.

Sequential versus Concurrent New-Product Development

The advantage a firm gains by being first to the market with a new product often depends on whether it follows a sequential or concurrent path when developing the product. Sequential new-product development utilizes a progressive sequence in which functional areas consecutively complete their development tasks. In a sample sequential path, the idea for a new product might be generated in marketing, passed on to R&D for prototype development, and then tested by manufacturing to see if it can be produced efficiently. This approach can help a firm control complex and risky projects by ensuring that it performs only one set of activities at a time, and the project can be easily tracked. However, sequential NPD can also be time-consuming. Since the product can only progress along one development path, a delay in one area holds up the whole process. Because of the importance of time to market, the sequential approach may prevent the product from achieving its full potential.

On the other hand, there is an alternate process. Concurrent new-product development uses cross-functional teams made up of representatives from various departments to develop goods and services. This is the approach most supply chain management professionals prefer. Teams typically include members from R&D, manufacturing, marketing, engineering, and purchasing and can also include suppliers and customers. In a concurrent approach, company departments complete tasks simultaneously rather than passing the product on after individual tasks are completed, so a problem that occurs in one area does not necessarily affect the overall project timeline. However, concurrent NPD can be more difficult to control and create more tension between departments than the more traditional sequential approach. For goods such as high-tech electronics,

sequential new-product development

New-product development that utilizes a progressive sequence in which functional areas consecutively complete their development tasks.

concurrent new-product development

New-product development that uses cross-functional teams made up of representatives from various departments to develop goods and services.

TABLE 6.1   Sequential versus Concurrent New-Product Development

Sequential New-Product Development	Concurrent New-Product Development
Advantages	*Advantages*
Company has more control over development of complex products.	Delays in one area do not hold up work in other areas.
Company can track project progress more easily.	Input from all areas happens throughout the process.
	Problems may be recognized earlier in the process.
Disadvantages	*Disadvantages*
It can be time-consuming.	It is more difficult to control.
It can be inefficient.	It may create tension between functional areas.
Delays in one area hold up work in other areas.	

the speed of a concurrent NPD process will likely outweigh the risk of any such issues. Table 6.1 outlines the advantages and disadvantages of the two processes. In the next section, we'll discuss some of the other risks involved in NPD.

LO 6-3
Summarize the major risks in new-product development and discuss ways to reduce those risks.

RISKS IN NEW-PRODUCT DEVELOPMENT

Firms that want to maintain or improve their competitive position in the marketplace generally must develop new products. Failure to do so carries tremendous risk, particularly for companies that develop products that quickly become obsolete. However, NPD does not come without its own risk to a company. Table 6.2 identifies some of these risks, where they fall in terms of severity, and what the consequences of the risks are to firms.[14] Companies need to understand both the types and severity of risks and how to mitigate those risks if they are going to succeed in introducing new products to the marketplace.

Categorizing Risks in New-Product Development

The highest level of risk occurs when products fail to generate sales or prove to be dangerous and defective. These risks can be devastating to a company if they permanently damage the firm's image or create legal liabilities, such as in the case of loss of life or injury to customers. Mattel had to recall over 18 million toys in 2007 due to lead in the paint and poorly designed magnets.[15] The recall severely damaged Mattel's image and resulted in a fine from the U.S. government. Beyond this, the firm lost sales and incurred the additional costs of removing the products from the marketplace and compensating consumers.

Organizations face significant risks when marketing new products internationally. Issues with product quality, supply, or marketing mix can lead to missed launch dates, dissatisfied customers, excessive returns, and lost profits. For example, Nokia's launch of its Lumia smartphone met with poor sales in some parts of the world, such as the Middle East, Africa, and Asia, because of a marketing mix issue: The prices that Nokia was charging were too high for most people in those regions.[16] As a result, Nokia had to substantially lower its prices to compete with rivals like Samsung, which sells less expensive models and has been catching up to Nokia as the world's largest maker of phones by volume.

Reducing Risks in New-Product Development

Companies can reduce the risk of new product failures by doing the following:

1. *Listening to the customer carefully.* The voice of the customer should always help guide idea generation and screening in a company because customer needs and wants drive purchasing.
2. *Making a commitment to the NPD process.* Every stage of the NPD process must be followed for the process to work correctly. Companies trying to launch a poorly conceived or executed product just to get a jump on the

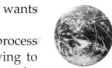

Introducing new products to international markets comes with added risks for firms, as Nokia's launch of the Lumia demonstrated. Nokia was forced to cut prices substantially after launching the product because it set the original price too high for consumers in the Middle East, Africa, and some parts of Asia.

TABLE 6.2 New-Product Development Risks and Related Outcomes

Severity of Risk	Types of Risk	Outcomes
Very high	Product fails to meet needs and wants of customers.	Costs are not recouped; company loses money.
	Product proves to be dangerous or defective.	Company suffers legal liabilities and product recalls.
High	Quality is not up to customer standards.	Customers are dissatisfied and there are excessive returns.
	Supply of product is inadequate to meet demand.	Company loses orders, sales, and customers.
	New product is not accepted well in the marketplace.	Company loses revenue and profits and is stuck with obsolete goods.
	Inadequate supply of materials delays production.	Product launch is delayed; first-to-market advantage is lost.
	Target price is not accepted by the market.	Company reduces price, meaning lost revenue and profits.
Moderate	Supplier cost savings are not achieved.	Profitability is reduced.
	Product takes sales from existing products.	Total company revenue and profits are less than expected.
	Competitors copy products and sell them at a lower price.	Company loses market share and profits.

market or to generate quick profits are likely to damage their brand image as well as lose money.

3. ***Understanding current market trends and anticipating changes in the market.*** Gathering data requires a commitment to both marketing and technical research. A firm must stay on top of changing economic, demographic, cultural, and technological conditions so it can anticipate market demand over time.

4. ***Asking the right questions.*** Some questions a firm should ask include: What is the expected demand for the good or service over time? How much will it cost to produce and distribute the good or service at varying levels of demand? What level of quality will be required for the product to be competitive? Are there any potential environmental and safety issues? What is the best pricing strategy to apply at the launch of the product?

5. ***Being willing to fail on occasion.*** Companies that develop new products sometimes will fail. However, firms must learn from past failures. Learning should come not only from products that failed after launch but also from those that failed along the NPD process.

 Interactive Assignment 6-4

|MARKETING   Please complete the *Connect* exercise for Chapter 6 that focuses on identifying risk levels for new products. By better understanding the risk factors, you will be able to judge which new products to develop.

Firms that take steps to reduce risk in new-product development, particularly by analyzing and learning from mistakes, are well positioned to see their new products adopted by consumers. Later in the chapter, we'll discuss the consumer adoption process. First, we'll discuss the ethical implications of new-product development and how ignoring ethical issues can also be risky for firms.

LO 6-4

Summarize the ethical issues in new-product development.

ETHICAL ISSUES IN NEW-PRODUCT DEVELOPMENT

Another type of risk that a company needs to be aware of in NPD is creating an ethical problem that may hurt the company's image. Several ethical issues can arise as firms develop new products.

- The most common ethical issue involves the FTC's definition of the term *new*. Firms may make only minor changes to a product and then try to claim that it is changed in a "functionally significant or substantial respect." Such actions result not only in ethical issues but also in legal issues if the FTC disagrees with the company's viewpoint.

- Ethical issues can also arise if a company chooses not to develop important new products until an existing product has become obsolete or its patent has expired. For example, pharmaceutical companies typically put a lot of resources into developing a drug and need many years of sales to recoup their development expenditures. As a result, they may want to hold off marketing new drugs until they've paid for development of an existing drug. Keeping new drugs out of the marketplace protects a company's stockholders and ensures that the company has sufficient funds to invest in

Marketers must ensure that revamped products that are introduced to the market as new and improved fit the Federal Trade Commission's definition of the term *new*.

new R&D. At the same time, however, the company could be holding back important innovations that may improve, and possibly save, lives.

- A third ethical issue related to new-product development is planned obsolescence. Planned obsolescence occurs when companies frequently come out with new models of a product that make existing models obsolete. An example is the projection TV. Companies were still producing projection TVs even though they were planning to launch flat screen plasma and liquid crystal display (LCD) TVs that they knew consumers would favor. Ethical issues aside, such behavior may damage a company's relationships with its business customers and potentially with individual consumers as well. However, there is a difference between planned obsolescence and products that change frequently due to changes in technology. People want the latest and greatest technology, which forces companies to constantly upgrade the functionality of their products to keep up with the competition. While this may mean that the Apple iPhone you carry is two generations old, it does not mean that Apple has used planned obsolescence as a strategy. In the world of high technology, Apple is simply doing what it must to maintain or gain market share.

planned obsolescence

A practice in which companies frequently come out with new models of a product that make existing models obsolete.

PRODUCT ADOPTION

When a consumer purchases and uses a product, the product has been adopted. The process through which a product is adopted and spreads across various types of adopters is called diffusion. Marketers who understand diffusion—how their new products are likely to be adopted, the rate at which they will be adopted, and the process through which their products will spread into markets—will have a better chance of successfully launching and sustaining new products. Diffusion gives marketers a way to figure out who will likely buy their product over a period of time, plan an appropriate marketing mix, and forecast potential sales.

Earlier in the chapter, we discussed the new-product development process. Customer adoption of new products also follows a process. The consumer adoption process includes the following five stages.[17]

1. *Awareness.* In this stage, the consumer has been exposed to the product and knows that it is available on the market.
2. *Interest.* Interest occurs when the product registers as a potential purchase in a consumer's mind and he or she begins to look for information concerning the product.
3. *Evaluation.* In the third stage, the customer thinks about the product's value and whether to try it out. The customer evaluates competing products as well to determine which product best satisfies his or her needs and wants.
4. *Trial.* In the trial stage the consumer tests or uses the product to see if it meets requirements. Trials include things like test driving an automobile, borrowing a new shampoo from a friend, or signing up for 30-day access to Hulu's online streaming services.
5. *Adoption.* In the final stage, the consumer buys and uses the product.

Adoption happens at different times depending on the type of adopter.

Types of Adopters

Customers, whether individual consumers or business customers, buy and use a new good or service at different times and at different rates following product launch. When a firm launches a new product, only a few people buy and use it, but

LO 6-5

Describe the consumer adoption process and explain how types of adopters and the characteristics of a new product affect product diffusion.

diffusion

The process by which new products are likely to be adopted, the rate at which they will be adopted, and the process through which the products will spread into markets.

consumer adoption process

The process by which customers formally accept and purchase products.

FIGURE 6.2   Percentage of Each Type of Adopter

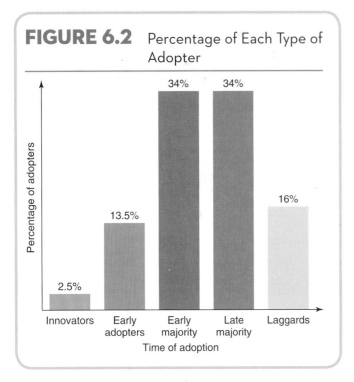

as word spreads, consumers purchase the product at an increasing rate for a period of time. Eventually, sales hit a peak and start to diminish. During this time period, various types of adopters purchase the product. We can group these types of adopters into five categories: innovators, early adopters, early majority, late majority, and laggards. Figure 6.2 shows the approximate percentage of the population that falls into each adopter category.

Innovators   Approximately 2.5 percent of those who adopt a product do so almost immediately after the product is launched. These people are called innovators. If you are always one of the first people you know to try a new product, you probably fall into this category. Innovators tend to be younger and more mobile than those who adopt a product later in the diffusion process. They are often obsessed with the idea of newness and unafraid to take risks when it comes to trying new products. In addition, they tend to be very knowledgeable, have higher-than-average incomes, possess self-confidence, and choose not to follow conventional norms. While only a small number of purchasers fit into this category, firms value innovators because they share information about the product with others, which can help the product gain market acceptance.

innovators

A category of consumer that adopts a product almost immediately after it is launched.

early adopters

A category of consumer that purchases and uses a product soon after it has been introduced, but not as quickly as innovators.

Early Adopters   Early adopters comprise roughly the next 13.5 percent of adopters after innovators. Early adopters purchase and use a product soon after it has been introduced, but not as quickly as innovators. They tend to conform to group norms and values more closely than innovators and have closer ties to social groups and their communities. Though they adopt products earlier than the remaining categories, unlike innovators, they wait for product reviews and further information concerning new products before purchasing them. Early adopters are typically well respected by their peers, and marketers seek to gain their acceptance because they tend to be opinion leaders who are willing to talk to other people about their experiences with their purchases. These individuals are therefore important to the diffusion of a new product.

Early adopters not only help marketers spread the message about a product to the rest of the population, they also provide valuable feedback to marketers about their products.

Early Majority   The next category of adopters comprises approximately 34 percent of the adopters of a new product. The early majority is careful in their approach, gathering more information and spending more time thinking about the purchasing decision than the previous two categories. Typically, by the time the early majority buys a product, more competitors have entered the market, so this group will have some choice as to which product to buy. Members of the early majority generally are not opinion leaders themselves, but they often are associated with such leaders. If this group does not purchase the product, the good or service will likely fail to be profitable. The early majority also serves as a bridge to the next group of adopters: the late majority.

Late Majority   The late majority also comprises about 34 percent of adopters. Members of the late majority tend to be cautious about new things and ideas. They often are older than members of the previous three categories and may not act on a new product without peer pressure. They often rely on others for information, buying a good or service because their friends have already done so. Members of this group tend to be below average in income and education. When the late majority purchases a product, the product has typically achieved all it can from a market in terms of profitability and growth.

Laggards   The final category of adopters is the laggards. These customers make up about 16 percent of the market. Laggards tend to be conservative and do not like change; they may remain loyal to a product until it is no longer available for sale. Laggards are typically older and less educated than members of the other four categories.[18] Many choose not to use the Internet. They tend to be tied to tradition and are not easily motivated by promotional strategies. In fact, marketers may never convince laggards to buy their good or service, making them a group on which marketers should not expend a great deal of time or effort. Individuals who have no access to the Internet are examples of laggards who will not be using Amazon as a source from which to buy products.

Product Characteristics

Categories of adopters aren't the only thing that affects the diffusion of a new product. New product characteristics, including the following, also impact the adoption rate.

- *Competitive advantage.* A product obtains a competitive advantage over competing products if consumers believe it has more value than other products in its category. If a product has a competitive advantage, it will be adopted quickly. The Apple iPhone had a competitive advantage over the original BlackBerry because its operating system used icons, which users were familiar and comfortable with.
- *Compatibility.* Compatibility refers to how well a new product fits into potential customers' needs, values, product knowledge, and past behaviors. For example, a new beer will not be a compatible product in countries that frown on alcoholic beverages due to religious taboos.
- *Observability.* When people can see others using a product and perceive value in its use, the product will diffuse quickly. Some products are naturally more visible than others. For example, consumers can observe others using smartphones in many public places, including restaurants, stores, and on the street. Personal products such as Banana Boat suntan lotions, on the other hand, are not as easily observed, and how well they work can be difficult to confirm.
- *Complexity.* Typically, the easier it is to understand and use a product, the faster it will diffuse. If the market finds a new product too difficult to use, as happened with the first video cassette recording (VCR) devices, sales often will not increase until the product is simplified. In the case of the VCR, the addition of on-screen programming made it possible for the average user to follow directions for recording a television show. The effect of complexity may

early majority
A category of consumer that gathers more information and spends more time deciding to make a purchase than innovators and early adopters.

late majority
A category of consumer that relies on others for information, buying a good or service because others have already done so.

laggards
A category of consumer that does not like change and may remain loyal to a product until it is no longer available for sale.

competitive advantage
The superior position a product enjoys over competing products if consumers believe it has more value than other products in its category.

High-end digital single lens reflex cameras with a multitude of functions like the Nikon D3100 might not be adopted quickly by the average consumer, but if the firm targets camera enthusiasts willing to spend the time to learn how to use the camera's features, the product can still be successful.

differ between regions of the world. In industrialized societies, consumers are exposed to and use more technologically complex products and therefore may accept and even desire intricate products that offer additional features.

- *Trialability.* Most of the time, products that consumers can try without significant expense will diffuse more quickly than others. For example, a GPS phone app like GPS Drive that costs 99 cents will diffuse a lot faster than a stand-alone GPS device costing $50. Similarly, consumers may adopt a product they are first exposed to through trial sizes, free-sampling programs, and in-store trials (e.g., taste testing food).

The rate at which a product is adopted based on its characteristics and the consumer adoption process influences the length of the product's life cycle, which we'll discuss in more depth in the next section.

THE PRODUCT LIFE CYCLE

LO 6-6

Illustrate the product life cycle and describe its stages and aspects.

product life cycle (PLC)

The series of stages a product goes through from the time it is launched into the market until the time it is removed from the market.

introduction stage

The stage of the product life cycle that occurs after the firm launches the product into the marketplace and innovators begin to buy it.

The launch of a new product begins that product's life. Just like humans, products go through various stages that mark their lifespan. This series of stages is called the product life cycle (PLC). Figure 6.3 illustrates the five stages of the PLC and the implications of the various stages on sales and profits during the life of a product. During the new-product development process, which the chapter has focused on up to this point, the product is actually costing the company money. Once the product is introduced to the market, sales increase slowly as the firm's marketing activities begin to raise awareness of the product. The growth stage brings a spike in sales and profits as consumers recognize the product's ability to satisfy their needs and wants. Sales and profits begin to drop in the maturity stage as competition increases and customers begin to look for the next big thing, then fall off completely during the decline stage.

We will discuss the introduction stage through the decline stage of the PLC in more depth in the sections that follow.

Introduction

Once the firm launches the product into the marketplace and innovators begin to buy it, it has entered the introduction stage of the PLC. This stage is characterized by few or no competitors if the product is new to the market, but sales are typically slow because customers are not yet accustomed to the product. If the firm is first to market, it may be able to capture a large percentage of the market early, giving it advantages in economies of scale and brand recognition. Also, if the product is a good, the company may be able to monopolize the capacity of available suppliers, making it more difficult for other companies to get supplies of components from which to make the product. However, due to the high cost of developing, advertising, manufacturing, and distributing a new product, profits are often low or negative at this point in the PLC. During this phase, the firm attempts few refinements. Firms tend to produce basic models until the product's sales improve to the point at which the product is profitable. Sales typically increase slowly, and companies may need to

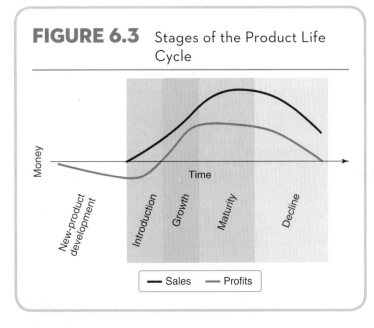

FIGURE 6.3   Stages of the Product Life Cycle

Money / Time

New-product development — Introduction — Growth — Maturity — Decline

— Sales   — Profits

Misti McCollum

Membership Marketing Specialist
Girl Scouts of Arkansas, Oklahoma and Texas

Misti McCollum
Membership Marketing Specialist

Girl Scouts of Arkansas, Oklahoma and Texas
http://www.girlscoutsdiamonds.org/

Girl Scouts of Arkansas, Oklahoma and Texas is a youth organization for girls focused on building character and self-esteem and encouraging community service.

Describe your job. My main job function is to recruit girls and adult volunteers into the Girl Scouts organization and to market recruitment events that will appeal to girls in kindergarten through twelfth grade. My other duties include volunteer management, community and public relations, and strategic implementation of events and programs in my assigned territory.

Describe how you got the job that you have. As my college graduation day approached, I applied for many jobs. I really do not recall applying for my job with Girl Scouts but when I received the call, I thought of it as a blessing. I had no specific plans to work for a nonprofit, but, by keeping my mind and options open, I found a wonderful opportunity to begin my career in marketing.

What has been the most important thing in making you successful at your job? I would definitely have to say the most important aspect of my success is great people skills. A positive attitude provides the basis for developing good people skills.

What advice would you give soon-to-be graduates? An internship in your field of study is very beneficial to your future. I completed a marketing internship for a local small business during my senior year that really helped me to develop my skills and understand what is expected of a marketing professional. Take time to seek and apply for any opportunities for hands-on experience that you can while you are in college. Don't wait until your graduation day approaches to apply for jobs. Start at the beginning of your last semester and make sure you seek out people and resources that can help you.

What do you consider your personal brand to be? My personal brand is lending a helping hand for the betterment of our youth. My personal experience makes me who I am! I am a single mother who cares about the world my daughter will grow up in. That makes me strive to do all I can to help the youth of today.

offer incentives to stores to get them to carry the product, thus limiting distribution. New services may require similar incentives. Companies might offer their customers a low introductory price to interest them in the service.

A number of factors influence how long the introduction stage lasts, including the product's relative advantage, the amount of resources the company puts into promoting the product, and the effort required to educate the market about the product's attributes. For example, high definition televisions moved slowly through the introduction stage; smartphones, on the other hand, moved quickly.

Growth

growth stage

The stage of the product life cycle characterized by increases in sales, profits, and competition.

Early adopters, followed by the early majority, begin to buy the product during the growth stage. Sales begin to rise, as do profits, as companies begin to take advantage of economies of scale in purchasing, manufacturing, and distribution. Competitors enter the market, which forces prices down. During this stage, the firm has to promote the differences between its brand and the competition's and may attempt to refine aspects of the product by improving quality or adding new features. Also during this phase, a company typically tries to focus its marketing efforts on showcasing the competitive advantage of its product over others. Although promotional costs will still be substantial due to these efforts, they generally drop from the high levels of the introduction phase. The firm also must concentrate on building the distribution of the good or service to increase market share. This is accomplished through intense efforts to enlist dealers, distributors, and retailers to carry the good or an expansion of the service distribution network through additional locations or personnel. If the product satisfies the market, repeat purchases help make the product profitable, and brand loyalty begins to develop.

Maturity

maturity stage

The stage of the product life cycle during which the firm focuses on profitability and maintaining the firm's market share for as long as possible.

In the maturity stage of the PLC, late majority and repeat buyers make up an increasing percentage of the customer base. The main objectives of the maturity stage are profitability and maintaining the firm's market share for as long as possible. Sales level off as the market becomes saturated and competition becomes fierce. Companies not doing well will drop out of the market. Marketing costs rise due to competition as each firm tries to find ways to gain market share. The firm may need to make large promotional expenditures to show the differences between the firm's product and the competition and feel pressure to reduce prices. As a result, profits typically begin to decline during this stage. If the product is a good, the company begins to offer more versions in different styles and with different features. It also may continue to improve the good's quality and performance features, which requires adjustments to the marketing mix to accommodate more product options. Price reductions, more effective advertising, and trade promotions may be used to generate demand. Promotion to resellers often increases during this stage to entice them to continue to buy the company's product rather than a competitor's. Customer service and repairs begin to take on significance and can serve as a source of differentiation from competing products. Services also attempt to differentiate themselves from competitors during this stage. For example, the airline industry promotes service quality through things like on-time deliveries, more favorable cancellation policies, and early boarding options. The maturity stage is usually the longest stage of the PLC.

Decline

The decline stage of the PLC is preceded by a falling off of sales and profits. Depending on the product, the decline in sales may be rapid or could occur over a long period of time. During the decline stage, competitors drop out of the market as the product becomes unprofitable. The firm will likely cut prices to generate sales, curtail advertising, eliminate unprofitable items from the product line, and reduce or eliminate promotion to individual consumers and resellers. Little or no effort is put into changing a good's appearance or functionality at this stage since consumers have moved on to other types of products. The good usually becomes obsolete at this point, and the firm may sell it off to discount retailers, such as Odd Lots. Coupons or buy-one-get-one-free promotions may be used to prolong sales and reduce existing inventories. If the firm keeps the product active, it may put little effort into selling or advertising it. At this point the firm must decide whether to discontinue the product, reposition it, or find a niche market that may be small but profitable. For example, travel agency services are in far less demand than they were a generation ago, before travelers could research and book and plan trips online. In response, many travel agencies have shifted their focus from general consumer markets to niche markets, such as horseback-riding trips in South America or wine-tasting tours in Europe. Such trips generate limited demand but can still earn profits for the agency.

New material technology in fly rods made bamboo rods much less attractive due to the superior performance of graphite and boron, yet the market for bamboo rods still exists. Though an R.L. Winston bamboo rod can cost $3,000, aficionados of this type of rod continue to purchase them even though more effective rods cost less.

decline stage
The stage of the product life cycle characterized by decreases in sales and profits.

ASPECTS OF THE PRODUCT LIFE CYCLE

Once firms understand the stages of the PLC, they can tailor the marketing mix for their new products appropriately at each stage.

Estimate the Length of the Product's Life

As a first step, marketers should estimate the length of the product's life, taking into account marketing research and analysis of any similar competitive products. For example, Apple could have used data from its personal computer products to estimate the PLC of an iPad model since the products have many similarities and possibly many of the same customers. Product life cycles can be of varying lengths, depending on the type of product. Technology-driven products like computers tend to have a short PLC because of rapid changes in computing power and features. Other products may remain viable in the marketplace for decades. For example, Wells Fargo has been offering banking services since its founding in 1852 and continues to be one of the largest suppliers of mortgage financing in the second decade of the twenty-first century. One general trend in marketing is that product life cycles are getting shorter. In addition to technology changes, which rapidly make products obsolete, firms now introduce new products at a faster rate, which pushes existing products into the mature and decline stages faster.

Organizations can combat shortening life cycles by developing a product mix that consists of various products at different stages of the PLC. A firm's product mix comprises all of the products that it sells. For example, Bank of America's product mix includes a variety of services—checking and savings accounts, credit cards, student banking, and online and mobile banking. The new mobile banking service might be the introduction stage, while basic savings accounts might, at the same time, be in the decline stage. Each of these items within the product mix provides Bank of America's marketers with unique opportunities. The new mobile banking product might include features and technology that create value for busy,

product mix
The combination of all of the products a company sells.

tech-savvy consumers, while a basic savings account, though in the decline stage, still allows marketers to serve more traditional consumers as well as young consumers who might be opening their first bank account and could develop a life-long relationship with Bank of America.

Project the Shape of the PLC Curve

high-learning products

Products that take longer for consumers to see the benefits of or that do not have a good infrastructure in place to support them.

low-learning products

Products with benefits customers can easily see.

fad product

A product that is very popular for a relatively short amount of time.

fashion product

A product that comes in and out of favor with consumers.

As a second step, firms should project the shape of the PLC curve for their product. Figure 6.4 shows four common PLC curves. Products that take longer for consumers to see the benefits of (e.g., the personal computer when it was introduced for home use), or that do not have a good infrastructure in place to support them (e.g., electric automobiles), will have a curve with a long, flat-shaped introductory and growth phase. These are called high-learning products. Products with benefits customers can easily see are called low-learning products. Low-learning products have a curve that is steep through the maturity phase. An example of a low-learning product is a free checking account at a local bank. A fad product, one that is very popular for a relatively short amount of time, will have a steep up-and-down curve as consumers rapidly adopt and then abandon the product. The Koosh ball is an example of a fad product that quickly gained then lost its appeal to the market. A fashion product comes in and out of favor with consumers. Men's hats were fashionable for decades but lost their appeal in the 1960s, only to recently start becoming fashionable again. Fashion life cycles typically last longer than fad products but are short compared to high-learning and low-learning product curves. Some companies, like athletic clothes manufacturer Lululemon Athletica, manage their new items with a short life cycle in mind. Lululemon Athletica comes out with new colors and seasonal items that have 3-, 6-, or 12-week life cycles to make its stores seem very up-to-date and fresh.

Understanding the PLC and its implications impacts how marketing professionals manage the marketing mix for products. In the next section, we'll discuss

Electric cars like the Tesla Model S are high-learning products because it takes longer for consumers to evaluate the benefits of owning one.

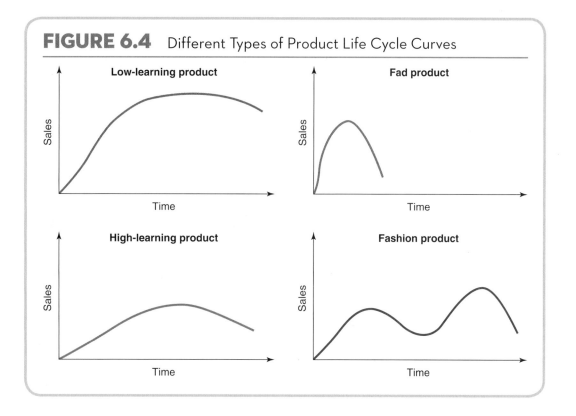

FIGURE 6.4   Different Types of Product Life Cycle Curves

how firms can modify their marketing mix strategies in response to what stage of life a product is in.

Implications for the Marketing Mix

Just as our interest, activities, and abilities change as we enter various stages of our life, the stage of a product's life has many implications for how a firm markets the product.

- Product strategies typically change from a small number of models or service offerings in the introductory stage, to an expanded number in the growth stage, to a full line of products in the maturity stage, then to a reduction in the number of models or service offerings during the decline stage so that only the best-selling products remain.
- Place (distribution) strategies generally include a change from limited distribution in the introductory phase, to an extensive number of distribution channels, to a reduction in the number of distribution channels as the product loses profitability.
- Promotional strategies usually involve making customers aware of the product and its attributes in the introductory stage, intensive advertising that stresses how the product differs from the competition in the growth stage, reminding consumers about the product and its value to them in the maturity stage, and minimal efforts or none at all in the decline stage.
- Price is usually higher in the introductory phase due to lack of competition and high launch costs, then starts to fall in the growth stage as competition becomes more intense. The price continues to fall through the maturity stage, when a firm must defend its market share, then levels out in the decline stage.

Table 6.3 lists the typical strategies a firm undertakes for each of the four Ps, depending on where the product is in its life cycle.

TABLE 6.3 Typical Marketing Mix Strategies during a Product's Life Cycle

Stage	Product Strategies	Place Strategies	Promotion Strategies	Price Strategies
Introduction	Small number of models	Limit distribution; attract channel partners	Promote to develop customer awareness	Price high
Growth	Variety of models; many modifications	Intensive effort to expand distribution	Promote to build awareness; increase personal selling	Price begins to fall as competition arrives
Maturity	Full line of products	Intensive effort to maintain distribution	Promote to point out brand attributes and differentiating features	Price equal or below competitors
Decline	Reduce number of products based on profitability	Phase out unprofitable outlets	Reduce promotion to a minimum or eliminate	Price to maintain small profit; can increase if product appeals to niche market

SUMMARY

LO 6-1 Distinguish among the different types of new products and describe the advantages and risks of each.

A new product is one that is new to a company in any way. If a product is functionally different from existing products in the market or is not marketed in its current form or manner by the company, it can be considered a new product. New products can be placed into the following categories: (1) new-to-the-market products, which are inventions that have never been seen before and that create a new market, (2) new category entries, which involve the introduction of products new to a company but *not* new to the marketplace, (3) product line extensions, which are products that extend and supplement a company's already-established product line, and (4) revamped products, which are existing products that have been changed in some way.

LO 6-2 Outline the various stages of new-product development.

The new-product development process consists of seven steps: (1) new-product strategy development involves determining the direction a company will take when (not if) it develops a new product; (2) idea generation involves coming up with a set of product concepts from which to identify potentially viable new products; (3) idea screening involves evaluating the idea to determine whether it fits into the new-product strategy; (4) business analysis is undertaken to determine profitability; (5) product development confirms that the product can be made in a way that meets customer needs and generates profits; (6) test marketing involves introducing a potential new product to a geographically limited market; and (7) product launch involves making the product available to the market.

LO 6-3 Summarize the major risks in new-product development and discuss ways to reduce those risks.

Failing to develop new products carries tremendous risk for companies, particularly those with products that quickly become obsolete. However, NPD comes with its own risks, including that the product will prove to be dangerous and defective or that the product will produce less-than-expected cost savings. Companies can reduce the risk of new product failures by doing the following: (1) listening to the customer carefully, (2) making a commitment to the NPD process, (3) understanding current market trends and anticipating changes in the market, (4) asking the right questions, and (5) being willing to fail on occasion.

LO 6-4 Summarize the ethical issues in new-product development.

Several ethical issues can arise as firms develop new products. The most common ethical issue involves the FTC's definition of the term *new*. To be called new, the product must be changed in a "functionally significant or substantial respect." Ethical issues can also arise if a company chooses not to develop important new products until an existing product has become obsolete or its patent has expired. A third ethical issue is planned obsolescence. Planned obsolescence occurs when companies frequently come out with new models of a product that make existing models obsolete.

 LO 6-5 Describe the consumer adoption process and explain how types of adopters and the characteristics of a new product affect product diffusion.

Product adoption includes the following five steps: (1) awareness, (2) interest, (3) evaluation, (4) trial, and (5) adoption. Adoption happens at different times during a product's lifespan, depending on the type of adopter buying the product. The characteristics of a new product, such as its relative advantage and complexity, also impact its diffusion rate, or how quickly the various categories of customers will adopt it.

 LO 6-6 Illustrate the product life cycle and describe its stages and aspects.

There are five stages in a product's life cycle: (1) product development, (2) introduction, (3) growth, (4) maturity, and (5) decline. Once the product is introduced to the market, sales increase slowly as the firm's marketing activities begin to raise awareness of the product. The growth stage brings a spike in sales and profits as consumers recognize the product's ability to satisfy their needs and wants. Sales and profits begin to decline in the maturity stage as competition increases and customers begin to look for the next big thing, then fall off completely during the decline stage. The length of a product's life and the shape of its PLC curve depend on whether the product is a high-learning product or a low-learning product.

KEY TERMS

business analysis (p. 167)
competitive advantage (p. 177)
concept test (p. 166)
concurrent new-product
    development (p. 171)
consumer adoption process (p. 175)
decline stage (p. 181)
diffusion (p. 175)
early adopters (p. 176)
early majority (p. 177)
fad product (p. 182)
fashion product (p. 182)
growth stage (p. 180)
high-learning products (p. 182)
idea generation (p. 165)

idea screening (p. 166)
innovators (p. 176)
introduction stage (p. 178)
laggards (p. 177)
late majority (p. 177)
low-learning products (p. 182)
maturity stage (p. 180)
new category entries (p. 162)
new-product development
    (NPD) (p. 165)
new-product strategy
    development (p. 165)
new-to-the-market products (p. 161)
offshore (p. 167)
outsource (p. 165)

planned obsolescence (p. 175)
product (p. 160)
product development (p. 168)
product launch (p. 169)
product life cycle (PLC) (p. 178)
product line (p. 163)
product line extensions (p. 163)
product mix (p. 181)
prototype (p. 168)
revamped product (p. 163)
sequential new-product
    development (p. 171)
simulated test markets (p. 169)
test marketing (p. 168)
time to market (p. 170)

MARKETING PLAN EXERCISE

In this chapter we talked about developing successful products. The next step in developing your personal marketing plan is to provide a concise description of the product you are offering the company or graduate school program you seek—you. Think through the SWOT analysis you completed in Chapter 2, and develop a two-paragraph personal product offering. Your description should focus on the specific value you would bring to the firm or graduate school. Think of the description as your elevator pitch, or 30- to 60-second description of the value you would bring to an organization. Formalizing this in your personal marketing plan will also help you identify specific jobs that match the skill sets that you offer. Your pitch might include answers to the following questions:

- What makes you different from other potential employees?
- Why is the company or graduate program better *with* you than *without* you?
- How do your skills and background fit into what the organization wants to do?

Your Task: Write a two-paragraph product description of yourself that you can read or present in less than 60 seconds. The description should highlight your value to a potential organization or graduate school. You only have a limited amount of time, so choose your words carefully to ensure they create the maximum impact.

DISCUSSION QUESTIONS

1. Assume that you are the vice president of marketing for a consumer packaged goods company like Procter & Gamble, one that produces everyday items at a low price. Your marketing team has expressed a desire to revamp one of its brands to appeal to younger buyers. Develop a list of questions to determine the risks and rewards this revamping strategy poses for the company.
2. Select a product, either a good or service, that you consider to be in the decline phase of the PLC. Discuss some of the options the company has for dealing with this product. What do you think is the best option, and why do you think so?
3. Discuss the advantages of a concurrent NPD process over a sequential process. What impact will a concurrent NPD process have on time to market, profits, and brand image? What are some of the issues a company might face when using a concurrent process?
4. Which product characteristics influence the length and shape of a product's PLC? What changes might a company make in its product design to lengthen its life cycle?
5. Assume you are in charge of the business analysis stage of a company's NPD process. What data will you need to collect to make an informed decision about whether product development should continue? What elements of bias might exist from the data you receive from the marketing department?

SOCIAL MEDIA APPLICATION

Pick a new product that has been launched in the past three months. This could be any type of new product, from a new menu item at a fast food restaurant to a new video game. Analyze how the organization has used social media to launch its new product using the following questions and activities as a guide:

1. How has the company used social media to make customers aware of the new product?
2. Explain what you like or dislike about how the company is using social media to promote the product.
3. If you worked in marketing at the company, what two specific suggestions would you have about how the company could use social media more effectively?

ETHICAL CHALLENGE

Consider a company that markets a men's cologne and aftershave product. Marketing has decided that the brand needs a makeover and determined that a product revamp would be a good way to generate excitement about the brand, which used to be a big seller but now looks as if it's headed toward the decline phase of the product life cycle. The company plans to redesign the label, deepen the color of the bottle to distinguish it from the older version, and reformulate the product by increasing its scent. The product will be re-launched with a new-and-improved sticker on the front of the bottle. Please use the ethical decision-making framework to answer the following questions:

1. Who are the stakeholders impacted by this decision, and how might they be affected?
2. Assume you are the vice president of marketing and have the final say as to whether the product will be advertised as new and improved. Would you feel comfortable making that claim?
3. What other changes could be made to the product to support the company's new-and-improved claim?

VIDEO CASE

Please go to *Connect* to access the video case featuring EA Sports that accompanies this chapter.

CAREER TIPS

Marketing Your Future

You have read in this chapter about the importance of developing your product. Good product managers are rare—they seldom want for work and they earn a good living. As you consider your future, Tom Payne, who was featured in the Executive Perspective at the beginning of the chapter, describes some of the intangible characteristics that good product managers share.

1. *A Positive Attitude.* What most of us learned in grade school is true: Attitude *is* everything. No one likes to work around a naysayer. If the product manager doesn't believe in the product and the outcome, who will? I have never known a sour, sarcastic, negative product manager; well, I have, but they don't stay in product marketing long.

2. *Responsibility.* Good product managers run toward problems not away from them. They understand that they are responsible for making sure that every task is identified and every issue is considered and resolved. They never say, that's not my job. That does not mean they do everything themselves. They just ensure that process problems are not ignored or passed around.

3. *Financial Understanding.* Why do companies hire product managers to create and manage products?

To make money of course! No matter what your product is, you will be expected to deliver it on time and on budget. As your product matures it will be expected to produce revenue for the company; if you are a "good" product manager, it will produce profits. Yes, products need to be of good quality and they need to work, but I have seen plenty of good products fail because they did not sell.

4. *Aptitude for Learning.* This is a hard one to say but dumb people don't make good product managers (nor do lazy people). As a product manager, you are often, by definition, creating something new. If you are developing a new product, you are both creating the questions (How will we do this? What should it look like? How should we package it?) and finding the answers. There are seldom easy answers and no one person you can go ask. So how do you answer these questions? You're the product manager, go figure it out! (That's probably what your boss will say when you ask her—at least, that's what mine said to me.)

5. *Understand Software Is a Tool Not a Solution.* Project management software is both a blessing and a curse. So many product management professionals believe that if they just put all the data into their planning software and check all the boxes, that will get the job done. Does buying MS Word write your term paper? Software organizes data, it helps track dates and budgets, but it does not create profitable products.

CHAPTER NOTES

1. Julianne Pepitone, "Atari U.S. Files for Bankruptcy but Plays On," *CNNMoney*, January 21, 2013, http://money.cnn.com/2013/01/21/technology/atari-bankrupt/index.html.

2. Justin Scheck and Paul Glader, "R&D Spending Holds Steady in Slump," *The Wall Street Journal*, April 6, 2009, http://online.wsj.com/article/SB123819035034460761.html.

3. Peter Whoriskey, "Chevy Volt Will Cost $41,000," *The Washington Post*, July 27, 2010, http://www.washingtonpost.com/wp-dyn/content/article/2010/07/27/AR2010072703364.html.

4. Ibid.

5. Bernie Woodall, Paul Lienert, and Ben Klayman, "GM's Volt: The Ugly Math of Low Sales and High Costs," *Reuters*, September 10, 2012, http://www.reuters.com/article/2012/09/10/us-generalmotors-autos-volt-idUSBRE88904J20120910.

6. Lisa McQuerrey, "Objectives of Revamping a Product," *Houston Chronicle*, n.d., http://smallbusiness.chron.com/objectives-revamping-product-50406.html.

7. Federal Trade Commission, *Code of Federal Regulations*, Title 16, Volume 1, Part 500, Rev. January 1, 2000.

8. Adam Bryant, "In the Idea Kitchen, Too Many Cooks Can Spoil the Broth," *The New York Times,* November 24, 2012, http://www.nytimes.com/2012/11/25/business/nottingham-spirks-co-presidents-on-cultivating-new-ideas.html?_r=0.

9. Lydia Dishman, "How Outsiders Get Their Products to the Innovation Big League at Procter & Gamble," July 13, 2012, http://www.fastcompany.com/1842577/how-outsiders-get-their-products-innovation-big-league-procter-gamble.

10. Melinda Emerson, "Using Social Media to Test Your Idea before You Try to Sell It," *The New York Times,* August 3, 2012, http://boss.blogs.nytimes.com/2012/08/03/using-social-media-to-test-your-idea-before-you-try-to-sell-it/.

11. Ibid.

12. Will Connors, "RIM's BlackBerry Delay Hits Stocks," *The Wall Street Journal,* June 28, 2012, http://online.wsj.com/article/SB10001424052702304058404577495013601177508.html.

13. David Fickling and Susanna Ray, "Boeing Loses Qantas Order for 35 Dreamliners after Delays," *Bloomberg,* August 23, 2012, http://www.bloomberg.com/news/2012-08-22/qantas-airways-has-first-annual-loss-as-fuel-costs-rise.html.

14. Omera Khan, Martin Christopher, and Bernard Burnes, "The Impact of Product Design on Supply Chain Risk: A Case Study," *International Journal of Physical Distribution and Logistics Management* 28, no. 5 (2008), pp. 412-432.

15. Louise Story and David Barboza, "Mattel Recalls 19 Million Toys Sent from China," *The New York Times,* August 15, 2007, http://www.nytimes.com/2007/08/15/business/worldbusiness/15imports.html?pagewanted=all&_r=0.

16. Kalyan Parbat, "Nokia to Lower Lumia Prices in India," *The Times of India,* February 18, 2013, http://articles.timesofindia.indiatimes.com/2013-02-18/strategy/37159401_1_lumia-range-nokia-plan-stephen-elop.

17. Jim Blythe, *Consumer Behaviour* (London: Thomson Learning, 2008), p. 284.

18. Wayne D. Hoyer and Debra MacInnis, *Consumer Behavior* (Mason, OH: South-Western Cengage Learning, 2008), p. 424.

Chapter 7

SEGMENTING, TARGETING, AND FINDING YOUR MARKET POSITION

LEARNING OBJECTIVES

After reading this chapter, you should be able to

LO 7-1 Explain the importance of effective market segmentation.

LO 7-2 Describe the four bases for segmenting markets.

LO 7-3 Summarize the elements of international market segmentation.

LO 7-4 Discuss the criteria for successful market segmentation.

LO 7-5 Describe the strategies for selecting target markets.

LO 7-6 Compare the most common target marketing strategies.

LO 7-7 Summarize the ethical issues in target marketing.

LO 7-8 Outline the three steps of effective market positioning and explain why firms may choose to use repositioning strategies.

EXECUTIVE PERSPECTIVE

Cornelius Lovelace
Executive Director
Fitness Bootcamp Unlimited

Although Cornelius Lovelace majored in biology and physical therapy in college, he soon discovered that marketing would be essential to achieving his goals of building a successful business and helping others. At Fitness Bootcamp Unlimited, Lovelace and his team help people across multiple age and income segments live healthier lives by positioning their services to meet their clients' specific goals. While numerous competitors offer similar services, Fitness Bootcamp Unlimited has succeeded by finding the right potential customers; tailoring its message, which emphasizes personal training and health education; and then providing a high-quality service that keeps clients coming back.

What has been the most important thing in making you successful at your job?

I would say listening and caring about my clients' goals. We are in the business of helping people sustain their health by eating better and exercising. I believe that customers of almost any business know when you genuinely care about them and when you are only providing lip service to that idea and don't really care. If you don't put your customers first, they will find a company that will.

What advice would you give soon-to-be graduates?

If word-of-mouth communication is the best form of advertising, make sure the word about you and your business is good, true, and honest! Every new professional should understand that customers are going to talk to friends, family, and often the world through Facebook, Twitter, or product reviews. Every consumer can potentially say something that will help or hurt your business, and business people must focus on making every single customer experience the best it can be. Good, true, and honest word-of-mouth advertising is perhaps the most powerful marketing tool, and negative reviews can be the most damaging.

How is marketing relevant to your role at Fitness Bootcamp Unlimited?

I am always marketing our business. I think this is true of most small businesses. I am always looking for ways to promote our company and share our message with potential customers. Every small decision, from our website design to what our business cards look like, represents an important marketing decision we have to make.

What do you consider your personal brand to be?

I like to say, teamwork makes your dream work! I think a big part of my personal brand is that I can work with a wide range of people effectively to drive results for our business and our clients. The best organizations are places where people work together to harness their talents and make the whole organization greater than the sum of its parts.

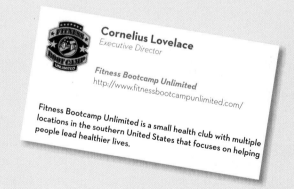

Cornelius Lovelace
Executive Director

Fitness Bootcamp Unlimited
http://www.fitnessbootcampunlimited.com/

Fitness Bootcamp Unlimited is a small health club with multiple locations in the southern United States that focuses on helping people lead healthier lives.

FORECAST

This chapter explores the importance of market segmentation, targeting, and positioning. You are highly unlikely to achieve marketing success trying to be all things to all consumers. Your ability to effectively segment and target specific markets with a positioning strategy that appeals to those targeted consumers is at the heart of marketing. This chapter discusses the bases for segmenting markets, the criteria for successful market segmentation, and strategies for targeting and positioning your organization's products. As you read through the chapter, consider the following key questions:

1. What is market segmentation and how does it affect marketing success?
2. How can I divide the marketplace into manageable parts?
3. How does international market segmentation differ from domestic market segmentation?
4. What makes a segment a viable option for me to target?

5. What strategies should I use when targeting where I want to work after college?
6. What strategies can I use to reach my target market?
7. Which target markets are most likely to create ethical challenges?
8. How am I positioning myself for the career that I want?

LO 7-1

Explain the importance of effective market segmentation.

market segmentation

The process of dividing a larger market into smaller groups, or market segments, based on meaningfully shared characteristics.

Thoughtful market segmentation allows Five Guys Burgers and Fries to enjoy success serving only a limited number of menu choices that it knows will satisfy its target market.

MARKET SEGMENTATION

The days of one-size-fits-all mass marketing are largely over. Marketers who try to be all things to all people typically end up serving no one well. Imagine going into a restaurant with 85 items on the menu, featuring everything from hamburgers to pasta to sushi. You may suspect that a restaurant offering such a wide range of diverse choices does not prepare any of them very well. Compare this strategy with that of restaurant chain Five Guys Burgers and Fries, which has consistently offered a very limited menu. Potential customers have a wide variety of tastes and preferences, but Five Guys focuses on serving what works best for its specific business. When Five Guys opened, people asked for coffee, so the company's restaurants began to serve it. Unfortunately, the young people working at the restaurants did not know anything about coffee. It tasted terrible, and Five Guys became concerned that negative word-of-mouth communication would hurt its core business. The restaurants stopped serving coffee. Five Guys tried a chicken sandwich once, too, but took that off the menu as well when sales failed to materialize. The menu does include hot dogs, which have been profitable, but other than that, all you can get at Five Guys Burgers and Fries is . . . burgers and fries. It has become the fastest growing restaurant chain in North America serving a limited menu of quality food.[1]

Rather than trying to offer a menu where every potential consumer can find something, Five Guys has chosen to segment the market and provide the best possible product to its target market. Market segmentation is the process of dividing a larger market into smaller groups, or market segments, based on meaningfully shared characteristics. Market segments are the relatively homogenous groups of consumers that result from the segmentation process. Market segmentation plays an important role in the success of almost every organization in the U.S. and throughout the world. There are over 7 billion people in the world with different needs and wants that are impossible to attract with a single marketing mix. Market segmentation helps firms like Five Guys navigate these various needs and wants in three major ways:

market segments

The relatively homogenous groups of consumers that result from the segmentation process.

1. Market segmentation helps firms define the needs and wants of the customers who are most interested in buying the firm's products. Five Guys customers typically pay more and wait longer than they would at other fast food hamburger restaurants.[2] The restaurant's target market values taste, freshness, and quality and is therefore willing to pay a premium for a more "gourmet" hamburger experience.

2. Market segmentation helps firms design specific marketing strategies for the characteristics of specific segments. This allows firms to increase revenues by gaining a much larger share of the market segments they target. For example, since the marketing department at Five Guys understands its customers' needs and wants, it is able to develop promotional campaigns and advertisements that focus on high-quality, fresh products rather than lower prices or quicker service, which are not high priorities for the targeted segment. Five Guys has capitalized on this knowledge, even using signs that urge people to seek their burgers elsewhere if they're in a hurry.[3] Such tactics reinforce that Five Guys focuses on preparing the best possible burger for customers rather than simply trying to get everyone through the line.

3. Market segmentation helps firms decide how to allocate their marketing resources in a way that maximizes profit. By understanding the needs and wants of its market segment, Five Guys has been able to funnel resources toward more profitable markets, such as those in which hamburgers and fries are purchased more often and those with higher family income levels like northern Virginia and Dallas, Texas.

Marketers use numerous variables to segment the market, which we can group into four main categories: demographic, geographic, psychographic, and behavioral.

SEGMENTATION BASES

Marketers use segmentation bases, which are characteristics of consumers that influence their buying behavior, to divide the market into segments. These bases help firms develop customer profiles that highlight the similarities within segments and the dissimilarities across segments. Figure 7.1 shows the four broad bases of segmentation—demographic, geographic, psychographic, and behavioral—and specific variables within each that can be used to segment the market. Each of the four bases is described in more detail in the sections that follow.

LO 7-2

Describe the four bases for segmenting markets.

Demographic

Companies divide markets using characteristics such as age, gender, income, education, and family size to achieve demographic segmentation. Age and gender are the most commonly used demographic variables because they are often the easiest to identify. A marketer does not have to be very skilled to recognize whether someone is young or old, male or female.

demographic segmentation

Segmentation that divides markets by characteristics such as age, gender, income, education, and family size.

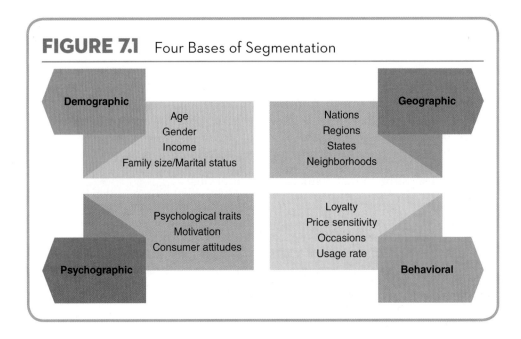

FIGURE 7.1   Four Bases of Segmentation

Demographic
- Age
- Gender
- Income
- Family size/Marital status

Geographic
- Nations
- Regions
- States
- Neighborhoods

Psychographic
- Psychological traits
- Motivation
- Consumer attitudes

Behavioral
- Loyalty
- Price sensitivity
- Occasions
- Usage rate

If less obvious information is required, firms can find demographic information that may be useful for market segmentation in a number of places. One of the most important is the U.S. Census Bureau. Small businesses and other organizations often have a very limited marketing research budget. For them, websites like www.census.gov, which provides large amounts of market information for free, are an increasingly valuable tool. The Census Bureau's website provides marketers with information such as the net worth and asset ownership of households segmented by race, education, age, and occupation.

Age   Age is an especially valuable segmentation tool in areas such as food, housing, and health care because older Americans spend significantly more than younger consumers. The median age for residents of the U.S. is the highest in the history of the country, providing marketers with expanding market segments of older Americans for their products that represent billions of dollars in potential sales.[4] Older consumers typically have two things that most of their younger counterparts do not: time and money. However, today's older consumers are not the same as older consumers from previous generations. Older consumers today want to stay active in retirement and seek out ways to look and feel younger.[5] Firms that develop marketing strategies for things like anti-aging products and natural and organic foods have found success appealing to older market segments. Products ranging from Viagra to Botox to Whole Foods have generated profits for their organizations by marketing the idea of youth to an aging population.

Marketers also have success targeting young consumers. For example, McDonald's developed a strategy focused on children whose appetites have outgrown Happy Meals. McDonald's marketing research found that children between ages 8 and 10 had growing appetites and didn't want to order a "little kids meal." In response, the company introduced Mighty Kids Meals. The meals offer this slightly older segment expanded menu choices and larger portions. McDonald's has been able to take existing products and repackage them in a way that appeals to kids at a variety of ages and helps drive additional revenues for the company.

Segmenting by age doesn't just help marketers develop a strategy aimed at a single age group, it also allows them to adapt their strategy to target multiple age segments with the same product. For example, Disney Cruise Line has developed strategies to appeal to consumers of varying ages. Young children are attracted to the cruise as a magical adventure where they get to meet their favorite characters, while teenagers like the unique interactive entertainment options that are just for them. Older consumers enjoy the food, scenery, and reduced physical toll of going on a cruise compared with walking long distances through a large amusement park. Disney marketers have successfully offered a single cruise vacation that members of multiple age segments feel is designed just for them.

Gender Men and women, of course, each make up approximately half of the U.S. population, and gender is a valuable segmentation variable for products ranging from clothing to soft drinks to medications. Marketers are also expanding beyond traditional gender segmentation as new trends shift marketing dollars away from male- or female-oriented marketing to try to appeal to both genders. For example, marketers for home improvement store Lowe's recognized that women were becoming an increasingly large part of their customer base but were largely being ignored by their promotional strategies. In an effort to target female consumers, Lowe's introduced a new line of Martha Stewart products and other home decor items such as mood lighting and chrome toilet paper holders.[6]

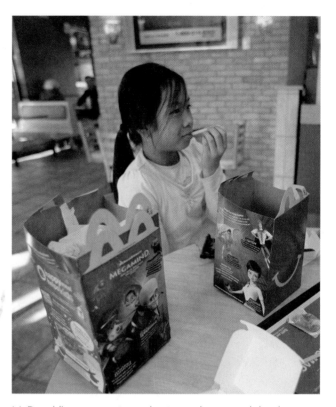

McDonald's segments its market in part by age and develops products that effectively target each age group it identifies, from Happy Meals for children, Mighty Kids Meals for older kids, and the Dollar Menu that appeals to high school and college students with limited cash flow.

Gender segmentation is evolving for younger consumers as well. After targeting boys almost exclusively for more than 20 years, Lego introduced the Lego Friends line for girls when marketing research showed that girls enjoyed playing with Legos in a distinctly different way than boys. The segmentation strategy has worked well and the Lego Friends line, which features pastel colors and sets that involve building cafes rather than battleships, has sold twice as much as the company originally anticipated.[7]

Income Income affects consumers' ability to buy goods and services and provides marketers with a valuable segmentation tool. For example, the demand for wealth management and financial planning services in the U.S. has risen dramatically in recent decades. Firms like Merrill Lynch target American households that are considered *mass affluent*, that is, those that have between $100,000 and $250,000 in investable assets.[8] Mass affluents are one of the fastest growing segments in the U.S. and many need the type of financial planning that Merrill Lynch offers. By segmenting the market in this way, Merrill Lynch can tailor its global investment advice and professional money management services to best meet the needs of these targeted consumers. Merrill Lynch now has over 11 million customers between its consumer banking and global wealth and investment management units.[9]

Family Size and Marital Status Family size and marital status can be helpful demographic segmentation tools. A company might discover that married individuals will pay higher prices than single individuals, or that single customers purchase a certain product more frequently than married customers do. A jewelry store can target married customers with promotions for anniversary bands, for

Family size can provide a good market segmentation tool for homebuilders like Lennar, which has developed a new type of home called Next Gen—The Home Within a Home that includes additional space for long-term guests, extended family, or adult children.

geographic segmentation

Segmentation that divides markets into groups such as nations, regions, states, and neighborhoods.

example, and target unmarried women with right-hand rings, which are often worn as a signal of independence.

In recent years, the size of families living under one roof has increased as more college-age students move back home and more adult couples take care of their elderly parents. Marketers at major U.S. homebuilders like Lennar hope to appeal to these larger family units by building and promoting houses that come with additional rooms or garage apartments with a separate entrance.[10]

Geographic

The value consumers place on a product can vary greatly by region. For this reason, marketers often find it helpful to segment on the basis of geography. Geographic segmentation divides markets into groups such as nations, regions, states, and neighborhoods. Marketers pay special attention to local variations in the types of goods and services offered in different geographic regions. A Walmart located near the beach in Southern California might sell surfboards to meet demand for a popular local sport. It is doubtful that a similarly sized Walmart store in Denver, Colorado, will offer surfboards due to the geographical differences. Walmart marketers empower local managers to stock products that are most appropriate for their local community.

Market Size The size of a market is an important geographic segmentation tool. IKEA marketers prefer to locate new stores in areas where at least 2 million people live within a 60-mile range.[11] This type of geographic segmentation requires information about the entire market, beyond just a city or county. The U.S. Census Bureau divides cities and urbanized areas into Metropolitan Statistical Areas (MSA), which are free-standing areas with a core urban population of at least 50,000. IKEA marketers generally target their stores to the largest MSAs in an attempt to reach the volume of consumers they desire. Figure 7.2 shows the 10 largest MSAs in the United States and all of the cities and areas that are included in each.

Customer Convenience Segmenting by geography also allows marketers to capitalize on convenience to the customer. Cracker Barrel Old Country Store® has developed a successful restaurant and retail business across the United States by locating its stores in convenient geographic locations. A major component of the Cracker Barrel Old Country Store marketing strategy has been to place locations along interstate highways. Consumers have almost come to expect a Cracker Barrel at major exits, especially in the southern United States. Travelers make up approximately one-third of the Cracker Barrel guest base, so statistics like miles driven and the percentage of people who travel mostly by automobile affect Cracker Barrel's revenue. In regions of the country where more families drive to their vacation destination, Cracker Barrel does particularly well. Cracker Barrel marketers have built on the need for traveler convenience by implementing

FIGURE 7.2   Ten Largest Metropolitan Statistical Areas in the U.S.

Rank	Core City	Metro Area Population	Metropolitan Statistical Area	Region
1	**New York City**	19,831,858	New York-Newark-Jersey City, NY-NJ-PA	Northeast
2	**Los Angeles**	13,052,921	Los Angeles-Long Beach-Anaheim, CA	West
3	**Chicago**	9,522,434	Chicago-Naperville-Elgin, IL-IN-WI	Midwest
4	**Dallas**	6,700,991	Dallas-Fort Worth-Arlington, TX	South
5	**Houston**	6,177,035	Houston-The Woodlands-Sugar Land, TX	South
6	**Philadelphia**	6,018,800	Philadelphia-Camden-Wilmington, PA-NJ-DE-MD	Northeast
7	**Washington, D.C.**	5,860,342	Washington-Arlington-Alexandria, DC-VA-MD-WV	South
8	**Miami**	5,762,717	Miami-Fort Lauderdale-West Palm Beach, FL	South
9	**Atlanta**	5,457,831	Atlanta-Sandy Springs-Roswell, GA	South
10	**Boston**	4,640,802	Boston-Cambridge-Newton, MA-NH	Northeast

Source: U.S. Census Bureau, "Annual Estimates of the Population of Metropolitan and Micropolitan Statistical Areas: April 1, 2010 to July 1, 2012," n.d., http://www.census.gov/popest/data/metro/totals/2012/.

an operating platform that focuses on getting customers through the door and eating in 14 minutes for those guests in a hurry.[12] Such convenience will also help make Cracker Barrel more attractive to consumers in certain geographic market segments.

Gas stations, banks, and retailers like Cracker Barrel Old Country Store make customer convenience based on geographic segmentation a central part of their marketing strategy.

Population Shifts Finally, geographic segmentation can be a valuable tool for understanding population changes across different regions of the country. The 2010 census illustrated a shifting population, with southern states like Texas and Florida growing substantially and many northern states, including Ohio, Michigan, and New York, growing at a slower rate or not at all.[13] The number of members each state has in the United States House of Representatives is determined by population and calculated every 10 years following the census. Figure 7.3 highlights the population shifts between 2000 and 2010 by illustrating which states have grown the most (and gained seats in the House of Representatives) and which states have seen the biggest population declines (and lost seats in the House).

The economic recession, retirement, and even natural disasters can cause people to move. For example, in Figure 7.3, you will notice that the only southern state that lost seats in the House of Representatives was Louisiana. That loss occurred

FIGURE 7.3   Seats Gained and Lost in the U.S. House of Representatives Due to Population Shifts

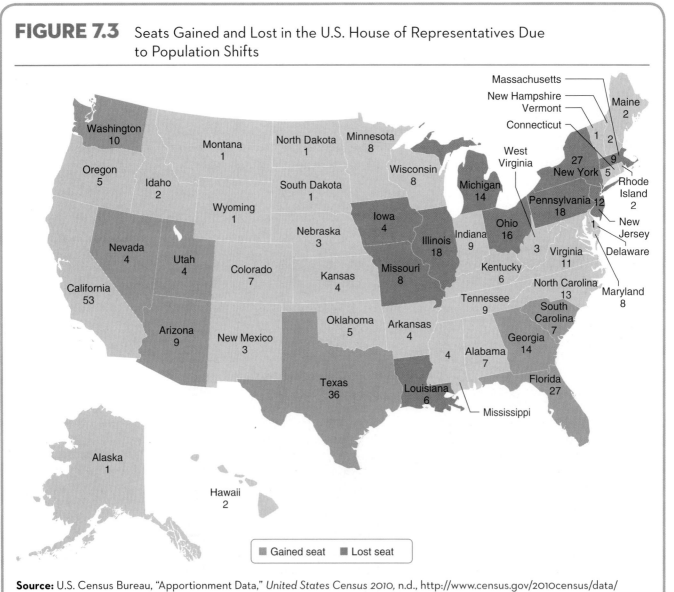

Source: U.S. Census Bureau, "Apportionment Data," *United States Census 2010,* n.d., http://www.census.gov/2010census/data/apportionment-data-text.php.

because Louisiana's largest city, New Orleans, lost 29 percent of its residents in the years following Hurricane Katrina.[14] It is important for marketers to research patterns of consumer movement to understand why and where they are moving. For example, real-estate marketers can use this information when selecting locations to build new housing developments. The growth in states like Texas provides marketers an opportunity to deliver products that meet the growing demand for houses that comes with a rapidly increasing population.

Psychographic

The science of using psychology and demographics to segment consumers is called psychographic segmentation. While demographic characteristics give us multiple ways to segment markets, consumers within the same demographic profile can have very different psychological or personality traits that influence their purchasing behavior. Psychographic segmentation allows marketing professionals to create a more meaningful profile of market segments by focusing on how those psychological traits intersect with demographic characteristics.

When marketers segment based on psychographics, the market is divided into groups according to the reason the consumer made the purchase. For example, consumers purchase a new Mercedes automobile for a variety of reasons. One segment of consumers may buy a Mercedes for the status that a luxury car will provide them. A different segment may buy the car because of its superior safety features. Mercedes salespeople who highlight specific features of their product based on an understanding of individual consumer motivations increase the likelihood of a sale because the features highlighted are more likely to match the customer's specific needs and wants.

Lifestyle   Many firms, including Kraft, have successfully segmented by lifestyle in recent years. Lifestyle segmentation divides people into groups based on their opinions and the interests and activities they pursue. While other companies were trying to connect with women by pushing messages to their mobile phones, Kraft implemented a different strategy to reach targeted female consumers. Instead of just pushing out a mobile message, Kraft created an iPhone app called "iFood Assistant" that actually made mealtime easier for consumers by putting 7,000 recipes at their fingertips. By effectively segmenting the market, Kraft was able to design a product that met the needs of its targeted consumers better than its competitors, thus increasing sales and customer loyalty.

VALS Network   Perhaps the most commonly used psychographic segmentation tool is the VALS™ framework. VALS, originally developed by SRI International, classifies U.S. and Canadian adults age 18 years of age and older on the basis of their responses to 34 attitudinal and 4 demographic questions into 8 psychographic groups—Innovators, Thinkers, Believers, Achievers, Strivers, Experiencers, Makers, and Survivors. VALS measures two dimensions: primary motivation and

EXECUTIVE PERSPECTIVE

Cornelius Lovelace
Executive Director
Fitness Bootcamp Unlimited

What is the most important part of segmentation in your business?

By far it is segmenting people based on why they want to pay us to help them get fit. The psychological motivation of someone who wants to get fit so they can have a more active social life differs from that of someone who needs our services because of high cholesterol. The great part about our business is that we can help both of these people achieve their goals, and we make sure to market to both with different advertisements and information on our website.

psychographic segmentation
The science of using psychology and demographics to segment consumers.

lifestyle segmentation
Segmentation that divides people into groups based on their opinions and the interests and activities they pursue.

Hunting, fishing, and outdoor gear retailer Cabela used lifestyle segmentation to develop a marketing campaign called "It's in Your Nature" that consisted of multiple videos promoting the various activities the retailer's customers pursue, including boating and camping.

resources. How motivation and resources combine explains why different consumer groups exhibit different behaviors, and why different consumer groups often exhibit the same behaviors for different reasons. Table 7.1 shows the eight VALS segments and provides a sample of the psychological attributes each possesses as well as some of the demographic and behavioral characteristics each displays.

As the table shows, VALS identifies three primary motivations: ideals, achievement, and self-expression. The abundance of resources (emotional and psychological resources, such as self-confidence, as well as key demographics, such as income and education) affects each group's ability to act on its primary motivation. For example, consumers who are motivated by achievement look to others for approval and acceptance. Resources determine how the motivation manifests itself. High-resource, achievement-motivated Achievers emulate the groups to which they aspire to belong; low-resource, achievement-motivated Strivers seek identification with others like them. Marketers use VALS to determine whether Achievers or Strivers, for example, are more likely to buy their product and then tailor the marketing mix accordingly.

Though segmenting by psychometric frameworks like VALS allows firms to understand consumer behavior better, psychographic segmentation can be more difficult and expensive than demographic or geographic segmentation. Firms will need to conduct surveys, with the VALS survey incorporated, to place consumers into VALS segments. In addition, if a firm is planning to market its products globally, it will need to reevaluate its segmentation to capture cultural differences. For example, Japan's VALS framework has 10 segments rather than 8. Different countries require different frameworks because of language and cultural differences. In addition to the U.S. and Japan, VALS frameworks are available for the U.K., Venezuela, the Dominican Republic, Nigeria, and China. We will discuss international market segmentation in more depth later in the chapter.

---

connect | MARKETING   **Interactive Assignment 7-1**

Please complete the *Connect* exercise for Chapter 7 that focuses on the eight VALS segments. By identifying which goods and services are most attractive to specific segments, you will better understand how segmentation provides useful insights that can impact marketing strategy.

Behavioral

behavioral segmentation

Segmentation that divides consumers according to how they behave with or act toward products.

80/20 rule

A theory that suggests that 20 percent of heavy users account for 80 percent of the total demand.

Segmentation by behavior involves categorizing customers based on what they actually do with their goods and services. Behavioral segmentation divides consumers according to how they behave with or act toward products. Behavioral segmentation variables include occasions (e.g., a wedding or business trip), loyalty, and usage rate. For example, marketers at Netflix might start with usage rate by segmenting the market into groups of users and nonusers. Next, they may further segment current Netflix users into groups such as heavy, moderate, or light users. Heavy users form the firm's profit core and should be treated accordingly. Many firms subscribe to the 80/20 rule, which suggests that 20 percent of heavy users account for 80 percent of the total demand. If a firm can identify its heavy users, it is in a better position to create an effective marketing strategy to reach those consumers who contribute most to the firm's success.

When done well, behavioral segmentation helps marketers clearly understand the benefits sought by different consumer segments. For example, if a customer

TABLE 7.1   Demographic and Behavioral Characteristics of VALS™ Consumer Groups (or Segments)

Primary Motivation		Ideals		Achievement		Self-Expression		
Psychographic Groups	Innovators	Thinkers	Believers	Achievers	Strivers	Experiencers	Makers	Survivors
Psychological Descriptors	Sophisticated In Charge Curious	Informed Reflective Content	Literal Loyal Moralistic	Goal Oriented Brand Conscious Conventional	Contemporary Imitative Style Conscious	Trend Seeking Impulsive Variety Seeking	Responsible Practical Self-Sufficient	Nostalgic Constrained Cautious
Demographic and Behavioral Characteristics	Percent of Innovators	Percent of Thinkers	Percent of Believers	Percent of Achievers	Percent of Strivers	Percent of Experiencers	Percent of Makers	Percent of Survivors
Total U.S. Population	10%	11.3%	16.5%	14%	11.5%	12.7%	11.8%	12%
Married	62	73	62	70	32	20	64	45
Work full time	67	52	40	65	45	42	56	13
Own a tablet or e-reader	36	25	9	19	6	14	7	4
Own a dog	39	40	43	52	44	41	57	38
Bought new or different auto-insurance policy in past year	17	16	16	18	15	16	22	14
Buy food labeled natural or organic	24	15	8	10	4	9	8	4
Media trusted the most:								
TV	11	25	43	26	38	24	33	54
Radio	15	11	7	7	7	6	12	11
Internet	42	30	21	35	32	48	26	4
Magazines	10	9	7	7	4	3	7	5
Newspapers	23	25	23	24	18	19	22	24

Source: Strategic Business Insights (SBI): www.strategicbusinessinsights.com/VALS.

Marketing efforts toward heavy users are the goal of loyalty programs such as the Holiday Inn Priority Club, which rewards frequent guests by giving them points to use toward future stays at Holiday Inn hotels.

has been using the same brand of toothpaste for 12 years and has had no cavities in that time period, a small price increase will most likely not be a problem for that customer. However, that same price increase might cause a less-committed user to change brands. Understanding how changes to marketing mix strategies affect different types of users allows the firm to evaluate the impact of such changes on sales and revenue.

Behavioral segmentation is often the most difficult of the four bases to use. The marketing research required to track and understand how consumers behave with a certain product is very expensive and time-consuming. Firms must weigh the benefits of such segmentation against the costs associated with obtaining the necessary information.

Business-to-Business Segmentation Bases

B2B firms generally segment their markets using three types of bases: demographic, geographic, and behavioral. While the names of these bases match those of the B2C bases discussed earlier, they apply differently.

- *Demographic.* The main B2B demographic variables include industry, size of the organization, and ownership structure. Segmenting by industry is an important first step that helps marketers determine which sectors of the economy might be most valuable to their business. The size of the organization is a critical variable because organizations of different sizes often have different needs and wants. In addition, large organizations like Cisco might have more complex buying processes that might require more salespeople compared to a small business. Finally, ownership structure can influence marketing decisions. For example, marketing a controversial product to a publicly traded company like Verizon may prove challenging because the organization may fear upsetting its shareholders. In contrast, a privately held firm might have fewer layers of management and be able to make decisions more quickly.

- *Geographic.* B2B geographic variables are similar to consumer variables and include things like country, region, state, and climate. Geographic segmentation allows marketers to group B2B customers by geography-related needs or headquarters location. This can help B2B marketers allocate resources to the parts of the country or the world with the highest concentration of economic- or climate-driven need.

- *Behavioral.* Behavioral segmentation might be the most beneficial variable to B2B marketers because it allows them to segment based on purchasing patterns, supplier requirements, and technological orientation. Purchasing patterns, such as the time of year contracts come up for bid, can be helpful in the segmentation process. Supplier requirements, which include things like whether the supplier has e-commerce functionality, can help marketers determine which segments' capabilities and technological orientation make them attractive.

Southwest, AirTran, Lufthansa, and Virgin Atlantic have launched their own social networking sites, allowing customers to interact and participate in contests and drawings.

In both B2B and B2C markets, social media present marketing professionals with additional options for segmenting the market and then reaching targeted segments.

THE ROLE OF SOCIAL MEDIA IN MARKET SEGMENTATION

Social media can be especially effective in market segmentation strategies. By segmenting the market by those who are active on social media, companies can, with minimal financial responsibility, engage and interact personally through individualized social media platforms such as Facebook and Twitter with a larger and more diverse consumer base. Nevertheless, questions remain as to exactly how to engage consumers on social networking sites and, more importantly, whom to engage.

Airlines are an example of one industry that has sought to answer such questions. Airlines increasingly use social media channels to address and target key market segments, with significant success. Several carriers, including AirTran, have taken advantage of college-aged consumers' familiarity with social media by posting videos on collegehumor.com.[15] They also promote the fact that consumers can view schedules and ticketing services on the airline's Facebook page. By engaging the college-age segment now, the airlines hope to develop a relationship with students who are likely to purchase significantly more airline tickets over the next decade of their lives as they begin their careers and travel with their young families.

---

connect |MARKETING

Interactive Assignment 7-2
Social Media in Action

The use of social media has grown significantly in recent years throughout the Middle East. Companies like Saudi Arabian telecommunications giant Mobily increasingly use Twitter instead of traditional advertising to reach customers. The impact of social media sites is especially powerful in Saudi Arabia. It has the highest number of Twitter followers of any country in the Arab world. Social media use has more than tripled in the region in recent years, partly because it gives Arab consumers a forum in which to talk to each other in a way that was not possible before.

Egypt has also jumped on the social media bandwagon. Twitter formed a partnership with the Egyptian digital advertising company Connect Ads to market and sell advertising services across the Middle East. These services offer marketers Twitter's products, including promoted tweets and promoted trends. Through these, a brand can reach broad Twitter audiences or more narrowly defined geographic or demographic segments. It can even target users of the Android or iPhone or other specific smartphone brands. Firms that have signed up for this service include Mobily, Pepsi Arabia, and the resort company Atlantis the Palm.

The Social Media in Action *Connect* exercise in Chapter 7 will let you develop social media strategies to target specific market segments in the U.S. and international markets. Segmentation and targeting are at the heart of successful marketing, and social media provide marketers from organizations of all sizes powerful tools to reach consumers more efficiently and effectively.

Source: See Sarah Hamdan, "Social Media Firms Move to Capitalize on Popularity in Middle East," *The New York Times*, February 7, 2013, http://www.nytimes.com/2013/02/07/world/middleeast/social-media-firms-move-to-capitalize-on-popularity-in-middle-east.html.

Summarize the elements of international market segmentation.

INTERNATIONAL MARKET SEGMENTATION

Even with the help social media platforms provide in reaching international markets, international market segmentation is a costly exercise, and often a very difficult one. First, accessing demographic, geographic, psychographic, and behavioral information can be challenging. Even demographic information, which is typically the easiest to acquire, may be slow in coming or completely unavailable. Canada conducts a census, which provides important demographic information to marketers, about every five years. France conducts a census about every seven years. However, many emerging nations might not conduct an accurate census for decades at a time. In addition, not all countries collect or classify their data in the same way, making it all but impossible to compare characteristics across nations. Even if marketing professionals obtain the information they seek, each nation and region has its own unique features that make establishing quality market segments problematic. When possible, companies may try to identify several markets that exhibit behavior similar enough to form a segment, allowing marketers to apply marketing research findings from one market to the rest of the segment.

International Segmentation Bases

Firms typically segment international markets using three general bases: global, regional, and unique.

global segmentation

Segmentation that is used when a firm can identify a group of consumers with common needs and wants that spans the entire globe.

1. Global segmentation is used when the firm can identify a group of consumers with common needs and wants that spans the entire globe. Global segmentation usually results in market segments made up of young

In Macau, China, McDonald's restaurants offer specialty food choices based on unique segmentation.

people, those that have more money to spend, or those with access to the Internet.

2. Regional segmentation may be used when the similarity in needs and wants only extends across the region or several countries. Firms will often use this when they want to capitalize on the financial savings of global segmentation but still adjust for local customs and culture.

3. If a firm wants to completely localize, it may choose unique segmentation, which targets the preferences of a segment within one country. Such segmentation usually becomes necessary for products like specialty foods.

All three types of segments offer potential profits depending on how consumers within the segment respond to the marketing mix.

regional segmentation
Segmentation that is used when the similarity in needs and wants only extends across the region or several countries.

unique segmentation
Segmentation that is used when the similarity in needs and wants exists only within one country.

International Market Segments and the Marketing Mix

International market segments can be used to group together countries with market conditions that are materially the same in relation to the company's product. This means that a marketing mix strategy that works well in one market may be successful for other markets in the same segment, allowing the firm to standardize the marketing mix across segments. However, marketers must also be mindful that, while segmentation allows them to standardize, there will often be instances where they need to localize within a segment. Some countries place a higher tariff on goods sold by foreign companies, which may make product pricing in those areas less competitive than they would be in other markets. Other aspects of the marketing mix can also fluctuate among markets in a segment. For example, advertising regulations and preferences vary substantially across Asia. Asian countries vary in their preference for which gender their promotional materials depict: In Malaysia, males are more likely to be seen in advertisements for food and soft drinks, whereas in Japan, females are more likely to appear in ads for the same products.[16]

Marketers in the U.S. and throughout the world can use a single segmentation base to divide the marketplace, or they can use multiple segmentation bases to provide a more complete picture of the consumers within each segment. Each has its own advantages and disadvantages depending on the firm, its products, and its budget. Marketers today use an increasingly large number of consumer characteristics to divide markets, both domestic and international, into useful segments that meet the five important criteria discussed in more detail in the next section.

LO 7-4

Discuss the criteria for successful market segmentation.

CRITERIA FOR EFFECTIVE MARKET SEGMENTATION

While there are multiple ways to segment markets, none of them are guaranteed to prove helpful to marketers. Simply dividing a larger group of consumers or businesses into smaller ones serves no purpose unless doing so improves how the firm markets its goods and services. To be effective, segmentation should create market segments that rate favorably on the following five criteria:

1. *Substantial.* The segments must be large enough for the firm to make a profit by serving them. For example, designing a cereal for people who are over 100 years of age or athletic shoes for people who wear larger than a size 24 shoe are not viable options because the market for each product is not substantial enough for the firm to make sustainable profits.
2. *Measurable.* The size and purchasing power of the segment should be clearly identified. Many successful marketers believe that if you cannot measure something you cannot manage it. Managers today demand high levels of accountability from marketers who must show measurable results of the success or failure of specific marketing strategies. For example, Nissan marketers researched the size and purchasing power of the market segment that desired an all-electric vehicle. A critical factor in the long-term success of the firm's Nissan Leaf product will be tied to how well the company estimated the number of consumers who want this type of car and how much those consumers are willing to pay for it.
3. *Differentiable.* Dividing the market into segments does no good if all the segments respond the same to different marketing strategies. Many marketers make this mistake. For example, segmenting students for a specific marketing class by gender or age would not provide a textbook firm any value since everyone in the class would be required to buy the book.
4. *Accessible.* Marketers must be able to reach and serve the segment. If the firm doesn't have the size, financial capital, expertise, or government permits to serve a certain market segment, all of the other criteria are irrelevant. It would be impossible for a small construction business to compete in the home building market if it did not have the financial capital to buy land and pay for expenses or the local permits necessary to legally build houses.
5. *Actionable.* Marketers should be able to develop strategies that can attract certain market segments to their firms' goods and services. A firm should be reasonably certain that its marketing mix can inform consumers about the product, how it adds value to the consumer, and ultimately how to purchase it. Subway has marketed its products to a wider market segment with campaigns featuring Jared, which appealed to more male consumers and informed them how the restaurant chain could help them lose weight.

Once a marketer has determined that a potential market segment meets these five criteria, the marketer can move on to the next step: choosing a strategy for targeting that market segment.

With the launch of its 550-calorie menu, Applebee's has implemented an actionable strategy to reach a substantial group of people looking for convenient, but still healthy, restaurant options.

---

connect | MARKETING   ## Interactive Assignment 7-3

Please complete the *Connect* exercise for Chapter 7 that focuses on identifying quality market segments. By understanding which segments are viable for a firm and why others are not, you will better understand the criteria and process for effectively segmenting the market.

SELECTING TARGET MARKETS

While market segmentation provides a good first step toward reaching potential consumers, the firm has more work to do. It must review the segments to determine which to target. Targeting occurs when marketers evaluate each market segment and determine which segment or segments present the most attractive opportunity to maximize sales. The segments selected are the firm's target markets. A target market is the group of customers toward which an organization has decided to direct its marketing efforts. Firms should consider the following three important factors during the targeting process:

1. *Growth potential.* Typically, the higher the future growth rate, the more attractive the segment is. For example, AT&T's existing residential landline business is still a multibillion-dollar market.[17] However, revenue and profits in the business have declined every year for the past decade as more and more consumers use their cell phones exclusively and get rid of their home phones. While a marketer would look at the residential phone business and see large sales potential, the growth potential is very limited, making the segment far less attractive.

2. *Level of competition.* The more intense the competition within a segment, the less attractive it is to marketers. Competitors will fight extremely hard to prevent market share loss, and the potential for price wars can negatively impact success. Generally, more competitors means a firm has to work

LO 7-5

Describe the strategies for selecting target markets.

targeting
The act of evaluating each market segment to determine which segment or segments present the most attractive opportunity to maximize sales.

target market
The group of customers toward which an organization has decided to direct its marketing efforts.

When looking to expand into a new target market, Olive Garden should evaluate the level of competition and consider selecting a market in which there is no major Italian food restaurant option to compete with.

harder and invest more in promotion to earn business and increase market share. When considering two market segments in which other factors, such as size and growth potential, are constant, the one with a less competitive environment is more attractive. For example, marketers of a Chinese fast food restaurant like Panda Express might want to reconsider entering a market where there are a high number of Chinese food restaurants offering all-you-can-eat buffets and delivery service. The increased level of competition will make it more expensive to reach consumers in that community and maintain high profits.

3. *Strategic fit.* Marketers should work to ensure that the target markets selected fit with what the organization is and wants to be as defined in its mission statement. The SWOT analysis provides an excellent framework to determine if a firm will be successful targeting a specific segment.

Selecting an appropriate target market is crucial to a successful marketing strategy. Regardless of how clever and innovative a firm's marketing mix may be, if it targets the wrong consumers, the product will fail. McDonald's introduced an Angus burger to its menu in 2009 as a premium choice at its restaurants. The Angus burger was one of the priciest menu items and did not fit well with the company's typical dollar-menu consumers. McDonald's target market did not want to pay four or five times more for a hamburger, even though the product was superior. McDonald's eventually removed the Angus burger from its menu in 2013.[18]

LO 7-6

TARGET MARKETING STRATEGIES

Compare the most common target marketing strategies.

The marketing department spends a great deal of time deciding which market segments are best to target. Once it has made that decision, the firm must develop a strategy for reaching those segments. The three basic strategies for targeting markets include: undifferentiated targeting, differentiated targeting, and niche marketing. Each of these is described in the sections that follow.

Undifferentiated Targeting

The major advantage of an undifferentiated targeting strategy is the potential savings in developing and marketing the product. An undifferentiated targeting strategy approaches the marketplace as one large segment. Because the firm doesn't segment the market further, it can approach all consumers with the same product offering and marketing mix. Undifferentiated targeting works best with uniform products, such as salt or bananas, for which the firm can develop a single marketing mix that satisfies the needs and wants of all customers. Only a limited number of products fall into this category; the majority of products satisfy very different needs and wants for different consumers.

Firms that offer only a general good or service are vulnerable to competitors that offer more specialized products that better meet consumer needs. The likelihood that a generic car or a restaurant that offers nothing unique or special will succeed in modern marketing is very small. Therefore, in most situations, marketers should use one of the more focused strategies described next.

undifferentiated targeting
A targeting strategy that approaches the marketplace as one large segment.

Differentiated Targeting

Typically, firms can provide increased levels of satisfaction and generate more sales using a differentiated targeting strategy rather than an undifferentiated targeting strategy. Differentiated targeting occurs when an organization simultaneously pursues several different market segments, usually with a different strategy for each. General Motors (GM) provides a classic example of successful differentiated targeting. Nearly a century ago, GM segmented consumers by the price they could afford and the quality they desired, then customized its products, messages, and promotions to the unique needs of each group. This practice was the beginning of the GM family—from Chevrolet to Buick to Cadillac.

Firms that market the same product to multiple regions with different preferences often use differentiated target marketing. In such cases, the product may be tweaked to ensure that it meets a need unique to each segment. For instance, some regions may prefer food flavors that won't sell in other areas. Frito-Lay offers more than 10 regional flavors, including Wavy Au Gratin in the Midwest and a ketchup-flavored chip that has gained a following in Buffalo, New York, but was originally targeted to the Canadian market.[19] While the core product remains the same, select flavors may be distributed to certain regions based on local preferences.

A firm marketing to a region outside the U.S. may also need to modify products according to local government regulations and cultural preferences. For example, Walmart initially offended Chinese consumers by selling fish and meat in Styrofoam and cellophane, the way the company sells these items in the U.S. Chinese consumers value fresh food and viewed the products that had been pre-wrapped as old merchandise.[20] Marketers responded quickly to this problem and differentiated their Chinese offerings by installing fish tanks and selling meat products uncovered. These moves, in combination with other differentiating strategies like elaborate cosmetics counters just inside the front door, have helped Walmart resonate with its target market in China.

differentiated targeting
A targeting strategy that simultaneously pursues several different market segments, usually with a different strategy for each.

niche marketing
A targeting strategy that involves pursuing a large share of a small market segment.

Frito-Lay has made use of differentiated targeting by developing various flavors of potato chips to appeal to different regions of the country.

Niche Marketing

Consumers of niche marketing products typically have very specialized needs and will pay higher prices to meet those needs. Niche marketing involves targeting a large share of a small market segment. Niche product

Pizza Patrón's has gained a following by implementing a niche marketing strategy specifically targeted toward the Hispanic population as a subset of the larger pizza-eating population.

firms possess a unique offering or specialization that is desirable to their targeted customers. Ties.com is a successful Internet-based niche retail company. The business, which shares its name with its website, has been in operation since 1998.[21] It focuses exclusively on men's neckties and related products. Fashion retailer Kathy Marrou founded the company, replacing her general clothing retail operation with one focused only on ties. The idea has been successful and the company has now added scarves to its lineup to target a niche market of female consumers who are passionate about neckwear. Whatever market niche a firm targets must still be a segment that is substantial enough to be successful. If Ties.com sold neckwear to only 10 people who liked exotic ties, it would be virtually impossible for the company to turn a profit and sustain itself as a business. The market segment for neckwear is substantial enough that Ties.com was able to generate $2.4 million in annual revenue in 2012, a 578 percent increase over just three years before.[22]

There can be multiple niche markets within the same product category. Pizza sales in the United States reached $32 billion annually in recent years, led by firms such as Pizza Hut, Domino's, and Papa John's. However, a number of pizza providers have found success targeting specific niche segments of the pizza market. Pizza Fusion targets consumers looking for a healthier and environmentally friendly alternative to the large pizza chains, Papa Murphy's leads the take-and-bake pizza niche, and Little Caesars's $5 Hot-N-Ready Pizza targets customers looking for value and time savings.

LO 7-7

Summarize the ethical issues in target marketing.

ETHICAL ISSUES IN TARGET MARKETING

Regardless of what target marketing strategy firms use, they must keep in mind the growing ethical concerns around targeting some market segments, in particular children, non-native language speakers, and the elderly. Beginning in the late 1990s and early 2000s a trend emerged in which marketers at Abercrombie and Fitch, Juicy Couture, and similar firms began targeting "tween" consumers, children between the ages of 8 and 12. The tween segment accounts for over $51 billion in direct consumer purchases and significantly influences another $170 billion

Jonathon Looney
Outside Sales Associate

ADP
http://www.adp.com/

ADP provides business outsourcing solutions in the areas of human resource, payroll, tax, and benefits administration as well as integrated computing solutions to auto, truck, motorcycle, marine, recreational vehicle, and heavy equipment dealers throughout the world.

Describe your job. My day-to-day tasks consist of effectively identifying existing and new businesses that may be facing cash flow management, people management, and risk and compliance issues and finding solutions to these issues using ADP's products. I offer a host of goods and services that streamline the day-to-day processes that our clients face around payroll, employee time management, and tax filing. Also, I help provide human resources outsourcing, retirement, and insurance services to small businesses.

Describe how you got the job that you have. I participated in a sales and marketing internship where I sold print, online, and mobile advertisement for local businesses to market directly to college students and faculty. My team and I finished 5 percent over goal and, because of my contributions, I was recruited by many of the internship's corporate partners. After several interviews from companies during my last semester in college, I accepted the offer from ADP and was employed before I walked the stage to graduate that year.

What has been the most important thing in making you successful at your job? I am younger than most of the current and potential clients I encounter, so I have to be knowledgeable and confident in myself and be prepared to handle all questions and objections. To accomplish this, I practice my personal five Ps—prior preparation prevents poor performance.

What advice would you give soon-to-be graduates? Being coachable has provided me with the map to success and achievement. I started seeing real results when I stopped trying to do things my way and sought advice from those with more experience.

What do you consider your personal brand to be? Adversity introduces a man to himself! I have realized that my real concern for the satisfaction of my clients has set me apart and made my business grow exponentially through referrals and positive word of mouth. In business something always will go wrong; it's how you respond to adversity that makes you better and builds your character.

spent by parents and family members.[23] This trend had the effect of causing firms to adjust the target age for their products downward until they were marketing tweens products like makeup and trendy clothing that had always been considered more appropriate for teenagers. In addition, embedded marketing programs in schools and product placements in popular television and movies by some of these companies made it difficult for tweens to differentiate between entertainment and a product promotion. An analysis of popular online children's retailers showed that almost 30 percent of children's clothes have sexualized characteristics and that the highest proportion of sexualized clothing came from stores aimed at tweens.[24] Several grassroots organizations have been formed to promote ethical marketing to children, and marketers should consider the ethical implications of any target marketing strategies they implement.

positioning

The activities a firm undertakes to create a certain perception of its product in the eyes of the target market.

 LO 7-8

Outline the three steps of effective market positioning and explain why firms may choose to use repositioning strategies.

MARKET POSITIONING

Success within the target market depends, to some degree, on how the firm positions its product. Positioning happens in many different ways and assumes that consumers compare goods and services on the basis of benefits. Positioning often takes into account the identity of the organization and where it fits relative to the competition. Successful positioning involves all of the marketing mix elements (price, product, promotion, and place). Marketers should follow three major steps to decide how to best position their product.

Step 1: Analyze Competitors' Positions

As a first step, firms must understand the position other competitors have taken in the marketplace. Positioning does not occur in isolation, and it is important for marketers to have a realistic view of how customers perceive competitive offerings. Competitive analysis becomes even more important when competitors all appear to offer a similar good or service. Financial institutions like banks and credit unions face this challenge; services like free checking and online banking are pretty much the same regardless of the type of bank. Bank of America has tried to overcome this obstacle by using advertising to emphasize its thousands of ATMs across the world and the fact that customers can scan and deposit a check using an ATM. In contrast, credit unions promote customer-friendly service—including lower fees and interest rates—and highlight that they are not designed to make a profit. By explaining to potential members that a credit union is not designed to extract profit from them, credit unions may be able to position themselves as more customer focused and convince individuals to switch from for-profit banks.

perceptual map

A competitive analysis tool that creates a visual picture of where products are located in consumers' minds.

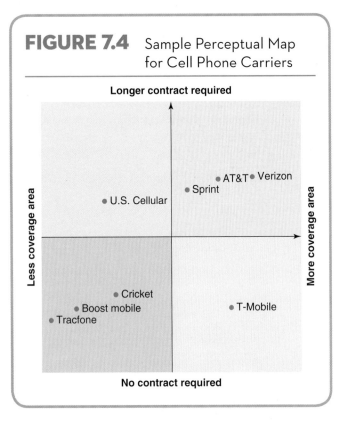

FIGURE 7.4   Sample Perceptual Map for Cell Phone Carriers

A perceptual map provides a valuable tool for understanding competitor positions in the marketplace. A perceptual map creates a visual picture of where products are located in consumers' minds. Marketers can develop a perceptual map based on marketing research or from their knowledge about a specific market. Figure 7.4 shows a sample perceptual map illustrating the domestic cell phone carrier market.

Perceptual maps provide guidance on potential market positions that might be underserved. For example, Figure 7.4 illustrates one of the reasons wireless provider T-Mobile decided to promote new service plans that did not require an annual contract in 2013.[25] In doing so, T-Mobile became the only major wireless provider occupying the position of offering nationwide coverage to consumers purchasing an iPhone or Android device with no contract required. Contrast this to the number of major providers offering nationwide coverage but requiring a contract of at least one year. AT&T, Verizon Wireless, and Sprint already compete in that market position, making it difficult for T-Mobile to succeed using the same positioning strategy.

Step 2: Clearly Define Your Competitive Advantage

Great marketers understand competitive advantage and why consumers buy their firm's goods and services. They know that consumers must have a clear answer to the question, Why should I buy this product? If a marketer cannot clearly establish an answer to this question in the mind of the consumer, the product may not realize its full potential. There are a number of positioning strategies available to highlight a firm's competitive advantage, including the following:

1. *Price/quality relationship.* Walmart is a great example of a low-cost retailer that has successfully positioned itself using a price/quality relationship strategy. Because of its thousands of stores globally, it can negotiate bulk discounts from wholesalers and keep its distribution costs low. These cost savings translate into low selling prices for goods with which rivals cannot compete. Shoppers know that Walmart offers the lowest prices, so they choose to shop there. This in turn enhances Walmart's brand, which only improves its competitive advantage.

2. *Attributes.* Often a product will have multiple attributes that create a unique position in the market. Marketers should evaluate those attributes that put its product in a special category of value to the customer. Successful attributes might include leadership, heritage, product manufacturing process, or the coolness factor. For example, Nike continued to have sales success marketing the Air Jordan line of shoes years after Michael Jordan retired from sports. The coolness factor of the shoes is an attribute that creates a unique position in the marketplace and resonates with consumers across generations.

3. *Application.* Apple has had success with its iPad product, in part, because of the competitive advantage it has when it comes to the application and use of the product. As new versions of the iPad have been introduced, Apple has had success emphasizing exclusive services like FaceTime and iCloud to further differentiate the iPad from competitors. In addition, Apple reminds customers that its app store is still the largest store of its type with the highest security standards.

Firms can choose to promote one or multiple competitive advantages, as long as they can clearly articulate those advantages to their target market.

Step 3: Evaluate Feedback

The third step in market positioning is constantly evaluating consumer feedback. Just as fashion styles change, consumer tastes for almost everything, including cars, food, and even educational learning formats, change. For example, as more students began to work while attending college, universities began offering a larger number of night classes than they had before. In recent years, to accommodate fluctuating student work schedules, high gas prices, and a

Evaluating feedback is essential for universities and other organizations as they seek to position themselves with a target market increasingly focused on digital products through online classes and digital learning formats.

weak economy, universities began offering more online courses. Universities continue to position themselves as providers of quality higher education programs even as they have shifted their product to accommodate the additional features and conveniences their target market requires.

Disney provides another example. Disney used feedback from consumers who were concerned about childhood health to further position itself. The company has announced that it will require food and beverage products advertised on its networks to meet its specific nutritional standards by 2015. In 2012, it began using a "Mickey Check" seal of approval to indicate that foods sold in its stores, theme parks, and resorts meet its nutritional standards.[26] The stated objective of these programs is combatting childhood obesity. Listening to customer feedback on this sensitive issue has allowed Disney to position itself as a partner for parents in ensuring healthy lives for children.

connect Interactive Assignment 7-4

|MARKETING Please complete the *Connect* exercise for Chapter 7 that focuses on the steps in the market positioning process. By understanding the decisions at each step of the process, you will better understand how to develop an effective market position.

Positioning Statement

positioning statement

A succinct description of the core target market to which a product is directed and a compelling picture of how the firm wants that core market to view the product.

Once a firm has completed the steps to decide how best to position its product, the hard part begins. The firm must determine how to succinctly communicate the market position it has chosen, first to its own organization and then to the world. A positioning statement consists of a succinct description of the core target market to which a product is directed and a compelling picture of how the firm wants that core market to view the product. A successful positioning statement should clearly reflect the steps of the positioning process, including the competitive advantages of the product. However, positioning statements should also be short to facilitate communication and enhance the likelihood that stakeholders and consumers will understand the desired message. Zipcar is a membership-based car-sharing company that provides automobile reservations to its members, billable by the hour or day. Its goal is to emphasize the superiority of its service in relation to the competitive alternative of owning one's own car. This approach is captured in the following positioning statement, which, in less than 30 words, outlines the target market, how Zipcar wants consumers to view its service, and how its service bests other options.

> To urban-dwelling, educated techno-savvy consumers **[target market]**, when you use Zipcar car-sharing service instead of owning a car **[picture of how they want consumers to view the service]**, you save money while reducing your carbon footprint **[how they are better]**. [27]

The positioning statement can be used as part of an external marketing strategy, but it should first serve as an internal guiding statement, keeping employees and other stakeholders aligned to the firm's guiding principles. The better all departments understand an organization's market positioning, the more likely it is to be communicated and executed throughout the organization.

Firms that maintain the same position year after year, even if it has been successful, can lose touch with changing customer preferences. Smart marketers realize that positioning doesn't just take place when launching new products, rather it is an ongoing process. Consumer feedback, declining sales, or reduced market share can all suggest that the firm needs to undertake a major change in strategy.

Repositioning

In this digital age, marketers have to change and adapt their strategies if they want to continue to reach their target market. Repositioning involves reestablishing a product's position to respond to changes in the marketplace. Dr Pepper Snapple Group, the Sunkist brand's licensee for soda in the U.S., initiated a repositioning strategy aimed at trend-savvy teens and young adults. The soda brand now utilizes YouTube and Facebook platforms to promote its products.

repositioning
The act of reestablishing a product's position to respond to changes in the marketplace.

Repositioning and the Marketing Mix
Repositioning typically involves changing one or more marketing mix elements, often product or promotion. Domino's Pizza's self-deprecating marketing campaign serves as a great example of how to reposition a brand. According to Domino's internal research, its biggest customer segment, college students, reject the brand as the students get older and care more about quality and taste than low prices. Domino's realized this attrition offered a sizable opportunity for growth and, because it has been transparent in its repositioning campaign, its story has caught the attention of lots of people. One key reason for the campaign's success is the advertising footage highlighting consumers' negative feelings toward the quality and taste of Domino's pizza. By acknowledging this part of the story and understanding the attitudes and opinions of its target audience, Domino's message resonated with consumers. Current and past customers bought into the first part of the story in which the company admitted its problems; because of this, Domino's was given permission to tell the rest of the story about how it has changed and improved.

Repositioning the Competition
Sometimes marketers choose to reposition the competition rather than change their own position. For example, Apple had success repositioning its PC competitors like Dell and Hewlett-Packard using the popular "I'm a Mac, I'm a PC" advertisements that compared the capabilities and attributes of Macs and PCs. The promotion succeeded in characterizing the PC as formal and stuffy, while portraying Apple's Mac as the relaxed, easy-to-use alternative. This type of repositioning strategy is also common in political marketing as strategists look to define their opponent negatively without changing their own candidate's positions. Check out any major election cycle in your state or region and you are likely to find plenty of examples of this type of repositioning strategy.

To reposition its product with younger consumers, Sunkist's marketers partnered with social media outlets to promote their "12 ounces of awesome" campaign and created several new YouTube videos featuring break dancers.

SUMMARY

LO 7-1 Explain the importance of effective market segmentation.

Market segmentation is the process of dividing a larger market into smaller groups, or market segments, based on meaningfully shared characteristics. Market segments are the relatively homogenous groups of consumers that result from the market segmentation process. Market segmentation plays an important role in the success of almost every organization in the U.S. and throughout the world. The process helps firms define the needs and wants of the customers the firm wants to target. Market segmentation also helps firms design specific marketing strategies for the characteristics of specific market segments.

LO 7-2 Describe the four bases for segmenting markets.

Marketers use segmentation bases, which are characteristics of consumers that influence their buying behavior, to divide the market into segments. There are four broad bases of segmentation—demographic, geographic, psychographic, and behavioral. Demographic characteristics include age, gender, income, education, and family size, among other things. Age and gender are the two most commonly used demographic variables. Geographic segmentation divides markets into nations, regions, states, and neighborhoods and other physical areas. Marketers pay special attention to local variations in the types of goods and services offered in different geographic regions. Psychographics is the science of using psychology and demographics to segment consumers. Psychographic segmentation focuses on the intersection between personality traits and demographic characteristics. Behavioral segmentation divides consumers according to how they behave with or act toward products. This type of segmentation is concerned with what consumers actually do with their goods and services.

LO 7-3 Summarize the elements of international market segmentation.

International market segmentation is a costly exercise, and often a very difficult task. Firms typically segment international markets using three general bases: global, regional, and unique. Global segmentation is used when the firm can identify a group of consumers with common needs and wants that spans the entire globe. Regional segmentation may be used when the similarity in needs and wants only extends across the region or several countries. If a firm wants to completely localize, it may choose unique segmentation, which targets the preferences of a segment within one country. All three types of segments offer potential profits depending on how consumers within the segment respond to the marketing mix.

LO 7-4 Discuss the criteria for successful market segmentation.

While there are multiple ways to segment markets, none of them are guaranteed to prove helpful to marketers. Simply dividing a larger group of consumers into smaller ones serves no purpose unless it helps marketers sell their firm's goods and services. To be effective tools, market segments should rate favorably on five criteria; they should be substantial, measurable, differentiable, accessible, and actionable.

LO 7-5 Describe the strategies for selecting target markets.

Targeting occurs when marketers evaluate each market segment and determine which segment (or segments) presents the most attractive opportunities. The segments they select are called their target markets. When determining which market segments to pursue, marketers should consider the following important factors: growth potential, level of competition, and strategic fit.

LO 7-6 Compare the most common target marketing strategies.

There are three general strategies for targeting markets. An undifferentiated targeting strategy approaches the marketplace as one large segment. Differentiated targeting occurs when an organization simultaneously pursues several different market segments, usually with a different strategy for each. Finally, a niche marketing strategy involves targeting a large share of a small market segment.

LO 7-7 Summarize the ethical issues in target marketing.

Regardless of what target marketing strategy firms use, they must keep in mind the growing ethical concerns around targeting some market segments, in particular children, non-native language speakers, and the elderly. Several grass-roots organizations have been formed to promote ethical marketing to children, and marketers should consider the ethical implications of any target marketing decisions they make.

 LO 7-8 Outline the three steps of effective market positioning and explain why firms may choose to use repositioning strategies.

Positioning is the act of designing the firm's offering and image to occupy a distinctive place in the minds of the target market and involves three major steps: (1) understand the position other competitors have taken in the marketplace, (2) clearly define a competitive advantage, and (3) constantly evaluate consumer feedback. Consumer feedback, declining sales, or reduced market share can all suggest that the firm needs to undertake a change in strategy. Repositioning involves reestablishing a product's position to respond to changes in the marketplace. Repositioning typically involves changing one or more marketing mix elements. Marketers can also choose to reposition the competition rather than change their own position.

KEY TERMS

behavioral segmentation (p. 200)
demographic segmentation (p. 193)
differentiated targeting (p. 209)
80/20 rule (p. 200)
geographic segmentation (p. 196)
global segmentation (p. 204)
lifestyle segmentation (p. 199)

market segmentation (p. 192)
market segments (p. 193)
niche marketing (p. 209)
perceptual map (p. 212)
positioning (p. 212)
positioning statement (p. 214)
psychographic segmentation (p. 199)

regional segmentation (p. 205)
repositioning (p. 215)
target market (p. 207)
targeting (p. 207)
undifferentiated targeting (p. 209)
unique segmentation (p. 205)

MARKETING PLAN EXERCISE

In this chapter, you read about the importance of targeting specific segments and developing a positioning strategy that appeals to those segments. Your assignment for this chapter is to apply these critical concepts to your marketing plan. First, refer back to the career objectives (what company you want to work for or what graduate school you want to attend) that you have already developed. Next, think about and clearly articulate how you will position yourself for your target market. There are a limited number of openings for good jobs and quality graduate schools. To maximize your chances of success, you must plan ahead and use the marketing strategies you have learned to position yourself properly in a very competitive environment. You should ask yourself questions such as:

- How can I best position myself for a job with one of these organizations?
- What classes have I taken or what experiences have I had that position me for the graduate school I want to attend?

Your Task: Write a one-paragraph personal positioning statement that includes succinct answers to these questions.

DISCUSSION QUESTIONS

1. Choose a company you have worked for or would like to work for and discuss how it could benefit from market segmentation. Does that company do a good job segmenting today? Why or why not?
2. Select a product that you use almost every day and explain how each of the major segmentation bases can be applied to you as a consumer of that product. What insights can each segmentation base provide to firms to help them develop a marketing mix that would win your business? (For example, you might say that geographic segmentation would help a firm market heavy coats to you because you live in a cold climate.)
3. Select a market segment for fast food. First, describe the segment. Then explain how the segment meets all five of the criteria to be considered an effective market segment.
4. Assume that your university is looking to increase enrollment. Choose the best targeting strategy (undifferentiated, differentiated, or niche) for achieving this goal and describe how it will be effective in bringing more students to your campus.

5. Select a company that you think has successfully positioned its products and describe why it has been successful. Next, select a company that you think has done a poor job positioning its products and explain why it hasn't been successful.

6. Select one firm that you think needs to reposition itself. Describe what you think isn't working about its current position and then provide three specific recommendations for how it could reposition itself for a successful future.

SOCIAL MEDIA APPLICATION

S Social Media Select a product that you like and that you would enjoy marketing. This could be a type of car, cell phone, or restaurant. Segment the market for this product using the following questions and activities as a guide:

1. Select 20 friends, followers, or connections that you have on any social media platform and segment them as if they are potential customers of the product you have chosen to market. You need to identify at least three different segments.

2. What variables did you use to segment the potential customers?

3. How were social media helpful to you in assigning each person to a specific segment?

4. Decide which segment of the three you are going to target your marketing efforts to. Why did you make that decision?

5. How can social media help you reach the targeted consumers with your marketing message?

ETHICAL CHALLENGE

Currently, users under the age of 13 are not permitted to create profiles on Facebook. Although many tweens lie about their age and create profiles (a ComScore survey indicated that 7.5 million Facebook users are younger than 13), because Facebook can't identify users under 13, advertisers can't use Facebook to reach this demographic.

Allowing tweens to create profiles could reinvigorate Facebook's slowing growth. But Facebook has already come under fire for privacy issues, and it may want to avoid exposing itself to potential allegations about exploiting or failing to protect children. In addition, The Children's Online Privacy Protection Act (COPPA) would require Facebook to allow parents to elect not to have their children's online activities tracked. If parents took advantage of this option, Facebook would have limited data and access to offer advertisers, compromising its ability to profit from the preteen demographic. As a result, Facebook must weigh many risks and potential benefits in deciding whether to open up to tweens.

Please use the ethical decision-making framework to answer the following questions:

1. Why do some people feel that Facebook shouldn't target children under 13? Do you agree?

2. Despite the current policy, surveys suggest that millions of children under the age of 13 lie about their age and use Facebook. How should Facebook, parents, and children share the responsibility for any adverse consequences the children might experience? Would the risk of such consequences be lessened if Facebook allowed children to have profiles?

3. What risks, costs, and benefits should Facebook consider in deciding whether to allow preteen users? To what extent should Internet companies be held accountable for children's online safety?

Source: See Jordan Roberston, "Will Facebook Friend Pre-Teens?" *Bloomberg Businessweek*, June 14, 2012, http://www.businessweek.com/articles/2012-06-14/will-facebook-friend-preteens.

VIDEO CASE

Please go to *Connect* to access the video case featuring Marriott that accompanies this chapter.

CAREER TIPS
Marketing Your Future

You have read in this chapter about the critical marketing concept of positioning. In a personal context, positioning involves how you are perceived by those people who can impact your career success, such as employers, coworkers, customers, and classmates. Author Shane Hunt would like to share with you three major stages of your life at which successfully positioning yourself will help you have the career you desire.

1. **Positioning yourself during college.** You should give careful consideration to how you position yourself in college. Part of this process involves asking yourself, What am I doing that will give me a competitive advantage over my classmates? Ask yourself how the classes you are taking are helping you to achieve your goals. Be selective in picking courses because, in addition to the time and money you spend completing them, through them you have the opportunity to acquire differentiating knowledge. A course in the marketing program or a foreign language class might be time-consuming, but these kinds of classes are far more likely to help you carve a unique position for yourself as you complete your degree. You need to be thoughtful in considering how specific course knowledge, leadership activities, and work experiences make your position unique.

2. **Positioning yourself as a problem solver.** Once you start your career, you should work to position yourself in the mind of your manager as someone who can be relied upon and, most importantly, can solve problems. Your ability to get paid more in your career is directly related to your ability to solve problems for your organization. Take on difficult assignments and volunteer for committees that might be stressful but that will raise your profile and advance your learning about the organization. If your manager perceives you as someone whose problem-solving ability and attitude are superior to your peers, your likelihood for promotion and raises increases substantially.

3. **Don't be afraid to reposition yourself.** There might come a time when the job or career you have chosen ceases to be as personally or financially fulfilling as you had hoped. If this is the case, you need to consider how you can reposition yourself. You might consider going to graduate school or learning a new skill at your current job. Sometimes repositioning is necessary because of technology or industry changes. Learn how to create an app for your small business or acquire new certifications relevant to your field. You must continue to learn when you finish college and develop new skills for the rest of your career so that you can reposition yourself to compete against future graduates.

CHAPTER NOTES

1. Monte Burk, "Five Guys Burgers: America's Fastest Growing Restaurant Chain," *Forbes*, July 18, 2012, http://www.forbes.com/forbes/2012/0806/restaurant-chefs-12-five-guys-jerry-murrell-all-in-the-family.html.
2. Rob Sachs, "High-End Burger Joints Raise the Stakes," *NPR*, April 21, 2011, http://www.npr.org/2011/04/21/135569985/high-end-burger-joints-raise-the-stakes.
3. Ibid.
4. Lindsay M. Howden and Julie A. Meyer, "Age and Sex Composition: 2010," *U.S. Census Bureau*, May 2011, http://www.census.gov/prod/cen2010/briefs/c2010br-03.pdf.
5. Kaylene C. Williams and Robert A. Page, "Marketing to the Generations," *Journal of Behavioral Studies in Business*, no. 3 (April 2011), pp. 1–17.
6. Stephanie Clifford, "Revamping, Home Depot Woos Women," *The New York Times*, January 28, 2011, http://www.nytimes.com/2011/01/29/business/29home.html.
7. Elizabeth Sweet, "Guys and Dolls No More?" *The New York Times*, December 21, 2012, http://www.nytimes.com/2012/12/23/opinion/sunday/gender-based-toy-marketing-returns.html?_r=0).
8. Colin Barr, "'Mass Affluent' Are Strapped Too, BofA finds," *CNNMoney*, January 24, 2011, http://finance.fortune.cnn.com/2011/01/24/mass-affluent-are-strapped-too-bofa-finds/.
9. Ibid.
10. Penelope Green, "Under One Roof, Building for Extended Families," *The New York Times*, November 29, 2012, http://www.nytimes.com/2012/11/30/us/building-homes-for-modern-multigenerational-families.html?pagewanted=1.
11. Ryan Poe, "Ikea in Birmingham? Metro Falls Short of Retailer's Population Target," *Birmingham Business Journal*, October 29, 2012, http://www.bizjournals.com/birmingham/blog/2012/10/ikea-in-birmingham-dont-hold-your.html.
12. Joshua Caucutt, "Cracker Barrel Is Cracklin'," *InvestorGuide*, May 25, 2010, http://www.investorguide.com/article/6467/cracker-barrel-is-cracklin-cbrl/.
13. U.S. Census Bureau. "Table 14, State Population—Rank, Percent Change, and Population Density: 1980–2010,"

Statistical Abstract of the United States: 2012, n.d., http://www.census.gov/compendia/statab/2012/tables/12s0014.pdf.

14. David Mildenburg, "Census finds Hurricane Katrina Left New Orleans Richer, Whiter, Emptier," *Bloomberg,* February 3, 2011, http://www.bloomberg.com/news/2011-02-04/census-finds-post-katrina-new-orleans-richer-whiter-emptier.html.

15. Mike Beirne, "AirTran Caters to College Crowd," *AdWeek,* April 9, 2008, http://www.adweek.com/news/advertising-branding/airtran-caters-college-crowd-95470.

16. Mary Jiang Bresnahan, Yasuhiro Inoue, Wen Ying Liu, and Tsukasa Nishida, "Changing Gender Roles in Prime Time Commercials in Malaysia, Japan, Taiwan, and the United States," *Sex Roles* 45, nos. 1–2 (July 2001), pp. 117–131.

17. Todd Haselton, "AT&T Revenue Up 2% in Q2; 3.6 Million iPhones Activated," *BGR,* July 21, 2011, http://bgr.com/2011/07/21/at-3-6-million-iphones-activated/.

18. NBC News Staff, "Where's the Beef? McDonald's Dropping Angus Burgers from U.S. Menu," *NBC News,* May 9, 2013, http://www.nbcnews.com/business/wheres-beef-mcdonalds-dropping-angus-burgers-us-menu-1C9864163.

19. Michele Kayal, "America's Patchwork of Potato Chip Varieties," *Huffington Post,* August 8, 2012, http://www.huffingtonpost.com/2012/08/14/regional-potato-chip-varieties_n_1775098.html.

20. Keith Naughton, "The Great Wal-Mart of China," *Newsweek,* October 29, 2006, http://www.thedailybeast.com/newsweek/2006/10/29/the-great-wal-mart-of-china.html.

21. Sebastian Weiss, "Husband and Wife Team Ties into Rising Tide of E-Business," *San Antonio Business Journal,* December 12, 1999, http://www.bizjournals.com/sanantonio/stories/1999/12/13/story5.html?page=all.

22. Inc., "2012 Inc.com 5000 List," n.d., http://www.inc.com/inc5000/list/2012/400/employees/ascend.

23. Leslie Jane Seymour, "Tween 'R' Shoppers," *The New York Times,* April 22, 2007, http://www.nytimes.com/2007/04/22/nyregion/nyregionspecial2/22RSHOP.html?pagewanted=all&_r=0.

24. Samantha M. Goodin, Alyssa Van Denburg, Sarah K. Murnen, and Linda Smolak, "Putting on Sexiness: A Content Analysis of the Presence of Sexualizing Characteristics in Girls' Clothing," *Sex Roles* 65 (2011), pp. 1–12.

25. David Pogue, "Breaking Free of the Cellphone Carrier Conspiracy," *The New York Times,* April 3, 2013, http://www.nytimes.com/2013/04/04/technology/personaltech/t-mobile-breaks-free-of-cellphone-contracts-and-penalties.html?pagewanted=all&_r=0.

26. Brooks Barnes, "Promoting Nutrition, Disney to Restrict Junk-Food Ads," *The New York Times,* June 5, 2012, http://www.nytimes.com/2012/06/05/business/media/in-nutrition-initiative-disney-to-restrict-advertising.html?pagewanted=all&_r=0.

27. Alice M. Tybout and Bobby J. Calder, eds., *Kellogg on Marketing,* 2nd ed. (Hoboken, NJ: John Wiley & Sons, 2010), p. 89.

PART THREE
Reaching Your Customer

Teresa Goodnight
Senior Director of Sales

zayo

Zayo Group
http://www.zayo.com/

Zayo Group is a global provider of data transfer infrastructure services used by wireless and wireline carriers; media and content companies; governments; and high-bandwidth enterprises, like health care, education, financial services, logistics, technology, and numerous other industries.

Terry Matthews
Executive Vice President and President of Intermodal

J.B. HUNT

J.B. Hunt Transport Services, Inc.
http://www.jbhunt.com/

J.B. Hunt is a Fortune 500 company and one of the largest transportation logistics companies in North America. It provides safe and reliable transportation services to a diverse group of customers throughout the continental United States, Canada, and Mexico.

Mark Duckworth
Chief Executive Officer and Founder

Optus Inc.
https://www.optusinc.com/

Optus provides customers with business telecommunications solutions, offering telephone hardware; engineering, training, and maintenance services; and complementary products.

Andrew Hicks
Law Firm Partner

Schiffer Odom Hicks
& Johnson PLLC
Trial Lawyers

Schiffer, Odom, Hicks, and Johnson
http://www.sohlawfirm.com/

Schiffer, Odom, Hicks, and Johnson is a boutique litigation firm with offices in Houston, Texas, and Seattle, Washington.

Chapter 8

PROMOTIONAL STRATEGIES

LEARNING OBJECTIVES

After reading this chapter, you should be able to

LO 8-1 Describe the elements of the promotion mix and how they relate to an integrated marketing communications strategy.

LO 8-2 Compare the advantages and disadvantages of different types of advertising.

LO 8-3 Summarize the various types of sales promotion.

LO 8-4 Explain the importance of personal selling.

LO 8-5 Outline the personal-selling process.

LO 8-6 Describe the role of public relations within the promotion mix.

LO 8-7 Summarize the promotion mix budgeting strategies.

EXECUTIVE PERSPECTIVE

Teresa Goodnight
Senior Director of Sales
Zayo Group

As a senior director of sales, Teresa Goodnight understands personal selling. Long before she managed a sales team at Zayo Group, she had to learn how to sell herself. Goodnight was an English major in college and intended to go to law school. But she grew disenchanted with the legal world and took a job answering phones until she could figure out a new career path. Rather than viewing the job as a way to bide her time, she took advantage of her new position to learn as much as she could about all aspects of marketing, from products to marketing communications to selling, by substituting for and shadowing other employees. After several years, she was hired into a marketing position in which she was responsible for handling trade shows and other events. This exposure awakened her to the excitement of sales. A few years later, Goodnight had the opportunity to join the sales team at Zayo. She quickly became one of the leading salespeople in the entire organization and eventually was promoted to lead the sales team.

What has been the most important thing in making you successful at your job?

Being dedicated to work and believing that passionate customer service makes a difference are two of my key elements for success. If you care more about the customer than yourself, it shows. They don't see that a lot. It's different. It evokes trust. (If it's real.)

What advice would you give soon-to-be graduates?

The closer you are to contributing to the bottom line of an organization and demonstrating your contribution through your metrics and deliverables, the more secure your position will be at the company. By choosing marketing, you are closer to the bottom line results of an organization than virtually any other area. I would also encourage you to not do something just because it has been done before. If you are doing something for "marketing's sake" because other people say you should do it, stop and think about how it will really help. Marketers today must be more thoughtful and strategic. I've seen money wasted on ridiculous campaigns and unnecessary research,

among other things, by companies who could have used those dollars in the end when they were failing. Focus on increasing value for your stakeholders and stay true to that measure and you will be in better shape.

How is marketing relevant to your role at Zayo?

There are a lot of people involved in marketing, and that runs the gamut from product development to marketing communications. That said, the primary focus of marketing at Zayo is generating shareholder value. Although that takes on many different meanings depending on your department, I am an avid believer that marketing's primary job is to support sales.

What do you consider your personal brand to be?

Passion. Integrity. Responsiveness. Listening. My customers know I don't have all the answers, but they always know I am dedicated to finding them. I don't really believe in sentiments like *we can't* or *we won't* or *no*. Almost every time I've pushed back on such statements, I've found that we can and we do. I'm also known to my CEO as the one he can receive a straight answer from, whether it's what he wants to hear or not. I'm not sure it's a compliment, but it is a big part of who I want to be. I think it's the backbone of my success with my customers as well.

Teresa Goodnight
Senior Director of Sales

Zayo Group
http://www.zayo.com/

Zayo Group is a global provider of data transfer infrastructure services used by wireless and wireline carriers; media and content companies; governments; and high-bandwidth enterprises, like health care, education, financial services, logistics, technology, and numerous other industries.

FORECAST

This chapter explores the importance of promoting goods, services, and ideas to communicate value to current and prospective customers. The promotion mix provides you with the tools to deliver a value-driven message across multiple types of media and organizational interactions. This chapter outlines the promotion mix elements of advertising, sales promotion, personal selling, and public relations and describes how marketers can integrate these tools into an integrated marketing communications strategy. As you read through the chapter, consider the following key questions:

1. What tools can I use to promote my products?
2. Why should I choose certain types of advertising over others?
3. How do different types of sales promotions benefit the organization?
4. Why does personal selling matter to an organization?

5. What are the steps involved in selling my product?
6. Why is the public relations function so important to organizations?
7. How do organizations determine their promotional budgets?

LO 8-1

Describe the elements of the promotion mix and how they relate to an integrated marketing communications strategy.

promotion

All the activities that communicate the value of a product and persuade customers to buy it.

PROMOTION MIX

Red Bull marketers were seeking a way to promote their brand and products that would communicate the firm's slogan, "Red Bull Gives You Wings," in a creative way. They developed a strategy that involved hiring extreme athlete Felix Baumgartner to break the world record for the longest free fall jump. Baumgartner jumped from 120,000 feet above the Earth, reaching a speed of 690 miles per hour during his descent.[1] The event promoted the Red Bull lifestyle and has been watched by over 50 million people on YouTube.[2] Images from the jump also became part of Red Bull's television advertising campaign. Red Bull marketers were able to integrate the success of the event to enhance the impact of their promotional strategy in everything from television to social media.

Promotion is one of the four marketing mix elements and where most of an organization's communications with the marketplace occur. Promotion is all the activities that communicate the value of a product and persuade customers

Athlete Felix Baumgartner's free fall jump from 23 miles above the earth generated significant publicity and free media for Red Bull, the company that sponsored the event, as it appeared on dozens of news programs and websites.

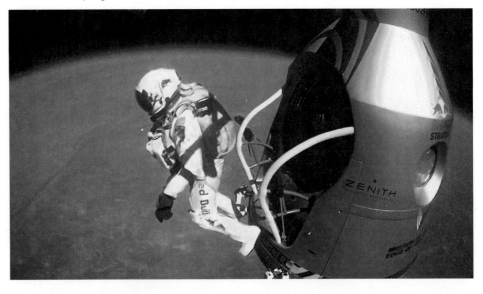

to buy it. The tools marketing professionals use to promote their products are referred to as the promotion mix. The promotion mix is a subset of the marketing mix and includes four main elements of marketing communication: advertising, sales promotion, personal selling, and public relations.

Elements of the Promotion Mix

Each element of the promotion mix shown in Figure 8.1 represents a different way for the organization to communicate with its customers.

1. *Advertising.* Nonpersonal promotional communication about goods, services, or ideas that is paid for by the firm identified in the communication.
2. *Sales promotion.* A set of nonpersonal communication tools designed to stimulate quicker and more frequent purchases of a product.
3. *Personal selling.* The two-way flow of personal communication between a salesperson and a customer that is paid for by the firm and seeks to influence the customer's purchase decision.
4. *Public relations.* Communication focused on promoting positive relations between a firm and its stakeholders.

FIGURE 8.1 Elements of the Promotion Mix

Historically, the four elements of the promotion mix were handled by self-contained areas within an organization, with very little attention paid to how the elements fit together. The advertising department would plan and implement advertising messages without coordinating with the sales force, which might be focusing on a different message during customer visits. Today, firms work to integrate the four elements so that the contribution from the whole promotion mix exceeds the sum of the individual elements.

Integrated Marketing Communications

An integrated communications solution involving multiple elements of the promotion mix allows a firm to effectively create and develop relationships with customers. An integrated marketing communications (IMC) strategy involves coordinating the various promotion mix elements to provide consumers with a clear and consistent message about a firm's products. For example, the brand essence of Taco Bell's IMC campaign that encourages consumers to *Live Más* (live more) reflects customers' evolving mindset of "food as fuel" to "food as an experience." Taco Bell's advertising, public relations, sales promotion, and in-store employees were all focused on the "Live Más" theme.[3] Taco Bell used a sales promotion sweepstakes in which the winner received a trip to the MTV Video Music Awards to promote its "Big Box Rewind" product. Consumers could enter the sweepstakes by liking the Taco Bell Facebook page. Marketers also tied this sales promotion to their "Feed the Beat" music program that helps feed and support up-and-coming bands on tour.

A major part of the "Live Más" strategy involved the launch of Locos Tacos, which leveraged IMC elements to become the most successful product launch in the history of the company.[4] Television advertising for the launch included the

promotion mix

A subset of the marketing mix that includes four main elements of marketing communication: advertising, sales promotion, personal selling, and public relations.

integrated marketing communications (IMC)

A promotional strategy that involves coordinating the various promotion mix elements to provide consumers with a clear and consistent message about a firm's products.

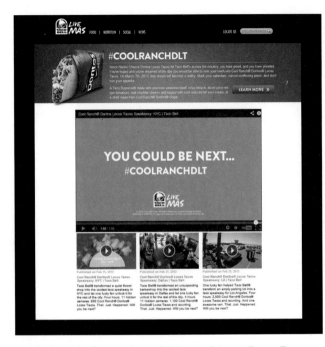

For the launch of its Cool Ranch® Doritos® Locos Tacos, Taco Bell, in partnership with Frito-Lay, used an integrated marketing communications strategy that included television, radio, outdoor, retail activation, and online advertising as well as public relations and social media promotions.

popular commercial titled "Road Trip." The commercial was inspired by the true story of a group of friends from New York who traveled to Ohio to try Taco Bell's Doritos Locos Tacos. The IMC strategy enjoyed almost immediate success; the company sold over 100 million Doritos Locos Tacos in the first 10 weeks.

Each of the promotion mix elements can exert influence on different segments of the target market, and marketers should try to understand the impact of each element within the IMC strategy. For the Locos Tacos launch, Taco Bell relied heavily on its television advertising. However, firms should use marketing research techniques to continuously assess which promotion mix elements have the most influence on different market segments at different points in the product life cycle. Based on this research, the marketing department can allocate more of its promotional budget to the elements that are most effective—those that can increase sales, build brand equity, and improve customer relationships when designed efficiently and implemented throughout the organization. Each promotion mix element has its own unique advantages and disadvantages, which are described in detail in the sections that follow.

ADVERTISING

LO 8-2

Compare the advantages and disadvantages of different types of advertising.

advertising

Nonpersonal promotional communication about goods, services, or ideas that is paid for by the firm identified in the communication.

advertising campaign

A collection of coordinated advertisements that share a single theme.

informative advertising

A type of advertising that attempts to develop initial demand for a product.

persuasive advertising

A type of advertising that attempts to increase demand for an existing product.

Advertising is the element of the promotion mix most consumers think of first. Advertising is nonpersonal promotional communication about goods, services, or ideas that is paid for by the firm identified in the communication. Two words in the definition, *paid* and *nonpersonal,* are key to understanding how advertising fits into the promotion mix. The paid aspect of the definition reflects that the time or space for an advertising message is purchased. Since it is paid for, advertising has the advantage of control; the purchaser decides how to present the message to the public. The nonpersonal component refers to the fact that advertising uses media (e.g., Internet, television, radio, print, etc.) to transmit a message to large numbers of individuals rather than marketing to consumers face-to-face.

Firms spend hundreds of billions of dollars on advertising campaigns each year in an effort to appeal to large numbers of individuals. An advertising campaign is a collection of coordinated advertisements that share a single theme. Marketers use advertising campaigns to achieve three primary objectives: to inform, to persuade, and to remind.

1. Informative advertising attempts to develop initial demand for a product. It's especially important in the introductory stage of the product life cycle. A flyer for an upcoming meeting of a new club at your college with the date, time, room number, and a description of the guest speaker classifies as informative advertising.

2. Persuasive advertising attempts to increase demand for an existing product. Persuasive advertising is common during the growth stage of the product life cycle as firms compete directly and attempt to take market share from one another. Persuasive advertising would include a speech from one of your professors that highlights the benefits of selecting a major in his or her course area.

3. Reminder advertising seeks to keep the product before the public in an effort to reinforce previous promotional activity. Reminder advertising is most common in the maturity and decline stages of the product life cycle. An e-mail prompting you to purchase season tickets to support one of your college's sports teams is an example of reminder advertising.

Depending on the firm's objective, marketers must also decide on the media to use to convey their message. Figure 8.2 illustrates the percentage of global advertising delivered via each major medium: the Internet, television, radio, magazines, newspapers, and outdoor (e.g., billboards; signs in sports arenas; skywriting; and ads on the side of buildings, buses, and cars). Notice that, though some forms are projected to remain relatively stable, newspaper advertising is expected to drop, while Internet advertising is expected to grow by approximately 5 percent. Each type of media has its own unique advantages and disadvantages that firms must understand if they want to determine the best fit for their specific product and budget.

Internet Advertising

Internet advertising takes many forms. Paid Internet advertising can be broken down into paid search and paid display advertising. Paid search advertising typically involves offering consumers advertising links to brand content based on what they're searching for. Paid display typically consists of banner advertising—a graphic display that appears on a website in an effort to get you to click on the content. For example, the 2013 movie *Olympus Has Fallen* was promoted using banner ads on sites like ESPN.com. Consumers could watch an extended movie trailer by clicking on the ad, which was located directly above the breaking news stories.

Social media platforms like Facebook are an ever more popular choice for Internet advertisers because they offer new strategies for online advertising. Facebook's sponsored stories feature posts from friends about a product, which firms pay to highlight to make them more visible to other potential consumers.[5] Coca-Cola, Levi's, UNICEF, and other organizations increasingly spend part of their ad budgets on these new strategies. Overall, the U.S. spends the most on online advertising, approximately $35.4 billion in 2012. However, Internet advertising is gaining popularity across the globe, with Asia-Pacific countries spending over $30 billion, while western European countries combined spent just under $27 billion.[6]

The Internet has also made it easier for organizations to advertise directly to consumers. Direct marketing is advertising that communicates directly with consumers and organizations in an effort to provoke a response. You have likely received an e-mail advertisement directed to you based on information that marketers have about you from your previous purchases or marketing research. The e-mail might contain information about a new product that might interest you or promote a special offer at a restaurant you frequent. By individually customizing their advertising using direct marketing strategies, firms seek to increase interest and awareness and, ultimately, generate additional revenue.

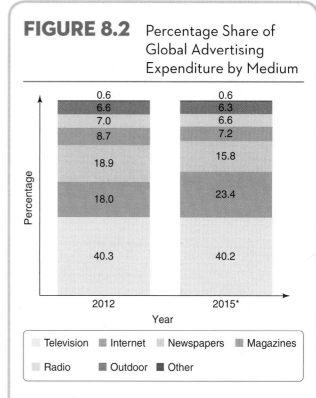

FIGURE 8.2   Percentage Share of Global Advertising Expenditure by Medium

*Projected.
Source: ZenithOptimedia, "Advertising Expenditure Forecasts, April 2013," http://www.zenithoptimedia.com/zenith/wp-content/uploads/2013/04/ZO-Adspend-Forecast-April-2013-executive-summary.pdf.

reminder advertising

A type of advertising that seeks to keep the product before the public in an effort to reinforce previous promotional activity.

direct marketing

Advertising that communicates directly with consumers and organizations in an effort to provoke a response.

Measurement tools like Google Analytics provide companies with data about their Internet advertising strategies, including how many people click on their advertising, visit their website, and purchase their products.

cost-per-thousand impressions (CPM)

What the firm pays for a thousand views of its ad.

cost per click (CPC)

The amount the firm pays each time a customer clicks on an ad.

click-through rate (CTR)

A ratio showing how often people who see an ad end up clicking on it.

Advantages of Internet Advertising One advantage of advertising via the Internet is the reduced cost relative to advertising on other media. Online video advertising rates have been falling 10–15 percent since 2011, and most social media ad content can be posted for almost nothing.[7] In addition, the effectiveness of Internet marketing is far more measurable than television, radio, or print options. Firms can use measurement tools like Google Analytics to closely monitor their return on investment, using metrics such as cost-per-thousand impressions, cost per click, and click-through rates to determine the success of their Internet advertising.

- Cost-per-thousand impressions (CPM) is what the firm pays for a thousand views of its ad. CPM exposes the firm and its products to potential customers.
- Cost per click (CPC) is the amount the firm pays each time a customer clicks on an ad. Monitoring CPC gives marketing professionals a more accurate picture of the effectiveness of their advertisement because the clicks represent some interest on the part of the customer.
- The click-through rate (CTR) is a ratio showing how often people who see an ad end up clicking on it. CTR can be used to gauge how well the firm's ads perform.

Firms that have access to such metrics and, more importantly, use them to determine the effectiveness of their marketing strategies are in a better position to modify those strategies as needed to increase sales.

Another major advantage of Internet advertising is the ability to target specific consumers. Marketers use cookies, which are small files on your computer that track information about the websites that you visit and the information that you share online, to collect data and design advertising based on those data. The average web page visit generates 50 data collection events that can provide direction to marketers in their efforts to segment and target specific consumers.[8]

Disadvantages of Internet Advertising For all its advantages, Internet advertising has drawbacks, including clutter and the difficulty of actually reaching consumers. Banner ads for example have an average CTR of around 0.1 percent, which means that if 1,000 people see a banner only one of them actually clicks on it.[9] Consumers have become so accustomed to seeing banner ads on websites that they no longer pay as much attention to them.

Another potential disadvantage of Internet advertising involves consumer privacy. Privacy advocates worry that data collection efforts by marketers will hurt consumers because information about their Internet habits could be released or used inappropriately. Privacy groups are pushing for new rules that would allow marketers to keep Internet data on consumers for only 24 hours unless consumers opt in and allow marketers to keep data for longer than that.[10] Privacy concerns have led marketers to use Internet advertising based on consumers' web-browsing habits 75 percent less than they would otherwise.[11] A major privacy breach could greatly harm an organization's image and the increased regulatory scrutiny gives Internet advertising an uncertain future that is troublesome for some marketers.

Television Advertising

People often think of television advertising first when they hear the term *marketing*. Television advertising is very different today than it was a generation ago. In the early 1980s, the most popular television show was "Dallas," and more than 30 million people tuned in every week to watch J.R. Ewing and the drama that surrounded his family.[12] Today, the most popular shows on television often average less than 10 million viewers per week, and running ads during such shows comes at an increasingly high cost to firms. Marketing professionals must understand the changing landscape of television advertising and consider the various advantages and disadvantages of trying to reach consumers in this way.

Advantages of TV Advertising

One reason for the decreased viewership of top-rated TV programs is the greater number of channels available to consumers. In the early 1980s the average American home had access to less than 20 channels. Today the average American household can choose from over 118 channels, plus a variety of pay-per-view and on-demand options.[14]

A large number of channels provides marketers an opportunity to target specific

When TNT revived the show "Dallas" in 2012, it became one of the most watched new shows of the year. Even with its success, the number of weekly viewers for the new show averaged less than 7 million viewers per week.[13]

markets through narrowcasting. Narrowcasting is the dissemination of information (often by television) to a fairly small, select audience that is defined by its shared values, preferences, or demographic attributes. For example, firms that marketed products to tennis fans a generation ago might have advertised heavily on ESPN, which at the time was the only all-sports channel on many basic cable subscriptions. Now these same firms can promote their equipment and tennis apparel on The Tennis Channel, which is broadcast to over 34 million households in the U.S.[15] While the average viewership of The Tennis Channel is far lower than ESPN, the audience is almost exclusively tennis enthusiasts, allowing marketers to reach their target market at a lower cost (ads on The Tennis Channel are far less expensive than on ESPN) and without wasting a significant amount of advertising on people who prefer other sports.

Another major advantage of television advertising is the ability to combine sight, sound, and motion to appeal to consumer senses. Television ads can develop messages that entertain or emotionally appeal to consumers in ways that radio and print media cannot. In addition, television ads can demonstrate a product in use, for example, a new Toyota product with a rear camera that allows drivers to see the child's bike sitting behind it or the absorption power of the ShamWow. Such demonstrations give consumers a better understanding of what owning the product would mean to their daily lives.

narrowcasting

The dissemination of information to a fairly small, select audience that is defined by its shared values, preferences, or demographic attributes.

Disadvantages of Television Advertising

Perhaps the biggest disadvantage of television advertising is cost. The cost to air a single 30-second ad on a major broadcast network (NBC, ABC, CBS, or Fox) during prime time averages well over $100,000.[16] Ads for special events, such as the Super Bowl or the Academy Awards, can cost significantly more. In recent years, a 30-second television ad during the Super Bowl cost over $3 million.[17] Creating television ads is also expensive relative to other types of advertising. Television commercials can cost tens or even hundreds of thousands of dollars to make, depending on the length, complexity, and method used.

Complicating the use of television advertising is the rapid growth of digital video recorders (DVRs). Over half of all American households that subscribe to cable or satellite television services now have some type of DVR for recording and watching

Hulu has experimented with allowing consumers to customize their ad-viewing experience. Though Hulu's technology prevents consumers from fast-forwarding through ads, it allows consumers to choose the ad they would prefer to watch from among three different options.

their favorite programs.[18] Consumers love the ability to skip or fast-forward through ads to reduce the time it takes to watch shows or events, which leaves marketing professionals paying for television ads that viewers aren't watching. In response, firms are exploring new technologies to ensure that viewers see their ad content. It has become common practice to hold the camera on a product for an extended period of time so that a viewer who is fast-forwarding through the commercial still has enough time to register the product. Firms are also implementing new strategies to put their ads directly into the program content using product placement.

Product Placement   The use of product placement has expanded in the past decade as marketers look for ways to get their products in front of their target audience despite the prevalence of DVRs. Product placement is an advertising technique in which a company promotes its products through appearances on television shows, movies, or other media. For example, Sony used the 2012 hit movie *The Amazing Spider-Man* to promote several of its consumer electronic products. In the movie, Spider-Man uses a Sony smartphone to make calls, check voicemail, and listen to police radio broadcasts.[19] Even the movie's villain, Dr. Curt Connors, stays connected using a Sony Vaio laptop and records his experiments with a Sony camcorder. Sony chose to place its products in *The Amazing Spider-Man* in an effort to increase its coolness factor with young consumers used to associating cool with companies like Apple.

Product placement has expanded beyond television and movies in recent years. In 2012, the National Basketball Association (NBA) developed a plan to become the first major North American sports association to allow teams to advertise on player jerseys.[20] The ads consist of 2.5-by-2.5-inch patches located on the left shoulder of the jersey, where the NBA logo used to be found. The ads allow marketers to feature their brand prominently during NBA games rather than only during commercials, which sports fans may not watch. The NBA estimates that this use of product placement will generate $100 million per year in new revenue in the coming years.

product placement

An advertising technique in which a company promotes its products through appearances on television shows, movies, or other media.

Interactive Assignment 8-1
Social Media in Action

The language of social media includes words such as *fans*, *friend request*, and *status update* that increasingly appear in all types of advertising. The starring role of social media phrases and buzzwords signals that marketers believe that a large segment of the population recognizes these terms. Marketers for the Toyota Venza used social media in an ad campaign centered on "the redefinition of social" that highlighted how the car could appeal to a wide range of demographic groups. A print ad read, "My mom hasn't accepted my friend request yet. What could she possibly be doing?" The ad then revealed that Mom had driven her Toyota Venza with non-virtual friends to go biking in the mountains. The ads were well received, indicating that the use of social media made the campaign very understandable for consumers.

Other firms have also used the language of social media in their advertising to communicate with consumers. Mars has created ads for Snickers Peanut Butter Squared candy in which the word *like* and a thumbs up, similar to what you would see on Facebook, appear over a competitor's product while a heart and the word *love* hover over the image of the Snickers product. Marketers for Chinet paper plates used advertisements that portrayed their product as "the official plate of logging on to something social." Positive response to the ads prompted Chinet to expand the ad campaign to include all of Chinet's products with the slogan "You're Invited."

The Social Media in Action *Connect* exercise in Chapter 8 will let you develop potential advertisements emphasizing social media to reach targeted consumers. By understanding strategies that can integrate social media tools and terminology, you will be prepared to develop effective advertising for consumers of various demographic groups and interests.

Source: See Stuart Elliott, "Ads That Speak the Language of Social Media," *The New York Times*, March 24, 2013, http://www.nytimes.com/2013/03/25/business/media/ads-that-speak-the-language-of-social-media.html?_r=0.

Radio Advertising

There are thousands of radio stations in the United States, ranging from satellite radio stations that reach consumers across the country to local terrestrial stations that reach only small, rural communities. Radio advertising remains a powerful promotional tool because consumers can listen to the radio in their cars, online, and virtually anywhere else through their smartphones. Marketers spend approximately $14 billion per year on radio advertising, which provides certain unique advantages and disadvantages.[21]

Advantages of Radio Advertising Radio advertising has two major advantages. First, radio advertising is often the most cost-effective medium available to a company. Not only is buying radio ad time far cheaper than buying television ad time, the production costs are comparatively low or even nonexistent if the ad is read live during a broadcast.

A second advantage is that radio advertising allows marketers to segment effectively based on the geographic location and type of format a radio station uses. The narrow transmission of terrestrial radio stations provides a great way to market to small geographic regions. While most regions of the country have a limited number of television markets that serve a large proportion of the population, each region has significantly more radio stations, including many that serve very small or rural communities. The local nature of radio makes it a perfect advertising medium for small merchants in the listening area. Marketers can also segment consumers by what they listen to: country, pop, gospel, hip-hop, heavy metal, sports talk, politics, and numerous other formats. Advertising on stations that cater to these different audiences is a form of narrowcasting that allows firms to target more effectively.

Disadvantages of Radio Advertising   Traditionally, the biggest disadvantage of radio advertising has been that radio ads are audio-only. Being able to appeal to only one sense makes it difficult for companies to illustrate the uses and benefits of their products. In recent years, technology advances have created several additional disadvantages for radio advertising. Most cars today have digital presets that allow listeners to switch stations when a commercial comes on simply by touching a button. For traditional music-based radio stations, the popularity of satellite radio represents an emerging challenge. Though satellite channels devoted to sports and news typically air ads, music stations on satellite radio are commercial-free. Finally, most new cars today come with the ability to plug in an MP3 player or smartphone. Over 38 percent of Americans listen to content on digital devices in their car and that number is expected to double by 2015, making it harder for traditional radio advertising to reach these customers.[22] In response to these challenges, firms like Subway are exploring creative ways to reach consumers listening to podcasts and other digital content. Subway has partnered with ESPN to sponsor several of its most popular podcasts, such as "The B.S. Report" with Bill Simmons. The podcast is free and averages over 600,000 downloads per episode.[23] Each podcast includes several mentions of Subway products, allowing the firm to reach listeners of the show in a new way.

SiriusXM, the leading satellite radio company in North America, represents a challenge to traditional radio advertising because of its paid subscriber base of over 20 million customers who get over 140 commercial-free music channels they can listen to anywhere in the country.[24]

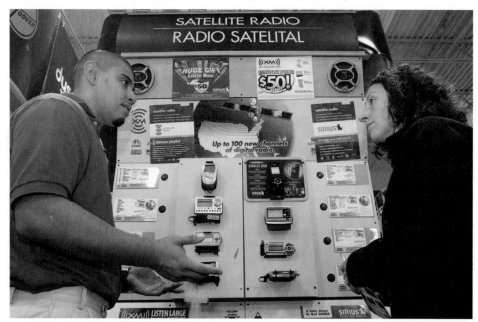

Print Advertising

Print media, which typically comprises newspapers and magazines, requires a greater degree of involvement on the part of the consumer than broadcast media. Readers choose what they want to read and then can spend as much time as they want reading it. This makes print advertising especially appealing for high-involvement (significant) consumer products, such as a house or a car.

Advantages of Print Advertising
Newspapers have been a valuable tool for marketers, especially retailers, for well over a century. Marketers spend over $20 billion each year on newspaper advertising, although that number is less than half of what it was in 2005.[25] Newspaper advertising has two major advantages. First, newspaper advertising is an effective way for small businesses to advertise their goods or services to the local community. Small-town newspapers or local community inserts in larger city (or even national) newspapers help marketers attract the local population that is most likely to buy their products. In addition, firms can run their ads in a particular section of the newspaper if their business or product is specific to that section. For example, if you run a sporting goods store you might specify that your ad should appear in the paper's sports section; if you are a financial advisor you can run your ad in the business section.

In addition to newspapers, there are thousands of special interest magazines in the U.S. and throughout the world covering almost every possible subject or interest. Approximately half of all U.S. adults look through at least one magazine on a regular basis.[26] Marketers divide magazines into two categories: business magazines (e.g., *Bloomberg Businessweek*, *Fortune*, and *Money*) and consumer magazines (e.g., *People*, *Better Homes and Gardens*, and *Sports Illustrated*). Consumer magazines have a wider audience and present subject matter using a more general approach than business magazines, as illustrated by the list of the most popular consumer magazines in Figure 8.3 on the next page.

Both business and consumer magazines allow firms to segment based on a variety of demographic, geographic, and behavioral variables to reach their target audience. For example, *AARP Bulletin*, *Cosmopolitan*, and *Parenting* offer marketers the ability to reach very precise target markets with their ads. Magazine advertisements also have a longer shelf life than daily newspapers. Imagine that a consumer is traveling for the weekend and gets home to find three editions of the daily newspaper waiting; it's unlikely that he or she will read any of them. Compare that to readers of *Bloomberg Businessweek* who have a full week to read the content before a new issue arrives.

Disadvantages of Print Advertising
The major disadvantage of advertising in print media is that fewer and fewer Americans use that as their primary information source. Younger consumers often receive news, entertainment, and employment information via computers and portable electronic devices. Even if they still rely on newspapers and magazines for information, they may choose to access the content online rather than buying the hard copy. An additional disadvantage for newspaper advertising is that newspaper ads compete with other ads and editorial content for the consumer's attention. Firms with small or unimaginative ads risk the possibility that readers will pass over them completely while they engage with larger or more interesting graphics. Readers viewing multiple ads may also subconsciously spend less time on each individual ad.

Magazine advertising has several disadvantages as well, beginning with the lead time necessary to place an ad. The timeframe for designing a magazine forces marketers to plan and prepare advertisements months in advance of publication. As a result, the target audience might not see the ad until after the firm has committed the time and resources to the advertisement. If you own a small start-up business, the amount of time you spend waiting for your ad to bring in revenue could determine whether the business succeeds or fails. Beyond this, events may

FIGURE 8.3   Most Popular U.S. Consumer Magazines

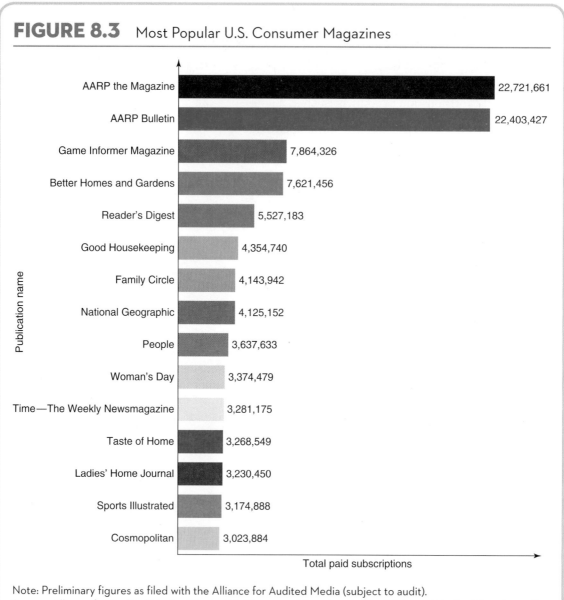

Note: Preliminary figures as filed with the Alliance for Audited Media (subject to audit).
Source: Alliance for Audited Media, "Top 25 U.S. Consumer Magazines by Total Paid and Verified Circulation," February 7, 2013, http://www.auditedmedia.com/news/blog/2013/february/top-25-us-consumer-magazines-by-total-paid-and-verified-circulation.aspx.

occur between when the ad is placed and when it is seen that limit the impact of the ad or affect the way readers perceive it. In addition, marketers typically do not control where their advertisements are placed in relation to the features and stories contained in the publication. Effective placement of an ad is essential to its success or failure. An advertisement placed in the back of the magazine may not receive the same attention as those at the front.

Outdoor Advertising

Outdoor advertising includes billboards, signs in sports arenas, skywriting, and ads on the sides of buildings, buses, and cars. Outdoor advertising has several advantages, including its flexibility and reduced costs, that are very appealing to marketers.

Advantages of Outdoor Advertising Outdoor ads can be located where they will most likely be seen. For example, a company selling organic foods might advertise on a billboard near a farmer's market. A new college night club might advertise outside of a popular restaurant to target diners looking for someplace to go later in the evening. These same ads, if placed in a newspaper or on the radio, may be missed altogether by the target market. Outdoor advertisements are also one of the most cost-efficient ways to reach potential customers and clients and are generally cheaper than television, radio, or print advertisements.[27]

Disadvantages of Outdoor Advertising Outdoor advertising also has several disadvantages. First, because of the speed people travel in cars, the exposure time for outdoor ads is generally very short. This limits the number of words or images that firms can use effectively. Too much information on an outdoor ad can make it difficult to see, read, and understand in the limited amount of time consumers have as they walk or drive by. The other major disadvantage is wasted coverage. While outdoor advertising allows companies to target specific areas, it is unlikely that everyone driving past an outdoor ad is part of the target market. An outdoor advertisement for a new local restaurant might look great, but its effect is wasted on those audiences who do not like the type of food or price range promoted.

mobile advertising

A form of advertising that is communicated to the consumer via a handheld device.

Nontraditional Advertising

Business spending on traditional advertising like television, radio, and newspapers has been declining over the past decade. However, spending on nontraditional advertising has increased as firms place messages on everything from valet tickets to hubcaps. KFC used nontraditional advertising to help an Indiana town in need of new fire hydrants. The firm paid the town to place Fiery Grilled Wing ads on three hydrants, helping to offset the cost of the new hydrants.

Mobile advertising is a form of advertising that is communicated to the consumer via a handheld device. It has experienced significant growth in recent years. Over 45 percent of U.S. adults use smartphones and most keep their devices within arm's reach the majority of the day, allowing tech-savvy marketers a way to reach consumers at virtually any time.[28] One of Chevrolet's recent Super Bowl mobile ads was a "Chevy Game Time" app. The app was designed to keep consumers' attention on the Chevy products on their phone or tablet computer and away from commercials from other companies on their television sets. It rewarded players who paid attention to the app and answered trivia questions to win prizes during the game. As many as 700,000 users signed into the Chevy app, and over 21 million trivia questions were answered.[29]

Another fast growing area for advertisers is video games. The global market for ads in video games is expected to grow from $3.1 billion in 2010 to $7.2 billion in 2016.[30] For example, the popular video game *FIFA International Soccer* prominently displays an Adidas ad on an onscreen billboard as users play. Video game

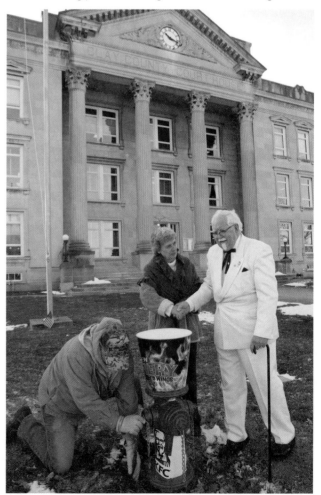

Nontraditional advertising strategies, such as KFC's fire hydrant promotion in Indiana, capture the attention of consumers, a task that's increasingly difficult through traditional advertising media.

advertising benefits from widespread Internet connectivity and larger bandwidth, both of which allow manufacturers to deliver advertisements remotely and update advertisements after the game is launched. In October 2008, then-U.S. presidential candidate Barack Obama placed advertisements in numerous Xbox games destined for sale in 10 swing states, including the racing game *Burnout Paradise.*

When implementing nontraditional advertising, marketers must avoid harming or offending consumers. In 2007 Dr Pepper held a promotional treasure hunt in Boston, Massachusetts, in which a $10,000 prize was hidden in a cemetery. The event would have ultimately led pickaxe-wielding consumers into a 350-year-old graveyard in search of the prize. Unsurprisingly, Dr Pepper was eventually forced to cancel the event.[31]

As consumer behavior continues to evolve, firms will turn more and more to nontraditional advertising at the expense of traditional advertising like television commercials or newspaper ads. Marketers must be on the lookout for new and better ways to get their message in front of their target consumers.

---

connect Interactive Assignment 8-2
| MARKETING

Please complete the *Connect* exercise for Chapter 8 that focuses on the advantages and disadvantages of different advertising media. By understanding the benefits and challenges of each form of advertising, you will be able to choose the appropriate advertising media to successfully execute your organization's marketing strategy.

---

sales promotion

A set of nonpersonal communication tools designed to stimulate quicker and more frequent purchases of a product.

LO 8-3

Summarize the various types of sales promotion.

coupons

Documents that entitle the customers who carry them to a discount on a product.

Coupons, whether in traditional or electronic form, for products such as cosmetics, hair care, and diapers continue to be in demand.

SALES PROMOTION

Sales promotion activities account for the bulk of most firms' promotional budgets. Firms often use sales promotion to support the other elements of their promotion mix. Sales promotion is a set of nonpersonal communication tools designed to stimulate quicker and more frequent purchases of a product. For example, in recent years McDonald's implemented a sales promotion in which young customers received plastic figures of the cartoon characters The Smurfs in their Happy Meals.[32] The promotion prompted more consumers to buy Happy Meals in an effort to add to their Smurf collections. Successful sales promotions like this have the potential to build short-term excitement and long-term customer relationships simultaneously. We'll discuss some common sales promotions in the sections that follow.

Coupons

Coupons remain the most common type of sales promotion. Coupons are documents that entitle the customers who carry them to a discount on a product. Traditionally, coupons have come in the form of printed vouchers that customers present to claim their discount. However, the expansion of mobile advertising and the popularity of websites like Groupon have allowed companies to distribute coupons digitally to a smartphone device that the targeted consumer can then redeem directly from that device at a specific business.

Coupons provide firms with an effective method for stimulating sales and encouraging customers to make additional or repeat purchases. In addition, a firm can control the timing and distribution of coupons in a way that does not dilute potential revenue from a customer who is happy paying full price. However, coupons also have several disadvantages. Coupon fraud is a serious problem in the form of misredemption practices. Misredemptions can range from illegal copying of coupons by the consumer to innocent mistakes by an employee who gives too large a discount or forgets to take the coupon from the customer after the purchase. All misredemptions have the effect of reducing the firm's profitability, so care must be taken to anticipate and discourage such practices.

Rebates

Many promotional strategies make use of rebates; marketing professionals offer over 400 million rebates each year.[33] Rebates allow consumers to recoup a specified amount of money after making a single purchase. While most customers prefer coupons because they're easier to use, most marketers prefer rebates. Rebates provide the incentive of a price decrease, but, since customers often fail to redeem them—statistics show that between 40 percent and 60 percent of all rebates are not redeemed[34]—the firm typically earns greater profits than it would by issuing coupons. Rebates work most effectively when offered in conjunction with a high-involvement purchase in which the perceived value of the rebate is magnified. A $200 rebate for a flat screen television or a $2,000 rebate for a new car typically generates more purchases than small rebates for everyday items that consumers tend to forget about.

rebates
Sales promotions that allow consumers to recoup a specified amount of money after making a single purchase.

Samples

Samples offer potential consumers the chance to actually try the product. They have been an effective sales promotion tool for decades and involve everything from trying a new type of sausage at your local grocery store to getting a free weekend of HBO's TV programming. Samples can be expensive, since marketers are giving away products in many cases, but they can also be a powerful tool for getting customers to actually buy the product. Marketers of baby formula often send samples to new mothers in the hopes that the family will like it and start using that brand of formula during the child's first years of life.

Contests and Sweepstakes

Firms spend approximately $2 billion per year on contests and sweepstakes. The terms *contest* and *sweepstakes* are often used interchangeably, but there is a distinct difference between the two.

- Contests are sales promotions in which consumers compete against one another and must demonstrate skill to win. Contests provide marketers with a way to engage consumers and empower them to promote an organization's products and brand. For example, Oreo sponsored an "Oreo and Milk Jingle" video contest that offered cash prizes and trips to the group who did the best job designing and singing the "Oreo and Milk" jingle.[35]
- Sweepstakes are sales promotions based on chance. The only requirement to win is that you enter. Every entry has an equal chance of being drawn as the winner. An example of sweepstakes includes the HGTV Dream Home Giveaway, in which HGTV randomly selected a viewer to win $500,000 and a cottage in Hawaii.[36] Sweepstakes like HGTV's have the advantage of creating interest and excitement from a broad group of consumers. This particular sweepstakes also helped bring HGTV to a wider audience.

contests
Sales promotions in which consumers compete against one another and must demonstrate skill to win.

sweepstakes
Sales promotions based on chance such that entry is the only requirement to win.

Both contests and sweepstakes have disadvantages. Contests can be expensive to administer because each entry must be judged, meaning firms can't rely on random selection. A potential disadvantage of sweepstakes is the legal and regulatory issues that can arise. Publishers Clearing House was fined millions of dollars to resolve allegations that it misled the public in its advertising campaign portraying average

Amazon Prime and other loyalty programs help companies retain customers even in the face of fierce competition and a decrease in the natural loyalty customers feel toward firms and products.

loyalty programs

Sales promotions that allow consumers to accumulate points or other benefits for doing business with the same company.

trade sales promotions

Sales promotions directed to B2B firms, including wholesalers, retailers, and distributors, rather than individual consumers.

allowances

Trade promotions that typically involve paying retailers for financial losses associated with consumer sales promotions or reimbursing a retailer for an in-store or local expense to promote a specific product.

Americans winning millions of dollars by participating in the company's well-known sweepstakes. Multiple federal and state government agencies monitor contests and sweepstakes to make sure they are fair and properly represented to the public.

Loyalty Programs

Designed to strengthen customer relationships, loyalty programs allow consumers to accumulate points or other benefits for doing business with the same company. Loyalty programs are especially popular in the airline and hotel businesses. Holiday Inn, for example, has had success with its Priority Club loyalty rewards program. Global membership in the loyalty club has reached over 65 million, and members are rewarded with points that increase more rapidly the more often they stay at a Holiday Inn hotel.[37] The points can then be turned into free hotel stays, gift cards, and even charitable contributions.

Loyalty programs have grown in importance as natural loyalty to products has decreased in many industries. Increasingly, consumers view things like flights to Boston or hotel rooms in Chicago as commodities and make their decision about which company to buy from based solely on price. Loyalty programs offer incentives that encourage satisfied consumers to go out of their way to fly Delta Airlines or stay at a Holiday Inn Express in an effort to receive additional rewards.

Trade Sales Promotions

The sales promotion tools discussed up to this point are often directed to individual consumers. Trade sales promotions are promotion tools directed to B2B firms, including wholesalers and retailers, rather than individual consumers. Trade sales promotions often include the same tools discussed earlier (coupons, rebates, contests and sweepstakes, and loyalty programs), plus two other major approaches:

1. *Allowances.* Allowances typically involve paying retailers for financial losses associated with consumer sales promotions or reimbursing a retailer for an in-store or local expense to promote a specific product. For example, a local grocery store might be reimbursed for a radio ad that mentions that Diet Dr Pepper is on sale over the next few days. Typically, the firm will only pay the retailer once it has proof of the financial loss or local promotion costs.
2. *Training.* The other major trade sale promotion is training the reseller's sales force. Training activities such as brochures or on-site demonstrations help retail and wholesale personnel understand the product's benefits. This in turn makes the resellers better equipped to speak with consumers and sell the firm's products. Training also helps to ensure that employees at every level understand the features, advantages, and benefits of the products they are trying to sell.

LO 8-4

Explain the importance of personal selling.

personal selling

The two-way flow of communication between a salesperson and a customer that is paid for by the firm and seeks to influence the customer's purchase decision.

PERSONAL SELLING

Personal selling takes many forms and can include someone trying to sell you insurance or a new car. It can even take the form of the person behind the fast food counter trying to get you to upsize your order. Personal selling is the two-way flow of communication between a salesperson and a customer that is paid for by the firm and seeks to influence the customer's purchase decision. Despite economic and technological changes, the role of personal selling is more important today than ever before. Salespeople often serve as the critical link between the firm and the customer. They are the eyes and ears of the organization and help marketers understand what customers like and dislike and what changes are happening within an industry. Personal selling differs from the other tools of the promotion mix because messages flow directly from the salesperson to the customer, often face-to-face.

A major challenge of personal selling is the cost involved. The average cost of a sales call varies across industries but almost always averages several hundred dollars per visit.[38] The costs are even higher when you consider that, for most products, one sales call will not result directly in an order. Historically, the other challenge for personal selling has been ensuring that each salesperson communicates a message that is consistent with other salespeople as well as the full integrated marketing communications strategy. Inconsistent messaging is the equivalent of a firm having as many marketing strategies as it does salespeople. Firms can overcome this challenge by offering information and training to the sales force.

While personal selling is one of the most expensive elements of the promotion mix, it offers two unique advantages over the other promotional elements:

1. Personal selling results in immediate feedback from the customer. Perhaps most importantly, the salesperson can see the nonverbal communication that might give insight into the customer's mindset and the likelihood that he or she will buy. In addition, the salesperson can listen directly to the feedback, objections, and concerns that the customer has. This allows the salesperson to adjust the sales presentation accordingly and provide detailed and customized solutions that can generate more sales.
2. Personal selling allows the firm to develop a personal relationship with the customer. Relationship selling involves building a trusting relationship with a customer over a long period of time. Relationship selling is increasingly important since very few firms can survive on the profits generated from one-time transactional sales.

relationship selling

Building a trusting relationship with a customer over a long period of time.

Personal selling is the single most effective approach for establishing and developing a personal relationship with the customer. While personal selling often involves face-to-face interaction, technology and social media can support and enhance that relationship.

The Impact of Social Media on Personal Selling

Social media have revolutionized the way customers gain access to and use information to make purchase decisions. Customers used to rely heavily on salespeople and other elements of the promotion mix for information about a company's products, but no longer. Today, customers can obtain information from a myriad of online sources, many of which are out of a firm's direct control. However, rather than fear the changing dynamic, companies can embrace all the tools at their disposal, including social media, and use them to their advantage. Ford incorporated social media during the launch of its 2010 Explorer by building relationships with customers early via an online community. The company

IBM salespeople reach their target market in a new way by gathering data from the Internet about what words potential customers use to search for solutions to their software problems and then posting inexpensive how-to videos addressing those problems to the Internet.

allowed the community to review and provide feedback on the plans for the new model. Enthusiastic customers were also invited to preview the car and test drive the new model. The company's outreach extended to dealers as well. By the time the car was officially launched, the company had already secured 10,000 pre-orders.[39]

Finally, social media allow salespeople to stay in close contact with their current and potential customers. A salesperson who is a Facebook friend of a customer can get a better understanding of what motivates that person and what's going on in his or her life. Social media have provided new tools to make personal selling easier and more effective. Whether a salesperson is using a new medium or interacting with a customer face-to-face, personal selling involves the same basic process.

THE PERSONAL-SELLING PROCESS

There are over 13 million Americans working as salespeople today. This means that salespeople comprise over 4 percent of the U.S. population.[40] Selling is a complex process that spans everything from initially searching for prospects to following up with customers after the sale. The specific process followed by each salesperson varies based on experience, selling situation, and individual firms; however, most move through the general sales process illustrated in Figure 8.4.

Step 1: Prospecting and Qualifying

Prospecting and qualifying are the lifeblood of the personal-selling process as firms constantly seek new customers for their business. Prospecting involves the search for potential customers—those who need or want a product and fit into a firm's target market. Potential customers can be found in a variety of ways, including from customer referrals, trade shows, industry directories, websites, and networking.

While merely finding potential customers is important, the main goal of this step is to find *qualified* prospects. Qualifying prospects involves identifying which potential customers within the firm's target market have not only a desire for the product but also the authority to purchase it and the resources to pay for it. Salespeople qualify prospects using a number of tools, including talking with the potential customer and conducting marketing research to better understand the target customer's needs, wants, and ability to pay. Once a salesperson qualifies a prospect, the prospect is further targeted based on how much income he or she may generate for the company and how probable it is that he or she will become a customer. This further targeting is an essential step. Firms will approach higher-rated prospects differently, with greater effort, than lower-rated prospects, who may only receive e-mails and a quarterly phone call.

Step 2: The Preapproach

Before engaging in the actual personal-selling process, sales professionals first analyze all the information available to them about a prospect. The preapproach involves identifying key decision makers, reviewing account histories, identifying product needs, and preparing sales presentations. Rather than traditional

LO 8-5
Outline the personal-selling process.

prospecting
The search for potential customers—those who need or want a product and fit into a firm's target market.

qualifying
A part of the personal-selling process that involves identifying which potential customers within the firm's target market have not only a desire for the product but also the authority to purchase it and the resources to pay for it.

preapproach
A part of the personal-selling process that involves identifying key decision makers, reviewing account histories, identifying product needs, and preparing sales presentations.

cold calling, which is the process of approaching unknown prospective customers or clients, salespeople today can use technology to understand customers and their needs and wants. Quality preapproach research focuses on a consumer or organization and the environmental forces at work in the consumer's life or the organization's industry. The entire personal-selling process can result in failure if the salesperson doesn't learn as much as possible about the prospect before approaching them to complete the sale.

Step 3: The Approach

The approach step includes the initial meeting between the salesperson and the prospect. During the approach, the sales professional meets and greets the prospect, provides an introduction, establishes a rapport that sets a foundation for the relationship, and asks open-ended questions to learn more about the prospect and his or her needs and wants. Ultimately, the customer must be convinced that the salesperson is offering something of value.

When approaching a customer, salespeople must understand any cultural protocols at play. For example, a salesperson approaching a U.S. prospect would likely begin with a firm handshake. In contrast, when approaching an international prospect, the custom would differ. A French prospect would expect a gentle handshake while Japanese prospects would expect an appropriate bow. Again, the success of the approach depends largely on the level of preparation the salesperson has achieved in the preapproach step.

Step 4: The Presentation

After the approach, the salesperson should be prepared to present the product's major features, describe its strengths, and detail how it will improve the business or life of the potential customer. In any situation, the sales presentation provides a forum to convey the organization's marketing message to the prospect. Authors Mark Johnston and Greg Marshall suggest that a great sales presentation displays the following four characteristics:[41]

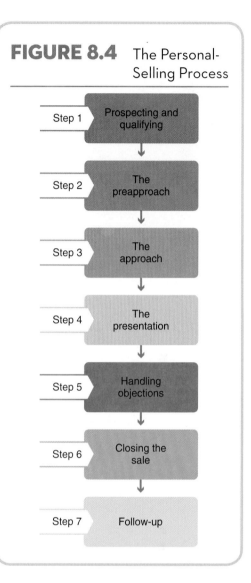

FIGURE 8.4   The Personal-Selling Process

Step 1 Prospecting and qualifying

Step 2 The preapproach

Step 3 The approach

Step 4 The presentation

Step 5 Handling objections

Step 6 Closing the sale

Step 7 Follow-up

1. *Explains the value proposition.* The sales presentation should make it very clear what value the product holds for the customer.
2. *Asserts the advantages and benefits of the product.* Each sales presentation should clearly state the advantages and benefits of the product relative to competing products or not purchasing a product at all.
3. *Enhances the customer's knowledge of the company and product.* Customers want to do business with organizations they like and trust. In addition to providing important information about the product, the sales presentation should also reinforce why the organization will be a good partner to the customer.
4. *Creates a memorable experience.* Salespeople should spend time thinking about what they want the customer to remember about the presentation. Customers will use these memories as they make purchase decisions, so focusing on key words, phrases, or images during the presentation can be critical.

Planning and preparation lead directly to successful sales presentations; however, salespeople should not underestimate the value of listening during the presentation. Talking too much can signal a lack of real interest in the prospect's needs and wants. In addition, presentations must be prepared with an understanding

cold calling

The process of approaching unknown prospective customers or clients.

approach

A part of the personal-selling process that involves meeting the prospect and learning more about his or her needs and wants.

sales presentation

A forum to convey the organization's marketing message to the prospect.

The sales presentation can range from a girl scout selling cookies at your door to you giving a PowerPoint presentation to a purchasing manager at a major firm.

of the value of the customer's time. They should quickly and efficiently link the firm's goods, services, and ideas to solutions that help the customer.

Step 5: Handling Objections

objections

The concerns or reasons customers offer for not buying a product.

Objections can be an opportunity to clarify and reassure the customer about pricing, features, and other potential issues. Objections are the concerns or reasons customers offer for not buying a product. Handling objections requires professionalism, strong communication skills, and a sincere respect for the prospect's concerns. Common techniques for overcoming objections include:

- *Acknowledging the objection.* "Yes, our prices are higher because our product is better." This allows the salesperson an additional opportunity to stress the benefits of the product. For example, consumers are willing to pay higher prices provided they've been given a clear reason (higher quality, better safety, more efficient, etc.) for spending more.
- *Postponing.* "We'll discuss the delivery option in a few minutes, but first let me ask about your needs in this area . . . ." Salespeople should postpone addressing objections if the full context of an appropriate answer has not been developed. This strategy works best if the salesperson plans to address an objection shortly. Postponing for too long will frustrate customers and reduce their level of trust.
- *Denial.* "That is not accurate. The truth is . . . ." If a customer mentions something that is completely false, the salesperson should strongly deny the point, but only in a way that is not offensive or insulting to the customer.

Young salespeople often make the mistake of striving to go through an entire sales presentation without any objections from the prospective customer. The ability to answer specific objections is one of the major advantages of personal selling compared to other elements of the promotion mix. Salespeople should make sure to validate the customer's objection, no matter how trivial it might seem, because the customer finds it important. Successfully dealing with objections, large and small, can strengthen the customer relationship and encourage sales now and in the future.

Step 6: Closing the Sale

closing

The point at which the salesperson asks the prospect for the sale.

The close is often the most difficult part of the personal-selling process because it requires the salesperson to overcome the basic human fear of being rejected. Closing the sale occurs at the point when the salesperson asks the prospect for the sale. The majority of customers will not take the initiative to close the sale, so the act of asking for the sale is very important to securing it.

Salespeople generally use one of the three major closing strategies that follow:

1. *Summarization close.* The salesperson summarizes the product's benefits and how it meets the customer's needs before asking for the sale.
2. *Trial method.* The salesperson solicits customer reaction without asking for the sale directly.
3. *Assumptive close.* The salesperson asks something like, "What date do you want those products delivered?" knowing that if the customer responds with a specific date, he or she has decided to make the purchase.

No salesperson can rely only on one closing strategy. Each can be used effectively, depending on the customer and the specific situation. Salespeople who listen closely to the clues given by the customer during the earlier steps of the personal-selling process will be best prepared to select the appropriate closing strategy.

Step 7: Follow-Up

After spending time and resources to close a new customer, it is essential to keep them as a customer as long as possible. Conventional wisdom says that it costs five times as much to acquire a new customer as to keep an existing one. Because of this, the follow-up stage is a critical step in creating customer satisfaction and building long-term relationships with customers. If the customer experienced any problems with the firm's product, the salesperson can intervene and become a customer advocate to ensure 100 percent satisfaction. A tremendous amount of activity happens after the sale. Most importantly, customers often share their experiences with others. They may talk with a few friends and family, or they may share their thoughts with hundreds, thousands, or even millions of others through social media. Diligent follow-up can also lead to uncovering new customer needs or wants, securing additional purchases, and obtaining referrals and testimonials that can be used as sales tools.

EXECUTIVE PERSPECTIVE

Teresa Goodnight
Senior Director of Sales
Zayo Group

What is the most important skill that salespeople need to be successful as they move through the personal-selling process?

Definitely the ability to listen. The best salespeople are *not* the people who can talk the most. In this day and age, they are often the ones who listen intently and collaborate with their prospects to generate a win-win solution. They close business with a real answer to a problem, and that real answer can only be found by listening and truly understanding the nature of the problem.

 Interactive Assignment 8-3

|MARKETING

Please complete the *Connect* exercise for Chapter 8 that focuses on the personal-selling process. By identifying the necessary actions and decisions at each step, you will understand how to successfully navigate the process and increase sales for your organization.

PUBLIC RELATIONS

Public relations strategies provide information and build a firm's image with the public, including customers, employees, stockholders, and communities. Public relations is nonpersonal communication focused on promoting positive relations between a firm and its stakeholders. Organizations use a variety of tools for public relations, including the following:

- *Annual reports* provide a forum for the organization to share with its stakeholders what it has achieved over the past year. They present the firm with an opportunity to highlight financial successes as well as charitable and philanthropic work that portray the organization in a positive light.

LO 8-6

Describe the role of public relations within the promotion mix.

public relations

Nonpersonal communication focused on promoting positive relations between a firm and its stakeholders.

- *Speeches* provide an avenue for members of an organization to market their message directly to a group in a longer form speech. These speeches, usually given by key members of the organization, can generate positive press and help to develop relationships with stakeholders and the public at large.
- *Blogs* are an emerging social media tool through which individuals can share their thoughts and knowledge with the public. Blogs can be a mix of insights, humor, or other personal interests and have become increasingly popular with marketers focused on public relations. Established industry executives also make use of blogs. Former CEO of Marriott International, Inc., Bill Marriott, who started his blog, "Marriott on the Move," in 2007, was ranked as having one of the best CEO blogs in 2012.[42,43] An executive at an organization of any size who blogs consistently and well can build goodwill for the company he or she leads.
- *Brochures* typically are intended to inform and/or engage the public. A modern public relations brochure can be on paper or online and provides a forum for educating the public about a firm, its mission, or a specific cause. Brochures often present information similar to that found in an annual report, but in a shorter, more accessible way. Marketers should ensure that the brochure contains useful information, is visually engaging, and is consistent with the rest of the company's promotion mix elements.

Each of these public relations tools promotes a positive image and serves as a way to educate stakeholders about company developments.

Another public relations tool is publicity. Publicity involves disseminating unpaid news items through some form of media (e.g., television story, newspaper article, etc.) to gain attention or support. The major advantage of publicity is that, when done well, it allows marketers to communicate with consumers at an extremely

publicity

Disseminating unpaid news items through some form of media (e.g., television story, newspaper article, etc.) to gain attention or support.

The sports-entertainment company WWE has received positive publicity for its charitable work, including its partnership with the Make-A-Wish foundation. During the foundation's World Wish Day initiative, WWE superstar John Cena agreed to personally match every frequent flier mile donated to help reduce travel expenses for the organization so that it can grant more wishes.

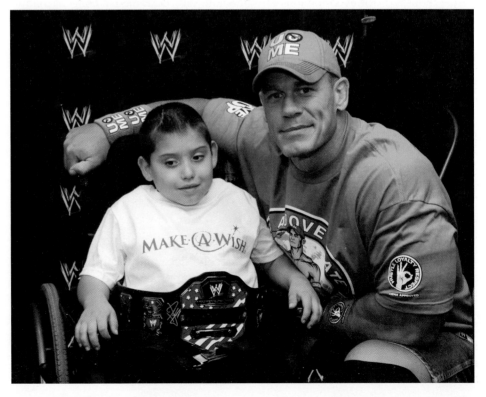

low cost. During the most recent economic recession, firms often used publicity as a way to lower the cost of their public relations efforts. The major disadvantage of publicity is that organizations have less control over how the information is presented because they don't pay for it. Bad publicity and negative news can harm an organization's reputation and image.

Crisis Management

Public relations can be especially important when an organization faces a crisis, as BP did during and after the 2010 oil spill in the Gulf of Mexico. In response to the negative publicity BP received due to the spill, the company filled its website with the typical press releases and financial statements you would expect to see on a corporate site as well as technical briefings with BP officials and maps and charts detailing the company's efforts to contain the leak. BP also produced and posted short films

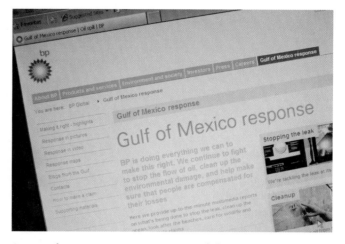

As part of its crisis management strategy following the oil spill in the Gulf of Mexico, BP posted to its website videos and briefings about cleanup and response efforts to help mitigate the effects of the negative publicity it received.

featuring BP officials, representatives of government agencies, and area residents helping in the Gulf cleanup effort. In addition, the company publicized other positive actions it was taking, such as donating $1 million to help a food bank feed people whose incomes were washed away by the spill[44] and actively hiring laid-off workers to clean beaches and animals contaminated with oil. Finally, BP gave the Gulf States money to promote the region's seafood industry in an effort to improve economic conditions in the area.

The Changing Face of Public Relations

Public relations today is a 24-hours-a-day, 7-days-a-week job for marketers across government entities, for-profit industries, and nonprofit organizations. Advances in technology cause information to spread faster than ever before and enhance the influence of that information on potential customers. Marketers should use all of the tools discussed, including social media, to make sure the public perceives the company in the most positive way possible. A simple truth in marketing is that people want to do business with organizations they like and respect. It is incumbent upon marketers to share the organization's actions with the public in a way that entices customers to buy from the company, give money to the charitable organization, or support a specific person or idea.

FINDING THE OPTIMAL PROMOTION MIX

Finding the optimal promotion mix presents a great challenge to marketers. The optimal mix might include additional advertising for new products or high levels of sales promotion for mature products. Other firms might decide the best way to leverage their promotion mix is by adding additional salespeople. Regardless of where a product is in its life cycle, public relations often requires significantly more marketing resources in the months following a crisis. The mix of promotional tools and how marketers integrate them can also change from year to year or even from week to week as environmental factors and consumer demands change. Marketers should thoughtfully consider what mix of promotional elements will be most effective for their target market and utilize marketing research to measure how successful each element of the promotion mix is, making adjustments as necessary to maximize the value of each promotional dollar spent.

Kimberly Winchester
Sales and Marketing Coordinator

Little Rock Marriott
www.marriott.com

Little Rock Marriott is a luxury, full-service Marriott that specializes in serving business events, social gatherings, and wedding receptions.

Describe your job. I have numerous duties, assisting the director of sales and marketing and seven sales managers with daily tasks; effectively arranging detailed accommodations and amenities for incoming guests; successfully assisting with diverse clientele, whether by taking sales inquiries, quoting rates, or developing sales contracts; coordinating, planning, and organizing large events for the greater Little Rock area; and actively participating in local outreach programs and initiatives.

Describe how you got the job that you have. After graduating with a marketing degree, I pursued a position that would fulfill my sales ambitions. I did a few job searches online and came across an opening for the sales and marketing coordinator at what was then called The Peabody Little Rock on indeed.com. I immediately decided to apply. The position had been revamped to include many new duties like updating the hotel's social media sites and assisting with the Peabody's large event planning, which fit with my personal experience in social media and passion for event planning. I interviewed with six different people and marketed myself by explaining to them that I had the dedication and skills to be a member of their sales team.

What has been the most important thing in making you successful at your job? The most important thing that has

made me successful at my job is the appropriate personal selling and sales promotion strategies that I learned in my many marketing classes. On many occasions at my job, I speak to clients and personally sell the benefits of our hotel as a host for groups and conferences. On the sales promotions side, we regularly attend exhibitions and I personally control aspects of our public relations by making sure the hotel is fairly represented on social media sites.

What advice would you give soon-to-be graduates? Be confident that you will find a job in your field and don't settle for anything less. I know that my current job will lead me down the right path in the sales industry or event planning field. It can be discouraging in these hard economic times to find a job in your field, but keep looking! Doing what you want to do will help you be happier and successful not only in your career but also in life.

What do you consider your personal brand to be? Extremely organized with excellent attention to detail and the ability to create special events and work well in a high-paced sales environment. I am a highly motivated person who can take on sales and event-planning projects with confidence and gusto.

PROMOTION MIX BUDGETING STRATEGIES

Determining the appropriate promotional budget is an important decision within any marketing strategy. Firms that set the budget too low risk blending into the competition and are often ineffective in communicating value to potential customers. Firms that set the budget too high open themselves up to waste and lower profits. Promotional budget decisions should consider a variety of factors, such as the types of products sold by the firm, the geographic location of the firm's customers, and the level of competition in the industry. Firms typically determine their promotional budget using one of three methods: the affordable method, the percentage-of-sales method, or the objective-and-task method.

Affordable Method

The affordable method is a top-down approach that is simple and fiscally conservative but offers no other benefits for the organization. Firms that use the affordable method set their promotion budget based on what they believe they can afford. The affordable method is particularly common in small businesses, but it can also occur when a firm does not view promotional strategies as an investment. A major disadvantage of the affordable method is that firms who allocate a random dollar amount to the promotion mix guarantee virtually nothing except that the money will be spent. There are countless stories of marketing departments spending money on promotion at the end of the fiscal year simply because it was there to spend rather than because it was helping them achieve organizational goals. Since the promotional budget is not tied to specific organizational objectives in this approach, the marketers tend to allocate dollars haphazardly with no real focus on what the promotional strategies should achieve.

affordable method

A promotion mix budgeting strategy in which firms set their promotion budget based on what they believe they can afford.

Percentage-of-Sales Method

One of the most widely used budgeting approaches is the percentage-of-sales method. Companies that use the percentage-of-sales method allocate a specific percentage of a period's total sales to the promotional budget for that period. The method has the advantage of being simple since the promotional budget increases at the same rate that firm sales increase. The primary disadvantage of the method arises when a firm's sales decline. Imagine that you own a car dealership and that your sales have declined 30 percent over the past year due to increased competition and economic concerns. It's not necessarily the case that your best promotional strategy for the following year is to reduce promotional expenditures by 30 percent. Quiznos, for example, saw its total sales decline by more than 50 percent between 2007 and 2011 as the company lost market share to competitors like Subway.[45] Quiznos marketers realized that reducing the promotional budget by more than half to match sales would not help to turn around their revenue or market share numbers. In 2012 they embarked on a new promotional campaign, allocating significant resources to advertising and sales promotion that focused on high-quality ingredients.

percentage-of-sales method

A promotion mix budgeting strategy in which firms allocate a specific percentage of a period's total sales to the promotional budget for that period.

Objective-and-Task Method

The objective-and-task approach is typically considered the best of the budgeting methods because it incorporates many of the strengths of the other budgeting methods without falling prey to their weaknesses. The objective-and-task method

objective-and-task method

A promotion mix budgeting strategy in which a firm defines specific objectives, determines the tasks required to achieve those objectives, and then estimates how much each task will cost.

takes a bottom-up approach to promotional budgeting by defining specific objectives, determining the tasks required to achieve those objectives, and then estimating how much each task will cost. By focusing on what the organization wants to achieve, the marketing department invests each dollar in the specific promotion mix elements that best deliver on those objectives. The only major disadvantage of this method is the time and judgment required to decide on the required tasks. However, firms should consider this time an investment that leads marketers to allocate resources in the best possible way to achieve the desired results.

Rather than using the percentage-of-sales budgeting method and cutting its promotional budget after a five-year period of disappointing sales, Quiznos embarked on a new promotional campaign to attract customers.

 connect | MARKETING

Interactive Assignment 8-4

Please complete the *Connect* exercise for Chapter 8 that focuses on the different promotion mix budgeting strategies. By identifying the rationale and benefit of each, you will understand which one is an appropriate budgeting strategy for your organization and how each will impact the success of your promotional strategy.

SUMMARY

LEARNSMART ADVANTAGE

LO 8-1 Describe the elements of the promotion mix and how they relate to an integrated marketing communications strategy.

Promotion is all the activities that communicate the value of a product and persuade customers to buy it. The promotion mix is a subset of the marketing mix and includes four main types of marketing communication: advertising, sales promotion, public relations, and personal selling. An integrated marketing communications (IMC) strategy involves coordinating the various promotion mix elements. Many firms have adopted the IMC perspective in an effort to provide consumers with a clear and consistent message about their products.

LO 8-2 Compare the advantages and disadvantages of different types of advertising.

Advertising is nonpersonal promotional communication about goods, services, or ideas that is paid for by the firm identified in the communication and comes in various forms, each of which has its own advantages and

disadvantages. Internet advertising is the fastest-growing type and holds the most promise for future innovation. Television advertising provides marketers with an opportunity to target specific markets as well as to combine sight, sound, and motion to appeal to consumer senses, while radio advertising is often the most cost-effective medium available to an advertiser. Although it's losing ground to other forms, print advertising continues to offer marketers the ability to reach local and narrowly segmented audiences. Outdoor advertising is flexible and relatively inexpensive but doesn't always reach the target market effectively. Nontraditional advertising, which includes ads on everything from valet tickets to hubcaps, has the advantage of attracting consumer attention in a way traditional advertising no longer does.

LO 8-3 Summarize the various types of sales promotion.

Sales promotion is a set of nonpersonal communication tools, including coupons, rebates, contests, sweepstakes, and loyalty programs, designed to stimulate quicker and more frequent purchases of a product. Trade sales promotions are promotion tools directed to B2B firms—wholesalers, retailers, and distributors—rather than individual consumers. Unique trade sales promotions include allowances and training. Most firms use sales promotion tools to support their advertising, public relations, and personal-selling activities.

LO 8-4 Explain the importance of personal selling.

Personal selling is the two-way flow of communication between a salesperson and a customer that is paid for by the firm and seeks to influence the customer's purchase decision. Salespeople often serve as the link between the firm and the consumer. A major challenge of personal selling is the cost involved, but it provides the firm with immediate feedback from the market and allows the firm to develop a personal relationship with the customer. Relationship selling is increasingly important as very few firms can survive on the profits generated from one-time transactional sales.

LO 8-5 Outline the personal-selling process.

The personal-selling process consists of seven steps: (1) Prospecting and qualifying involves the search for and qualification of potential customers, (2) the preapproach involves identifying key decision makers, reviewing account histories, identifying product needs, and preparing sales presentations, (3) the approach is the initial meeting between the salesperson and the prospect, (4) the sales presentation provides a forum to convey the organization's marketing message, (5) handling objections involves anticipating and responding to the concerns or reasons consumers offer for not buying a product, (6) closing occurs when the salesperson asks the prospect for the sale, and (7) follow-up is a critical step

in creating customer satisfaction and building long-term relationships with customers.

LO 8-6 Describe the role of public relations within the promotion mix.

Public relations is nonpersonal communication focused on promoting positive relations between a firm and its stakeholders. Organizations use a variety of tools for public relations, including annual reports, speeches, blogs, brochures, and magazines. Publicity involves disseminating unpaid news items through some form of media (e.g., television story, newspaper article, etc.). The major advantage of publicity is that, when done well, it allows marketers to communicate with consumers at an extremely low cost.

LO 8-7 Summarize the promotion mix budgeting strategies.

Promotional budget decisions should consider a variety of factors, including the types of products sold by the firm, the geographic location of the firm's customers, and the level of competition in the industry. Firms typically determine their promotional budget using one of three methods. Firms using the affordable method set their promotion budget based on what they believe they can afford. The percentage-of-sales method allocates a specific percentage of a period's total sales for the promotional budget for that period and is the most widely used approach. The objective-and-task method takes a bottom-up approach by defining specific objectives, determining the tasks required to achieve those objectives, and then estimating how much each task will cost.

KEY TERMS

advertising (p. 226)
advertising campaign (p. 226)
affordable method (p. 247)
allowances (p. 238)
approach (p. 241)
click-through rate (CTR) (p. 228)
closing (p. 242)
cold calling (p. 241)
contests (p. 237)
cost per click (CPC) (p. 228)
cost-per-thousand impressions (CPM) (p. 228)
coupons (p. 236)
direct marketing (p. 227)

informative advertising (p. 226)
integrated marketing communications (IMC) (p. 225)
loyalty programs (p. 238)
mobile advertising (p. 235)
narrowcasting (p. 229)
objections (p. 242)
objective-and-task method (p. 247)
percentage-of-sales method (p. 247)
personal selling (p. 238)
persuasive advertising (p. 226)
preapproach (p. 240)
product placement (p. 230)
promotion (p. 224)

promotion mix (p. 225)
prospecting (p. 240)
public relations (p. 243)
publicity (p. 244)
qualifying (p. 240)
rebates (p. 237)
relationship selling (p. 239)
reminder advertising (p. 227)
sales presentation (p. 241)
sales promotion (p. 236)
sweepstakes (p. 237)
trade sales promotions (p. 238)

MARKETING PLAN EXERCISE

The marketing plan exercise for this chapter focuses on developing your own promotional strategy. You can think about this using the same four promotion mix elements discussed in this chapter: advertising, sales promotion, personal selling, and public relations. First, how are you advertising yourself? For example, what does your resume look like? What does it say about you? If your resume is the same basic template that looks just like everyone else's, how will you stand out from others competing for the same job? Please read the Career Tips at the end of this chapter for suggestions. Also consider what your social media profile says about you. If a prospective employer were to look at your Facebook, LinkedIn, or Twitter profile, would they like what they saw? Would it reflect the image of a thoughtful, driven professional?

Next, consider using a sales promotion tool such as sampling. Unpaid internships give firms an opportunity to sample your work, increasing the likelihood that you could be hired there on a permanent and paid basis. Do the companies you want to work for offer unpaid internships? If so, how do you go about applying for them? How can you

adjust your personal financial situation to take an unpaid internship if it helps to advance your career?

Next, consider your ability to personally sell yourself. What will you say in an interview that will convince a prospective employer that they are better off with you than without you? The same strategies salespeople use to make a good first impression, such as appearance, grooming, professional dress, and a firm handshake are all things you want to fine-tune as you get ready for the job market.

Finally, public relations are essential as you start to develop your career. What do your colleagues think about you? Would your professors or classmates recommend you? Think about what you can do to improve or enhance others' perceptions of you.

Your Task: Create an outline of the specific advertising, sales promotion, public relations, and personal-selling strategies you plan to use as you begin your career. For each type of promotion, answer the questions posed in the Exercise and summarize how each can help you market yourself.

DISCUSSION QUESTIONS

1. What advertising medium is most effective for reaching you as a consumer? Has that changed in the past five years? What do you think the most effective medium for advertising to you will be five years from now?
2. If you had to advertise a new product to your marketing classmates, what media would you choose and why?
3. Describe a company that you think does a poor job advertising. Why is the advertising ineffective? Anyone can criticize something that is not working, but those who offer creative solutions to fix advertising strategies that are broken have a very bright future ahead. With this in mind, make two specific suggestions about how the company could improve its advertising.

4. Imagine you are in charge of getting students at your school to attend a lecture on campus. Would you choose a contest or a sweepstakes as a tool for promoting the event and increasing attendance? Explain your answer.
5. Sales jobs are one of the fastest-growing areas for new college graduates. Are you considering a job in sales after graduation? Please explain why or why not.
6. List two organizations that you think do a good job handling public relations and explain why you think this. List two organizations that you think do a poor job handling public relations and make specific suggestions as to how they might improve.

SOCIAL MEDIA APPLICATION

Select two firms that offer sales promotions through social media. These could include any of the strategies discussed in this chapter—coupons, rebates, contests, or sweepstakes. Describe which sales promotions each firm offers through which social media platforms and then analyze those promotions using the following questions and activities as a guide:

1. In your opinion, which firm is doing a better job using social media to enhance its sales promotions? Explain your answer.

2. Who are the target markets for these social media sales promotions? Are the sales promotions an effective way to generate additional sales and profits from these target markets? Explain your answer.
3. Provide at least two specific recommendations for sales promotion strategies that each of these firms can implement through social media. Be sure to discuss why you think your recommendations would succeed in generating additional sales and profits from the firm's target markets.

ETHICAL CHALLENGE

There is an increasing public backlash over marketers who make false or misleading statements about their products. In recent years, numerous consumer lawsuits have resulted in multimillion-dollar settlements for several major companies. Dannon made claims that its yogurt products prevent sickness. Kellogg claimed that Rice Krispies help immunity. Ferrero USA made false claims about the healthiness and sugar content of Nutella. These claims have led to financial losses for the firms involved and also have the potential of eroding consumer trust. The U.S. Food and Drug Administration (FDA) is responsible for enforcing truthful labeling for food products, and some believe that these lawsuits are an effective way to improve the truth and transparency of food labeling and advertising. However, some marketers have fought back, suggesting that many of these cases are "silly" and that consumers don't care that Quaker Oats calls its granola products "wholesome," even though they contain some trans fats. This leaves food marketers with an ethical dilemma. On the one hand, they want to promote their product in the best, most persuasive way possible, but they must balance that with the risks of saying something on the label that might potentially open the firm up to a consumer lawsuit. Please use the ethical decision-making framework to complete the following:

1. Consider the various claims being made in consumer lawsuits against food companies. Do you consider the claims legitimate or "silly"?
2. What might be motivating the growing number of consumer lawsuits against food companies?
3. Many of the lawsuits against food companies described involve foods consumed by children. Do food companies have more responsibility for the truth and transparency of their advertising and labeling when their products are consumed by children?

Source: See Katherine Campbell, Education Resource Center, "Mom and Dad vs. Snap, Crackle, and Pop," *Bloomberg Businessweek*, June 25, 2012, http://resourcecenter.businessweek.com/reviews/mom-and-dad-vs-snap-crackle-and-pop.

VIDEO CASE

Please go to *Connect* to access the video case featuring the Memphis Grizzlies of the NBA that accompanies this chapter.

CAREER TIPS

Marketing Your Future

You have read in this chapter about the importance of promoting products to communicate value to current and prospective customers. Similarly, as you embark on your career, you will need to be comfortable promoting yourself to prospective employers. Debbie Pilgrim is the executive vice president of PeopleSource, a staffing and recruiting service with offices located throughout the central United States. She has spent nearly a quarter century helping people find jobs and careers. She offers the following advice for ensuring your resume serves as an effective promotional tool:

In today's job market, it sometimes takes a little extra personal marketing to get noticed. Stacks of resumes make it difficult for a plain, basic resume to stand out, regardless of what the candidate's accomplishments are. Soon-to-be college graduates should view their resume as a marketing tool to creatively communicate why they bring value to a potential employer.

The question I get from most job seekers is, How do I get organizations to notice my resume? A resume not only reflects your personality, it also speaks to your capability and creativity. Your resume is usually the first thing any employer sees, and if it is not good, the *only* thing they will see, so putting more effort and thought into creating an impressive resume is definitely worthwhile. I have heard of people printing their resume on florescent paper, sending baked goods along with a cover letter, or buying online ads to promote themselves. You can search online to find examples and ideas of possible resume templates. I strongly encourage you to choose one that reflects your personality. Don't try to be something you are not. The worst possible career path in my opinion is to market yourself as something you are not and then, if you get that job, have to be that other person every day. I encourage you to search sites like Pinterest or Business Insider to get ideas for creative resumes that can help you stand out and communicate your value.

CHAPTER NOTES

1. Red Bull, "Red Bull Stratos," October 14, 2012, http://www.redbull.ca/cs/Satellite/en_CA/Article/Red-Bull-Stratos-Watch-the-mission-LIVE-NOW-021243270035378.

2. Mallory Russell, "Fearless Felix Baumgartner Is Second Fastest to 50 Million Views," *Advertising Age*, October 19, 2012, http://adage.com/article/the-viral-video-chart/fearless-felix-baumgartner-fastest-50-million-views/237870/.

3. Shirley Brady, "Taco Bell Promotes New 'Live Más' Tagline in New Campaign," February 24, 2012, http://www.brandchannel.com/home/post/2012/02/24/Taco-Bell-Live-Mas-Doritos-Locos-Tacos-Spots-022412.aspx.

4. Taco Bell Press Release, "It's About Time: Taco Bell's Cool Ranch Doritos Tacos Available Nationwide Today, March 7," March 7, 2013, http://www.tacobell.com/Company/newsreleases/cool_ranch_doritos_locos_tacos.

5. Geoffrey Fowler, "Facebook Friends Used in Ads," *The Wall Street Journal*, January 26, 2011, http://online.wsj.com/article/SB10001424052748704013604576104532107484922.html.

6. WPP, "Global Internet Ad Spend Hit $99bn in 2012, Almost 20% of Total Investment," March 27, 2013, http://www.wpp.com/wpp/press/2013/mar/27/global-internet-ad-spend-hit-99bn-in-2012/.

7. Suzanne Vranica, "Bigger and Less Profitable," *The Wall Street Journal*, March 14, 2013, http://online.wsj.com/article/SB10001424127887324034804578346540295942824.html.

8. Chuck Hemann and Ken Burbary, *Digital Marketing Analytics* (Indianapolis, IN: Pearson, 2013), p. 4.

9. Ibid.

10. Steve Lohr, "Privacy Concerns Limit Online Ads, Study Says," *The New York Times*, April 30, 2010, http://bits.blogs.nytimes.com/2010/04/30/privacy-concerns-limit-online-ads-study-says/.

11. Ibid.

12. Michael O'Connell, "TNT's Dallas Premiere Scores just South (Fork) of 7 Million Viewers," June 14, 2012, http://www.hollywoodreporter.com/live-feed/dallas-premiere-ratings-tnt-337831.

13. Ibid.

14. Nielsen, "Average U.S. Home Now Receives a Record 118.6 TV Channels, According to Nielsen," June 6, 2008, http://www.nielsen.com/us/en/press-room/2008/average_u_s_home.html.

15. Matt Cronin, "Tennis Channel's Complaint against Comcast in Jeopardy," *Tennis*, February 26, 2013, http://www.tennis.com/pro-game/2013/02/tennis-channels-complaint-against-comcast-jeopardy/46604/.

16. Anthony Crupi, "In Their Prime: Broadcast Spot Costs Soar," *Adweek*, June 22, 2011, http://www.adweek.com/news/television/their-prime-broadcast-spot-costs-soar-132805.

17. Suzanne Vranica, "Costly Super Bowl Ads Pay Publicity Dividend," *The Wall Street Journal*, February 3, 2013, http://online.wsj.com/article/SB10001424127887324900204578282360008085752.html.

18. Associated Press, "Study: DVRs Now in Half of US Pay-TV Homes," *USA Today*, November 30, 2012, http://www.usatoday.com/story/tech/2012/11/30/study-dvrs-now-in-half-of-us-pay-tv-homes/1737637/.

19. Mark Milian, "Spiderman Spins Web of Sony Products and Bing Searches," *Bloomberg*, July 6, 2012, http://go.bloomberg.com/tech-blog/2012-07-06-spider-man-spins-web-of-sony-products-and-bing-searches/.

20. Steve Olenski, "Marketers and Advertisers: The NBA Is for Sale, Sort Of," *Forbes*, July 25, 2012, http://www.forbes.com/sites/marketshare/2012/07/25/marketers-advertisers-nba-for-sale/.

21. Andy Fixme, "Pandora Gains Access to $14 Billion Radio Ad-Sales Market," *Bloomberg*, March 5, 2013, http://www.bloomberg.com/news/2013-03-05/pandora-gains-access-to-14-billion-radio-ad-sales-market.html.

22. Laura Houston Santhanam, Amy Mitchell, and Tom Rosenstiel for the Pew Research Center, "Audio: How Far Will Digital Go?" *The State of the News Media 2012*, http://stateofthemedia.org/2012/audio-how-far-will-digital-go/.

23. Karl Tero Greenfeld, "ESPN: Everywhere Sports Profit Network," *Bloomberg Businessweek*, August 30, 2012, http://www.businessweek.com/articles/2012-08-30/espn-everywhere-sports-profit-network#p1.

24. SiriusXM, "Corporate Overview," n.d., http://www.siriusxm.com/corporate.

25. Erik Sass, "Newspaper Ad Spending Now Half What It Was in 2005," March 26, 2012, http://www.mediapost.com/publications/article/171052/newspaper-ad-spending-now-half-what-it-was-in-2005.html#axzz2R2AgIwGT.

26. Carolyn Miller, Kristen Purcell, and Lee Rainee, "Reading Habits in Different Communities," *Pew Internet*, December 20, 2012, http://libraries.pewinternet.org/2012/12/20/reading-habits-in-different-communities/.

27. Paul R. Lamonica, "Look Up: Big Bucks in Billboards," *CNN Money*, April 5, 2006, http://money.cnn.com/2006/04/05/news/companies/billboards/.

28. Joanna Brenner, "Internet," *PewInternet*, January 31, 2013, http://pewinternet.org/Commentary/2012/February/Pew-Internet-Mobile.aspx.

29. Laura Stampler, "These Are the 11 Best Mobile Ads in the World," *Business Insider*, June 21, 2012, http://www.businessinsider.com/these-are-the-11-best-mobile-ads-in-the-world-2012-6?op=1.

30. Dean Takahashi, "Global Ad Spending in Video Games to top $7.2B in 2016," September 12, 2011, http://venturebeat.com/2011/09/12/global-ad-spending-in-video-games-to-top-7-2b-in-2016/.

31. CNBC, "10 Massive Advertising Failures," n.d., http://www.cnbc.com/id/41624240/page/10.

32. PR Newswire, "McDonalds Goes Blue This Summer with the Launch of The Smurfs," *Bloomberg*, July 29, 2011, http://www.bloomberg.com/apps/news?pid=conewsstory&tkr=MCD:US&sid=aaBly7NcIp98.

33. Brian Grow, "The Great Rebate Runaround," *Bloomberg Businessweek*, November 22, 2005, http://www.businessweek.com/stories/2005-11-22/the-great-rebate-runaround.

34. Patrick M. Dunne, Robert F. Lusch, and James R. Carver, *Retailing*, 7th ed. (Mason, OH: South-Western Cengage, 2011), p. 295.

35. Oreo Press Release, "Oreo Announces Casting Call for National 'Milk's Favorite Jingle' Contest," June 7, 2005, http://www.prnewswire.com/news-releases/oreor-announces-casting-call-for-national-milks-favorite-jingle-contest-54538802.html.

36. HGTV, "Congrats to the HGTV Dream Home 2013 Winner!" n.d., http://www.hgtv.com/hgtv-dream-home-2013-giveaway/package/index.html.

37. Barbara De Lollis, "IHG's Loyalty Club to Raise Point Rates for 25% of Hotels," *USA Today*, January 6, 2012, http://travel.usatoday.com/hotels/post/2012/01/ihg-priority-club-to-raise-point-rates-but-phase-in-change/591898/1.

38. Mark W. Johnston and Greg W. Marshall, *Relationship Selling,* 3rd ed. (New York: McGraw-Hill, 2010).

39. Brian Featherstonhaugh, "The Future of Selling: It's Social," *Forbes,* December 3, 2010, http://www.forbes.com/2010/12/03/future-of-selling-leadership-sales-leadership-ogilvyone.html.

40. Bureau of Labor Statistics, "Occupational Employment and Wages: Sales and Related Occupations," May 2012, http://www.bls.gov/oes/current/oes410000.htm.

41. Johnston and Marshall, *Relationship Selling.*

42. Marty Duren, "9 CEO Blogs to Watch," *SocialMedia Today,* February 12, 2013, http://socialmediatoday.com/martyduren/1235491/nine-ceo-blogs-watch-2013.

43. Michael S. Rosenwald, "An Old Dog Learns to Write a New Blog," *The Washington Post,* January 16, 2007, http://www.washingtonpost.com/wp-dyn/content/article/2007/01/15/AR2007011501348.html.

44. Betsy Rate, "Spinning the Spill: BP's PR Ballet," *Need to Know on PBS,* June 14, 2010, http://www.pbs.org/wnet/need-to-know/environment/spinning-the-spill-bps-pr-ballet/1460/.

45. Steve Raabe, "Denver-Based Quiznos Seeks Recovery with New Marketing Strategy," *Denver Post,* July 8, 2012, http://www.denverpost.com/business/ci_21025259/quiznos-recovery-new-marketing-strategy.

Chapter 9

SUPPLY CHAIN AND LOGISTICS MANAGEMENT

LEARNING OBJECTIVES

After reading this chapter, you should be able to

LO 9-1 Structure the various flows within a supply chain.

LO 9-2 Explain the importance of supply chain orientation and supply chain management to organizations.

LO 9-3 Compare the various types of supply chain strategies firms use.

LO 9-4 Describe how logistics activities add value to products.

LO 9-5 Describe how the primary logistics functions support a firm's supply chain strategy.

LO 9-6 Explain the importance of mode and carrier selection in domestic and international supply chains.

EXECUTIVE PERSPECTIVE

Terry Matthews

Executive Vice President and President of Intermodal

J.B. Hunt Transport Services, Inc.

Terry Matthews graduated from college in the early 1980s with a major in economics. Following graduation, Matthews went to 22 on-campus interviews but received no job offers. He moved back home and entered graduate school, where he learned more about marketing and discovered logistics and supply chain management. Matthews realized quickly that logistics was a critical element for virtually every business and also a career field with great growth potential. Eventually, he got a job at North American Van Lines and held various positions there before moving to J.B. Hunt. Today, as a J.B. Hunt executive, he oversees a $2.7 billion intermodal company and focuses on three- to five-year strategies, financial results, safety, service, and company culture.

What has been the most important thing in making you successful at your job?

Fear of failure, competitive persistence, and long hours.

What advice would you give soon-to-be graduates?

First, find an industry that's growing and try to find a position with a company within that industry. A growing industry and growing company will give you more opportunity for upward mobility. Second, build a base of experience by doing as many different jobs as possible early in your career. Don't be afraid of a lateral move if it broadens your knowledge of the company or industry.

How is marketing relevant to your role at J.B. Hunt?

I focus on the place element of the four Ps. We are one of the best companies in the world at getting products to the places they need to be in a timely and affordable way. Our ability to be a great logistics company helps us market our services each day and also helps our customers succeed in their businesses.

What do you consider your personal brand to be?

High ethics and morals. Don't take no for an answer because there's usually an angle that somebody has not yet followed.

Terry Matthews
Executive Vice President and
President of Intermodal

J.B. Hunt Transport Services, Inc.
http://www.jbhunt.com/

J.B. Hunt is a Fortune 500 company and one of the largest transportation logistics companies in North America. It provides safe and reliable transportation services to a diverse group of customers throughout the continental United States, Canada, and Mexico.

This chapter explores the concepts of supply chains and logistics. It discusses the importance of supply chain management, the trade-offs involved in managing the supply chain, and various supply chain strategies. The chapter also discusses the impact of logistics on the supply chain. You will learn the importance of aligning logistics operations with a firm's supply chain strategies and become familiar with the various modes of transportation, their strengths and weaknesses, and where they fit into supply chain strategies. As you read through the chapter, consider the following key questions:

1. What are the important flows in a supply chain?
2. How does an organization benefit from a supply chain orientation?
3. What supply chain strategies could my firm pursue?

4. How do logistics functions add value to my products?
5. What are the primary logistics functions?
6. Why are transportation mode and carrier selection important to organizations?

LO 9-1

Structure the various flows within a supply chain.

SUPPLY CHAINS

Have you ever passed a truck on the highway and wondered where it was headed and what it was carrying? Chances are it was carrying finished goods toward the end of a journey that originated halfway across the world. The truck is performing one of many functions necessary for companies to operate a supply chain. Organizations make use of and are part of many supply chains, without which they cannot survive. Regardless of your job title, if you work for an organization, it's likely you will take part in some way in its supply chain. A supply chain delivers value to the end customer by leveraging the resources and skills of its various component firms. Value can be added in many different ways by many different parts of a company. For example, research and development adds value by designing a product that meets or exceeds the needs of customers. Purchasing adds value by finding the best suppliers of components and raw materials for the product. Whatever functional area you end up working in, you will benefit from understanding the various trade-offs involved in a successful supply chain strategy.

supply chain

A set of three or more companies directly linked by one or more of the upstream and downstream flows of products, services, finances, and information from a source to a customer.

Supply Chain Flows through Marketing Channels

A supply chain is "a set of three or more companies directly linked by one or more of the upstream and downstream flows of products, services, finances, and information from a source to a customer."[1] Figure 9.1 illustrates the flow of a supply chain. The image of a stream can help you visualize these flows.

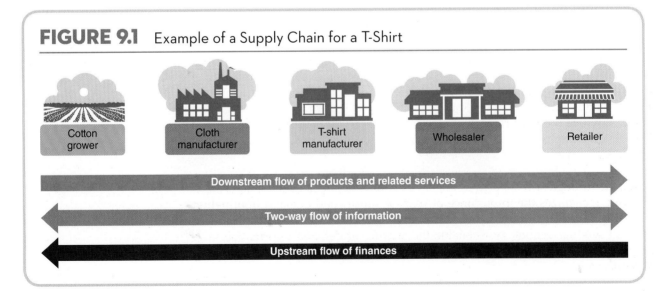

FIGURE 9.1   Example of a Supply Chain for a T-Shirt

Cotton grower — Cloth manufacturer — T-shirt manufacturer — Wholesaler — Retailer

Downstream flow of products and related services →

← Two-way flow of information →

← Upstream flow of finances

Imagine that you are standing in the middle of a stream (fly fishing, perhaps). The source of the water flowing toward you is upstream, and the water flowing away from you is moving downstream toward its eventual destination in the ocean. Products and the services involved in getting them to customers primarily move downstream from a supplier to a customer (an exception is when a customer returns goods). On their way downstream, they pass through distribution channels. Distribution channels or marketing channels are intermediaries, such as whole-salers, distributors, and retailers, through which the flow of products travels.[2] All along the supply chain, distribution channels add value to the product by changing its form and location. For example, the cloth manufacturer converts cotton to cloth. A truck delivers the finished T-shirt from the wholesaler to a store where a consumer like you can buy it. Finances, on the other hand, flow upstream in a supply chain. When you purchase a T-shirt, the money flows out of your pocket to the retailer. Likewise, the retailer paid the wholesaler, who paid the T-shirt manufacturer, who paid the cloth manufacturer, and so on upstream through the chain.

Information flows both upstream and downstream. A retailer may pass its sales forecast for T-shirts upstream to its wholesaler, who then passes the information to the T-shirt supplier. In return, the T-shirt supplier might pass information about when the T-shirts will be available for delivery downstream to the retailer. The flow of information impacts all members of a supply chain because without accurate, timely information companies cannot make good decisions.

Supply Chain Network

The concept of a supply chain is actually a simplified version of what is, in actuality, a network of companies made up of many suppliers and customers. A company producing cosmetics may have hundreds of suppliers, some of which may be selling the same or similar raw and packaging materials to other cosmetics manufacturing companies. In addition, that same cosmetics manufacturer may sell to a retailer that buys similar cosmetics from a number of other manufacturers. Figure 9.2 on page 258 illustrates how a company can be a member of a number of competing supply chains. Though Smith's and Kennedy's drugstores compete for customers, they both count cosmetics manufacturer B as a member of their supply chain. Ultimately, the supply chain that provides the most value to its customers will succeed. This is where the concepts of supply chain orientation and supply chain management come in.

SUPPLY CHAIN ORIENTATION

A firm that recognizes and responds to the impact supply chain flows have on its business possesses a supply chain orientation.[3] A supply chain orientation is a management philosophy that guides the actions of company members toward the goal of actively managing the upstream and downstream flows of goods, services, finances, and information across the supply chain. This implies an outward focus on the activities and performance of other companies, rather than an inward focus on one's own company. It also implies a willingness to get involved in coordinating those activities to add value to the end customer.

Firms that seek to implement the supply chain orientation across suppliers and customers through specific actions engage in supply chain management.[4] When a company recognizes the importance of sharing supply and demand information with suppliers and customers, it exhibits a supply chain *orientation*. When management sets up technology to enable the sharing of demand information with suppliers, such as Walmart's Retail Link program, it is practicing supply chain *management*.

distribution channels (marketing channels)

Intermediaries—wholesalers, distributors, and retailers—through which the flow of products travels.

LO 9-2

Explain the importance of supply chain orientation and supply chain management to organizations.

supply chain orientation

A management philosophy that guides the actions of company members toward the goal of actively managing the upstream and downstream flows of goods, services, finances, and information across the supply chain.

FIGURE 9.2   Two Competing Supply Chains

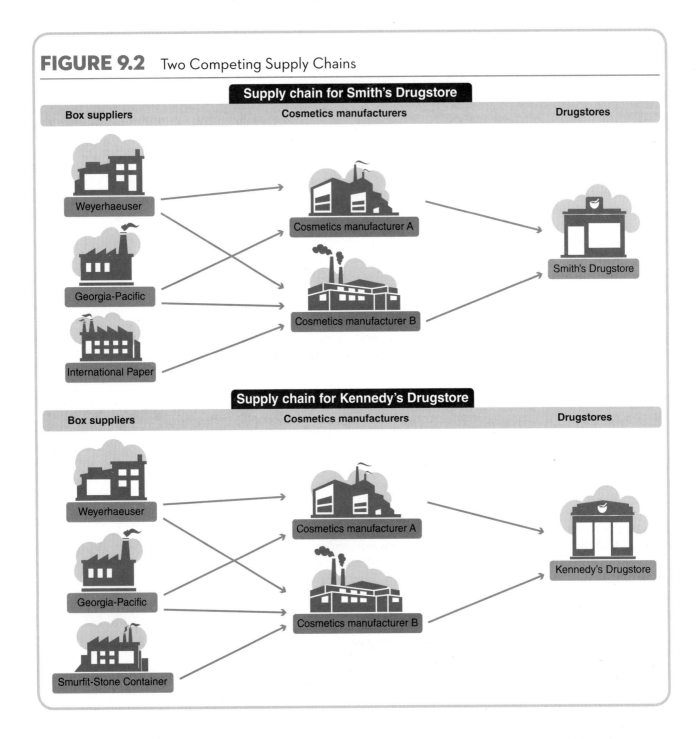

Supply Chain Management

supply chain management

The actions the firm takes to coordinate the various flows within a supply chain.

The term *supply chain management* became common in the 1990s as organizations began to look for additional ways to create customer value. Supply chain management refers to the actions the firm takes to coordinate the various flows within a supply chain. Companies that view the total system of interrelated companies that make up the supply chain as something to manage have greater control over the customer value they provide. This in turn generates higher revenue for the company. The underlying philosophy behind this concept is that no company is an island. All companies rely on related companies whose activities add value to the final product. This reliance can take the form of sharing sales forecasts and product delivery information or enlisting another company to perform a function if the other company can do it more efficiently or effectively than the firm itself.

Supply chain management decisions often involve trade-offs. Decisions made about one area of the supply chain will affect other areas, sometimes negatively. For example, when sales personnel offer a volume discount to a customer without knowing whether that amount of product can be produced and delivered on time without incurring extra cost, the sale may actually end up costing the company money. Another important trade-off exists between inventory and customer service. When there is not enough inventory to satisfy customer demand, the firm may incur additional costs or lose sales or both. To combat such situations, companies sometimes store (carry) extra inventory. However, any money tied up in inventory is not available to the company to use for other things, such as capital investments, advertising, or paying bills. Additionally, inventory costs money, both to purchase (or produce) and to store. Inventory carrying costs are the costs required to make or buy a product, including risk of obsolescence, taxes, insurance, and warehousing space used to store the goods. These examples show the importance of understanding supply chain trade-offs and their implications for supply chain management decisions.

Supply chain management involves making decisions that involve trade-offs, for example, about how much inventory to keep in stock. Too much extra stock can end up costing the company a great deal of money over time, but too little can leave the company unprepared to meet demand.

inventory carrying costs

The costs required to make or buy a product, including risk of obsolescence, taxes, insurance, and warehousing space used to store the goods.

Supply Chain Integration

The ultimate objective of supply chain management is to integrate related companies, thus facilitating the coordination of activities across the supply chain in a manner that improves the entire chain's performance. In essence, the supply chain becomes an extended enterprise. Individual firms integrate their activities to such a degree that they function as one organization.[5] Integrated supply chains typically benefit from reduced costs, better customer service, efficient use of resources, and an increased ability to respond to changes in the marketplace.[6]

For an integrated supply chain to work, companies must be willing to embrace relationship-based strategies that involve close, long-term collaboration for mutual benefit. For example, if a materials manager in a manufacturing facility establishes a close relationship with a box supplier that handles the plant's box inventory, the manufacturing plant could share production schedules with the supplier. The supplier then would be able to efficiently schedule the delivery of boxes, and the plant would not have to expend any manpower determining when they need boxes and how many they need or ordering them from the supplier. Both members of a supply chain gain from such a relationship-based strategy. In the next section, we will investigate some of the supply chain strategies that firms can use to achieve effective integration.

Today's global business environment makes supply chain integration even more of an imperative for firms trying to overcome the time and distance obstacles that can stand in the way of efficient supply chain operations.

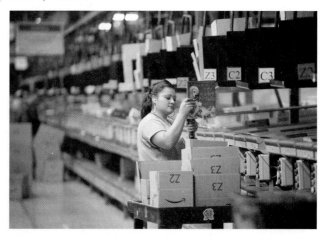

LO 9-3

Compare the various types of supply chain strategies firms use.

SUPPLY CHAIN STRATEGY

Effective supply chain management and integration require a thoughtful supply chain strategy that helps the firm establish the right network of suppliers and customers to meet its objectives. Supply chain objectives should be based on the firm's marketing objectives and can include such things as the types and locations of markets to be served, the market share and customer service desired, the speed with which new products should be developed, and cost reduction and profitability goals.[7] In the sections that follow, we will focus on three supply chain strategies: push, pull, and hybrid (push-pull).

Push Strategy

If a company's marketing strategy includes objectives related to cost competitiveness and good customer service, it should consider a push supply chain strategy. A push strategy (also known as a *speculation strategy)* is one in which a company builds goods based on a sales forecast, puts those goods into storage, and waits for a customer to order the product. The automotive industry, for example, relies on sales forecasts to plan production well in advance. The main advantage of this type of strategy is that it allows firms to achieve economies of scale; because the firm makes large batches of one good at a time, it can reduce manufacturing, transportation, and other costs. Placing large orders of raw and packaging materials, such as steel or glass for a car manufacturer, drives down the cost. Additionally, push strategies often positively impact customer service because the goods are already in stock, awaiting the customer's order.

However, there are disadvantages to using a push strategy. First, sales forecasts must be accurate. If they're not, the company will have too much of a product no one wants or not enough of a product consumers do want. Second, production facilities set up to manufacture one good over a period of time will respond slowly to changing demand patterns. For example, it is extremely expensive and time-consuming to retool an automotive plant to produce a small, fuel-efficient car instead of an SUV if gasoline prices suddenly increase and demand for SUVs slows. Third, inventory carrying costs are expensive, typically 25–30 percent of the cost to produce and deliver the goods. This can cut into the cost savings achieved through economies of scale in manufacturing, purchasing, and transportation. The ability to accurately forecast customer sales therefore becomes a priority for companies utilizing a push strategy.

Pull Strategy

Firms whose marketing strategy requires the kind of agility and product customization push strategies can't accommodate may choose to pursue a pull supply chain strategy instead. In a pull strategy (also known as a *responsive supply chain)*, customer orders drive manufacturing and distribution operations. In a pure pull system, the good is not made until a customer order is received. Postponing manufacturing until an order is received eliminates the risks associated with producing unwanted product. In addition, such a strategy reduces inventory carrying costs, allows the firm to customize products specifically to customer requirements, and gives firms the ability to respond rapidly to changing market conditions. Boeing uses a pull system. It builds aircraft to customer specifications and only when an order is received. Imagine the millions of dollars Boeing would tie up if it built aircraft to hold in inventory until an order came through.

The additional flexibility and customization a pull strategy offers comes with a price. A pull strategy doesn't often allow firms to take advantage of economies of scale. Because the company only orders what it needs immediately to meet its production requirements, it typically orders small quantities, eliminating the possibility of quantity discounts. In addition, to effectively implement this strategy, firms

push strategy

A supply chain strategy in which a company builds goods based on a sales forecast, puts those goods into storage, and waits for a customer to order the product.

pull strategy

A supply chain strategy in which customer orders drive manufacturing and distribution operations.

need a production facility that can change rapidly to produce different products and a distribution system that can deliver the product quickly once it's made. This is why few companies practice a pure pull system.

Push-Pull Strategy

A third strategy is a hybrid of the other two strategies. In a push-pull strategy, the initial stages of the supply chain operate on a push system, but completion of the product is based on a pull system. Thus a company may forecast sales, build an inventory of components based on the forecast, and hold those components in inventory until a customer order is received, as they would using a push strategy. Then, as in a pull strategy, they finalize the product based on the order. Dell, for example, builds component inventory based on its sales forecast but doesn't completely assemble computers until a customer order is received. A push-pull strategy combines the key advantages of the other two methods: companies can achieve economies of scale in purchasing, while engineering flexibility into manufacturing. The hybrid strategy also takes advantage of the fact that sales forecasts tend to be more accurate at an aggregate level than at a specific product level. Dell can more accurately forecast the number of computers it will sell in a given period than the number of each type of computer it will sell.

push-pull strategy
A supply chain strategy in which the initial stages of the supply chain operate on a push system, but completion of the product is based on a pull system.

As with the other methods, a push-pull system does have drawbacks. It may not be as cost competitive as a push system since the firm cannot take advantage of manufacturing and transportation economies of scale. In addition, the firm will still incur costs to store components in inventory. Finally, as in a pure pull system, the company will need to develop a distribution system that can deliver products quickly to avoid customer service complaints. Figure 9.3 on page 262 illustrates the three different types of supply chain strategies.

Selecting the Appropriate Strategy

Which of the three supply chain strategies is appropriate for a company? The answer depends on several things, including the following factors:[8]

1. *How stable demand is.* If a firm can't predict demand for its product, it can't create an accurate sales forecast that would allow it to enjoy the benefits of a pure push system. Demand uncertainty often occurs when products are in the introductory and growth stage of the product life cycle. During these stages, a firm may want to stick with the maximum flexibility a pull strategy allows or follow a hybrid strategy that commits to inventory of raw and packaging materials without committing to a large amount of finished goods inventory.

2. *How cost competitive a firm needs to be.* If cost reduction is part of a firm's strategy, a pure push system will allow it to achieve cost savings through economies of scale in purchasing, manufacturing, and transportation.

3. *How customized products need to be.* If a company competes on its ability to deliver customized products and a high level of customer service built on manufacturing and distribution flexibility, then a pull or hybrid strategy would be a good choice.

4. *How quickly customers need the product.* If customers want a short lead time—the time it takes from the placement of an order to the delivery of the goods—the company will need to have products already made and ready to deliver. A push strategy is best for this scenario.

Dell uses UPS to ensure speedy delivery of its computers. The partnership keeps customer service levels high and allows Dell to concentrate on its core competency—building computers to customer specifications.

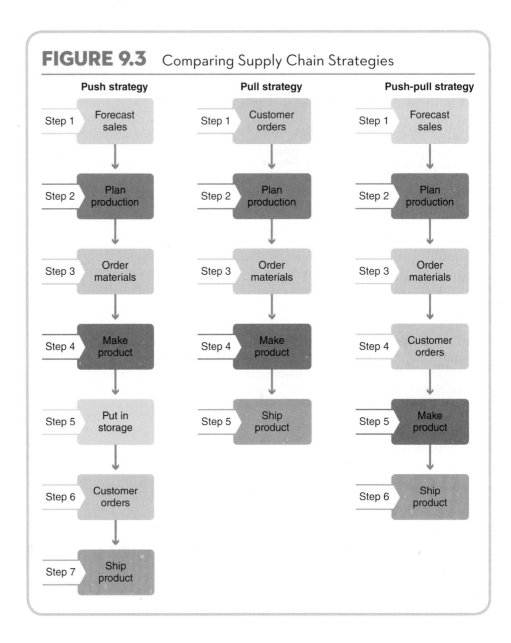

FIGURE 9.3 Comparing Supply Chain Strategies

A firm's overall marketing strategy dictates where it fits according to all of these considerations and, ultimately, which supply chain strategy it should pursue. Companies that are significantly affected by all of the factors listed may choose to take advantage of both the cost savings of a push system and the flexibility of a pull system by employing a push-pull system. Whichever supply chain strategy a firm chooses, effective implementation is impacted by logistics operations, which we will discuss in the next section.

connect | MARKETING   Interactive Assignment 9-1

Please complete the *Connect* exercise in Chapter 9 that focuses on supply chain strategies. By identifying the appropriate strategy, you will be able to establish the right network of suppliers and customers necessary to meet your objectives.

WHAT IS LOGISTICS?

Although the term *logistics* has been around a long time, it only recently entered the public consciousness. UPS ads proclaiming "We Love Logistics" and signs on trucks promoting logistics solutions have made the term more popular but not necessarily better understood. While most recognize that logistics relates to the place aspect of the marketing mix, logistics operations provide more than just the truck that delivers T-shirts to the retailer that sells them to you. Logistics is that part of supply chain management that plans, implements, and controls the flow of goods, services, and information between the point of origin and the final customer.[9] Due to the increased complexity of supply chains, logistics is a growing field. The U.S. Department of Labor expects employment in the sector to grow by 25.5 percent through 2020.[10] And *U.S. News and World Report* ranked logistician as one of the top 20 best business jobs in the country.

Logistics is an important part of supply chain management, not supply chain management itself, as some people think. Logistics comprises some specific functions that enable a supply chain to operate smoothly and effectively. Through these various functions, logistics adds value to products moving through the supply chain.[11] How well companies provide value by performing the seven Rs of logistics—delivering the *right* product, to the *right* place, to the *right* customer, at the *right* time, in the *right* quantity, in the *right* condition, and at the *right* price— will determine how satisfied their customers are. Executing logistics functions successfully can serve as a competitive advantage for some companies. We will discuss most of these functions later in this chapter. First, we will discuss how these functions impact the four Ps.

The Impact of Logistics

Managers from all areas of business should be aware of the impact logistics operations and personnel have on their own functional areas. Arguably the biggest impact is on the four Ps of marketing.[12] It's easy to see how logistics operations impact the place aspect of the marketing mix. Logistics provides distribution activities, such as fulfilling customer orders, and makes decisions about where to place distribution facilities, what modes of transportation to employ, and which carriers to use. However, logistics activities also have an effect on price, product, and promotion.

Price is affected by logistics operations in several ways. Purchasing activities impact the cost of buying or making goods through volume discounts, reliability of suppliers, and the quality of the goods procured. Decisions regarding the amount of inventory to hold will also affect costs since inventory carrying costs add to the cost of goods. Transportation planning by logistics personnel can affect the price of products. Shipping goods in full vehicles, rather than partially loaded vehicles, lowers transportation costs, savings the firm can pass along to the customer in the form of lower prices. Logistics managers affect the product aspect of the marketing mix through feedback on packaging. Too much packaging adds weight and bulk to the product, driving costs up; too little packaging may cause the good to be damaged in transit, leading to dissatisfied customers and costly returns. Finally, when marketers plan a promotion, they must make logistics managers aware of any increase in expected sales so that sufficient inventory, equipment, and personnel are available to handle increased volumes.

FedEx's express shipping services provide value by offering companies a variety of options for getting their products to customers, including same-day delivery service across the United States.

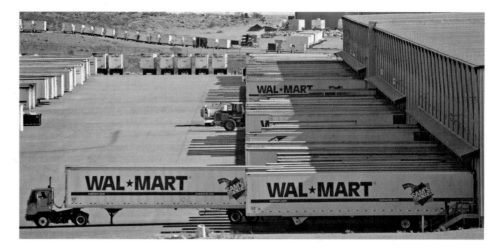

Walmart saves money not only by moving goods using its own fleet of trucks but also by encouraging its suppliers to use Walmart trucks when shipping goods to Walmart facilities.

While the impact of logistics on the marketing mix may be the most obvious, marketing is not the only area of an organization affected by logistics.[13] Logistics personnel support manufacturing operations by receiving, storing, and retrieving materials needed in production. Coordination between the two operations is critical to ensure a smoothly running manufacturing facility. Logistics affects finance activities because the amount of inventory a company holds and the costs of warehousing and transportation impact return on investment (ROI). In addition, how well the logistics managers perform affects customer service, which ultimately can impact revenue positively or negatively. Logistics operations affect and are affected by all areas of a company. As a result, regardless of your major or what type of job you plan to pursue after you graduate, you will benefit from understanding what logistics is and what it does.

Aligning Logistics with Supply Chain Strategies

As we saw earlier, firms can employ push, pull, or push-pull supply chain strategies depending on their objectives. As an important aspect of supply chain management, logistics operations have to be properly configured to meet the different challenges presented by each type of supply chain strategy. A company pursuing the economies of scale that come with a push strategy will have to set up logistics operations that can handle large volumes of product. They will need to select modes of transportation that can inexpensively handle large amounts of product and have large warehouses equipped to efficiently store, retrieve, and load goods onto vehicles at a fast pace. Companies looking for efficiency will have fewer, but larger, facilities to take advantage of economies of scale.

Companies that employ a pull or push-pull strategy typically establish logistics operations based on service quality, innovation, and flexibility. Purchasing managers select suppliers that produce quickly. Transportation managers use the firm's own fleet of trucks to ensure on-time delivery and accommodate special customer requirements. Firms can also utilize advanced technology to increase the responsiveness and flexibility of logistics operations. For example, enterprise resource planning (ERP) systems are data management systems that integrate information across all the departments of an organization. ERP systems give logisticians access to the most recent data from which to plan and implement their operations. ERP systems also can be used to communicate with the information technology (IT) systems of other companies through electronic data interchange (EDI). EDI enables an almost instantaneous transfer of information

enterprise resource planning (ERP) systems

Data management systems that integrate information across all the departments of an organization.

from one company's computer to another. Thus an advance ship notice can be sent to a customer alerting the warehouse that a shipment is planned, what will be on that shipment, and when it will arrive, speeding up the receiving process for both companies.

Logistics functions support supply chain strategies to achieve cost containment, innovativeness, flexibility, customer satisfaction, and other important marketing objectives. Next, we will investigate the important operational aspects of logistics functions in detail to get a fuller understanding of how logistics managers and personnel add value for customers and help achieve company goals.

LOGISTICS FUNCTIONS

LO 9-5

Describe how the primary logistics functions support a firm's supply chain strategy.

When you go to a store to purchase a product, you expect that it will be on the shelf. If you order an item from an online site, you expect it to be delivered to you fairly quickly. However, you may not have given much thought to all that goes into ensuring the product's availability or shipping it to customers like you. Logistics personnel are a big part of making that happen. A breakdown in any logistics function will result in back orders, empty shelves, and customer dissatisfaction. We'll discuss each of these functions in more depth in the sections that follow.

Managing Inventories

Suppose you really like Dr Pepper and drink three cans a day that you buy from the store around the corner from your dorm. You can easily track how much Dr Pepper you should keep in stock in your room—you buy a six-pack every other day and maybe keep an extra six-pack in case some friends come over. Now imagine that you were in charge of stocking Dr Pepper for the entire dorm. You would need to know how much your dorm mates consume on average every day. You would also need to know if consumption changes daily and within what range it changes so that you have enough Dr Pepper to satisfy demand even on days of heavy consumption. Now imagine that you are in charge of stocking enough Dr Pepper, Dr Pepper 10, and Diet Dr Pepper to satisfy demand in your entire state. The problem becomes even more complex since you must handle multiple varieties of Dr Pepper correctly to keep everyone satisfied. This example illustrates the difficulties companies face managing their inventories.

just-in-time (JIT)

A manufacturing process that seeks to make products based on customer orders rather than in anticipation of orders and to receive components from suppliers only when they are needed for production.

Firms rely on inventory management for several reasons, but primarily because, unless the right amount of inventory is available at the right location, customer service will suffer. The challenge of inventory management is to manage inventories in a way that balances supply and demand in a cost-effective manner. Some companies have moved to a just-in-time (JIT) manufacturing process that allows them to greatly reduce inventories. The JIT approach seeks to make products based on customer orders rather than in anticipation of orders and to receive components from suppliers only when they are needed for production. It relies on short and consistent delivery lead times from suppliers, a high level of quality from both suppliers and the manufacturing process itself, elimination of waste, and small production runs of product. These factors combine to eliminate any unnecessary inventories in the process, saving money in inventory costs, space, and labor.

While satisfying your own demand for Diet Dr Pepper is relatively easy, satisfying demand for customers around the world is much more complex, requiring thoughtful and efficient inventory management.

Types of Inventories   Firms must manage a number of types of inventories, including the following:[14]

cyclical inventory

Inventory a firm needs to meet average demand.

pipeline inventory

Inventory that is in transit between suppliers and customers.

anticipative stock

Inventory that is produced or purchased when a company expects something to occur in the future that will negatively affect stock availability.

seasonal stock

The goods a firm sells only at certain times of the year.

obsolete inventory

Inventory that can no longer be sold because the product has expired, been redesigned, was over-ordered, or is at the end of its product life.

1. Cyclical inventory is inventory a firm needs to meet average demand. If the firm produces the stock, the production lot sizes—that is, the quantity a firm determines is most economical to produce at one time—determine the cyclical inventory. If the firm purchases the stock (as a retailer would), quantity discounts, economical transportation quantities, and storage space availability regulate the amount of cycle stock. Inventory carrying costs and the time it takes to replenish stock influence both produced and purchased cyclical inventories.

2. Pipeline inventory refers to inventory that is in transit between suppliers and customers. Pipeline inventory is unavailable for sale or use in production and adds to inventory carrying costs. Firms with products in the introductory stage of the product life cycle often rely on pipeline inventories as producers attempt to keep up with demand that may exceed the supplier's ability to produce.

3. Anticipative stock is inventory that is produced or purchased when a company expects something to occur in the future that will negatively affect stock availability. An example is when a supplier announces a plant shutdown for maintenance two months before the actual shutdown. This gives the company adequate time to buy additional stock to last during the shutdown.

4. Seasonal stock refers to goods a firm sells only at certain times of the year (for example, the oranges used to make orange juice), or during certain seasons (for example, sunscreen). Manufacturing companies often have to start production of seasonal goods early so they can manufacture products fast enough to meet demand.

5. Firms end up with obsolete inventory when goods undergo design changes, are near the end of their product life cycles, have been over-ordered, or have

Supply chain disruptions that occur unexpectedly and last for extensive periods of time, like the Tsunami in Japan in 2011 that affected a number of major industries, cannot be overcome easily without the existence of anticipative stock.

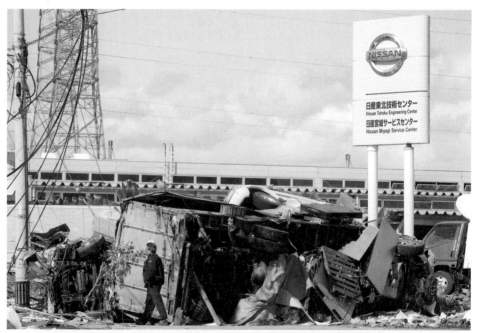

expired. An example of this might be a company that had an entire warehouse full of useless corrugated boxes because of product design changes that made the boxes obsolete.

Companies need most of these inventory types to support their marketing and supply chain strategies. The only exception is obsolete inventory, which is simply a drain on company finances and may need to be sold at an extreme discount or disposed of, either of which can actually cost a company money.

Inventory Costs Effective inventory management policies balance product availability with the costs of carrying inventory. A firm must track three types of costs to determine the correct level of inventory to keep in stock: purchasing costs, inventory carrying costs, and the costs incurred by stockouts.

1. Purchasing costs include order-processing and placement costs, and transportation charges if the purchasing company pays freight charges. The more often a company places orders for an item, the higher the annual purchasing costs.
2. Inventory carrying costs include storage and handling expenses, capital costs in tying up money, service costs such as property taxes and insurance, and costs associated with damage to or obsolescence of the good while it is in storage.
3. A stockout occurs when a company does not have enough inventory available to fill an order. In such cases, a customer can either place a back order or cancel the order. There are costs associated with processing the back order and making sure the product is delivered as soon as it is available. A lost sale means lost revenue. In more serious situations, the customer not only cancels the order but also decides not to buy from the firm any longer, costing the company future revenue.

stockout

A situation in which a company does not have enough inventory available to fill an order.

inventory turns

The number of times a firm's entire inventory is sold and replaced; calculated by dividing the cost of goods sold by the company's average inventory.

Figure 9.4 illustrates the relationships among the three costs. As order quantities increase, inventory carrying costs increase because the larger the order the more average inventory a firm will have on hand. Meanwhile, purchasing costs decrease because the firm will need to place fewer orders, and costs associated with stockouts decrease because the average inventory will be larger, making a stockout less likely.

Fortunately, firms can calculate all of these costs with some degree of accuracy by establishing models that take into account customer demand, replenishment lead time, order and inventory carrying costs, and service level requirements.[15] Sales forecasts are critical to this process since the firms base the models on anticipated customer orders over a period of time.

Evaluating Inventory Management Companies that successfully implement effective inventory management policies can not only keep their customers satisfied but also reduce product costs. Perhaps the most common measure of inventory management is inventory turns. Inventory turns refers to the number of times a firm's entire inventory is sold and replaced. It can be calculated by dividing the cost of goods sold by the company's average inventory level. The higher the turn ratio, the faster the company is converting

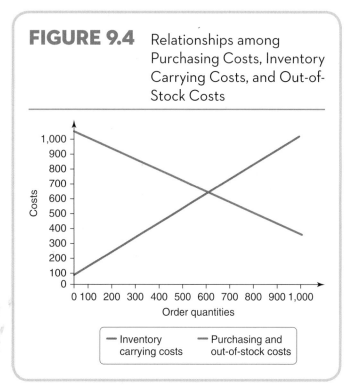

FIGURE 9.4 Relationships among Purchasing Costs, Inventory Carrying Costs, and Out-of-Stock Costs

inventory into revenue and the lower the chance that inventory will become obsolete. This calculation is usually performed annually for finished goods.

Another indication of effective inventory management is days of supply (or *days of coverage*). Days of supply estimates how many days the firm's current inventory will last and is calculated by dividing the inventory on hand by the average daily usage or sales. This calculation can be used to estimate days of supply for both finished goods and raw or packaging materials. Even with these measurements in hand, the impact of inventory investment on customer service should still be the firm's paramount consideration. A company with high inventory turns may also suffer poor customer service because inventory is not always available to ship to customers when ordered.

days of supply

An estimate of how many days the firm's current inventory will last; calculated by dividing the inventory on hand by the average daily usage or sales.

---

connect |MARKETING Interactive Assignment 9-2

Please complete the *Connect* exercise in Chapter 9 that focuses on inventory management. By understanding the key metrics of inventory management, you will be able to carry out this logistics function in the most cost-effective manner.

Purchasing

Purchasing involves the sourcing and procurement of raw materials, component parts, components, finished goods, and services for companies. Purchasing is an important logistical function in all organizations for a number of reasons. First, materials purchased for manufacturing typically account for 40 to 60 percent of the product costs, meaning that any savings in purchase costs can add significantly to a company's profits. Second, purchasing is a major factor in good and service quality. Selecting suppliers that can provide high-quality goods and services enables companies to compete with or even surpass the quality of other companies. Third, purchasing can help improve product design and time to market for new products by involving appropriate suppliers early in the product design process. Fourth, sourcing materials and products from reliable suppliers ensures that the flow of goods in a firm's supply chain meets demand, leading to superior customer service.

Purchasing Activities   To carry out the purchasing strategy of a company, purchasing managers perform a variety of activities, including

- *Selecting and qualifying appropriate suppliers.* Appropriate suppliers are critical to a company's success. A company selects suitable suppliers based on criteria, such as cost or service capability, established by the purchasing manager to fit the company's needs.[16] Given the global nature of businesses, some or all of the suppliers may be from a different country or region.
- *Negotiating contracts and placing purchase orders.* When an important good or service requires a new contract or contract renewal, the company will negotiate with a supplier over contract terms and conditions. Negotiations can occur over a number of aspects of a contract, including specific quantities to be delivered, quality factors, price, credit terms, and delivery terms. Based on the terms of the negotiations, the purchasing manager writes a purchase order, which is a legal obligation to buy a certain amount of product at a certain price from a supplier to be delivered at a specified date. Not all suppliers and buyers go through a negotiation phase. When a number of suppliers can provide goods or services that are not critical to the buyer, the purchasing manager may issue a purchase order for a one-time delivery of goods or performance of a service.

purchase order

A legal obligation to buy a certain amount of product at a certain price from a supplier to be delivered at a specified date.

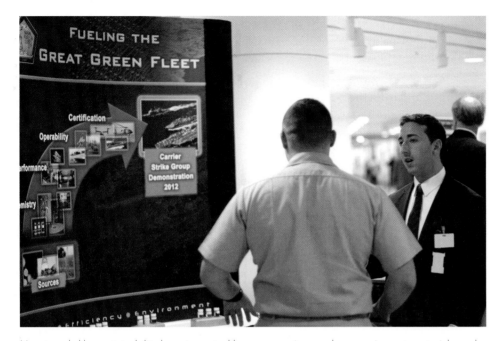

New trends like sustainability have impacted how companies purchase equipment, materials, and components from suppliers. The military is only one of many organizations whose procurement personnel increasingly seek out environmentally friendly products.

- *Monitoring supplier performance.* Purchasing managers establish performance expectations for suppliers and develop ways to measure their performance. Expectations often relate to quality, on-time delivery, rapid response to problems, and accuracy of invoices, but they can be customized to the needs of the buyer. A firm that relies on innovation as a competitive advantage may establish criteria related to the delivery of newly designed components within a short timeframe. As part of their monitoring activities, purchasing managers meet regularly with suppliers to discuss their performance. They may reduce the business awarded to the supplier, levy monetary fines, or refuse to do business with the supplier in the future if it does not meet expectations.

- *Supplier development.* Sometimes suppliers need extra help in meeting the expectations of the buying company. Purchasing managers can help develop supplier capabilities by visiting the supplier's operations to better understand issues, organizing supplier training by company experts, and providing financial assistance to suppliers for needed equipment purchases. Firms typically reserve this type of approach for critical suppliers due to its high cost.

Ultimately, managers want to create a world-class supply chain. To achieve this objective, many companies rely on global sourcing, which gives them access to the highest quality materials, goods, and services at the lowest possible price. Although there are a number of additional costs involved in sourcing goods and services from other countries—transportation costs, inventory carrying costs for goods in transit, and customs duties (tariffs), among other things—inexpensive labor and materials and high-quality goods and services often offset these costs. However, the cost of labor in and transportation from international sources has begun to rise. As a result, some companies now source goods and services domestically again. It is up to the purchasing manager to find the best suppliers, wherever they are located, and to understand the trade-offs involved in global sourcing.

Purchasing Ethics

Purchasing managers are in a unique ethical position in organizations due to their ability to award business to other companies. Unethical behavior in purchasing takes many forms.[17]

reciprocity
Purchasing goods and services from suppliers only if they buy from the purchasing manager's company.

personal buying
When a purchasing manager buys items for the personal use of employees rather than for business use.

- **Reciprocity** involves purchasing goods and services from suppliers only if they buy from the purchasing manager's company. This is an illegal practice and is monitored by the Federal Trade Commission (FTC).
- **Personal buying** occurs when a purchasing manager buys items for the personal use of employees rather than for business use. Some states have laws against this type of buying. Where such laws do not exist, personal buying represents a gray area, and the purchasing manager must determine the legality and company position on such behavior.
- **Accepting gifts and favors** from suppliers is a common ethical problem for purchasing managers and should be covered in a company's ethics policy. Some companies set a monetary limit on such gifts; some companies do not allow gifts of any kind. Regardless of the policy, accepting gifts from suppliers is a highly questionable activity and should be avoided.
- **Financial conflicts of interest** involve giving business to a supplier when the purchasing manager or relatives of the purchasing manager have a financial interest in the supplier. While not illegal, this act is considered unethical since it gives the impression that the purchasing manager is practicing favoritism, and may even be receiving financial gain from the arrangement.

Materials Management, Warehousing, and Distribution

Once purchasing managers procure raw and packaging materials or component parts, logistics personnel must manage them in a cost-efficient manner that supports manufacturing operations. Materials management involves the inbound movement and storage of materials in preparation for those materials to enter and flow through the manufacturing process. Effective materials management benefits the company in the following four ways:[18]

materials management
The inbound movement and storage of materials in preparation for those materials to enter and flow through the manufacturing process.

1. Reduces procurement, transportation, and production costs through economies of scale.
2. Coordinates supply and demand for materials. Warehouses can be used to store the various types of inventory—cyclical, safety, and anticipative stocks—until needed.
3. Supports manufacturing activities. Materials management ensures that stored or recently received materials get to the production floor when they are needed.
4. Supports marketing objectives by making sure that goods are available to ship to customers in an efficient and effective manner.

Materials management typically occurs in a warehouse. To maximize the benefits of materials management, logistics personnel must effectively coordinate various warehouse functions.

Warehouse Functions

Warehouses perform a number of different types of activities. These activities can be organized into three basic functions: storage, movement, and production.[19]

Storage   Storage involves holding inventories until they are needed. Storage may be temporary or semipermanent. Temporary storage implies that the goods are warehoused for a short period of time. Temporary storage can also be used to accumulate goods from small shipments for consolidation into larger shipments to reduce transportation costs. Semipermanent storage is used to warehouse inventory needed to meet demand over and above normal replenishment, such as seasonal stock, or to house extra inventory purchased as part of a push strategy or through volume discounts.

Movement The movement functions of a warehouse include receiving, put-away, picking, shipping, and delivery to a production area. Receiving involves unloading goods from a carrier, updating inventory records, and quality inspection, if required. Put-away refers to moving goods to their temporary or semipermanent storage location and updating inventory records. Picking involves retrieving materials from storage and bringing them to manufacturing to fulfill a production order, or retrieving finished goods from storage and preparing them for shipment to fulfill a customer order. Shipping involves loading picked items onto transportation vehicles, updating inventory records, and preparing the necessary documents to transport the items.

Activities like picking—retrieving and delivering materials or goods to fulfill production or shipment orders—make up one of the movement functions provided by warehouses.

Production Some warehouses also perform a production function. This may include such activities as light assembly of products like store displays, customizing products for customers (e.g., mixing different products into a shipment for customers that do not need large quantities of any one product), and refurbishing returned goods.

Distribution Centers
Distribution occurs when a company ships its goods to its customers. This activity is performed by distribution centers. A distribution center (DC) is a type of warehouse used specifically to store and ship finished goods to customers. Distribution centers perform all of the same storage and movement functions as warehouses, as well as additional activities to support company and marketing objectives. The four additional functions DCs perform include product accumulation, sortation, allocation, and assortment.[20]

- Product accumulation involves receiving goods from various suppliers, storing the goods until they're ordered by a customer or other company-owned facility, and consolidating orders to achieve transportation economies of scale. Orders from customers are collected until enough goods are ordered to fill vehicles, which reduces transportation costs. Figure 9.5 illustrates the product accumulation role of a distribution center.
- Product sortation refers to gathering goods with similar characteristics in one area of the DC to facilitate proper inventory controls and effectively provide customer service. For example, a company that sells sunscreen, which is regulated by the United States Food and Drug Administration (FDA), must keep expired products off store shelves. Product sortation enables such companies to maintain control over their inventory and avoid accidently shipping goods that are no longer fit for sale.
- The product allocation process involves picking available goods to fill customer orders. Distribution centers can be set up to pick full pallets of goods, full cases of goods, or individual goods. The ability of a DC to allocate goods down to a single piece allows customers to buy in quantities that make sense for their business. Walgreens, for example, would not want to order a full pallet of ruby red lipstick that would take years to sell. The DC's allocation function enables Walgreens to order only the quantities it needs.

put-away

Moving goods to their temporary or semipermanent storage location and updating inventory records.

picking

Retrieving materials from storage and bringing them to manufacturing to fulfill a production order, or retrieving finished goods from storage and preparing them for shipment to fulfill a customer order.

distribution center (DC)

A type of warehouse used specifically to store and ship finished goods to customers.

product accumulation

Receiving goods from various suppliers, storing the goods until they're ordered by a customer or other company-owned facility, and consolidating orders to achieve transportation economies of scale.

product sortation

Gathering goods with similar characteristics in one area of the distribution center to facilitate proper inventory controls and effectively provide customer service.

product allocation

Picking available goods to fill customer orders.

FIGURE 9.5   Accumulation Role of a Distribution Center

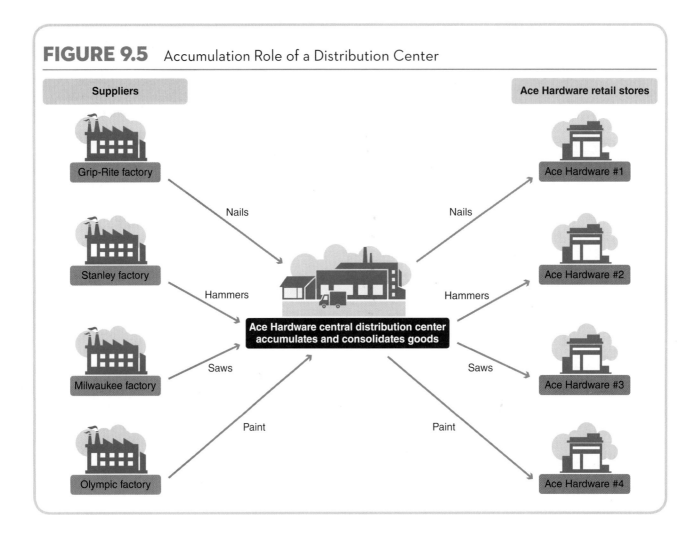

product assortment

Mixing goods coming from multiple suppliers into outgoing orders so that each order includes a variety of goods rather than just one type of good.

- A distribution center's product assortment function also supports ordering smaller, more economic quantities of goods. Product assortment occurs when the DC mixes goods coming from multiple suppliers into outgoing orders so that each order includes a variety of goods rather than just one type of good. As shown in Figure 9.6, customers often require small quantities of goods from a variety of suppliers. The product assortment function of a distribution center allows companies to meet this need in a cost-effective way by combining orders for a variety of products going to the same location in the same truck to save money.

Distribution Network Design   The number and location of DCs are among the strategies a company can use to support its marketing objectives. Should the firm establish a few, large centralized DCs, or more DCs that are closer to the customer but hold less inventory? The answer has to be based on the company's marketing and supply chain strategies. Some of the factors a company needs to consider when designing its distribution network include:[21]

- *Inventory levels.* The more facilities in the network, the higher the overall inventory in the system. The additional inventory can benefit the company if demand unexpectedly increases, but it adds to inventory carrying costs.
- *Operating expenses.* The fewer facilities in the network, the less operating expense incurred. With fewer facilities, the company will require fewer

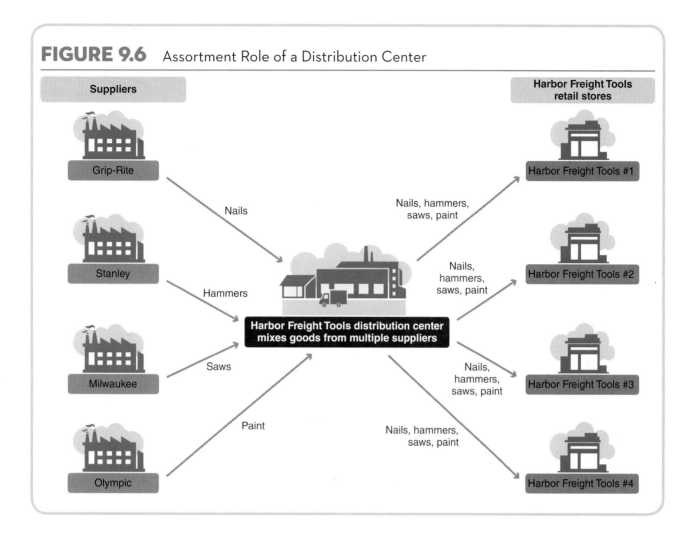

FIGURE 9.6 Assortment Role of a Distribution Center

management and clerical employees and less information technology equipment to conduct distribution activities.

- *Customer service.* More facilities result in faster delivery to customers since facilities will be closer to markets. However, centralized facilities generally result in better product availability, leading to superior customer service with less inventory investment.

- *Transportation costs.* More facilities lead to higher transportation costs from production sites and suppliers to the warehouses or DCs. However, transportation costs between the facilities and customers may be lower due to their close proximity.

In addition to these factors, distribution network decisions will be heavily influenced by the structure of a company's distribution channels. How a company uses these intermediaries, where they are located, their inventory and customer service expectations, and the extent of business the company does with them will influence distribution network decisions. For example, a company that counts Walmart or another very large company as a customer will likely want to place its own DCs close to those owned by the large company to service them faster.

Distribution channel members like Walmart and Target have a disproportionate influence on distribution network decisions due to their large share of the retail business.

Retailers Retailers like Walmart represent an important distribution channel. A retailer is a firm that sells mainly to end-user consumers. Retailers can take the form of large chain stores directed by corporate offices that centralize purchasing, advertising, human resources, and other functions. Walmart, as well as Target and Dillard's, are examples of chain stores. Independent retailers, such as a local book store or gift shop, may have only one or a few stores. Retailers can also be franchised from a large corporation. In such a case, the corporation sells the franchise store to an individual or individuals to operate, while maintaining control over management training, advertising, the supply of products being sold, and many other aspects of the store. Sonic and Radio Shack are examples of franchises.

Not all retailers operate brick-and-mortar stores. Some companies perform direct retailing, selling to customers at their homes, at their offices, or through parties at a customer's home at which the customer's friends and family watch product demonstrations by a company representative. Mary Kay Cosmetics is an example of a direct retailer. Telemarketing and mail order retailing are other nonstore forms of retailing. Mail order retailing relies on purchases made from catalogs mailed to customers' homes. Bass Pro Shops is an example of a company that has practiced catalogue sales successfully for many years. Online retailing (sometimes called *e-tailing*), or purchasing through a computer, tablet, or smartphone, is the fastest growing retailer category. Online retailers such as Amazon have taken advantage of the spread of electronic devices and the Internet throughout the world to sell goods anywhere there is an Internet connection. Because of the convenience consumers expect from online retailers, the decisions they make with regard to their distribution network design are especially critical to their ultimate success.

Interactive Assignment 9-3
Social Media in Action

As consumers shift their shopping experience from brick-and-mortar to online stores, retailers must increasingly embrace social media sites as a tool for reaching their target market. Firms ranging from Starwood Hotels to nutrition store GNC have invited customers to spend money through company fan pages on social media platforms. Retailers like JCPenney allow their customers to shop directly from their social media platforms and offer customers the added bonus of being able to share items they like instantaneously with their social media community.

Retailers want to go where their customers are and, increasingly, those places are social media platforms. The average consumer now spends more time each month on social media than on the top 500 online shopping sites combined. The popularity of social commerce also provides the added benefit of generating marketing research that helps retailers and their entire supply chain track trends and manage inventories.

The Social Media in Action *Connect* exercise in Chapter 9 will let you make decisions about social commerce strategies for retailers and use customer-generated marketing research to manage the supply chain. Social media tools can not only help retailers sell more but also create a more efficient supply chain.

Source: See Dana Mattioli, "Retailers Embrace Social Commerce," *The Wall Street Journal*, May 19, 2011, http://online.wsj.com/article/SB10001424052748703367004576289461779663904.html.

Ryan Burks
Network Manager
Frito-Lay Corporation

Describe your job. I manage the process of aligning inbound and outbound freight for our warehouse, which involves making the best use of our trucks to handle goods coming into and out of our manufacturing facility. My job is to ensure that, as an operation, we make the best decisions about transportation modes, cost trade-offs, the safety of our fleet and drivers, and operations efficiency.

Describe how you got the job that you have. I was hired as a result of a summer internship with Frito-Lay. I was made aware of the internship by a professor during my junior year. Because of the results I achieved during the internship, I was hired full time as a manager after my graduation.

What has been the most important thing in making you successful at your job? The most important aspect of my job is the people I manage. To be a successful manager, you must make your team successful. I strive to do everything I can to ensure that my team is successful.

What advice would you give soon-to-be graduates? Be willing to get out of your comfort zone and push yourself. Tackle public speaking or give a presentation. By doing so, you force yourself to become better at what makes you uncomfortable.

What do you consider your personal brand to be? I'm a "developer." I think the most important aspect of being successful is developing your team and those around you. By working to develop my team, I help equip them to handle issues and make the right decisions.

Managing Transportation

Transportation management is one of the most important logistics functions, for retailers and every other member of the supply chain. Effective transportation management creates value that is essential to keeping customers satisfied. Cost-effective transportation allows companies to market goods to greater distances, helping companies build global supply chains and compete in new markets. We'll discuss the various types of transportation modes and the factors firms should consider when choosing a mode and carrier in the next section.

LO 9-6

Explain the importance of mode and carrier selection in domestic and international supply chains.

MODE AND CARRIER SELECTION

Transportation plays a critical role in the logistics function of supply chain management, particularly in an increasingly interconnected world that allows companies to form a supply chain that spans the globe. A company can transport goods in a number of ways, but not all forms of transportation (modes) are suitable for every type of product. Highly profitable items like fashionable clothing or perishable goods like exotic fruit tend to be shipped by air because of its speed and expense. On the other hand, crude oil is most efficiently transported by pipeline. As with other supply chain decisions, mode selection involves trade-offs.

Transportation Modes

There are six types of transportation modes, each of which has advantages and disadvantages. Understanding these modes is essential to building an efficient and effective transportation network.

Intermodal transport allows shipments to be transferred easily from mode to mode, expediting delivery times.

Railroads Railroads transport a wide variety of products over long distances. Almost half of the ton-miles (one ton of goods carried one mile) moved in the United States are moved by rail. Historically, railroads have carried bulk products such as chemicals, coal, produce, and automobiles. However, with the advent of intermodal transportation, which we'll discuss in more depth in a later section, railroads commonly transport a variety of consumer goods. The primary advantage of rail transport is that it enables firms to convey a wide variety of goods in large quantities at a low cost. The disadvantages of rail transport include damages, inconsistent service, and accessibility. Accessibility refers to a carrier's ability to transport goods from the source of the shipment to their final destination. Typically, goods must be transferred from railcars to trucks for the end of the journey.[22]

Trucks Trucks (motor carriers) account for approximately one-third of the ton-miles of U.S. cargo movement and 84 percent of the money spent on transporting goods in the country. Trucks primarily move small- to mid-size shipments. Companies can either hire carriers or maintain their own fleet of trucks. For-hire carriers fall into two categories: common carriers, which sell their services to any business, and contract carriers, which move goods exclusively for certain customers. Trucks are accessible, reliable, and fast, but they charge a fairly high cost per ton-mile and have limited vehicle capacity. Due to the universal accessibility of motor carriers, for most shipments, some part of the journey will be completed by a truck.[23]

Air Transportation Air transportation accounts for less than 1 percent of the intercity ton-miles in the U.S., yet the speed with which goods can be transported via air secures its important role in logistics operations. For certain types of goods and shipments, air is the only viable option. For flowers to arrive fresh in New York City from South America they must be flown in; no other mode will do. Emergency medical shipments provide another example. When a life hangs in the balance airfreight may be the only viable option. Another advantage to air transportation is that the risk of damage is low, making it a good candidate for shipping fragile, expensive goods. The main reason airfreight is used sparingly is its cost. It is far and away the most expensive way to move goods. Another issue is accessibility. With very few exceptions, the final delivery of a shipment initiated by air will be made by a truck. Airfreight only makes sense for expensive goods that can bear the high cost of transportation or those that have to be there overnight.

Water Transportation Water transportation has taken on great significance as production has moved to low-cost producers in Asia and other parts of the world. Ships cross oceans on regular schedules, carrying thousands of containers of goods across thousands of miles each trip. Containers can be loaded and unloaded from ships quickly and efficiently, making ocean transport the mode of choice for international transportation of not only traditional products like raw materials and other bulk commodities but consumer products as

EXECUTIVE PERSPECTIVE

Terry Matthews
Executive Vice President and President of Intermodal
J.B. Hunt Transport Services, Inc.

Why is trucking so important to marketing?

For marketers to be successful, they have to get their products to customers in the fastest, safest, most cost-efficient way possible. For all of the changes in the economy, most of the products you use were still on a truck at some point in the supply chain. Marketers who understand the transportation opportunities that trucking provides will have an advantage in developing solutions to get products to their customers quickly and efficiently.

common carriers

For-hire truck companies that sell their services to any business.

contract carriers

For-hire truck companies that move goods exclusively for certain customers.

New models of TVs, game consoles, and Blu-ray players allow customers to purchase digital content that can be delivered via cyberspace.

well. Goods are also transported on lakes, rivers, and inland waterways. These shipments tend to be bulk commodities, such as farm products and minerals, rather than finished goods. Water transportation's advantages are its low cost and high capacity, but it takes longer than other modes. Additionally, cold weather can freeze water routes, eliminating this mode as an alternative for months at a time.

Pipelines Pipelines make up a very specialized mode that services only a few industries. Nevertheless, pipelines account for approximately 20 percent of the total ton-miles shipped in the United States.[24] Pipelines transport oil, oil products, and natural gas. Pipelines have a huge impact on national economies and play an important role in providing fuel for industrial, personal, and utility use. This mode is very efficient and low cost, but, in addition to being able to carry only a few types of products, it is slow.

Cyberspace A sixth mode of transportation, one you likely use frequently but may not think of as a transportation mode, is cyberspace.[25] Anything that can be digitized can be sent through the Internet and delivered to businesses and homes. Software, documents, and media (e.g., music, pictures, and film) can all be sent electronically. Once a firm sets up the technology to transmit data over the Internet, the shipment costs little and products arrive at their destination almost instantaneously. Retailers such as Amazon, with its wide selection of Kindle-ready digitized books, make transportation in cyberspace part of their supply chain strategy.

Firms must match the modes of transportation they choose to use with their overall marketing strategy to get the most advantage from their logistics operations. Global operations add complexity to the choices since the supply chain of a global company covers vast distances and will require several modes of transportation.

Mode Selection

Companies must consider many factors when choosing transportation modes, including transit times, mode accessibility, the ability of the mode to handle necessary volumes (capacity), and the ability of the mode to consistently service customers.[26] Cost will always be a factor in mode choice but will influence the decision more for certain products than others. Table 9.1 on page 279 lists the key factors that influence mode selection and how the modes compare across those factors.

Many firms, particularly those with global supply chains, rely on intermodal transportation, which involves using several types of transportation for the same shipment, for example, a truck to bring goods from a factory in China to a port, an ocean liner to carry the goods to a port on the west coast of the United States, a train to take the goods to an intermodal switching yard in Tennessee, and a truck

intermodal transportation

Using several types of transportation for the same shipment.

TABLE 9.1   Comparing the Six Modes of Transportation

Mode	Accessibility	Speed	Capacity	Cost	Service	International Capabilities
Rail	Low	Moderate	High	Moderate	Moderate	Intermodal
Truck	High	Moderate	Low	Moderate	High	Intermodal
Water	Low	Slow	Very High	Low	Moderate	Intermodal
Air	Low	Fast	Low	High	High	Intermodal
Pipeline	Low	Very Slow	Very High	Very Low	High	Limited
Cyberspace	Very High	Very Fast	Very Limited	Very Low	Very Limited	Very High

to deliver the goods to a retailer in Mississippi. The advent of intermodal transportation began with an important transportation innovation from the 1950s: the container. Containers are steel boxes used to transport goods, usually internationally. Containers can be loaded and unloaded from ships very quickly, which has greatly sped up the process of moving large amounts of goods between continents such as Asia and North America. Containers have also made intermodal transportation efficient since ships can transport thousands of containers at a time, which is highly cost effective.

container

Steel boxes used to transport goods, usually internationally.

Ultimately, modal capabilities should be matched to products. Not all of a company's goods may be transported with the same combination of modes. Where the product falls in its product life cycle (PLC) will also impact modal selection. Consider a new electronics product the size of a tablet computer sourced out of China that costs $100 to manufacture and will sell for $500. The product's design makes it far superior to competing products, leading to high demand. Getting the product to customers quickly is essential and, because the product is highly profitable, the cost of transportation will not be an issue. In this case, the company will want to use air transportation from China to minimize transit time and reduce the damage risks, then use a motor carrier from the airport to the final destination.

Connect |MARKETING **Interactive Assignment 9-4**

Please complete the *Connect* exercise in Chapter 9 that focuses on choosing modes of transportation. By understanding how to match the mode of transportation to the products a firm is selling, you will be able to efficiently deliver value to customers.

International Mode Selection

Globalization makes international transportation an increasingly important topic, particularly because efficient and effective international transportation has, in part, contributed to the rise of outsourcing and offshoring. Modern international transportation has enabled companies to source materials and goods from low-cost producers wherever they are found. However, companies must analyze the

Containers have been a driving factor in the globalization of supply chains because they allow a large amount of goods to be shipped inexpensively and can be quickly and easily loaded and removed from ships.

costs involved in moving goods between countries and continents. The cost of international shipments generally makes up a much higher percentage of the product costs than domestic transportation due to the longer routes, use of multiple modes, and administrative costs. In addition, the complexities of international transportation—volatile fuel prices, congested ports, piracy, union strikes, and inland transportation delays—affect a company's ability to ship goods in a cost-effective and reliable manner. To effectively market goods in a global environment, companies must empower logistics professionals to navigate the maze of transportation choices and develop solutions that support the firm's marketing strategy. The factors logistics professionals consider include the availability of modes, transportation rates, service capabilities, reliability, and government regulatory restrictions.[27]

Carrier Selection

After a firm chooses a mode for its goods, it must decide which carrier to use. Most carriers within a mode can provide similar service at a similar cost. However, a company needs to thoroughly investigate the individual service capabilities and rates among companies, which will vary geographically depending on the carrier's presence in a region. The ability of a carrier to track and trace a shipment, provide around-the-clock customer service, transport products safely and reliably, and deliver products within a specified time also impact carrier selection. Companies often adopt a core carrier strategy as opposed to using a large number of different carriers. A firm with a core carrier strategy selects a small number of carriers that offer volume discounts and quality service, which gives the company control and negotiating leverage when it comes to cost.

core carrier
A strategy in which a firm selects a small number of carriers as opposed to using a large number of different carriers.

SUMMARY

LO 9-1 Structure the various flows within a supply chain.

A supply chain is a set of three or more companies directly linked by one or more of the upstream and downstream flows of products, services, finances, and information from a source to a customer. Products primarily move downstream from a supplier to a customer, adding value to the final customer along the way. On their way downstream, they pass through distribution channels (or marketing channels), which are intermediaries such as wholesalers, distributors, and retailers. Finances, on the other hand, flow upstream in a supply chain. Information flows both upstream and downstream. Real-world supply chains typically involve a complex network made up of many suppliers and customers. A company can be a member of a number of supply chains.

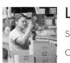

LO 9-2 Explain the importance of supply chain orientation and supply chain management to organizations.

A supply chain orientation is a management philosophy that guides the actions of company members toward the goal of actively managing the upstream and downstream flows of goods, services, finances, and information across the supply chain. Supply chain management involves the actions the firm takes to implement the supply chain orientation and coordinate the various flows within a supply chain. Looking at the total system of interrelated companies as something that can be influenced and managed gives companies control over the value they provide for their customers, which in turn should provide higher revenue to the company.

LO 9-3 Compare the various types of supply chain strategies firms use.

To effectively perform supply chain management firms must first develop a supply chain strategy. The chapter focuses on three types of strategies: push, pull, and hybrid (push-pull). A push supply chain strategy is one in which a company builds goods based on a sales forecast, puts the goods into storage, and waits for a customer to order them. In a pull supply chain, production and distribution operations are driven by customer orders. In a push-pull supply chain, the initial stages of the supply chain operate on a push system, but the finalization of the product is based on a pull system.

LO 9-4 Describe how logistics activities add value to products.

Logistics is that part of supply chain management that plans, implements, and controls the flow of goods, services, and information between the point of origin and the point of consumption to meet customers' requirements. Logistics operations add value to products moving through the supply chain. Though logistics is often associated with the place aspect of the four Ps, it impacts all aspects of the marketing mix. By aligning logistics activities with its supply chain strategies, a firm can ensure that it adds value to a customer at all stages.

LO 9-5 Describe how the primary logistics functions support a firm's supply chain strategy.

The primary logistics functions include inventory management, purchasing, materials management, warehousing, distribution, and transportation. Inventory management allows companies to maintain as low an inventory carrying cost as possible while still maintaining good customer service. Purchasing provides materials and goods at the lowest cost and highest quality needed to meet a company's marketing strategy. Materials management, warehousing, and distribution functions store goods until needed by manufacturing or a customer, then pick those goods and prepare them for delivery. Transportation delivers goods to customers at the right time, to the right place, and in the right condition.

LO 9-6 Explain the importance of mode and carrier selection in domestic and international supply chains.

Firms must match the modes of transportation they choose to use with the types of products they sell and the firm's marketing strategy. Global operations add complexity to the choices since the supply chain of a global company covers vast distances and typically requires several modes of transportation. Factors companies must consider when choosing transportation modes include cost, transit times, mode accessibility, the ability of the mode to handle necessary volumes (capacity), and the ability of the mode to consistently meet lead time requirements (reliability). Most carriers within a mode can provide similar service and costs. However, a company needs to thoroughly investigate the individual service capabilities and rates among companies.

KEY TERMS

anticipative stock (p. 266)
common carriers (p. 277)
container (p. 279)
contract carriers (p. 277)
core carrier (p. 280)
cyclical inventory (p. 266)
days of supply (p. 268)
distribution center (DC) (p. 271)
distribution channels (marketing channels) (p. 257)
enterprise resource planning (ERP) systems (p. 264)
intermodal transportation (p. 278)

inventory carrying costs (p. 259)
inventory turns (p. 267)
just-in-time (JIT) (p. 265)
logistics (p. 263)
materials management (p. 270)
obsolete inventory (p. 266)
personal buying (p. 270)
picking (p. 271)
pipeline inventory (p. 266)
product accumulation (p. 271)
product allocation (p. 271)
product assortment (p. 272)
product sortation (p. 271)

pull strategy (p. 260)
purchase order (p. 268)
push strategy (p. 260)
push-pull strategy (p. 261)
put-away (p. 271)
reciprocity (p. 270)
seasonal stock (p. 266)
stockout (p. 267)
supply chain (p. 256)
supply chain management (p. 258)
supply chain orientation (p. 257)

MARKETING PLAN EXERCISE

In this chapter, we discussed the importance of distribution. Getting your name, skills, and profile in front of decision makers is critical for you to achieve career success. In the next section of the marketing plan exercise, your assignment is to create a specific plan for how you will distribute your information and qualifications to reach your career objectives.

Job seekers upload and share millions of resumes every day on the Internet, even though the success rate of finding a job online is less than 20 percent in the U.S. What do you plan to do to increase your success rate using this distribution channel? A growing number of professionals use online services like LinkedIn. If you are thinking about LinkedIn or other social media distribution methods, which sites are best for your specific career path? What strategies should you employ on each site to maximize your efforts? Are there specific keywords you should use? Are there resume formats that work better on specific job sites?

If your career goals focus on graduate school, this process is equally important. Many graduate school entrance

exams allow you to select a limited number of schools to send your scores to. Which schools will you choose? If you plan to seek a job or graduate school opportunity using e-mail, what is the best strategy for designing that e-mail? Hiring managers and admissions personnel will pay attention to the e-mail text, the subject line, and even the time of day that you sent the e-mail (what would a manager think if your resume arrives at 2:30 a.m.?). Spending time now planning a personal distribution strategy will help as you prepare for your job or graduate school search.

Your Task: Write a one- to two-paragraph explanation of how you will distribute your information and qualifications. Your answer should include the websites or companies to which you plan to distribute your resume or the five schools to which you will send your graduate entrance exam scores. Also include any social media platforms you plan to use as part of your distribution strategy and how you plan to utilize them.

DISCUSSION QUESTIONS

1. Acme Manufacturing buys raw materials from Apex Unlimited. Acme gives Apex a monthly forecast of what it thinks it will buy and pays for the goods within 30 days of receipt. Better Retailing, Inc., is one of Acme's customers. It provides Acme with data that record the sales of Acme's products at Better Retailing's checkout counters. Better Retailing pays for the goods it receives from Acme within 30 days of when the products sell. Do Acme, Apex, and Better Retailing constitute a supply chain? Explain your answer.

2. Mumbai Grocery in India buys produce directly from farmers. It provides the farmers with information regarding the amount it would like the farmers to harvest each day to avoid having too little, thus losing sales, or too much, causing some of the produce to spoil and become unsellable. Does Mumbai Grocery have a supply chain orientation? Is it practicing supply chain management? Defend your answers.

3. Shanghai Computers uses a sales forecast to purchase components for desktop and laptop computers. The firm also uses the sales forecast to schedule the

production of partially assembled computers that are missing random-access memory (RAM), hard drives, and other components. Shanghai Computers waits until it receives a customer order, then finishes assembling the computers to the configuration ordered by the customer. What supply chain strategy is Shanghai Computers using? Explain why you chose that answer.

4. How do the various types of utilities provided by logistics operations help companies achieve their marketing objectives?

5. Explain the various types of inventories and how each type is used by companies to meet their marketing objectives.

6. Just-a-Buck is a low-cost retailer that sources its goods from factories in Asia. Just-a-Buck built its competitive strategy around providing products for exactly one dollar. Just-a-Buck has a distribution center located in Los Angeles that services the western half of the United States and another distribution center in Atlanta that services the eastern half of the U.S. What modes of transportation would Just-a-Buck logically want to use to transport the goods it purchases from Asia to the U.S.? What modes would it use to get the goods to its distribution centers? What modes would it use to get the goods to its stores? Explain your answers.

SOCIAL MEDIA APPLICATION

Assume that you are hired by the purchasing department at your university and your first task is to decide what type of PCs, laptops, or tablet computers the university is going to buy for its students. Analyze the social media presence of potential suppliers using the following questions and activities as a guide:

1. Decide on a list of three to five potential suppliers. What criteria, such as cost or service capability, did you use to determine the list?

2. Carefully read through the social media platforms used by each of the potential suppliers that the university might purchase from. Based only on what you read across the social media platforms, how would you rank the potential suppliers in terms of which you would most like to purchase from? Explain your answer.

3. Is there anything that you have found on your preferred suppliers' social media presence that can help you in negotiating with those firms? For example, do any of them appear to be having any customer service issues that you might be able to use as leverage to negotiate a lower price?

ETHICAL CHALLENGE

Tony Dauginas is a purchasing agent for a consumer packaged goods company based in the U.S. His company manufactures various goods in the health and beauty industry, such as cosmetics, skin lotions, toothpaste, and shampoo. Tony's company has come under assault from another, much larger company that can use its large purchasing volume as leverage to buy components for its products much less expensively than Tony's company can. This has put a lot of pressure on Tony's purchasing group to get the best price possible on the components it buys for manufacturing.

One of the types of materials that Tony buys is corrugated boxes. The boxes are used as secondary packaging for all his company's goods. The price of wood pulp used to make the boxes has been steadily rising, causing prices of corrugated boxes to rise along with it. Tony has been very concerned about this price trend because a

large percentage of the company's product-related costs is spent on boxes.

Tony just got back from a trade show, during which he received some interesting insider information about one of his suppliers. While talking to a fellow purchasing manager at a noncompeting company he found out that the other purchasing manager's company was terminating its contract with one of Tony's corrugated box suppliers, Amalgamated Boxes, Inc. The company Tony's friend works for is Amalgamated's biggest customer, constituting about 50 percent of its business. The loss of this business will likely be a damaging, if not fatal, blow to Amalgamated.

Tony is considering calling on Amalgamated's sales office and chatting with the vice president of sales. He figures that Amalgamated will be desperate for business and will be willing to do just about anything to secure Tony's company as a customer. Tony is thinking that he might be able to negotiate a long-term contract that locks in prices over several years, preventing Amalgamated from passing on rising wood pulp prices to his company. He is also thinking about making a deep reduction in Amalgamated's prices a condition of the contract. Please use the ethical decision-making framework to answer the following questions related to this scenario:

1. What are the ethical implications of Tony's plan to negotiate a long-term contract under the conditions presented in the scenario? Explain your answer.
2. What other approaches could Tony take with Amalgamated?
3. If you were in Tony's shoes, what would you do, and why?

VIDEO CASE

Please go to *Connect* to access the video case featuring FedEx that accompanies this chapter.

CAREER TIPS

Marketing Your Future

You have read in this chapter about supply chain management and logistics functions. This area of marketing is rapidly growing and can be a great career path for recent graduates. Author John Mello spent over 25 years as an employee and manager in the field of logistics and supply chain management. Based on his experience, he has provided four important tips to consider if you choose to pursue a career in this field.

1. **Be flexible.** Be willing to relocate to a new city or state when applying for a job. You will greatly limit your chances for getting a good job if you tell the employer that you are not willing to move. In addition, be flexible about what type of job you are willing to do. An offer for an off-shift job or one that involves working in an area open to the elements may not seem appealing; however, such jobs usually lead to higher-paying and more prestigious positions because they give you invaluable operations experience.

2. **Be collaborative.** If you cultivate good relationships with the people you work with, they will cooperate with you when you need them to. You will also develop a reputation as someone with whom it is easy to work. Beyond this, if you attempt to make someone else's job easier, you will gain their admiration and respect. This applies to your employees, your peers, your boss, and the people you are in contact with outside the company such as suppliers or customers. Do what you can to help others. You never know when you will need their help to get something done. Personal relationships are key to your success and ultimately your career.

3. **Be honest.** First, be honest with yourself. Ask yourself whether you are a person others would like to be around. If the answer is no, work on improving your interpersonal skills. Second, be honest with others. Don't tell people just what they want to hear. That may make them feel better, but it doesn't help them solve personal or company problems.

4. **Keep learning.** The more you know about your job and your industry, the more valuable you will be to the firm and to yourself. Learning includes asking questions on the job, shadowing experienced professionals, reading information about your field, and obtaining additional certifications and degrees. Find out what certifications are available in your field of interest. Once you're established in a company, look for opportunities to further your formal education with a master's degree. Often, your company will pay for all or part of your continuing education.

CHAPTER NOTES

1. John T. Mentzer, ed., *Supply Chain Management* (Thousand Oaks, CA: Sage Publications, 2001), p. 14.
2. John J. Coyle, John C. Langley, Jr., Robert Novack, and Brian J. Gibson, *Supply Chain Management: A Logistics Perspective,* 9th ed. (Mason, OH: South-Western Cengage Learning, 2013).
3. Mentzer, *Supply Chain Management.*
4. Ibid.

5. Coyle et al., *Supply Chain Management: A Logistics Perspective.*
6. David Simchi-Levi, Philip Kaminsky, and Edith Simchi-Levi, *Designing and Managing the Supply Chain: Concepts, Strategies and Case Studies,* 3rd ed. (New York: McGraw-Hill, 2008).
7. James R. Stock and Douglas M. Lambert, *Strategic Logistics Management,* 4th ed. (New York: McGraw-Hill, 2001).
8. Simchi-Levi et al., *Designing and Managing the Supply Chain,* pp. 191–193.
9. Council of Supply Chain Management Professionals, "Supply Chain Management Terms and Glossary," February 2010, http://cscmp.org.
10. *U.S. News and World Report,* "Best Business Jobs, 2013," n.d., http://money.usnews.com/careers/best-jobs/logistician.
11. Coyle et al., *Supply Chain Management: A Logistics Perspective.*
12. Ibid.
13. Ibid.
14. Ballou, Ronald H., *Business Logistics/Supply Chain Management,* 5th Edition. Copyright © 2004, pp. 330–331, 470. Reprinted by permission of Pearson Education, Inc., Upper Saddle River, NJ.
15. Simchi-Levi et al., *Designing and Managing the Supply Chain.*
16. W. C. Benton, Jr., *Purchasing and Supply Management,* 2nd ed. (New York: McGraw-Hill, 2010).
17. Robert M. Monczka, Robert B. Handfield, Larry C. Ginipero, and James L. Patterson, *Purchasing and Supply Chain Management* (Mason, OH: South-Western Cengage Learning, 2012).
18. Ballou, Ronald H., *Business Logistics/Supply Chain Management,* 5th Edition. Copyright © 2004, pp. 330–331, 470. Reprinted by permission of Pearson Education, Inc., Upper Saddle River, NJ.
19. Stock and Lambert, *Strategic Logistics Management.*
20. Simchi-Levi et al., *Designing and Managing the Supply Chain,* p. 80.
21. Ibid.
22. Coyle et al., *Supply Chain Management: A Logistics Perspective.*
23. Ibid.
24. Ibid.
25. Stanley E. Fawcett, Lisa M. Ellram, and Jeffrey A. Ogden, *Supply Chain Management: From Vision to Implementation* (Upper Saddle River, NJ: Pearson/Prentice Hall, 2007).
26. Coyle et al., *Supply Chain Management: A Logistics Perspective.*
27. Stock and Lambert, *Strategic Logistics Management.*

Chapter 10

PRICING FOR PROFIT AND CUSTOMER VALUE

LEARNING OBJECTIVES

After reading this chapter, you should be able to

LO 10-1 Explain the importance of pricing strategy to every organization.

LO 10-2 Outline the steps in setting a price.

LO 10-3 Compare the pricing tactics marketers can use.

LO 10-4 Explain the influence of technology on pricing.

LO 10-5 Summarize the major challenges of pricing for international markets.

LO 10-6 Explain the major legal and ethical issues associated with pricing.

EXECUTIVE PERSPECTIVE

Mark Duckworth
Chief Executive Officer and Founder
Optus Inc.

Mark Duckworth did not want to waste time as he pursued his dream of becoming a successful entrepreneur. As an accounting major in college, Duckworth took a part-time job performing basic accounting functions but realized that his real love was sales and working directly with people to put deals together. His first real job was as a salesperson. After gaining experience in the business world, Duckworth decided to establish Optus, a telecommunications firm, in a rural community. As CEO and founder, Duckworth is instrumental in setting the rates the company charges customers to ensure that his company makes a profit. Today, Optus has over 100 employees and Duckworth spends his days providing strategic oversight and direction to his executive team.

What has been the most important thing in making you successful at your job?

There are many explanations for the success I have enjoyed. One of the most important factors has been creating genuine relationships with employees, customers, and vendors. Also, I personally believe that sales success is usually created because of purchasing efforts beforehand. I have made a lot of money based on what I buy something for. I take chances on good deals because I know there is a market or I can create demand. Lastly, I am always optimistic, focused on the possibilities ahead but trying to balance that with a healthy dose of realism. Never underestimate the value of tenacity and a positive attitude.

What advice would you give soon-to-be graduates?

Get a robust education as a solid foundation and consider graduate school if it will help give you an advantage in your specific area of focus. If you have dreams of becoming an entrepreneur and starting a business, consider working in a related industry for a year or two, but pursue starting the business early in your career. It is much easier to focus on making such

an investment before you have a family and your risk tolerance changes. When I started my business, I was single and could fail because I knew I would always land on my feet and get a job. Later in life, once I was married and had a child, that changed. If I'd waited, I would not have been able to take such a risk and possibly would have never started a business.

How is marketing relevant to your role at Optus?

I am the CEO of a marketing- and sales-driven company, so it is extremely relevant to me. Our ability to be successful starts with our ability to have great products, price them in a way that provides maximum value to us and our customers, and promote and deliver them in a way that brings value to those customers. We work in a very competitive industry, and our ability to make good strategic marketing decisions and execute on those strategies is essential to our success in the short and long term.

What do you consider your personal brand to be?

I provide unique value not offered in the marketplace by the competition: a passion to out-serve any of my competitors and to create genuine relationships with others.

Mark Duckworth
Chief Executive Officer and Founder

OPTUS

Optus Inc.
https://www.optusinc.com/

Optus provides customers with business telecommunications solutions, offering telephone hardware; engineering, training, and maintenance services; and complementary products.

FORECAST

This chapter explores the importance of pricing, which is one of the most important strategic decisions a firm faces. Think about how many firms are impacted by how much they charge for their goods or services. Our guess is your list includes nearly every firm you know. Firms that set prices too high risk losing customers to competitors, but keeping prices lower than what customers are willing to pay leaves additional profits on the table that can never be recovered. In this chapter you will learn about the price-setting process, specific pricing tactics you can use to maximize profits, and important laws and regulations you must consider when pricing your products. As you read through the chapter, consider the following key questions:

1. Why is pricing important to my organization?
2. How do firms set prices?
3. What are specific pricing tactics that can be used by an organization?
4. How has technology changed pricing?

5. What are the challenges associated with pricing products in international markets?
6. What are the laws that I should be aware of when setting prices for my organization?

LO 10-1

Explain the importance of pricing strategy to every organization.

THE IMPORTANCE OF PRICING

Pricing affects your life each day and is part of almost every consumer decision that you make. Whether you are buying a new car or ordering lunch, the prices of the products you are considering typically factor into your decision about what to purchase. If the price for a lunch special is too high, you may buy something else to eat. But consider that, if the restaurant charges less than you would have been willing to pay, it has reduced its profit. You should be mindful of these factors when, after you graduate, you negotiate the price an organization is willing to pay you as an employee. If the price to hire you is too high, the company you are interviewing with may hire someone else. However, if you ask for a lower salary than what the company is willing to pay you, you have sacrificed initial earnings potential. This, in turn, could affect your earnings for years to come if your raises are based on percentage increases in your initial salary. Thus it is critical that you understand the strategy and tactics of pricing and how they impact your future and the future of the organizations you work for.

The other three elements of the marketing mix—product, promotion, and place—come together to determine how marketers capture value through pricing. Price is the amount of something—money, time, or effort—that a buyer exchanges with a seller to obtain a product. Pricing is one of the most important strategic decisions a firm faces because it reflects the value the product delivers to consumers as well as the value it captures for the firm. When used correctly, pricing strategies can maximize profits and help the firm take a commanding market position. When used incorrectly, pricing strategies can limit revenue, profits, and brand perceptions.

Pricing is the essential element for capturing revenue and profits. Revenue is the result of the price charged to customers multiplied by the number of units sold. Profits are simply revenue minus total costs. These two calculations, represented in the following equations, underlie the firm's entire marketing strategy:

$$\text{revenue} = \text{units sold} \times \text{price}$$

$$\text{profits} = \text{revenue} - \text{cost}$$

The objective of strategic pricing is profitability. The majority of marketers and firms throughout the world seek to increase revenue, which can ultimately lead to increased profits. There are only two ways to increase revenue: sell more products or sell them at a higher price. As a result of this reality, marketers must make strategic trade-offs between volume and price to maximize profits.

price

The amount of something—money, time, or effort—that a buyer exchanges with a seller to obtain a product.

revenue

The result of the price charged to customers multiplied by the number of units sold.

profits

Revenue minus total costs.

Ultimately, marketers want to charge as much as they possibly can as long as the consumer still perceives value in the product at that price. Integrating the pricing strategy with other marketing mix elements ensures that the firm's products include only those features that add value to customers. For example, consider customers who stop buying cable television or combo meals at a certain fast food restaurant because the price included channels or menu items they didn't want to pay for. If the price is set too high, customers will simply choose another good or service. To avoid such pitfalls, marketers use a systematic process to evaluate relevant factors when setting a price.

THE PRICE-SETTING PROCESS

Many factors influence how a firm sets prices. A firm's various stakeholders may voice a preference for higher or lower prices depending on their point of view. Marketing executives in search of substantial profits typically want high prices across the products they sell, while customers and salespeople often want low prices to increase the perceived customer value and ultimately the number of units sold. Thoughtful consideration of the impact on all stakeholders at each step in the price-setting process, illustrated in Figure 10.1, increases the likelihood that the final price captures value for the firm and delivers value to the customer.

Companies that charge a higher price than the value the customer places on a product run the risk that the customer will choose another good or service. In recent years, some cable customers have disconnected their service in favor of less-costly alternatives like streaming Netflix or Google TV.

Step 1: Define the Pricing Objectives

The first step in setting a price is to clearly define the pricing objectives. Pricing objectives should be an extension of the firm's marketing objectives. They should describe what a firm hopes to achieve through pricing and, similar to the firm's marketing objectives, should be specific, measurable, and reflect the market realities the firm faces. Common pricing objectives include profit maximization, volume maximization, and survival.

Profit Maximization Profit maximization is designed to maximize profits on each unit sold. Profit maximization, or *price skimming*, involves setting a relatively high price for a period of time after the product launches. Over time, the firm often decreases the price to a level designed to be more sustainable over the long term. Profit maximization assumes that customers value a product's

LO 10-2

Outline the steps in setting a price.

profit maximization (price skimming)

A pricing strategy that involves setting a relatively high price for a period of time after the product launches.

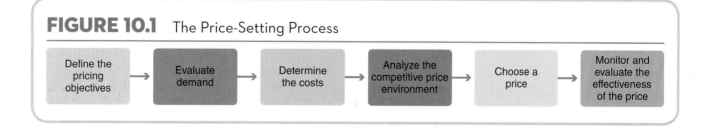

FIGURE 10.1   The Price-Setting Process

Define the pricing objectives → Evaluate demand → Determine the costs → Analyze the competitive price environment → Choose a price → Monitor and evaluate the effectiveness of the price

Luxury brands like Rolex charge high prices as part of a profit maximization strategy that relies on a customer's willingness to pay more for a product they attach more value to.

differentiating attributes and are willing to pay a higher price to take advantage of those attributes, especially early in a product's life cycle. Apple's pricing of a newly released iPad model provides a good example of profit maximization.

For a profit maximization strategy to work, firms must use the other marketing mix elements to make sure the product is produced, delivered, and promoted in a way that clearly differentiates it from competing alternatives. For example, a luxury brand like Mercedes-Benz does not sell inexpensive products or use promotional gimmicks in an effort to increase the volume of its sales because the firm wants customers to associate Mercedes-Benz with higher levels of quality and elegance than a regular car company. By consistently selling at a higher price, Mercedes-Benz maximizes profits and reinforces the added value and superior experience of buying its cars.

Volume Maximization Volume maximization is designed to maximize volume and revenue for a firm. Volume maximization, often referred to as *penetration pricing*, is the process of setting prices low to encourage a greater volume of purchases. By lowering prices, marketers lower the level of involvement for the consumer. DirecTV, for example, aggressively promotes a pricing strategy in which customers get access to over 150 channels for less than $40 per month during their first year of service. While the pricing package requires a two-year contract (and prices typically increase in the second year to a specified rate), consumers see immediate savings in their monthly bill and receive a whole home digital video recorder (DVR) and other added features. The penetration pricing strategy has increased the volume of DirecTV customers to more than 20 million subscribers.[1]

volume maximization (penetration pricing)

A pricing strategy that involves setting prices low to encourage a greater volume of purchases.

For this type of strategy to work over the long term, the firm must have a significant cost or resource advantage over competitors. For example, Walmart has become the largest retailer in the world largely because it leverages its bulk buying power and efficient supply chain to reduce costs as part of a volume maximization strategy.

Survival Pricing The survival objective is designed to maximize cash flow over the short term and is typically implemented by a struggling firm. Survival pricing is the process of lowering prices to the point at which revenue just covers costs, allowing the firm to endure during a difficult time. It should not be a permanent pricing objective, but it can be useful as a temporary means of staying in business. During the recession that began in late 2007, General Motors (as well as a number of other companies) reduced prices in an effort to avoid bankruptcy and sustain the firm.[2]

survival pricing

A pricing strategy that involves lowering prices to the point at which revenue just covers costs, allowing the firm to endure during a difficult time.

Step 2: Evaluate Demand

The second step in setting a price is evaluating demand for the product at various price levels. The concept of supply and demand sits at the heart of setting prices. According to traditional economic theory, setting prices is as simple as finding the point at which marginal revenues equal marginal costs. Marginal revenue is the change in total revenue that results from selling one additional unit of product, while marginal cost is the change in total cost that results from producing one additional unit of product. Unfortunately, pricing in today's market is much more

marginal revenue

The change in total revenue that results from selling one additional unit of product.

marginal cost

The change in total cost that results from producing one additional unit of product.

complicated. To start, environmental forces can significantly impact demand for products. For example, during the recession, demand for houses declined significantly due to high unemployment, reduced consumer confidence, and tight lending standards by banks that made it difficult for consumers to get home loans. The economic situation reduced demand to such a degree that house prices in many parts of the country declined by more than 15 percent from their previous values.[3]

In addition to assessing the impact of environmental factors, marketers have to project not only the overall product demand but also the specific demand at various price points. This requires an understanding of consumers' price sensitivity, which is the degree to which the price of a product affects consumers' purchasing behavior. The degree of price sensitivity varies from product to product and from consumer to consumer. A number of factors influence price sensitivity, as shown in Table 10.1. A consumer shopping for a new car who cannot afford to spend more than a certain amount on such a large purchase will be more price sensitive than a consumer with more money to spend on a car or a consumer shopping for a smaller purchase like a new piece of clothing. Consumers are also more price sensitive if the price they see for a new car at the dealership is higher than they anticipated. Regardless of the car's features, a consumer is less likely to pay the price if it's more than he or she expected to spend. Marketers consider each of the factors during the price-setting process to understand the impact of specific price-sensitivity drivers. Once marketers understand the price sensitivity exhibited by members of their target market, they can use this measure to calculate how changes in price will impact demand for a product and thus the amount of product the firm can sell at various price levels.

price sensitivity
The degree to which the price of a product affects consumers' purchasing behavior.

TABLE 10.1   Factors Influencing Price Sensitivity

Factor	Description
Size of expenditure	Customers are less sensitive to the prices of small expenditures which, in the case of households, are defined relative to income.
Shared costs	Customers are less price sensitive when some or all of the purchase price is paid by others.
Switching costs	Customers are less sensitive to the price of a product if there is added cost (both monetary and non-monetary) associated with switching to a competitor.
Perceived risk	Customers are less price sensitive when it is difficult to compare competing products and the cost of not getting the expected benefits of a purchase is high.
Importance of end-benefit	Customers are less price sensitive when the product is a small part of the cost of a benefit with high economic or psychological importance.
Price–quality perceptions	Customers are less sensitive to a product's price to the extent that price is a proxy for the likely quality of the purchase.
Reference prices	Customers are more price sensitive the higher the product's price relative to the customers' price expectation.
Perceived fairness	Customers are more sensitive to a product's price when it is outside the range that they perceive as "fair" or "reasonable."
Price framing	Customers are more price sensitive when they perceive the price as a "loss" rather than as a forgone "gain." They are more price sensitive when the price is paid separately rather than as part of a bundle.

Source: Thomas Nagle, John Hogan, and Joseph Zale, *The Strategy and Tactics of Pricing,* 5th ed. (Upper Saddle River, NJ: Pearson, 2011), pp. 132–133.

price elasticity of demand

A measure of price sensitivity that gives the percentage change in quantity demanded in response to a percentage change in price (holding constant all the other determinants of demand, such as income).

inelastic demand

A situation in which a specific change in price causes only a small change in the amount purchased.

elastic demand

A scenario in which demand changes significantly due to a small change in price.

Because demand for Netflix's DVD and online streaming services is inelastic—not significantly affected by changes in price—the additional revenue it earned when it increased prices for each service more than outweighed the revenue it lost due to unhappy customers.

Price elasticity of demand is a measure of price sensitivity that gives the percentage change in quantity demanded in response to a percentage change in price (holding constant all the other determinants of demand, such as income). It is one of the most important concepts in marketing and should be considered when pricing any product. Consider the following example: Suppose a car dealership reduces prices on its entire stock of new inventory by 10 percent. You would expect demand and, consequently, the number of cars sold to increase. But by what percentage would sales increase? Would they increase enough to offset the decrease in price? If the dealership reduced prices by 10 percent but sold only 4 percent more cars, it would be worse off than it was initially, as the following equations illustrate:

March: 1,000 cars sold × $20,000 (average price for new cars) = $20,000,000
April: 1,040 cars sold (4% increase) × $18,000 (10% price decrease) = $18,720,000

This scenario happens all too often and illustrates the concept of inelastic demand. Inelastic demand refers to a situation in which a specific change in price causes only a small change in the amount purchased.[4] As a marketing professional, if salespeople or others in an organization approach you asking for a price reduction to sell more units, your first question should be how many more units do they expect to sell at the reduced price. If the additional sales don't offset the price reduction, you would not want to approve their request.

Now consider a different scenario. Suppose the car dealership's 10 percent reduction in price leads to a 20 percent increase in the number of cars sold. In that case the firm would be better off than it was originally, as shown in the following equations:

March: 1,000 cars sold × $20,000 (average price for new cars) = $20,000,000
April: 1,200 cars sold (20% increase) × $18,000 (10% price decrease) = $21,600,000

In this scenario, the car market demonstrated elastic demand. Elastic demand is a scenario in which demand changes significantly due to a small change in price. Prices are generally more elastic in the early stages of the product life cycle and increasingly inelastic in the later stages of the product life cycle.

To see these concepts at work in the real world, consider how the principle applies to cost increases at Netflix. In 2011, Netflix raised prices on its DVD and online streaming services by over 50 percent.[5] While the company received a significant amount of negative publicity, less than 4 percent of paid subscribers stopped using the service. In fact, Netflix's quarterly revenue and profit after the change were both significantly higher. If we plug these percentages into our fictional car example, look at what the equivalent results would be:

March: 1,000 cars sold × $20,000 (average price for new cars) = $20,000,000
April: 960 cars sold (4% decrease) × $30,000 (50% price increase) = $28,800,000

In the case of Netflix, because of inelastic demand, the firm could raise prices significantly and realize only a small reduction in units sold. In light of this, the company's decision to raise prices to increase profitability was a good one.

Step 3: Determine the Costs

Accurately determining the costs of a product sets a lower price limit for marketers and ensures that they will not lose money by pricing their products too low. While a firm may temporarily sell products below cost to generate sales as part of a survival pricing strategy, it cannot endure for very long employing this tactic. A marketer should understand all of the costs associated with its product offering, whether the product is a good, service, idea, or some combination of these. Calculating the total cost of a product begins with an understanding of the two major types of costs: fixed and variable.

Fixed Costs versus Variable Costs

Costs that remain constant and do not vary based on the number of units produced or sold are called fixed costs. Examples of fixed costs include salaries, rent, insurance, and advertising costs. Since these costs will be incurred regardless of the level of production or sales activity, they must be recovered during the course of doing business. Marketers must set a final price that allows the firm to cover fixed costs over the long term.

Costs that vary depending on the number of units produced or sold are called variable costs. Variable costs include things such as material, sales commissions, utilities, and delivery costs. To illustrate the difference between the two types of costs, let's use our car dealership example again. Fixed costs for a car dealership include rent for the offices and showroom and employee salaries and benefits. These costs exist each month and do not change even if, for example, an additional 10 cars are sold in one month. Variable costs for a car dealership would include things like commissions for the dealership's salespeople. The organization must ensure that prices generate profits after accounting for *both* fixed and variable costs. A $20,000 car might generate an $800 per-car profit for the dealership after all of the fixed costs are accounted for. However, if the dealership offers its salespeople a 5 percent commission ($1,000) on each new car sold, the dealership would actually lose money on sales of the car. Marketing professionals must watch costs closely and set prices accordingly to avoid such scenarios.

Break-Even Analysis

Once a company estimates fixed and variable costs, it can incorporate them into a break-even analysis to determine how much it would need to sell to make the product profitable. Break-even analysis is the process of calculating the break-even point, which equals the sales volume needed to achieve a profit of zero. Specifically, the break-even point is the point at which the costs of producing a product equal the revenue made from selling the product. Once the firm has established the break-even point, it has a starting point for estimating how much revenue it must generate to earn a profit. To calculate the break-even point, we divide total fixed costs by the unit contribution margin, which is determined by subtracting the variable cost per unit from the selling price per unit. Figure 10.2 on page 294 illustrates break-even analysis and the influence of fixed and variable costs. Notice that fixed costs remain flat while variable costs increase as the amount of sales increases. Once unit sales pass the break-even point, the firm begins to generate a profit.

Consider this simple example of break-even analysis: If it costs $50 to produce a widget, and fixed costs are $1,000, we can calculate the break-even point at a price of $100 and a price of $250 as follows.

$$\frac{\$1,000}{\text{fixed costs}} \div \left(\frac{\$100 \text{ selling}}{\text{price per unit}} - \frac{\$50 \text{ variable}}{\text{cost per unit}} \right) = \frac{20}{\text{widgets}}$$

$$\frac{\$1,000}{\text{fixed costs}} \div \left(\frac{\$250 \text{ selling}}{\text{price per unit}} - \frac{\$50 \text{ variable}}{\text{cost per unit}} \right) = \frac{5}{\text{widgets}}$$

EXECUTIVE PERSPECTIVE

Mark Duckworth
Chief Executive Officer and Founder
Optus Inc.

What step in the price-setting process do you think is most problematic for marketers?

I would say it is determining costs. I have seen too many businesses over the years that don't have an accurate picture of how much each unit of product actually costs. In order to make sure that you are pricing in a way that can keep your business profitable, you have to make sure all of the fixed and variable costs, whether that be the rent for the warehouse, salaries for the human resources team, or the cost of staples at your desk, are accounted for in each product price.

fixed costs
Costs that remain constant and do not vary based on the number of units produced or sold.

variable costs
Costs that vary depending on the number of units produced or sold.

break-even analysis
The process of calculating the break-even point, which equals the sales volume needed to achieve a profit of zero.

break-even point
The point at which the costs of producing a product equal the revenue made from selling the product.

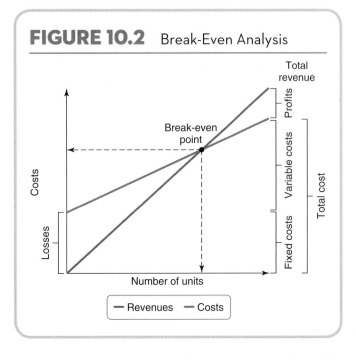

FIGURE 10.2 Break-Even Analysis

Note that break-even analysis only analyzes the costs of the sales; it does not reflect how demand may be affected at different price levels. In other words, it doesn't measure price sensitivity. Just because the firm will break even selling 5 widgets at a price of $200 each doesn't mean customers are willing to buy widgets at that price.

While marketers must understand a firm's costs to set prices effectively, costs should never dictate price. Strategic pricing requires firms to integrate costs into other aspects of the marketing mix, including what value the customer places on the product and the price environment in the industry.

Step 4: Analyze the Competitive Price Environment

Pricing does not occur in a vacuum. Marketers must consider what competitors charge for their products. Setting prices to compete against other firms is challenging and complex. Marketers can choose to match competitor prices, price lower than competitors thus offering customers greater value, or price higher because the firm offers a superior product. This decision should be consistent with the overall marketing objectives of the firm and the other three marketing mix elements. Industry structure plays an important role in this process. For example, in a market structure in which there are a large number of buyers and sellers, as is the case for our car dealership, the pricing impact of any single firm will be fairly small. If a car dealership in Dallas reduced or raised prices on certain types of cars, it is doubtful the change in price would significantly influence pricing at other car dealerships in the area. However, in an industry in which a small number of firms

Marketers in industries with few competitors like the domestic airline industry increasingly look to avoid price wars by competing based on rewards programs, enhanced flight offerings, and other nonprice strategies.

compete, firms will typically match the price of competitors. A common example of this is the wireless phone industry, in which only a few major competitors fight for market share in a multibillion-dollar industry. Marketers at AT&T, Verizon Wireless, and other firms compete on nonprice strategies, such as rollover minutes and better product features.

Marketers also should consider how competitors might respond to their pricing. Pricing can resemble a game of chess. You should always be thinking about what your opponents' future moves might be. How a firm reacts to a change in a competitor's prices depends on whether the competitor is a stronger or weaker rival and whether the price reduction is cost justified, that is, if the lower price will allow the firm to remain profitable. For example, if a weaker competitor initiates a price decrease that would leave the firm unable to cover its costs if adopted, it will likely simply ignore the competitor's price cut and maintain its current pricing. However, if the price cut is initiated by a stronger competitor and is cost justified, the firm will likely reduce prices to defend its existing customer base and market share.

Marketers must also take online competitors into account when determining the initial prices for both in-store and online-only items. Recently, retailer Brookstone separated its team of pricing employees into an in-store group and an online-commerce group. Every day the online team scours competitors' websites to check the prices of their online electronics and then adjusts the prices of thousands of Brookstone's online-only items accordingly.[6]

Step 5: Choose a Price

Determining the costs provides a lower price limit. Analyzing the competition narrows the range of prices that can be charged. After completing these two steps, it is time for marketers to choose a price. Again, the pricing decision should be made with the goal of maximizing long-term, sustainable profits. Choosing a price is a complicated process and marketers rarely do it perfectly. The next section of the chapter will discuss the most common tactical strategies for determining price. First, we'll discuss two often overlooked factors that influence price: reference prices and underpricing.

Reference Prices Chances are you compare the prices of almost everything you buy, from textbooks to coffee to gasoline, on a daily basis. Marketers can capitalize on this tendency by identifying the reference prices of their targeted consumers when setting their own prices. Reference prices are the prices that consumers consider reasonable and fair for a product. Reference prices matter to marketers because consumers are typically more price sensitive the higher a product's price is relative to expectations. Salespeople can be a valuable tool when identifying reference prices. In most cases, salespeople have the most direct contact with customers and thus a good sense of what customers are willing to pay. Salespeople who have developed relationships with customers often understand the most attractive price points and can leverage the quality of their relationship with the customer to obtain higher profits. Marketers should work closely with the sales force to understand how high they can price a product before customers stop considering the product a good value. Customer surveys, focus groups, and other forms of marketing research also are helpful in understanding how consumers view a certain product and how much they are willing to pay for it.

Instead of just seeking to identify reference prices, marketers can also seek to establish reference prices for consumers. Apple, for example, launches a variety of products at various price points so that buyers can compare the products and begin to associate features with dollars. As a result of this strategy, customers don't mind paying a higher price for a product with more capacity or better

reference prices
The prices that consumers consider reasonable and fair for a product.

Retailers like T.J. Maxx and Loehmann's use reference prices to illustrate the savings they offer customers by listing both the original price of the good and the retailer's discount price on the merchandise tags.

underpricing

Charging someone less than they are willing to pay.

features. They are willing to pay $199 for the iPod Touch with 8 gigabytes (GB) of storage because it has high-definition recording, the iCloud, and many other sought-after features that earlier versions of the iPod, such as the 8GB Nano (priced at $129), don't have. If customers are willing to pay an even higher price for more storage capacity, they may choose the 32GB iPod Touch for $299. Even if a firm doesn't seek to establish reference prices as Apple does, its marketers should always question what reference prices potential customers will compare the firm's prices with.

Underpricing One of the most common mistakes in modern pricing is charging someone less than they are willing to pay, or underpricing. Customers place different values on the goods and services they buy. As Charlie Sheen's character Budd Foxx famously said in the movie *Wall Street*, "You should not charge a guy $30 for an airline ticket if he is willing to pay $300."

Because revenue is simply the number of units sold multiplied by the price per item, marketers too often make the mistake of setting prices too low in an effort to increase the units sold side of the equation, without considering all of the other factors that contribute to the value a customer places on a product.

Airlines have considered the ramifications of underpricing for years in their pricing strategies. If you purchased an airline ticket today for a flight three months from now from Dallas to Los Angeles, you might pay $500. However, if you wait until the day before that flight to buy the same ticket, you may pay something in the range of $1,500. The customer buying three months in advance, whether he or she is attending a conference or taking a family trip to Disneyland, has plenty of time to comparison shop. However, the person who needs to fly to Los Angeles tomorrow may have an urgent business meeting or a new baby in the family, either of which increases the value of the airline ticket. Could the airline charge the last-minute customer the same price as the recreational traveler? Yes, but why should it if the value the customer places on the ticket differs?

Step 6: Monitor and Evaluate the Effectiveness of the Price

Choosing a price is not a one-time decision and should be monitored and evaluated to determine how effectively the strategy meets the pricing objectives. Pricing strategy evolves and should be reevaluated throughout the product life cycle. Marketers in the introduction stage for a new type of smartphone might select a price-skimming strategy to achieve maximum profits from the innovators and early adopters who are most excited about the product. As the product enters the growth stage and the customer base expands, a firm will often gradually lower prices as it achieves economies of scale and more competitors enter the market. Once the product enters the decline stage of the product life cycle, the firm may decide to use survival pricing to clear out remaining inventories and sustain the product for as long as possible.

One of the most challenging aspects of pricing is initiating price increases. It is hard to imagine a customer being excited about paying more for the same product. However, in an effort to recover increasing costs or improve profits, firms often face situations that require price increases. For example, restaurants Wendy's and Arby's were both forced to raise prices after the cost of beef and other key ingredients increased by more than 5 percent.[7] Two of the most common and effective strategies for raising prices are unbundling and escalator clauses. When undertaking either strategy, the firm must take the time to clearly explain the price change to customers so they understand why it's being done and believe it to be fair, even if they still may not be happy with the change. If the firm doesn't communicate the purpose of the increase effectively, customers who are unwilling to accept the increase may use social media platforms or other word-of-mouth strategies to protest against the new policies.

Unbundling

Unbundling provides value for customers who are focused on a specific price point rather than the complete product offering. Unbundling involves separating out the individual goods, services, or ideas that make up a product and pricing each one individually. Such a strategy allows marketers to maintain a similar price on the core product but recover costs in other ways on related goods and services. For example, a restaurant might unbundle a meal so that the hamburger sells for the same price, but the customer now must pay extra for the french fries. Airlines have pursued an unbundling strategy over the course of the last decade. They now charge separate fees for baggage rather than bundling luggage fees into the cost of the ticket. Netflix used an unbundling strategy when it separated its streaming service from its DVD-by-mail service. Customers could still get one service or the other for less than $10 per month, but not both, which amounted to a price increase for those customers who wanted to continue utilizing both services.

Escalator Clauses

An escalator clause in an agreement provides for price increases depending on certain conditions. The escalator clause ensures that providers of goods and services do not encounter unreasonable financial hardship as a result of uncontrollable increases in the costs of or decreases in the availability of something required to deliver products to customers. An escalator clause in

unbundling

Separating out the individual goods, services, or ideas that make up a product and pricing each one individually.

escalator clause

A section in a contract that ensures that providers of goods and services do not encounter unreasonable financial hardship as a result of uncontrollable increases in the costs of or decreases in the availability of something required to deliver products to customers.

Construction contracts often have built-in escalator clauses to protect construction firms in the event of increases in the price of materials like copper, asphalt, lumber, and concrete.

logistics can take the form of a fuel surcharge that allows carriers, such as trucking companies, to adjust prices based on the current price of fuel, which tends to fluctuate daily. Many rental agreements provide a good example of how an escalator clause can be enacted. Landlords often include an escalator clause within the body of a rental contract that makes it possible to increase the monthly rent if taxes on the property go up. Firms that decide to use escalator clauses should make them as transparent as possible and specify whether price adjustments will be made at fixed intervals (e.g., quarterly, semi-annually, or annually) or only at the expiration of the contract.

---

connect Interactive Assignment 10-1
|MARKETING Please complete the *Connect* exercise for Chapter 10 that focuses on the price-setting process. By understanding the dynamics of each step of the process, you will gain insight into how marketers set prices that maximize both profits and customer value.

LO 10-3
Compare the pricing tactics marketers can use.

PRICING TACTICS

Once marketers have completed their analysis of demand, costs, and the competitive environment, they can use a number of different tactics to choose a final price. In this section, we will discuss several of the most common methods and discuss the advantages and disadvantages of each. Which tactic to use depends on the value customers perceive the product to have, their ability to pay, and how they intend to use the product.

Markup Pricing

markup pricing

A pricing method in which a certain amount is added to the cost of the product to set the final price.

Markup pricing (also known as *cost-plus pricing*) is one of the most commonly used pricing tactics, largely because it is easy. In markup pricing, marketers add a certain amount to the cost of the product to set the final price. A pricing analyst can implement a markup pricing strategy easily by reviewing a spreadsheet and adding 20 percent to the cost of each item, such as a lawn chair, as illustrated in the following equation:

$$\text{markup price} = \$10 \text{ unit cost of lawn chair} + (\$10 \times 0.2) = \$12$$

Though markup pricing has the advantage of being easy, it's not very effective at maximizing profits, which is the ultimate objective of a good pricing strategy. Let's look at an example of how markup pricing does *not* capture value for our lawn chair. As we have discussed, different customers place different values on the products they purchase. Marketing research, salespeople, and other sources of data should help marketers better understand the value that each customer places on the lawn chair in our example. Imagine we have four target customers who personally value the lawn chair at $10, $14, $15, and $20, respectively. Table 10.2 shows how much profit margin the firm can expect to earn on each lawn chair if it uses a markup pricing strategy. Profit margin is the amount a product sells for above the total cost of the product itself. Notice that the profit margin for each customer who purchases a lawn chair will always be $2 ($12 selling price − $10 unit cost) due to the 20 percent markup, giving the firm a total profit of $6.

profit margin

The amount a product sells for above the total cost of the product itself.

Now compare this to a firm that uses the price-setting process more effectively. The cost of producing the product is still $10 per lawn chair, but marketing research has told the company that competitors charge $16 or more per chair and

TABLE 10.2   The Profit Implications of Using a Markup Pricing Strategy

	Perceived Value of the Lawn Chair to the Customer	Does the Customer Purchase at the 20% Markup Price ($12)?	Profit Margin for Firm
Customer #1	$10	No	$0
Customer #2	$14	Yes	$2
Customer #3	$15	Yes	$2
Customer #4	$20	Yes	$2

TABLE 10.3   The Profit Implications of Using a Research-Based Pricing Strategy

	Perceived Value of the Lawn Chair to the Customer	Does the Customer Purchase at the Research-Based Price ($15)?	Profit Margin for Firm
Customer #1	$10	No	$0
Customer #2	$14	No	$0
Customer #3	$15	Yes	$5
Customer #4	$20	Yes	$5

that many customers value their lawn chairs at $15 or more. As a result, the firm sets its price at $15. Table 10.3 shows the firm's improved outcomes using this alternate pricing strategy. Even though the firm ends up with one less sale because customer #2 perceives the price to be too high, the total profit of $10 is close to 50 percent higher than the $6 total profit the firm earned using a simple markup strategy.

Odd Pricing

Have you ever seen a product sitting on a shelf at Target with a price of $19.95 and wondered why the price wasn't set at an even $20.00? Chances are it's because Target is pursuing an odd-pricing strategy. Odd pricing is a pricing tactic in which a firm prices products a few cents below the next dollar amount. For the strategy to succeed, customers must perceive a product priced at $19.95 as offering more value than a product priced at $20.00. Though the price difference seems immaterial, if customers feel they received a deal, they are more likely to share that with others, which can lead to additional sales.

Firms that use odd pricing still need to consider the impact of price elasticity of demand at odd-pricing points. For example, would a fast food restaurant that offers a value meal for $4.95 see any decrease in sales if it raised the price to $4.99? Probably not, and the resulting $0.04 increase could result in significant profits over millions of customer transactions throughout the year.

Prestige Pricing

Firms that want to promote an image of superior quality and exclusivity to customers may pursue a strategy of prestige pricing. Prestige pricing is a pricing strategy that involves pricing a product higher than competitors to signal that it

odd pricing

A pricing tactic in which a firm prices products a few cents below the next dollar amount.

prestige pricing

A pricing strategy that involves pricing a product higher than competitors to signal that it is of higher quality.

Starbucks pursues a prestige pricing strategy by setting its prices high to convey increased value compared to other coffee purveyors like Dunkin' Donuts.

is of higher quality. Luxury brands, such as Louis Vuitton, Cartier, and Mercedes-Benz, provide perfect examples of this strategy. Such companies use high prices to suggest their products are high quality and stylish. Simply improving the look, packaging, delivery, or promise of a product can justify a higher price and support a prestige pricing strategy.

Seasonal Discounts

seasonal discounts

Price reductions given to customers purchasing goods or services out of season.

Price reductions given to customers purchasing goods or services out of season are called seasonal discounts. Disney World pursues this strategy by offering its best rates in months like February, when demand is at its lowest due to cold weather and the fact that children are in school. Disney World promotes this time of year as its value season, which typically includes January, February, and the first three weeks of December.[8] Seasonal discounts allow Disney World to maintain a steady stream of visitors to its parks year round. The strategy also exposes new customers to the brand. Young families (those with children younger than school age) can afford to try Disney World during its value season and many go on to become loyal customers, purchasing Disney vacations during the peak summer seasons once their children start school.

Price Bundling

price bundling

A strategy in which two or more products are packaged together and sold at a single price.

There are usually two ways to purchase products: à la carte (individually) or as a bundle. Price bundling is a strategy in which two or more products are packaged together and sold at a single price. Marketers often use bundling as a tool because they can charge higher prices for the bundle than they could for the elements individually. Assume you are buying a new Ford Escape SUV. Would you prefer to purchase the base model and then handpick options, such as a moon roof or satellite radio, or are you better off buying the vehicle as one all-inclusive bundle? Conventional wisdom says that à la carte pricing benefits the customer and bundled pricing benefits the firm. Undoubtedly, price bundling simplifies things for marketers. The company can sell the same bundle to everyone leading to reduced advertising and selling costs. Think of the success bundled software packages such as Microsoft Office enjoy, despite the fact that many of the software's users need only a fraction of the available functionality.

Such success aside, price bundling has come up against increased customer resistance in some industries in recent decades. Cable television providers have always relied on a bundling strategy in which customers have to buy a package of channels rather than paying individually for the channels they want. In recent years, as the price of those channel bundles keeps rising, the practice has come under fire. Consumer advocates point out that, if you're watching only 10 channels, why should you pay for 85? They've begun pushing for a system of à la carte pricing in the hopes that such a move will drive down prices for consumers.

---

connect |MARKETING **Interactive Assignment 10-2**

Please complete the *Connect* exercise for Chapter 10 that focuses on pricing tactics. By understanding the dynamics of different tactics and being able to perform the necessary pricing calculations, you should gain insight into how marketers choose specific prices and when those tactics will be most effective.

TECHNOLOGY AND PRICING

LO 10-4
Explain the influence of technology on pricing.

Technology influences pricing strategy in a significant and growing way. Technology has helped to shift the balance of power from companies to customers, who are better informed about prices than ever before. The Internet has made it possible for customers to comparison shop for products literally around the world. If you had taken this course a generation ago, your pricing options for buying this product would have been whatever the campus bookstore charged. Today, you can comparison shop at bookstores throughout the U.S. and online marketplaces such as Amazon or buy digital copies directly from the publisher. In addition to the power of the Internet, mobile applications and dynamic pricing are rapidly changing the nature of pricing.

Mobile Applications

Smartphone and tablet technology has unleashed a new era of pricing transparency as consumers use wireless apps and search engines on their mobile devices in stores to compare prices. In response, marketers at traditional brick-and-mortar stores more aggressively review the prices of online stores when setting the initial price of an item as part of their analysis of the competitive price environment.

Since more people use their mobile phones and tablets to order products, apps are becoming increasingly important in directing users to online sites to complete a purchase. Popular price comparison apps like eBay Inc.'s RedLaser and TheFind had 16 million and 1.4 million downloads in 2011, respectively, up from 6 million downloads for RedLaser and 1 million downloads for TheFind the year before.[9] Both apps allow users to scan barcodes, take a photo, or search a product while in a store. The app then displays how much online competitors charge for that product and allows customers to immediately purchase the product through their mobile device. TheFind says its mobile app averages between 18 million and 20 million price checks each month, up from 13 million to 15 million checks per month last year. Recent research suggests that over 40 percent of consumers search for and purchase a low-priced product using an in-store shopping app or online search engine.

Dynamic Pricing

dynamic pricing
A pricing strategy that involves constantly updating prices to reflect changes in supply, demand, or market conditions.

While dynamic pricing is not new, its popularity has grown explosively due to improving and readily available technological tools that facilitate its use. Dynamic pricing is a pricing strategy that involves constantly updating prices to reflect changes in supply, demand, or market conditions. Dynamic pricing helps

During the run-up to the winter holidays, gift items like DVD box sets can fluctuate significantly in price as firms use a dynamic pricing strategy to attract customers on the hunt for sales on Black Friday as well as customers willing to pay a premium for last-minute gifts.

yield management

A strategy for maximizing revenue even when a firm has a fixed amount of something (goods, services, or capacity).

marketers emphasize yield management, which is a strategy for maximizing revenue even when a firm has a fixed amount of something (goods, services, or capacity), such as a sports team that has only a finite number of seats in its stadium.

To simplify the introduction of dynamic pricing, more and more companies use data management systems from firms like SAP and Oracle that provide marketers with more data and enhanced ways of estimating price elasticity. Sports leagues have always faced the dilemma of balancing ticket prices with actual attendance and the possibility that such pressures will lead to unhappy fans. A team might want to charge the maximum possible price for a ticket, but if the price is too high, actual attendance at the game might suffer. In contrast, if prices are set too low, the team's marketers have missed an opportunity to improve their profits through yield management by selling the finite number of tickets they have available for less than what people are willing to pay. To solve this problem, some sports leagues have instituted dynamic pricing to sell tickets at the price that reflects the true value to fans for a specific event. For example, baseball's San Diego Padres began using dynamic pricing earlier this decade. The team sets a ticket price for each baseball game played at home before the season begins. However, as the season progresses, fans may lose interest in a scheduled home game with another team, perhaps because the visiting team is not playing well or has lost a star player to injury. In such cases, the Padres try to gauge the level of demand and adjust ticket prices accordingly. For example, outfielder for the Los Angeles Dodgers Matt Kemp, considered one of the best players in the League, was on the disabled list twice in 2012, reducing the value associated with watching the Padres play the Dodgers that season.

LO 10-5

Summarize the major challenges of pricing for international markets.

GLOBAL PRICING

Pricing is a critical component of a successful global marketing strategy. Historically, companies have set prices for products sold internationally higher than the same products sold domestically. However, technological advancements and growing Internet access throughout the world have made global pricing more transparent and, in many cases, more competitive. In addition, challenging economic conditions over the past decade have impacted pricing in a global context. China experienced an economic slowdown beginning in 2011 that impacted pricing strategy, both for Chinese companies selling to other nations and for firms selling to Chinese consumers. The slowdown forced U.S. marketers to modify their prices to reach increasingly price-sensitive Chinese shoppers.[10] For example, McDonald's introduced a value dinner starting at 15 yuan (approximately $2.40, at the time) to combat declining sales. In addition to technological and economic factors, firms seeking additional revenue and profits by marketing their products globally encounter unique challenges related to global pricing, including the gray market, tariffs, and dumping.

Gray Market

gray market

The sale of branded products through legal but unauthorized distribution channels.

You have probably heard of the *black market*, which refers to the illegal buying and selling of products outside of sanctioned channels. A lesser-known relative of the black market is the gray market. The gray market consists of branded products sold through legal but unauthorized distribution channels. This form of buying and selling often occurs when the price of an item is significantly higher in one country than another. Individuals or groups buy new or used products for a lower price in a foreign country and import them legally back into the domestic market, where they sell them for less than the normal market price. Gray market goods can be a boon for consumers, allowing them to obtain legally produced items for less than they could normally. However, gray market goods cut into a firm's revenue and profits, leaving marketers looking for ways to control and repress such activity. The increasingly interconnected nature of world economies makes gray market exchanges easier than ever, and firms find it difficult, if not impossible, to track exactly how much of their products sell in this manner. As they set international prices, U.S. marketers must be cognizant of the potential for gray market exchanges. If they price their smartphones or books significantly lower in foreign countries than in the domestic market, they may open the door to gray-market buyers who, using modern technology, will buy the products internationally and then sell them in the U.S. at a price that undercuts the standard rate paid by American consumers.

Tariffs levied on products can impact the overall price of a product in other countries and thus how companies set their baseline prices. An American-made surfboard that carries a 20 percent tariff in another country may need to be priced lower to be competitive in that market.

Tariffs

Many nations place tariffs on a variety of products, especially fruits and vegetables, which have tariffs in some countries of over 25 percent.[11] Tariffs are taxes on imports and exports between countries. For example, in 2012, the United States levied tariffs ranging from 2.9 percent to 4.7 percent on Chinese-made solar panels to make American-produced solar panels more price competitive.[12] Similarly, tariffs may raise the price that foreign customers must pay for goods produced in the U.S., negatively impacting a U.S. firm's ability to be price competitive in those markets. The international pricing strategy of any U.S. firm must take into account the potential tariffs foreign countries will place on its goods. Marketers typically prefer targeting international markets with low tariffs or with which the U.S. has an international agreement, such as the North American Free Trade Agreement (NAFTA), to lower tariffs. The absence of tariffs among the U.S., Mexico, and Canada allows for easier transactions between companies and customers in those countries.

tariffs

Taxes on imports and exports between countries.

Dumping

In recent years, the removal of tariffs due to international agreements has caused countries to switch to nontariff barriers, such as anti-dumping laws, to protect their local industries. Dumping occurs when a company sells its exports to another country at a lower price than it sells the same product in its domestic market.[13] For example, in the last decade Indian silk producers claimed that the price of Chinese-produced silk sold in India was so cheap that Indian firms could not compete. The Indian silk producers declared that Chinese producers must be dumping the products. Indian companies complained that, by selling silk at an unreasonably low price, Chinese companies were negatively impacting Indian firms, leaving them with only two options: losing customers to the Chinese producers or selling their silk at a loss.[14] Though the World Trade Organization hasn't classified dumping as illegal, many countries enact their own laws to curb the strategy. As they develop their international pricing strategy, companies must monitor how anti-dumping laws affect similar companies in the industry and calculate the potential impact of anti-dumping regulations on sales.

dumping

A protectionist strategy in which a company sells its exports to another country at a lower price than it sells the same product in its domestic market.

Ken Sage

Senior Carrier Sales Coordinator
J.B. Hunt Transport Services, Inc.

Describe your job. My main responsibility is to bridge the gap between customers and our partner carriers. Each and every day, I am on the phone with our partner carriers negotiating prices. Our primary goal is to drive down the cost of transportation so we can maximize profit. To give an example, let's say I get a load of goods that needs to be shipped from a customer who is willing to pay $1,000 for the shipment. It is now my job to reach out to our partner carrier network and fulfill the customer request at the lowest price possible to ensure I make the most profit. In a single day, I could touch base with 100 different carriers looking for and negotiating the best price.

Describe how you got the job you have. I was unsure what I wanted to do after college. I did internships in sales and manufacturing, but realized that wasn't the path I wanted to take. I wanted to do something new and out of the ordinary. Every day you can see a J.B. Hunt truck out on the road nationwide. I grew curious about what else the company had to offer. I decided to look into the careers they had open to recent graduates and discovered the position I am in now. I was lucky enough to make it through the interview process and get a job offer to work for this terrific company.

What has been the most important thing in making you successful at your job? I believe I have been successful in my job because of my competitive spirit. Not only am I competing on an individual level, but I am competing as a team within my branch, and, more importantly, competing against other companies as part of J.B. Hunt. It was always

my goal to out-negotiate the next person or offer the best price I could to a customer. I not only pushed myself to do better, but pushed the people around me to do better, too. This helped with my success because I positioned myself to be the go-to person for my team members and my customers.

What advice would you give soon-to-be graduates? Think outside the box and don't be scared to try something new. There are going to be thousands of recent graduates just like you looking for the same jobs that we all first think of when applying after graduation. Don't be scared to look into the trucking company that you think only hires dispatchers and drivers. Remember, there are always things going on behind the scenes you may not know about until you look into them. Don't be scared to do something you are not familiar with. You may stumble across a career in pricing that you didn't know was out there. I know I did.

What do you consider your personal brand to be? I am a yes-man. Many people think that being a yes-man means being a pushover. To me, being a yes-man means thinking nothing is impossible. I learned a long time ago that it is easy to say, "No, I can't do that." I always look for ways to make things happen. Every problem has a solution; one just has to work to find it. I believe by being a yes-man I have shown that I am willing to work hard, never give up, and always try to solve the problem. I believe my personal brand has gotten me where I am today and that it will continue to help me succeed.

LEGAL AND ETHICAL ISSUES IN PRICING

Many legal and ethical issues impact pricing decisions. Pricing is one of the most watched and regulated marketing activities because it directly impacts the financial viability of both organizations and individuals. In the sections that follow, we'll discuss some of the ethical issues marketers may face as they seek to set prices for their products, including price discrimination, price fixing, predatory pricing, and deceptive pricing. We'll then look into some of the regulations the American government has put into place to combat such practices.

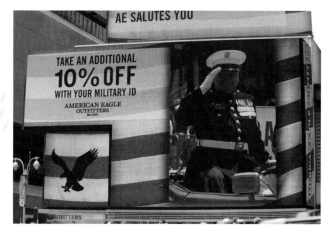

Companies ranging from AMC Theaters to Lowes to American Eagle Outfitters engage in legitimate price discrimination by offering goods and services to active military personnel and veterans for a lower price than other customers.

Price Discrimination

You may be surprised to hear that you have likely benefited from discriminatory pricing in various ways. If you've paid student prices at a movie theater or an introductory price to switch cell phone or cable providers, you've taken advantage of price discrimination. Price discrimination is the practice of charging different customers different prices for the same product. Price discrimination sounds negative, but it is illegal only if it injures competition. Organizations can charge customers different amounts for legitimate reasons. This is especially common in B2B settings in which different customers might be charged different rates due to the quantities they buy, the strategic value of the company, or simply because one firm did a better job negotiating the contract. Note that later in this section, we'll discuss the Robinson-Patman Act, which has helped to clarify when price discrimination can and cannot be used.

LO 10-6

Explain the major legal and ethical issues associated with pricing.

price discrimination

The practice of charging different customers different prices for the same product.

  Interactive Assignment 10-3

Social Media in Action

Social media are influencing the prices consumers see when buying products online. Rosetta Stone, which sells language-learning products, varies the prices for some of its products and the product bundles offered depending on whether or not a consumer comes to its site through a social media link. However, marketers should be careful as studies suggest that over 75 percent of consumers say they would be bothered if they knew that someone paid a lower price for the same product.

Some organizations also offer different online prices based on what type of mobile device consumers use to access the site and where consumers are located. Office supply company Staples discounted the price of its online products for consumers who lived within a 20-mile range of major competitors. Some firms, such as travel website Orbitz, modified the prices consumers saw depending on whether the customer was using a specific type of mobile device. Consumers using an iPhone or Android phone saw discounts of up to 50 percent compared to what a person searching the site on a traditional computer saw.

The Social Media in Action *Connect* exercise in Chapter 10 will let you make decisions about setting consumer prices based on the social media profiles of consumers. By understanding the insights that social media can provide, you will be able to develop pricing strategies that maximize profits from each individual consumer.

Source: See Jennifer Valentino-Devries, Jeremy Singer-Vine, and Ashkan Soltani, "Websites Vary Prices, Deals Based on Users' Information," *The Wall Street Journal,* December 24, 2012, http://online.wsj.com/article/SB10001424127887323777204578189391813881534.html.

Price Fixing

price fixing

When two or more companies collude to set a product's price.

When two or more companies collude to set a product's price, they are engaging in price fixing. Price fixing is illegal under the Sherman Antitrust Act of 1890 and the Federal Trade Commission Act, which we will discuss later in the chapter. An example of price fixing occurred when British Airways and its rival Virgin Atlantic agreed to simultaneously increase their fuel surcharges.[15] Over the next two years, fuel surcharges increased from an average of five British pounds a ticket to over 60 pounds. When the price-fixing scheme was reported by Virgin, British Airways was punished with record fines. The British Office of Fair Trading fined the airline £121.5 million and the American Department of Justice levied an additional $300 million fine. Virgin was given immunity for reporting the collusion and was not fined.

Predatory Pricing

predatory pricing

The practice of first setting prices low with the intention of pushing competitors out of the market or keeping new competitors from entering the market, and then raising prices to normal levels.

Consider a situation in which a chain supermarket opens across the street from a locally owned grocery store. Theoretically, the prices at both stores should be similar because the costs and customer demand will be similar. However, because the chain supermarket can rely on corporate backing for support, it makes the decision to radically lower prices, attracting more customers to its facility and eventually driving the competition out of business. This example illustrates a strategy called predatory pricing. Predatory pricing is the practice of first setting prices low with the intention of pushing competitors out of the market or keeping new competitors from entering the market, and then raising prices to normal levels. This type of long-term aggressive pricing strategy could be considered an attempt to create a monopoly and is therefore illegal under U.S. law; however, predatory pricing is difficult to prove. The Supreme Court has ruled that the victim must prove that the company being accused of predatory pricing (the chain supermarket in our example) would be able to recoup its initial losses by charging higher prices later on, once it has driven others out of business.[16]

Deceptive Pricing

deceptive pricing

An illegal practice that involves intentionally misleading customers with price promotions.

Deceptive pricing practices can lead to price confusion, where consumers have difficulty discerning what they are actually paying. Deceptive pricing is an illegal practice that involves intentionally misleading customers with price promotions. The most common examples of deceptive pricing involve firms that falsely advertise wholesale pricing or promise a significant price reduction on an artificially high retail price. These types of deceptive pricing practices have come under fire in recent years in industries ranging from credit cards to home loans, where important information was often buried deep within little-noticed and hard-to-read disclaimers and information. In 2011, China accused Walmart and its French competitor Carrefour of deceptive pricing.[17] The Chinese cited examples in which Carrefour and Walmart overcharged their consumers or quoted a higher original price to make the discounts they offered on products seem more substantial. For example, a Walmart store in the city of Nanning priced Nescafe coffee at $5.44, discounted from an advertised price of $6.67; in fact, the original price was $5.66. Similarly, a Carrefour store in Changchun, the capital of Jilin province, allegedly discounted men's cotton undershirts to around $7 from an advertised original price of just over $25. The original price was verified by regulators to be $18.07.

U.S. Laws Impacting Pricing

The United States government and other major economies, such as Japan and the European Union, are committed to stopping and punishing anticompetitive and harmful pricing behavior through a variety of laws and regulations, including the following:

- To combat price discrimination that injures competition, the United States government passed the Robinson-Patman Act as an amendment to the Clayton Antitrust Act of 1914. The Robinson–Patman Act (also called the *Anti-Price Discrimination Act*) was made into law in 1936 with the goal of requiring sellers to charge everyone the same price.[18] It grew out of concerns that large companies would leverage their buying power to purchase goods at lower prices than smaller companies could. Though the purpose of the act was to reduce injurious price discrimination, it did provide for three scenarios in which price discrimination may be allowed:

    - A firm can charge different prices if it is part of a quantity or manufacturing discount program. For example, a company selling 5,000 laptops to a Fortune 500 company in Oklahoma can charge less per unit than if it sells the same laptop to an individual consumer buying just one.
    - A firm can lower prices for certain customers if a competitor undercuts the originally quoted price. This impacts Walmart and several large retailers that promise to match any competitor's price if the consumer produces proof of the lower price. These retailers are not legally required to extend this same discount to customers who do not present proof of the lower price, effectively resulting in different prices for different customers.
    - Finally, market conditions such as going-out-of-business sales or situations in which the quality of products has changed give firms the opportunity to charge different prices for the same product. For example, a bakery may sell loaves of French bread for $3 each on the day it bakes them. However, it would be allowed to sell the same loaves the next day at a steep discount since the quality and freshness of the bread has deteriorated.

- The Federal Trade Commission Act (FTCA) was passed in 1914. It established the Federal Trade Commission (FTC), which had the authority to enforce laws aimed at prohibiting unfair methods of competition.[19] The FTCA was later

Robinson–Patman Act

A law passed in 1936 that requires sellers to charge everyone the same price for a product.

Federal Trade Commission Act (FTCA)

A law passed in 1914 that established the Federal Trade Commission and sought to prevent practices that may cause injury to customers, that cannot be reasonably avoided by customers, and that cannot be justified by other outcomes that may benefit the consumer or the idea of free competition.

Walmart's price match guarantee provides an example of price discrimination sanctioned by the Robinson–Patman Act. It allows Walmart to offer a different price only to those customers who can prove that a competing retailer is offering the same product for a lower price.

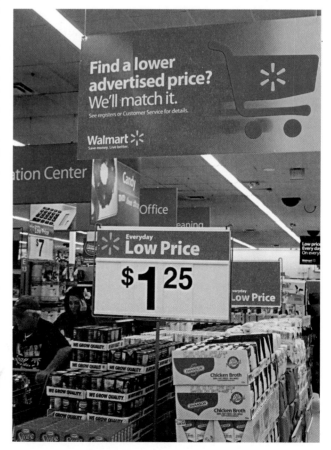

broadened to prevent practices, such as price fixing and deceptive pricing, that may cause injury to customers, that cannot be reasonably avoided by customers, and that cannot be justified by other outcomes that may benefit the consumer or the idea of free competition.

Wheeler-Lea Act

An amendment to the Federal Trade Commission Act passed in 1938 that removed the burden of proving that unfair and deceptive practices had to injure competition.

- The Wheeler-Lea Act of 1938 (also called the *Advertising Act*) is an amendment to the FTCA.[20] Its passage removed the burden of proving that unfair and deceptive practices had to injure competition as well as customers and broadened the FTC's powers to include protecting consumers from false advertising practices.

These laws provide much of the regulatory framework for the most common legal challenges associated with price discrimination, price fixing, predatory pricing, and deceptive pricing.

---

connect |MARKETING **Interactive Assignment 10-4**

Please complete the *Connect* exercise for Chapter 10 that focuses on important laws that impact pricing. By recognizing the specific requirements of each law, you will understand the legal requirements of pricing decisions and be able to help your firm avoid violating pricing rules and regulations.

SUMMARY

LO 10-1 Explain the importance of pricing strategy to every organization.

Price is the amount of something—money, time, or effort—that a buyer exchanges with a seller to obtain a product. It is the essential element for capturing revenue and profits. Revenue is the result of the price charged to customers multiplied by the number of units sold. Profits equal revenue minus total costs. The objective of strategic pricing is to maximize profits. If the price is set too high, customers will simply buy another product. If the price is set too low, the firm loses revenue it can never recover.

LO 10-2 Outline the steps in setting a price.

Marketers use a systematic six-step process to evaluate relevant factors when setting a price and should thoughtfully consider the decisions at each step in the price-setting process to increase the likelihood that the final price captures value for the firm and delivers value to the customer. The six steps include the following: (1) Select the pricing objective, (2) evaluate demand, (3) determine the costs, (4) analyze the competitive price environment,

(5) choose a price, and (6) monitor and evaluate the effectiveness of the price.

LO 10-3 Compare the pricing tactics marketers can use.

Markup pricing is a pricing method in which a certain amount is added to the cost of the product to set the final price. It is one of the most common pricing tactics used, largely because it is easy, but it's not very effective at maximizing profits. Odd pricing is a tactic in which a firm prices products a few cents below the next dollar amount. This strategy is effective with customers who perceive they are getting a good value for their money when a product is priced slightly below a whole number value. Prestige pricing involves pricing a product high to signal that it is of high quality. Seasonal discounts involve price reductions given to customers purchasing goods or services out of season. Price bundling involves packaging two or more products together to be sold at a single price, allowing marketers to earn greater profits than if they priced the elements individually.

LO 10-4 Explain the influence of technology on pricing.

Technology has helped to shift the balance of power from companies to customers, who are better informed about prices than ever before. The Internet has made it possible for buyers to comparison shop for products literally around the world. Smartphone technology allows consumers to use wireless apps and search engines in stores to compare prices. In response, marketers at traditional brick-and-mortar stores review prices at online stores when setting the initial price of an item. Technology has also increased the role of dynamic pricing, a strategy that involves constantly updating prices to reflect changes in supply, demand, or market conditions.

 LO 10-5 Summarize the major challenges of pricing for international markets.

Firms that price their products to be sold internationally face several unique challenges. The gray market, which involves the sale of branded products through legal but unauthorized distribution channels, continues to expand. Tariffs, taxes on imports and exports between countries, raise the prices that customers must pay for goods, thus negatively impacting a company's ability to be price competitive in countries that impose tariffs. Dumping occurs when a company sells its exports to another country at a lower price than it sells the same product in its domestic market. Dumping and the laws imposed to prevent it are increasingly important to multinational corporations as they determine their global pricing policy.

 LO 10-6 Explain the major legal and ethical issues associated with pricing.

There are many laws, regulations, and ethical issues that impact pricing decisions. Price discrimination is the practice of charging different customers different prices for the same product. It is only illegal if it injures competition. Price fixing occurs when two or more companies collude to set a product's price. Price fixing is illegal under the Sherman Antitrust Act and the Federal Trade Commission Act. Predatory pricing is the practice of first setting prices low with the intention of pushing competitors out of the market or keeping new competitors from entering the market, and then raising prices to normal levels. Deceptive pricing involves intentionally misleading customers with price promotions and is illegal under the Wheeler-Lea Act and the Federal Trade Commission Act.

KEY TERMS

MARKETING PLAN EXERCISE

In this chapter you learned about setting prices based on costs and market conditions. For the next part of your marketing plan exercise, you will conduct a pricing analysis of your future career plans. First, you should consider the costs you expect to have in the next decade, including things like repaying your student loans, paying your rent, saving for a house, or starting a family. Take time to consider the potential costs of these things on a monthly and annual basis. Then compare these costs with the career information you put together in an earlier chapter. How do they match up?

Next, consider your market value within your company or industry either now or after graduate school. The price elasticity you inspire in future employers will be an important consideration as you develop in your career. For example, if you possess a unique combination of experience, education, personality, and work ethic, demand for your services might well be inelastic. In this scenario, you might be able to negotiate a higher salary because the demand for your services is high. Knowing whether demand for your personal brand is inelastic or elastic is essential. Too many employees undervalue their brand and work for less than what market prices would dictate, leaving money on the table over a significant period of their career. Conversely, if demand for your brand is elastic, you should understand your lessened bargaining power and work to develop unique skills or take on difficult assignments within your company to increase the value others place on your brand.

Your Task: Develop a detailed list of the costs necessary to have the career you desire 10 years from now (e.g., student loans, training seminars, graduate school costs, or any fixed or variable costs). Next, compare these costs with the prices that organizations are paying for people with your skill set. Finally, determine your own personal break-even point for your salary level. Also, identify when you expect to reach the salary that you desire.

DISCUSSION QUESTIONS

1. Why is it difficult to determine reference prices? Consider a new pizza restaurant opening near your campus. What challenges would the restaurant's marketers encounter as they attempt to determine their customers' reference prices? How could they find this information?
2. What is the problem with standard markup pricing? How do buyers and sellers lose from this type of pricing strategy?
3. Name a product that you think is underpriced. What price do you think should be charged and what would be the benefits of that higher price for the company that produces the product?
4. Name one product for which your demand is elastic and one product for which your demand is inelastic. For example, if Subway raised its prices by 10 percent,

would you reduce the number of times you eat there by 10 percent, by more than 10 percent, or would the price increase not change your purchases at Subway at all? Do you think most other consumers of these two products feel the same way? How should this information impact the pricing of those products?
5. Go to the Stubhub website (www.stubhub.com) and find an event for which you might be interested in buying tickets. Are prices higher or lower than you could buy directly from the venue? Why do you think that is? Why is Stubhub not violating price discrimination laws?
6. Think of your favorite brand of potato chip and then discuss what considerations would affect how you would price that product in a neighboring country such as Mexico or Canada.

SOCIAL MEDIA APPLICATION

Pick two companies that you currently buy products from and look at all of the social media platforms the company employs (for example, Facebook, Twitter, YouTube, etc.). Analyze what is being said about pricing either by the company or customers on these platforms using the following questions and activities as a guide:

1. How much is pricing discussed? Provide specific examples.

2. Is pricing mentioned by the company, social media users, or both?
3. Is pricing discussed on social media by one company more than the other? If so, why do you think this is?
4. If you worked in marketing for either firm, is there anything you have read on social media that would make you consider changing the price of that company's products? Explain your answer.

ETHICAL CHALLENGE

National Basketball Association (NBA) teams play an exhausting 82-game regular season before they reach the playoffs, if they're lucky enough to do so. The playoffs are not just a reward for the organization but also for its fans. Playoff tickets are generally in far more demand than regular season tickets, and marketers for a number of teams attempt to use pricing strategies to improve their yield management. For example, many teams require that fans make a deposit to secure season tickets for the following year before they can buy playoff tickets at face value. Or teams might offer single game playoff tickets to those who don't hold season tickets, but at a price that runs from between 200 and 400 percent more than what season ticket holders would pay. While such tactics can generate additional revenue and increase a team's season ticket holder base, the team also risks alienating nonseason ticket holders who may only be able to attend a few games a year but who follow the team faithfully on television and the Internet. Please use the ethical decision-making framework to answer the following questions:

1. Is an NBA team charging nonseason ticket holders more than season ticket holders an example of price discrimination? Explain your answer.
2. Do you agree with the idea of NBA teams requiring fans to place deposits for season tickets for the following year? What about the NBA charging higher single game prices to nonseason ticket holders? Explain your answers.
3. Since season ticket holders probably represent a team's most devoted fans, would it make sense to charge them the higher playoff ticket prices on the assumption that, because their demand is inelastic, they will pay almost any price?

VIDEO CASE

Please go to *Connect* to access the video case featuring Amy's Candy Bar that accompanies this chapter.

CAREER TIPS
Marketing Your Future

You have read in this chapter about the importance of developing an effective pricing strategy. Author Shane Hunt began his career as a pricing analyst for The Williams Companies, a Fortune 500 company specializing in energy and telecommunications based in Tulsa, Oklahoma, and considers it one of the best things that ever happened to him. Based on his experience, he has provided three things to remember if you are considering a job in pricing:

1. **Supply and demand works in your favor.** Some jobs in marketing are highly sought after because they are glamorous or sound cool to new graduates. Everyone wants to be the salesperson who accompanies clients to the Super Bowl or the event planner who throws elaborate parties for important people. Product manager and brand manager jobs have impressive sounding titles. In my years as a professor, I have taught thousands of students with all kinds of career goals, and not one has come to me on the first day of class and said, "Dr. Hunt, I want to be a pricing analyst." This is a good thing. This chapter talks about the fact that pricing is an essential element for virtually every organization on the planet, yet most new graduates don't consider working in pricing. When demand for a job is high, and the supply is low, the wages for that job increase. I encourage you to consider pricing as a career in this challenging economic environment.

2. **Pricing is a great way to combine marketing with other disciplines.** Perhaps you are pursuing a major other than marketing but think marketing might make for a great career. I want to especially encourage you to consider pricing, which requires a combination of skills in addition to marketing, such as a knowledge of finance and psychology. Pricing jobs also can lead to career paths in marketing or finance, which will give you increased flexibility as your career develops.

3. **Develop your skills using Excel.** One important piece of career advice I would give you, regardless of your major, is to become proficient at using Excel. While PowerPoint, Word, and other products may be most common in your college courses, Excel is by far the most frequently used tool in day-to-day pricing jobs (and many other jobs as well). I would encourage you to take courses that utilize Excel and develop skills that will help your career in pricing and many other areas.

CHAPTER NOTES

1. Alex Sherman, "DirecTV Spurns Dish's View that Wireless Is Satellite TV Savior," *Bloomberg Businessweek,* May 6, 2013, http://www.businessweek.com/news/2013-05-06/directv-spurns-dish-s-view-that-wireless-is-satellite-tv-savior.

2. Nick Bunkley, "Sales Decline 20%, but GM Sees a Bright Spot," *The New York Times,* September 3, 2008, http://www.nytimes.com/2008/09/04/business/04auto.html.

3. Nick Timiraos and Kelly Evans, "Home Prices Rise Across the U.S.," *The Wall Street Journal,* July 29, 2009, http://online.wsj.com/article/SB124878477560186517.html.

4. Campbell R. McConnell, Stanley L. Brue, and Sean M. Flynn, *Economics* (New York: McGraw-Hill, 2012), p. 76.

5. Cliff Edwards, "Netflix Seen Cracking Down on Sharing to Bolster Profit," *Bloomberg,* April 22, 2013, http://www.bloomberg.com/news/2013-04-22/netflix-seen-cracking-down-on-sharing-to-bolster-profit.html.

6. Dana Mattioli, "Retailers Try to Thwart Price Apps," *The Wall Street Journal,* December 23, 2011, http://online.wsj.com/article/SB10001424052970203686204577114901480554444.html.

7. Lisa Baertlein, "Wendy's/Arby's Mulls Price Increases," *Reuters,* May 10, 2011, http://www.reuters.com/article/2011/05/10/us-wendysarbys-idUSTRE74935120110510.

8. Isaiah David, "Tips to Save Money on a Disney Vacation," *USA Today,* http://traveltips.usatoday.com/tips-save-money-disney-vacation-14495.html.

9. Mattioli, "Retailers Try to Thwart Price Apps."

10. Justina Lee, "China Slowdown Forcing Discounting at McDonald's," *Bloomberg,* August 1, 2012, http://www.bloomberg.com/news/2012-08-01/china-slowdown-forcing-discounting-at-gome-to-mcdonald-s.html.

11. Renee Johnson, "The U.S. Trade Situation for Fruits and Vegetable Products," *Congressional Research Service,* December 17, 2012, http://www.nationalaglawcenter.org/assets/crs/RL34468.pdf.

12. James O'Toole, "U.S. to Impose Tariffs on Chinese Solar Panels," *CNN Money,* March 20, 2012, http://money.cnn.com/2012/03/20/markets/chinese-solar/index.htm.

13. World Trade Organization, "Anti-Dumping," n.d., http://www.wto.org/english/tratop_e/adp_e/adp_e.htm.

14. Charlotte Windle, "China Faces Indian Dumping Allegations," *BBC News,* July 31, 2006, http://news.bbc.co.uk/2/hi/business/5224370.stm.

15. BBC News, "BA's Price-Fix Fine Reaches £270m," August 1, 2007, http://news.bbc.co.uk/2/hi/business/6925397.stm.

16. Thomas T. Nagle, John E. Hogan, and Joseph Zale, *The Strategy and Tactics of Pricing,* 5th ed. (Upper Saddle River, NJ: Pearson, 2011).

17. Parija Kavilanz, "China Accuses Wal-Mart of Deceptive Prices," *CNN Money,* January 26, 2011, http://money.cnn.com/2011/01/26/news/international/walmart_china_fines/index.htm.

18. Robert J. Toth, "A Powerful Law Has Been Losing a Lot of Its Punch," *The Wall Street Journal,* May 21, 2012, http://online.wsj.com/article/SB10001424052702304746604577380172754953842.html.

19. Federal Trade Commission, "FTC Fact Sheet: Antitrust Laws: A Brief History," n.d., http://www.ftc.gov/bcp/edu/microsites/youarehere/pages/pdf/FTC-Competition_Antitrust-Laws.pdf.

20. Federal Trade Commission, "Appendix 1—Laws Enforced by the FTC," n.d., http://www.ftc.gov/opp/gpra/append1.shtm.

Chapter 11

BUILDING SUCCESSFUL BRANDS

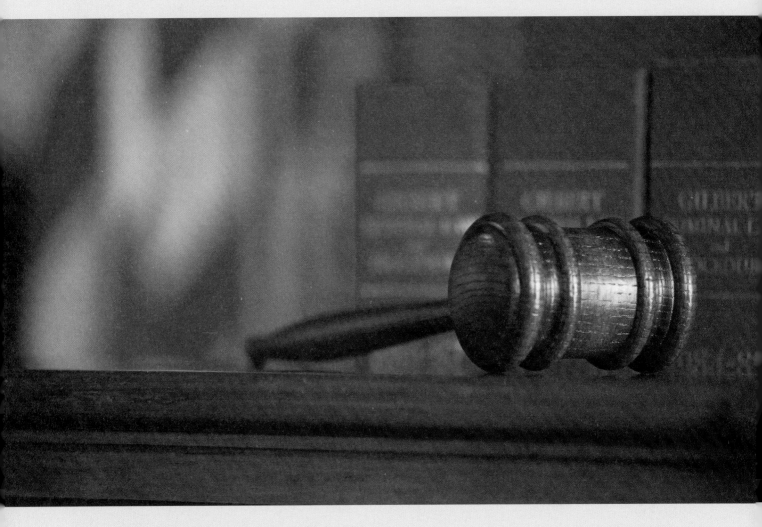

LEARNING OBJECTIVES
After reading this chapter, you should be able to

LO 11-1 Explain the importance of building a successful brand.

LO 11-2 Describe the relevance of brand equity for marketers.

LO 11-3 Compare some common strategies for developing brands.

LO 11-4 Summarize the impact of packaging on brand building.

LO 11-5 Summarize the impact of social media on brand management.

LO 11-6 Discuss the major branding challenges facing global marketers.

LO 11-7 Explain the role of branding in nonprofit organizations.

EXECUTIVE PERSPECTIVE

Andrew Hicks
Law Firm Partner
Schiffer, Odom, Hicks, and Johnson

Andrew Hicks majored in political science in school with an eye toward attending a top law school upon graduation. Following his law school graduation, Hicks went to work for a nationally recognized law firm located in the state of Texas. After a few years, Hicks was recognized as one of the top young lawyers in the state and, with such validation in hand, decided to start a new firm with several law partners. Hicks soon realized that building a brand for his organization would be critical to its success. Hicks and his partners contemplated the brand they wanted the firm to have. They began to execute a strategy based on personal attention and aligning their interests with their clients through efficient, effective representation. As a lawyer in the firm, Hicks practices commercial litigation and international arbitration, but as a founding partner, Hicks takes a lead role in continuing to build and manage the organization's brand.

What has been the most important thing in making you successful at your job?

Hard work. Sometimes we overanalyze what it takes to be successful; much of it comes down to simply outworking your competition. Whether it is college or your career, the harder you work the greater your likelihood for success. If you look around and others are consistently outworking you, then your goals are going to be much harder to achieve.

What advice would you give soon-to-be graduates?

I have worked with many people at all levels (from factory workers to hedge fund managers to chief executive officers) in a number of different industries, and some principles simply apply universally. Business is built on personal relationships. No matter what

your particular product may be, ultimately it is the relationships you create and your personal integrity that count.

How is marketing relevant to your role at Schiffer, Odom, Hicks, and Johnson?

The core elements of marketing are critical to our success as a firm. Our brand image has to be that of a firm comprised of great litigation attorneys who operate efficiently and ethically. Our product is a service, and we have to deliver a quality service that provides value for our clients. Not only do we want to retain our current clients, but to grow the firm we must also attract new ones. We do this by communicating our message to prospective clients. Marketing is an important part of our firm and every successful organization.

What do you consider your personal brand to be?

I work hard to ensure the brand that bears my name is one of hard work, integrity, and passion about the clients I represent.

Schiffer Odom Hicks
& Johnson PLLC
Trial Lawyers

Andrew Hicks
Law Firm Partner

Schiffer, Odom, Hicks, and Johnson
http://www.sohlawfirm.com/

Schiffer, Odom, Hicks, and Johnson is a boutique litigation firm with offices in Houston, Texas, and Seattle, Washington.

FORECAST

This chapter explores the importance of building a successful brand. Branding is the primary strategy marketers use to differentiate their goods, services, and ideas from the competition. Building a successful brand is critically important for marketers trying to improve the profitability of their organization and for you as a college graduate looking to develop a successful and rewarding career. As you read through the chapter, consider the following key questions:

1. Why do brands matter?
2. How does brand equity add value to my organization?
3. How can I develop a brand?
4. How can packaging help build a brand?
5. Why are social media important to my brand?

6. What factors must be considered when building a brand globally?
7. What impact does branding have on nonprofit organizations?

LO 11-1

Explain the importance of building a successful brand.

BRANDING

For current, former, and potential customers, a brand represents everything that a good, service, or idea means to them. Think about brands ranging from Apple to Disney to Ford and consider what they mean to you. The differentiating characteristics of the brands that matter to you might be tangible and related to the product (such as the towing capacity of a Ford F-150 truck) or they might be emotional and focused on a special memory (such as your memories of Disney World). Specifically, a brand is the name, term, symbol, design, or any combination of these that identifies and differentiates a firm's products. A successful brand adds value to organizations in numerous ways, including through loyal customers and recognizable goods and services, both of which lead to more revenue for for-profit firms and more donations and support for nonprofit organizations.

brand

The name, term, symbol, design, or any combination of these that identifies and differentiates a firm's products.

brand loyalty

When a consumer displays a steadfast allegiance to a brand by repeatedly purchasing it.

brand recognition

The degree to which customers can identify the brand under a variety of circumstances.

- Brand loyalty is when a consumer displays a steadfast allegiance to a brand by repeatedly purchasing it. Brand loyalty typically develops because of a customer's satisfaction with an organization's products.[1] Brand-loyal customers typically exhibit less sensitivity to price, making them an important contributor to a firm's long-term success and profitability. Coca-Cola enjoys millions of brand-loyal customers who actively seek Coca-Cola products and will purchase them even if they are priced higher than the Pepsi products on sale down the aisle. Such brand loyalty adds to Coca-Cola's pricing power and thus its ability to maintain higher profits.

- Brand recognition is the degree to which customers can identify the brand under a variety of circumstances. Firms like Nike and McDonald's employ brand marks, which are the elements of a brand not expressed in words that a consumer instantly recognizes, such as a symbol, color, or design. The Nike swoosh and McDonald's golden arches are brand marks that have become powerful marketing tools for those companies. The importance of brand recognition can perhaps best be seen when a company changes or updates its symbol or logo in an attempt to better resonate with customers. Consumers often grow attached to certain brand logos or symbols and changes can cause a backlash.

Gap learned how attached consumers can become to a brand mark when it tried to replace its logo (on the left) with a modified version (on the right) to represent the company's modern edge.

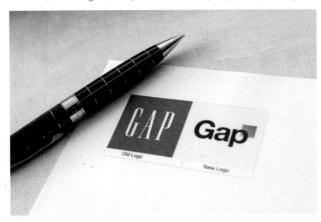

For example, Gap was forced to abandon a new logo only a week after it was launched due to thousands of complaints online and throughout social media from unhappy consumers.[2]

Developing Your Personal Brand

Branding doesn't only benefit organizations. Regardless of what you do after graduation, you will engage in branding. The most important brand you will ever manage is your personal brand. Responsibility for building and managing the brand image that bears your name is a 24-hours-a-day, 7-days-a-week, 365-days-a-year job. Brand image is the unique set of associations target customers or stakeholders make with a brand. It signifies what the brand presently stands for in the minds of others. For example, Mountain Dew marketers built a brand image of a youthful, fun product that represents energy and excitement. Today, Mountain Dew products are associated with extreme sports, video gaming, and other youth activities. As you develop in your career, you should identify and monitor your brand image. What do managers and coworkers think when they hear your name? What associations do they make with your brand? Do they consider you a hard worker, a team leader, and a thoughtful employee, or do they think of you as smart, but lazy and difficult to work with?

Throughout this book, you have had the opportunity to read the personal brand statements of executives across a variety of industries. For example, successful small business owner Erin Brewer described her personal brand this way: "I strive to enjoy the moment, make decisions that leave me without regret, treat others with courtesy and respect, learn something every day, and be comfortable in my own skin. I love asking and trying to answer tough questions! I'm getting more and more comfortable not knowing all the answers. I believe people, me included, can change if they choose. I have a running list of things to improve within myself. I proudly own my own history with all the failures, successes, decisions, friends and experiences that have shaped me. In short, I'm trying to be the best me I can be." Establishing a brand image, like Brewer has, in the minds of peers, colleagues, or customers begins with understanding the components of a successful brand.

brand marks
The elements of a brand not expressed in words that a consumer instantly recognizes, such as a symbol, color, or design.

brand image
The unique set of associations target customers or stakeholders make with a brand.

Components of a Successful Brand

Whether you are building the brand for your firm's product or your personal brand, the process involves the following four essential components:

1. *Deliver a quality product.* The product should attract a positive reaction from consumers, whether that's achieved through packaging, delivery, or the value it offers to users. If a consumer does not perceive value in using a particular product, he or she will not remain a customer for very long. A strong brand provides continued value and quality to customers over time. Southwest Airlines has accomplished this by consistently offering low fares and refusing to charge baggage fees, even as other airlines have begun doing so.

2. *Create a consistent brand image.* All of the firm's marketing decisions, promotions, and employees should reinforce the brand by providing a consistent experience in the minds of

EXECUTIVE PERSPECTIVE

Andrew Hicks
Law Firm Partner
Schiffer, Odom, Hicks, and Johnson

What are the most important components of building a successful brand?

I would say there are two. First, you have to deliver a quality product. Without a quality product, it will be all but impossible to build a quality brand. Second, you need to capture feedback. Find out what your clients are thinking and look for ways to learn from that feedback and use it to improve your organization.

consumers. Mountain Dew's efforts to be seen as a youthful, energetic, and extreme brand would be compromised if it began promoting its image by sponsoring senior golf tournaments and advertising in business trade magazines. For your personal brand, this step is equally important. How you dress for work, how you treat others at your office, and the quality of the work you produce combine to create a narrative that becomes your brand. An inconsistent brand image, such as doing a great job on a presentation but then showing up 10 minutes late to the office or dressing unprofessionally, will reduce the likelihood that your organization views you as someone on the fast track toward advancement and promotion.

GEICO has had several slogans and commercials featuring different characters, from a talking gecko to a pig named Maxwell, but each drives home the same message of value and cost savings for current and potential customers.

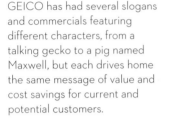

3. *Create consistent brand messaging.* As with brand image, brand messaging should be consistent and concise. It should be easy to remember and remind consumers about the product attributes they care about most. Marketers commonly make the mistake of trying to share all of the individual good things about their organization's product. Too many different messages can potentially confuse customers as to why they should purchase a specific brand. Auto insurance company GEICO has succeeded in providing one consistent brand message through a variety of ad concepts: a promise to save consumers money on their car insurance.

4. *Capture feedback.* Since the real power of a brand exists in the minds of consumers, marketers must always capture and analyze customer feedback. Companies with strong brands are typically great listeners and use a variety of marketing research to better understand the thoughts, feelings, and concerns of their customers. For example, Chick-Fil-A offers random customers the opportunity to receive a free chicken sandwich if they go online and fill out a survey about their experience with the restaurant within 48 hours of their visit. The survey captures feedback on the quality of the food, the portion size of the order, the cleanliness of the restaurant, and the friendliness of the employees, all of which impact the company's brand image. Chick-Fil-A then uses these data, which are tied to a specific restaurant and time of day, to identify potential problems and improve every part of the dining experience. Capturing and responding to feedback contributed to Chick-Fil-A being recognized as a top restaurant brand in customer satisfaction by research firm J.D. Power.[3] Firms can also use social media tools to gather data about their brand. We'll discuss the social media tools firms can use later in the chapter.

You will receive feedback on the success of your personal brand from various stakeholders in your life, including your friends, family, classmates, managers, coworkers, and professors. Consistently monitoring your personal brand will allow you to see what changes need to be made. For example, if your firm continues to pass you over for a promotion, you should ask what it is about your brand that might be keeping you from a higher position. Is it the way you approach your job or perhaps how you dress (think of this as personal packaging) that might be sending the wrong message? In the same way that a firm analyzes both the positive and negative feedback it receives for a product, so should you reflect on the feedback you are getting throughout your academic and professional career.

Understanding the components of a successful brand is important for a firm both internally and externally. Internally, a strong brand drives cohesion and helps an organization build the capacity and skills to implement its mission. Externally, a strong brand results in trust among the firm's many constituents, be they customers, donors to a nonprofit organization, suppliers, or communities. If a firm successfully executes on these four components and develops a successful brand, it can begin to benefit from the brand equity it creates. We'll discuss brand equity and the benefits it provides in the next section.

brand equity

The value the firm derives from consumers' positive perception of its products.

Interactive Assignment 11-1

Please complete the *Connect* exercise for Chapter 11 that focuses on the steps to building a successful brand. By understanding different strategies and the importance of each step, you will gain insight into how to effectively build a brand, whether it is a firm's, a nonprofit's, or your personal brand.

BRAND EQUITY

LO 11-2

Describe the relevance of brand equity for marketers.

Large U.S. firms typically spend millions of dollars each year developing and promoting their brand in an effort to increase brand equity. Brand equity is the value the firm derives from consumers' positive perception of its products. Brand equity increases the likelihood that the consumer will purchase the firm's brand rather than a competing brand. Young and Rubicam, a global advertising agency, developed the BrandAsset Valuator, which suggests that brand equity is based on four dimensions: differentiation, relevance, esteem, and knowledge.[4] Firms with high brand equity like Apple and Disney reflect these dimensions (illustrated in Figure 11.1); they clearly stand apart from competitors, are relevant to a large segment of consumers, and are well known and positively thought of by the majority of their target markets. Organizations with high brand equity enjoy significant advantages over other firms.

Benefits of Brand Equity

High brand equity is an asset to an organization and provides three major benefits to marketers.

1. *Brand equity increases a firm's ability to succeed in a difficult competitive environment.* Competitors of all sizes will try to tempt consumers with new features, catchy slogans, and reduced prices. A consumer who has tried and likes a product is more likely to continue to buy it regardless of outside influences.

2. *Brand equity facilitates a brand's expansion into new markets.* For example, Microsoft's brand equity helped facilitate its move into the video game industry with the introduction of its Xbox gaming system. Microsoft's relevance and knowledge as a technology leader helped the Xbox gain popularity and vault ahead of established gaming-focused companies like Nintendo in a relatively short time.[5]

3. *Brand equity can contribute to positive perceptions of product quality.* Mercedes-Benz is also near the top of brand-equity rankings and benefits from the fact that most consumers consider a new automobile introduced by the company to be of the highest quality, even before they have had any interaction with it.[6]

Each of the benefits of brand equity discussed also applies to your personal brand. If the work you produce for your employer is of significant value and builds your personal brand equity, the firm will be much more willing to promote you to a new position over another candidate and view your future work as high quality. High personal brand equity translates into a larger salary and more career opportunities

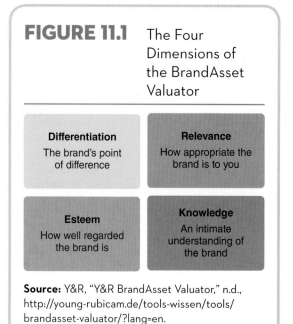

FIGURE 11.1   The Four Dimensions of the BrandAsset Valuator

Differentiation
The brand's point of difference

Relevance
How appropriate the brand is to you

Esteem
How well regarded the brand is

Knowledge
An intimate understanding of the brand

Source: Y&R, "Y&R BrandAsset Valuator," n.d., http://young-rubicam.de/tools-wissen/tools/brandasset-valuator/?lang=en.

smarter together

IBM

IBM has been ranked near the top of a list of firms with the highest brand equity and sees many benefits as a result, including the ability to succeed in a competitive industry like technology.

than you might have received otherwise. As you seek to establish brand equity, you must have a way to identify it and measure it. You may do so through formal performance reviews with your supervisor as well as casual conversations with colleagues. Similarly, firms looking to create brand equity use various techniques to define and quantify it. We'll discuss some of the common qualitative and quantitative techniques firms use in the next section.

Measuring Brand Equity

Measuring brand equity is fundamental to understanding how to build and manage a brand over time. Companies use several qualitative and quantitative research methods to measure brand equity. Qualitative research is particularly helpful in identifying the sources of brand equity and its role in consumer decisions.[7] Two important qualitative research methods are free association and projective techniques.

- Free association involves asking consumers what comes to mind when they think about the brand.[8] For example, consumers participating in a focus group who are asked to list what comes to mind when they hear the word *Lexus* may respond with words and phrases such as *luxury, high quality,* or *very stylish.* These responses give marketers insight into what consumers think of the firm's brand and whether those associations are consistent with the firm's marketing mix strategies.

- Projective techniques are tools used to uncover the true opinions and feelings of consumers when they are unwilling or otherwise unable to express themselves.[9] A common projective strategy involves asking a consumer to compare a brand to a person, animal, car, or country. For example, a consumer may be asked, If Microsoft was a car, what kind of car would it be? If the consumer likens Microsoft to a sports car, it might suggest that the consumer considers Microsoft a fast-moving, exciting brand. However, if the consumer compares Microsoft to a minivan, the consumer may believe Microsoft is a conservative, reliable brand that's less exciting than other tech firms like Apple or Google.

While qualitative techniques provide in-depth consumer insights, they typically involve very small samples of consumers that may not be generalizable to the perception of the larger population. In an effort to get a more complete understanding of brand equity, marketers also use several quantitative research techniques. Two common quantitative research techniques focus on measuring consumers' recognition and recall of specific brands.

Companies like Taco Bell can measure their brand equity using free association or projective techniques. Consider for a moment what comes to your mind when you hear the name *Taco Bell*.

- Brand recognition research helps marketers understand which brands stand out in a consumer's memory and what the strength of his or her association is with the brand. One basic type of recognition measure gives consumers a set of single product names, images, or slogans (e.g., State Farm Insurance's "discount double check") in a survey and asks them to identify which items they've previously seen or heard of. Marketers typically include decoys in the list, items that consumers could not possibly have seen. The decoys allow marketers to tell if consumers are truly able to identify the brands they have seen and distinguish between those and brands that they have not been exposed to.

- Brand recall refers to consumers' ability to identify the brand under a variety of circumstances.[10] Researchers often use cues to understand brand recall, such as, When you think of great pizza, what brands come to mind? Recall measures can be used to determine whether consumers consider the firm's brand when they are planning to make a purchase and, if so, whether they think of the firm's brand before they think of competing brands.

As with any kind of marketing research, the tools for measuring brand equity come with both advantages and disadvantages. Which method a company chooses to use depends on the costs of pursuing the research relative to the benefits the firm will gain from any insights uncovered. Firms use these insights to gauge not only the strength of the brand now but also how they may need to modify their brand strategy to be more successful in the future.

BRAND STRATEGIES

When choosing a brand strategy, marketers seek to maximize their brand equity without diluting profits or damaging the attractiveness of the brand. As always, the brand strategy should align with the overall marketing strategy the firm established in its marketing plan and be implemented with the goal of helping the firm accomplish its marketing objectives. Companies have a number of choices as they decide which brand strategies are best for their organization. We'll discuss some common strategies—including brand extensions, brand revitalization, co-branding, and private label brands—in the sections that follow.

LO 11-3

Compare some common strategies for developing brands.

Brand Extension

Companies that already possess a strong brand and high brand equity may pursue a brand extension strategy. Brand extension is the process of broadening the use of an organization's current brand to include new products. Unlike product extensions, in which a firm expands within the same product category (e.g., Coke and Coke Zero are both soft drinks), brand extensions typically involve taking a brand

brand extension

The process of broadening the use of an organization's current brand to include new products.

name into a different product category. A brand extension strategy enables new products to profit from the recognition and acceptance the brand already enjoys. For example, McDonald's extended its brand beyond convenience and Happy Meals to include healthier items such as salads, yogurt parfaits, and premium coffee. Crest extended its brand beyond toothpaste to include dental floss, mouthwash, and toothbrushes. Dove has extended its brand from traditional soap products into new product categories like hair care. Because Dove customers already associate the Dove brand with quality, they were able to extend that association to shampoo and other hair care products. The company employed this same strategy to enter into the lotion and deodorant markets as well.

As a company implements a brand extension strategy, it must remain mindful of the following two potential concerns:

cannibalization

When new products take sales away from the firm's existing products rather than generating additional revenues or profits through new sales.

1. It must ensure that the extension lives up to the quality consumers expect from the brand. If the quality of the extension products does not meet customer expectations, the firm jeopardizes sales, consumer trust, and brand loyalty.
2. Brand extensions must be implemented with an eye toward avoiding cannibalization. Cannibalization occurs when new products take sales away from the firm's existing products rather than generating additional revenues or profits through new sales. For example, when KFC introduced its new grilled chicken products, the company was targeting customers looking for great taste and healthier options. But rather than winning over new customers, KFC soon realized that the grilled chicken seemed to be purchased mostly by existing KFC customers, who were buying it instead of the fried version. Despite a major promotional push, sales fell by 4 percent at some KFC locations in the first full year after the launch of the product, in part due to the cannibalizing effect it had on the company's traditional products.[11]

Brand Revitalization

brand revitalization (rebranding)

A strategy to recapture lost sources of brand equity and identify and establish new sources of brand equity.

Brands do not die natural deaths. However, they can be destroyed through mismanagement. Some firms mismanage brands into a position from which they cannot recover, but others can be revitalized. Brand revitalization, or *rebranding*, is a strategy to recapture lost sources of brand equity and identify and establish new sources of brand equity. Revitalization often begins with an investment in

Dove used a brand extension strategy to leverage its reputation for quality into new product categories, including hair care, lotion, deodorant, and others.

rebuilding trust with consumers. Following the major scandals from the past decade related to the Deep Water Horizon oil spill in the Gulf of Mexico, marketers at BP responded to consumer demand for more openness, more social responsibility, and more integrity. They did so by instituting a long-term strategy to rebuild trust that included donating millions of dollars to help the environment and promote tourism in the Gulf region.[12]

Similarly, Toyota marketers embarked on a brand revitalization campaign with the motto "Moving Forward," following the largest recall in the history of the company.[13] Their efforts included advertisements communicating the company's desire to start fresh with consumers. By fixing defective products and promoting a brighter future, Toyota was able to begin rebuilding its brand image and was successful in increasing positive perceptions of the brand in the year following the start of the revitalization campaign.[14]

Co-Branding

As an alternative to extending its brand through new product development, a firm can choose to increase its own brand equity by leveraging the equity of another brand using a co-branding strategy. Co-branding is a strategy in which two or more companies issue a single product in an effort to capitalize on the equity of each company's brand. For example, the menu at casual dining restaurant T.G.I. Friday's has an entire section dedicated to Jack Daniel's-flavored food. The partnership started in 1997 and continues to be a customer favorite.[15] Another example involves Betty Crocker, the brand introduced in 1921 and owned by General Mills, which has been involved in numerous successful co-branding campaigns. The company has issued new products with the likes of Hershey's and Sunkist to create easy-to-make food products that leverage the equity of multiple brands to attract customers.

Cold Stone Creamery® restaurants and the Canadian restaurant chain Tim Hortons have co-branded nearly 150 restaurant locations in the U.S. and Canada.[16] The co-branding initiative aims to leverage the complementary strengths of each partner to provide value for customers and generate profits for both companies. The Cold Stone Creamery desserts sell mostly during the evening hours, while Tim Hortons, known for its coffee and baked goods, is popular in the morning and over the lunch hour. Their partnership has allowed Tim Hortons, which faced stiff

co-branding

A strategy in which two or more companies issue a single product in an effort to capitalize on the equity of each company's brand.

A co-branding strategy, such as that pursued by Tim Hortons and Cold Stone Creamery, aims to leverage the strengths of two complementary brands to generate new revenue and profit sources for both companies.

competition from Starbucks, Dunkin' Donuts, and McDonald's, to expand into the American market and given Cold Stone Creamery a new way to entice customers into its stores in the morning and afternoon hours.[17]

Co-branding has many benefits, but if one of the brands involved receives negative publicity, it could impact the co-branding partner in a negative way. For example, consider a rental car company that enters into a co-branding agreement with a hotel chain to provide additional value for business travelers. If the hotel chain receives negative publicity because of poor customer service, the co-branded rental car company is likely to be negatively impacted in the minds of consumers because of its association with the underperforming brand. To avoid potential pitfalls, marketers should develop processes to select appropriate co-branding partners. Organizations like AT&T have developed a co-branding decision tool that helps guide the firm's marketers as they make decisions related to co-branding opportunities.[18]

Private Label Brands

private label brands

Products developed by a retailer and sold only by that specific retailer.

manufacturer brands

Brands that are managed and owned by the manufacturer rather than a reseller.

In recent years, as a sluggish economy forced consumers to closely monitor their spending, more and more retailers have begun pursuing their own branding strategy—private label brands. Private label brands, sometimes referred to as *store brands*, are products developed by a retailer and sold only by that specific retailer. For example, Walgreens has developed its own private label aspirin that competes against the well-known Bayer brand. Private label goods and services are available in a wide range of industries, from food to cosmetics to web hosting. They are often positioned as lower cost alternatives to well-known manufacturer brands, which are managed and owned by the manufacturer. Private label brands like Walgreens's aspirin can cost up to 50 percent less than Bayer aspirin.[19] Table 11.1 provides examples of private label brands across several different types of products.

TABLE 11.1   Examples of Private Label Brands

Bagels	Kirkland Signature Plain (Costco)
Beer	Big Flats Lager 1901 (Walgreens), Name Tag Classic Lager (Trader Joe's)
Frozen fruit bars	365 Everyday Value Strawberry (Whole Foods)
Kitchen trash bags	CVS Odor Control Drawstring, Kirkland Signature Drawstring Trash 50787 (Costco)
Laundry detergents	Kirkland Signature Ultra HE liquid (Costco), Sears Ultra Plus Concentrated 9879 powder, Up & Up HE Fresh Breeze liquid and Up & Up Ultra Concentrated conventional powder (both Target)
Lightbulbs	EcoSmart 100W Soft White CFL (Home Depot), Utilitech 100W Soft White CFL (Lowe's)
Paper towels	CVS Big Quilts, Great Value (Walmart), Kirkland Signature (Costco), Up & Up (Target, Eastern U.S.), Walgreens Ultra
Pickles	365 Everyday Value Organic Kosher Dill (Whole Foods)
Sunscreen	Walgreens Continuous Spray Sport SPF 50
Toilet paper	CVS Premium Ultra, Great Value Ultra Strong (Walmart), White Cloud 3-Ply Ultra Soft and Thick and White Cloud Soft and Thick (both Walmart)

Source: "Store-Brand vs. Name-Brand Taste-Off" Copyright 2012 Consumers Union of U.S., Inc. Yonkers, NY 10703-1057, a non-profit organization. Reprinted with permission from the October 2012 issue of *Consumer Reports*® for educational purposes only. www.ConsumerReports.org.

Over the past decade, annual sales of private label products have increased by 40 percent in U.S. supermarkets. In addition, over 40 percent of U.S. shoppers now say that at least half of the groceries they buy are private label brands.[20] Walmart's Great Value brand, and others like it, are even more popular in Europe, where private label brands account for 35 percent of retail sales, a significantly higher market penetration than in the United States.[21]

One of the ways that Walmart promotes its low-cost Great Value brand is through its packaging. The simple designs featuring the Great Value logo in blue and a picture of the product signal to customers that this is a no-frills product that delivers value for their dollar. Whatever brand image a firm is trying to establish, it should understand the powerful tool that packaging can be in building a successful brand.

PACKAGING

When you consider how many advertisements every consumer is exposed to (TV, radio, billboards, newspapers, online, etc.), you may assume that virtually every product you buy is heavily promoted. The truth is that we all buy many products for which we never see, hear, or read a promotional message. For such products, the only tool marketers have at their disposal to catch our attention, provide information, and build their brand is packaging. Packaging is all of the activities of designing and producing the container for a product. It is one of the most underappreciated tools in marketing. While virtually every good comes in a package, many marketers do not take advantage of the opportunity to use packaging to promote the brand and cut through the growing amount of clutter faced by consumers. Packaging gives the product a chance to stand out among the other 30,000 items that are stocked at an average American retailer.[22] Companies use words, symbols, colors, pictures, and other brand marks on their packages to help communicate the brand attributes to consumers. In addition, packaging promotes and reinforces brand image.

Promoting Brand Image

Many organizations only consider packaging in the basic terms of containing, protecting, and shipping packages. This is a short-sided view. Packaging provides marketers with an opportunity to promote the image they want others to associate with the brand. For example, packaging allows premium products to communicate class and sophistication. A classic Tiffany gift box indicates quality and suggests a lavish lifestyle, both to the person receiving the gift and the rest of the world. The Tiffany's box and shopping bag one consumer carries out of the store are seen by other consumers, particularly in large metropolitan cities, and serve as a type of mobile billboard. The shopping bag may also remain in a consumer's home for some time after the purchase, offering a constant reminder of the luxury experience, which can increase brand recall. Packaging is one of the few points of contact upscale firms have with customers that they can directly control. As a result, they cannot afford to miss the chance to extend the luxury experience beyond the store's walls.

Reinforcing Brand Image

Marketers also can utilize packaging to reinforce their brand image with consumers. For example, demand for environmentally friendly packaging has changed the marketing landscape for U.S. consumer

---

LO 11-4
Summarize the impact of packaging on brand building.

packaging
All of the activities of designing and producing the container for a product.

The simple elegance of Tiffany's packaging is reminiscent of the luxury of the brand's physical store and reminds consumers of their in-store experience.

goods in many categories. Research suggests that a growing number of consumers are *green motivated*, or driven to make decisions based on concern about the environment.[23] They make purchasing decisions based not only on environmentally friendly ingredients and manufacturing procedures but also on packaging materials. In response to this trend, Coca-Cola launched PlantBottle, a recyclable plastic bottle made partly of plants, in 2009. It has plans to offer all of its beverages in the sustainable packaging by 2020.[24]

Regardless of the industry, packaging is considered an important indicator of brand quality. The quality of the brand therefore has to be communicated by good packaging and not just by promises of quality made in the text on the packaging. Effective packaging results in an engaging and persuasive marketing tool in which the product and its packaging form a coherent whole, and the consumer forms his or her image of the brand based on this consistency. The same holds true when it comes to branding yourself. From a self-branding perspective, the way you package your ideas, thoughts, and accomplishments influences others to listen to what you have to say. Consider the way you package yourself for an interview. Your resume and clothing project your brand image. Ineffective packaging of your personal brand could include typographical errors on your resume, poor grammar in your e-mails, or unprofessional attire for an interview. Your ideas and potential may be phenomenal, but no one will listen to you if you package yourself the wrong way. Therefore, invest time and resources into packaging your personal brand in a way that promotes and reinforces your brand image.

---

 connect |MARKETING   ## Interactive Assignment 11-2

Please complete the *Connect* exercise for Chapter 11 that focuses on packaging. By analyzing different packaging strategies, you should gain insights into which strategies work and don't work and how packaging can play an important role in building a strong brand.

LO 11-5

Summarize the impact of social media on brand management.

Jell-O engaged consumers with its brand by installing a billboard that analyzes the number of happy and sad emoticons used on Twitter at any given time.

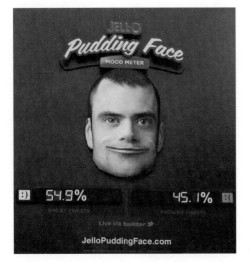

THE ROLE OF SOCIAL MEDIA IN BRANDING

The idea that firms can manage their brands by simply crafting messages onto print and digital materials and then handing them down from the corporate office is becoming more outdated every day. Consumers spend more time than ever using social media, trading opinions and feedback on everything they come into contact with. Marketing professionals who understand the impact social media can have on building their brands and connecting directly with their audience will be positioned for success. Understanding the impact of social media also involves understanding the risks that accompany implementing such strategies. McDonald's discovered this firsthand when it launched #McDStories on Twitter as a way to encourage customers to share fun or heart-warming stories about their experiences at the restaurant. What McDonald's marketers did not expect, and thus were not prepared for, was people sharing negative stories about the McDonald's brand. Any consumer who searched for "McDStories" immediately saw thousands of tweets describing awful experiences users had with McDonald's.[25]

Customer Engagement through Social Media

Figure 11.2 lists the top reasons social media users engage with brands via social media.

Consumers as Brand Advocates Despite the potential for customers to use social media as a way to disparage a brand, as Figure 11.2 indicates, among consumers who write product reviews online, a majority say they share their experiences to recognize the company for a job well done. In light of this, companies increasingly recruit their fans and followers to spread word-of-mouth recommendations about their products and act as ambassadors and advocates for the brands they like. Red Bull has been a leader in this area and has one of the largest follower bases on the social media site Instagram. Red Bull encourages customers and fans to post fun and action-packed images promoting the brand and the lifestyle it reflects.

Consumers Sharing Brand Information Social media play an important role in how consumers discover, research, and share information about brands and products. Recent data from the Nielsen research firm provide striking evidence of the growing role of social media in brand building, including the fact that 60 percent of consumers researching products through online sources learned about a specific brand or retailer through social networking sites.[26] Active social media users are more likely to read product reviews online, and three out of five create their own reviews of products. Female consumers are more likely than male consumers to tell others about products that they like (81 percent of females versus 72 percent of males).

Figure 11.3 on page 328 lists the most common sources of product information and the percentage of social media users that prefer each source. Overall, users prefer consumer-generated reviews and product ratings to other sources of product

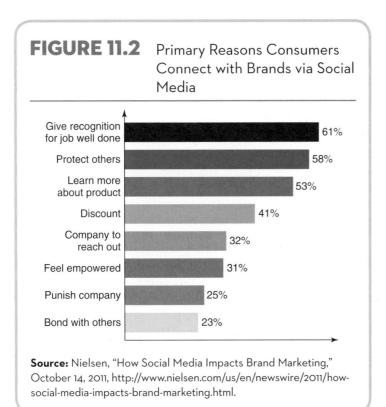

FIGURE 11.2   Primary Reasons Consumers Connect with Brands via Social Media

Give recognition for job well done — 61%
Protect others — 58%
Learn more about product — 53%
Discount — 41%
Company to reach out — 32%
Feel empowered — 31%
Punish company — 25%
Bond with others — 23%

Source: Nielsen, "How Social Media Impacts Brand Marketing," October 14, 2011, http://www.nielsen.com/us/en/newswire/2011/how-social-media-impacts-brand-marketing.html.

Videos posted to social media sites demonstrating the ease with which Kryptonite bike locks could be opened with a pen prompted Kryptonite to redesign its product.

information. Though firms can't control such content, they must be aware of it and respond to it as part of their branding strategy. One of the earliest examples of social media's impact on a brand occurred with Kryptonite, which has been a leading producer of bicycle locks for more than three decades. Several consumer-produced videos appeared on YouTube and other sites showing how to open a Kryptonite bike lock with a common Bic pen. The video spread rapidly and negative consumer reviews began to appear as a result. Kryptonite responded to these reviews by redesigning its product and offering free upgrades to those who purchased vulnerable locks to protect its brand equity.[27]

When researching products, social media users tend to trust the recommendations of their friends and family most. Firms like Starbucks are aware of the influence these personal recommendations can have and make a concerted effort to reach *super influencers*, or men and women typically between 18 and 49 years old who reach a large number of potential consumers through social media. Social media users with a high Klout score are especially appealing. A Klout score measures, on a scale of 1 to 100, a user's influence based on his or her ability to drive other people to act on social media sites. The score is calculated by looking at the number of people a specific user influences, how much influence the user holds, and how influential the user's network is. In 2012, the individuals with the highest Klout score included a wide array of people, from President Obama and Sarah Palin to Kim Kardashian and Justin Bieber.[28]

Consumers Seeking Discounts Research shows that consumers increasingly use social media to express their brand loyalty in the hopes of reaping benefits from firms. Among those who share their brand experiences through social media, at least 41 percent say they do so to receive discounts.[29] Starbucks was ranked as the most "loved" brand on social media in 2012, in part because of the specials it offers to its most loyal customers.[30] Starbucks-specific apps allow customers to pay by smartphone and earn customers stars in the My Starbucks Rewards program. Though offering special discounts can increase positive feedback, marketers should be aware of the potential risks of continually using this kind of promotional activity. Constantly offering discounts and specials has the potential to devalue the brand and its relationship with its customers. It can also have the effect of underpricing the product, thereby reducing profits. Marketers must balance the desire to have a significantly positive social media presence with the brand equity measures discussed earlier in this chapter. When asked to describe a brand, if consumers' free association responses include "constant discounts" or "wait for special promotions," such responses should be consistent with the firm's desired brand image. If they're not, the company may need to rethink how it's using social media tools.

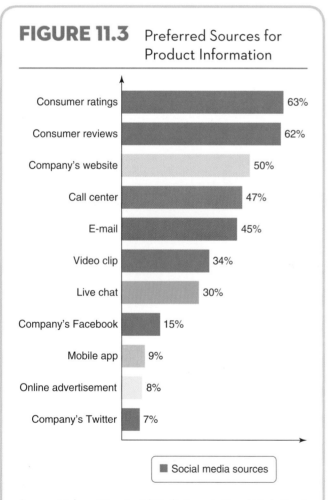

FIGURE 11.3   Preferred Sources for Product Information

Source	Percentage
Consumer ratings	63%
Consumer reviews	62%
Company's website	50%
Call center	47%
E-mail	45%
Video clip	34%
Live chat	30%
Company's Facebook	15%
Mobile app	9%
Online advertisement	8%
Company's Twitter	7%

■ Social media sources

Source: Nielsen, "How Social Media Impacts Brand Marketing," October 14, 2011, http://www.nielsen.com/us/en/newswire/2011/how-social-media-impacts-brand-marketing.html.

Branding through Customer Service

Many customers use social media to engage with brands on a customer-service level. Questions from customers on social media sites allow companies to provide direct feedback and potentially resolve a specific problem faster than they could have otherwise. While social media can spread complaints like wildfire, responding in a timely fashion can showcase the company's commitment to excellence. For example, review the exchange in Figure 11.4 between American Express and a customer. Notice the dates of the question and feedback and how timely American Express was in responding to the customer and resolving the situation.

Though social media facilitate the speed and efficiency with which firms can respond to customer service issues, they also raise the expectations customers have for how quickly their problems should be resolved. According to Nielsen, 42 percent of 18–34 year olds acknowledge that they expect customer support within 12 hours of a question or complaint.[31]

Social Media Branding Goals

Social media can support the goal of building a successful brand in two main ways:

1. By allowing the firm to develop deeper relationships with customers.
2. By generating positive word-of-mouth communication about the brand across social networks.

Mexican-style fast food chain Chipotle has kept these two goals in mind as it implements social media activities as part of its marketing strategy. Chipotle has developed a robust online following, and its active social media team interacts regularly with those followers. The team responds promptly to questions posed via the company's website and on its Facebook page. It thanks people with positive feedback and assists with resolving customer service issues. In addition, the company has made its mission of "food with integrity" apparent on its Facebook page by creating events for dates when it will visit farmers' markets. Chipotle also sponsors events such as the Cultivate Festival, an outdoor party focused on food, music, and ideas, with demos by nationally known chefs.[32] The company posts photos of the traveling festival to Facebook, which helps cultivate interest in the event. Marketers should consistently evaluate their social media presence to determine if these two key goals are being achieved, and if not, what strategies they can take to use social media more effectively.

Companies like Macy's, Old Navy, and Wendy's offer discounts to consumers on Facebook and other social media sites. While customers benefit from the bargains, the companies benefit from the online endorsement they receive when customers redeem the discount.

Klout score
A measure, on a scale of 1 to 100, of a user's influence based on his or her ability to drive other people to act on social media sites.

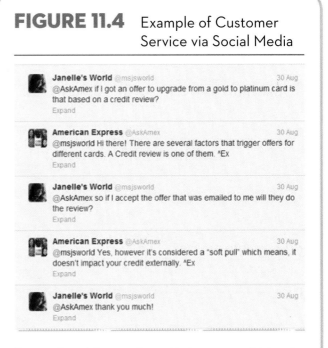

FIGURE 11.4 Example of Customer Service via Social Media

> **Janelle's World** @msjsworld   30 Aug
> @AskAmex if I got an offer to upgrade from a gold to platinum card is that based on a credit review?
> Expand

> **American Express** @AskAmex   30 Aug
> @msjsworld Hi there! There are several factors that trigger offers for different cards. A Credit review is one of them. ^Ex
> Expand

> **Janelle's World** @msjsworld   30 Aug
> @AskAmex so if I accept the offer that was emailed to me will they do the review?
> Expand

> **American Express** @AskAmex   30 Aug
> @msjsworld Yes, however it's considered a "soft pull" which means, it doesn't impact your credit externally. ^Ex
> Expand

> **Janelle's World** @msjsworld   30 Aug
> @AskAmex thank you much!
> Expand

Source: Copyright © 2008–2012 Hashtags.org, a division of Web X.o Media LLC - All Rights Reserved. Reproduced with Permission of Hashtags.org.

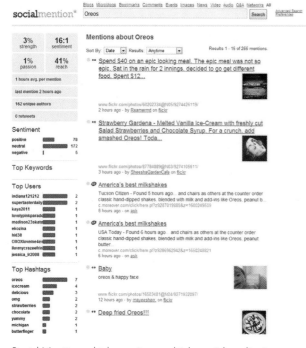

Social Mention, which monitors multiple social media sites, is one of various tools firms can use to measure social media activity that affects their product, brand, or industry.

Monitoring a Social Brand

Regardless of what prompts consumers to follow and engage with a brand, marketers should closely monitor what is being said about their brands on social media. Companies can use a number of tools to monitor their social media presence, whether they're a Fortune 500 firm, a small business, or a local nonprofit organization. Some of the most commonly used tools include the following:

- *Google Alerts.* Firms can set up alerts about their company, good, service, or brand and receive an e-mail whenever they appear online. Firms can also set up alerts to be notified when consumers search the Internet using keywords or industry terminology that is important to their business.
- *Social Mention.* While firms can set up individual tools for specific forums like Technorati, which functions as a search engine for blogs, Social Mention captures a brand across most social media sites. The Social Mention search engine monitors over 100 platforms, isolating relevant keywords and measuring a brand's impact online.
- *Twitter Search.* Tweeters don't necessarily use hashtags or handles when they talk about a company or brand. Searching Twitter by good, service, or company name may prove more fruitful than relying on mention alerts and will allow the firm to remain informed and focused on customers' conversations and experiences.

These and other tools are relatively inexpensive and easy to set up. Marketers who use these tools to monitor their brands are able to recognize potential threats to their brand equity quickly and develop solutions. They are also better prepared to facilitate an ongoing dialogue with customers to strengthen brand loyalty over time. Firms that monitor the social profiles they build and integrate the various ways they communicate with customers online can successfully leverage social media to help build a successful brand.

 ## Interactive Assignment 11-3

Social Media in Action

The speed with which brands are forced to react to negative events has increased dramatically because of social media. For example, Reebok made the decision to end its relationship with rapper Rick Ross after a social media outcry from consumers due to offensive lyrics in one of his songs. Within weeks of when consumers began complaining about Ross's song via social media platforms, Reebok had severed all ties with Ross and his music. A generation ago unhappy customers may have sent a protest letter to a brand and action could have taken months or even years. Today social media allow protests to occur almost in real time. Social media have allowed consumers to mobilize much more quickly, and brands must show that they are listening to customer complaints and responding accordingly. Brands that respond appropriately and quickly can also be rewarded with consumer appreciation. Within a week of

Reebok's action, a digital thank-you card for Reebok's response had gathered over 10,000 virtual signatures.

Social media's impact on brands extends beyond the U.S. For example, Ford apologized for an online advertisement the firm ran in India that featured three bound and gagged women in the rear of a vehicle driven by European politician Silvio Berlusconi. The apology came quickly from Ford after consumers and women's advocacy groups complained on Ford's Facebook page. India is an important market for Ford, and the potential loss of brand equity required that Ford respond quickly to the concerns expressed through social media.

The Social Media in Action *Connect* exercise in Chapter 11 will let you evaluate social media feedback on a variety of marketing topics and make decisions to strengthen your organization's brand. Brands can be built or destroyed faster than ever before due to the power of social media, and it will be important for you to consider consumer input captured on social media when making marketing decisions.

Source: See Tanzina Vega and James C. McKinley, Jr., "Social Media, Pushing Reebok to Drop a Rapper," *The New York Times*, April 12, 2013, http://www.nytimes.com/2013/04/13/arts/music/reebok-drops-rick-ross-after-social-media-protest.html?pagewanted=all&_r=0.

global brand
A brand that is marketed under the same name in multiple countries.

GLOBAL BRANDING

LO 11-6
Discuss the major branding challenges facing global marketers.

Building a strong brand is a complicated task, and the challenge is even greater when the branding becomes global. A global brand is a brand that is marketed under the same name in multiple countries. Table 11.2 lists the most valuable global brands in 2012 based on three criteria: (1) the financial performance of the branded product, (2) the role the brand plays in influencing consumers, and (3) the ability of the brand to draw a premium price or significantly impact the company's profits.

Coca-Cola ranks at the top of the list as the most valuable global brand. The Atlanta-based company has had marketing success throughout the world, including in Mexico, where it was introduced back in 1898 and registered as a brand in 1903. To expedite its entry into the Mexican market, Coca-Cola provided free refrigerators to restaurants and taco restaurants to encourage distribution and trial. The strategy worked as increasing numbers of Mexican consumers tried the product and Coke became widely distributed even in the remotest parts of Mexico. Coca-Cola has used a similar strategy for success in many developed and emerging economies.

The Global Strength of U.S. Brands

The fact that the American economy rebounded from the financial crisis that began in December 2007 at a slightly faster pace than many European countries enhanced the marketing value of U.S. brands in the global marketplace. In addition, American companies in general benefit from the collective success of U.S. tech companies like Apple, Facebook, and Google, due to the cachet of Silicon Valley in the global imagination. The Internet and the language associated with it are rooted in American brands and American imagery,

TABLE 11.2   The Top 10 Most Valuable Global Brands

1. Coca-Cola	6. GE
2. Apple	7. McDonald's
3. IBM	8. Intel
4. Google	9. Samsung
5. Microsoft	10. Toyota

Source: Manish Modi, "Coca-Cola Retains Title as World's Most Valuable Brand," *Bloomberg*, October 2, 2012, http://www.bloomberg.com/news/2012-10-03/coca-cola-retains-title-as-world-s-most-valuable-brand-table-.html.

increasing marketers' success building American brands globally. Also, social networking sites such as Facebook and Twitter have been important tools in promoting American brands internationally. Research indicates that emerging middle-class consumers in developing countries desire American-sounding brand names. These socio-economic groups in China, India, Brazil, Russia, and other developing countries associate status with American brands. Consumers in China, for example, seek brands such as Budweiser, General Motors, Tiffany, Jack Daniels, Levi's, Harley-Davidson, KFC, and Pizza Hut.[33]

Adapting Brands to the Global Market

Even with the strength of U.S. brands overseas, global branding is mainly about finding the right balance between being global and being local. With the abundance of digital platforms, companies can no longer follow different brand strategies in different countries. They must adopt a more unified branding approach. While the brand image has to remain unaltered, the ways to communicate it and make it relevant to local consumers should adapt to each specific context. The biggest challenge in global branding is to remain easily recognizable at any location and, at the same time, be compatible with the local culture and traditions.

Marketing professionals often appeal to local culture through packaging. Cultural differences can greatly affect how product packaging is perceived. For example, mayonnaise is often sold in large two-pound bags in Chile since the average consumer there eats several pounds of mayonnaise each year, much more than the average U.S. consumer.[34] When KFC first entered the Japanese market, its traditional "bucket" packaging did not meet the higher standards of Japanese consumers for food packaging and presentation. In response, KFC modified its packaging and presentation strategy, laying the chicken neatly in wide boxes.[35]

A common mistake U.S. marketers make is to group nations, for example, Asian countries, together and assume that those consumers have similar tastes and brand preferences. Such a short-sighted view can cause problems as brands enter international markets. For example, Japanese consumers are

Gucci, Chanel, and other luxury brands typically succeed in countries like Japan in which consumers accept, and sometimes prefer, foreign brands that project a particular self-image.

Lindsey Hawkins
Marketing and Business Development Officer
First Security Bank

Lindsey Hawkins
Marketing and Business Development Officer

First Security Bank
http://www.fsbank.com/

First Security Bank offers solutions for the financial needs of individuals, businesses, and the public sector, including a network of local community banks, investment banking and wealth management services, public finance, real estate development and revitalization, leasing, and mortgage services.

Describe your job. I am primarily responsible for three key areas that are critical in building the brand of our bank—advertising, public relations, and business development. Under the advertising umbrella, I manage all external media relationships, schedule ads, place ads, and prepare and maintain the advertising budget. I also manage relationships with our advertising agency. My public relations responsibilities include being active in the community through volunteer work, serving on boards, and simply having a presence at community-based events. Business development can mean different things in different places, but at First Security Bank it can best be defined as building and cultivating relationships with key people in order to grow the business and increase sales. As a bank, our brand image and how people see us is critical to our ability to succeed. I know that if I am successful in the three areas of my job, our brand will be stronger and our future brighter as a company.

Describe how you got the job you have. Toward the end of my freshman year in college, it occurred to me that I needed to have some real-life business experience to build my personal brand. I volunteered to work at our Chamber of Commerce business expo where I was introduced to a couple of key people who worked at First Security Bank. They let me know they had a part-time teller position open. I worked as a teller for two years. After taking a full-time position with

the bank after graduation, I eventually was promoted to the marketing and business development officer position.

What has been the most important thing in making you successful at your job? Building relationships, in my opinion, is the key to being successful at any job. It was once put to me like this by a mentor of mine: "People have to get to know you to like you, they have to like you to trust you, and they have to trust you to do business with you." So the key is just getting to know people.

What advice would you give soon-to-be graduates? My first advice would be to get some kind of experience, if you haven't already. Even if you aren't sure what you want to do or where you want to be, getting out there and trying to build your brand is going to benefit you more than you realize. Never underestimate the power of getting involved, through the Chamber of Commerce, civic clubs, on-campus organizations, or anything else that will allow you to get to know people and give you experience.

What do you consider your personal brand to be? I am a very positive person with lots of energy and enthusiasm. I am an approachable leader; I like for people to feel comfortable sharing ideas and giving feedback. As I develop in my career, I want my brand to be that I'm someone who listens, collaborates, and inspires people.

the most brand conscious and status conscious of all developed countries and are generally accepting of foreign brands. Research suggests that Japanese consumers prefer global brands that contribute to their sense of identity and self-expression.[36] Many of the most successful brands in Japan are Gucci, Coach, Chanel, and other prestigious names. Korean consumers share a preference for premium brands, but, in contrast to Japanese consumers, they hold relatively more negative attitudes toward foreign brands. For U.S. brands to be successful in Korea, marketers often look to rebrand their products or even pursue a co-branding strategy with a local brand.

The coming decade is likely to bring continued economic challenges to many parts of the world, making it increasingly necessary for marketers to establish truly global brands that help them attract and retain customers, mitigate potential risks, and successfully manage their brand in whatever geographic location offers their firm the greatest chance for growth and success.

---

connect |MARKETING **Interactive Assignment 11-4**

Please complete the *Connect* exercise for Chapter 11 that focuses on strategies for localizing a global brand to maximize success in different international markets. By understanding the branding decisions required to best appeal to a particular country and culture, you should gain insights into how to market your brand in different regions of the world.

LO 11-7

Explain the role of branding in nonprofit organizations.

BRANDING FOR NONPROFIT ORGANIZATIONS

When it comes to building a strong brand, for-profit firms like Gucci have a clear reason for doing so— they need to generate profits by satisfying customer needs and wants with products that customers perceive as better than competing products. On the other hand, United Way, Big Brothers Big Sisters, and other nonprofit organizations have complex missions that are hard to achieve, difficult to measure directly, and typically require a number of partners. Nonprofits also have many customers, or stakeholder groups, that are critical to their success. The complexity of both the goals and the audiences that nonprofit marketers have to address makes branding even more critical for them. The organization's brand has to help motivate donors, staff, volunteers, beneficiaries, and partners.

An effective nonprofit brand should be unique, pleasing to the eye and ear, easy to remember, and, perhaps most importantly, reflective of the work the organization does. The World Wildlife Fund (WWF) provides an example of successful branding by a nonprofit organization. It has a portfolio of activities and partners, with programs spanning advocacy, market transformation, community-based conservation, and climate change; however, the brand image it established with its panda logo has been tied most closely to only its most well-known activity: species

The World Wildlife Fund has worked hard to ensure that its panda brand mark reflects the work the organization does in conservation, climate change, and species protection.

conservation. WWF marketers addressed this by developing internal story themes to help align the brand image with the brand mark so that the recognizable panda conveys the breadth of the organization's work beyond species conservation without compromising both clarity and emotional pull.

Nonprofit Brand Equity

Like a for-profit firm, once a nonprofit organization creates a brand image that matches its mission, it should seek to establish and increase its brand equity. A nonprofit with high brand equity can use the value stakeholders associate with the organization to raise the funds and support it needs to accomplish its mission. The Girl Scouts and the Make a Wish Foundation are examples of nonprofit organizations that command high brand equity. They were named the top nonprofit brands in their respective categories in 2012.[37] Table 11.3 lists the most valuable nonprofit brands in 2012 across several categories, including youth interest, animal welfare, health, social service, disability, international aid, and environmental. The analysis, by the marketing firm Harris Interactive, used surveys to determine how well the public knows a brand, how positively they think of the brand, and whether they would do business with or donate to the brand.

Measuring Nonprofit Brand Equity

Similar to for-profit firms, nonprofit marketers should regularly measure their brand equity using the tools described earlier in this chapter. Social media tools are particularly important for nonprofit marketers because of their low cost relative to other traditional brand-building media, such as television advertising. While nonprofit organizations often do not have the resources to enhance their brand image through expensive ad campaigns or sponsorships, social media help to level the playing field by offering nonprofit marketers low-cost (and often free) tools to communicate with followers and potential donors about their work. A nonprofit organization that can develop a strong brand image is far more likely to align supporters with the organization's mission and deepen their commitment as donors, volunteers, and advocates.

TABLE 11.3   The Most Valuable Nonprofit Brands

Category	Most Valuable Nonprofit Brand
Youth Interest	Girl Scouts of the USA
Animal Welfare	Best Friends Animal Society
Health	Stand Up To Cancer
Social Service	American Red Cross
Disability	Goodwill
International Aid	Food for the Poor
Environmental	Wildlife Conservation Society

Source: Harris Interactive, "2012 Harris Poll Non-Profit EquiTrend," June 28, 2012, http:// www.harrisinteractive.com/NewsRoom/PressReleases/tabid/446/mid/1506/articleId/1042/ ctl/ReadCustom%20Default/Default.aspx.

SUMMARY

LO 11-1 Explain the importance of building a successful brand.

A brand is the name, term, symbol, design, or any combination of these that identifies and differentiates a firm's products. For many current, former, and potential customers, a brand represents everything that a good, service, or idea means to a customer. A successful brand leads to increased brand loyalty and more recognizable products. Brand loyal customers exhibit less sensitivity to price, making them an important contributor to a firm's long-term success and profitability. Brand recognition based on symbols and logos can be a powerful marketing tool. Developing a successful brand involves four essential components: (1) deliver a quality product, (2) create a consistent brand image, (3) create consistent brand messaging, and (4) capture feedback.

LO 11-2 Describe the relevance of brand equity for marketers.

Brand equity is the value the firm derives from consumers' positive perception of its products. Brand equity is based on four dimensions: differentiation, relevance, esteem, and knowledge. High brand equity provides three major benefits to marketers. First, it increases a firm's ability to succeed in a difficult competitive environment. Second, it can facilitate a brand's expansion into new markets. Third, it can contribute to positive perceptions of product quality. Measuring brand equity is fundamental to understanding how to build and manage equity over time. There are several qualitative (e.g., free association and projective techniques) and quantitative (e.g., brand recognition and recall) research techniques that marketers use to measure brand equity.

LO 11-3 Compare some common strategies for developing brands.

Marketers should choose a brand strategy that increases their brand equity without diluting profits or damaging the attractiveness of the brand. A brand extension is the process of broadening the use of an organization's current brand to include new products. Many new products are brand extensions, which provide the new good or service increased recognition and faster acceptance. Brand revitalization is a strategy to recapture lost sources of brand equity and identify and establish new sources of brand equity. Co-branding is a strategy in which two or more companies issue a single product in an effort to capitalize on the equity of each company's brand.

Private label brands are products developed by retailers. They are often positioned as lower cost alternatives to well-known manufacturer brands.

LO 11-4 Summarize the impact of packaging on brand building.

Packaging is all of the activities of designing and producing the container for a product and is one of the most underappreciated tools in marketing. Packaging uses words, symbols, colors, pictures, and designs to help communicate the brand's attributes to consumers. Packaging promotes and reinforces brand image. The quality of the brand has to be communicated by good packaging and not just by promises of quality made in the text on the packaging.

LO 11-5 Summarize the impact of social media on brand management.

Social media play an important role in how consumers discover, research, and share information about brands and products. Research shows that consumers increasingly use social media to express their loyalty to their favorite brands, and many seek to reap benefits from brands for helping promote their products. In addition, many customers use social media to engage with brands on a customer-service level. Two common ways social media support brand building across industries are by helping the company deepen its relationships with customers and generating positive word-of-mouth communication that can spread across social networks.

LO 11-6 Discuss the major branding challenges facing global marketers.

Building a strong brand is a complicated task, and the challenge is even greater when the branding becomes global. A global brand is a brand that sells at least 20 percent of its product outside of the country where the firm's headquarters is located. Global branding is mainly about finding the right balance between being global and being local. U.S. firms should understand and seek to capitalize on the strength of their brands in global markets. They should focus on the factors that drive consumers to pay a premium price for global brands, including the conviction that global brands represent better quality and the latest innovations.

LO 11-7 Explain the role of branding in nonprofit organizations.

The complexity of both the goals and the audiences that nonprofit organizations have to address makes branding perhaps even more critical in the nonprofit sector. An effective nonprofit brand should be unique, pleasing to the eye and ear, easy to remember, and reflective of the work the organization does. The nonprofit organization's brand has to further the mission at every step and motivate donors, staff, volunteers, beneficiaries, and partners to contribute funds and support.

KEY TERMS

brand (p. 316)
brand equity (p. 318)
brand extension (p. 321)
brand image (p. 317)
brand loyalty (p. 316)

brand marks (p. 317)
brand recognition (p. 316)
brand revitalization (rebranding) (p. 322)
cannibalization (p. 322)
co-branding (p. 323)

global brand (p. 331)
Klout score (p. 329)
manufacturer brands (p. 324)
packaging (p. 325)
private label brands (p. 324)

MARKETING PLAN EXERCISE

In this chapter we discussed the importance of building a strong personal brand. The next step in developing your personal marketing plan is to establish a strategy for building your personal brand that will help you achieve the objectives you identified in Chapter 1. First, think about what your personal brand is now. What do people think of when they hear your name? Are you happy with the answer to that question? Remember that not having a brand at all can negatively influence your success, too. It prevents you from standing out from your classmates and others who will be applying for the same job or graduate school opening.

Next, develop specific brand-building action items for the next year that will help build, strengthen, or revitalize your personal brand. You might include things like running for office in a club or organization on campus or targeting a specific type of internship. You could also include things like going to your professors during their office hours to make yourself more than a face in the crowd, which can be very beneficial when it is time to list references or ask for letters of recommendation. Make sure to give this exercise careful thought. Being aware of your current brand and planning specific actions to develop that brand will be one of the most important career steps you can take over the next year.

Your Task: Develop three to five specific brand-building action items for the next year. For each, clearly define the action you plan to take and set a deadline for taking that action. Finally, provide a description of what the expected outcomes will be for each brand-building action.

DISCUSSION QUESTIONS

1. Think of a brand to which you, as a consumer, are loyal. Why are you loyal to that brand? Does your brand loyalty extend to paying more if the price increases? Next, think of a type of product for which you feel no loyalty to any one brand. How does not being loyal to any brand change your buying patterns for that type of product?

2. Name a specific brand that you think needs to be revitalized. Why do you think this? What specific advice and suggestions would you give the company as it embarks on the brand revitalization process?

3. How high would you consider your personal brand equity to be? If you used the tools discussed in this chapter to measure brand equity, how might others in your life respond? For example, ask a friend, family member, or professor what they think of when they hear your name or, if you were a car, what kind of car you would be and why. Based on these responses, are you satisfied with your current level of brand equity? If not, what are you planning to do in the next 12 months to build more equity?

4. Look at your home or at a grocery store and identify two brands that you think use packaging in an effective way. Explain specifically why you think the packaging is effective. Then, reverse this and identify two brands that you think do not use packaging effectively. Again, explain specifically why you feel this way.

5. Consider a nonprofit organization in your life (this could be your church, a charity, an organization on

campus, etc.) and analyze whether it does a good job of building its brand. Does it have high brand equity? If you chose to measure the organization's equity, how do you think people in your community would answer the qualitative and quantitative questions referenced in this chapter? Give two recommendations to help the nonprofit build its brand (or further enhance it if you feel it already has a strong brand).

6. Think of a global brand headquartered outside of your home country that you are loyal to (e.g., Honda if you live in the U.S. or Coca-Cola if you live in South Africa). Why are you loyal to that brand? Why do you choose that brand over domestic brands?

SOCIAL MEDIA APPLICATION

Select a public figure (celebrity, politician, professional athlete, etc.) that you are familiar with who effectively leverages social media to build his or her personal brand. Analyze the person's efforts to build brand equity via social media using the following questions and activities as a guide:

1. What specific activities does the person engage in via social media to build his or her brand?

2. Give two potential strategies for how you can use social media to build your personal brand.

3. Briefly summarize how social media can potentially harm the public figure discussed earlier or your own personal brand.

ETHICAL CHALLENGE

A university's brand is critical to how it is perceived by students, alumni, faculty, and staff. In 2013, marketers at Florida Atlantic University (FAU) were looking for new revenue to support its athletic teams and agreed to a deal with GEO Group in which the school received $6 million in exchange for allowing GEO to put its name on the FAU football stadium. The practice of putting a brand name on athletic facilities has become commonplace in recent years; however, the difference in this case was that GEO's business is running for-profit prisons.

Within months of the announcement, the deal was terminated. The termination quelled the negative backlash FAU had begun to receive on campus and from the community and media for agreeing to the deal. However, without the deal, FAU lost a substantial revenue source, making it more difficult for the school to compete on the field. The dilemma presented an ethical challenge to the FAU brand. Which is more damaging: a stadium named for a prison or a losing football team? Please use the ethical decision-making framework to answer the following questions:

1. Do you think FAU made a mistake in agreeing to a naming-rights deal with a company that runs prisons? Explain your answer.

2. What value would putting its name on the stadium hold for GEO Group's brand?

3. What types of companies would you not want associated with your university, even if those companies were willing to give money to your school?

Source: See Ira Boudway, "Florida Atlantic University Backs Off on Naming Its Stadium After a Prison Company," *Bloomberg Businessweek,* April 02, 2013, http://www.businessweek.com/articles/2013-04-02/florida-atlantic-university-backs-off-on-naming-its-stadium-after-a-prison-company.

VIDEO CASE

Please go to *Connect* to access the video case featuring the American Red Cross that accompanies this chapter.

CAREER TIPS
Marketing Your Future

In this chapter and throughout this product, you learned that one of the most important contributors to a successful career is having a strong personal brand. As you build your personal brand, author Shane Hunt urges you to focus on the following two key elements:

1. ***What do you want your brand to be?*** This is a personal question and focuses on who you are and what you want from your life. If you want your brand image to be that of a hard-working, responsible person, you have to make the decision not to be late for work, not to miss class, and not to forget to do things when others are counting on you. Just wanting your brand to be characterized by descriptors like *hard working* and *responsible* is not enough if your actions day to day do not support them. Similarly, if you want to be considered a problem solver, find problems to solve. Simply sitting in your office doing the bare minimum will not

convince anyone. I would encourage each of you to think about your own personal strengths and weaknesses, and decide while you are in college what you want your personal brand to be as you embark on your career.

2. ***How do you build your brand image?*** Your brand image involves how others see you and it is being shaped every second of every day. Your brand does not take a day off. If someone from your office sees you on the weekend acting markedly different than you do in the office, they will see you in a different light and your brand will be forever changed in their eyes. How you treat a stranger at a grocery store can impact your brand image just as much as how you treat someone in a college class. Every assignment you turn in, every project you work on, every job you complete builds your brand; however, each also can be an opportunity to damage your brand if handled improperly. Remember to build and protect your brand image in everything you do.

CHAPTER NOTES

1. D. E. Schultz, "The Loyalty Paradox," *Marketing Management* 14, no. 5 (2005), pp. 10–11.
2. Joseph Schumpeter, "Logoland: Why Consumers Balk at Companies' Efforts to Rebrand Themselves," *The Economist*, January 13, 2011, http://www.economist.com/node/17900472.
3. J.D. Power, "North America Restaurant Customer Satisfaction Study," September 17, 2010, http://www.jdpower.com/content/press-release/MQ401AS/north-america-restaurant-customer-satisfaction-study.htm.
4. Giep Franzen and Sandra Moriarty, *The Science and Art of Branding* (New York: M.E. Sharp, 2009), p. 427.
5. Don Reisinger, "Xbox 360 Again the Most Popular Gaming Console among U.S. Gamers," *CNET*, February 15, 2013, http://news.cnet.com/8301-10797_3-57569574-235/xbox-360-again-the-most-popular-console-among-u.s-gamers/.
6. Harris Interactive, "2012 Harris Poll EquiTrend Automotive Scorecard," June 25, 2012, http://www.harrisinteractive.com/NewsRoom/PressReleases/tabid/446/mid/1506/articleId/1035/ctl/ReadCustom%20Default/Default.aspx.
7. Kevin Lane Keller, "Measuring Brand Equity," in *Handbook of Marketing Research—Do's and Don'ts*, Rajiv Grover and Marco Vriens, eds. (Thousand Oaks, CA: Sage Publications, 2006), pp. 546–568.
8. Ibid.
9. Ibid.
10. Ibid.
11. Emily Bryson York, "KFC's Stunts Make Nightly News, but Don't Stop Sales Slide," *Advertising Age*, April 19, 2010, http://adage.com/article/news/fast-food-kfc-s-stunts-stop-sales-slide/143359/.
12. Kathy Finn, "Two Years After BP Oil Spill, Tourists Back in U.S. Gulf," *Reuters*, May 27, 2012, http://www.reuters.com/article/2012/05/27/usa-bpspill-tourism-idUSL1E8GP15X20120527.
13. Anne Marie Kelly, "Has Toyota's Image Recovered from the Brand's Recall Crisis?" *Forbes*, March 5, 2012, http://www.forbes.com/sites/annemariekelly/2012/03/05/has-toyotas-image-recovered-from-the-brands-recall-crisis/.
14. Ibid.
15. *Bloomberg Businessweek*, "Twenty Co-Branding Examples," n.d., http://images.businessweek.com/ss/09/07/0710_cobranded/16.htm.
16. *Bloomberg Businessweek*, "Tim Hortons and Cold Stone: Co-Branding Strategies," July 10, 2009, http://www.businessweek.com/smallbiz/content/jul2009/sb20090710_574574.htm.
17. Courtney Dentch, "Tim Hortons, Cold Stone to Form 100 Co-Branded Stores," *Bloomberg*, February 6, 2009, http://www.bloomberg.com/apps/news?pid=newsarchive&sid=amENTv5wwAcU.

18. Steve McKee, "The Pros and Cons of Co-Branding," *Bloomberg Businessweek,* July 10, 2009, http://www.businessweek.com/smallbiz/content/jul2009/sb20090710_255169.htm.

19. Walgreens, n.d., http://www.walgreens.com/store/c/genuine-bayer-aspirin-325-mg-tablets/ID=prod5589359-product.

20. E. J. Schultz, "Grocery Shoppers Continue to Spend Less, Embrace Private Label," *Advertising Age,* June 10, 2011, http://adage.com/article/news/grocery-shoppers-spend-embrace-private-label/228107/.

21. Nielsen, "The Rise of the Value-Conscious Shopper," March 2011, http://hk.nielsen.com/documents/PrivateLabelGlobalReport.pdf.

22. *The Economist,* "The Tyranny of Choice: You Choose," December 16, 2010, http://www.economist.com/node/17723028.

23. Ernest Beck, "Do You Need to Be Green?" *Bloomberg Businessweek,* June 18, 2006, http://www.businessweek.com/stories/2006-06-18/do-you-need-to-be-green.

24. Coca-Cola, "PlantBottle: Frequently Asked Questions," January 1, 2012, http://www.coca-colacompany.com/stories/plantbottle-frequently-asked-questions.

25. Kashmir Hill, "#McDStories: When a Hashtag Becomes a Bashtag," *Forbes,* January 24, 2012, http://www.forbes.com/sites/kashmirhill/2012/01/24/mcdstories-when-a-hashtag-becomes-a-bashtag/.

26. Nielsen, "How Social Media Impacts Brand Marketing," October 14, 2011, http://www.nielsen.com/us/en/newswire/2011/how-social-media-impacts-brand-marketing.html.

27. Griff Witte, "Flaw Makes Bike Locks Easy to Crack," *The Washington Post,* September 18, 2004, http://www.washingtonpost.com/wp-dyn/articles/A30149-2004Sep17.html.

28. Seth Stevenson, "What Your Klout Score Really Means," *Wired,* April 24, 2012, http://www.wired.com/business/2012/04/ff_klout/all/.

29. Nielsen, "How Social Media Impacts Brand Marketing."

30. Richard Satran, "Starbucks Is the Best Loved Food Brand on Social Media," NBC News, September 5, 2012, http://www.nbcnews.com/business/starbucks-best-loved-food-brand-social-media-981100.

31. Nielsen, "How Social Media Impacts Brand Marketing."

32. Chipotle Mexican Grill, "Chipotle to Host Cultivate Festivals in San Francisco, Denver, and Chicago," April 8, 2013, http://ir.chipotle.com/phoenix.zhtml?c=194775&p=irol-newsArticle&id=1804146.

33. Felix Gillette, "Made in USA Still Sells," *Bloomberg Businessweek,* October 11, 2012, http://www.businessweek.com/articles/2012-10-11/made-in-usa-still-sells.

34. Adam Wooten, "International Business: Cultural Tastes Affect International Food Packaging," *Deseret News,* June 17, 2011, http://www.deseretnews.com/article/705374644/Cultural-tastes-affect-international-food-packaging.html?pg=all.

35. Ibid.

36. Masaaki Kotabe and Crystal Jiang, "Three Dimensional," *Marketing Management* 15, no. 2 (March/April 2006), p. 39.

37. Harris Interactive, "2012 Harris Poll Non-Profit EquiTrend," June 28, 2012, http://www.harrisinteractive.com/NewsRoom/PressReleases/tabid/446/mid/1506/articleId/1042/ctl/ReadCustom%20Default/Default.aspx.

PART FOUR
Responding to Your Customer

Gina Gomez
Executive Director

Hispanic Community Services, Inc.
http://www.jhcsi.org/

Hispanic Community Services, Inc., is a nonprofit organization that supports the integration of the Hispanic population into their local communities by providing assistance through social, educational, legal, health, and other referral services.

HOLT CAT

Edward Craner
Vice President, Strategy and Marketing

Holt Cat Companies
www.holtcat.com

Holt Cat is one of the largest Caterpillar heavy equipment and engine dealers in the U.S. It sells, services, and rents Caterpillar equipment, engines, and generators for construction, mining, industrial, petroleum, and agricultural applications.

Dean Lee
Athletic Director

Arkansas State University
http://www.astate.edu/

Arkansas State University is a public institution of higher education that enrolls over 20,000 students as part of the Arkansas State University system. As a teaching, research, and service institution, the university seeks to provide students with a broad educational foundation. The university's athletics program supports 16 NCAA-level sports.

Chapter 12

MANAGING YOUR CUSTOMER RELATIONSHIPS

LEARNING OBJECTIVES

After reading this chapter, you should be able to

LO 12-1 Explain the importance of effective customer service to organizations.

LO 12-2 Explain how companies cultivate loyalty in their customers.

LO 12-3 Describe how to develop good customer relationships.

LO 12-4 Outline the customer relationship management process and describe how it uses customer information.

LO 12-5 Discuss the security and ethical issues involved in using customer relationship management systems.

LO 12-6 Describe how companies can judge the effectiveness of their customer relationship management efforts.

EXECUTIVE PERSPECTIVE

Edward Craner
Vice President, Strategy and Marketing
Holt Cat Companies

Edward Craner had a nontraditional, or perhaps more accurately, nonlinear, career. As an undergraduate student pursuing a degree in radio and television production, he started his own plumbing business and followed that up with a stint as a program director at a church while obtaining an MBA. In such service-oriented roles, he learned the importance of customer satisfaction and effectively managing customer relationships. After accepting a position in the procurement department with AT&T (SBC Communications, at the time), Craner held positions in supply chain management, supplier quality, sales operations, strategic projects, and customer experience, all of which provided him with invaluable experience and insights into the complexity of business operations and the importance of encouraging brand loyalty in all aspects of those operations. With these insights in hand, he eventually joined Holt Cat as the director of strategic marketing and was promoted four years later to his current position of vice president, strategy and marketing. In this role, Craner oversees all aspects of marketing for Holt's dealerships. In addition, he leads the strategic planning and execution process for Holt Companies.

What has been the most important thing in making you successful at your job?

The unending quest to learn from all the outstanding people I have had the privilege to work alongside. I have often worked with coworkers or managers who had a trait or skill that made them particularly effective at their job or appealing to others. I would challenge myself to emulate that trait or skill and adopt it as my own, things like building presentations, effective communication across company levels, idea articulation, data analysis, active listening, holding eye contact, showing authentic smiles (key to this: smile with your eyes!), and exhibiting consistent behavior (regardless of the circumstances). The key for me has been to make sure my learning and adopting of traits, skills, and behaviors is done in an authentic manner and with the proper motivation: to get better and be better.

What advice would you give soon-to-be graduates?

Regardless of what job you are in, make yourself invaluable through your individual contribution. Each one of us has something valuable and unique to bring to a job . . . something we do well that can set us apart. Identify your unique contribution, hone it to make it better, and then make it available often to help your team, department, or company succeed. By doing so, you'll be the go-to person for that certain skill or contribution.

How is marketing relevant to your role at Holt?

Marketing is essential to almost everything I do at Holt. From targeting new markets to developing pricing strategies to making sure our team provides excellent customer service, marketing is very critical to our success as an organization.

What do you consider your personal brand to be?

Inquisitive. Everything has an optimum manner in which to function. Whether it is a business, a relationship, a team, a product, or a process, I'm the guy who wonders what the secret sauce is to achieve optimum performance. This creates a continual learning environment and an ongoing state of "becoming." Trying to figure it all out can drive me batty at times. But hey, everyone needs a batty guy around occasionally!

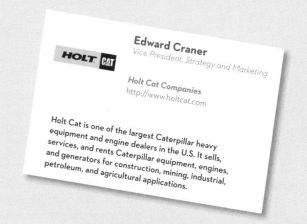

Edward Craner
Vice President, Strategy and Marketing

Holt Cat Companies
http://www.holtcat.com

Holt Cat is one of the largest Caterpillar heavy equipment and engine dealers in the U.S. It sells, services, and rents Caterpillar equipment, engines, and generators for construction, mining, industrial, petroleum, and agricultural applications.

343

Marketers across the globe need to have an in-depth understanding of how to develop and enhance customer relationships through customer relationship management. This chapter will explain how companies provide outstanding service through managing their customer relationships. Regardless of your chosen profession, you need to understand the value of maintaining good relationships with customers because the decisions and actions of almost every employee in the firm affect a company's customers. Without good customer relationships, your company can easily lose business to competitors. This chapter will discuss the concepts of customer service and customer satisfaction, explore customer relationship management (CRM) and CRM systems, and describe customer retention and recovering customers when things go wrong. As you read through the chapter, consider the following key questions:

1. Why is customer service so important to organizations?
2. How do loyal customers benefit my organization?
3. How can my organization develop good customer relationships?
4. What is customer relationship management and why does it matter to me?
5. What are the ethical issues involved in customer relationship management?
6. How do I know if my organization's customer relationship management strategy is working?

WHAT IS CUSTOMER SERVICE?

LO 12-1
Explain the importance of effective customer service to organizations.

During the course of your life you have probably experienced good and bad customer service. Perhaps you were in Best Buy trying to figure out what laptop to buy for school on a tight budget, and a friendly and knowledgeable customer service representative (CSR) helped you select just the right computer for your needs and pocketbook. Or perhaps you went through the frustrating experience of trying to return a defective good to a store with a no-returns policy and were told to deal directly with the product's manufacturer. Businesses, as well as consumers like you, experience both good and bad customer service. Transportation firms like trucking companies that can track goods in transit provide that extra bit of service that makes their customers happy. On the other hand, poor customer service from suppliers may force manufacturers to shut down production due to the late delivery of parts or result in the delivery of the wrong product to retailers.

While poor customer service is almost guaranteed to frustrate customers, good customer service alone doesn't make customers happy. Even if a company offers good customer service, it can still lose customers if it doesn't provide service that differs significantly from that provided by another company. Research suggests that it takes more money to acquire a new customer than to keep a current one since current customers tend to be less expensive to market to than new ones. Sometimes a customer is simply irreplaceable. A mid-size company that receives half of its revenue from Home Depot may well go out of business if it loses Home Depot as a customer. To maintain current customers, as well as gain new ones, firms must provide customer service that makes them stand out among competitors. Firms like the Temkin Group and J.D. Power provide customer service rankings for a variety of companies. Table 12.1 lists the top- and bottom-rated organizations according to Temkin. Smart consumers use these ratings to select whom to buy goods and services from. Therefore, it is important for companies to maintain a good reputation for customer service.

Defining Customer Service

customer service
All of the activities a firm engages in to satisfy the needs and wants of its customers.

Anything a company does that directly touches the customer falls under the realm of customer service. Customer service involves all of the activities a firm engages in to satisfy the needs and wants of its customers. These activities comprise both human methods (for example, placing an order for a catalogue item directly with

TABLE 12.1   Best and Worst Customer Experience Ratings

2013 Temkin Experience Ratings: Best and Worst Organizations					
Top-Rated Organizations			**Bottom-Rated Organizations**		
Rank	**Company**	**Industry**	**Rank**	**Company**	**Industry**
1	Publix	Grocery	232	Charter Comm.	Internet service
2	Trader Joe's	Grocery	232	AT&T	TV service
3	Aldi	Grocery	232	Blue Shield of California	Heath plan
3	Chick-fil-A	Fast food	232	Health Net	Health plan
5	Amazon.com	Retailer	239	Charter Comm.	TV service
5	Sam's Club	Retailer	239	Highmark (BCBS)	Health plan
7	H.E.B.	Grocery	239	Medicaid	Health plan
7	Dunkin' Donuts	Fast food	242	21st Century	Insurance
7	Save-a-Lot	Grocery	242	Empire (BCBS)	Heath plan
7	Sonic Drive-In	Fast food	244	Days Inn	Hotel chain
7	Little Caesar's	Fast food	244	Time Warner Cable	TV service
7	Ace Hardware	Retailer	246	US Airways	Airline

Base: 10,000 U.S. consumers.
Source: Temkin Group Q1 2013 Consumer Benchmark Study, Copyright © 2013 Temkin Group. All rights reserved.

a CSR) and mechanical methods (for example, placing an order for a product on a company's web page) for direct customer interaction. The company's philosophy toward dealing with its customers drives such activities. When companies commit to fostering customer satisfaction by providing uniquely outstanding customer service, they enact a philosophy that elevates customer service to the highest priority level for the company. A strategy for dealing with customers will follow from this philosophy.

A company's customer service strategy guides the establishment of policies and procedures that ensure the strategy is enacted and followed. Such policies might set rules for allowing customers to return unwanted goods, dictate how often a salesperson should call on a customer in a given period of time, determine the amount of discretion an employee has in handling a customer complaint, or establish the hours of a firm's customer service department. For example, some companies provide directions and shipping labels for returning unwanted products to customers up-front to make it easier to get replacements or refunds. High rates of returns for products ordered over the Internet make this an effective part of a customer service strategy for many companies. Beyond this, specific procedures for dealing with returns might define what information may be given to a customer, how customer returns are processed, or methods for dealing with complaints.

In addition, firms that want to improve their customer service strategy put measurements in place to track how well they are satisfying their customers. Companies that understand the importance of customer service will develop such

Online retailer Zappos.com has made free, fast, and easy returns a major part of its customer service strategy.

measures with input from their customers. What might seem like good service to the company may seem like poor service to important customers. For example, does a 96 percent customer satisfaction rate seem like a good goal to you? While 96 percent on an exam is an excellent score, if a company didn't deliver 4 percent of the items a customer ordered, the customer may consider it an excessive amount of missed orders and stop doing business with the company.

The ultimate goal of delivering superior customer service is to increase brand loyalty. Customers will usually remain loyal to a company or brand if they feel they receive more value from that company's goods and services than they do from its competitors. Offering superior customer service goes a long way toward ensuring that the company's customers will stay loyal.

Establishing Customer Service Policies

A firm builds an effective customer service strategy around a set of common objectives for all company employees. These objectives dictate the firm's policies for interacting with and treating its customers. Whether a company sells to other businesses (B2B) or directly to consumers (B2C), the following objectives remain the same:

- Deliver the good or service completely and in a timely manner.
- Ensure that the process for taking and fulfilling customer orders is reliable.
- Establish convenient customer communication channels.
- Encourage ease of doing business, so that the customer finds it convenient and pleasant to deal with the firm.

These four factors are critical to delivering customer service and, ultimately, maintaining brand loyalty.

timeliness
The ability of a company to deliver a good or service by the time a customer expects to have it available for sale or consumption.

order cycle
The total amount of time that elapses from the time a customer places an order until the time the product is delivered to the customer.

Timeliness Consumers don't want to wait long for their products to arrive. Timeliness concerns the ability of a company to deliver a good or service by the time a customer expects to have it available for sale or consumption. The process companies use to take a customer order and deliver goods to a customer is referred to as the order cycle. The order cycle is the total amount of time that

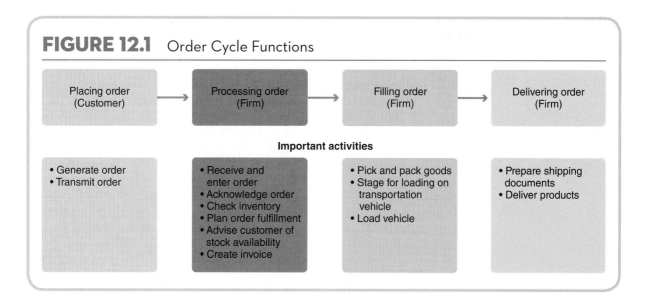

FIGURE 12.1   Order Cycle Functions

| Placing order (Customer) | → | Processing order (Firm) | → | Filling order (Firm) | → | Delivering order (Firm) |

Important activities

Placing order	Processing order	Filling order	Delivering order
• Generate order • Transmit order	• Receive and enter order • Acknowledge order • Check inventory • Plan order fulfillment • Advise customer of stock availability • Create invoice	• Pick and pack goods • Stage for loading on transportation vehicle • Load vehicle	• Prepare shipping documents • Deliver products

elapses from the time a customer places an order until the time the product is delivered to the customer. The order cycle involves a number of activities, as shown in Figure 12.1.

Inventory reduction due to lean manufacturing principles and good inventory management practices represent major trends in business, and these trends drive the desire for shortened order cycles. Distribution systems that can quickly and efficiently get the product to a customer help firms satisfy this desire. In addition, firms must put in place efficient order processing systems. These systems take in the order, check for stock availability, and print pick tickets for warehouse workers to reference as they select products from warehouse locations and load orders onto transportation vehicles. Order processing plays an integral role in timely delivery; thus companies must maintain their order processing system and ensure that it utilizes good data.

reliability

The company's ability to ensure that customers will receive a good or service within a stated lead time and that there will be no problems with the order.

customer communication

The two-way information flow between the firm and its customer.

Reliability   A second customer service objective that guides the firm's policies and procedures is reliability. Reliability involves ensuring that customers can depend on receiving a good or service within a stated lead time and that there will be no problems with the order. Reliability becomes a particularly important objective in B2B transactions. Business customers may accept a longer lead time from a reliable supplier because it involves less uncertainty. When business customers can depend on the delivery of products, they can hold less inventory, thus reducing their inventory carrying costs. Firms develop a reputation for reliability by establishing effective inventory management policies, performing accurate sales forecasts, and maintaining effective transportation and distribution operations (or hiring reliable third parties to perform those functions).

Customer Communication   Firms that fail to communicate with customers and provide convenient ways for customers to communicate with them likely will not perform well in the marketplace. Customer communication involves the two-way information

EXECUTIVE PERSPECTIVE

Edward Craner
Vice President, Strategy and Marketing
Holt Cat Companies

What is the most important aspect of providing great customer service?

At Holt, we are passionate about all aspects of customer service, as I think you have to be to be truly successful. If I had to pick one, I would say it is reliability. Our customers know that they can always count on us, and that, when challenges arise, Holt will be there to help. Many of our customers are small business owners themselves, and our reliability helps them run their operations more efficiently and also builds brand loyalty with Holt.

Companies communicate important information to customers in many ways, including via shipment tracking capability.

ease of doing business

The amount of effort required on the part of a customer when dealing with a firm.

flow between the firm and its customer. A number of important types of information can flow between the firm and the customer, and this information must be accurate and timely. Order status communication provides the customer with information concerning the completeness of the order, when it will ship from the firm, and when it will arrive to the customer. An example of order status communication is the tracking number for a carrier (e.g., UPS or the U.S. Postal Service) you receive from a firm like Amazon allowing you to trace the delivery status of your order. Shipment tracking capability is particularly important to business customers that might need to know the status of the materials required to keep a production line running, for example. Customer service departments can also provide information to the customer concerning back-order status, inventory availability, and pricing, as well as answer questions from customers concerning their orders. Communication may be done by computer-to-computer links (e.g., via an electronic data interchange that automatically sends data about an order), by e-mail, or by telephone. All of these types of communications help a firm maintain customer satisfaction.

Ease of Doing Business Convenience is a major part of ease of doing business. Ease of doing business is the amount of effort required on the part of a customer when dealing with a firm. For example, having a help line available to answer customer questions anytime provides a great deal of convenience to customers who may need answers right away. At stores like Academy Sports + Outdoors, salespeople on the store floor armed with a smartphone can place an order for a customer, take a credit card payment, and have merchandise delivered at no additional charge without the customer having to go through a checkout line. Websites also offer consumers convenience. They supply information about the product, the ability to compare products and prices quickly, and a simple checkout process.

In addition to convenience, ease of doing business extends to the financial aspect of a purchase. Offering favorable payment terms and discounts for quick payment can differentiate a firm from competitors that are less flexible in their approach to getting paid for their goods or services. Simple things like training customer-facing employees, such as customer service representatives and salespeople, to treat customers professionally and in a friendly manner can make doing business with that firm easy for customers. Liberal return policies represent another way to enhance convenience. In short, anything a company can do to make a sales transaction go smoothly will help it gain loyal customers.

The Role of Social Media in Customer Service

In today's world of instant communication and social media, customers expect help immediately, at any hour of the day, on any day of the week. Customers also expect to be able to communicate with brands using the method of their choice, which increasingly involves social media tools. Many of the world's companies use social media for activities that include some form of customer service. Activities include responding to customer comments about a good or service, resolving problems customers encounter with products, answering requests for information, addressing complaints, gathering competitive information and new product ideas, and quantifying the number of people who like or show interest in the firm's products.

Many large companies, including FedEx, have adopted social media as a way to enhance their customer service capabilities. FedEx offers its customers a number of ways to interact with the company, including through online chats, blogs, and Facebook and Twitter pages. The company has a dedicated team responsible for handling requests for customer care and following up with customers to help solve problems or answer questions. The team's goal is to respond to customers in a matter of minutes. It also tracks online conversations to follow what customers say about the company and its products.[1] Though such activities are also supported by more traditional customer service activities, social media have become the front line for many companies as they deal with customers.

Interactive Assignment 12-1
Social Media in Action

Citibank, one of the five largest banks in the U.S., has spent several years working to improve how it provides customer service using social media. The owner of a California-based small business who had been on hold for 40 minutes waiting for help from the bank decided to tweet her displeasure to the firm's @AskCiti Twitter account. She received a tweet back almost immediately asking for her phone number so a service representative could call her directly. Her problem was quickly resolved, and the small business owner now goes directly to Twitter when she has a problem. As a result of Citigroup's efforts, it has resolved the highest percentage of customer complaints through social media of any of the large U.S. banks.

Large banks have a history of scoring poorly on customer service, with nearly one out of five customers having a problem with their bank, according to J.D. Power. To combat this reality, other major banks, such as Wells Fargo, Chase, and Bank of America, have joined Citibank in dedicating teams to quickly respond to both complaints and praise from customers on social media sites. While regulations and privacy issues restrict the ease with which banks can resolve customer issues via social media, marketers at large banks continue to search for ways to balance such concerns with the positive impact of social media on customer service.

The Social Media in Action *Connect* exercise in Chapter 12 will let you develop strategies for improving customer service through social media. Utilizing the unique characteristics of different social media platforms to improve customer responsiveness can be a powerful tool in the effort to provide excellent customer service and increase brand loyalty.

Source: See Suzanne Kapner, "Citi Won't Sleep on Customer Tweets," *The Wall Street Journal*, October 4, 2012, http://online.wsj.com/article.

Tracking Customer Service Performance

How do companies know if they are doing a good job servicing their customer? Primarily, they do so by establishing performance measurements, also known as metrics, that tie to the four objectives of customer service discussed in the previous section. Commonly used metrics for tracking customer service performance include the following:

- Fill rate is the percentage of an order shipped on time and complete. Fill rate can be measured in several ways, as shown in the calculations provided in Table 12.2 on page 350 and described in more detail in the following list:
  - Item fill rate measures the percentage of the total number of items on the order that the firm shipped on time. Thus if there are a total of

fill rate

A metric that measures the percentage of an order shipped on time and complete.

item fill rate

A metric that measures the percentage of the total number of items on the order that the firm shipped on time.

TABLE 12.2 Fill Rate Calculations

SKU	Items Ordered	Items Shipped	Dollars Ordered ($)	Dollars Shipped ($)	Line Fill Rate (%)
1	10	10	$ 150	$ 150	100%
2	15	12	300	240	0
3	5	5	75	75	100
4	25	22	475	418	0
5	75	75	1,500	1,500	100
6	66	66	1,250	1,250	100
7	100	99	2,500	2,475	0
8	6	6	250	250	100
9	79	74	790	740	0
10	120	120	5,000	5,000	100
	501	489	$12,290	$12,098	

Item Fill Rate: 489/501 = 97.6%
Dollar Fill Rate: 12,098/12,290 = 98.4%
Line Fill Rate: 6/10 = 60.0%
Perfect Order Rate: 0.0%

dollar fill rate

A metric that measures the value of goods shipped on time versus the total value of the order.

line fill rate

A metric that measures the percentage of item types (SKUs) on the order shipped on time and complete.

perfect order rate

A metric that measures how many orders have been filled, delivered, and billed without error.

on-time delivery

A metric that measures how many shipments are delivered per the requested delivery date.

501 items on the order, and the firm ships 489 on time, the item fill rate is 97.6 percent.

- Dollar fill rate measures the value of goods shipped on time versus the total value of the order. If the items ordered are worth $12,290, and the items shipped are worth $12,098, then the dollar fill rate is 98.4 percent.
- Line fill rate measures the percentage of item stocking types, known as stock-keeping units (SKUs), on the order shipped on time and complete. The SKU helps the company differentiate among similar items that may be stocked in various ways. For example, a promotional twin-pack of Pantene Lively Clean shampoo takes a different SKU than a single bottle of the same product. If there are 10 different SKUs on the order, and the firm fills 6 completely with 4 on back order, then the line fill rate is 60 percent.
- Perfect order rate judges the reliability of the order system. As the name implies, the metric measures how many orders have been filled perfectly. It leaves no room for error. A perfect order must be delivered to the right place, on the correct due date, with the right items in the right quantity, and with no damage. It also must be billed correctly. Any deviation from these requirements constitutes a failure and receives a zero. If the company fills 2 out of 10 orders perfectly, but the other 8 have errors, the perfect order fill rate is 0 percent. This metric has become important as customer expectations for exceptional service have increased over time.
- On-time delivery recognizes that it is not enough just to ship the goods on time; they must *arrive* on time as well. The only date that matters is the due date for the order to arrive at the customer's location. Firms base the on-time delivery measure on the actual delivery date versus the requested delivery date. In today's business world, in which firms watch inventories

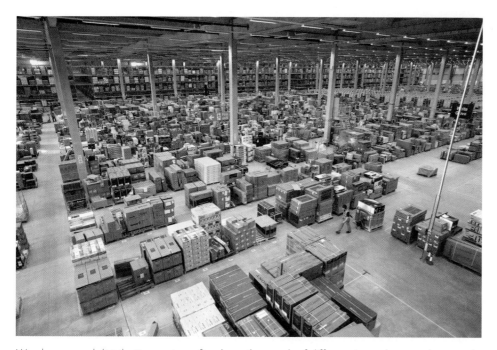

Warehouses and distribution centers often have thousands of different items that must be stored, picked, and shipped, making the perfect order metric difficult to achieve; however, companies that do achieve this level of excellence satisfy customers in a way that differentiates the company from competitors.

closely, delivering earlier than the requested date as well as later constitutes a failure for this metric.

- The order cycle time metric measures the length of the order cycle, or the ability of the order system to react to customer orders. Both B2B and B2C customers increasingly seek shortened order cycles.

- Measuring customer communication involves reviewing communication at three stages. At the pre-transaction point, the firm measures the accuracy and timeliness of the information fed back to a customer concerning product availability and delivery dates. This aspect of the metric relates to being proactive with customers and keeping them informed. The second communication point occurs at the transaction and measures the ability of the firm to accurately provide shipment status and order tracking. The third stage is post-transaction and measures the ability of the firm to answer questions concerning the use of the product or to process returned goods in a timely manner.

- The responsiveness metric measures the firm's flexibility. Flexibility can involve the firm's ability and willingness to provide fast service, answer customer inquiries, and resolve problems.

These metrics cannot be developed in a vacuum; customer input is critical to customer satisfaction. It does a company no good to establish a line-fill-rate goal of 95 percent if the company's customers expect perfect orders and know that another firm can deliver that.

order cycle time
A metric that measures the length of the order cycle, or the ability of the order system to react to customer orders.

responsiveness
A metric that measures the firm's ability and willingness to provide fast service, answer customer inquiries, and resolve problems.

---

connect |MARKETING **Interactive Assignment 12-2**

Please complete the *Connect* exercise for Chapter 12 that focuses on analyzing customer service metrics. By being able to calculate various fill and perfect order rates, you will be prepared to evaluate and manage customer service at your organization.

LO 12-2
Explain how companies cultivate loyalty in their customers.

customer satisfaction

A state that is achieved when companies meet the needs and expectations customers have for their goods or services.

GAINING AND KEEPING LOYAL CUSTOMERS

The ultimate goal of achieving customer satisfaction is to promote brand loyalty, which, if done in a cost-effective manner, will drive long-term profitability. Companies achieve customer satisfaction when they meet the needs and expectations their customers have for their goods or services. In today's business climate, customer satisfaction is merely a first step to ensuring that customers will remain loyal to the company or brand. Think of a good or service you regularly buy. How happy are you with it? If the product satisfies you, but you discover that another company's good or service can provide additional value, you probably would consider switching. In response to this reality, customer-driven companies strive to delight, rather than simply satisfy, their customers. Delighted customers obtain more value than they had expected to from their purchase. A company that can make a customer's shopping experience easier, offer a significantly superior product, sell its product at a lower price, provide follow-up customer service, or make an around-the-clock customer help line available provides extra value when compared with competitors. As a result, customers are likely to be delighted with the exchange. Not only do delighted customers tend to become loyal customers, they also may tell friends and family of their experience, post favorable reviews on social media, and rate the firm highly on websites such as Amazon and eBay. All of these positive actions help companies gain new customers in addition to retaining existing customers.

The Bases of Customer Satisfaction

A company's emphasis on customer satisfaction develops as a consequence of a customer orientation. Firms with a customer orientation set an expectation that all employees should seek to provide value to the customer in a way that meets, or hopefully exceeds, the customer's expectations. A customer orientation makes up a part of the marketing concept, which reflects the idea that a firm's long-term success must include a company-wide effort to satisfy customer needs and wants. The marketing concept is based on the following principles:[2]

1. A company-wide managerial awareness and appreciation of the consumer's role in the firm's existence, growth, and stability.
2. An active company-wide managerial awareness of and concern with the interdepartmental implication of decisions and actions of an individual department with regard to the customer.
3. An active company-wide managerial concern with innovation of goods and services designed to solve select customer problems.
4. A general managerial concern with the effect of the introduction of new goods and services for the firm's profit position, both present and future.
5. A general managerial appreciation of the role of marketing intelligence in determining the needs and wants of customers.
6. A company-wide managerial effort in determining corporate and departmental objectives based on customer satisfaction.

Companies that base their business on the marketing concept maintain a focus on delivering value to the customer in any profitable way they can; they put the customer in the center of the firm's thinking in terms of both strategy and operations. In such a company, all areas of the firm should be customer oriented, not just sales and marketing. Purchasing, finance, engineering, manufacturing, and logistics

marketing concept

A marketing strategy that reflects the idea that a firm's long-term success must include a company-wide effort to satisfy customer needs and wants.

Companies seek to delight customers so that, in addition to becoming loyal, they also will become advocates for the brand to family, friends, and their online community.

This member is an eBay Top-rated seller

Top-rated seller

✓ Consistently receives highest buyer ratings
✓ Dispatches items quickly
✓ Has earned a track record of excellent service

Learn more

Detailed Seller Ratings   (last 12 months)
                          Average rating   Number of rat...
Criteria   ★★★★★   42486

also focus on promoting customer satisfaction, not just meeting their own individual department objectives.

Limitations on Customer Satisfaction

An aspect of adopting a customer orientation that emphasizes customer satisfaction is recognizing the things that limit satisfaction. As noted previously, just meeting a customer's expectations does not always lead to loyalty. Satisfaction ties into customer perceptions. If a gap exists between the company's capabilities and the customer's true needs and wants, other firms can exploit that gap. For example, a customer may want perfect orders but realize that the firm achieves a perfect order only occasionally. The company can meet the customer's expectations but the customer isn't completely happy with the relationship, just satisfied that the firm is doing its best to provide good service. If the customer finds another firm that can provide a higher percentage of perfect orders for a similar product, the customer likely will buy from it instead. Similarly, if a customer wants consistent mobile phone coverage, but knows his or her mobile carrier only delivers spotty coverage in certain areas, the customer may switch to another carrier that offers better coverage, even though the original carrier has met the customer's expectation. Customer satisfaction doesn't always lead to brand loyalty.

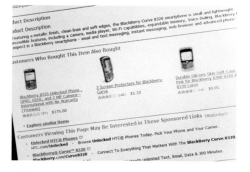

Direct marketing, which Amazon engages in when it suggests products based on a customer's browsing history, offers individualized value that can build brand loyalty.

Beyond this, one customer's needs and wants must be treated separately from those of other customers. What delights one customer does not necessarily satisfy others. A one-size-fits-all customer service policy isn't likely to lead to a great many loyal customers if customer perceptions of value differ widely. Direct marketing (also referred to as *one-to-one marketing*) individualizes the relationship between the firm and customer by gathering and using specific customer information to understand what will delight the customer. Through personalized communication and customized product offerings, companies can improve customer satisfaction and loyalty. For example, Amazon sends out messages to buyers of a particular item pointing out that others who purchased the same item also purchased other, similar products. This offers individualized value to Amazon customers that can lead to high levels of satisfaction.

IMPROVING CUSTOMER RELATIONSHIPS

LO 12-3
Describe how to develop good customer relationships.

While a customer orientation should be a primary focus for businesses, maximizing customer satisfaction must remain in balance with profitability. Providing too much value in terms of low prices, extra features, or custom services may lead to an unprofitable situation in which the company's efforts actually cost it money. Companies want to capture and retain customers that will be not only loyal but also profitable, which often means targeting fewer customers with whom to do business. After a firm screens out potentially unprofitable customers, it can focus its efforts on the specific customers with which it most wants to develop good relationships.

Relationship Marketing

Once a company identifies those customers that will contribute most to its long-term profitability, it can devote its resources to building brand loyalty through relationship marketing. Relationship marketing is a strategy that focuses on attracting, maintaining, and enhancing customer relationships, thus building

relationship marketing
A strategy that focuses on attracting, maintaining, and enhancing customer relationships.

Third-party logistics provider C.H. Robinson engages in relationship marketing by leveraging its expertise in the shipping business to offer customer value that differentiates it from competitors.

customer value

The perceived benefits, both monetary and nonmonetary, that a customer receives from a product compared to the cost associated with obtaining it.

brand loyalty. The following represent two basic keys to building good relationships with customers:

1. First, the company must establish the ways in which it will provide more value in its exchange with the customer than its competitors do. Customer value refers to the perceived benefits, both monetary and nonmonetary, that a customer receives from a product compared to the cost associated with obtaining it. The firm can understand customer value by making a special effort to stay in tune with the needs of the customer. This attention often leads to trust and commitment between the two parties that can result in a long-term, mutually beneficial relationship. For example, vendors that subscribe to Walmart's Retail Link software get daily updates on sales of their products, which allow them to better anticipate the retailer's needs and offer better customer service that results in fewer stock shortages at Walmart stores.[3]

2. Second, the firm must deliver its goods or services in ways that meet or exceed the expectations of the customer. This involves not only knowing what the customer wants but also knowing what the company can consistently deliver in terms of value. It does the firm no good to make promises it cannot keep consistently. Sometimes companies want a customer's business so badly they offer prices, order cycles, or special features that cannot be reliably and profitably delivered, leading to dissatisfaction for both parties in the exchange. It is not enough to merely understand what the customer perceives as value; it is just as important to understand the capabilities of the company in delivering that value.

Empowering Service Employees

Despite a company's best efforts to deliver value according to the key strategies discussed, customers may still have problems with a company's products. Negative experiences customers have with a company can damage the customer relationship and future business opportunities. Negative experiences carry more weight than positive ones when it comes to a customer's decision to do business with a company again. Word-of-mouth criticisms to a customer's friends and relatives can also damage future sales. Effectively resolving a customer's problem, therefore, is critical to repairing any damage that was done to the customer relationship as a result of a negative experience.

empowerment

Giving employees permission to make decisions and take action on their own to help customers.

Have you ever been in a situation in which you complained to a service employee and he or she was able to resolve your problem without asking for permission from a supervisor? If so, you were lucky enough to be dealing with a company that believes in empowering its service employees. Empowerment means giving employees permission to make decisions and take action on their own to help their customers. The approach is most commonly implemented with salespeople, retail employees, and others who have direct contact with customers and the public. Empowerment usually involves training employees in what they should do to satisfy customers and setting boundaries beyond which the employee will need to ask for permission from a supervisor to address a customer's issue. If the job is routine or the issue is minor, the company can develop a set of rules to guide the employee on the appropriate response. For example, Applebee's may put in place a policy that states that, if it takes longer than 20 minutes for food to reach a table in a restaurant, the server can automatically offer a free dessert or subtract a percentage off the bill. Similarly, retail employees at a store like Nordstrom may be empowered to offer damaged goods at a reduced price of 10 percent or extend the merchandise hold policy for a profitable customer.

Empowerment programs have an added bonus: employee satisfaction. Empowered employees take on a sense of ownership for how well they do their jobs, have a strong affinity for their company, and are happier in their jobs. Also, customers who deal with empowered employees experience high rates of satisfaction because their issues are resolved quickly and with little to no hassle. Happy employees and customers provide a good basis for company success in the marketplace.

CUSTOMER RELATIONSHIP MANAGEMENT

Companies interested in improving customer relationships and empowering their employees to support that effort often formalize the process by making customer relationship management a large part of their marketing strategy. Customer relationship management (CRM) is the process by which companies get new customers, keep the customers they already have, and grow the business by increasing their share of customers' purchases. It is an overall strategy that unifies all of a company's activities under the overarching goal of achieving customer satisfaction through the right actions, attitudes, and systems. Companies that adopt CRM use data to understand customer needs and wants. Based on that understanding, they respond to and anticipate customer expectations in a way that delivers value to the customer. These activities, if done well, can foster favorable impressions of the company and its goods or services.

In modern times, CRM software aids in this process by capturing consumer data, storing that data, and performing analysis of the data to create and maintain customer profiles, including buying habits and purchasing patterns. The company can then leverage the information to help marketers design individualized fulfillment strategies for their customers. Such systems have been augmented by companies with Internet sites through which they can track how customers navigate their websites, what customers look at, and what customers ultimately buy. Companies with both a physical and an Internet presence (sometimes called *click-and-mortar companies*) thus have the ability to track customers through various means: capturing point-of-sale data, cataloguing direct interaction with salespeople, and monitoring traffic on the firm's website. Each of these opportunities represents a touch point. A touch point is any point at which a customer and the company come into contact. Best Buy, for example, has a touch point when customers create an online account and order merchandise, a touch point when a customer goes to a store and talks to a salesperson, and another touch point when the customer purchases goods at a store.

Customer Relationship Management Objectives

CRM entails gathering data from all touch points (e.g., face-to-face, telephone, and Internet) and using those data to understand the customer's needs and wants. This enables the firm to develop tactics for building a long-term, mutually beneficial relationship with the customer. CRM technologies support this effort by allowing marketers to do the following:

1. Track consumer behavior over time.
2. Capture data that allow the firm to identify customers who are likely to be profitable.

LO 12-4

Outline the customer relationship management process and describe how it uses customer information.

customer relationship management (CRM)

The process by which companies get new customers, keep the customers they already have, and grow the business by increasing their share of customers' purchases.

touch point

Any point at which a customer and the company come into contact.

Companies use data collection and analysis technologies like Salesforce.com to support their customer relationship management efforts.

3. Interact with customers to learn what they need and want.
4. Take the information gathered and tailor goods and services accordingly.

The Internet, in particular, has proven invaluable in allowing companies to collect individualized data to use to send personalized messages that market directly to individual consumers. For example, J. Crew offers its customers advice via e-mail from Jack O'Connor, a real stylist, in a friendly and conversational manner. Macy's tracks its customers' shopping patterns and sends them sales offers that complement their previous purchases. Neiman Marcus sends an e-mail to its customers called a *gift dash* that offers big discounts for items not advertised through any other medium.[4]

CRM provides a structure for a company to establish and maintain valuable relationships with customers that should prove profitable over the long term. Using CRM, companies can readily develop a customer orientation because they focus on gathering data that allow them to understand the needs of individual customers rather than an entire market segment, as in a traditional marketing approach. This narrower focus allows companies to obtain maximum profits from customers they already have rather than spending time and money prospecting for new customers.

The Customer Relationship Management Process

The CRM process revolves around a cycle of activities. As Figure 12.2 illustrates, CRM is an iterative rather than a linear process; the firm repeats the sequence of steps as necessary to reach the desired result.

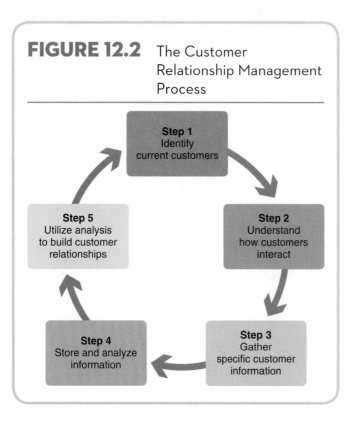

FIGURE 12.2 The Customer Relationship Management Process

- **Step 1** Identify current customers
- **Step 2** Understand how customers interact
- **Step 3** Gather specific customer information
- **Step 4** Store and analyze information
- **Step 5** Utilize analysis to build customer relationships

Step 1: Identify Current Customers The company initiates the CRM process by identifying its current customers. For example, a company like Dell that has both business customers and individual customers would identify its customers by finding out their locations, breaking down computer purchases by customer type, quantifying the frequency of both individual and business purchases, and determining how many computers each type of customer typically purchases. Even within each type of customer, Dell would want to note distinctions. Though they both fall into the category of business customer, Arkansas State University might differ from the Department of Defense when it comes to the type and number of computers purchased.

Step 2: Understand How Customers Interact Next, the company seeks to understand how customers interact with the firm, that is, how they purchase from (e.g., via the Internet, in brick-and-mortar stores, through a salesperson) and communicate with the firm. Interaction between the company and its customers serves as the basis for a CRM system. Dell has several channels through which it sells computers to individuals. It would probably want to know which types of customers are more likely to order a computer on the company's website, and which would prefer to go to a retail store to buy one. Interactions can take many forms: phone calls and e-mails to customer service, conversations with salespeople, purchases, questionnaire responses, coupon redemption, requests for information, and repair or product return requests. Kroger's use of free customer loyalty cards, for example, helps the company track information about customers. Purchase information is collected at the counter and tagged directly to the customer through the loyalty card.

Grocery stores and other companies use customer loyalty cards to understand how customers interact with the firm as part of the customer relationship management process.

Step 3: Gather Specific Customer Information
Previous steps involved gathering general customer information. The next step is to gather specific information on each individual customer's touch points with the company, such as website visits, purchase history, use of coupons or promotional codes when purchasing a good or service, warranty card submissions, point-of-sale data, customer inquiries, or any other time the customer has had contact with the company in any way. A salesperson serves as an excellent source of information about in-person customer interactions. He or she can record information, including the customer's contact information and good or service preferences into a CRM system. Internet interactions in which a customer goes on a company's website for information, purchases goods or services, or provides feedback on a good or service are an increasingly popular way for companies to gather information. For example, Dell uses software called *Dell Premier* to track purchase information. Additionally, Facebook, Twitter, and other social media sites offer avenues for companies to interact with individual customers.

Step 4: Store and Analyze Information
After the company has gathered the appropriate data, it must store the data so that CRM data analysis applications can access it. CRM databases store the information for individual or business customers, depending on the needs of the firm. CRM data analysis applications can only work with the data stored. Consequently, the information input into the CRM database must be accurate if the company hopes to use it later to take action that will create and maintain satisfied, profitable long-term customers.

The analysis that leads to such action is accomplished through data mining techniques within the CRM system. Data mining is a process that involves the computerized search for meaningful trends in a large amount of data. Using data mining software like ProClarity, marketers at Dell can search for relevant data, organize the data based on select criteria, and create customer profiles that can be used to analyze customers. Analysis can include one or more of the following techniques:

data mining
A process that involves the computerized search for meaningful trends in a large amount of data.

customer segmentation analysis
A method of analyzing data that creates customer profiles and categorizes them.

recency-frequency-monetary analysis
A method of analyzing data that categorizes customers by their buying patterns.

- Customer segmentation analysis involves creating customer profiles based on demographic characteristics, purchase patterns, and other criteria and placing them into various categories.
- Recency-frequency-monetary analysis involves categorizing customers by their buying patterns, such as how recently they have purchased a good or service, how often they purchase from the company, and how much money they spend on the company's products. Based on this analysis, the system ranks customers according to how profitable they are (or their profitability potential), so the firm can target them for marketing efforts.

lifetime value (LTV) analysis

A comparison of the costs of retaining customers and the costs of acquiring new customers with the goal of determining how much money each type of customer requires.

predictive modeling

Analysis that uses sophisticated algorithms based on patterns of previous buying behavior to try to determine the future actions of customers.

- Lifetime value analysis allows the company to monitor the actual costs of doing business with customers to ensure that it is focusing on the most profitable customers. In lifetime value (LTV) analysis, the system compares the costs of retaining customers with the costs of acquiring new customers to determine how much money each type of customer requires. With this analysis in hand, a company can predict how valuable a customer will be over a period of time. The system can also help a company identify potential customers on whom it may be worth spending money to develop a long-term relationship.
- Predictive modeling uses sophisticated algorithms to try to determine the future actions of customers. Based on patterns of previous buying behavior, the system attempts to predict how customers will act given a current or past action. For example, Norwegian Cruise Lines might use its CRM system to predict whether a customer will purchase a cruise in the future based on the timing and frequency of previous cruise purchases. The company could use the results of its predictive modeling to identify the customers who are likely to purchase a cruise in the near future, enabling marketers to focus on them for promotional activities.

Step 5: Utilize Analysis to Build Customer Relationships

The fifth step in the CRM process is to utilize the information gathered and analyzed in the previous steps to build customer relationships. At this stage, information is sent to functional areas within the company, like sales and marketing, that then use it to customize their activities to target specific customers. Norwegian Cruise Lines, for example, may offer a discount or cabin upgrade to customers who have frequented its cruises. We'll discuss these types of tailored examples, as well as additional ways a firm can leverage the information obtained through the CRM process, in the next section.

Predictive modeling identifies patterns in past behavior to help firms, such as cruise lines, anticipate the future actions of customers and adapt their marketing activities accordingly.

Leveraging Customer Information

A firm can use customer information obtained from CRM systems to its advantage in a number of ways beyond those already discussed.

Tailor Customer Promotions Perhaps the most obvious use of CRM data is to tailor promotions to match customer profiles. For example, Kroger offers discounts on gasoline purchases for members of its loyalty card program. Based on past purchases and the customer's receipt, Kroger generates discount coupons to send to customers, creating an incentive for the customer to return to the store. While repeat customers might be targeted for such loyalty programs, infrequent buyers could receive different incentives, such as a coupon good for their next purchase. Similarly, a Dell customer who mainly shops on the company's website might receive promotional materials through an e-mail, while another who purchases a computer from a store might be targeted for mailed coupons or catalogues.

CRM databases also can be leveraged to target specific customers for direct-mail advertising. Mail-order companies can track purchases and inquiries from customers and use that information to predict how various customers would react to a particular catalog sent to their residences. Through CRM systems, companies gain efficiencies in their promotional efforts, thus maximizing the ratio of promotional spending to profitability. Additionally, companies can monitor the success of such tailored promotional efforts through a CRM system by cross-referencing promotions to specific categories of customers and making adjustments as needed.

Companies can leverage data collected through customer relationship management to alleviate customers' post-purchase cognitive dissonance by reminding customers of the superiority of their purchase.

Combat Cognitive Dissonance Firms also can use CRM information to combat cognitive dissonance (buyer's remorse) by congratulating the buyer on his or her choice and reinforcing the best aspects of the good or service. A car manufacturer could send an e-mail to a customer congratulating them for purchasing a car that was rated the highest in its class for initial customer satisfaction by J.D. Power.

Improve Business-to-Business Relationships Firms that sell to other businesses can use CRM systems to improve the profitability of their customer relationships in much the same way B2C companies do with individual consumers. They can cross-sell their products (promoting other products they sell that might be purchased by an existing business customer), track customer service complaints and returned goods, and tailor promotional programs to specific business customers based on classification. Beyond this, CRM systems offer several unique advantages to B2B firms. Suppliers can generate sales forecasts from information in CRM systems like past and current orders. The system also can provide product availability information to manufacturers as they establish production runs or to retailers as they plan sales.

Companies that collect and store customer information, such as Living Social, must be vigilant about identifying and addressing cyber-attacks that compromise customer data.

LO 12-5

Discuss the security and ethical issues involved in using customer relationship management systems.

SECURITY AND ETHICAL ISSUES IN CUSTOMER RELATIONSHIP MANAGEMENT

Not all customers feel comfortable having their information accumulated and stored in a company's computer system. The issue of privacy is becoming increasingly acute as instances of hacking into computers to steal personal information have been made public and customers realize that any computer security system that stores birth dates, credit card numbers, addresses, and other personal information can be breached. Additionally, because companies can capitalize on information about a customer's buying habits and product preferences, among other things, a general discomfort with invasion of privacy has become widespread. Such information could be sold to or traded between companies. Since good customer relationships are built in part on trust, any doubt about the security of personal data can lead the customer to take his or her business elsewhere.

To guard against a breach of security, CRM systems must have robust firewalls to protect the privacy of customers. While all CRM applications are vulnerable to security breaches, companies using cloud computing CRM applications should understand the increased risks involved in entrusting data to a third party and require the third-party vendor to employ protective measures to discourage and prevent data hacking. Safeguarding the privacy and trust of a company's customers requires constant vigilance and regular upgrading of security systems. The U.S. government has put in place laws for protecting the financial, health, telephone, and e-mail information of citizens. Still, companies should supplement these laws with company policies that govern how the company can collect information, how it can use the information it collects, whether it may share the information with other companies, and how it will protect the information. Though almost all companies have such policies, firms also must fully train employees in their application and monitor and enforce the policies. The possibility of unethical behavior by employees always exists. Companies interested in protecting the privacy of their customer information must therefore make a concerted effort not only to develop such policies but also to make sure they are followed every day. Failure to do so could lead consumers to lose trust in the company and, as a result, switch to a competitor.

LO 12-6

Describe how companies can judge the effectiveness of their customer relationship management efforts.

DETERMINING THE EFFECTIVENESS OF CUSTOMER RELATIONSHIP MANAGEMENT

How can a company determine whether its CRM strategy is working? There are four basic criteria a company can use to judge the effectiveness of its CRM program.

share of customer

A measure of the quantity of purchase dollars each customer spends on the company's products.

1. *Share of customer.* Share of customer differs from market share in that it measures the quantity of purchase dollars each customer spends on the company's products rather than the number of customers. If a company's CRM efforts lead to an increase in the number of goods or services purchased by a consumer, then it has been successful in increasing its share of customer. As share

Logan Hawley
Store Manager

Textbook Brokers
http://www.textbookbrokers.com/

Textbook Brokers and its partner stores buy, sell, and rent college textbooks and supplies at a reduced cost.

Describe your job. As a store manager for Textbook Brokers, my job is to develop customer relationships and make our store as profitable as it can be. I am in charge of hiring a staff and overseeing day-to-day operations. My job is part marketing, part human resources, part merchandising, and a ton of customer service.

Describe how you got the job that you have. I had a friend who had gone to work for Textbook Brokers in another state. He kept telling me what a great place it was to work and about all of the advancement possibilities there were. I gave him my resume to send in, and I got an interview. The company liked my background as a nontraditional student, the leadership experience I had in the Army, and the fact that I had a marketing degree from a good school. I have been here almost a year now, and I love what I get to do.

What has been the most important thing in making you successful at your job? I spent several years serving in the United States Army before I returned to college. My background has helped me develop my leadership skills, and those have been incredibly important

since I manage a location and about a dozen employees. I think my ability to execute on my company's strategies and lead by example has been the most helpful. My degree in marketing has also helped a lot, especially the courses in professional selling and consumer behavior.

What advice would you give soon-to-be graduates? Develop your people skills. The better you can get along with customers of all types, the more likely you are to solve their problems and win them over. We sell pretty much the same textbooks and merchandise as every other book store, but what makes us different and drives our success is that we put customer relationships first. That starts with my boss and it carries through even to the part-time people I hire. Because we put customers first, they put us first when it comes time to buy.

What do you consider your personal brand to be? A leader, and someone who is dedicated to serving others. I was fortunate to serve with some great people in the Army, and the lessons they taught me about work ethic and serving others stays with me every day of my life.

A firm can measure various criteria to determine the success of its CRM program, including share of customer, customer equity, customer focus, and the lifetime value of the customer.

customer equity

A ratio that compares the financial investments a company puts into gaining and keeping customers to the financial return on those investments.

of customer increases, so do the company's profits. If the CRM efforts do not increase the company's share of customer, the company must evaluate them to determine why and apply corrective measures. For example, if a customer buys a Nissan Altima, the company contacts him or her when the warranty is about to run out with an offer for an extended warranty. If Nissan does not follow up, the company misses an opportunity to gain share of customer.

2. *Customer equity.* Customer equity is a ratio that compares the financial investments a company puts into gaining and keeping customers to the financial return on those investments. A company can determine the value of its CRM program from this ratio. If a company determines that it is spending more on CRM than it is getting back in profit, it needs to evaluate the program and correct the problems. For example, if a salesperson neglects to follow up with B2B customers to offer post-sales service that other companies do not offer, the company has given up the chance to increase the financial return on its investment in those customers.

3. *Customer focus.* Customer focus measures how well a CRM program prioritizes customers based on each customer's profitability. A CRM program that enables marketers to identify and focus on highly profitable customers will likely yield more profit for a company than one that only allows a company to communicate equally to all customers. If a CRM system can properly identify highly profitable customers, the company can direct its personal selling efforts, which can be time-consuming and expensive, only to those customers who are or are likely to become profitable in the future.

4. *Lifetime value.* As discussed earlier in the chapter, LTV is measured by the total profit a customer brings to a company during the time that the individual or firm is a customer. The CRM efforts of a company, if done right, should be able to maximize the lifetime value of customers large and small. Companies that can predict which customers will generate the most profit over a long period of time can eliminate or reduce services to customers with low LTV, thereby reducing customer service costs, while maintaining or even increasing services to customers with high LTV.

Understanding the criteria for measuring the effectiveness of a CRM strategy is important because, unless a firm knows the extent to which any aspect of its business is succeeding, it cannot identify and address problems that may affect its profitability. Successful CRM programs require monitoring and assessment to adequately support the firm's overall marketing efforts.

---

connect | MARKETING   Interactive Assignment 12-4

Please complete the *Connect* exercise for Chapter 12 that focuses on determining the effectiveness of customer relationship management. By understanding these criteria, you can improve CRM outcomes and increase the likelihood that your organization's CRM program will be successful.

SUMMARY

LEARNSMART™
ADVANTAGE

LO 12-1 Explain the importance of effective customer service to organizations.

Customer service involves all of the activities, both human and mechanical, a firm engages in to satisfy the needs and wants of its customers. A company's customer service strategy must be built around a set of common objectives for all company employees: deliver the good or service completely and in a timely manner, ensure that the process for taking and fulfilling customer orders is reliable, establish convenient communication channels between the company and its customers regarding the product, and establish ease of doing business so that the customer finds it convenient and pleasant to deal with the firm. Some of the most common metrics companies use to track how well they are meeting these objectives include line fill rate, item fill rate, dollar fill rate, on-time delivery, perfect order rate, order cycle time, communication, and responsiveness. These metrics must be developed with customer input for customer satisfaction to be achieved.

LO 12-2 Explain how companies cultivate loyalty in their customers.

Customer satisfaction is achieved when companies meet the needs and expectations customers have for their goods or services. The ultimate objective behind achieving customer satisfaction is to promote brand loyalty, which, if done in a cost-effective manner, will drive long-term profitability. While customer satisfaction is important, maximizing customer satisfaction must remain in balance with profitability, especially since customer satisfaction does not always lead to loyalty. Firms must seek to delight, not just satisfy, their customers. Direct marketing individualizes the relationship between the firm and customer by gathering and using specific customer information to better understand what will delight the customer.

LO 12-3 Describe how to develop good customer relationships.

Relationship marketing refers to long-term arrangements in which a firm seeks to build mutually beneficial exchanges with a customer. Its objective is to find ways to keep and build upon good relationships with current customers to keep them loyal to the firm. Loyal customers mean consistent profits and potential growth in sales. The first key to building customer relationships is to establish ways in which the customer receives more value from an exchange with the company than with other firms. The second key is for the firm to deliver its goods or services in ways that meet or exceed customer expectations. If it does not, the customer may have a negative experience, which can damage the relationship. Empowerment means giving employees permission to make decisions and take action on their own to help customers who've had negative experiences.

LO 12-4 Outline the customer relationship management process and describe how it uses customer information.

Customer relationship management (CRM) is the process by which companies obtain new customers, keep the customers they already have, and grow the business by increasing their share of customers' purchases. Companies that adopt CRM use software to gather information about customers to understand what the customer needs and wants. They then utilize that understanding to respond to and anticipate customer expectations in a way that delivers customer value. The cyclical CRM process includes identifying current customers, understanding how they interact with the firm, gathering specific information about individual customer interactions with the company, and then analyzing the information using CRM data analysis applications. Finally, the firm uses the analysis to build customer relationships by sending it to functional areas within the company, like sales and marketing, that can use it to customize their activities.

LO 12-5 Discuss the security and ethical issues involved in using customer relationship management systems.

The issue of privacy is becoming increasingly acute as instances of hacking into computers to steal personal information have been made public, and a general discomfort with invasion of privacy from companies has become widespread. Because good customer relationships are built in part on trust, any doubt about the security of personal data can prompt a customer to take his or her business elsewhere. To guard against a breach of security, CRM systems must employ protective measures to protect the privacy of customers. In addition, companies interested in ensuring the privacy of their customer information must make a concerted effort not only to develop such policies but to make sure they are followed every day by all employees.

LO 12-6 Describe how companies can judge the effectiveness of their customer relationship management efforts.

There are four basic criteria a company can use to judge the effectiveness of its CRM program. The first is share of customer, which differs from market share in that it measures purchase dollars from each customer rather than number of customers. A second criterion is customer equity, determined by comparing the financial investments a company puts into gaining and keeping customers to the financial return on those investments. A third way is customer focus, which measures how well the CRM programs prioritize customers based on the profitability of the customer. A fourth criterion is lifetime value of the customer, which measures the total profit a customer brings to a company during the time that the individual or firm is a customer.

KEY TERMS

customer communication (p. 347)
customer equity (p. 362)
customer relationship management (CRM) (p. 355)
customer satisfaction (p. 352)
customer segmentation analysis (p. 357)
customer service (p. 344)
customer value (p. 354)
data mining (p. 357)
dollar fill rate (p. 350)

ease of doing business (p. 348)
empowerment (p. 354)
fill rate (p. 349)
item fill rate (p. 349)
lifetime value (LTV) analysis (p. 358)
line fill rate (p. 350)
marketing concept (p. 352)
on-time delivery (p. 350)
order cycle (p. 346)
order cycle time (p. 351)
perfect order rate (p. 350)

predictive modeling (p. 358)
recency-frequency-monetary analysis (p. 357)
relationship marketing (p. 353)
reliability (p. 347)
responsiveness (p. 351)
share of customer (p. 360)
timeliness (p. 346)
touch point (p. 355)

MARKETING PLAN EXERCISE

This chapter focused on customer service and developing customer relationships. As you develop your personal marketing plan, you should ask yourself how good you are at developing relationships. We live in an age in which we text or tweet more than we write notes or have conversations. Some might think they are great at developing relationships because they have 2,000 friends on Facebook. But are those really relationships? Consider your Facebook friends. What would those people say about you and your brand if you asked them? Do they even know you well?

For the marketing plan exercise in this chapter, your assignment is to plan a strategy to improve the most important relationships in your life. Even if they are good, there are always things you can do better. Think about how you can improve your relationship with your current boss, professors, classmates, and group members. These people are likely to be important as you seek a job or apply to graduate school. (Relationship development with professors is especially important when it comes time to request letters of recommendation for graduate school.) Next, consider how you can improve your personal customer service. Are you an ideal group member, or do you look for excuses to miss team meetings? Do you thank people who help you? Do you try to help others solve problems in a positive way? Providing great service to the people in your life, both personally and professionally, will help you to build the type of relationships that will provide a rich future in every way possible.

Your Task: Select three to five professional relationships in your life, such as a manager, professor, classmate, or group member, and then identify one or two specific actions you can take in the next three months to strengthen each of those relationships. Next, explain in one paragraph how you have delivered excellent customer service sometime in your life, whether it was on the job, in school, or in your personal life. This will help you articulate your customer service skills in an interview.

DISCUSSION QUESTIONS

1. Discuss an experience you had as a customer in which you were either very satisfied or very dissatisfied with the customer service of a company. What were the circumstances that made this particular incident stand out to you as memorable? How did this experience affect your future purchases with this company? What did you learn about customer service from this experience that you could apply to your current or future career?

2. Imagine you work as a buyer for a large consumer electronics retail company that purchases its goods mainly from Asia. Of the four factors critical to delivering customer service discussed in this chapter, select the two most important for your type of business. Why did you select those two before the others? Would your choices change if you were purchasing fresh fruit for a grocery store chain? Explain your answer.

3. Discuss a time when a company used direct marketing to communicate with you. What did the company do? How did you feel about this tactic as a consumer? How did this tactic affect your plans to purchase more goods or services from this company in the future?

4. Assume you are about to purchase a new television. What attributes of this particular product contribute to your perception of customer value, and why? What attributes do not contribute to your perception of customer value, and why? In your responses, consider both the attributes of the good itself and the accompanying services the manufacturer offers in your analysis.

5. In this chapter you learned about employee empowerment as it relates to customer service. Assume that you are the director of customer service for a cell-phone service provider. What types of decisions concerning customer service issues would you allow your employees to make on their own without having to check with their supervisor? What decisions would you not allow your service representatives to make? Explain your answers.

6. How does the concept *share of customer* differ from the concept of market share? What types of things does a company have to do differently to increase its share of customer versus increasing its market share?

SOCIAL MEDIA APPLICATION

Analyze how social media impact the way that your university provides customer service to its students using the following questions and activities as a guide:

1. If you have an issue with some part of your educational experience, such as housing, financial aid, or career services, can you get help and answers through some social media platform? If so, which platform(s) does your school use? How convenient and timely are the responses? If your school does not use a social media platform for these issues, what platform would you suggest it use? Why?

2. Discuss two ways that your college or university can improve its efforts to communicate and respond to students via social media. Explain your answer.

3. If you were put in charge of increasing student satisfaction at your school, how would you specifically use social media to help achieve your goal?

ETHICAL CHALLENGE

Imagine that you work for a company that has had only brick-and-mortar stores but is just starting a website for customers who wish to shop online. Your CEO is concerned about some of the bad press she has seen concerning consumer privacy and wants to make sure that the company is not unduly intruding on the privacy of its customers through its website. The CEO has asked you, as the chief information officer (CIO) of the company, to ensure that the firm is operating in an ethical manner. As CIO, it is your responsibility to devise a set of policies for the company to follow. Please use the ethical decision-making framework to complete the following:

1. Write a set of rules (a minimum of five) that all company employees who deal directly with customers must follow in order to protect the privacy of your online customers.

2. Next, write a set of rules (a minimum of five) that the information technology employees must follow for obtaining information and describe how that information should be handled once it is obtained.

3. Finally, explain why you selected those particular rules.

VIDEO CASE

Please go to *Connect* to access the video case featuring Edward Craner that accompanies this chapter.

CAREER TIPS
Marketing Your Future

You have read in this chapter about the importance of managing customer relationships. Whatever course of study you pursue, you likely will work in a variety of jobs and industries during your career in which you will need to deal with customers in one form or another. With that in mind, Edward Craner, who was featured in the Executive Perspective at the beginning of the chapter, shares the following career advice to help you position yourself for a career that may take you in many different directions.

Your credentials (e.g., education, previous job experience, and industry knowledge) will help you get a job. They're easy to quantify and help employers quickly screen candidates. But what if you lack experience or want to move into a new industry? Though they may not explicitly state it, every employer wants, even more than credentials, the unique transferrable skills a job candidate can bring to a position. Showcase your expertise and competence related to transferrable skills and provide context for how those skills can help a prospective employer. Assure the employer that you can learn the job requirements and the industry. What they would get by hiring you is a set of well-developed skills that may include the following:

- *Writing expertise.* Bring a customized example of what the company can expect from you in the way of written communication.
- *Oral communication.* Ask the employer for a topic (or come prepared with one) and do an ad hoc persuasive presentation (no longer than 3 minutes in length).
- *Creative design.* Most employers appreciate creativity in a job applicant. Describe a situation from your previous work or school experience that displays your original thinking.
- *Microsoft Office competency.* The majority of businesses consider Microsoft Office a valuable tool. Showcase an example of a data analysis, database framework, or PowerPoint presentation you've developed.
- *Organizational skills.* Don't talk about being highly organized—show it! Describe a complex project you've managed, or describe processes related to the company or industry that you've observed and how they could be improved.
- *Results-oriented outlook.* Provide specific examples of results you've achieved that the interviewer will remember.

This is only a small sampling of the things you, as a job candidate, might bring to an interview. Identify your unique transferrable skills and then leverage them by showing prospective employers how they apply to the job you want.

CHAPTER NOTES

1. Ekaterina Walter, "The Big Brand Theory: How FedEx Achieves Social Customer Service Success," *SocialMedia Today,* May 27, 2013, http://socialmediatoday.com/ekaterinawalter/1494726/big-brand-theory-how-fedex-achieves-social-customer-service-success.

2. George Schwartz, ed., *Science in Marketing* (New York: John Wiley & Sons, 1965), pp. 70–97.

3. Sam Hornblower, "Always Low Prices," *Frontline,* November 16, 2004, http://www.pbs.org/wgbh/pages/frontline/shows/walmart/secrets/pricing.html.

4. Elizabeth Holmes, "Dark Art of Store Emails," *The Wall Street Journal,* December 19, 2012, http://online.wsj.com/article/SB10001424127887323723104578187450253813668.html.

Chapter 13

SOCIAL RESPONSIBILITY AND SUSTAINABILITY

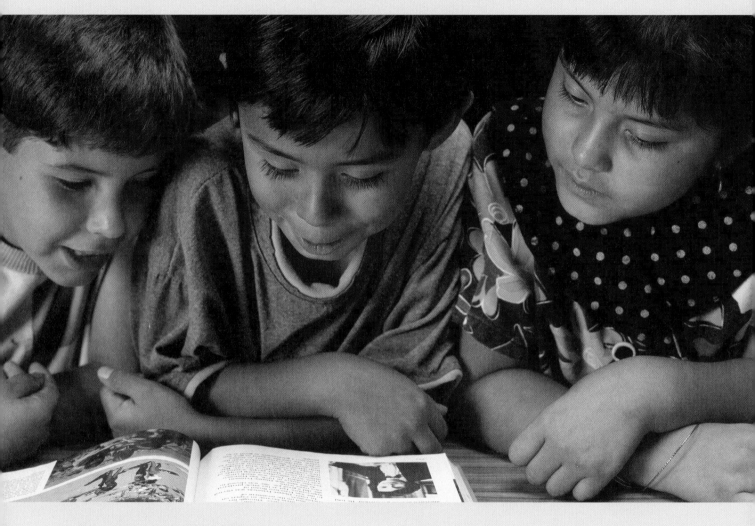

LEARNING OBJECTIVES

After reading this chapter, you should be able to

LO 13-1 Describe the features of a successful corporate social responsibility program.

LO 13-2 Explain how sustainable marketing contributes to a firm's corporate social responsibility efforts.

LO 13-3 Explain the impact of environmentalism on marketing success.

LO 13-4 Describe the challenges of environmental and sustainable marketing on a global scale.

LO 13-5 Analyze how firms use social media to support their corporate social responsibility efforts.

EXECUTIVE PERSPECTIVE

Gina Gomez
Executive Director
Hispanic Community Services, Inc.

Those who work for nonprofit organizations feel the impact of corporate social responsibility in a unique way. Gina Gomez is no exception. As a psychology major, she discovered how much she enjoyed working with people, trying to understand their behavior, and developing programs and activities that empower them and contribute to the improvement of their quality of life. Today, as the executive director of Hispanic Community Services, Inc. (HCSI), she is responsible for making sure the organization functions well from a management, public relations, and fundraising perspective. In addition, she leads the organization's efforts to develop relationships with socially responsible firms interested in supporting their local community and its citizens. She is also responsible for establishing working relationships with organizations and community groups. Firms that recognize the positive effect a focus on corporate social responsibility can have on their business, both from an image and an economic standpoint, increasingly seek to partner with nonprofit organizations like Gomez's that can help them make a greater impact on social and global problems. With an eye to the future, executives like Gomez seek to take advantage of this trend by identifying the challenges a firm faces that their nonprofit can help address.

What has been the most important thing in making you successful at your job?

I think passion for what you do is the key to success in any job. When you are passionate about what you do, you do your best and obtain the best results. I believe loving what you do is essential not just to be a good employee but also to be satisfied with your life. I never take anything for granted. Everything has a cost. When HCSI became a nonprofit organization back in 2004, things were not easy. The struggle for funds was tough, but you know what? It gets easier with time. I stick to my principles. My motto is never give up, always keep trying.

What advice would you give soon-to-be graduates?

My first advice would be not to underestimate your studies. Books have always been a good inspiration for new and great ideas, and the knowledge and expertise provided by your professors is priceless. Then, persevere and always keep trying, never give up. Business life is not easy; it gets very competitive and complicated sometimes, but with your best effort and sacrifice, you will be able to reach the top.

How is marketing relevant to your role at Hispanic Community Services, Inc.?

I spend a significant portion of my time promoting events we have through our website, social media, and traditional marketing tools. I also work on developing products and programs that will help our community succeed and then presenting those ideas to our board of directors for approval. Finally, I work hard to communicate the value of HCSI to individuals, business community members, and potential supporters throughout the region.

What do you consider your personal brand to be?

I was raised in the Hispanic culture with a good education. I left home and moved to the U.S. looking for new opportunities in life and obtained my first job in the U.S. at the Hispanic Center. All this has combined with my natural talents, education, and experiences to make me a very compassionate, strong, and determined person. So I think that it would be true to say that my personal brand is defined by the work I have done motivating others and spending my life helping everyone around me improve their situation in life. I have also tried to encourage people to take advantage of the opportunities given to them in this country. I hope I've set an example of how honesty, loyalty, hard work, and passion for what you do can bring you success in life.

Gina Gomez
Executive Director

Hispanic Community Services, Inc.
http://www.jhcsi.org/

Hispanic Community Services, Inc., is a nonprofit organization that supports the integration of the Hispanic population into their local communities by providing assistance through social, educational, legal, health, and other referral services.

This chapter explores the importance of social responsibility, sustainability, and environmentalism in today's marketplace. Organizations around the world are adopting active corporate social responsibility and sustainability programs. As a result, it is likely that the organization you work for will seek some of the financial and social benefits of instituting such programs. In this chapter, you will learn how sustainability and environmental programs contribute to a firm's corporate social responsibility efforts, how those efforts apply domestically and globally, and how social media can impact the success of those efforts. As you read through the chapter, consider the following key questions:

1. Why does corporate social responsibility matter to my organization?
2. What is a sustainability vision?
3. How does environmental sustainability impact marketing?

4. What unique challenges does sustainable marketing pose globally?
5. How can social media strategies help my organization's corporate social responsibility initiatives succeed?

LO 13-1

Describe the features of a successful corporate social responsibility program.

corporate social responsibility (CSR)

An organization's obligation to maximize its positive impact and minimize its negative impact on society.

stakeholder responsibility

The obligations an organization has to those who can affect the achievement of its objectives.

Organizations like Junior Achievement, which is dedicated to preparing students for the workplace, allow individuals from all organizational areas and backgrounds to participate in their firms' corporate social responsibility efforts.

CORPORATE SOCIAL RESPONSIBILITY

Have you ever bought a pair of Toms shoes or chosen to spend more on an organic apple from Whole Foods than you would have at the grocery store down the street? If so, you are part of an ever-growing group of consumers that makes purchase decisions in part because of a firm's reputation for corporate social responsibility. Organizations today are forced to confront a new economic reality: that it is no longer acceptable to experience economic prosperity in isolation from those stakeholders (customers, communities, employees, etc.) who are impacted by the organization's decisions. In the same way that firms choose to hire new employees they like and respect, consumers increasingly choose to buy from firms that value and support the same causes they do. As a result, firms have begun to accept responsibility for balancing profitability with social well-being when determining their success. Success begins with the quality of the relationships that a company develops with its customers and other stakeholders. These relationships are at the heart of corporate social responsibility.

Corporate social responsibility (CSR) refers to an organization's obligation to maximize its positive impact and minimize its negative impact on society. CSR has been shown to benefit companies in many ways, including by improving employee retention as well as the company's brand image.[1] Within many organizations, the marketing department is primarily responsible for the ideas and strategies that comprise a CSR program, making this topic an important part of your marketing education. However, to succeed, a CSR focus must be adopted and enacted by all of the functional areas within a firm. Accountants who offer free tax preparation to low-income or elderly citizens and managers who work with students to develop future business leaders in the community also have a CSR focus.

CSR includes not only economic and legal issues but also a focus on ethics and accountability to stakeholders. Stakeholder responsibility, which focuses on the obligations an organization has to those who can affect the achievement of its objectives, has received significant attention in recent years. Stakeholder responsibility is the driving consideration across the four dimensions of corporate social responsibility: economic, legal, ethical, and philanthropic. As you can see in Figure 13.1, economic and legal considerations form the foundation of CSR. The ethical and philanthropic aspects go further to encompass actions that, while not required of the firm, meet stakeholders' expectations for how the firm should act. We'll discuss each of these dimensions in more depth in the sections that follow.

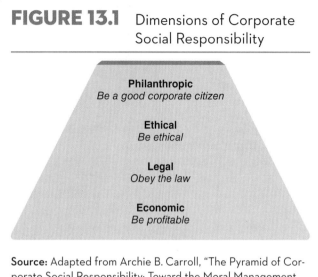

FIGURE 13.1 Dimensions of Corporate Social Responsibility

Source: Adapted from Archie B. Carroll, "The Pyramid of Corporate Social Responsibility: Toward the Moral Management of Organizational Stakeholders," *Business Horizons* 34, no. 4 (July–August 1991), p. 39.

Economic Dimension

For-profit firms have a responsibility to their stakeholders to be profitable. Without profits, a business cannot survive. A failed business hurts employees, investors, and communities. In addition, it can no longer engage in any type of philanthropy, which has economic consequences for the causes the company supported. Publicly traded firms have a unique responsibility to investors. These shareholders have invested in the firm with the expectation that they'll receive high share prices and dividends to fund their retirement or college education in return. Over 50 percent of Americans invest in the stock market in the U.S. alone, making the economic dimension critical not just to the firm's success but to the overall economic wealth of the country as well.[2]

Legal Dimension

Marketers have a responsibility to understand and obey the laws and regulations of the communities in which they do business. They must follow local, state, and federal laws. Beyond this, U.S. companies are also subject to the laws and regulations of the foreign countries in which they do business. CSR programs often begin as a way of reducing the likelihood of legal problems and public relations disasters, either at home or abroad. The past two decades are littered with examples of firms—Enron, Arthur Andersen, and WorldCom, to name a few—whose failure to obey the appropriate laws and regulations led to their demise. Such examples prove that the short-term benefits from the economic dimension will be erased if the firm eschews responsibility in the legal dimension. Despite years of economic success, the failure of these companies to obey the law hurt every stakeholder group. Thousands of employees lost their jobs, customers and suppliers lost an important business partner, and shareholders lost virtually their entire investment.

Marketers must take a broad view of the legal dimension and its relationship to ethics. In the years leading up to the recession that began in late 2007, many firms, in industries ranging from banking to real estate, marketed products that, while legal at the time, were highly questionable ethically. After the recession hit, outraged consumers demanded action. The result was new laws and regulations, such as the Dodd-Frank Wall Street Reform and Consumer Protection Act of 2010, which have altered the legal dimension for firms for years to come. Because of Dodd-Frank, real estate transactions involve more steps, stricter due diligence, and longer timeframes than they did previously. These additional complexities can delay or reduce the revenue a firm might generate from the transaction. In addition, bank marketers face new pricing restrictions on debit cards and other bank

The Dodd-Frank Wall Street Reform and Consumer Protection Act, signed into law in 2010, was passed to improve accountability and transparency in the financial system and, ultimately, to protect consumers from abusive financial service practices.

ethics
The moral standards expected by a society.

corporate philanthropy
The act of organizations voluntarily donating some of their profits or resources to charitable causes.

The Pepsi Refresh Project, an example of corporate philanthropy, awarded grants based on customer votes via social media to individuals and organizations who submitted innovative ideas to better the world.

services. Such new restrictions could require banks to raise fees in other areas (e.g., through the elimination of free checking accounts) to maintain revenue and profit.

Ethical Dimension

The ethical challenges facing marketers come from many different places. Inevitably, they involve more gray areas than the legal dimension. Ethics are the moral standards expected by a society. Marketers are responsible for a number of choices with an ethical dimension and will be held accountable for making the right decision. The ethical decision-making framework described in the chapter "Why Marketing Matters to You" provides a systematic tool for thinking about and making ethical decisions. Marketers who take the time to identify the ethical issue at hand and consider how their decision will impact each of the firm's stakeholders are far more likely to make the right decision and successfully resolve the problem.

Philanthropic Dimension

Marketers understand that giving back to the community is not only the right thing to do but also a great way to get the firm's name, product, or promotion out to consumers at a reasonable cost. Corporate philanthropy is the act of organizations voluntarily donating some of their profits or resources to charitable causes. In recent years, companies have looked for new and innovative ways to engage in corporate philanthropy. For example, Pepsi marketers experimented with a program that combined philanthropy and social media in its Pepsi Refresh Project. Instead of spending millions of dollars on traditional advertising, the beverage maker set out to award grants to "people, businesses and non-profits with ideas that will have a positive impact."[3] Consumers were engaged through social media and could vote for up to 10 of their favorite ideas every day. The Pepsi Refresh Project searched for 1,000 ideas every month and allowed the company to positively impact society. At the same time, the campaign engaged potential customers and enhanced the image of the firm.

|MARKETING

Interactive Assignment 13-1

Please complete the *Connect* exercise for Chapter 13 that focuses on the different dimensions of corporate social responsibility. By understanding the dynamics of each dimension, you should gain insight into how marketers can make strategic decisions to benefit the largest group of organizational stakeholders.

Developing a Successful Corporate Social Responsibility Program

The marketing department is typically responsible for developing an organization's corporate social responsibility program. The process begins when a firm incorporates a focus on fulfilling the economic, legal, ethical, and philanthropic dimensions into its marketing strategy. This focus is often expressed through a formal corporate social responsibility statement. The CSR statement for Toyota in Table 13.1 provides an example. The task of implementing this type of broad focus through specific action is often difficult, but firms can use the following key elements to guide them through the process:[4]

1. *Good stakeholder management.* Marketers should seek significant interaction with the stakeholders who influence the decisions and behavior of the company. For example, Toyota might meet with investors, environmentalists, regulators, and customers to gather ideas for ensuring that the plastic resources used in manufacturing will be discarded in an environmentally friendly way. The company could also work with the community to understand the impact of water usage by its manufacturing plant on surrounding areas.

2. *Good corporate leadership.* The firm's leaders play a vital role in guiding their organization's business practices toward social responsibility. Success requires them to demonstrate a unique array of skills and competencies. The emphasis in business thinking has shifted from process to people.[5] Today, leaders who can thoughtfully balance the four dimensions of CSR and communicate their intentions accordingly generally succeed at implementing socially responsible behaviors.

3. *Integration of CSR into corporate policy at all levels and in all divisions of the firm.* CSR policies and procedures are most useful when they are written down, well understood, and endorsed by affected employees. These

---

TABLE 13.1   Toyota's Corporate Social Responsibility Statement

We, TOYOTA MOTOR CORPORATION and our subsidiaries, take initiative to contribute to harmonious and sustainable development of society and the earth through all business activities that we carry out in each country and region, based on our Guiding Principles.

We comply with local, national and international laws and regulations as well as the spirit thereof and we conduct our business operations with honesty and integrity.

In order to contribute to sustainable development, we believe that management interacting with its stakeholders ... is of considerable importance, and we will endeavor to build and maintain sound relationships with our stakeholders through open and fair communication.

We expect our business partners to support this initiative and act in accordance with it.

Source: Toyota, "Toyota's CSR Concepts: CSR Policy," n.d., http://www.toyota-global.com/sustainability/csr_initiatives/csr_concepts/policy.html.

FIGURE 13.2   The Framework for CSR-Informed Policy at Toyota

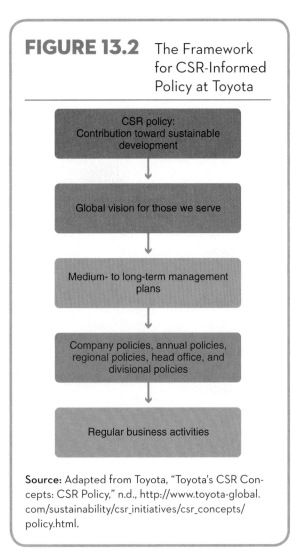

Source: Adapted from Toyota, "Toyota's CSR Concepts: CSR Policy," n.d., http://www.toyota-global.com/sustainability/csr_initiatives/csr_concepts/policy.html.

procedures could vary from strategic decisions about the treatment of foreign workers to smaller initiatives such as establishing procedures that require employees to shut off the lights before leaving work. Figure 13.2 illustrates how the CSR policy at Toyota guides decisions across the firm and throughout the world.

Toyota has been able to build strong connections with its stakeholders by focusing on these three key elements as it developed a CSR policy. The company's shift to a stakeholder-centric approach has brought it observable benefits, including improved customer and employee loyalty at all levels of the company.

Auditing a Corporate Social Responsibility Program

Once an organization has developed a corporate social responsibility program, the focus shifts to how well it is working. This can be accomplished through an audit that considers the following crucial points as it measures the program's effectiveness:[6]

- *The inclusion of all significant stakeholder groups in the auditing process.* Not considering this point is perhaps the biggest misstep marketers can make when evaluating the success of their CSR programs. The wide variety of stakeholder interests makes it challenging, but imperative, for a firm to get feedback from each stakeholder group in evaluating the program. For example, if a CSR program is having a positive philanthropic impact in the community at the expense of stockholder return, the long-term viability of the program, and the firm, may be at risk.

- *Measurements should be both quantitative and qualitative in nature.* Companies must undertake quantitative measures as part of their audit, including the return on investment (ROI) and any changes in employee turnover and brand image associated with the CSR program. Marketers should also ask questions and measure what consumers and employees really know about the organization's CSR efforts. Research involving Procter & Gamble, General Mills, Timberland, and others revealed that many of their stakeholders had only a limited understanding of the companies' corporate social responsibility initiatives.[7] Stakeholders of those companies often questioned the motivation for engaging in CSR activities. Such qualitative research highlights the necessity of effectively communicating the firm's CSR initiatives and the rationale for engaging in those initiatives if the firm wants to maximize their benefits. Companies can use this research to refine the CSR program to make it more successful going forward.

VOLUNTEERISM

The Civic 50 is a scorecard of America's community-minded companies produced by Bloomberg LP in partnership with the National Conference on Citizenship and Points of Light.[8] Firms like IBM rank near the top in this list, in part because they lead the way when it comes to promoting volunteerism. Corporate volunteerism is the policy or practice of employees volunteering their time or talents for charitable, educational, or other worthwhile activities, especially in the community. Volunteer projects, such as FedEx delivering emergency medicine to disaster areas or Aetna tackling the health ailments of underserved communities, achieve maximum impact when they draw on a company's strengths.[9] For example, Campbell Soup Company launched a bold initiative to curb obesity in its hometown of Camden, New Jersey. It freed up staff to help design school menus and fresh produce displays for local stores. In addition, Campbell granted a food bank access to its production lines to turn spoiling perishable donations into 54,000 jars of peach salsa. Sales of the salsa raised $100,000 for the food bank.[10] Companies like Campbell, which was recognized in the inaugural Civic 50 in 2012 (see Table 13.2), contributed a remarkable amount of time and resources to improve the communities they serve. The top five companies alone provided $1.5 billion in grant support to community organizations, 17.5 million volunteer hours valued at over $375 million, and $150 million in matching donations.[11]

As part of its corporate volunteerism efforts, FedEx partners with nonprofit organization Direct Relief to deliver emergency medicine to disaster areas.

corporate volunteerism

The policy or practice of employees volunteering their time or talents for charitable, educational, or other worthwhile activities, especially in the community.

SUSTAINABLE MARKETING

LO 13-2

Explain how sustainable marketing contributes to a firm's corporate social responsibility efforts.

Today more than ever, marketers recognize that, beyond the moral and ethical implications, adopting sustainable strategies has become an essential element of a firm's CSR efforts and one that contributes to long-term competitive advantage. The concept of sustainability first came to international attention in the 1987 United Nations report *Our Common Future*. The report laid the groundwork for a modern understanding of sustainability as a commitment to adopting a lifestyle that meets the needs of the present without compromising the ability of future generations to meet their own needs.[12] Marketers looking to enhance the sustainability of their firm's goods and services need to form a partnership with customers, suppliers, and communities to increase the likelihood that the firm makes socially responsible marketing decisions.

Sustainable marketing is the process of creating, communicating, and delivering value to customers in a way that recognizes and incorporates the concept of sustainability. One of the easiest ways for marketers to engage in sustainable marketing is to seek ways to cut costs using sustainable practices as a guideline. Firms can choose from a wide range of strategies and ideas, from developing different packaging to using less energy. For example, General Mills is on a path to reduce its energy consumption by 20 percent by 2015 as a result of its sustainability initiatives.[13] The company made several sustainable business changes. It installed energy monitoring meters on several pieces

EXECUTIVE PERSPECTIVE

Gina Gomez
Executive Director
Hispanic Community Services, Inc.

What impact does corporate volunteerism have on a nonprofit organization?

We have so many great corporate volunteer partners that help us raise money and put together a number of events for the Hispanic Center. There is something very special about seeing volunteers putting in the time and effort to help nonprofit organizations in our community. I also think there is a benefit for the businesses, because I know that I try and support and purchase items from companies that I see volunteering to make our community better.

TABLE 13.2   The Top 20 Companies from the Civic 50 Rankings

1. IBM	11. Western Union
2. Citigroup	12. FedEx Corporation
3. AT&T Inc.	13. Allstate
4. Aetna	14. Microsoft
5. Capital One Financial Corporation	15. Bank of America
6. Morgan Stanley	16. Target Corp.
7. Campbell Soup Company	17. Intel Corporation
8. The McGraw-Hill Companies	18. UnitedHealth Group
9. General Electric	19. Abbott
10. Hasbro, Inc.	20. Southwest Airlines

Source: "The Civic 50," *Bloomberg Businessweek*, December 7, 2012, http://www.businessweek.com/articles/2012-12-07/the-civic-50.

sustainability

A commitment to adopting a lifestyle that meets the needs of the present without compromising the ability of future generations to meet their own needs.

sustainable marketing

The process of creating, communicating, and delivering value to customers in a way that recognizes and incorporates the concept of sustainability.

of equipment at its Covington, Georgia, plant that saved the company $600,000 in the first year.[14] These types of savings add up quickly, improving a firm's overall economic performance.

You may have owned a pair of Levi's jeans, but did you know that the company is very active in sustainable marketing? Marketers at Levi's were one of the first in the apparel industry to conduct a life cycle assessment of the firm's major products. Between when the cotton was grown in the fields and the end of the product's life, they found that manufacturing had the least impact on water and energy use. Meanwhile, growing the cotton used a great deal of water. With that knowledge in hand, Levi's joined a consortium of organizations known as the Better Cotton Initiative to teach an important stakeholder, farmers, how to grow cotton with less water. Today, each pair of Levi's jeans is made of about 5 percent of the low-water cotton. Levi's goal is to use a 20 percent blend of the new cotton in its products by 2015.[15]

Marketers at Levi's were one of the first in the apparel industry to conduct a life cycle assessment of the firm's major products to identify opportunities for improving sustainability.

Sustainability Vision

To get stakeholders to agree to sustainability initiatives, marketers must communicate a sustainability vision. That vision should highlight the importance of the organization's efforts and the potential benefits for each stakeholder. Having a vision of sustainability begins by communicating how the company's industry and specific organization work within the larger social and natural world. A sustainability vision should answer important questions: How is the world enriched or diminished by our goods or services? What is our major impact on society? How does our overall business strategy reflect that impact?[16]

As part of its sustainability efforts, Coca-Cola helped citizens of Montreal, Canada, harvest rainwater by donating 100 rain barrels to Regroupement des éco-quartiers, an educational program dedicated to the environment.

Sustainability Vision Statement Many organizations find it useful to articulate the answers to these questions through a sustainability vision statement. For example, DuPont's statement highlights the company's commitment to "creating shareholder and societal value, while reducing our footprint throughout the value chain."[17] PepsiCo's sustainability statement is to "continually improve all aspects of the world in which we operate—environmental, social, economic—creating a better tomorrow than today."[18] Both of these clearly articulate each company's sustainability mission. Not coincidentally, these firms are two of the leaders in sustainable marketing throughout the world.

The Benefits of a Sustainability Vision A sustainability vision can drive innovation within an organization. For example, Unilever PLC used the lens of sustainability as a way to design and produce new products, such as a hair conditioner that uses less water.[19] Without sustainable marketing, the company's research and development efforts may not have led to the product, which has been well received by consumers and helped to improve the firm's profit.

A commitment to sustainability also benefits employees. They tend to be engaged when they work for a company that expresses sustainability goals and holds itself accountable to its stakeholders. In addition, they believe they are part of something bigger than just their job or department. At Coca-Cola in Great Britain, for example, an appointed Green Team encourages employees to live more sustainably. Among other things, the group coordinates initiatives focused on reducing water usage in the workplace and discouraging activities that emit substantial amounts of carbon into the atmosphere. Shortly after starting the Green Team program, Coca-Cola was ranked as one of the top 30 great places to work in Britain by the Great Place To Work Institute.[20]

Consumerism

A new generation of consumers concerned with sustainability has begun to demand more from companies and marketers than just low prices. These consumers also seek a higher meaning in the products they purchase. Consumerism is a movement made up of citizens and government entities that focuses on protecting consumers and promoting their interests. The movement's activities include anti-consumption campaigns, such as those against drinking carbonated soft drinks or wearing fur coats, staged as a form of resistance to a commodity culture and corporate brands.[21] Marketers should be aware of the power of these campaigns and the potential harm they can do to their products and brands.

consumerism

A movement made up of citizens and government entities that focuses on protecting consumers and promoting their interests.

Consumerism also includes an effort on the part of consumers to avoid purchasing goods and services that have been produced in a way that is inconsistent with sustainable business practices.[22] Consumerism efforts increasingly occur both domestically and in international markets. Despite this trend, firms seeking to market sustainable products face roadblocks when it comes to reaching the larger population. Marketers face the following five major barriers to encouraging sustainable consumer behavior:[23]

1. *Lack of awareness and knowledge.* Many consumers don't know how to reduce the social and environmental impact of their purchasing behavior. Marketers can play an important role in overcoming this barrier. Advertising, websites, social media, and other tools can educate consumers about how they can make a difference by consuming the company's products over those of competitors. In addition to traditional advertisements, Pepsi used the power of social media sites to promote its "Performance with Purpose" strategy. The strategy focused on delivering sustainable products and investing in a healthy future for consumers and society as a whole.

2. *Negative perceptions.* Some consumers have negative perceptions of sustainable products. They tend to believe that, while the products might be produced in a more sustainable way, they are inferior in quality. To combat this barrier, firms must design and produce sustainable products of high quality. Equally important, they must use the various promotional tools at their disposal to communicate that quality to customers.

3. *Distrust.* Some consumers simply do not believe the sustainability claims made by marketers, and thus it is essential for marketers to promote their products in an honest and ethical manner. Walmart has promoted its sustainability focus heavily in recent years, but found itself in a difficult position when the government fined the company $81 million after it was discovered that Walmart employees improperly handled and disposed of hazardous materials at stores across the country.[24] A firm caught misleading consumers over sustainability claims could damage its reputation for years to come, reducing profit and hurting the firm's long-term viability.

4. *High prices.* Consumers also have come to believe that the cost of producing a sustainable product translates into higher prices. One of the earliest complaints customers had against hybrid and electric cars was the high cost associated with the purchase. Technological improvements and economies of scale as well as increasingly efficient supply chains gradually brought prices down. Beyond this, however, marketers used promotional tools to demonstrate how gas savings offset the high prices. Marketing environmentally friendly products can lead to higher prices due to the additional costs the firm incurs. In such cases, marketers must ensure that their customers understand the genesis of the high prices. If the firm can communicate the additional value the product offers, customers will be more willing to pay a high price for it.

5. *Low availability.* Consumers in small communities or developing parts of the world may have a hard time finding sustainable products to buy. The place element of the marketing mix becomes critical in overcoming this barrier. Marketing professionals must find ways to deliver products to the sustainability-minded customers who want to buy them.

A critical component of overcoming all of these barriers is communication. Marketers must effectively communicate that sustainable consumer behavior doesn't always require sacrificing current needs and wants for some distant benefit. As firms continue to develop sustainable goods and services that add value to consumers' lives, marketers must communicate this balance to consumers.

 Interactive Assignment 13-2

Please complete the *Connect* exercise for Chapter 13 that focuses on marketing strategies that promote sustainable consumer behavior. By understanding the major barriers to sustainable consumer behavior and how to overcome them, you should gain insight into how marketers can most effectively influence consumer decisions and support sustainable behaviors.

ENVIRONMENTAL MARKETING

Historically, customers bought products solely on the bases of price, performance, and convenience. Today, customers also care about a product's origins and how it is manufactured, packaged, and disposed of. Firms sometimes mistake these emerging concerns as the domain of younger generations. In reality, over half of all baby boomers consider themselves environmentally conscious shoppers.[25] That's 40 million customers who choose to buy resource-conserving products from the shelves and boycott the products of companies that pollute or engage in other activities that could damage the environment. These baby boomers represent a segment of the green market. The green market is a group of sustainability-oriented customers and the businesses that serve them.

More and more, marketers face scrutiny from the green market related to whether they conduct business in an environmentally responsible way. Environmentalism is a movement of citizens, government agencies, and the business community that advocates the preservation, restoration, and improvement of the environment. Its mission impacts firms large and small and cuts across numerous industries and geographic locations. For example, 96 percent of European consumers say that protecting the environment is important to them.[26] Increasingly,

LO 13-3

Explain the impact of environmentalism on marketing success.

green market

A group of sustainability-oriented customers and the businesses that serve them.

environmentalism

A movement of citizens, government agencies, and the business community that advocates the preservation, restoration, and improvement of the environment.

Kohl's is one of a number of companies recognized by the Environmental Protection Agency's Green Power Partnership for steps it's taken to power its stores and operations in an environmentally friendly way.

Chinese consumers purchase products based on concerns about climate change. In the U.S., 80 percent of customers claim to act on environmental concerns. In response to these trends, Walmart, the world's largest retailer, ran a global ad campaign designed to highlight its sustainability efforts and raise awareness about the environment and the product choices consumers could make. In addition, Walmart initiated a $30 million project, the first of its kind, focused on lifestyle and environmental improvements.[27] Walmart employees who chose to participate in the voluntary program learned in company-sponsored workshops about the benefits of carpooling to work, discontinuing cigarette smoking, and turning off the television. They also learned about the importance of embracing environmental sustainability, reducing carbon emissions, and consuming healthy and environmentally friendly (green) food. About 50 percent of Walmart's employees worldwide opted to participate in the program.[28]

The green market doesn't seek only environmentally friendly goods. Its members also want environmentally friendly services. Service providers ranging from doctors to electricians to universities have made efforts to protect the environment part of their service offering. Some utility companies now offer customers the opportunity to purchase their energy needs from wind, solar energy, and other renewable sources.[29]

Environmental Marketing Strategies

Environmental marketing (also called *green marketing*) activities can be divided into three levels: tactical greening, quasi-strategic greening, and strategic greening.[30]

tactical greening

A type of environmental marketing activity that involves implementing limited change within a single area of the organization.

quasi-strategic greening

A type of environmental marketing activity that involves substantive changes in marketing actions as well as broad-based coordination among non-marketing activities.

strategic greening

A type of environmental marketing activity that integrates and coordinates all of the firm's activities on environmental issues across every functional area.

1. Tactical greening involves implementing limited change within a single area of the organization, such as purchasing or advertising. Tactical activities represent relatively small actions aimed at instituting environmentally friendly practices within an organization. For example, JC Penney might decide to stop doing business with suppliers that do not meet the company's environmental or recycling requirements.

2. Quasi-strategic greening usually involves more substantive changes, for example, redesigning the firm's logo or overhauling a product's packaging, in marketing actions. Telecommunications provider Sprint engaged in quasi-strategic greening when it began using 100 percent recycled materials in all its branded packaging. In addition, it now uses soy inks and environmentally friendly adhesives and coatings. The new packaging is also 60 percent smaller in volume and 50 percent lighter in weight than the old packaging, which has saved Sprint money.[31]

3. Strategic greening requires a holistic approach that integrates and coordinates all of the firm's activities on environmental issues across every functional area. It represents a fundamental shift in the way the firm markets its products. For example, Nestlé has reformulated certain products to decrease their environmental impact without affecting their taste, nutrition, or consumer appeal. Beyond this, the company has begun training farmers on good environmental stewardship and funding scientific research into producing sustainable cocoa and coffee. Such moves contribute to Nestlé's bottom line in many ways; because of its research efforts, the company now harvests from trees that produce more than regular, existing trees.[32]

These three categories of marketing activities represent the various degrees to which a firm can adopt an environmental focus. The categories are governed by the overall environmental strategy a company chooses to implement. Figure 13.3 shows five types of environmental marketing strategies marketers can choose to

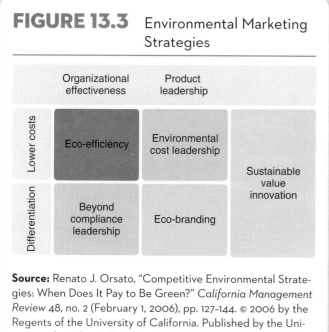

FIGURE 13.3   Environmental Marketing Strategies

	Organizational effectiveness	Product leadership	
Lower costs	Eco-efficiency	Environmental cost leadership	Sustainable value innovation
Differentiation	Beyond compliance leadership	Eco-branding	

Source: Renato J. Orsato, "Competitive Environmental Strategies: When Does It Pay to Be Green?" *California Management Review* 48, no. 2 (February 1, 2006), pp. 127–144. © 2006 by the Regents of the University of California. Published by the University of California Press.

implement, depending on their competitive advantage and the overall marketing strategy they have adopted.[33] Firms that emphasize differentiation and organizational effectiveness will pursue a different environmental marketing strategy than firms that want to lower costs but lead the market in terms of their good or service.

Each of the strategies is discussed in more detail in the sections that follow.

Strategy 1: Eco-Efficiency   Marketers seeking to reduce costs and the environmental impact of their activities typically pursue a strategy of eco-efficiency. This strategy involves identifying environmentally friendly practices that also have the effect of creating cost savings and driving efficiencies throughout the organization. Transportation companies like J.B. Hunt, for example, look for ways to increase fuel efficiency. Fuel efficiency both saves the firm money and decreases the environmental impact of the company's services.

Strategy 2: Beyond Compliance Leadership   Most marketers who adopt a beyond compliance leadership strategy focus on communicating to stakeholders the company's attempts to adopt environmentally friendly practices. Marketers who select this strategy want to show customers that the company does more than the competition to implement an environmental strategy. Unlike with an eco-efficiency strategy, companies that employ a beyond compliance leadership strategy typically care more about differentiating themselves from competitors than about keeping costs low. The Pepsi Refresh Project discussed earlier in this chapter provides an example of this strategy at work in the marketplace.

Strategy 3: Eco-Branding   An eco-branding strategy focuses on creating a credible green brand. For this strategy to be effective, consumers must recognize a noticeable benefit from their purchase. For example, the Chevy Volt electric car

To increase fuel efficiency, transportation companies like C.R. England have reconfigured their trucks by adding extenders from the cab to the trailer and side skirts that allow for easy air flow to decrease drag on the vehicle.

provides an immediate and sizeable savings on monthly gasoline purchases. The eco-branding strategy tends to succeed in industries in which significant barriers to imitation exist. To achieve differentiation as part of an eco-branding strategy, the environmental improvement, such as the technology involved in developing a desirable electric car, should be difficult to imitate.

Strategy 4: Environmental Cost Leadership

Firms seeking a price premium for their environmentally friendly products often adopt an environmental cost leadership strategy. Green products sometimes cost more to produce than traditional products. Thus a leadership strategy that also seeks to lower costs may be the only way for a company to pay for its ecological investments and generate a profit for its other stakeholders. Green and organic grocery stores, such as Whole Foods, have been able to demand a price premium for their products. This, in turn, has allowed these types of organizations to recover the additional costs of selling only fresh, organic products to consumers.

Strategy 5: Sustainable Value Innovation

A final strategy firms can pursue is sustainable value innovation. This strategy entails re-shaping the industry through the creation of differential value for consumers and through making contributions to society in the form of both reduced costs and reduced environmental impact. Firms that engage in this strategy do not aim to outperform the competition in an existing industry but to create a new market space. In doing so, they hope to make the competition irrelevant by giving the consumer more value per product at a lower price. Examples of this strategy in action include solar-tracking skylights designed to follow the sun and maximize daylight harvesting and walls built from straw, channel glass, and other energy-efficient materials.

Interactive Assignment 13-3

Please complete the *Connect* exercise for Chapter 13 that focuses on environmental marketing strategies. By understanding the types of strategies that might fit best with different products and market segments, you should be able to make better marketing strategy decisions for your organization.

Benefits of Environmental Marketing

The benefits of an environmental marketing strategy extend to virtually all of a firm's stakeholders when the strategy is effectively integrated with the firm's general marketing plan. For example, the online retail and auction site eBay makes it easy for people all over the world to exchange and reuse goods rather than throwing them away, thereby lengthening the life cycle of the products. The company also introduced an eBay Classifieds section that allows individuals to buy and sell used household appliances, furniture, and other hard-to-ship items within their local community. The Classifieds section eliminates the need for shipping and packaging and keeps functional items out of landfills. Such efforts have allowed eBay to help the environment while earning a significant profit and employing thousands of workers throughout the world.

With many consumers committed to "going green," environmentally focused organizations often benefit from favorable public opinion and loyal customers. Dell has received favorable feedback in response to its commitment to use 50 percent recycled paper for printed marketing materials. Through this commitment, Dell hopes to avoid using approximately 35,000 tons of virgin fiber annually.[34] In addition, Dell's office printers now default to double-sided printing. Finally, the company has initiated a modification of its packaging policy that is designed to cut the size of its product packaging and increase the amount of recycled content inside. All of these small marketing decisions add real value in the minds of environmentally conscious consumers and, ultimately, contribute favorably to the bottom line.

environmental regulations
The laws designed to protect the natural environment against undue harm by individuals and organizations.

Environmental Regulation

In addition to meeting consumer demand for green products, marketers must also consider new and changing environmental regulations. Environmental regulations are the laws designed to protect the natural environment against undue harm by individuals and organizations.[35] Regulations range from the 1972 Clean Water Act, which was designed to reduce industrial pollution in U.S. waters, to the Clean Air Act, which places limits on the emission of greenhouse gases. Such regulations, though they may limit firms in some regard, provide marketers with opportunities. For example, when the 1992 Energy Policy Act limited the amount of water showerheads could deliver, firms like Teledyne Technologies developed a new line of products, the Shower Massage showerheads. The showerheads met this standard and captured sales and profit for the firm.[36]

Dell hopes to reap the benefits of environmental marketing by implementing new environmentally friendly policies, such as using recyclable and rapidly renewable bamboo to package and protect certain products.

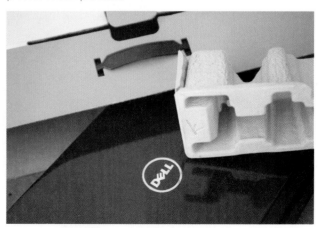

Describe the challenges
of environmental and
sustainable marketing on a
global scale.

GLOBAL ENVIRONMENTALISM AND SUSTAINABILITY

As globalization brings the world closer together, marketers must develop strategies that fit with expectations in both domestic and international markets. The strategic choice to become environmentally conscious and sustainable has proven to be profitable and a good public relations decision not just in the U.S. but across the globe. For example, the U.K. retailer Marks & Spencer spent $323 million over five years on sustainability strategies and then reported, just two years into implementing the initiatives, that its investment had already paid for itself.[37] In addition to saving on its energy costs, the company's initiative appealed to customers seeking to purchase more sustainable products.

Global Challenges and Opportunities

Management consulting firm McKinsey found that, of the nearly 2,000 executives it surveyed from around the world, 50 percent considered sustainability very or extremely important in new product development, reputation building, and overall corporate strategy.[38] However, implementing sustainability efforts on a global scale comes with its own unique set of challenges. Political barriers in some countries, including a lack of political will on the part of leaders to enact sustainability-focused legislation, can limit the availability of or increase prices on sustainable goods for consumers. Elections, changes in consumer sentiment, and other external factors can increase or decrease such political barriers. On the bright side, marketers who actively scan the global environment can find foreign governments and policies that provide new opportunities for marketing sustainable products to global customers. For example, a ban on incandescent light bulbs that took effect in the European Union made efficient lighting technologies, including compact fluorescent light bulbs (CFLs) and light-emitting diodes (LEDs), standard across Europe.[39] This political shift, driven by regulation and

To capitalize on the interest emerging economies show in sustainability, Vodafone markets its mobile technologies to farmers in rural areas of sub-Saharan Africa who use the technology to communicate easily with prospective buyers, thus boosting their income.

Kristina Myers

Director of Business Development
Jonesboro Regional Chamber of Commerce

Describe your job. I am responsible for communicating the numerous diverse marketing opportunities that are available to members of the Jonesboro Chamber of Commerce. I help to promote a unified business community through heavy relationship management with new or prospective members, as well as current members of the Chamber of Commerce. We are fortunate in this region to have a large number of very socially responsible firms who place a tremendous value on the work we are doing at the chamber to help our entire business community, and it is a privilege to get to work with them each day.

Describe how you got the job that you have. While attending college, I learned to come out of my shell and express my thoughts without worrying what people thought. During this process of becoming more extroverted, my efforts to network with others were noticed by one of my professors who, in time, asked me for my resume to pass on to potential employers. I received a phone call from the Chamber of Commerce and interviewed with the Chamber's president and vice president, one of whom was a customer of mine from a previous job and already knew my personality and work ethic. Shortly after my interview, I was offered the position.

What has been the most important thing in making you successful at your job? I would consider my ability to be empathetic and understanding to be the most important thing that has made me successful at my job. I have to put myself in others' positions to really understand what members of the Chamber of Commerce need from my organization, as well as the community. The ability to empathize with business owners and prospective newcomers to the community allows me to comprehend the marketing opportunities that would benefit them the most.

What advice would give soon-to-be graduates? First, and foremost, do not limit yourself because of fear. Be proud of all that you have accomplished and know that, through strong intrinsic motivation and determination, you can be successful! Also, the idea of continuous improvement is important to apply to not only your professional but your personal life as well. Reflect on your experiences and learn as much as you can from them.

What do you consider your personal brand to be? I am a supportive, professional relationship manager. I try to reinforce this brand in every action I take professionally and personally.

innovation, opened up new opportunities for marketers to sell green products to European consumers.

The divergence in how different geographic regions perceive sustainability also provides both challenges and opportunities for marketers. While a majority of global business executives believe that sustainability is of significant importance to their business, marketers should be aware of how the location of those executives affects their opinion. Breaking the numbers down further reveals that almost two-thirds of decision makers in emerging markets, such as India and South Africa, consider sustainability critical to business.[40] Meanwhile, just under a third of decision makers in Japan and a quarter in the largest European markets (Germany, France, and the United Kingdom) feel the same. In response to this divergence, many organizations that engage in sustainable marketing focus a disproportionate amount of their efforts on emerging economies, where they tend to find more supportive consumer and political environments.

Rationalizing Global Sustainability

The way marketers justify sustainable marketing varies in different parts of the world. For example, U.S. marketers rationalize sustainability strategies using economics or bottom-line terms and arguments, whereas companies owned by members of the European Union rely more heavily on language related to the idea of citizenship, corporate accountability, or moral commitment. While European companies do not value sustainability to the exclusion of financial elements, they instead project a commitment to sustainability in addition to their commitment to financial success. Regardless of the justification, sustainable and environmental strategies tend to work best when firms can maximize the benefits for all stakeholders concerned.

LO 13-5

Analyze how firms use social media to support their corporate social responsibility efforts.

THE IMPACT OF SOCIAL MEDIA ON CORPORATE SOCIAL RESPONSIBILITY

In the end, corporate social responsibility, sustainability, and environmentalism, whether they are implemented domestically or globally, are about communication. Marketing professionals who genuinely consider the impact of their business need to listen, consider what they hear, and respond appropriately to the widest group of stakeholders possible. Social media provide a means for communicating with an enthusiastic group of consumers. Social media allow people to organize, collaborate, and accomplish shared goals in ways that would have been unimaginable several decades ago. In response, companies have evolved from a reactive state, in which they responded to customer feedback about their CSR-related strategies, to a proactive approach, in which they make their CSR activities known to customers through the various online tools at their disposal. Social media play an increasingly important role in how companies shape their CSR policies and present themselves as good corporate citizens to consumers and other stakeholders.

Social Media–Based Corporate Social Responsibility Initiatives

To capitalize on the opportunity social media provide, marketers must be consistent in their social media presence and make each digital communication (tweet, Facebook post, etc.) something of value to their digital community. The companies leading the way in merging CSR and social media include some of the largest and most successful firms in the world, such as GE, IBM, and Target. IBM's Smarter Planet, for example, is a website devoted to communicating the firm's sustainability initiatives. It uses compelling storytelling that showcases its work in communities and cities around the world. Meanwhile, GE's Ecomagination Challenge is a $200 million experiment in which businesses, venture capital firms, entrepreneurs, innovators, and students develop clean energy ideas and submit them for funding.[41]

Target uses social media to further its long-standing commitment to schools and education. Target partnered with Search Institute, a nonprofit organization devoted to improving the lives of children, to develop the "Turn Summer Play into Summer Learning" series on its Facebook page. The campaign provided parents with fun weekly tips about how to keep their child's mind active during the summer as well as supporting research into how summer learning positively impacts child development.[42] The series illustrated Target's commitment to education and promoted the brand in a positive way to consumers. In addition, it allowed Target to connect with parents, including many current and future Target consumers.

Social Media and Global Sustainability

The global arena also provides a good opportunity for using social media to highlight and support CSR initiatives. Figure 13.4 illustrates the impact of social media on sustainability throughout the world. In Japan, for example, over 80 percent of firms use social media and digital technology tools to engage with customers on the sustainability of their goods and services.[43] The Global Sustainable Tourism Council (GSTC), a global coalition formed under the umbrella of the United Nations, made a significant commitment to social media in an effort to achieve its goal of promoting best practices in sustainable tourism around the world. Sustainable tourism is the practice of recreational traveling in a way that maximizes the social and economic benefits to the local community and minimizes the negative impact on cultural heritage and the environment. The GSTC's Facebook page and Twitter feed are filled with content and conversations related to sustainable travel in a range of countries, from Greece to Mexico to Argentina.

sustainable tourism
The practice of recreational traveling in a way that maximizes the social and economic benefits to the local community and minimizes the negative impact on cultural heritage and the environment.

GE uses a number of social media tools, including a blog and a Facebook page, to list the hundreds of ideas that have been submitted as part of its Ecomagination Challenge campaign.

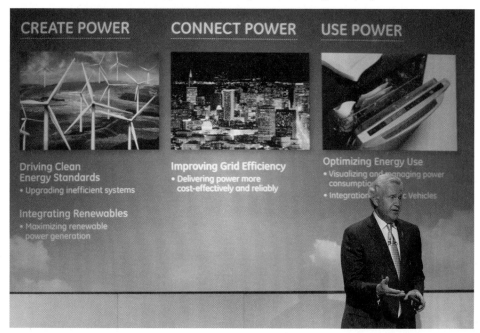

FIGURE 13.4   Percentage of Global Companies Using Social Media in Their Sustainability Efforts

To what extent are you using social media and digital technology to directly engage with your customers on the sustainability of your products?

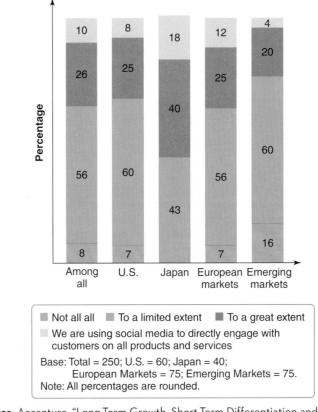

Percentage

Among all	U.S.	Japan	European markets	Emerging markets
10	8	18	12	4
26	25	40	25	20
56	60	43	56	60
8	7		7	16

■ Not all all   ■ To a limited extent   ■ To a great extent
☐ We are using social media to directly engage with customers on all products and services

Base: Total = 250; U.S. = 60; Japan = 40;
          European Markets = 75; Emerging Markets = 75.
Note: All percentages are rounded.

Source: Accenture, "Long-Term Growth, Short-Term Differentiation and Profits from Sustainable Products and Services," 2012, p. 9, http://www.accenture.com/SiteCollectionDocuments/PDF/Accenture-Long-Term-Growth-Short-Term-Differentiation-and-Profits-from-Sustainable-Products-and-Services.pdf. Copyright © 2012 Accenture. All rights reserved.

Whether focused on the domestic or the global marketplace, the central tenets of social media—transparency, authenticity, and engaging with the community to build a strong and profitable organization—reflect the same strengths that make corporate social responsibility and sustainability such compelling business philosophies. Marketing professionals at all types of firms, from Fortune 500 companies to local small businesses, recognize that social media can serve as valuable tools in the effort to create, communicate, and deliver sustainable products and solutions to their stakeholders.

McGraw Hill Education connect |MARKETING   **Interactive Assignment 13-4**

Social Media in Action

More and more firms turn to social media to convince potential customers that the organization operates in a socially responsible manner. This marketing action is in direct response to the growing number of consumers who say that what a company stands for affects what they buy. Panera Bread, a national restaurant chain, used social media platforms to promote its marketing campaign "Live consciously. Eat deliciously." Panera allowed some of its fans to preview the campaign several days before the general public. By interacting with consumers and spreading its message through social media, Panera's marketers advanced their goal of being an important part of the communities in which they operate.

Well-established companies that have been in business for decades increasingly use social media to promote their CSR initiatives. For example, Bumble Bee Foods (founded in 1899) replaced much of its traditional promotional tools (e.g., television, radio, print advertising) with social media to promote its CSR theme "BeeWell for Life®." Bumble Bee Foods marketers used social media tools such as Facebook and blogs to engage consumers in their CSR activities in a more meaningful way.

The Social Media in Action *Connect* exercise in Chapter 13 will let you develop specific social media strategies to promote the corporate social responsibility initiatives of an organization. By understanding the benefits and tools of different social media platforms, you will be able to spread the CSR activities of your organization and connect to consumers who pay attention to what a company stands for.

Source: See Stuart Elliott, "Selling Products by Selling Shared Values," *The New York Times*, February 13, 2013, http://www.nytimes.com/2013/02/14/business/media/panera-to-advertise-its-social-consciousness-advertising.html?pagewanted=all&_r=0.

SUMMARY

LEARNSMART™ ADVANTAGE

 LO 13-1 Describe the features of a successful corporate social responsibility program.

Corporate social responsibility (CSR) refers to an organization's obligation to maximize its positive impact and minimize its negative impact on society. Communities, investors, employees, and other stakeholders demand that firms take a proactive stance in terms of social responsibility. Stakeholder responsibility focuses on the obligations an organization has to those who can affect achievement of its objectives. It is the driving consideration across the four dimensions of corporate social responsibility: economic, legal, ethical, and philanthropic. There are several key elements to developing a successful CSR program, including good stakeholder management, good corporate leadership, and the integration of CSR into corporate policy at all levels of the organization.

 LO 13-2 Explain how sustainable marketing contributes to a firm's corporate social responsibility efforts.

Sustainability refers to pursuing a lifestyle that meets the needs of the present without compromising the ability of future generations to meet their own needs. Sustainable marketing is the process of creating, communicating, and delivering value to customers in a way that recognizes and incorporates the concept of sustainability. One of the easiest ways for marketers to engage in sustainability is to use it as a guideline for cutting costs, for example, by developing different packaging or using less energy.

 LO 13-3 Explain the impact of environmentalism on marketing success.

Environmentalism is a movement of citizens, government agencies, and the business community that advocates the preservation, restoration, and improvement of the environment. Environmental marketing activities can be divided into three categories: tactical greening, quasi-strategic greening, and strategic greening. Tactical greening involves implementing limited change within a single area of the organization. Quasi-strategic greening usually involves more substantive changes in marketing activities by various functional areas. Strategic greening integrates and coordinates the environmental initiatives of a firm with all actions across every functional area. Firms may choose which category of activities to pursue based on their environmental marketing strategy. Environmental strategies include eco-efficiency, beyond compliance leadership, environmental cost leadership, and sustainable value innovation.

 LO 13-4 Describe the challenges of environmental and sustainable marketing on a global scale.

Marketers at an increasing number of firms look to promote their sustainability efforts and to preserve and replenish the natural environment throughout the world. However, a lack of political will on the part of leaders in some countries to enact sustainability-focused legislation presents challenges to firms that may result in the reduced availability of sustainable products and high prices. The way marketers justify sustainable marketing also varies in different parts of the world. U.S. marketers justify sustainability strategies using economic arguments, whereas European Union companies rely more heavily on language focused on citizenship, corporate accountability, or moral commitment.

 LO 13-5 Analyze how firms use social media to support their corporate social responsibility efforts.

Corporate social responsibility, sustainability, and environmentalism are about communication. Marketers who genuinely consider the impact of their activities need to listen, consider, and respond to the widest group of stakeholders possible. To capitalize on the opportunity social media present, marketers should be consistent in their social media presence. In addition, they should make each digital communication something of value that holds meaning for their digital community. Regardless of the industry, the central tenets of a social media philosophy—transparency, authenticity, and learning from the community to build a stronger and more profitable organization—are the same strengths that make corporate social responsibility and sustainability such compelling business philosophies.

KEY TERMS

consumerism (p. 377)
corporate philanthropy (p. 373)
corporate social responsibility (CSR) (p. 370)
corporate volunteerism (p. 375)
environmentalism (p. 379)

environmental regulations (p. 383)
ethics (p. 372)
green market (p. 379)
quasi-strategic greening (p. 380)
stakeholder responsibility (p. 370)
strategic greening (p. 380)

sustainability (p. 376)
sustainable marketing (p. 376)
sustainable tourism (p. 387)
tactical greening (p. 380)

MARKETING PLAN EXERCISE

In this chapter, we have explored the impact corporate social responsibility has on organizations and marketing decisions. As part of developing your personal marketing plan, you will consider and develop a vision of your own social responsibilities. First you must understand who you're responsible to. Who are the stakeholders in your career success? Your list might include those who are impacted by your career path, including a current or future spouse, children, parents, or even the U.S. government that wants you to make enough money to pay back your student loans.

Also think about places of worship, charitable causes, communities, and other entities your choices affect.

Next, consider whether a firm or school's corporate social responsibility policies matter to you when choosing where to work or study. If they do, you should think about how you can best market yourself as the type of socially responsible professional that would be of interest to a company or school committed to corporate social responsibility. Being able to connect your socially responsible activities to those of a potential employer or graduate school program can be a subtle way to differentiate yourself from those competing against you for a position.

Your Task: List the stakeholders in your career success. Next, list three to five social responsibilities that you consider part of your professional career, explain each, and discuss the specific actions you would like to take relative to each over the next 5–10 years.

DISCUSSION QUESTIONS

1. Identify a Fortune 500 company that you think is socially responsible. Why do you think this way about the company? Does your opinion impact your decision to purchase from the company? Are you willing to pay more to buy from a socially responsible firm? Why or why not?
2. Imagine that you were put in charge of marketing at a small business in your hometown. What CSR or sustainability strategies would you consider for that business? Why did you select these strategies?
3. What is the social responsibility of colleges and universities in the United States? Using the ethical decision-making framework, analyze a hypothetical decision your college or university made to raise tuition 10 percent next year. Use each of the elements of the framework in your analysis. How would you, as a marketer for your university, present the reasons for the tuition increase to your stakeholders (students, legislators, communities, etc.)?
4. Which of the five barriers to sustainable consumer behavior discussed in this chapter most prevents you from engaging in more sustainable consumer behavior? Do you think your answer will be different in 25 years?
5. Provide two examples of organizations that use social media as part of their corporate social responsibility actions. What do they do well through social media? What would you suggest they improve? Based on your experience as a consumer, what social media outlet is most effective for communicating a firm's CSR efforts (e.g., Twitter, Facebook, YouTube, etc.)? Why?

SOCIAL MEDIA APPLICATION

Pick a for-profit firm that you have bought something from in the past month and a non-profit organization to which you might consider donating money (a charity, church, hospital, etc.). Analyze the social media presence of both organizations across all of the platforms that they employ using the following questions and activities as a guide:

1. What does the for-profit company do on social media to promote its corporate social responsibility activities? Is it enough to influence you to become a customer of the firm? Explain your answer.
2. What does the nonprofit organization do across its social media platforms to inform potential donors about its cause? Is it enough to influence your decision to donate to the organization? Explain your answer.
3. If you were the marketing manager for both organizations, what two specific things would you recommend each do to improve their social media efforts?

ETHICAL CHALLENGE

One of the most complex ethical challenges facing for-profit organizations today is balancing their goal of being socially responsible with their obligation to shareholders to earn a profit. Firms generally hire executives to increase profits. No matter how much good a firm does in its community, if it doesn't have a healthy bottom line, the executive may not be seen as a success. This is not unlike a college football coach who makes sure his players graduate every year, but consistently has a losing record. Odds are he won't remain the coach very long, even though he does a number of socially responsible things.

While executives at privately held companies have the right to make socially responsible decisions that might sacrifice revenue, executives at publicly held companies have to answer to their shareholders who expect firm profits and share prices to grow. Marketing executives at public companies frequently face situations that force them to choose between responsible action and the bottom line. Please use the ethical decision-making framework to answer the following questions:

1. Assume you are a shareholder in a publicly traded retail firm. Would you want that firm to raise pay rates for its employees to stay on pace with the inflation rate even if doing so would drive product prices up and profit margins down? Explain your answer.

2. Assume you are a shareholder for a manufacturing company in a small town far from your home. Would you be willing to trade polluting the environment in that one town for an increase in firm profits? Explain your answer. If the CEO of the company decided not to pollute the environment and profits decreased as a result, how should the firm market that decision to you and other stakeholders?

3. Assume you are a shareholder in a publicly traded beverage company. Would you support the company's plan to advertise to children even if its beverage is unhealthy for children? Explain your answer.

VIDEO CASE

Please go to *Connect* to access the video case featuring Williams, a Fortune 500 energy company, that accompanies this chapter.

McGraw Hill Education **connect** | MARKETING

CAREER TIPS
Marketing Your Future

You have read in this chapter about the important role corporate social responsibility plays in a firm's ultimate success. As you begin your career, few things will be as important as picking a successful organization to work for. Choosing an employer that stresses CSR as well as financial gain can get your career off to a great start through training, experience, and networking. Author C. Shane Hunt has seen too many students make poor career decisions because they decide to take their first job out of school simply on the basis of money rather than the potential for career growth and success. In an effort to help you choose the right company to work for after graduation, he offers the following four career tips:

1. *Research the best companies to work for.* There are all kinds of lists out there ranking the best companies to work for in different industries (see the Civic 50 rankings earlier in the chapter for an example). These lists can be great resources for helping you understand how the company ranks on corporate social responsibility, salary, benefits, advancement opportunities, and other important factors.

2. *Talk to employees of the organization.* This can be especially valuable if you are going to work for a small organization that may not be included in national rankings. Try to talk to current or former employees of the organization. This gives you an understanding of how your day-to-day life with the organization might be as well as how working there can help (or possibly hurt) you in your career going forward.

3. *Ask good questions.* Once you get to the interview stage, almost all employers will tell you that they promote employees from within. Ask them in an interview to give an example of someone that they have promoted from within. If they struggle to think of a specific example, they may not be as dedicated to the practice as they would have you believe.

4. *Understand the different benefit packages.* This is incredibly important and, unfortunately, something that many new graduates overlook. Check to see how much your health insurance benefits will cost with the organization. How does that compare to other places that you might work? If a company offers you $5,000 more per year in salary than another company, but you're going to have to pay $600 more per month (or $7,200 per year) for health benefits, the trade-off may not be worth it. Similarly, if you go to work for a company that provides a 6 percent matching contribution to your 401(k), that translates to an extra $3,000 per year if you make $50,000 a year, which you should take into account as you evaluate opportunities. Compare the retirement plans of organizations you might work for to make sure you are getting your financial future off to the best possible start.

CHAPTER NOTES

1. Sankar Sen and C. B. Bhattacharya, "Does Doing Good Always Lead to Doing Better? Consumer Reactions to Corporate Social Responsibility," *Journal of Marketing Research* 38, no. 2 (2001), pp. 225–244.

2. Dennis Jacobe, "In U.S., 54% Have Stock Market Investments, Lowest Since 1999," *Gallup*, April 20, 2011, http://www.gallup.com/poll/147206/stock-market-investments-lowest-1999.aspx.

3. Claire Grinton, "Pepsi's Refresh Everything vs. Coke's Live Positively: Which Soda Wins the War?" *Huffington Post*, April 19, 2010, http://www.huffingtonpost.com/2010/02/17/pepsis-refresh-everything_n_464712.html.

4. R. Morimoto et al., "Corporate Social Responsibility Audit: From Theory to Practice," *Journal of Business Ethics* 62, no. 4 (2005), pp. 315–325.

5. C. Kennedy, "The Great and the Good," *Director* 61, no. 3 (2007), pp. 102–106.

6. Morimoto et al., "Corporate Social Responsibility Audit: From Theory to Practice."

7. C. B. Bhattacharya, "Corporate Social Responsibility: It's All About Marketing," *Forbes*, November 20, 2009, http://www.forbes.com/2009/11/20/corporate-social-responsibility-leadership-citizenship-marketing.html.

8. "The Civic 50," *Bloomberg Businessweek*, December 7, 2012, http://www.businessweek.com/articles/2012-12-07/the-civic-50.

9. Diane Brady, "Volunteerism as a Core Competency," *Bloomberg Businessweek*, November 8, 2012, http://www.businessweek.com/articles/2012-11-08/volunteerism-as-a-core-competency.

10. Ibid.

11. Mei Cobb, "Corporate Volunteering: The Civic 50," *United Way*, March 15, 2013, http://www.unitedway.org/blog/entry/corporate-volunteering-the-civic-50/.

12. United Nations, "Report of the World Commission on Environment and Development: Our Common Future," 1987, p. 16, http://www.un-documents.net/our-common-future.pdf.

13. General Mills, "Environmental Sustainability: Energy," n.d., http://www.generalmills.com/~/media/Files/sustainability/GM_energy.ashx.

14. James Epstein Reeves, "Six Reasons Companies Should Embrace CSR," *Forbes*, February 21, 2012, http://www.forbes.com/sites/csr/2012/02/21/six-reasons-companies-should-embrace-csr/.

15. Susan Berfield, "Levis Goes Green with Waste‹Less Jeans," *Bloomberg Businessweek*, October 18, 2012, http://www.businessweek.com/articles/2012-10-18/levis-goes-green-with-waste-less-jeans.

16. Andrew Savitz, *The Triple Bottom Line: How Today's Best-Run Companies Are Achieving Economic, Social and Environmental Success—And How You Can Too* (San Francisco: Jossey-Bass, 2006).

17. DuPont, "2012 Sustainability Progress Report," http://www2.dupont.com/inclusive-innovations/en-us/sites/default/files/DuPont%20Sustainability%20Report%2012%20111612.pdf.

18. PepsiCo, "Global Sustainable Agriculture Policy," January 2009, http://www.pepsico.com/Download/PEP_Global_SAG_Policy_FINAL_Jan_2009.pdf.

19. Reeves, "Six Reasons Companies Should Embrace CSR."

20. Coca-Cola Great Britain, "Employment: Our People," n.d., http://www.coca-cola.co.uk/about-us/employment-our-people.html.

21. Diane Martin and John Schouten, *Sustainable Marketing* (Upper Saddle River, NJ: Pearson, 2012).

22. Ibid.

23. Ibid.

24. Tiffany Hsu, "Wal-Mart Pleads Guilty in Hazardous Waste Cases, to Pay $81 Million," *Los Angeles Times*, May 28,

2013, http://articles.latimes.com/2013/may/28/business/la-fi-mo-walmart-guilty-hazardous-waste-20130528.

25. Jacquelyn A. Ottman, *The New Rules of Green Marketing: Strategies, Tools, and Inspiration for Sustainable Branding* (Sheffield, UK: Greenleaf Publishing, 2011).

26. European Commission, "Attitudes of European Citizens towards the Environment," March 2008, p. 3, http://ec.europa.eu/environment/archives/barometer/pdf/summary2008_environment_en.pdf.

27. Jennifer Blackhurst and David Cantor, "Developing Sustainable Supply Chains: An Organizational and Supply Chain Employee View," *Center for Industrial Research and Service*, July 2012, http://www.ciras.iastate.edu/publications/Sustainable_Supply_Chains-Employee_View.pdf.

28. Michael Barbaro, "At Wal-Mart, Lessons in Self-Help," *The New York Times*, April 5, 2007, http://www.nytimes.com/2007/04/05/business/05improve.html?pagewanted=all.

29. Martin and Schouten, *Sustainable Marketing*.

30. M. J. Polonsky and P. J. Rosenberger, III, "Reevaluating Green Marketing: Strategic Approach," *Business Horizons*, 9–10 (2001), pp. 21–30.

31. Sprint, "White Paper: Sprint Improved Packaging Sustainability 55 Percent in Three Years," *The New York Times*, May 8, 2013, http://markets.on.nytimes.com/research/stocks/news/press_release.asp?docTag=201305081030BIZWIRE_USPRX__BW6064&feedID=600&press_symbol=109153.

32. Nestlé, "Nestlé and Sustainable Cocoa and Coffee," September 26, 2012, http://www.nestle.com/csv/case-studies/AllCaseStudies/Nestl%C3%A9-sustainable-cocoa-coffee.

33. Renato J. Orsato, "Competitive Environmental Strategies: When Does It Pay to Be Green?" *California Management Review* 48, no. 2 (2006), pp. 127–144.

34. Dell Press Release, "Dell Joins Prince's Rainforest Project," June 5, 2009, http://www.dell.com/learn/us/en/uscorp1/press-releases/DELLJOINSTHEPRINCESRAINFORESTSPROJECT?c=us&l=en&s=corp.

35. Martin and Schouten, *Sustainable Marketing*.

36. Ibid.

37. Julian Evans, "Good Intentions," *The Wall Street Journal*, February 3, 2010, http://online.wsj.com/article/SB10001424052748704878904575031330905332468.html.

38. Michael Adams, Barry Thornton, and Mohammad Sepehri, "The Impact of the Pursuit of Sustainability on the Financial Performance of the Firm," *Journal of Sustainability and Green Business* 1 (April 2012), pp. 1–14.

39. Eoin O'Carroll, "EU Bans Incandescent Light Bulbs," *Christian Science Monitor*, October 15, 2008, http://www.csmonitor.com/Environment/Bright-Green/2008/1015/eu-bans-incandescent-light-bulbs.

40. Accenture, "Long-Term Growth, Short-Term Differentiation and Profits from Sustainable Products and Services: A Global Survey of Business Executives," 2012, http://www.accenture.com/SiteCollectionDocuments/PDF/Accenture-Long-Term-Growth-Short-Term-Differentiation-and-Profits-from-Susvtainable-Products-and-Services.pdf.

41. Martin Lamonica, "GE, VCs Offer $200 Million in Smart-Grid Challenge," July 13, 2010, http://news.cnet.com/8301-11128_3-20010378-54.html.

42. Tamara Gillis, ed., *The IABC Handbook of Organizational Communication* (San Francisco: John Wiley and Sons, 2011), p. 77.

43. Accenture, "Long-Term Growth, Short-Term Differentiation and Profits from Sustainable Products and Services."

Chapter 14

MEASURING MARKETING PERFORMANCE

LEARNING OBJECTIVES

After reading this chapter, you should be able to

LO 14-1 Implement the key marketing performance metrics.

LO 14-2 Explain the importance of analyzing the performance of each marketing mix element.

LO 14-3 Discuss best practices for motivating and compensating marketing employees.

LO 14-4 Describe the barriers to implementing change in an organization.

EXECUTIVE PERSPECTIVE

Dean Lee
Athletic Director
Arkansas State University

Few areas are as steeped in the idea of performance metrics as athletics. Both fans and participants live by statistics and what those statistics convey about the player, the team, and the game. Dr. Dean Lee, athletic director at Arkansas State University, has been involved with performance metrics, both setting them and meeting them, since his undergraduate days as a physical education major. Lee began coaching immediately after graduating from college. As an athletic director at Arkansas State University, he manages 16 sports, 325 student-athletes, and a staff of 85 people. Every day is different, and the job requires him, at times, to be a salesman, a counselor, a fundraiser, an event manager, a referee, a judge, a father figure, an entertainer, a cheerleader, and an accountant. His success is measured not only by the performance of the teams under his management but also in attendance records and fundraising goals. Measuring his teams and himself against metrics gives him the opportunity to celebrate successes as well as learn from failures.

What has been the most important thing in making you successful at your job?

Hard work. I have always tried to never let anybody out-work me. I was born on a dairy farm and was the son of a bricklayer, so hard work was all I knew. Whatever commitment it took, that was the effort I was going to put forth. I was always one to hang around and pitch in with whatever needed to be done. Additionally, I have been fortunate to develop a host of friends in the industry. Through the years, these relationships have provided a strong network. My friends have served as my advisors, providing wise counsel in the field of athletics, and played a big part in how I operate and manage during difficult times. My marketing and sales experience has been beneficial to the athletic department's ability to sell tickets, fundraise, and obtain sponsorship.

What advice would you give soon-to-be graduates?

Jump head first into something you like. Get involved and give it your all. Get as much experience as possible whenever possible. Consider every opportunity a growing experience. Realize that your job is not a popularity contest. When you have tough decisions to make, make them with the best interest of the organization in mind. Whatever you do, always strive to do it the right way.

How is marketing relevant to your role at Arkansas State University?

I make decisions about advertising, ticket pricing, sponsorships, and logistical issues on a consistent basis. Athletics can be a great way to promote the university as a whole. Promoting our athletic programs brings positive attention to the entire campus.

What do you consider your personal brand to be?

Determined, committed, visionary, honest, innovative, and big-picture oriented.

Dean Lee
Athletic Director

Arkansas State University
http://www.astate.edu/

Arkansas State University is a public institution of higher education that enrolls over 20,000 students as part of the Arkansas State University system. As a teaching, research, and service institution, the university seeks to provide students with a broad educational foundation. The university's athletics program supports 16 NCAA-level sports.

FORECAST

This chapter explores the importance of measuring marketing performance. Marketers face an uncertain and rapidly changing environment that can render a good idea irrelevant in a short period of time. To make the best possible strategic decisions, you must be able to use the tools discussed in this chapter to analyze the effect of the different marketing mix elements on your organization's revenue, market share, and profitability. Once problems have been identified, you and your colleagues have a responsibility to make the necessary strategic changes to set the organization on a new course for success.

1. What performance metrics do marketers utilize?

2. How do I measure the success of each element of the marketing mix?

3. What are the best ways to compensate marketing employees?

4. What barriers am I most likely to face when trying to implement change in my organization?

LO 14-1

Implement the key marketing performance metrics.

THE IMPORTANCE OF MEASUREMENT

One thing you can be sure of as you finish this course and embark on your career is that, somewhere along the way, you will make a mistake. As a marketer, you might choose an advertising strategy that doesn't reach the targeted consumer or a pricing plan that is too high to gain market share. If you are a financial advisor, you might choose an investment that ends up losing your clients money. Whatever the mistake, the key to successfully overcoming it is, first, realizing that you made a mistake at all and, second, understanding specifically what that mistake was. Organizations and individuals who fail to recognize that they've made a mistake are doomed to repeat that mistake over and over again.

Building a great organization depends on the firm's ability to focus on the controls section of the marketing plan and measure and evaluate the success of its marketing strategy. Though success can take many forms, for both for-profit and nonprofit organizations, efficiency in financial matters often determines whether the organization survives. Effective metrics that measure the financial viability of a firm's marketing strategy provide a roadmap to guide the direction the company should take to ensure its survival. Performance metrics are measures that assist in ascertaining the extent to which objectives have been attained. We will discuss many specific measurement tools in this chapter, but let's begin with the five general principles you will want to follow as you implement marketing performance metrics.

performance metrics

Measures that assist in ascertaining the extent to which objectives have been attained.

1. *Know Your Business.* Before you measure anything, you need to understand your company's marketing strategy and objectives. Performance metrics at Southwest Airlines will differ substantially from those at Campbell Soup Company. Southwest's metrics may focus on customer service and measure flight delays and lost luggage, while Campbell is more likely to be concerned with production- and inventory-related measures. Marketers must develop metrics with their organization's revenue and profitability goals and mission statement in mind.

2. *Measure What You Can Modify.* When developing metrics, focus on what can actually be changed as a result of what you find. For example, if you are responsible for developing an online ad for a specific product, measure the click-through rate and modify the ad as necessary. However, if your company's tagline, brand mark, or pricing strategy fall outside your control, it may not make sense for you to spend a lot of time measuring their effectiveness.

Successfully measuring the efficacy of a firm's marketing strategy begins with understanding the business. Success looks very different if you work for John Deere or Major League Baseball.

3. ***Don't Cut Corners.*** Think through what needs to be measured and dedicate the resources to measuring it accurately. Once you start cutting corners, perhaps by not taking the time to collect enough data, your company will start to question your metrics and your conclusions based on them. For example, if you work in the restaurant industry, asking three people at a restaurant about a menu item does not give you enough data to determine whether you should eliminate the item. For fully accurate results, you need to provide segmented data that is broken down into actionable detail. It is not enough to supply data about how much a web page has been accessed or how many times an advertisement ran on television. To truly impact the company's performance, you will need to provide data about which customers are using the page or seeing the ad. From there, the company can determine whether it's reaching its target market and link the results to performance in other areas of the organization.

4. ***Make It Clear.*** Measurement reports tend to be lengthy. Make every effort to simplify and clarify the main point of your report. Be sure to present the metrics that actually measure business outcomes and improve marketing performance and profitability, rather than metrics that just sound good or support the results the company may have been hoping to achieve. Marketers should present their findings in a way that prioritizes the most important results (e.g., customers don't like the taste of the new chicken item on the menu) and make sure they clearly share the strongest conclusions derived from the metrics with the decision makers (e.g., the firm needs to develop a better chicken product to compete).

5. ***Start Measuring as Soon as Possible.*** Most companies do not begin measuring outcomes early enough in the product's life cycle, and they pay for it later. Even if the firm doesn't use the data right away, it will become invaluable down the road when marketers attempt to analyze and modify the marketing strategies. Information can be stored in anything from a marketing database to a simple spreadsheet hosted on a shared drive for a small business. The most important thing is to build the data history as early as possible.

With an understanding of these five principles, marketing professionals can begin to evaluate the various types of performance metrics available to them and identify those that will provide the most relevant and appropriate data to support their marketing efforts.

Marketing Return on Investment

Marketing represents one of the biggest expenditures for most organizations. More than ever, organizations calculate marketing return on investment to ensure that their expenditures produce results. Marketing return on investment (ROI) is a measure of the firm's effectiveness in using the resources allocated to its marketing effort. Marketing ROI is calculated as follows:

$$\text{marketing ROI} = \left(\text{sales} \times \text{gross margin \%} - \text{marketing expenditures} \right) \div \text{marketing expenditures}$$

In the calculation, sales include all of the revenue generated by core and non-core business activities. Gross margin equals the difference between price and cost and is calculated by subtracting the cost of goods sold per unit from the selling price of the item. For example, let's suppose that Best Buy sells flat-screen televisions for $1,000 and has a cost of goods sold of $500 per TV. Using the gross margin calculation, Best Buy generates a gross margin of 50 percent on each TV. Marketing expenditures is the amount of money spent on all marketing activities during a specified period of time. Continuing with our Best Buy example, assume that the company has sales of $200,000 and total marketing expenditures of $70,000. Given all of this information, we can calculate the marketing ROI as follows:

$$\text{marketing ROI} = (\$200,000 \times 0.50\% - \$70,000) \div \$70,000$$
$$= \$30,000 \div \$70,000$$
$$= 42.9\%$$

The marketing ROI in this scenario is 42.9 percent, which is a good number for most industries. It means that Best Buy has put its marketing resources to good use. Marketing ROI tells only part of the story, however. Companies often need to undertake further analysis to measure the success of specific aspects of their marketing strategy. We'll discuss three of these—revenue analysis, market share analysis, and profitability analysis—in the sections that follow.

Revenue Analysis

Firms that only look at marketing ROI may fall into the common trap of thinking all is well. In fact, it may be that one successful product line has masked failures in other parts of the company. Quantifying the sources of revenue can yield a wealth of information, which results in a more targeted and more efficient deployment of resources than the firm had been pursuing, ultimately increasing marketing ROI. Revenue analysis measures and evaluates actual revenue relative to the objectives of the organization. Using this measure, marketers analyze the success of specific products and regions to pinpoint what is working and what is not. For example, Target might see from its revenue analysis that a new line of women's clothing is meeting the firm's objectives at midwestern stores but falling short of objectives in the Southeast. This type of information can help Target's marketers as they select what merchandise to sell at each of their stores and how to allocate promotional resources.

Revenue Analysis in For-Profit Firms

Analyzing revenue is critical to both for-profit and nonprofit organizations. For-profit firms generally focus their revenue analysis on whether the firm is meeting sales objectives. They typically break sales down into the following three different revenue sources:

1. **Continuing sales to established customers.** Analyzing this measure helps marketing professionals determine if existing products have gained or lost ground in established markets. For example, McDonald's closely monitors the growth of stores that have been open more than 13 months in both the

---

marketing return on investment (ROI)

A measure of the firm's effectiveness in using the resources allocated to its marketing effort.

gross margin

The difference between price and cost.

marketing expenditures

The amount of money spent on all marketing activities during a specified period of time.

revenue analysis

A measure of actual revenue relative to the objectives of the organization.

U.S. and internationally. Even if the company's overall revenue increases, marketers at McDonald's have cause to become concerned if numbers at established stores remain flat or decrease. It could mean the company is losing members of its core target market.

2. *New sales from expanding markets.* Total revenue may increase for McDonald's even if sales at established stores haven't if the firm has continued to expand and open new stores at home and overseas. But the revenue associated with this growth should be analyzed in a different light than same-store sales. Doing so allows McDonald's to make necessary changes to improve revenue at its existing stores. Companies that don't understand the true source of their revenue growth can be lulled into a sense of complacency. Once their market matures and expansion, and the revenue related to it, slows, they're left unprepared. Beyond this, understanding how new sales contribute to overall revenue allows marketers to evaluate their expansion efforts and may highlight additional expansion opportunities.

3. *Entirely new lines of business unrelated to the core.* PepsiCo's revenue for much of the past two decades trended higher than the revenue generated by its beverage products because of its large restaurant conglomerate, which included Pizza Hut, KFC, and Taco Bell. Such unrelated businesses can be profitable for a firm, but their revenue should be viewed through a different lens than the firm's core business. Analysis may reveal that they should be eliminated, as PepsiCo did with its restaurant assets, if they direct focus away from core activities.

Based on revenue analysis, PepsiCo made a strategic decision to divest itself of its restaurant assets, and the revenue those assets generated, to focus on its core beverage business.

Revenue Analysis in Nonprofit Firms For nonprofit firms, revenue analysis typically focuses on the money raised by the organization. While many new revenue streams might be accessible, the organization should constrain its pursuit of new revenue by its ability to establish a plan, execute the plan, and survive to see what return the plan yields. Similar to for-profit firms, nonprofit organizations should seek to understand the funding source of their revenue. A nonprofit organization like the American Heart Association might see that its "Jump Rope for Heart" fundraising program, which encourages school children to raise money by jumping rope, is meeting objectives in rural schools but falling short of objectives in large, urban school districts. Revenue analysis can help the Association's marketers develop new promotional materials or incentives to motivate students in urban school districts to engage with the program.

Figure 14.1 shows the source of contributions to U.S. nonprofits in 2012. Around 72 percent of the $316 billion contributed to nonprofit firms came from individuals. While this is a general view, specific nonprofits should measure each potential revenue stream and look for ways to maximize contributions from each.

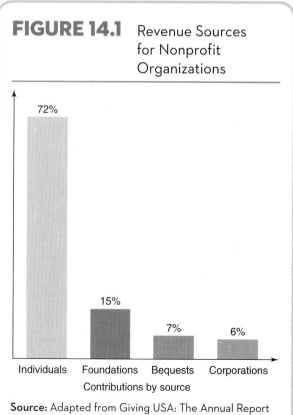

FIGURE 14.1 Revenue Sources for Nonprofit Organizations

Source: Adapted from Giving USA: The Annual Report on Philanthropy for the Year 2012 (2013). Chicago: Giving USA Foundation, www.givingUSAreports.org.

As helpful as revenue analysis can be in helping firms isolate the major sources of their sales or funding, it alone does not provide a complete measure of the firm's success. During the late 1990s and early 2000s, numerous technology companies saw their revenue and stock price grow exponentially. Williams Communications Group (WCG), which marketed the largest next-generation telecommunications network in the U.S., provides a case in point. WCG enjoyed substantial revenue growth beginning in the late 1990s, often exceeding 25 percent growth from one quarter to the next. By 2001, its annual revenue had grown to approximately $1.3 billion.[1] Unfortunately, market share challenges and lack of profits forced the company to file Chapter 11 bankruptcy in April of 2002, despite the fact that revenue had increased more than 500 percent over the previous four years.[2] While revenue growth had been high, the costs to build and maintain the network and run the day-to-day business were much higher. Marketing professionals must understand the limitations of simply measuring revenue. They must combine this analysis with an evaluation of market share and profitability before making decisions.

Market Share Analysis

market share analysis

A measure that reflects the firm's sales as a percentage of total market sales.

profitability analysis

A measure of how much profit the firm generates as well as how much profit certain aspects of the firm, including regions, channels, and customer segments, contribute.

Market share provides marketers with a quick look at how they are performing relative to their competitors. Market share analysis reflects the firm's sales as a percentage of total market sales. For example, Apple became the largest company in the world in terms of the total value of the company's stock partly because it captured substantial market share across its product lines. The iPad rapidly gained market share in the years after its debut; it accounted for 50 percent of global tablet shipments by 2012.[3] Apple's tablet market share was evidence that it was pulling away from Amazon's Kindle Fire and other competitors.

Market share is especially important to industries, such as auto manufacturing, in which total market share can increase or decrease significantly. In 2009, as the U.S. economy was in recession, total U.S. sales of new cars, trucks, and SUVs fell to 10.4 million, down from 16 million sold annually less than a decade before.[4] Market share is typically depicted using a pie graph, and auto manufacturers were forced to deal with a shrinking pie. As the economy began to recover, the pie grew again, but not immediately to its pre-recession levels. All auto manufacturers were forced to make do with a smaller piece of the pie than they enjoyed at the start of the century. Figure 14.2 illustrates a market share graph for automobile sales in the U.S. in May of 2013.

As with revenue, firms should not analyze market share data in isolation, but examine it relative to revenue and profitability. A firm can gain market share by drastically reducing prices, but such action will likely lead to decreased revenue and profitability. Ultimately, for-profit marketers should seek a revenue and market share level that maximizes profits for the firm.

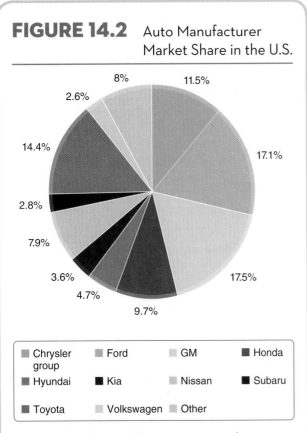

FIGURE 14.2 Auto Manufacturer Market Share in the U.S.

8%   11.5%
2.6%
14.4%   17.1%
2.8%
7.9%
3.6%   17.5%
4.7%
9.7%

- Chrysler group
- Ford
- GM
- Honda
- Hyundai
- Kia
- Nissan
- Subaru
- Toyota
- Volkswagen
- Other

Note: Numbers do not add up to 100 percent due to rounding.
Source: Edmunds.com, "Market Share by Manufacturer, May 5, 2013, http://www.edmunds.com/industry-center/data/market-share-by-manufacturer.html.

Profitability Analysis

Profits are the positive gain from a business operation after all of the expenses have been subtracted. Profitability analysis measures how much profit the firm generates as well as how much profit certain aspects of the firm, including regions, channels, and customer segments, contribute. Similar to revenue analysis, profitability analysis should examine more than just a single number. Marketers often use two important metrics to evaluate profitability.

Companies like Groupon must evaluate the cost of acquiring new customers against the amount of revenue each newly acquired customer contributes to the firm as part of their profitability analysis.

- *Customer acquisition* measures how much was spent on marketing (advertising, public relations, sales, etc.) to gain new customers. Additional customers don't necessarily equal additional profit. The firm's goal should be to obtain additional customers at a low cost, which provides evidence that they allocated marketing resources in an efficient way. However, a firm's marketing strategy sometimes makes this goal impossible or prevents it from being a short-term focus of the organization. For example, Groupon's cost of customer acquisition grew 485 percent between the first quarter of 2010 and the first quarter of 2011 to more than $52 per customer.[5] Groupon marketers made a strategic choice to accept the higher acquisition costs because they believed that, once they acquired customers, those customers would become profitable repeat purchasers in the months and years ahead.
- Marketers also measure *individual customer profitability.* As part of their profitability analysis, Groupon marketers evaluated data across the organization and attributed lower-than-expected profits to refunds associated with a specific customer segment that displayed higher-than-average customer dissatisfaction rates.[6] Their analysis enabled them to allocate additional resources to the most profitable segments and territories while reducing resources and costs in less profitable areas.

Marketing professionals throughout the world monitor revenue, market share, and profitability on a monthly, weekly, and sometimes even a daily basis. One of the most popular tools for quickly reviewing these metrics is a marketing dashboard, which is a collection of what the marketer identifies as the most critical diagnostic and predictive metrics organized to promote the recognition of patterns in performance. Figure 14.3 on page 402 provides an example of a marketing dashboard that displays important marketing metrics so they can be read and understood easily.

marketing dashboard
A collection of what the marketer identifies as the most critical diagnostic and predictive metrics organized to promote the recognition of patterns in performance.

---

connect | MARKETING   ## Interactive Assignment 14-1

Please complete the *Connect* exercise for Chapter 14 that focuses on the different measures of marketing performance. Being able to analyze and determine the importance of each type of measurement will allow you to evaluate the success of your marketing organization and the types of changes you may need to make to achieve success.

THE MARKETING AUDIT

Marketers often use a marketing audit to determine the specific changes that need to be made within the marketing mix. A marketing audit is a comprehensive examination of the objectives, strategies, and success of each element of the marketing mix. Marketing audits should include quantitative and qualitative data from

LO 14-2

Explain the importance of analyzing the performance of each marketing mix element.

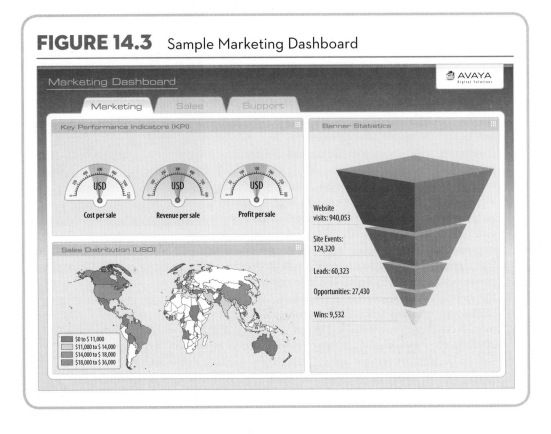

FIGURE 14.3 Sample Marketing Dashboard

marketing audit

A comprehensive examination of the objectives, strategies, and success of each element of the marketing mix.

rate of trial

A measure that indicates the success of the launch of a new product.

employees, customers, suppliers, and other stakeholders to measure the success of each marketing mix element. In addition to the kind of general metrics like marketing ROI and profitability analysis discussed earlier in the chapter, firms can employ other metrics specific to each marketing mix element as part of a marketing audit.

Measuring Product

Measuring the success of a product and its contribution to business performance is a complex process, especially with new products. Often, the organization has not defined what constitutes new product success, leading to fundamental problems when it comes to measuring that success. In addition to revenue, market share, and profitability analysis, firms can choose from among several other common techniques to measure the success of new products. The rate of trial is a measure that indicates the success of the launch of a new product. It provides a quick snapshot of the marketing team's success at enticing potential customers to try a new product for the first time. Taco Bell used the rate-of-trial method to measure the number of customers who tried its new Doritos Locos Tacos after the menu item launched in 2012. By this measure Taco Bell was wildly successful; it sold over 100 million Locos Tacos in the first 10 weeks and increased sales in its established stores by over 6 percent.[7] However, the more important metric for Taco Bell, and for other marketers launching a new product, is the repeat purchase rate, which measures how many initial customers came back. A high repeat purchase rate indicates that consumers enjoy the product and believe it to be a value at its current price point. A low repeat purchase rate may signal that, after the initial buzz about the product faded, consumers either did not like the product or thought it was overpriced.

Large companies like Taco Bell often find the rate of trial and other quantitative methods appropriate. However, because of the cost associated with such metrics, marketing professionals at small businesses and nonprofit organizations often focus on low-cost qualitative research. These types of measures include talking to buyers and consumers about product satisfaction and purchases. Nobody knows what the consumer wants better than the consumer. Though such qualitative research may suffer from bias, especially without standard interview controls, it supplies the company with timely information and, in many cases, cheap and actionable information about its products.

Measuring Price

In this part of the marketing audit, marketers analyze the price sensitivity of customers. Marketers generally focus on one of two measures for the analysis: actual purchases or consumers' preferences and intentions.[8] Actual purchases can be measured using historical sales data. More and more firms employ retail scanners and customer databases. The historical data those tools provide allow firms to generate excellent real-time estimates of consumers' price sensitivity and what they are willing to pay. For example, a grocery store like Safeway can use retail scanners to understand whether dropping the price of Sunkist soft drinks 10 percent generates additional sales on a weekday. The downside to measuring the success of a particular pricing strategy this way is that price changes by competitors such as Crush Orange, different promotional budgets, and general economic conditions can undermine the ability of historical data to predict the impact of a price change.

Historical sales data, collected through retail scanners and customer databases, provide firms with a way to measure the effectiveness of their pricing strategy.

To measure customers' preferences and intentions, firms can conduct simulated purchase experiments. In such experiments, marketers ask consumers to choose among various products at different price points. They can use actual products to measure the success of current prices, or simply use descriptions if they want to test different pricing strategies for a new product. For example, fast food restaurant Long John Silver's might recognize that a new fish combo meal with one side item priced at $3.99 will sell well, while a larger version with more side items will not sell well priced at $5.99. As with other methods, bias can play a role in simulated experiments; thus marketers should avoid letting the customer know too much about the goals of the experiment before they participate.

sales and operations planning (S&OP)

The process of creating one unified operating plan that ensures a company-wide focus on achieving the same goals and objectives

Measuring Place

As part of the marketing audit, marketers measure the success of their logistics functions across their organization. They also evaluate performance throughout the supply chain using on-time delivery percentage, inventory carrying costs, inventory turns, and other important metrics. Increasingly, marketers engage in sales and operations planning and collaborative planning, forecasting, and replenishment to measure and manage the place element of the marketing mix.

Companies use the sales and operations planning process to measure and balance supply and demand. Sales and operations planning (S&OP) is the process of creating one unified operating plan that ensures a company-wide focus on achieving the same goals and objectives.[9] It involves the coordination of

EXECUTIVE PERSPECTIVE

Dean Lee
Athletic Director
Arkansas State University

For what element of the marketing mix do you primarily use metrics?

Metrics are a critical part of how we evaluate everything in our athletic department. From a marketing standpoint, it would be pricing. We use a number of sophisticated tools to measure whether we are charging the right amount for tickets to our events. We might set different prices for different games at different times of the year to generate maximum revenue for the athletic department while also delivering maximum value for the team's fans.

sales, production, and distribution to develop consensus-based plans to best meet customer demand. For example, when discrepancies exist at auto manufacturer BMW between the ability of production to supply new cars and the level of customer demand to buy those cars, the company may decide to institute manufacturing plant overtime or outsource some of its production activities. Executives at BMW may also approve long-term plans to increase production and distribution capacity, perhaps through opening additional production facilities to make more cars, based on the metrics used to measure this marketing mix element.

Companies also use collaborative planning, forecasting, and replenishment to measure and manage demand. Collaborative planning, forecasting, and replenishment (CPFR) is the process of coordinating with other companies in the supply chain to create a sales forecast. The process begins with the sharing of marketing plans between companies, for example BMW and its suppliers. The companies create a sales forecast by agreeing on the timing of sales and make a commitment to follow the plan. Manufacturers throughout the supply chain use this forecast to schedule production to meet demand for tires, windshields, and other necessary components of BMW automobiles.

Measuring Promotion

Advertising and personal selling represent the most common elements of the promotional mix that firms measure during a marketing audit.

Measuring Advertising
Companies should measure the effectiveness of advertising before and after a campaign to understand its impact. Marketers typically conduct a pretest in which a sample of targeted consumers evaluates advertisements before the ad campaign begins. Pretests help to set a baseline measure for marketers to evaluate the success or failure of the subsequent campaign. After the campaign, marketers conduct a posttest, which involves an evaluation of the advertisements after the campaign by the same targeted segment of consumers. These two measures together help the firm gauge the ad campaign's success.

Companies often measure print and digital advertising based on whether consumers see the ads and how well they recognize and remember them. A recognition test involves showing consumers the print advertisement and asking if they recognize the ad. While recognition tests can help the firm determine whether its ad has caught the attention of the target market, recognition alone may not prompt consumers to buy a product. Marketing professionals often go a step further and assess what consumers recall about an advertisement using either unaided or aided recall tests. Unaided recall tests require consumers to recall ads from memory, without any clues. In aided recall tests, respondents receive clues to help stimulate their memory. If consumers don't recognize or recall the firm's print advertisements, marketers may change the size or message of the ad or deliver it through an alternative medium.

Marketers also measure how many consumers have been exposed to their various promotional efforts. Reach is the percentage of the target market that has been exposed to a promotional message (television advertisement, online advertisement, billboard, etc.) at least once during a specific time period. The Super Bowl serves as a powerful tool to increase reach. The game typically garners the highest ratings of any television program of the year and is one of the few televised events during which viewers actively watch the commercials. Marketers annually pay over $3 million per 30-second commercial to advertise during the Super Bowl in an attempt to reach as many people as possible.[10] Unfortunately, no matter how effective a single advertisement might be, it generally takes multiple exposures to move a consumer to make a purchase or change his or her buying habits in some

collaborative planning, forecasting, and replenishment (CPFR)

The process of coordinating with other companies in the supply chain to create a sales forecast.

pretest

An evaluation of advertisements before the ad campaign begins by a sample of targeted consumers.

posttest

An evaluation of advertisements after the ad campaign is launched by a sample of targeted consumers.

recognition test

A performance metric that involves showing consumers an advertisement and asking if they recognize it.

unaided recall tests

A performance metric that requires consumers to recall advertisements from memory, without any clues.

aided recall tests

A performance metric in which respondents are asked to recall advertisements based on clues they receive to help stimulate their memory.

reach

A measure of the percentage of the target market that has been exposed to a promotional message at least once during a specific time period.

To maximize the frequency of customer exposure to a promotion, a company may choose to run a large number of relatively inexpensive ads on a specialty channel like the Food Network that serves the company's target market rather than a smaller number of pricier ads on a major network that reaches more customers.

way. Therefore, marketers seek to increase both the reach and the frequency of their promotional exposure to their target market.

Frequency measures how often the audience is exposed to a promotional message during a specific time period. An old adage remains true in marketing today: a person has to hear something multiple times to remember it. Imagine that you sell tennis equipment and have a $100,000 television advertising budget. If you choose to advertise on ESPN (the largest sports cable network in the U.S.), you might be able to run approximately five commercials for that investment. However, you could choose to take those same dollars and advertise on the Tennis Channel. On the Tennis Channel, you could run dozens of commercials for less than the price of five ads on ESPN. While the Tennis Channel has lower average viewership ratings than ESPN, the frequency of your target market's exposure to the ad may outweigh its limited reach. This strategy of cultivating high-frequency advertising at a low cost can improve revenue per ad dollar, which is calculated by comparing total revenue to the amount of money spent on advertising. If your strategy of running ads on the Tennis Channel increases revenue for your tennis products without your having to spend any additional dollars on advertising, you have increased your revenue per ad dollar.

Companies should also explore the use of qualitative research tools as a way of understanding the effectiveness of their advertising, public relations, and other promotional programs. Techniques like focus groups and consumer interviews often generate in-depth responses. These give marketers insight into consumers' subtle likes and dislikes and can be valuable as the firm refines its promotional message.

Measuring Personal Selling

Evaluating salespeople, though a common way to measure promotional success, presents challenges for the firm. A salesperson with a large territory might sell more than a salesperson in a smaller territory with fewer customers or greater economic challenges. Does that mean that the salesperson who sells more in the large territory is better? Not necessarily. How then can organizations measure the effectiveness of their salespeople?

frequency

A measure of how often the target market has been exposed to a promotional message during a specific time period.

revenue per ad dollar

A performance metric that is calculated by comparing total revenue to the amount of money spent on advertising.

objective measures

A way of evaluating salespeople that relies on statistics that can be gathered from the firm's internal data, such as sales revenue, gross profit, and total expenses.

sales quotas

Specified sales or profit targets that the firm expects salespeople to meet.

subjective measures

A way of evaluating salespeople that relies on personal evaluations of a salesperson's performance based on observation by managers and executives.

Measures to evaluate salespeople generally fall into two categories: objective measures and subjective measures. Objective measures reflect statistics that can be gathered from the firm's internal data, such as sales revenue, gross profit, and total expenses. One of the most common objective measures for measuring personal selling is a sales quota. Sales quotas are specified sales or profit targets that the firm expects salespeople to meet. Measuring salespeople often begins by assessing whether or not they have met their sales quota. Subjective measures rely on personal evaluations of the salesperson's performance based on observation by managers and executives. Subjective measures might include job knowledge, sales territory, and customer relationships. Firms typically evaluate salespeople on subjective measures in the U.S. Still, salespeople who perform well according to subjective measures often still need to meet objective goals to remain in their position.

Measuring Social Media

Companies increasingly make investments in social media that require measurement to determine their success. Marketers use a variety of tools, including the following, to evaluate the success of their social media marketing strategies and guide their decisions going forward.

1. *Google Analytics.* Google has a comprehensive analytics service that helps track user activity on an organization's website in real time. A company can set up Google Analytics quickly and easily and receive a variety of useful data, including the number of daily visits to its site, the demographics of its users, how users got to the site, how long they stayed, and the relative popularity of each piece of content on the site.
2. *Klout.* Klout scores measure influence, defined as the ability to drive action on social networks. This measure tells marketers how many people the organization influences, how much it influences them, and the influence of its customer network across social media platforms. Klout allows marketers to see a map of their social media activity over the past 90 days, enabling them to cross-reference the exact moments their score increased. Such data provide important insight into which content most effectively engaged consumers.
3. *Wildfire's Social Media Monitor.* Social media marketing company Wildfire offers a free social media monitor that can help firms understand their Twitter and Facebook presence versus that of the competition. Wildfire's tools allow marketers to easily compare the number of likes, check-ins, and followers on each of the company's pages.
4. *My Top Tweet.* My Top Tweet ranks an organization's top 10 most-shared tweets and the number of times they were retweeted. Twitter is an increasingly powerful business tool. This measure allows marketers to understand what types of tweets are spreading throughout the social network. Not only does such a metric help a company manage its own brand but it also allows marketers to educate themselves about what works well for other brands, including their competitors.

---

 connect |MARKETING **Interactive Assignment 14-2**

Social Media in Action

In recognition of the prevalence of social media as a marketing tool, companies such as marketing research firm Nielsen and Internet-technology firm ComScore have partnered with Facebook to offer organizations analytical tools to support their measurement efforts.

ComScore began offering a service in 2011 that allows marketers to measure the number of people who view and interact with the company's products on Facebook. ComScore's system focuses on how big companies, such as Southwest Airlines or Starbucks, use Facebook fan pages and like buttons. In addition, it offers metrics that assess what individuals say about specific products on their personal Facebook pages. ComScore's tools allow firms to track how positive or negative word of mouth about their brand spreads through social media. Nielsen also teamed up with Facebook to offer a rating metric that measures the success of online marketing campaigns.

Large organizations have made use of these tools. Microsoft's Bing search engine was a pioneer in using these new metrics to evaluate its marketing efforts. Marketers at Microsoft have greatly increased their expenditures for social media marketing because of its impact on sales and brand loyalty, which the data and metrics gathered by these new analytical tools have validated.

The Social Media in Action *Connect* exercise in Chapter 14 will let you utilize social media metrics to assess the success of a promotional campaign. As social media become a large part of modern promotional strategies, you must be able to understand and evaluate the success or failure of your organization's efforts using available analytical tools.

Source: See Shayndi Raice, "New Metrics Gauge Heft of Facebook Ads," *The Wall Street Journal*, August 3, 2011, http://online.wsj.com/article/SB1000142405311190363 5604576474452983044810.html.

MEASURING INDIVIDUAL MARKETING PERFORMANCE

LO 14-3
Discuss best practices for motivating and compensating marketing employees.

In addition to measuring the effect of its marketing strategy, a firm must also measure the performance of those developing and executing the marketing plan. As with the objectives outlined in the marketing plan, marketing employees should each have clear, specific objectives for their performance. These objectives could include things such as the amount of time a pricing analyst averages in returning a price quote or the amount of new donors a nonprofit marketing manager should enlist in the coming year. Specific objectives for marketing employees differ based on the size and type of the firm, but all organizations must measure employee performance against them to ensure that the work of each employee helps the organization meet its overall objectives. Quality objectives for a marketing employee drive the evaluation of the success of that employee and often form the basis for rewarding him or her appropriately.

One of the biggest factors in the success of any organization's marketing efforts is the level of motivation of its employees. Motivated employees will initiate action on a certain task, expend a certain amount of effort on that task, and persist in expending effort over a period of time. Marketers can use both financial and nonfinancial rewards to motivate their marketing employees to deliver great results.

Nonfinancial Rewards

Nonfinancial rewards are a powerful tool for motivating employees. Virtually any firm can employ them regardless of its size or profitability. We all realize

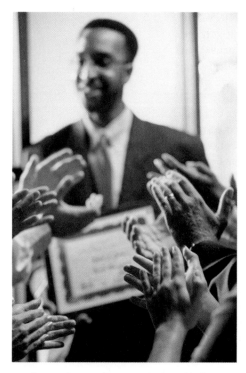

Nonfinancial rewards, particularly in the form of recognition for a job done well, provide firms with a means for motivating marketing professionals who meet or exceed established performance metrics.

that certificates, trophies, public recognition, and other nonfinancial rewards motivate children. Too often, companies forget that they can motivate adult employees through similar means, such as by recognizing an employee of the month or bestowing a department innovation award on an individual or team. Recognition can not only motivate the individual recognized but can also indirectly motivate the employee's peers as they become aware of their colleague's outstanding performance. The positive impact of recognition extends throughout the marketing mix. For example, nonfinancial rewards for truck drivers in the form of safety certificates and praise given in company newsletters is a critical part of many firms' supply chains. It can significantly motivate drivers in the areas of safety and on-time delivery.[11]

Promotions and advancement within the company also serve as powerful nonfinancial rewards for marketing employees. Young, well-educated marketing professionals want to work for firms that offer the opportunity to advance within the organization. These employees seek to grow their knowledge and experience as part of developing their career. Organizations (especially nonprofit firms who tend to offer employees less compensation than for-profit firms in exchange for a better title and more hands-on experience) that provide such nonfinancial rewards often find it to be a productive way to motivate marketing employees.

Financial Rewards

One of the most important reasons to effectively measure performance at the firm and individual level is to determine financial compensation. Despite the power of nonfinancial rewards, all employees seek fair pay in exchange for the work they do. Great organizations employ performance measurements that allow them to determine who is most valuable to the organization and then pay those employees accordingly.

Compensating Marketing Employees

Compensation for most marketing employees takes the form of a fixed salary. A fixed salary is a payment made at specific intervals to an employee (e.g., every other Friday or on the first and fifteenth of the month). In addition to a fixed salary, firms also typically offer a mix of health benefits and retirement plans to compensate marketing employees.

Today, firms around the world rely less on fixed salaries. Instead, they have adopted a pay-for-performance compensation system, which compensates employees only when they meet the certain objectives the organization has set for them. In conjunction with either fixed salaries or pay-for-performance compensation, firms may offer bonuses, which consist of payments made at the discretion of management if a marketing employee achieves or surpasses some established performance metrics. Typically, marketing employee bonuses tie to performance appraisals. For performance appraisals to succeed, firms emphasize the relevance, fairness, and rewards associated with them. Employees who can see the link between excellent job performance and a high bonus tend to be motivated to excel at their job and believe that the organization values their efforts.

As they make decisions about their compensation programs, firms should avoid the trap of feeling they need to treat everyone the same. If the company gives bonuses and salary increases at the same level to all of its marketing employees, it runs the risk of demotivating its best marketing staff. If a highly dedicated, productive employee who is doing great things and going the extra mile receives the exact same bonus as someone not contributing to the company in any tangible

fixed salary

A form of employee compensation in which payment is made at specific intervals to an employee.

pay-for-performance compensation

A form of employee compensation in which payment is made only when employees meet the certain objectives the organization has set for them.

bonuses

A form of employee compensation in which payments are made at the discretion of management if an employee achieves or surpasses some established performance metrics.

way, what would you expect to happen? In most cases, the superior employee's performance will decline because it hasn't been rewarded. If a company does not link performance evaluations to compensation in a recognizable way, employees may become comfortable with mediocrity and less motivated to do great things in their jobs.

Compensating Salespeople   Compensating salespeople offers some different challenges compared to compensating other marketing employees. Some companies compensate salespeople using a straight commission system in which the company pays salespeople only based on what they sell. A commission is a payment tied directly to the sales or profit a salesperson captures for the company. For example, a salesperson at Best Buy might receive 10 percent of the total price of a new television he or she sells as a commission. If the television was sold for $700, then the salesperson would receive a commission of $70. Firms that offer a commission based on the price of the product sold must take precautions to ensure that they earn enough profit on the sale to cover the commission and contribute to the company's bottom line. Imagine if Best Buy made only a $50 profit on each television sold. After subtracting a $70 commission, that profit would turn into a loss for the company. To avoid this pitfall, marketers today often base sales commissions on profit rather than sales. For example, Best Buy might offer a 25 percent commission on the profit it earns from each television sold. If the $700 sales price results in a $200 profit for Best Buy, the salesperson would receive 25 percent of that profit as a commission, which translates to $50 per television. This method aligns salesperson compensation with company profit and incentivizes the sales team to push for higher profit margins.

> **commission**
> A payment tied directly to the sales or profit a salesperson captures for the company.

A straight commission compensation structure can motivate salespeople since they do not make any money if they do not sell. Marketers like the strategy because it ties a salesperson's success to the success of the company. However, marketers have recently begun to recognize a couple of major disadvantages of a straight commission system.

1. Salespeople have little financial security in this type of compensation plan, which often means the firm gains and loses employees quickly and thus has less predictable selling costs.
2. Organizations also face an ethical risk: salespeople may make unethical or, potentially, even illegal short-term decisions to increase their commission so they can pay their rent or feed their family. Such decisions could open up the firm to future liabilities.

Most salespeople in the U.S. are compensated using a combination system made up of a fixed salary and commission. The salary component provides salespeople with some financial stability, while the commission offers the incentive of additional pay in exchange for hard work. A combination plan allows managers to focus on both the objective and subjective measures of performance when compensating salespeople. However, a combination plan can be difficult to administer. Firms also may have trouble choosing the appropriate size of the incentive relative to the base salary. The ratio of base salary to incentive pay matters. A compensation system in which 95 percent of salespeople's earnings comes from base salary presents different incentives and challenges for the firm than a plan in which 95 percent comes from commissions. A mix of 30 percent base salary and 70 percent commission is fairly typical in the U.S. today, but companies should

In addition to a fixed salary, salespeople are often paid a commission based on the sales or profit they generate for the company through their selling activities.

TABLE 14.1 Compensation Methods for Salespeople

Compensation Method	Especially Useful for	Advantages	Disadvantages
Straight Commission	When highly aggressive selling is required	Maximum incentive	Little security
	When minimal nonselling tasks are required	Managers can encourage sales of certain items	Little control over sales force
	When company can't closely control sales force	Selling expenses relate directly to selling resources	Sales force may provide inadequate service to smaller accounts
			Selling costs less predictable
Combination	When sales potential is similar across territories	Some security	Selling expenses less predictable
	When company wants to offer incentive but maintain some control	Some incentive	May be difficult to administer
		Selling expenses vary with revenue	
		Manager has some control over nonselling activities	

Source: Adapted from Mark W. Johnston and Greg W. Marshall, *Relationship Selling*, 3rd ed. (New York: McGraw Hill, 2009), p. 367.

use the specific dynamics of their organization and industry to adjust from there as appropriate. Table 14.1 highlights the advantages and disadvantages of the straight commission method versus the combination method of compensating salespeople.

connect | MARKETING Interactive Assignment 14-3

Please complete the *Connect* exercise for Chapter 14 that focuses on compensation strategies for marketing employees. By understanding how different compensation methods influence employee motivation, you will be prepared to choose the best compensation strategies to meet your organizational objectives.

BARRIERS TO CHANGE

LO 14-4

Describe the barriers to implementing change in an organization.

As we discussed at the beginning of this chapter, some of the marketing strategies and tactics your organization implements will fail in the years ahead. This chapter highlights strategies for measuring the performance of your marketing organization and identifying where changes need to be made. Unfortunately, knowing you are doing something wrong is only half the battle. Once metrics have identified

Nelson Taylor
Ticket Manager

Loyola University
http://www.luc.edu/

Loyola University is a private Jesuit institution of higher education in Chicago, Illinois, that serves approximately 16,040 students. It has been recognized for community service and engagement and offers undergraduate, graduate, professional, and continuing studies in a variety of fields. The university's athletics program supports multiple NCAA-level sports.

Describe your job. I have multiple responsibilities related to ticket sales and operations. My main goal is to generate revenue for the athletic department by selling season and group ticket packages. As such, I am responsible for setting departmental revenue goals, identifying new sales opportunities and expanding current sales programs, establishing ticket prices and packages, and developing marketing strategies to promote these packages. My job also requires me to work across multiple departments. We are constantly exploring new ways to generate student interest in athletic events, which requires me to work internally with our marketing and external operations staff and externally with other university groups. We also work closely with our alumni office to engage alumni onsite at athletics events.

Describe how you got the job that you have. The short answer is networking and persistence. Prior to starting at Loyola, I had experience in sports ticket sales and operations in both minor league baseball and the National Basketball Association. When I relocated to Chicago, I reached out to several collegiate athletics departments to introduce myself and offer to help in any paid or unpaid capacity. Helping in this way allowed me to gain an understanding of working in intercollegiate athletics. When my current position opened up, I applied through Loyola's jobs website, was offered an interview, and went into the interview with a written sales plan to show my interviewers exactly what I would bring to the table.

What has been the most important thing in making you successful at your job? Time management, flexibility, and relationship building. Every day is a new challenge. It's very rare that I get into the office and accomplish everything on my to-do list because new tasks or problems always present themselves. I believe that successful time management has allowed me to accomplish the most important things on that to-do list while still being able to address other issues as they pop up throughout the day.

What advice would you give soon-to-be graduates? My first boss always asked for out-of-the-box ideas for generating sales revenue and that's stuck with me. I am consistently searching for new and different ways to achieve departmental goals. Also, don't be afraid to ask questions. You don't have all the answers. There's a sharp learning curve as you enter the business world. Businesspeople have been in your shoes before, and it has been my experience that those same people are more than willing to answer your questions.

What do you consider your personal brand to be? My personal brand is built on consistently searching for new and different ways to achieve departmental goals. I want to be a problem solver at my organization and someone who will be there to help develop solutions when difficult situations arise.

the problem, the firm must make the changes necessary for success. The options for change can range from repositioning a brand to raising prices, but any decision will face obstacles. Some of the most common barriers to change include organizational structure, complacency, poor communication, and bankruptcy. Each of these is described in more detail in the sections that follow.

Organizational Structure

A firm's structure plays an important role in how quickly it can initiate change in response to measurement data. Organizational structure refers to the relationship among individuals and teams within an organization. Two broad categories of variables related to structure impact an organization's ability to make necessary changes. Formalization is the extent to which established rules and processes direct marketing decisions and activities. Centralization refers to the location of decision-making authority within a marketing organization. Highly formalized or centralized organizations often have a difficult time maximizing performance in response to rapid changes in the marketplace or customer preferences. In centralized companies, for example, individuals at high levels make most of the important decisions. This can slow the process of change and not address problems marketers see on the front lines of customer service. In decentralized companies, low-level employees closer to the problem in question make decisions and develop solutions. Firms increasingly implement a decentralized organizational structure in an effort to solve customer issues quickly and effectively as part of a customer orientation.

Complacency

Another barrier to change for an organization, and for each of us individually, is complacency. Good becomes the enemy of great as marketers rationalize their organization's performance and choose simply to stay the course rather than make changes. Today's rapidly changing global economy makes organizational failure due to complacency easier than ever before. For example, Kodak, which filed for Chapter 11 bankruptcy in 2012, did not move into the digital world skillfully enough or fast enough.[12] The roots of Kodak's complacency were planted in the organization during more prosperous times. In the late 1970s, Kodak claimed over 80 percent of the market share for camera and film sales in the United States.[13] Kodak already was failing to keep up in the late 1980s, even before the digital revolution. At that time, competitors like Fuji began doing a superior job squeezing profits out of an existing technology, the roll-film business, while also preparing for the switch to digital images.[14] Marketers at Kodak did not devote the necessary resources to addressing the impending shift. Ultimately, years of complacency can have a similar negative impact on almost any organization unless marketers work to overcome it.

Poor Communication

Failing to communicate with marketing employees invites rumors and fear to surround the change process, particularly if an organization faces major changes, such as downsizing or changing product lines. Employees want to know what's going on, whether it affects them positively or negatively. The feeling of uncertainty that comes from a lack of communication disrupts work and lowers productivity. It can also make employees feel as if they aren't part of the decision. Companies should use all the communication tools at their disposal to update employees regularly about any change and any process modifications the change requires. In addition, they should involve all employees as

organizational structure

The relationship among individuals and teams within an organization.

formalization

The extent to which established rules and processes direct marketing decisions and activities.

centralization

The location of decision-making authority within a marketing organization.

Companies, particularly successful companies, can all too easily become complacent about their marketing strategy, as Kodak did in recent years, thus allowing competitors like Fuji to gain a foothold in the marketplace.

much as possible, through meetings or question-and-answer sessions, to facilitate open communication during the change.

Failure to communicate the need for change also can result in a firm falling out of touch with its customers. National bookstore chain Borders filed for bankruptcy after years of not effectively communicating the need for change across the organization or executing on that change fast enough. The bookseller's poor communication was especially harmful because disruptive technology was shifting consumers from print to electronic books. Amazon was the first in the book-selling business to make the shift to eBooks, followed by Barnes and Noble. These competitor moves left Borders lagging too far behind to shift to eBooks and develop its own platform for distributing them. As eBooks began to make up an increasingly large portion of the industry's sales, Borders was unable to recoup its lost revenue, market share, and profitability.[15] Borders failed to communicate to its marketing department and other employees the need to change strategy quickly enough to adapt and succeed in a transforming marketplace.

A lack of internal communication about shifting trends from print books to digital books contributed to Borders's decision to file for bankruptcy.

Bankruptcy

Following the recession that began in 2007, many firms faced the difficult challenge of marketing during a bankruptcy. Bankruptcy does not necessarily mean the end of a firm. Marketers should understand the differences between the two most common types of corporate bankruptcies. Chapter 7 bankruptcy typically means that the business ceases operation immediately. Circuit City filed for Chapter 7 bankruptcy in 2009 and began the painful process of liquidating all of the merchandise from its 567 stores and laying off 30,000 employees.[16] A firm filing for Chapter 11 bankruptcy protection must reorganize its affairs and assets in accordance with specific terms. Firms can generally emerge from Chapter 11 bankruptcy with a fresh start as long as they have met the terms of their reorganization. General Motors filed for Chapter 11 bankruptcy protection in 2009 after years of losses.[17] The company's reorganization terms included making tough marketing decisions to eliminate less profitable brands like Saturn and Hummer. GM emerged from bankruptcy less than a year later and posted a profit for the first time in years in the spring of 2010.

Six Flags also successfully marketed itself through a Chapter 11 bankruptcy. During restructuring, the firm focused its marketing efforts on making its most loyal guests aware that it was business as usual at its various parks.[18] Six Flags leveraged e-mail marketing and social media and empowered its customers to become marketers by encouraging them to share the word with their friends and family. By laying a foundation that let people know that it was business as usual, Six Flags's marketers then could use traditional advertising to sell the brand and the park experience. The firm's emphasis on social media ensured that its 379,101 fans on Facebook and its 13,288 Twitter followers at the time were aware that it was a good day to have fun at Six Flags.[19]

Chapter 7 bankruptcy

Bankruptcy proceedings in which the business ceases operation immediately.

Chapter 11 bankruptcy

Bankruptcy proceedings in which a firm must reorganize its affairs and assets in accordance with specific terms.

After it filed for bankruptcy, Six Flags leveraged e-mail marketing and social media to empower its customers to market on behalf of the company.

---

connect | MARKETING   ## Interactive Assignment 14-4

Please complete the Connect exercise for Chapter 14 that focuses on barriers to change within a marketing organization. By understanding the major obstacles to strategic change, you should better understand how to overcome each barrier and make the marketing adjustments necessary for success.

SUMMARY

LEARNSMART™ ADVANTAGE

LO 14-1 Implement the key marketing performance metrics.

The need to measure and evaluate the success of marketing activities is essential to building a great organization. Organizations focus now more than ever on marketing return on investment, which is a measure of the firm's effectiveness in using the resources allocated to its marketing effort. Marketers should also use metrics like revenue analysis, market share analysis, and profitability analysis to evaluate success across the whole organization as well as in specific regions, channels, and customer segments. None of these measures should be viewed in isolation; one measure alone may not give an accurate picture of the health of an organization. A marketing dashboard, a collection of what are believed to be the most critical diagnostic and predictive metrics, provides a simple tool for quickly reviewing the metrics in combination.

LO 14-2 Explain the importance of analyzing the performance of each marketing mix element.

Marketers seeking to identify specific changes that need to be made within the marketing mix often use a marketing audit. A marketing audit is a comprehensive examination of the objectives, strategies, and success of each element of the marketing mix. Marketing audits should include quantitative and qualitative data from employees, customers, suppliers, and other stakeholders to measure the success of each marketing mix element. Two particularly important measures are reach and frequency. Reach is the percentage of the target population that is exposed to a promotional message (e.g., television advertisement, online advertisement, billboard, etc.) at least once during a specific time period. Frequency measures how often the

audience is exposed to a promotional message during a specific time period.

LO 14-3 Discuss best practices for motivating and compensating marketing employees.

Motivated employees will initiate action on a certain task, expend a certain amount of effort on that task, and persist in expending effort over a period of time. Firms can use both financial and nonfinancial rewards to motivate their employees to deliver great results. Most marketing employees' compensation takes the form of a fixed salary. Firms increasingly offer bonus programs to supplement fixed salaries to incentivize employees. Most salespeople in the U.S. receive a fixed salary and commission. The salary component provides salespeople with some financial stability, while the commission offers the incentive of additional pay.

LO 14-4 Describe the barriers to implementing change in an organization.

Some of the most common barriers to organizational change include organizational structure, complacency, poor communication, and bankruptcy. Highly formalized or centralized organizations often have a difficult time maximizing performance in response to rapid changes in the marketplace or in customer preferences. Good can become the enemy of great if marketers rationalize their organization's performance and choose simply to stay the course rather than make changes. Failure to communicate the need for change can result in a firm becoming out of touch with its customers. Bankruptcy represents an extreme barrier to change. Chapter 7 bankruptcy generally means that the business ceases operation immediately. Chapter 11 bankruptcy involves a reorganization of the firm's affairs and assets.

KEY TERMS

aided recall tests (p. 404)
bonuses (p. 408)
centralization (p. 412)
Chapter 11 bankruptcy (p. 413)
Chapter 7 bankruptcy (p. 413)
collaborative planning, forecasting, and replenishment (CPFR) (p. 404)

commission (p. 409)
fixed salary (p. 408)
formalization (p. 412)
frequency (p. 405)
gross margin (p. 398)
market share analysis (p. 400)
marketing audit (p. 402)
marketing dashboard (p. 401)

marketing expenditures (p. 398)
marketing return on investment (ROI) (p. 398)
objective measures (p. 406)
organizational structure (p. 412)
pay-for-performance compensation (p. 408)
performance metrics (p. 396)

MARKETING PLAN EXERCISE

The final section in most marketing plans outlines the controls that will be put in place for monitoring and adjusting implementation of the plan. The implementation section outlines how the specifics of the marketing plan will be carried out and who will carry them out. You have put a lot of ideas down on paper analyzing your strengths and weaknesses and where you want to go in your career. It is now time to implement those strategies and see if they work. There is no organizational structure to this marketing plan or question about who is accountable for which items. This marketing plan is about your career. In creating it, you have developed strategies intended to drive positive results in your life.

Your assignment for this chapter is to put measures in place to determine whether or not you are hitting your goals over the next three to five years, and beyond. Some parts of your personal marketing plan likely will not work. Conventional wisdom holds that over 70 percent of new business initiatives fail and over 90 percent of people never carry through on their planned New Year's resolution. You have outlined your contingency plans in a previous part of your personal marketing plan, but what measures will trigger the contingency plan? If your contingency plans involve attending graduate school sometime in the future, what will make you begin to look for a program? If you are not being compensated in a way that matches your market value, what will you do? How long are you willing to be underpaid?

Finally, consider contingency plans for further out in your career. Is it likely that you will move to another city in the next five years? Could family changes, such as getting married or needing to take care of an aging parent, impact the career path you should take? The more scenarios you can put down on paper, think about, and plan for, the greater the chance that you will successfully navigate the most important product launch of your career: you as a college graduate. Never forget that you are managing your personal brand every minute of every day. Never forget that you will make mistakes marketing yourself. That is ok as long as you learn from them. And never forget that, whether you are marketing cars, a non-profit organization, or yourself, planning increases the likelihood of success.

Your Task: List at least three specific professional objectives for yourself at each of the following key points in your career: at the one-, three-, and five-year marks after you graduate from college. Include your targeted industry, graduate school program (if applicable), level of employment (manager, director, etc.), and expected salary and benefits at each year. Then make specific contingency plans for each time period if you have not reached the objectives listed. Finally, write a one-paragraph description of how potential developments in your personal life over the next five years will impact the objectives you've listed.

DISCUSSION QUESTIONS

1. Based on your understanding of reach and frequency, would you recommend a company advertise during the Super Bowl? Why or why not? Would your answer vary depending on the type of business running the ad?
2. Based on what you have read about compensating salespeople, do you think salespeople should be compensated using only fixed salary, only commission, or a combination of the two? Please explain your answer. If you chose the combined approach, what would you consider the optimal ratio of fixed salary to commission?
3. List and describe two compensation strategies for marketing employees. How effective do you think

each strategy is? As you look for a job after graduation, what things about a job or compensation would most motivate you?
4. Do you think that bonuses should be tied to performance evaluations? Why or why not? What bonus percentage is high enough to motivate you personally? Would it make financial sense for a marketing executive to offer this level of performance bonus? Why or why not?
5. Think about a place that you have worked in the past. What kind of organizational structure did the organization have with regard to formalization and centralization? Do you think that was an effective structure for the organization? Why or why not?

SOCIAL MEDIA APPLICATION

Review your entire social media portfolio and consider how each of the social media platforms you use personally can impact your career positively or negatively as you move forward. Analyze your efforts to build your brand via social media using the following questions and activities as a guide:

1. List the social media platforms on which you have any type of presence. How many of those platforms do you check or use at least once per week?

2. Is the content you provide across each platform consistent? Do you have the same image across platforms? What grade would you give your overall social media portfolio? Explain your answer.

3. Use metrics to justify the overall grade you gave yourself. You can use any type of analytical tools (e.g., number of friends, followers, likes, Klout score, etc.) to provide support for your overall grade.

ETHICAL CHALLENGE

The National Football League (NFL) generates the most television revenue of any major North American professional sport. In addition to network deals with broadcast partners Fox, NBC, CBS, and ESPN, which generate $6 billion annually in rights fees for the NFL, the League decided to run 13 Thursday night games on its own NFL Network cable channel. *Thursday Night Football* on the NFL Network, which is available in over 78 million U.S. homes, averaged more than 7 million viewers a night during its first full season. Its success negatively impacted the ratings of the prime-time comedy and drama shows that air on NBC, CBS, and the NFL's other broadcast partners on Thursday evenings. While *Thursday Night Football* is bringing more viewers to the NFL's cable channel, marketers at the League's broadcast partners might be wondering why they are paying $6 billion a year to an organization that is stealing television viewers on what had been traditionally one of the broadcast networks' best nights. Please

use the ethical decision-making framework to complete the following related to this scenario:

1. Analyze the NFL's decision to play more Thursday night games on the NFL Network. What are the ethical implications of this decision?

2. If you were a marketer at a broadcast network partner of the NFL, what action might you take in response to the fact that Thursday night games have hurt the television ratings and advertising revenue of your Thursday night programming?

3. If you were a marketer for the NFL, why would you not put televised games on every night of the week? Are there any advertising or marketing concerns about showing football games on Tuesday, Wednesday, or Friday night?

Source: See Andy Fixmer, "Thursday Night Football Scores Big for the NFL," *Bloomberg Businessweek*, November 29, 2012, http://www.businessweek.com/articles/2012-11-29/thursday-night-football-scores-big-for-the-nfl.

VIDEO CASE

Please go to *Connect* to access the video case featuring Arkansas State University that accompanies this chapter.

CAREER TIPS

Marketing Your Future

And now, a word from your authors. . . . "Be quick. Don't hurry." This quote from legendary UCLA college basketball coach John Wooden is important for you to think about as you go through your career journey. You need to be quick as a new graduate. You need to quickly learn that if you don't think, solve problems, and work hard, your career will show it. We have seen countless new graduates waste their first year or two after graduation, ruin their

personal brand, and incur lots of debt. You must be quick in adjusting from the protective structure of school to the self-accountability of professional life. You are responsible for your actions, and as long as you embrace that, you can have a fulfilling career and life.

But don't try to hurry through life, taking the shortest route you can find. Despite what anyone may have told you, your college degree doesn't entitle you to anything. It doesn't guarantee you a job, a career, or the life you want. Your ability to succeed in your career is directly tied to your ability to solve problems for organizations and customers. There are no scantron tests or study guides as you begin your career. You will not be judged by whether you make a 91 percent or a 78 percent, but rather by how much better your organization is because you are there. Be quick to engage in the incredible experience of building a career and a life, but don't hurry, because you may miss out on the skills, relationships, and experiences that will give you the best memories and the highest quality career going forward.

Be quick to find something you are passionate about. We love being marketing professors, and we have loved creating the materials you have read and engaged with this semester. Our lives are better in every way because we love what we do. Your career will consume over half of your life; if you are doing something you hate, we doubt

that the money you make from it will ever be enough. Once you find the career you are passionate about, don't hurry, because the best, most meaningful parts of your career are ahead.

Good luck to you.

C. Shane Hunt and John Mello

CHAPTER NOTES

1. Tiffany Kary, "Williams Communications Beats 3Q Estimates; Sees Strong 4Q," *CNet News*, October 25, 2000, http://news.cnet.com/Williams-Communications-beats-3Q-estimates-sees-strong-4Q/2100-12_3-267220.html.
2. Elliot Spagat and Mitchell Pachell, "Williams Seeks Chapter 11 Protection, Strikes Deal to Distribute All Equity," *The Wall Street Journal*, April 23, 2002, http://online.wsj.com/article/0,,SB1019527209607062520-search,00.html.
3. Claire Cain Miller and Brian X. Chen, "The Tablet Market Grows Cluttered," *The New York Times*, November 18, 2012, http://www.nytimes.com/2012/11/19/technology/which-tablet-to-buy-among-dozens-confuses-shoppers.html?pagewanted=all.
4. Bill Vlasic and Nick Bunkley, "Sales Fell in August for Carmakers," *The New York Times*, September 1, 2010, http://www.nytimes.com/2010/09/02/business/02auto.html.
5. Peter Cohan, "Groupon Fires Its CEO, Andrew Mason," *Forbes*, March 1, 2013, http://www.forbes.com/sites/petercohan/2013/03/01/groupon-fires-its-ceo-andrew-mason/.
6. Brid-Aine Parnell, "Groupon Bungles Figures, Slides $65m into the Red," *The Register*, April 2, 2012, http://www.theregister.co.uk/2012/04/02/groupon_revises_q4_results/.
7. Stacy Curtin, "Taco Bell on Verge of Comeback: Sells 100 Million Doritos Tacos in 10 Weeks," June 6, 2012, http://finance.yahoo.com/blogs/daily-ticker/taco-bell-verge-comeback-sells-100-million-doritos-181206461.html.
8. Thomas T. Nagle, John E. Hogan, and Joseph Zale, *The Strategy and Tactics of Pricing*, 5th ed. (Upper Saddle River, NJ: Pearson, 2011), p. 274.
9. Larry Lapide, "New Developments in Business Forecasting," *Journal of Business Forecasting* (Summer 2002), pp. 11–14.
10. Stuart Elliott, "Super Bowl Commercial Time Is a Sellout," *The New York Times*, January 8, 2013, http://www.nytimes.com/2013/01/09/business/media/a-sellout-for-super-bowl-commercial-time.html?_r=0.
11. John Mello and C. Shane Hunt, "Developing a Theoretical Framework for Research into Current Driver Control Practices in the Trucking Industry," *Transportation Journal* 48, no. 4 (2009).
12. Joan Lappin, "Bad Choices, Not Just Photography Going Digital, Put Eastman Kodak into Bankruptcy," *Forbes*, January 19, 2012, http://www.forbes.com/sites/joanlappin/2012/01/19/bad-choices-not-just-photography-going-digital-put-eastman-kodak-into-bankruptcy/.
13. "The Last Kodak Moment?" *The Economist*, January 14, 2012, http://www.economist.com/node/21542796.
14. Ibid.
15. Ben Austen, "The End of Borders and the Future of Books," *Bloomberg Businessweek*, November 10, 2011, http://www.businessweek.com/magazine/the-end-of-borders-and-the-future-of-books-11102011.html.
16. Matthew Bandyk, "Circuit City to Liquidate in the Latest Massive Business Failure," *U.S. News & World Report*, January 16, 2009, http://money.usnews.com/money/blogs/risky-business/2009/01/16/circuit-city-liquidates-in-the-latest-massive-business-failure.
17. Scott Gamm, "GM Makes Rare Round Trip: Bankruptcy and Back to the S&P 500," *Forbes*, June 6, 2013, http://www.forbes.com/sites/scottgamm/2013/06/06/gm-makes-rare-trip-from-bankruptcy-back-to-the-sp-500/.
18. Jennifer Rooney, "How Six Flags Markets through Its Bankruptcy," *Ad Age*, November 9, 2009, http://adage.com/article/cmo-interviews/marketing-flags-markets-bankruptcy/140358/.
19. Ibid.

SAMPLE MARKETING PLAN

Personal Marketing Plan: Courtney Ewing

Throughout the chapters, you completed a personal marketing plan exercise that asked you to apply the concepts you have learned to the product you will market every day of your life: you. After going through each exercise, you have gained not only experience thinking about the various aspects of a marketing plan but also a roadmap for pursuing your professional objectives after graduation. This appendix provides a sample of what your completed personal marketing plan might look like.

MARKETING STRATEGY
    Future Objectives (Chapter 1)
SITUATION ANALYSIS
    Strengths, Weaknesses, Opportunities, and Threats (SWOT) Analysis (Chapter 2)
    Market Summary (Chapter 3)
    Marketing Research (Chapter 4)
TARGET MARKET (Chapter 5)
PRODUCT DESCRIPTION (Chapter 6)
POSITIONING MYSELF (Chapter 7)
PROMOTING MYSELF (Chapter 8)
DISTRIBUTION (Chapter 9)
PRICING (Chapter 10)
BRANDING (Chapter 11)
RELATIONSHIP DEVELOPMENT (Chapter 12)
SOCIAL RESPONSIBILITY (Chapter 13)
CONTROLS (Chapter 14)

MARKETING STRATEGY

Future Objectives (Chapter 1)

1. Attend an accredited law school somewhere in the southwestern United States, preferably Oklahoma or Texas. My top three choices are the University of Oklahoma, University of Tulsa, and Texas Tech University.
2. After law school graduation, I want to work in an established law firm, preferably in Tulsa, Oklahoma. My parents and much of my family live near Tulsa, and it would be my first choice as a home after law school graduation.

3. I want to live comfortably and have enough money to enjoy the time I have with my family. I will be 25 years old when I graduate law school, and it is my goal to make $100,000 in annual salary by the time I am 32 years old. I arrived at that number because that is what I will need to be able to pay for the things my family would want, for example, a nice home, two cars, and an annual vacation.

SITUATION ANALYSIS

SWOT Analysis (Chapter 2)

Strengths

- I am an extremely dedicated employee. I put 110 percent into any task or assignment that I undertake.
- I possess the analytical and creative skills necessary to succeed in law school, to strategically formulate plans, to design them, and to effectively implement them.
- I am a quick learner and not afraid to operate outside of my comfort zone. I am able to quickly adapt to new situations and to learn new skills.

Weaknesses

- I can be too detail oriented and it may take me longer to accomplish tasks or to be completely satisfied with my performance. By recognizing these weaknesses and taking on more school projects with short deadlines, I can improve the skills necessary to ensure quality work.
- I am often impatient, and a lack of patience can sometimes be a negative characteristic in an employee. However, I am working to never allow my impatience to affect my job performance or behavior.
- I do not have any real professional experience. While I have worked at a restaurant, I need more professional experience working for either a major business or a law firm. I plan to fix this by pursuing an internship this summer, even if it is unpaid, to gain experience that will build my skills and resume.

Opportunities

- My uncle is an attorney and has let me job shadow him on several occasions. This has been a great learning opportunity, and one that can help me articulate to schools why I want to be a lawyer.
- My education is both broad and versatile. With a degree in marketing, as well as a minor in history, I have learned a unique set of skills. I believe this degree, combined with my high grades and LSAT score, will position me very well for the law schools I want to attend.

- Due to the recent state of the economy, some law firms are opting to hire less experienced attorneys for less pay. This is a great way for companies to cut costs and allows young people like me an opportunity to prove themselves.

Threats

- While my targeted potential job market is pretty broad, the competition is extremely high. I will look to create a niche for myself by specializing in a particular area of the legal profession, perhaps oil and gas law.
- Although the economy could provide entry-level job seekers like me better opportunities, it could also be a threat. Many firms are eliminating positions and reducing the number of new associates that they hire. I may have to expand my search to places outside of Tulsa, and also consider working for a smaller practice when I first get out of law school.
- There could be an increase in law school applications at my targeted schools, reducing my chances for admission to my top choices for law school. I will research all of my targeted law schools to check the acceptance rates and admission requirements to make sure that I fully understand my chances of getting in.
- Personal financial issues are also a potential threat. In particular, I am concerned that national economic problems could reduce the amount of student financial aid that I can get. I plan to talk with my parents and develop a plan that sets the minimum amount of financial aid I could get and still get through law school.

Market Summary (Chapter 3)

The market for attorneys is competitive, and salaries have been generally lower in recent years. I was surprised to see that only 55 percent of law school graduates from the most recent year had full-time, long-term jobs that required a law degree within 9 months of graduation. The market is not in as good shape as I expected. It appears that more than 40,000 new law school graduates enter the job market each year, with almost half not finding jobs in the first year.

I will need to be prepared to face a difficult market upon graduation. I will need to understand the market for specific areas of specialty. For example, in recent years, law school graduates with an expertise in oil and gas, financial services, and cyber crime have been more likely to be hired by established firms.

Marketing Research (Chapter 4)

My marketing research, which included online information searches and speaking with a couple of admissions counselors at potential schools, was very helpful in better understanding where I stood in my effort to be accepted to law school. There are over 175 law schools in the United States, but there are 3 that I most want to attend: University of Oklahoma, University of Tulsa, and Texas Tech University. At Oklahoma, the acceptance rate is 32 percent, the median LSAT score is 158 and the average GPA is 3.48. At Tulsa, the acceptance rate is 40 percent, the median LSAT is 155, and the average GPA is 3.32. At Texas Tech, the acceptance rate is 47 percent, the median LSAT is 155, and the average GPA is 3.45. The median starting salary for graduates from all three schools is around $55,000 per year.

My LSAT score of 156 is a little low for Oklahoma, but above the median for the other two schools. My GPA of 3.59 is ahead of the average at all of the schools. I think my chances of getting into the University of Oklahoma are a little questionable, but I feel pretty confident about the University of Tulsa and Texas Tech. I need to improve my experience and extracurricular activities during the next year so that I can market myself as the best possible candidate to these law schools. Because my scores are close to the median at all of the schools, I also am going to apply to a couple of law schools with lower averages where I am very certain I will be accepted, just in case.

TARGET MARKET (Chapter 5)

My preference would be to work in a B2B environment in which my clients are companies. I have seen my uncle work in this environment, and he enjoys his job very much. Since my focus is likely to be oil and gas law, I will work primarily with other businesses, rather than individuals. There are three law firms in Tulsa that work in this B2B area that would make ideal employers when I finish law school. They are:

Hatteberg, Gonzales, and Xu
Basu, Hughes, Kieffer, and Ducham
Penn and Associates

PRODUCT DESCRIPTION (Chapter 6)

I would love the opportunity to be part of your law school program. I have excelled during my undergraduate career with a GPA above 3.59 as a marketing major with a history minor. I am a hard-working person with incredible attention to detail. I am confident but personable. I follow direction very well, and I make others around me better.

I am president of the Marketing Club at my university and have been a leader in other student organizations on campus. Perhaps most importantly, I am passionate about being a lawyer and want to do great things in this profession. I have talked with and job shadowed successful attorneys. These opportunities have given me experience and reinforced that I have what it takes to be successful as a lawyer. I know that the job market for attorneys is challenging, but I have confidence in my ability to succeed and make a difference. I believe that I will be a great addition to your law school and a source of pride for the university after my graduation.

POSITIONING MYSELF (Chapter 7)

I am positioning myself as a candidate for law school who has a high GPA as a college of business major, and who also is a leader among my peers. I received the highest grade in my business law class of 70 students. I also have taken two courses in constitutional law as part of my history minor. This has given me the opportunity, as an undergraduate, to study legal cases and write arguments for and against different rulings. I will arrive at law school on day one with a track record of academic success and a background in coursework that has prepared me to think in a legal way.

PROMOTING MYSELF (Chapter 8)

Advertising. I plan to develop a professional two-page resume that reflects my desire to work for an established law firm. I plan to join professional social networking organizations like LinkedIn and build my profile. I will eliminate or make private all of my personal social media pages, as I want employers to focus on me as a professional candidate for their law school and eventually their law firm. I also plan to use the same professional photo across all of the social media sites that I use to make me more recognizable to prospective employers, as well as to project a consistent image.

Sales promotion. Two of the firms I want to work for in Tulsa offer unpaid internships. I plan to apply to both this summer. Not only will this give me a sample of what it would be like to work for the firm, but it also will allow the firm to see my work ethic and recognize my potential. Because the internship is unpaid, I have started saving money now from my current job at a restaurant, and I will live at home with my parents during the summer to cut costs while I complete the internship. I believe these short-term sacrifices are a great long-term investment.

Personal selling. I try to always be professionally dressed and well groomed. When I was a freshman or sophomore, I would often just wake up and go to class, not looking my best. Now, as I get closer to graduation and law school, I am very conscious of my appearance and what that appearance says about my personal brand. I also plan to take advantage of the mock interview program offered at my university's career services department. The program is free and will allow me to participate in and then review a fake interview with a career services representative, which will prepare me to sell myself to future employers.

Public relations. I have always tried to be aware of how my actions may be perceived by others in my professional and personal life. When I decided I was going to go to law school, I knew that I would need recommendations from my professors. I worked very hard to do well in my classes and took the time to develop relationships with my professors. I make it a point to stop by during their office hours at the beginning of, as well as several times during, each semester, and I am confident that they would say very positive things about me. I also continue to try to be a good classmate. Many of my business courses require group projects, and I have worked with some terrible group members. Through that experience, I've learned that I don't want to be a terrible group member myself and work hard to do my part on group projects. I will continue to be a personable, helpful member of any team.

DISTRIBUTION (Chapter 9)

I plan to distribute my information through applications to five law schools, which are listed below:

1. The University of Oklahoma
2. The University of Tulsa
3. Texas Tech University
4. Oklahoma City University
5. The University of Houston

I also plan to distribute information about myself professionally through social networking sites like LinkedIn. I plan to follow each of the schools that I am applying to on all of the social media platforms that they use. I also plan to join a networking group in Tulsa comprised of people who work in oil and gas law to start making connections that could help me in the law school application process as well with future employment.

PRICING (Chapter 10)

My goal is to make a $100,000 per year annual salary by the time I am 32, which is roughly 10 years after I finish my bachelor's degree. Here are the costs that I anticipate upon my law school graduation:

Undergraduate student loans: $21,000
Law school student loans: $47,000

When taken together, I expect to pay around $600 per month in student loan payments. In addition, I expect that my mortgage or rent payment after graduating from law school will be around $900 per month in Tulsa. When I factor in car payments, insurance, groceries, and social activities, I estimate that I will need about $3,000 per month or $36,000 after taxes to live the way I want.

Based on my research and conversations with working attorneys, I project that about one-third of my total salary will not show up in my paycheck as it will be deducted for taxes, health insurance, and 401(k) retirement plan contributions. Considering this, my total starting salary will need to be $54,000 per year or more to cover my costs and to have the chance to hit my 10-year salary goal of $100,000 per year. Since the starting salary for graduates at my targeted law schools is $55,000, I feel good about my chances. However, I need to make sure to do well in law school and take advantage of every networking opportunity. If I make anything below the average salary, I will have to cut things out of my life (e.g., a nice home or a new car) that I would prefer to have.

BRANDING (Chapter 11)

In the next 12 months, I plan to do the following things to build my brand:

1. Work as a summer intern for an established law firm (in the next six months). This will help me build my brand as someone who is serious about a legal career. It also will increase my knowledge and improve my chances of success in law school.
2. Become an officer of another student organization on campus (in the next eight months). I currently serve as the president of the Marketing Club, but I would like to be an officer of a different organization, probably Phi Beta Lambda, which is for future business leaders, so that I can list that on my law school applications. I think this will help to build my brand as a leader among my peers, which is an attribute that top law schools are looking for.
3. I am going to take two of my free elective classes in Spanish (starting in three months). A foreign language is a great differentiator and taking these as electives, as opposed to easier classes I could take, helps to illustrate my brand of hard work and professional development.

RELATIONSHIP DEVELOPMENT (Chapter 12)

Working at a restaurant provides a large number of opportunities to deliver customer service. One of the things I pride myself on in my job is getting to know my customers and what they like. I think I am good at recognizing which customers want very attentive service and which prefer privacy. As a team lead server, I am usually brought in to talk with an unhappy customer.

I have been very successful in resolving situations, mostly because I listen to what has made the customer unhappy and then find a solution. I think this skill set of providing great customer service will help me as a lawyer and throughout my life.

In the next 12 months, I plan to strengthen relationships with the following three people:

1. *Dr. Tew.* He is a finance professor at my school and also a lawyer. He is a brilliant man and potentially would be a great person to provide me with a letter of recommendation. I plan to take a course with him next semester to get to know him. I am also going to attend the next monthly meeting of our Phi Beta Lambda business organization. He serves as the faculty advisor for the organization, which would provide me with an opportunity to get to know him in a different setting.
2. *Bob Tinker.* He is an oil and gas attorney my uncle knows. He could be a great contact to have during and after law school. He has lunch with my uncle about once per month, and I am going to join them in the next two months. I also am going to ask Mr. Tinker if I can job shadow him for a day sometime in the next year. Because he knows my uncle and is an alumnus of my university, I think he will be willing to do this.
3. *Leigh Manly.* She is the director of admissions at one of my top choices for law school. Ms. Manly is very active in organizing the local Heart Walk fundraiser for the American Heart Association. This is a great cause that I am passionate about. I plan to volunteer at the fundraiser in two months. This experience will improve my resume and also make a positive impression on Ms. Manly about how I would represent the school's law school program.

SOCIAL RESPONSIBILITY (Chapter 13)

The main stakeholders in my professional success are the following:

1. *My parents.* They have invested thousands of dollars in my education to reduce the amount of my student loans. They have been supportive and loving, and they are invested in my success. Plus, as an only child, I want to be able to assist them as they get older.
2. *My future spouse and children.* I have been dating someone seriously for more than a year. If we decide to get married and someday start a family, I want to be able to earn a good salary so that we can enjoy our lives and provide for our children.
3. *The U.S. government.* As I mentioned earlier, I expect to have $68,000 or more in student loan debt by the time I finish law school. I appreciate the great opportunities that student loans have given me, and I want to make sure I can pay them back with interest.

The main social responsibilities I feel will be part of my career and life going forward:

1. I feel a great responsibility to help the kids in my community. Tulsa has a high percentage of children living under the poverty line. Regardless of anything else in their lives, those children deserve to have enough to eat. A great program in my area called Kans 4 Kids provides students who are on free lunch programs with food for the weekend or school breaks when they otherwise would not have enough to eat. I plan to give money and raise money for this outstanding cause over the next decade.
2. As an attorney, I want to take time to offer a few hours every month of pro-bono services to help with programs such as children's legal services where I would represent and serve as an advocate for children in welfare and other types of cases before the court.
3. I want to support my university. I have had a lot of great opportunities here at school, and I want to give back both financially and with my time after I graduate. I am a first-generation college student whose life has been transformed by my experience, and I want to share that message with future students who are considering attending my school over the next decade.
4. I also want to help and support my local church. I have attended this church since I was seven years old, and I have developed many terrific relationships there. I want to help financially and also serve as a young leader, helping to mentor the youth in our church over the next decade.

CONTROLS (Chapter 14)

Here are my objectives for the next one, three, and five years:

One year after graduation

- I plan to complete my bachelor's degree.
- I plan to be accepted at one of my top law school choices.
- I plan to apply for scholarships to reduce my student loan burden in graduate school.

Contingency plan. I will take summer courses, if necessary, to complete my degree on time. I may have to take online classes if I am interning during the day, so I should plan ahead to see what classes are offered online and plan accordingly. If I do not get into one of my top law school choices, I plan to stay in school another year and get a second major in finance, and potentially a second minor in Spanish. I will also retake the LSAT in an effort to improve my score and chances for admission to law school.

Three years after graduation

- I plan to have a summer clerkship with an established law firm near Tulsa.
- I plan to have completed two years of law school.
- I plan to be interviewing for jobs as an associate once I finish my law degree.

Contingency plan. If I cannot find a clerkship in Tulsa, I will try and find one in a nearby metro area, such as Oklahoma City; Dallas, Texas; or Kansas City, Missouri. If I am unable to complete law school for any reason, I will pursue a job in marketing in Tulsa. I love marketing and think I would be successful in a career in sales or pricing. If I cannot find a job in Tulsa, I will pursue jobs throughout the country, since I know that it is critical that I start my career with a good company where I can gain experience.

Five years after graduation

- I plan to be an attorney in Tulsa.
- I plan to be making approximately $60,000 per year.
- Between my contribution and the company contribution (which I expect to be at least 3 percent of my annual salary), I expect to be saving at least $7,000 per year through my 401(k) benefit plan.
- I plan to own a home.
- I plan to have an affordable health care policy that my firm helps to pay for and that provides me and my family with excellent care.

Contingency plan. If I am not an attorney in Tulsa, I will evaluate how well I like the city I am living and working in. It is possible I will like that new city better, but, if not, I will consider what I am willing to trade as far as money to be closer to home. If I am well below my targeted salary, I will consider why that is. If my performance is poor, I will look for ways to improve at what I am doing. If I am doing well, I will consider other opportunities at firms that might pay me better or even consider the possibility of starting my own small law firm.

Personal contingency plan. There are definitely personal developments that could change my plans in the next five years. I may be married and my spouse will have a significant influence on where we work and live. I do not expect to be a parent in the next five years, but if I am, that will impact the type of law firm I choose to work for. One of my main personal goals for the rest of my life is to be a great parent, and I want to choose an employer that respects and appreciates that.

GLOSSARY

advertising Nonpersonal promotional communication about goods, services, or ideas that is paid for by the firm identified in the communication.

advertising campaign A collection of coordinated advertisements that share a single theme.

advertising effectiveness studies A type of research that measures how well an advertising campaign meets marketing objectives.

affordable method A promotion mix budgeting strategy in which firms set their promotion budget based on what they believe they can afford.

aided recall tests A performance metric in which respondents are asked to recall advertisements based on clues they receive to help stimulate their memory.

allowances Trade promotions that typically involve paying retailers for financial losses associated with consumer sales promotions or reimbursing a retailer for an in-store or local expense to promote a specific product.

anticipative stock Inventory that is produced or purchased when a company expects something to occur in the future that will negatively affect stock availability.

approach A part of the personal-selling process that involves meeting the prospect and learning more about his or her needs and wants.

aspirational reference group The individuals a consumer would like to emulate.

attitude A person's overall evaluation of an object involving general feelings of like or dislike.

baby boomers The generation born between 1946 and 1964.

behavioral segmentation Segmentation that divides consumers according to how they behave with or act toward products.

bonuses A form of employee compensation in which payments are made at the discretion of management if an employee achieves or surpasses some established performance metrics.

brand The name, term, symbol, design, or any combination of these that identifies and differentiates a firm's products.

brand equity The value the firm derives from consumers' positive perception of its products.

brand extension The process of broadening the use of an organization's current brand to include new products.

brand image The unique set of associations target customers or stakeholders make with a brand.

brand loyalty When a consumer displays a steadfast allegiance to a brand by repeatedly purchasing it.

brand marks The elements of a brand not expressed in words that a consumer instantly recognizes, such as a symbol, color, or design.

brand recognition The degree to which customers can identify the brand under a variety of circumstances.

brand revitalization (rebranding) A strategy to recapture lost sources of brand equity and identify and establish new sources of brand equity.

break-even analysis The process of calculating the break-even point, which equals the sales volume needed to achieve a profit of zero.

break-even point The point at which the costs of producing a product equal the revenue made from selling the product.

business analysis The process of analyzing a new product to determine its profitability.

business-to-business marketing (B2B) Marketing to organizations that acquire goods and services in the production of other goods and services that are then sold or supplied to others.

business-to-consumer marketing (B2C) Selling goods and services to end-user customers.

cannibalization When new products take sales away from the firm's existing products rather than generating additional revenues or profits through new sales.

causal research A type of research used to understand the cause-and-effect relationships among variables.

centralization The location of decision-making authority within a marketing organization.

Chapter 11 bankruptcy Bankruptcy proceedings in which a firm must reorganize its affairs and assets in accordance with specific terms.

Chapter 7 bankruptcy Bankruptcy proceedings in which the business ceases operation immediately.

click-through rate (CTR) A ratio showing how often people who see an ad end up clicking on it.

closing The point at which the salesperson asks the prospect for the sale.

co-branding A strategy in which two or more companies issue a single product in an effort to capitalize on the equity of each company's brand.

cognitive dissonance The mental conflict that people undergo when they acquire new information that contradicts their beliefs or assumptions.

cold calling The process of approaching unknown prospective customers or clients.

collaborative planning, forecasting, and replenishment (CPFR) The process of coordinating with other companies in the supply chain to create a sales forecast.

commission A payment tied directly to the sales or profit a salesperson captures for the company.

common carriers For-hire truck companies that sell their services to any business.

competitive advantage The superior position a product enjoys over competing products if consumers believe it has more value than other products in its category.

competitive intelligence Involves systematically gathering data about what strategies direct and indirect competitors are pursuing in terms of new product development and the marketing mix.

concept test A procedure in which marketing professionals ask consumers for their reactions to verbal descriptions and rough visual models of a potential product.

concurrent new-product development New-product development that uses cross-functional teams made up of representatives from various departments to develop goods and services.

consumer adoption process The process by which customers formally accept and purchase products.

consumer behavior The way in which individuals and organizations make decisions to spend their available resources, such as time or money.

consumer confidence A measure of how optimistic consumers are about the overall state of the economy and their own personal finances.

consumer ethnocentrism A belief by residents of a country that it is inappropriate or immoral to purchase foreign-made goods and services.

consumerism A movement made up of citizens and government entities that focuses on protecting consumers and promoting their interests.

container Steel boxes used to transport goods, usually internationally.

contests Sales promotions in which consumers compete against one another and must demonstrate skill to win.

contract carriers For-hire truck companies that move goods exclusively for certain customers.

core carrier A strategy in which a firm selects a small number of carriers as opposed to using a large number of different carriers.

corporate philanthropy The act of organizations voluntarily donating some of their profits or resources to charitable causes.

corporate social responsibility (CSR) An organization's obligation to maximize its positive impact and minimize its negative impact on society.

corporate volunteerism The policy or practice of employees volunteering their time or talents for charitable, educational, or other worthwhile activities, especially in the community.

cost per click (CPC) The amount the firm pays each time a customer clicks on an ad.

cost-per-thousand impressions (CPM) What the firm pays for a thousand views of its ad.

country-of-origin effects The beliefs and associations people have about a country.

coupons Documents that entitle the customers who carry them to a discount on a product.

currency exchange rate The price of one country's currency in terms of another country's currency.

customer communication The two-way information flow between the firm and its customer.

customer equity A ratio that compares the financial investments a company puts into gaining and keeping customers to the financial return on those investments.

customer relationship management (CRM) The process by which companies get new customers, keep the customers they already have, and grow the business by increasing their share of customers' purchases.

customer satisfaction A state that is achieved when companies meet the needs and expectations customers have for their goods or services.

customer segmentation analysis A method of analyzing data that creates customer profiles and categorizes them.

customer service All of the activities a firm engages in to satisfy the needs and wants of its customers.

customer value The perceived benefits, both monetary and non-monetary, that customers receive from a product compared to the cost associated with obtaining it.

customized research firms Research providers that offer services designed specifically for their customers.

cyclical inventory Inventory a firm needs to meet average demand.

data mining A process that involves the computerized search for meaningful trends in a large amount of data.

days of supply An estimate of how many days the firm's current inventory will last; calculated by dividing the inventory on hand by the average daily usage or sales.

deceptive pricing An illegal practice that involves intentionally misleading customers with price promotions.

decision support system (DSS) A computer program that enables access and use of the information stored in the data warehouse.

decline stage The stage of the product life cycle characterized by decreases in sales and profits.

demand analysis A type of research used to estimate how much customer demand there is for a particular product and understand the factors driving that demand.

demographics The characteristics of human populations that can be used to identify consumer markets.

demographic segmentation Segmentation that divides markets by characteristics such as age, gender, income, education, and family size.

derived demand When demand for one product occurs because of demand for a related product.

descriptive research A type of research that seeks to understand consumer behavior by answering the questions who, what, when, where, and how.

differentiated targeting A targeting strategy that simultaneously pursues several different market segments, usually with a different strategy for each.

diffusion The process by which new products are likely to be adopted, the rate at which they will be adopted, and the process through which the products will spread into markets.

direct competition A situation in which products that perform the same function compete against one another.

direct marketing Advertising that communicates directly with consumers and organizations in an effort to provoke a response.

direct ownership A method of entering an international market in which a domestic firm actively manages a foreign company or overseas facilities.

disposable income The amount of spending money available to households after paying taxes.

dissociative reference groups The people that the individual would *not* like to be like.

distribution center (DC) A type of warehouse used specifically to store and ship finished goods to customers.

distribution channels (marketing channels) Intermediaries—wholesalers, distributors, and retailers—through which the flow of products travels.

diversification A marketing strategy that seeks to attract new customers by offering new products that are unrelated to the existing products produced by the organization.

dollar fill rate A metric that measures the value of goods shipped on time versus the total value of the order.

Dominican Republic–Central America Free Trade Agreement (DR-CAFTA) An international agreement that eliminated tariffs, reduced nontariff barriers, and facilitated investment among the United States, Costa Rica, El Salvador, Guatemala, Honduras, Nicaragua, and the Dominican Republic.

dumping A protectionist strategy in which a company sells its exports to another country at a lower price than it sells the same product in its domestic market.

dynamic pricing A pricing strategy that involves constantly updating prices to reflect changes in supply, demand, or market conditions.

early adopters A category of consumer that purchases and uses a product soon after it has been introduced, but not as quickly as innovators.

early majority A category of consumer that gathers more information and spends more time deciding to make a purchase than innovators and early adopters.

ease of doing business The amount of effort required on the part of a customer when dealing with a firm.

80/20 rule A theory that suggests that 20 percent of heavy users account for 80 percent of the total demand.

elastic demand A scenario in which demand changes significantly due to a small change in price.

empowerment Giving employees permission to make decisions and take action on their own to help customers.

enterprise resource planning (ERP) systems Data management systems that integrate information across all the departments of an organization.

environmentalism A movement of citizens, government agencies, and the business community that advocates the preservation, restoration, and improvement of the environment.

environmental regulations The laws designed to protect the natural environment against undue harm by individuals and organizations.

environmental scanning The act of monitoring developments outside of the firm's control with the goal of detecting and responding to threats and opportunities.

escalator clause A section in a contract that ensures that providers of goods and services do not encounter unreasonable financial hardship as a result of uncontrollable increases in the costs of or decreases in the availability of something required to deliver products to customers.

esteem The need all humans have to be respected by others as well as by themselves.

ethics Moral standards expected by a society.

European Union (EU) An economic, political, and monetary union among 27 European nations that created a single European market by reducing barriers to the free trade of goods, services, and finances.

evaluative criteria The attributes a consumer considers important about a certain product.

exchange An activity that occurs when a buyer and seller trade things of value so that each is better off as a result.

experiments Procedures undertaken to test a hypothesis.

exploratory research A type of research that seeks to discover new insights that will help the firm better understand the problem or consumer thoughts, needs, and behavior.

exporting Selling domestically produced products to foreign markets.

external information search When consumers seek information beyond their personal knowledge and experience to support them in their buying decision.

fad product A product that is very popular for a relatively short amount of time.

family life cycle The distinct family-related phases that an individual progresses through over the course of his or her life.

fashion product A product that comes in and out of favor with consumers.

Federal Trade Commission (FTC) The consumer protection agency for the United States.

Federal Trade Commission Act (FTCA) A law passed in 1914 that established the Federal Trade Commission and sought to prevent practices that may cause injury to customers, that cannot be reasonably avoided by customers, and that cannot be justified by other outcomes that may benefit the consumer or the idea of free competition.

field experiments Experiments performed in natural settings like stores or malls.

fill rate A metric that measures the percentage of an order shipped on time and complete.

financial projections A bottom-line estimate of the organization's profitability.

fixed costs Costs that remain constant and do not vary based on the number of units produced or sold.

fixed salary A form of employee compensation in which payment is made at specific intervals to an employee.

focus groups Data collection tool in which a moderator engages a small group of people as they discuss a particular topic or concept with each other in a spontaneous way.

formalization The extent to which established rules and processes direct marketing decisions and activities.

franchising A contractual arrangement in which the franchisor provides a franchisee the right to use its name and marketing and operational support in exchange for a fee and, typically, a share of the profits.

frequency A measure of how often the target market has been exposed to a promotional message during a specific time period.

geographic segmentation Segmentation that divides markets into groups such as nations, regions, states, and neighborhoods.

global brand A brand that is marketed under the same name in multiple countries.

global marketing A marketing strategy that consciously addresses customers, markets, and competition throughout the world.

global segmentation Segmentation that is used when a firm can identify a group of consumers with common needs and wants that spans the entire globe.

gray market The sale of branded products through legal but unauthorized distribution channels.

green market A group of sustainability-oriented customers and the businesses that serve them.

gross domestic product (GDP) A measure of the market value of all officially recognized final goods and services produced within a country in a given period.

gross margin The difference between price and cost.

growth stage The stage of the product life cycle characterized by increases in sales, profits, and competition.

high-involvement products Significant purchases that carry a greater risk to consumers if they fail.

high-learning products Products that take longer for consumers to see the benefits of or that do not have a good infrastructure in place to support them.

hypothesis An educated guess based on previous knowledge or research about the cause of the problem under investigation.

idea generation The stage of new-product development in which a set of product concepts is generated from which to identify potentially viable new products.

idea screening The stage of new-product development in which the firm evaluates an idea to determine whether it fits into the new-product strategy.

impulse buying Purchasing a product with no planning or forethought.

indirect competition A process in which products provide alternative solutions to the same market.

inelastic demand A situation in which a specific change in price causes only a small change in the amount purchased.

inflation An increase in the general level of prices of products in an economy over a period of time.

informative advertising A type of advertising that attempts to develop initial demand for a product.

innovators A category of consumer that adopts a product almost immediately after it is launched.

integrated marketing communications (IMC) A promotional strategy that involves coordinating the various promotion mix elements to provide consumers with a clear and consistent message about a firm's products.

intermodal transportation Using several types of transportation for the same shipment.

internal information search When consumers use their past experiences with items from the same brand or product class as sources of information.

International Monetary Fund (IMF) An international organization that works to foster international monetary cooperation, secure financial stability, facilitate international trade, promote high employment and sustainable economic growth, and reduce poverty around the world.

interview A data collection tool in which the researcher works with one participant at a time, asking open-ended questions about how the individual perceives and uses various products or brands.

introduction stage The stage of the product life cycle that occurs after the firm launches the product into the marketplace and innovators begin to buy it.

inventory carrying costs The costs required to make or buy a product, including risk of obsolescence, taxes, insurance, and warehousing space used to store the goods.

inventory turns The number of times a firm's entire inventory is sold and replaced; calculated by dividing the cost of goods sold by the company's average inventory.

involvement The personal, financial, and social significance of the decision being made.

item fill rate A metric that measures the percentage of the total number of items on the order that the firm shipped on time.

joint venture An arrangement in which a domestic firm partners with a foreign company to create a new entity, thus allowing the domestic firm to enter the foreign company's market.

judgmental forecasting A method that involves asking experienced company personnel such as salespersons, marketers, and senior managers to give their best estimate of future sales.

just-in-time (JIT) A manufacturing process that seeks to make products based on customer orders rather than in anticipation of orders and to receive components from suppliers only when they are needed for production.

Klout score A measure, on a scale of 1 to 100, of a user's influence based on his or her ability to drive other people to act on social media sites.

laggards A category of consumer that does not like change and may remain loyal to a product until it is no longer available for sale.

late majority A category of consumer that relies on others for information, buying a good or service because others have already done so.

learning The modification of behavior that occurs over time due to experiences and other external stimuli.

level What sales would be without the influence of a trend or seasonality.

licensing A legal process in which one firm pays to use or distribute another firm's resources, including products, trademarks, patents, intellectual property, or other proprietary knowledge.

lifestyle A person's typical way of life as expressed by his or her activities, interests, and opinions.

lifestyle segmentation Segmentation that divides people into groups based on their opinions and the interests and activities they pursue.

lifetime value (LTV) analysis A comparison of the costs of retaining customers and the costs of acquiring new customers with the goal of determining how much money each type of customer requires.

line fill rate A metric that measures the percentage of item types (SKUs) on the order shipped on time and complete.

logistics That part of supply chain management that plans, implements, and controls the flow of goods, services, and information between the point of origin and the final customer.

low-involvement products Inexpensive products that can be purchased without much forethought and that are purchased with some frequency.

low-learning products Products with benefits customers can easily see.

loyalty programs Sales promotions that allow consumers to accumulate points or other benefits for doing business with the same company.

manufacturer brands Brands that are managed and owned by the manufacturer rather than a reseller.

marginal cost The change in total cost that results from producing one additional unit of product.

marginal revenue The change in total revenue that results from selling one additional unit of product.

market The group of consumers or organizations that is interested in and able to buy a particular product.

market development A marketing strategy that focuses on selling existing goods and services to new customers.

marketing An organizational function and set of processes for creating, communicating, and delivering value to customers and managing customer relationships in ways that benefit the organization and its employees, customers, investors, and society as a whole.

marketing audit A comprehensive examination of the objectives, strategies, and success of each element of the marketing mix.

marketing concept A marketing strategy that reflects the idea that a firm's long-term success must include a company-wide effort to satisfy customer needs and wants.

marketing dashboard A collection of what the marketer identifies as the most critical diagnostic and predictive metrics organized to promote the recognition of patterns in performance.

marketing expenditures The amount of money spent on all marketing activities during a specified period of time.

marketing information system (MIS) Computer software that helps companies continuously capture information and store it in a way that makes it accessible to researchers and decision makers.

marketing mix A combination of activities that represent everything a firm can do to influence demand for its good, service, or idea; often referred to as the four Ps of marketing.

marketing plan An action-oriented document or playbook that guides the analysis, implementation, and control of the firm's marketing strategy.

marketing research The act of collecting, interpreting, and reporting information concerning a clearly defined marketing problem.

marketing return on investment (ROI) A measure of the firm's effectiveness in using the resources allocated to its marketing effort.

market penetration A marketing strategy that emphasizes selling more of existing goods and services to existing customers.

market segmentation The process of dividing a larger market into smaller groups, or market segments, based on meaningfully shared characteristics.

market segments The relatively homogenous groups of consumers that result from the segmentation process.

market share analysis A measure that reflects the firm's sales as a percentage of total market sales.

market summary A description of the current state of the market.

markup pricing A pricing method in which a certain amount is added to the cost of the product to set the final price.

materials management The inbound movement and storage of materials in preparation for those materials to enter and flow through the manufacturing process.

mathematical modeling A type of causal research that involves using equations to model the relationships between variables.

maturity stage The stage of the product life cycle during which the firm focuses on profitability and maintaining the firm's market share for as long as possible.

membership reference group The group to which a consumer actually belongs.

millennials The generation born between 1978 and the late twentieth century.

mission statement A concise affirmation of the firm's long-term purpose.

mobile advertising A form of advertising that is communicated to the consumer via a handheld device.

modified rebuy A buying situation in which the customer's needs change slightly or they are not completely satisfied with the product they purchased.

motivation The inward drive we have to get what we need or want.

multinational company A firm that operates in two or more countries.

narrowcasting The dissemination of information to a fairly small, select audience that is defined by its shared values, preferences, or demographic attributes.

needs States of felt deprivation. Consumers feel deprived when they lack something useful or desirable like food, clothing, shelter, transportation, and safety.

neuromarketing A technique that measures brain activity when a participant is subjected to a particular stimulant to understand how consumers feel about products, packaging, and advertisements.

new buy A buying situation in which a business customer is purchasing a product for the very first time.

new category entries Products that are new to a company but not new to the marketplace.

new-product development (NPD) The process of conceiving, testing, and launching a new product in the marketplace.

new-product strategy development The stage of new product development in which the company determines the direction it will take when it develops a new product.

new-to-the-market products Inventions that have never been seen before and create a new market.

niche marketing A targeting strategy that involves pursuing a large share of a small market segment.

nonprobability sampling A type of sampling that does not attempt to ensure that every member of the target population has a chance of being selected.

North American Free Trade Agreement (NAFTA) An international agreement that established a free trade zone among the United States, Canada, and Mexico.

North American Industry Classification System (NAICS) A single industry classification system used by the members of the North American Free Trade Agreement—the United States, Canada, and Mexico—to generate comparable statistics for businesses and industries across the three countries.

objections The concerns or reasons customers offer for not buying a product.

objective-and-task method A promotion mix budgeting strategy in which a firm defines specific objectives, determines the tasks required to achieve those objectives, and then estimates how much each task will cost.

objective measures A way of evaluating salespeople that relies on statistics that can be gathered from the firm's internal data, such as sales revenue, gross profit, and total expenses.

observation A data collection tool that involves watching how people behave and recording anything about that behavior that might be relevant to the research objective.

obsolete inventory Inventory that can no longer be sold because the product has expired, been redesigned, was over-ordered, or is at the end of its product life.

odd pricing A pricing tactic in which a firm prices products a few cents below the next dollar amount.

offshore An organization that is located or based in a foreign country.

on-time delivery A metric that measures how many shipments are delivered per the requested delivery date.

opinion leaders Individuals who exert an unequal amount of influence on the decisions of others because they are considered knowledgeable about particular products.

opportunities External factors that the firm may be able to capitalize on to meet or exceed its stated objectives.

order cycle The total amount of time that elapses from the time a customer places an order until the time the product is delivered to the customer.

order cycle time A metric that measures the length of the order cycle, or the ability of the order system to react to customer orders.

organizational structure The relationship among individuals and teams within an organization.

outsource To procure goods, services, or ideas from a third-party supplier rather than from an internal source.

packaging All of the activities of designing and producing the container for a product.

pay-for-performance compensation A form of employee compensation in which payment is made only when employees meet the certain objectives the organization has set for them.

percentage-of-sales method A promotion mix budgeting strategy in which firms allocate a specific percentage of a period's total sales to the promotional budget for that period.

perceptual map A competitive analysis tool that creates a visual picture of where products are located in consumers' minds.

perfect order rate A metric that measures how many orders have been filled, delivered, and billed without error.

performance metrics Measures that assist in ascertaining the extent to which objectives have been attained.

personal buying When a purchasing manager buys items for the personal use of employees rather than for business use.

personality The set of distinctive characteristics that lead an individual to respond in a consistent way to certain situations.

personal selling The two-way flow of communication between a salesperson and a customer that is paid for by the firm and seeks to influence the customer's purchase decision.

persuasive advertising A type of advertising that attempts to increase demand for an existing product.

picking Retrieving materials from storage and bringing them to manufacturing to fulfill a production order, or retrieving finished goods from storage and preparing them for shipment to fulfill a customer order.

pipeline inventory Inventory that is in transit between suppliers and customers.

planned obsolescence A practice in which companies frequently come out with new models of a product that make existing models obsolete.

positioning The activities a firm undertakes to create a certain perception of its product in the eyes of the target market.

positioning statement A succinct description of the core target market to which a product is directed and a compelling picture of how the firm wants that core market to view the product.

posttest An evaluation of advertisements after the ad campaign is launched by a sample of targeted consumers.

preapproach A part of the personal-selling process that involves identifying key decision makers, reviewing account histories, identifying product needs, and preparing sales presentations.

predatory pricing The practice of first setting prices low with the intention of pushing competitors out of the market or keeping new competitors from entering the market, and then raising prices to normal levels.

predictive modeling Analysis that uses sophisticated algorithms based on patterns of previous buying behavior to try to determine the future actions of customers.

prestige pricing A pricing strategy that involves pricing a product higher than competitors to signal that it is of higher quality.

pretest An evaluation of advertisements before the ad campaign begins by a sample of targeted consumers.

price The amount of something—money, time, or effort—that a buyer exchanges with a seller to obtain a product.

price bundling A strategy in which two or more products are packaged together and sold at a single price.

price discrimination The practice of charging different customers different prices for the same product.

price elasticity of demand A measure of price sensitivity that gives the percentage change in quantity demanded in response to a percentage change in price (holding constant all the other determinants of demand, such as income).

price fixing When two or more companies collude to set a product's price.

price sensitivity The degree to which the price of a product affects consumers' purchasing behavior.

primary data Data collected specifically for the research problem at hand.

private label brands Products developed by a retailer and sold only by that specific retailer.

probability sampling A type of sampling in which every person in the target population has a chance of being selected, and the probability of each person being selected is known.

problem recognition The stage of the buying process in which consumers recognize they have a need to satisfy.

product The specific combination of goods, services, or ideas that a firm offers to its target market.

product accumulation Receiving goods from various suppliers, storing the goods until they're ordered by a customer or other company-owned facility, and consolidating orders to achieve transportation economies of scale.

product allocation Picking available goods to fill customer orders.

product assortment Mixing goods coming from multiple suppliers into outgoing orders so that each order includes a variety of goods rather than just one type of good.

product development A marketing strategy that involves creating new goods and services for existing markets. Also, the stage of new-product development at which a firm determines that the good can be produced or the service can be offered in a way that meets customer needs and generates profits.

product launch Completing all the final preparations for making the fully tested product available to the market.

product life cycle (PLC) The series of stages a product goes through from the time it is launched into the market until the time it is removed from the market.

product line A group of related products marketed by the same firm.

product line extensions Products that extend and supplement a company's established product line.

production orientation A marketing strategy in which the firm focused on efficient processes and production to create quality products and reduce unit costs.

product mix The combination of all of the products a company sells.

product placement An advertising technique in which a company promotes its products through appearances on television shows, movies, or other media.

product sortation Gathering goods with similar characteristics in one area of the distribution center to facilitate proper inventory controls and effectively provide customer service.

profitability analysis A measure of how much profit the firm generates as well as how much profit certain aspects of the firm, including regions, channels, and customer segments, contribute.

profit margin The amount a product sells for above the total cost of the product itself.

profit maximization (price skimming) A pricing strategy that involves setting a relatively high price for a period of time after the product launches.

profits Revenue minus total costs.

promotion All the activities that communicate the value of a product and persuade customers to buy it.

promotion mix A subset of the marketing mix that includes four main elements of marketing communication: advertising, sales promotion, personal selling, and public relations.

prospecting The search for potential customers—those who need or want a product and fit into a firm's target market.

prototype A mockup of a good, often created individually with the materials the firm expects to use in the final product.

psychographic segmentation The science of using psychology and demographics to segment consumers.

psychological processes The underlying psychological mechanisms that can influence consumer behavior.

publicity Disseminating unpaid news items through some form of media (e.g., television story, newspaper article, etc.) to gain attention or support.

public relations Nonpersonal communication focused on promoting positive relations between a firm and its stakeholders.

pull strategy A supply chain strategy in which customer orders drive manufacturing and distribution operations.

purchase order A legal obligation to buy a certain amount of product at a certain price from a supplier to be delivered at a specified date.

purchasing power A measure of the amount of goods and services that can be purchased for a specific amount of money.

push-pull strategy A supply chain strategy in which the initial stages of the supply chain operate on a push system, but completion of the product is based on a pull system.

push strategy A supply chain strategy in which a company builds goods based on a sales forecast, puts those goods into storage, and waits for a customer to order the product.

put-away Moving goods to their temporary or semipermanent storage location and updating inventory records.

qualifying A part of the personal-selling process that involves identifying which potential customers within the firm's target market have not only a desire for the product but also the authority to purchase it and the resources to pay for it.

quasi-strategic greening A type of environmental marketing activity that involves substantive changes in marketing actions as well as broad-based coordination among non-marketing activities.

quota sampling A type of sampling in which a certain number of participants is picked based on selection criteria such as demographics.

rate of trial A measure that indicates the success of the launch of a new product.

reach A measure of the percentage of the target market that has been exposed to a promotional message at least once during a specific time period.

rebates Sales promotions that allow consumers to recoup a specified amount of money after making a single purchase.

recency-frequency-monetary analysis A method of analyzing data that categorizes customers by their buying patterns.

recession A period of time during which overall gross domestic product (GDP) declines for two or more consecutive quarters.

reciprocity Purchasing goods and services from suppliers only if they buy from the purchasing manager's company.

recognition test A performance metric that involves showing consumers an advertisement and asking if they recognize it.

reference group A collection of people to whom a consumer compares himself or herself.

reference prices The prices that consumers consider reasonable and fair for a product.

regional segmentation Segmentation that is used when the similarity in needs and wants only extends across the region or several countries.

regression A forecasting method that attempts to draw relationships between the sales of a product and some other variable or variables that may be affecting those sales.

relationship marketing A marketing strategy that focuses on attracting, maintaining, and enhancing customer relationships.

relationship selling Building a trusting relationship with a customer over a long period of time.

reliability The company's ability to ensure that customers will receive a good or service within a stated lead time and that there will be no problems with the order.

reminder advertising A type of advertising that seeks to keep the product before the public in an effort to reinforce previous promotional activity.

repositioning The act of reestablishing a product's position to respond to changes in the marketplace.

resellers Retailers and wholesalers who buy finished goods and resell them for a profit.

responsiveness A metric that measures the firm's ability and willingness to provide fast service, answer customer inquiries, and resolve problems.

retailer A firm that sells mainly to end-user consumers.

revamped product A product that has new packaging, different features, and updated designs and functions.

revenue The result of the price charged to customers multiplied by the number of units sold.

revenue analysis A measure of actual revenue relative to the objectives of the organization.

revenue per ad dollar A performance metric that is calculated by comparing total revenue to the amount of money spent on advertising.

ritual consumption Patterns of consumption that are repeated with regularity.

Robinson–Patman Act A law passed in 1936 that requires sellers to charge everyone the same price for a product.

sales and operations planning (S&OP) The process of creating one unified operating plan that ensures a company-wide focus on achieving the same goals and objectives.

sales forecasting A form of research that estimates how much of a product will sell over a given period of time.

sales orientation A marketing strategy in which personal selling and advertising are used to persuade consumers to buy new products and more of existing products.

sales presentation A forum to convey the organization's marketing message to the prospect.

sales promotion A set of nonpersonal communication tools designed to stimulate quicker and more frequent purchases of a product.

sales quotas Specified sales or profit targets that the firm expects salespeople to meet.

sales tracking A type of research that follows changes in sales during and after promotional programs to see how the marketing efforts affected the company's sales.

sample A representative subset of the larger population.

sampling The process of selecting a subset of the population that is representative of the population as a whole.

seasonality A regularly repeating pattern of sales centered on a particular period of the year.

seasonal stock The goods a firm sells only at certain times of the year.

seasonal discounts Price reductions given to customers purchasing goods or services out of season.

secondary data Data collected for purposes other than answering the firm's research questions.

self-actualization A consumer's full potential and the need to realize that potential.

sequential new-product development New-product development that utilizes a progressive sequence in which functional areas consecutively complete their development tasks.

share of customer A measure of the quantity of purchase dollars each customer spends on the company's products.

simple random sampling A type of sampling in which everyone in the target population has an equal chance of being selected.

simulated test markets A procedure in which the firm builds a mock shopping experience for participants to observe their response to marketing stimuli.

situation analysis The systematic collection of data to identify the trends, conditions, and competitive forces that have the potential to influence the performance of the firm and the choice of appropriate strategies.

situational influences Factors like time and social surroundings that serve as an interface between the consumers and their decision-making process.

snowball sampling A type of sampling in which a set of participants is selected based on the referral of other participants who know they have some knowledge of the subject in question.

social media A group of Internet-based applications that allow the creation and exchange of user-generated content.

sociocultural The combination of social and cultural factors that affect individual development.

stakeholder responsibility The obligations an organization has to those who can affect whether or not it achieves its objectives.

standardized research firms Research providers that use common research designs that may apply to the research needs of many firms.

stockout A situation in which a company does not have enough inventory available to fill an order.

straight rebuy A buying situation in which a business customer signals its satisfaction by agreeing to purchase the same product at the same price.

strategic greening A type of environmental marketing activity that integrates and coordinates all of the firm's activities on environmental issues across every functional area.

strategic planning The process of thoughtfully defining a firm's objectives and developing a method for achieving those objectives.

strategy The set of actions taken to accomplish organizational objectives.

strengths Internal capabilities that help the company achieve its objectives.

subjective measures A way of evaluating salespeople that relies on personal evaluations of a salesperson's performance based on observation by managers and executives.

substitute products Goods and services that perform very similar functions and can be used in place of one another.

supply chain A set of three or more companies directly linked by one or more of the upstream and downstream flows of products, services, finances, and information from a source to a customer.

supply chain management The actions the firm takes to coordinate the various flows within a supply chain.

supply chain orientation A management philosophy that guides the actions of company members toward the goal of actively managing the upstream and downstream flows of goods, services, finances, and information across the supply chain.

surveys A data collection tool that poses a sequence of questions to respondents.

survival pricing A pricing strategy that involves lowering prices to the point at which revenue just covers costs, allowing the firm to endure during a difficult time.

sustainability A commitment to adopting a lifestyle that meets the needs of the present without compromising the ability of future generations to meet their own needs.

sustainable marketing The process of creating, communicating, and delivering value to customers in a way that recognizes and incorporates the concept of sustainability.

sustainable tourism The practice of recreational traveling in a way that maximizes the social and economic benefits to the local community and minimizes the negative impact on cultural heritage and the environment.

sweepstakes Sales promotions based on chance such that entry is the only requirement to win.

SWOT analysis An evaluation of a firm's **s**trengths, **w**eaknesses, **o**pportunities, and **t**hreats.

tactical greening A type of environmental marketing activity that involves implementing limited change within a single area of the organization.

targeting The act of evaluating each market segment to determine which segment or segments present the most attractive opportunity to maximize sales.

target market The group of customers toward which an organization has decided to direct its marketing efforts.

tariffs Taxes on imports and exports between countries.

test marketing Introducing a new product in its final form to a geographically limited market to see how well the product sells and get reactions from potential users.

threats Current and potential external factors that may challenge the firm's short- and long-term performance.

timeliness The ability of a company to deliver a good or service by the time a customer expects to have it available for sale or consumption.

time series techniques A forecasting method that seeks to establish the level, trend, and seasonality of a product's sales.

time to market The speed with which a company launches a product.

touch point Any point at which a customer and the company come into contact.

trade sales promotions Sales promotions directed to B2B firms, including wholesalers, retailers, and distributors—rather than individual consumers.

trend A pattern characterized by increasing or decreasing sales.

unaided recall tests A performance metric that requires consumers to recall advertisements from memory, without any clues.

unbundling Separating out the individual goods, services, or ideas that make up a product and pricing each one individually.

undifferentiated targeting A targeting strategy that approaches the marketplace as one large segment.

unique segmentation Segmentation that is used when the similarity in needs and wants exists only within one country.

underpricing Charging someone less than they are willing to pay.

validity The extent to which data measure what the researcher intended to measure.

values A consumer's belief that specific behaviors are socially or personally preferable to other behaviors.

variable costs Costs that vary depending on the number of units produced or sold.

volume maximization (penetration pricing) A pricing strategy that involves setting prices low to encourage a greater volume of purchases.

wants The form that human needs take as they are shaped by personality, culture, and buying situation.

weaknesses Internal limitations that may prevent or disrupt the firm's ability to meet its stated objectives.

Wheeler-Lea Act An amendment to the Federal Trade Commission Act passed in 1938 that removed the burden of proving that unfair and deceptive practices had to injure competition.

wholesaler A firm that sells goods to anyone other than an end-user consumer.

wholesaling The sale of goods or merchandise to retailers; industrial, commercial, institutional, or other professional business users; or other wholesalers.

World Trade Organization (WTO) An international organization that regulates trade among participating countries and helps importers and exporters conduct their business.

yield management A strategy for maximizing revenue even when a firm has a fixed amount of something (goods, services, or capacity).

CREDITS

Detailed Contents

p. xxvii: © Anna Zielinska/E+/Getty Images RF; p. xxviii(top): © John Lund/Digital Vision/Getty Images RF; p. xxviii(bottom): © Design Pics/Don Hammond RF; p. xxix: © Marmaduke St. John/Alamy RF; p. xxx: © Blend Images/Alamy RF; p. xxxi: © Richard Newstead/Flickr/Getty Images RF; p. xxxii(top): © Getty Images RF; p. xxxii(bottom): © Corbis RF; p. xxxiii: © Jeremy Woodhouse/Photodisc/Getty Images RF; p. xxxiv: © sot/Taxi Japan/Getty Images; p. xxxv: © Comstock/PunchStock RF; p. xxxvi(top): © Seth Perlman/AP Images; p. xxxvi(bottom): © 10000/Photolibrary/Getty Images; p. xxxvii: © Royalty-Free/Corbis RF.

Part 1 Opener

p. 1(top): © Anna Zielinska/E+/Getty Images RF; p. 1(center): © John Lund/Digital Vision/Getty Images RF; p. 1(bottom): © Design Pics/Don Hammond RF.

Chapter 1

Opener: © Anna Zielinska/E+/Getty Images RF; p. 3: Photo provided by Steve DeVore; p. 4: © Scott Eells/Bloomberg/Getty Images; p. 5: © Justin Sullivan/Getty Images News/Getty Images; p. 6: © Omikron/Photo Researchers/Getty Images; p. 9(top): © pumkinpie/Alamy; p. 9(bottom): © Blend Images/Getty Images RF; p. 11(top): Courtesy of GoodGuide, Inc.; p. 11(bottom): Photo provided by Steve DeVore; p. 14: © Dave Moyer RF; p. 16(left): © Kevin Winter/Getty Images Entertainment/Getty Images; p. 16(right): © Michael Neelon(misc)/Alamy; p.20: Photo provided by Steve DeVore; p. 21: Photo provided by Lance Gooch; p. 22: Courtesy of Brinker International; p. 26: Photo provided by Steve DeVore.

Chapter 2

Opener: © John Lund/Digital Vision/Getty Images RF; p. 29: Photo provided by Michael Friloux; p. 30: © Robert Churchill/the Agency Collection/Getty Images RF; p.31: Photo provided by Michael Friloux; p. 33: Courtesy of Ben & Jerry's Homemade, Inc.; p. 35: © Tim Boyle/Getty Images News/Getty Images; p. 37: Courtesy of SUBWAY® restaurants; p. 38: Photo provided by Michael Friloux; p. 39: Courtesy of Dr Pepper Snapple Group; p. 40: © Kevin Lee/Bloomberg/Getty Images; p. 42: Courtesy of McDonald's Europe Ltd.; p. 45: © Koichi Kamoshida/Getty Images Sport/Getty Images; p. 47: Photo provided by Erin Blankenship; p. 48: © Paul J. Richards/AFP/Getty Images; p. 52: Photo provided by Michael Friloux.

Chapter 3

Opener: © Design Pics/Don Hammond RF; p. 67: Photo provided by Erin Brewer; p. 68: © Gerardo Mora/Getty Images Entertainment/Getty Images; p. 69(top): © Scott Olson/Getty Images News/Getty Images; p. 69(bottom): © Nicolas Asfouri/AFP/Getty Images; p. 71(left): Courtesy of Dollar General Corporation; p. 71(right): © VIEW Pictures Ltd/Alamy; p. 73: © Lisa Poole/AP Images; p. 72: Photo provided by Erin Brewer; p. 74: Courtesy of SUBWAY® restaurants; p. 79: © Michael Neelon(misc)/Alamy; p. 81: © Matt Stroshane/Bloomberg/Getty Images; p. 86: © Nicolas Khayat/Newscom; p. 87: Photo provided by Halsey Ward; p. 90: Courtesy Big Brothers Big Sisters of America; p. 93: Photo provided by Erin Brewer.

Part 2 Opener

p. 95(top): © Marmaduke St. John/Alamy RF; p. 95(center left): © Blend Images/Alamy RF; p. 95(center right): © Richard Newstead/Flickr/Getty Images RF; p. 95(bottom): © Getty Images RF.

Chapter 4

Opener: © Marmaduke St. John/Alamy RF; p. 97: Photo provided by Dr. Judy Reed Smith; p. 99: © Dadang Tri/Bloomberg/Getty Images; p. 100: © Timothy A. Clary/AFP/Getty Images; p. 104: © ZUMA Press, Inc./Alamy; p. 106: Image courtesy of User Centric, a division of GfK Custom Research LLC; p. 107: Courtesy of SurveyMonkey; p. 110: Photo provided by Dr. Judy Reed Smith; p. 112: © Justin Sullivan/Getty Images News/Getty Images; p. 113: Courtesy of Glassdoor; p. 114: Photo provided by Dr. Judy Reed Smith; p. 116: © enis izgi/E+/Getty Images RF; p. 117: © Iain Masterton/Alamy; p. 118: Photo provided by Ashlyn Kohler; p. 120: Source: The Federal Trade Commission, http://www.consumer.ftc.gov/blog/wrong-path; p. 124: Photo provided by Dr. Judy Reed Smith.

Chapter 5

Opener: © Blend Images/Alamy RF; p. 127: Photo provided by Tracey Rogers; p. 129: Courtesy of TeamDetroit on behalf of Ford Motor Company; p. 131: © Sebastien Feval/AFP/Getty Images; p.132: © Ian Dagnall/Alamy; p. 135(top left and right): Used with permission of State Farm Insurance; p. 135(bottom right): Photo provided by Tracey Rogers; p. 137(top): Courtesy of Northern Illinois University Campus Recreation; p. 137(bottom): Property of Patagonia, Inc. Used with permission; p. 139: © Ramin Talaie/Bloomberg/Getty Images; p. 141: © NetPhotos/Alamy; p. 143: © Roger Kisby/Getty Images Entertainment/Getty Images; p. 145(top): © Buda Mendes/LatinContent WO/Getty Images; p. 145(bottom): Photo provided by Tracey Rogers; p. 146: U.S. Navy photo by Mass Communication Specialist 2nd Class John P. Curtis; p. 149: Photo provided by Caitlin Winey; p. 150: © Mario Tama/Getty Images News/Getty Images; p. 155: Photo provided by Tracey Rogers.

Chapter 6

Opener: © Richard Newstead/Flickr/Getty Images RF; p. 159: Photo provided by Tom Payne; p.161: Courtesy of Lytro, Inc.; p.162: © W. G. Murray/Alamy; p. 165: Courtesy of Keck Graduate Institute (KGI) and used with permission of Jamie Dananberg, Selena Gunggavakin, and Ryan McComb; p. 166: © 2015 The Clorox Company, Inc. Reprinted with permission. CLOROXCONNECTS is a registered trademark of The Clorox Company and is used with permission; p. 168(top left): © Toru Yamanaka/AFP/Getty Images; p. 168(top right): © Andrew Harrer/Bloomberg/Getty Images; p. 169: Photo provided by Tom Payne; p. 170: © Kevin P. Casey/Bloomberg/Getty Images; p. 173: © Aijaz Rahi/AP Images; p. 174: © studiomode/Alamy; p. 176: © Jack Plunkett/AP Images for LG Electronics USA; p. 177: © Joseph Branston/Digital Camera Magazine/Getty Images; p. 179: Photo provided by Misti McCollum; p. 181: © Dale Spartas/Corbis; p. 182: © Mark Elias/Bloomberg/Getty Images; p. 187: Photo provided by Tom Payne.

Chapter 7

Opener: © Getty Images RF; p. 191: Photo provided by Cornelius Lovelace; p. 192: © Crista Jeremiason/ZUMA Press/Corbis; p. 195: © Eric Risberg/AP Images; p. 196: Courtesy of Lennar Corporation; p. 197: Courtesy of Cracker Barrel Old Country Store, Inc.; p. 199(top): Photo provided by Cornelius Lovelace;

COMPANY INDEX

NAME INDEX

SUBJECT INDEX

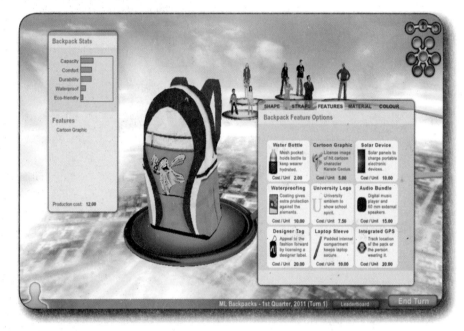